THE POWER OF ART

FOR OUR PARENTS

James Warren Ingalls
Flora Salvador Ingalls
Henry L. Lewis
and Joan Lewis

who first opened our eyes to the power of art

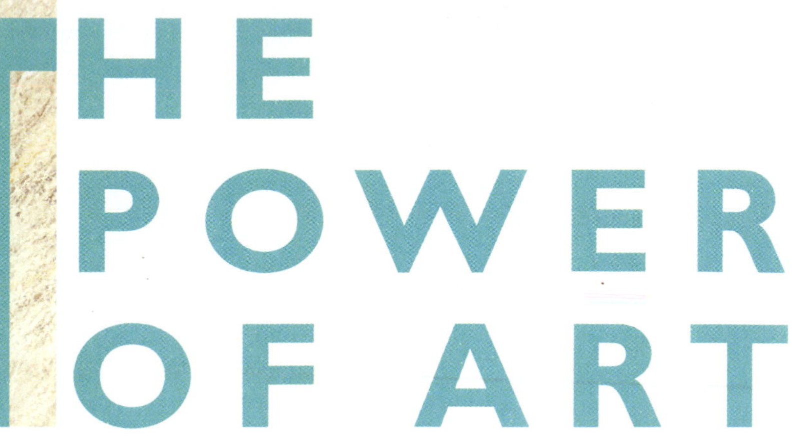

THE POWER OF ART

SECOND EDITION

Richard Lewis
MARIST COLLEGE

Susan I. Lewis
STATE UNIVERSITY OF NEW YORK
AT NEW PALTZ

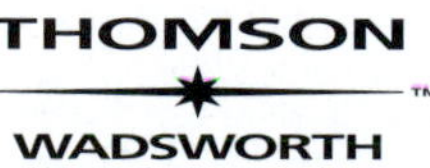

Australia • Brazil • Canada • Mexico • Singapore
Spain • United Kingdom • United States

THOMSON

WADSWORTH™

The Power of Art, Second Edition

Richard Lewis Susan I. Lewis

Publisher: Clark Baxter

Senior Development Editor: Sharon Adams Poore

Assistant Editor: Erikka Adams

Editorial Assistant: Nell Pepper

Managing Technology Project Manager: Wendy Constantine

Executive Marketing Manager: Diane Wenckebach

Marketing Assistant: Aimee Lewis

Lead Marketing Communications Manager: Heather Baxley

Senior Production Manager: Michael Burggren

Senior Content Project Manager: Lauren Wheelock

Senior Art Directors: Cate Rickard Barr and Maria Epes

Print Buyer: Becky Cross

Permissions Editor: Tim Sisler

Production Service: Lachina Publishing Services

Text Designer: Lee Anne Dollison

Photo Researcher: Sarah Evertson

Cover Designer: tani hasegawa

Cover Image: Art Resource, NY. Katsushika Hokusai (1760-1849). *The Great Wave of Kanagawa.* From the series "36 Views of Fuji." Color woodblock print.

Cover/Text Printer: Quebecor World - Versailles

Compositor: Lachina Publishing Services

Printed in the United States of America

1 2 3 4 5 6 7 11 10 09 08

Library of Congress Control Number: 2007935155

Student Edition:
ISBN-13: 978-0-534-64103-0
ISBN-10: 0-534-64103-2

Thomson Higher Education
10 Davis Drive
Belmont, CA 94002-3098
USA

PREFACE

Recently, while finishing the second edition of *The Power of Art,* we visited the Museum of Modern Art in New York City. As we walked through its galleries, filled with brilliant works of art, we saw a crowd gathered in front of a relatively small picture, towards one side of a long wall. Moving closer, we could see people crowded in front of a world famous masterpiece—Vincent van Gogh's *Starry Night* (**17-30**). Many appeared overwhelmed, though smiling. Young and old had difficulty leaving the spot where they were standing. Newcomers to the crowd experienced a sudden jolt of recognition. At times, strangers turned to each other and just nodded happily. Some even had tears running down their cheeks. Listening in, we heard many accents and many languages. One comment we overheard seemed to represent everyone's thoughts (as well as the title of this book)—"No matter how many times I see it, I never get over it."

People all over the globe are drawn to art for just such an experience. Museum attendance is at an all-time high. At Italy's Accademia Gallery in Florence, crowds of people line up for hours in the hot Tuscan sun for the opportunity to enter the museum. Once inside, one can hear viewers gasp in pleasure as they have their first look at Michelangelo's *David* (**14-16**). Similar reactions can be observed in Tokyo, Cairo, Melbourne, and Moscow.

Today, we and the art world are in the midst of both a Digital and Global Age. In the first edition of this book, we called the contemporary chapter A Storm of Images. The title is even more apt now. Since the arrival of the World Wide Web in the mid-1990s, the storm has become a virtual monsoon. But this deluge of imagery makes the need for a book like this even more important. How can a newcomer to art sift through the vast amount of art available online, on television, in magazines, and in books, much less than in the many art fairs, galleries and museums around the world? An internet search for a picture of the *Mona Lisa* will yield not only the famous masterpiece at www.louvre.fr, but a half-million other results. These include parodies, cartoons, posters, movies, recordings, a typeface, a condominium unit, and someone's dog. A search for background information on the painting will only be more confounding; a list of four-million choices from sites around the world will arrive in seconds.

To reflect these changes, *The Power of Art* has evolved to help students sort through the art of the past and today. A new chapter on the Principles of Design will help students understand the underlying principles behind all visual art. The Digital Arts are now featured in a separate chapter on New Media, with concrete explanations of the newest tools for artists. Global coverage has expanded with the presentation of many more individual nonwestern artists, particularly those from Asia and the Americas, along with added cultural and historical context. Discussion of contemporary issues has been, of course, updated and is now integrated throughout the book. Many images by twenty-first century artists in a wide range of media have been added. As befits an up-to-date book on art, almost every image is in color.

Yet we hope much of what made the first edition successful remains. We continue to believe that an art appreciation textbook is not meant to impress scholars with the erudition of its authors, but to inspire in its readers a lifelong love of art. Our goal, as before, has been to write a clear, concise, coherent, yet enjoyable book that educates by pleasure.

Since the first edition of the book was published, we have tested it on art appreciation classes of our own. We learned that students not only found the text accessible, but that they shared it (and especially the pictures) with their family, friends, and coworkers. Questions like "What is art?," "Should art be beautiful?," and "Who is your favorite artist?" have come alive for our students and thousands of others. These students, who often began by feeling confused, and even a little defensive, as they embarked on their academic exposure to the visual arts, quickly gained confidence and enthusiasm. Visits to galleries and museums became meaningful in new ways. Not that the students approved of everything about the original edition! Their critiques have been taken into account and, we trust, helped make this edition even better.

We are fortunate to live in an age of superb color reproductions, but it is worth remembering that no matter how well this book introduces one to the world of the visual arts, no matter how beautiful are the color images on its pages, nothing can replace being in the presence of the original. Books and websites, videos and magazines, are just starting places to begin one's appreciation of art. *The Power of Art* was designed only to open the door to a rich new world to be discovered and enjoyed for a lifetime.

We hope that the readers of this edition will find themselves one day, like the crowd in front of Van Gogh's *Starry Night,* smiling and a little short of breath in front of one of the many masterpieces that are our global heritage of art.

ACKNOWLEDGEMENTS

This book is the product of years of teaching—our own as well as that we received as students. We would like to acknowledge the excellence, dedication, and influence of Abe Ajay, Rudolf Arnheim, George Bayliss, Antonio Frasconi, Al Hinton, Gerome Kamrowski, Al Mullen, and Leonard Stokes, as well as Paul Berry, Dorothea Fisher, Eugenia Janis, Kenworth Moffet, and Clara Tucker. The following colleagues at Marist College, Scuola Lorenzo de Medici, and SUNY New Paltz were especially supportive during this revision of *The Power of Art:* Artin Arslanian, Fabrizio Guarducci, Guy Lometti, Dennis Murray, Steven Poskanzer, and John Ritschdorff.

As we revised the manuscript, many friends and colleagues offered advice, inspiration, perceptive comments and analysis that aided us immensely. We are indebted to Lorenzo Casamenti, Donise English, Kit French, Thomas Goldpaugh, David Krikun, James Luciana, Michele Rowe-Shields, Steve Vinson, and Beth Wilson.

We were also encouraged by enthusiastic readers among younger friends like Sarah and Amy Gross, Hannah Shreefter, Alison Oldehoff, and Elizabeth Moskowitz; and older art aficionados like Belle Bennett, Marjorie Brockman, Dr. Jay Levine, Edward Lewis, Ruth Page, Abby Schlossberg, and Scott Skodnek.

In developing the second edition, we responded to the recommendations of the many instructors who used the first one. We would like to thank in particular the following reviewers whose perceptive comments and analysis were extremely helpful in the preparation of this book:

William P. Andrews, Mississippi State University; Steven Bule, Utah Valley State College; Alisia G. Chase, SUNY Brockport; Patricia Cosper, University of Alabama at Birmingham; Michel Demanche, University of Maryland; Andree Flageolle, Pittsburg State University; Paul Greco, Collin County Community College; Soo Y. Kang, Chicago State University; Pamela A. Lee, Washington State University; Lynn Mackenzie, College of DuPage; Daniel Mason, North Hennepin Community College; Susan P. McKiernan, University of Akron; Anita L. Monsebroten, University of North Dakota; Richard Scott Parker, Tarrant County College; Barbara G. Pogue, Essex County College; Scott Robinson, North Central Texas College; Carey C. Rote, Texas A&M University-Corpus Christi; L. Dennis Sears, Gadsden State Community College; William Hunter Stamps, University of Central Arkansas; Steve D. Stones, Weber State University; Derrick White, Tyler Junior College; Jessie L. Whitehead, Southern Connecticut State University; and Linda Woodward, Montgomery College.

Like the art world, the publishing world is in the midst of both a Digital and Global Age, too. The way this text was produced reflects these important changes. The publishing team for Wadsworth was not located in an office building, but was spread across the United States and worked with sources all over the world. Despite the distances, we always felt a part of a talented and dedicated team. We want to thank our publisher, Clark Baxter, who contributed good spirits and his keen judgment to the entire project; our acquisitions editor, John Swanson, whose faith in this book and persistence made the second edition possible; our development editor, Sharon Adams Poore, who managed to be both the voice of reason and faith in the long process of revision and production; our project manager, Lauren Wheelock, who kept a steady hand on the steering wheel during the obstacle course that is publishing today; our production manager, Sheila McGill, who calmly managed the complicated production process; and our superb and ingenious photo researcher, Sarah Evertson, who constantly surprised us with her ability to find the most challenging images. We also want to thank Julie Iannacchino, the development project manager on the web and digital image library; Erikka Adams, the assistant editor for the supplements; Nell Pepper, our talented editorial assistant; Lois Walsh, for her invaluable and timely efforts on the supplements; and Diane Wenckebach, our enthusiastic and very nice executive marketing manager.

Finally, we would like to thank our students, many of whom sent us links and brought us articles and catalogs, but more importantly, who showed us the way to create a book that could transmit the power of art. The enthusiastic love for art of Erich Alejandro, Nicholas Baish, Joe Chiellini, Joe Concra, Rich Dachtera, Matt Daly, Stefanie DeRario, Kim

Dowd, Jessica Friedlander, Ryan Khoury, Jonathan Kiselik, Heather Krumm, Kevin McKiernan, Mike Milano, Joe Molloy, Danielle Morrison, Caitlin O'Hare, Matthew O'Neill, Christopher Perry, David Restiano, Richard Santiago, Nik Sardos, Joe Ventura, and many more students like them, is what encouraged us in the many years it took to bring this text to completion.

Last, but certainly not least, we would like to express love and appreciation to our son, Rob, for putting up with constantly busy parents and a really messy house for the past two years. Some day, we hope you will think it was worth it.

Richard and Susan Lewis

INSTRUCTOR RESOURCES

PowerLecture

This all-in-one presentation tool makes it easy to incorporate high-resolution digital images into your lectures. You can assemble, edit, and present customized lectures with the **Digital Image Library** that provides high-resolution images—maps, diagrams, and most of the fine art images from the text. A zoom feature enables you to magnify selected portions of an image for more detailed display in class. PowerLecture also includes a comparison-and-contrast feature, PowerPoint lecture outlines, an Instructor's Manual and ExamView computerized testing.

JoinIn Student Response System

Turn your lecture into a personal, interactive experience for your students. These text-specific slides are created for use with JoinIn™ software for classroom personal response systems ("clickers").

STUDENT RESOURCES

ArtExperience Online

This interactive website gives students access to useful technology resources that reinforce and complement topics in the textbook. ArtExperience Online features **flashcards** of images from the text, video demonstrations of studio art techniques, interactive exercises that explore the foundations of art, project ideas, and more.

SlideGuide

Help students study with this note-taking organizer that contains reproductions of the images from the book with captions and page numbers and space to take notes in class.

ArtBasics: An Illustrated Glossary and Timeline

Full-color images and high-quality line art make this brief introduction to the basic terms, styles, and time periods an excellent reference for beginning students.

Museum Experience Handbooks

Available by regions; East, Southeast, Southwest, West, and Midwest, these handbooks provide students with information about museum going and museums in their area.

CONTENTS IN BRIEF

CONTENTS

CHAPTER 1

The Power of Art

Among the treasures of the Louvre Museum in Paris is probably the best known work of art in the Western world, Leonardo da Vinci's *Mona Lisa* **(1-1)**. Signs are posted throughout the vast museum, marking the way to its most famous masterpiece. In the gallery where it hangs, there are other paintings by some of the most talented artists in history, but viewers surround only one, jostling each other to get better views. Tourists treat the painting like a famous landmark, posing for their pictures beside it. Guards are always nearby, and a wooden barrier keeps viewers at a distance. Deep within a massive case of bulletproof glass that dwarfs the small painting, the same elegant woman who has captivated generations of art lovers regards them with her inscrutable smile.

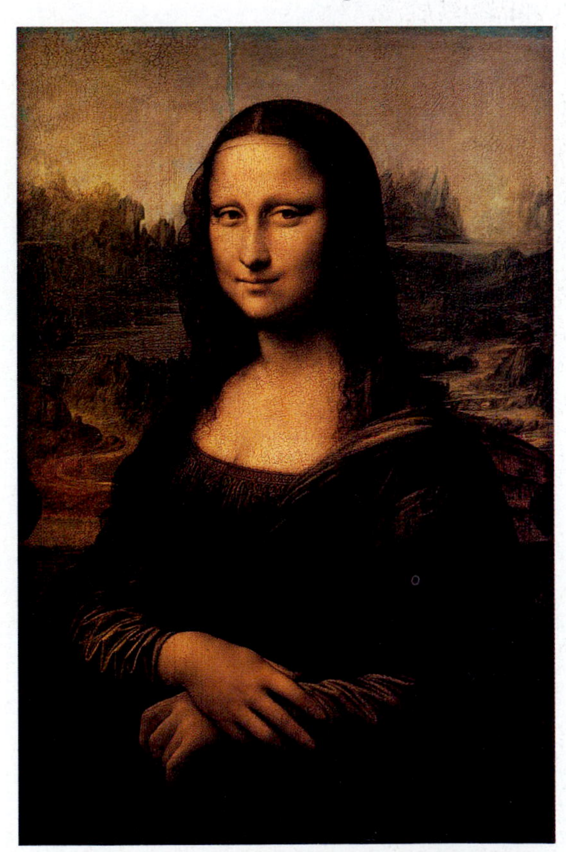

1-1 Leonardo da Vinci, *Mona Lisa,* c. 1503–1505. Oil on wood, approximately 30″ × 21″. Louvre, Paris.

Painted at the height of the Italian Renaissance, this fascinating portrait of a woman has attracted attention for hundreds of years. Poems and songs have been written, essays and scholarly works composed, about an oil painting that measures less than two feet by three feet. Even in our contemporary world of space travel and digital images, the power of da Vinci's portrait continues to transcend time. Legends have grown up around the picture—for instance, that the *Mona Lisa*'s eyes follow one around the room. Another legend suggests that the painting on display is no longer the genuine *Mona Lisa* (see "Art News" box).

What is it about this painting that has elevated it, not simply to the height of a masterpiece but to the symbolic pinnacle of Western art? How can a work of art become so valuable that it is seen as priceless? What gives the *Mona Lisa* its power over people from different centuries and cultures? Although many people have spoken of the air of mystery that surrounds the picture of the woman with the haunting smile, on first viewing it is common to find the picture a disappointment. The glass makes it difficult to see, and what we see is not exactly what Leonardo painted. The art historian Kenneth Clark described the *Mona Lisa* as "the submarine goddess of the Louvre," a phrase that accurately reflects the dominant greenish tone of the painting as well as its aquarium-like casing. Yet the earliest known description of the portrait raves about the warmth of the colors, the rosy nostrils and red lips, as well as the overall tone of the face that "seemed not to be colored but to be living flesh." Not only has the color faded, but also at some point in its history the painting was made smaller, probably to fit into a frame, slicing off a pair of columns that once surrounded her.

LOOKING AT ART

Learning How To See

Despite these ravages of time, it is possible to consider what makes the *Mona Lisa* a masterpiece. Whatever the type of art in question, the first step in learning to appreciate art is simply learning to *look*. This is more challenging than is usually believed. Often we think of looking as a passive act, as in watching TV or clicking through pictures on a webpage. But studying the visual arts requires more than empty viewing; seeing can be *active* rather than passive. When primitive people looked at the world, they had to *observe* nature because they were hunters and gatherers; they depended on their eyes for survival. In their world everything was natural and real; very little was made by man. We, on the other hand, live among literally millions of images, not only in books or on a screen but also on almost everything we touch—from cereal boxes to printed T-shirts. As opposed to primitive cultures, most of what we see and interact with is human-made. This constant bombardment by printed, video, and digital images has made us visually sophisticated, but can also leave our eyes numb.

Artists often say that someone can really "see" as if most people cannot. What an artist means by **seeing**

ART NEWS

The *Mona Lisa* has Been Stolen!

The *Mona Lisa was* actually stolen from the Louvre in 1911, causing a national scandal. While the complete story will never be known, it is believed that the theft was an attempt not only to sell the *Mona Lisa* but also many forged copies. The forger's plan was that upon the shocking announcement of the painting's theft, unscrupulous wealthy collectors around the world could be easily duped into buying his forgeries of the masterpiece.

The forger contacted a former employee of the Louvre, Vincenzo Peruggia, to arrange the theft. Peruggia and his accomplices, dressed as staff, entered the museum as it closed Sunday afternoon, August 20, 1911. The museum would not open again until Tuesday. The thieves slept overnight in the museum. Early the next morning, they carried the painting through the many galleries, planning to tell anyone who saw them that they were bringing the *Mona Lisa* to the staff photography lab. The only one who did see them was a plumber, who helped them open a stuck exit door.

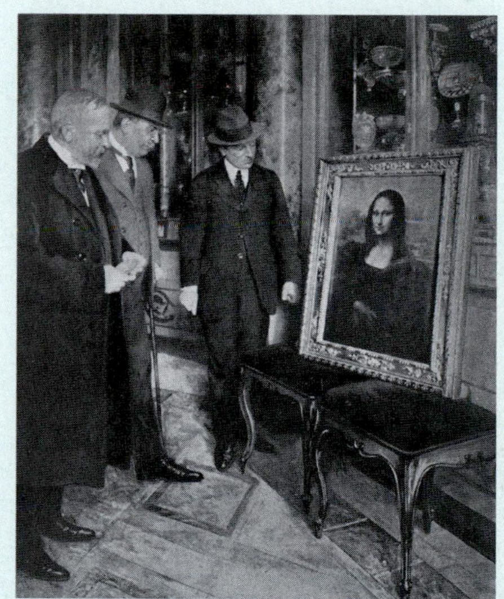

1-2 French officials examine the *Mona Lisa* after its return.

No one knew the painting was missing until the next day, and it took two years for it to reappear in Italy. Vincenzo Peruggia had tried to sell it and was turned over to the authorities. At the trial, the thief, who was born in Italy, claimed that he had stolen Leonardo's masterpiece to return it to its rightful place in his own country. A sympathetic Italian jury sentenced Peruggia to only a few months in jail. After the trial, the *Mona Lisa* was displayed briefly in Florence (where Leonardo had begun it in 1503) and then was returned to its home in the Louvre (**1-2**).

is hard to explain, but it is something like the totally involved gaze of a newborn child, hungrily looking at everything as if it had never been seen before, not blinded by preconceptions. All of us like to see new things, but in the midst of a busy life our seeing becomes stale, our eyes jaded. Art can renew the pleasure of seeing and help us feel more alive. Many people have had the exhilarating experience after leaving a museum of noticing that the world outside looks much more interesting and beautiful.

Let's return to the *Mona Lisa* and look at her carefully. First, the image is beautiful. It is not simply that this is the portrait of a beautiful woman—in fact, *La Gioconda* (Lisa del Giocondo) looks less than ideal to contemporary eyes. Although it is safe to assume that she was considered attractive by the standards of the sixteenth century, Leonardo did not give her face (see detail, **1-3**) the same perfect beauty he gave to his drawings of angels, for example. But what makes a work of art famous is less the quality of the subject than the way it is interpreted by the artist. The *Mona Lisa* is beautifully and gracefully painted. Viewers are attracted to da Vinci's work through the power of his skill as a draftsman and painter and his remarkable ability to bring his subject to life.

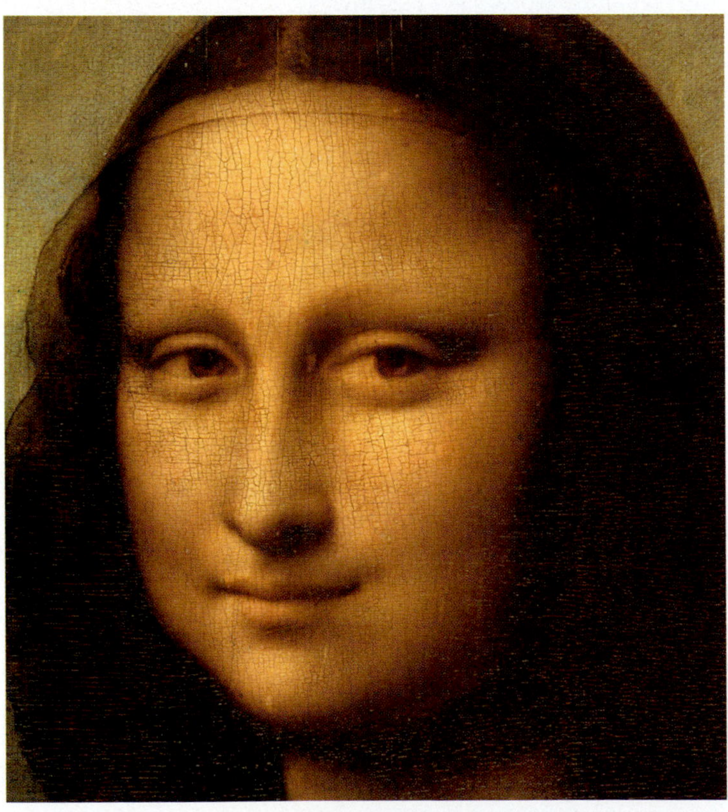

1-3 Detail of figure 1-1: face of *Mona Lisa*.

This lifelike quality made the *Mona Lisa* famous in its own time. According to the painter Giorgio Vasari, Leonardo's contemporary:

> Altogether this picture was painted in a manner to make the most confident artists—no matter who—despair and lose heart . . . in this painting of Leonardo's there was a smile so pleasing that it seemed divine rather than human; and those who saw it were amazed to find that it was as alive as the original.

As Vasari recognized, the *Mona Lisa* revolutionized the art of portraiture, adding movement and life in a way never seen before.

Methods and Materials

Leonardo wrote in his notebooks, "moderated light will add charm to every face," as anyone who has been with a date in a candle-lit restaurant knows. Leonardo used oil paint to recreate this effect, which he called **sfumato lighting** (in Italian, "the soft mist of a fountain"), a soft light that dissolved edges and made details unclear. The *Mona Lisa*'s eyes and mouth were bathed in sfumato light by Leonardo because he knew those are the two most important areas we look at on a face. Because they are left unclear, our imagination fills them in; the lips seem to move and give the *Mona Lisa* life. So it is Leonardo's use of sfumato lighting that is responsible for the legends surrounding this painting—her inscrutable smile, the eyes that look at you and then away.

Leonardo generated a sense of movement in another way. Notice how the background (**1-4**) does not line up on either side of the *Mona Lisa*'s shoulders. This was intentional—Leonardo wanted to create the illusion that his subject is shifting her shoulder while we are looking at her. Leonardo understood how people *see,* perhaps better than anyone who had ever lived, and he used this knowledge in subtle ways to create the illusion that his *Mona Lisa* was a real person. In fact, this is how viewers have always responded to her.

Placing Art and Artist in Historical Context

Great art reveals the spirit of the age that produced it. Therefore, we need to know when and who made a work of art so we can begin to consider how this affected its form. The grace and beauty of Leonardo's *Mona Lisa,* for example, reflects the value placed on these qualities during the Italian Renaissance.

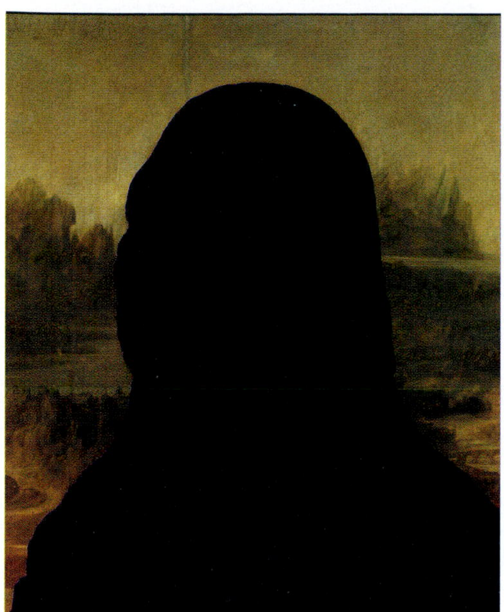

1-4 Detail of figure 1-1: background of *Mona Lisa.*

She also illustrates the highly prized attribute of aloofness—what the Italians called *sprezzatura,* a kind of aristocratic refinement and calm.

The life of Leonardo da Vinci represents many other Renaissance values as well. Leonardo was an independent thinker, a scientific observer of nature, an imaginative inventor, and a delightful conversationalist, as well as a talented artist. He filled many notebooks (**1-5**) with his observations, drawings, poems, and philosophical theories. Above all, he exemplifies a crucial Renaissance idea credited with giving birth to the modern age—*individualism.* Renaissance thinkers conceived of human beings as potentially godlike creatures with immense physical, intellectual, and creative powers. Part of the mystique of Leonardo's art is that it was done by one of the first individuals to be considered a creative genius in the modern sense.

No one can really be sure why Leonardo painted this portrait of twenty-four-year-old Lisa del Giocondo, the wife of an important Florentine merchant, at the same time the artist was refusing paid commissions from more notable persons. We do know that Leonardo worked on the *Mona Lisa* for decades and never considered it finished. Because he reworked the image over and over, carrying it with him on his travels, the painting must have exerted the same endless fascination over the artist as it has over its viewers. Leonardo died in France, the guest of King Francis I (who moved his mother and sisters out of a chateau so da Vinci could take up residence there), so the *Mona Lisa* became part of the royal art collection. That is

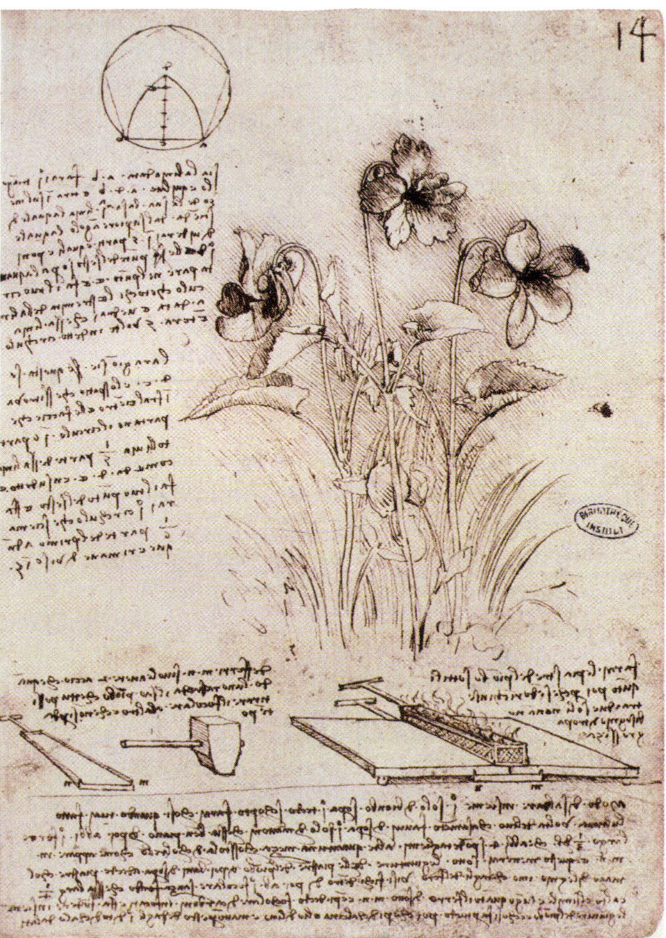

1-5 Leonardo da Vinci, *Drawing of Flowers and Diagrams.* Study from the notebooks, c. 1490–1519. Pen and ink.

how it came to be in the Louvre Museum in Paris, and why it eventually became identified as not only a part of Italian culture but French culture as well.

Art and Culture

Western cultures are not the only ones to see works of art as priceless. The Japanese, for example, have an elaborate system of rating works of art and their value to national heritage. The most valuable artworks are designated as Japanese **National Treasures,** while other significant works of art are categorized as **Important Cultural Properties.** Because of their historic and aesthetic importance, National Treasures (ranging from huge statues and painted screens to fragile decorated boxes and ceramic vessels, such as teacups) cannot be sold or taken out of the country. In Japan, even people—such as the most famous and accomplished living artists—can be given the official title of National Treasure.

One of the works of art designated as a Japanese National Treasure is the wooden statue of the *Amida Buddha* (the Buddha of the West, **1-6**), carved by the sculptor Jocho in the eleventh century. This statue is part of an entire sculptured environment, a grouping of many gilded wooden figures that decorate the central hall of a Buddhist temple designed for an aristocratic family of the period. Because of their great age and the high quality of their design and carving, all of the figures in this sculptural group qualify as National Treasures—considered as valuable to Japanese heritage as the Statue of Liberty is to Americans.

Even if we know little about Buddhism, we can be impressed by the elaborate carving and huge scale of this sculptural group. The *Amida Buddha* on his throne is almost twelve feet high, and the music-making angels that hang on the walls number in the dozens. One is also impressed by the excellent preservation of statues that will soon be a thousand years old. But imagine how powerful this vision of paradise must have seemed to the followers of the Pure Land Buddhist sect, who believed that when they died, their God would descend and lead their souls to a blissful paradise. It is this very descent, the floating of the Amida to earth, and the celestial paradise of dancing and music-making angels, that Jocho brought to life in the Phoenix Hall.

Just as the *Mona Lisa* reflects the ideals of Renaissance Italy, this Japanese sculptural group reflects the taste and beliefs of the world in which it was created. Eleventh-century Japan was dominated by a ruling class that valued elegance and courtly manners above all. The Amida cult appealed particularly to the upper classes because its promised paradise resembled a continuation of the luxurious life of beauty and ease they knew on earth. The Buddha, as seen by Jocho, is as refined and aloof as a prince who

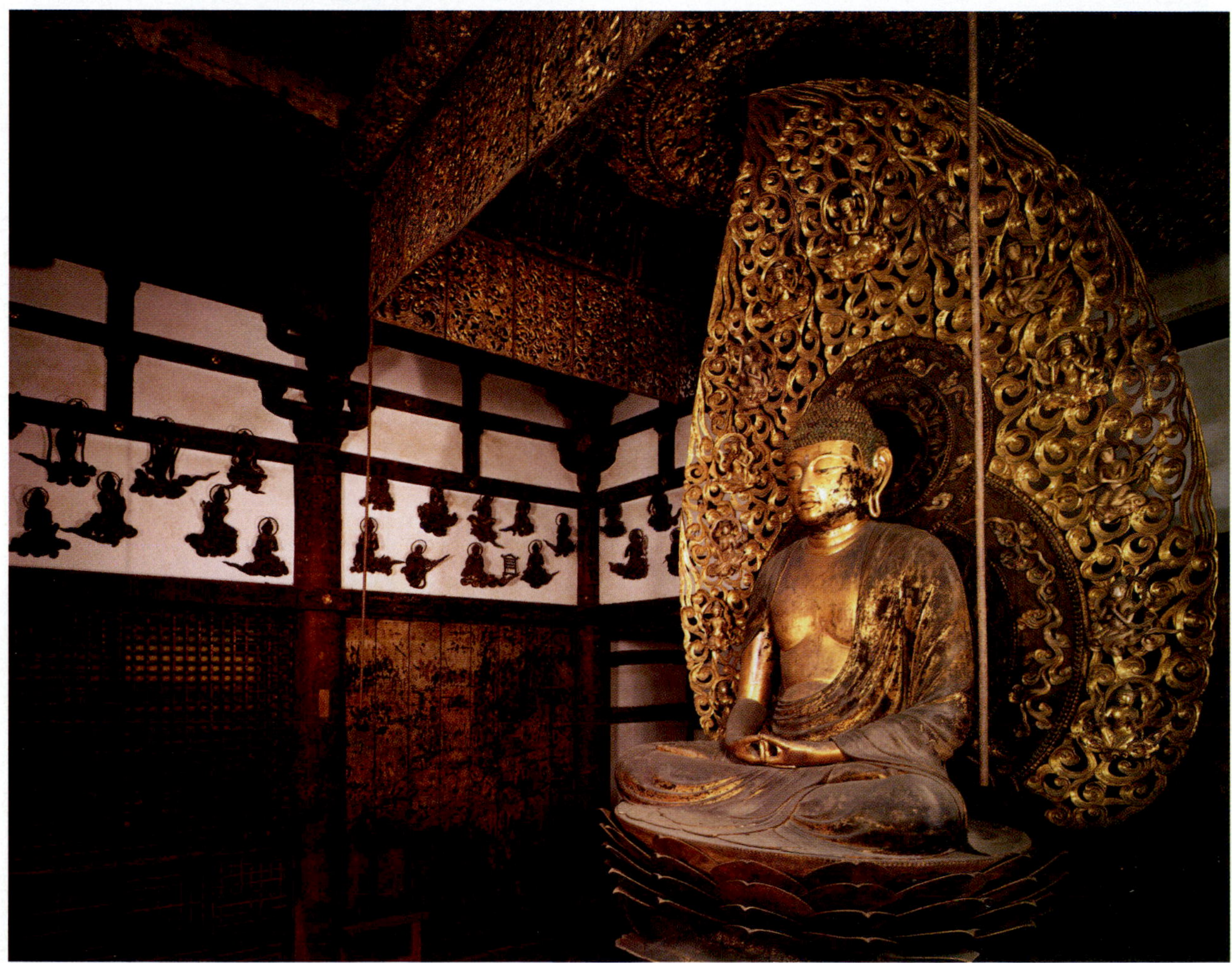

1-6 Interior of the Ho-o-do or Phoenix Hall, 1053. Byodo-in Temple at Uji, Japan.

looks down graciously at his worshippers; the dancing angels are like so many well-bred royal attendants. The slimness and delicacy of the carvings, the richness of the shimmering gold with which they were painted (now somewhat worn), were perfectly in tune with both the subject they represented and the patrons for whom they were made. Yet even today, in a completely changed world, embracing different religious beliefs, brought up in a different culture, we can appreciate the skill and genius that make Jocho's sculptural grouping a great work of art.

The setting for the *Amida Buddha* and dancing celestial angels is a fitting one, and its architecture reflects the same beliefs and taste as the decorated interior. The Buddha is housed within the Ho-o-do, or Phoenix Hall (**1-7**). Note how the delicate elegance of the celestial vision within the hall is echoed by the shape of the entire wooden structure. With its open, airy side pavilions spread out like the wings of a bird, and its roof corners pointed upward, the whole temple appears to be about to lift up off the ground. The impression of hovering weightlessness is enhanced by its mirrored reflection in a pond. Once again, the message of immortality and courtly beauty are merged in both the form and function of this thousand-year-old building. While great European structures—like the Louvre Palace that houses the *Mona Lisa*—are almost always made of stone, the lighter quality of wood greatly influences our aesthetic experience of the Phoenix Hall and its interior decoration.

THE POWERS OF ART: BRINGING FAITH TO LIFE

Through art, the deepest and most intangible beliefs of a culture can be translated into powerful images that communicate specific spiritual messages to the people who view them as part of their religious rituals. From the beginning of humanity, people have expressed their beliefs in material form. They pictured their gods and goddesses in statues and paintings; they built places for worship and religious rites. The *Amida Buddha* is an excellent example of how art brings religious beliefs to life. In some periods, such as the Middle Ages in the Western world, most art was religious in character. So much visual art is related to human beliefs and rituals of worship that it would be easy to fill an entire library with books exploring the relationship between art and faith in different cultures.

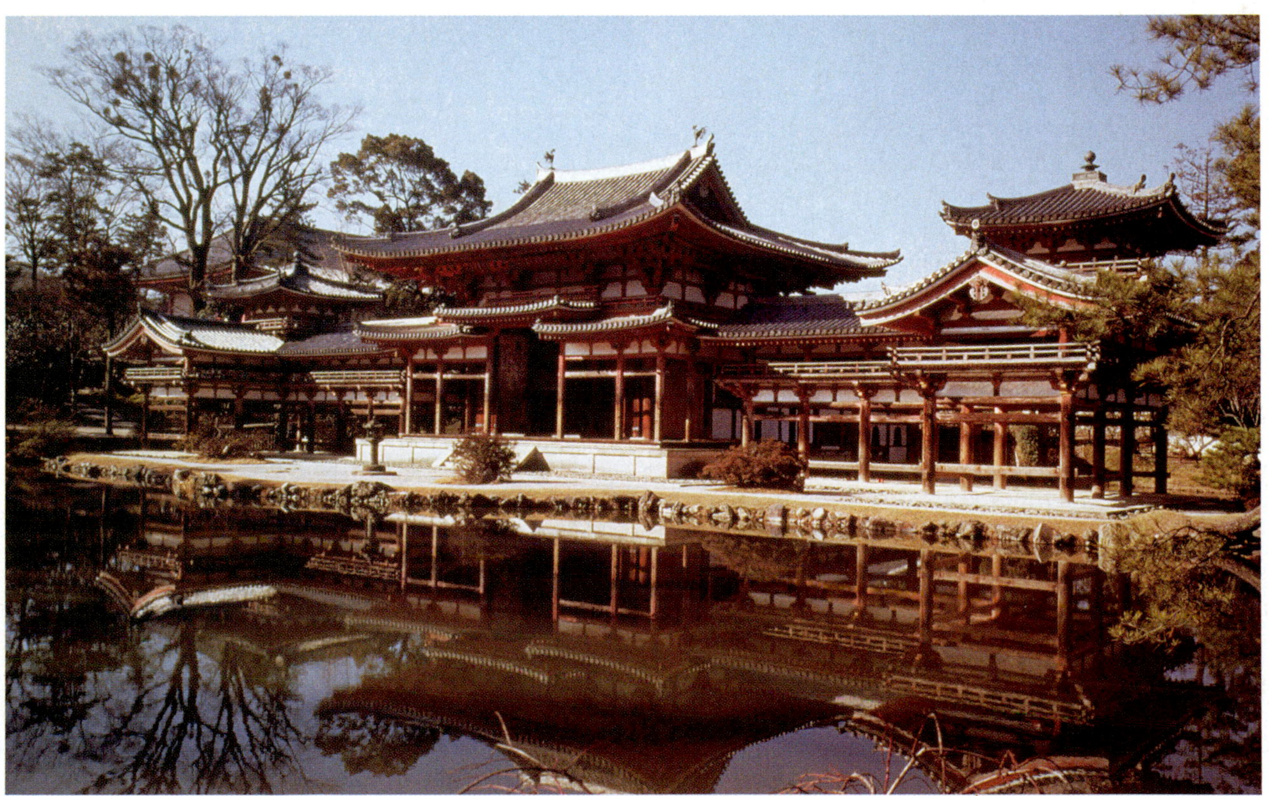

1-7 Exterior of the Ho-o-do or Phoenix Hall, 1053. Byodo-in Temple at Uji, Japan.

Prehistoric Art and Magical Powers

Art need not be as beautiful as the *Mona Lisa* or as elegant and sophisticated as Japanese sculpture to be considered great art. Some of the most powerful art ever made was done more than ten thousand years ago by the prehistoric hunting tribes who inhabited Europe before and during the last Ice Age. One of the very earliest known artworks of this period is a tiny (4-1/8 inch) carved stone figurine known as the *Venus of Willendorf* (**1-8**): *Venus* because it is obviously female, *Willendorf* after the town in Austria where it was found. Although its exact purpose and meaning remain shrouded in the mists of time, scholars have surmised that this female fertility figure was used as some kind of magical charm. With her exaggerated breasts, belly, and buttocks, this faceless Stone-Age Venus provides a powerful visual image of the life-giving earth mother. Such fertility symbols were repeated in many different materials and locations throughout Europe and were probably connected with rituals that associated human fertility with the survival of the Ice-Age clan or tribe. For the Stone-Age people who made and used them, these were not works of art in the same sense we understand the term. These amulets were made to be touched, held, carried, stroked, and worshipped—not to be viewed as beautiful objects in a glass cabinet, or admired as the works of individual artists.

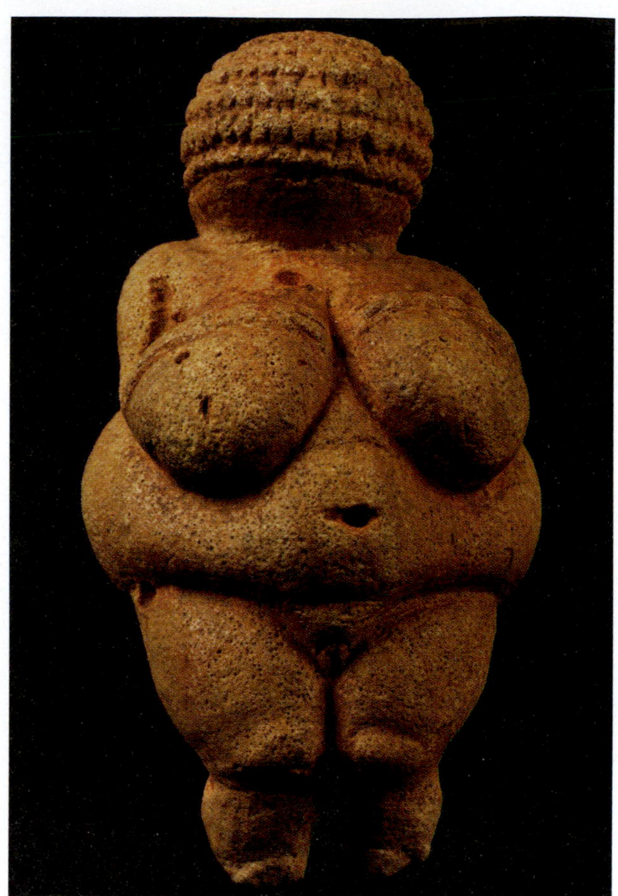

1-8 *Venus of Willendorf*, c. 30,000–25,000 BCE. Limestone, 4 1/8″ high. Naturhistorisches Museum, Vienna.

The earliest known paintings (**1-9**) were also creations of European hunting peoples, but they date from a period ten to fifteen thousand years later than early sculptures. Popularly known as cave paintings, these dramatic prehistoric pictures were done by Ice-Age tribes living in areas of what is now France and Spain around 15,000 BC. When the decorated caves at Lascaux, France, were discovered (accidentally in 1940 by some boys looking for an underground entrance to an old chateau), they caused a sensation throughout the worlds of history, archeology, and art. On these rocky walls, viewers can gaze back at the handiwork of peoples whose culture remains shrouded in mystery. Entering into the eerie, dark caves, viewers find pictures of huge Ice-Age beasts. The primary subjects of these early cave paintings are animals—most often bulls, horses, and bison, sometimes mammoths and woolly rhinoceroses. Humans were rarely shown. The depiction of these wild animals was not simplified or awkward; the cave paintings do not resemble the art of children. They are *naturalistic,* because the animals were drawn in motion, as if they were alive. Even without photographic details, contemporary viewers have no problem telling that one form is a horse, another a bull (**1-10**).

Were these images meant as records of successful hunts, or were they part of magical rituals meant to ensure success for future hunting parties? We cannot be absolutely sure of their purpose, but the most common explanation for the cave paintings is that they were used by their creators in magical rites. It is certainly unlikely that these pictures were simply decoration for people's living quarters. Most are painted in dark, difficult to reach parts of the caves, portions that show no archeological evidence of having been lived in. We do know that the artists came to these special caves to paint on scaffolds by the light of oil lamps; remnants of the lamps and their palettes, along with the holes for their scaffolds, have been found. After the paintings were completed, the caves and their images seem to have been used in ceremonies for thousands of years.

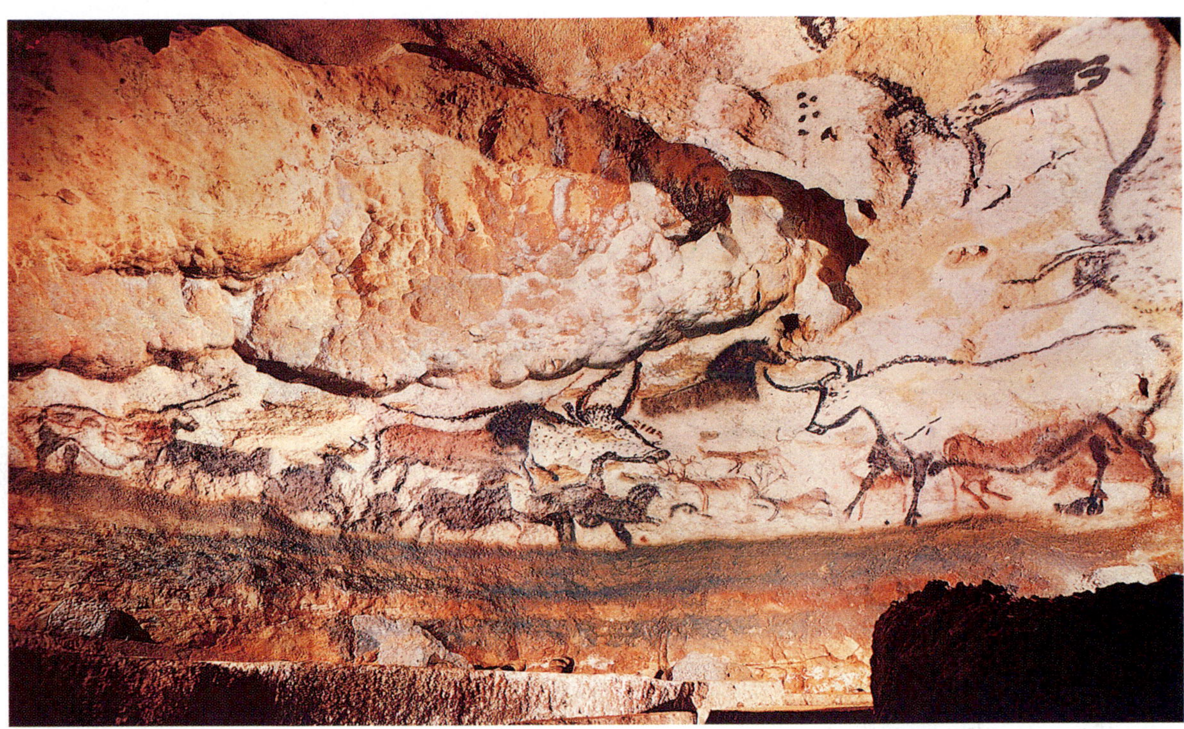

1-9 *Hall of the Bulls* (left wall), Lascaux, c. 13,000 BCE. Dordogne, France.

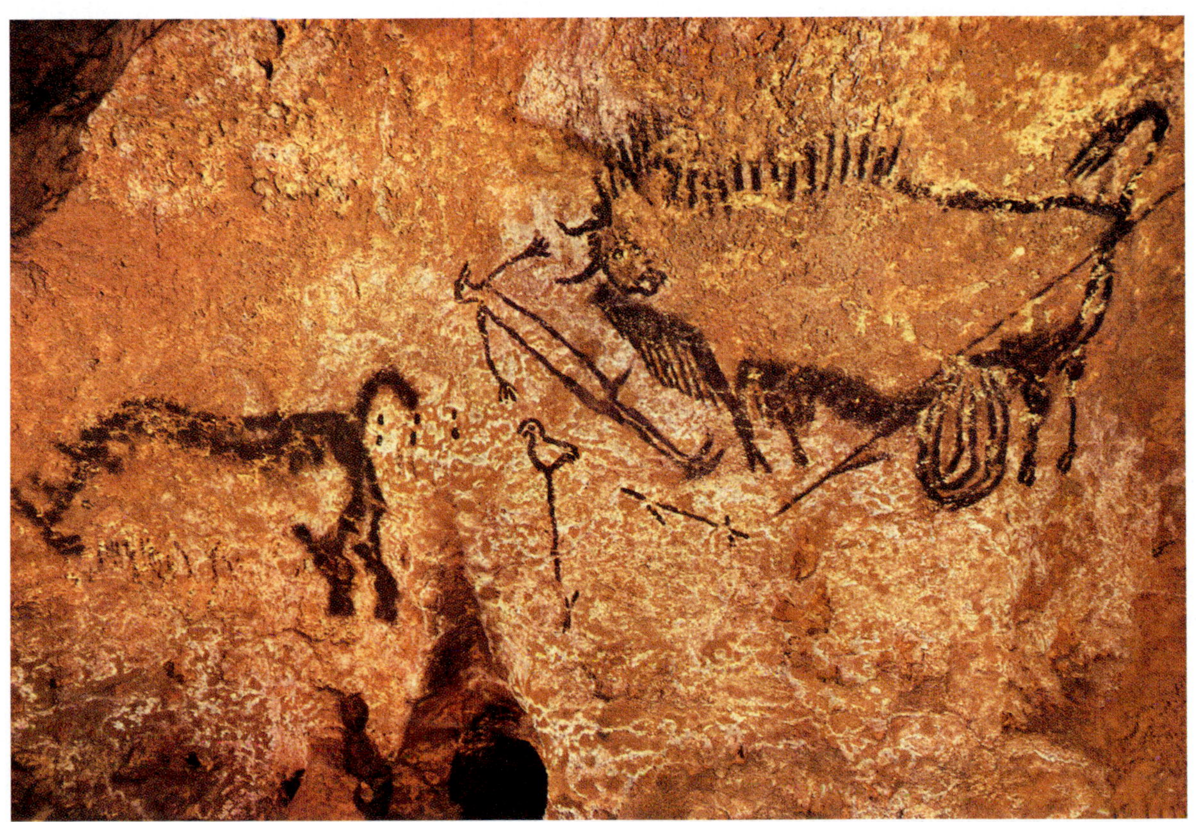

1-10 *Well Scene,* Lascaux, c. 13,000 BCE. Bison 55″ high. Dordogne, France.

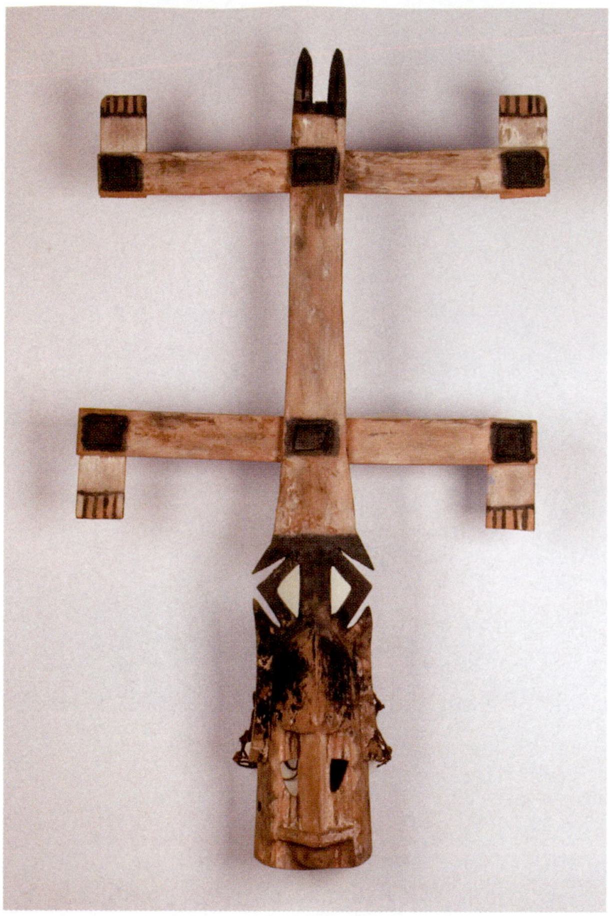

1-11 Mask (Kanaga). Dogon, Mali, twentieth century. Wood, polychrome, fiber, 43 1⁄16″ high. Gift of James M. Osbarn for the Linton Collection of African Art. Yale University Art Gallery, New Haven, CT.

The Power of Art for Tribal Peoples

Painting and carving in rock walls, known as **rock art,** was not simply a prehistoric European phenomenon. Rock art can be found in North America, Asia, Australia, and all across Africa. These sites reveal that art played a vital role in the rituals of tribal peoples for tens of thousands of years. In fact, this role remained uninterrupted until well into the twentieth century. Not only does African rock art depict long-extinct animals, but it also includes images of European colonists and their wagons alongside tribal hunters.

Tribal art is the art of any area of the world where people lived or still live in a preindustrial or preagricultural state—generally without permanent buildings, written language, or modern technology. Such art is what art historians once called primitive art and was originally considered crude and uncivilized by Western Europeans and Americans who came in contact with the "undeveloped" cultures that produced it. But at the turn of the nineteenth century, their attitude changed. Tribal art was seen as new and exotic, valued by collectors and artists for its immediacy and impact. More recently there has been an attempt to appreciate and understand the arts of tribal peoples living around the world as an expression of the cultures and beliefs that produced them.

For instance, African masks have been popular with European and American art collectors for more than a century and had a dramatic impact on the development of modern art. In Western museums, these sculptural masks are usually displayed as isolated art objects (1-11), hung in tasteful arrangements on

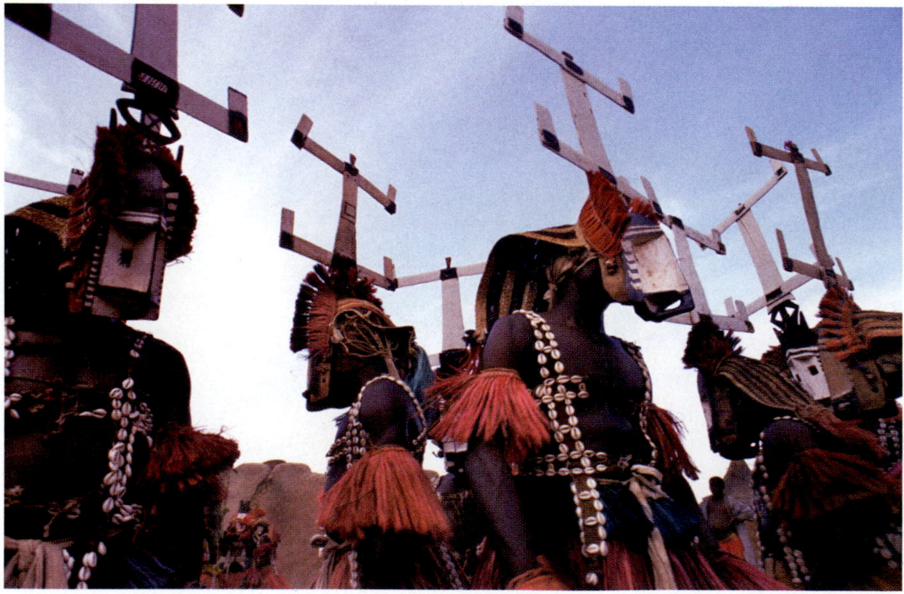

1-12 Dogon ceremony, Mali.

white gallery walls. Because of their strong sense of design, masks exhibited even in this static way retain their visual power, but the power of their original meaning has been lost. Within the culture and religion for which they were created, masks convey a variety of complex messages that are unknown to most museum viewers and are often obscure even to the collectors who purchase them. The mask is meant to be worn in association with an elaborate costume, during ceremonies where traditional songs and dances are performed (**1-12**). Within these ceremonies, which can last for several days, the masks have magical functions. For instance, some masks are supposed to transmit the spirits of the gods or ancestors they represent to the dancers, enabling them to dance for hours (see box).

A GLOBAL VIEW

Journeys to the Spirit Worlds

Although it is not possible to travel back in time to research the mythology of early humans, we can look at the beliefs of tribal societies today. For example, the Eskimos of the Arctic Circle live in an incredibly harsh environment, surrounded by many natural dangers. According to their beliefs, everything—animate beings like animals and inanimate objects like stones—has a spirit. These spirits can be contacted by a *shaman,* or magician/priest. Eskimos believe in an undersea kingdom of supernatural beings as well as a heavenly realm. Their gods include both helpful and destructive spirits, such as the kindly spirit of icebergs and the goddess Sedna, who controls all marine life. Shamans, besides acting as spiritual advisers and doctors to the community, intercede in times of trouble on behalf of the community with the spirits who control the Eskimo world. Illustrated here is a shaman's mask (**1-13**), most likely a report of a shaman's spiritual adventure. The face at the center represents the shaman's soul. Eskimo peoples believe that these souls can fly around the world and even the universe. Shaman stories often tell of flying to distant lands, the moon, and the Land of the Dead.

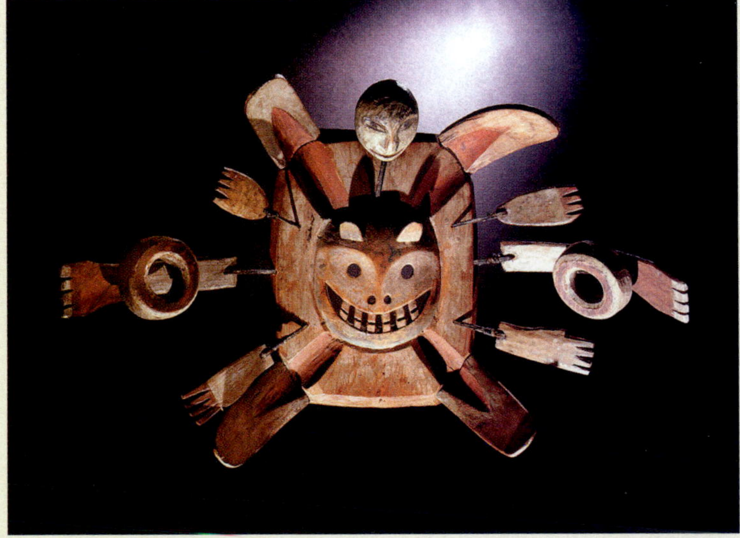

1-13 Eskimo mask depicting the spirit flight of a shaman, Alaska. Wood, metal, and paint.

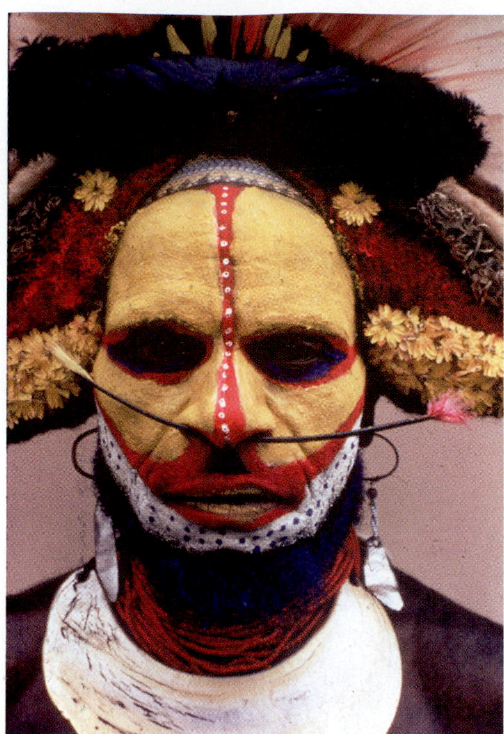

1-14 Face painting, Huli tribesman, from the Southern Highlands Province, Papua, New Guinea.

The peoples of New Guinea, in the South Pacific, still create elaborate costumes that include face and body painting (**1-14**). Like African masks, these self-decorations are part of ceremonies that have magical implications for the people who participate in them. Costumes include both headdresses and "aprons"; the traditional dances require that both headdress and apron sway in time to the music. If viewers see the dance and decorations as pleasing—if the plumes are shiny, the furs glossy, the face paint bright—they are pleased. But if the dance is poorly done and the decorations are second rate—the feathers and face seem dull and dusty, for instance—it is considered a sign of very bad luck, of coming troubles, even death.

The magical powers attributed to art by prehistoric peoples and "primitive" tribes are not generally accepted in our modern scientific and industrialized world. Still, even if we do not believe that works of art can cure sickness, placate dead spirits, assist us in predicting and controlling the future, or put us in direct touch with supernatural forces, we are not totally immune to the magical power in art. Imagine how you would feel if you discovered someone had poked holes in a photograph of your grandmother's face. Would you calmly reflect that it was only a damaged piece of paper? Or would you consider it an unjustifiable attack on a dearly loved person?

The Power of Religious Art

Religious art gives visual expression to inner belief and has the ability to raise people's spirits above the problems of daily life. For centuries, humans have created special places to worship with art. Such temples or churches are designed to convey particular religious messages and spiritual values. These places of devotion often share some of the magical quality of prehistoric caves. Both magical and religious art express human belief in a spiritual world. Magical art, however, supposes that images have a living power, while religious art is more often simply the visual expression of an inner belief.

Just as the Phoenix Hall (1-6) embodies the beliefs of Japanese Buddhism, the Gothic cathedral of *Notre Dame* (**1-15**) in Paris is a visual expression of the Christian faith of the medieval era. With its soaring vertical lines, the cathedral seems to lift the soul heavenward, toward God. Its stained glass windows tell biblical stories (**1-16**); its paintings and statues can instruct and even inspire the viewer. By transforming a material

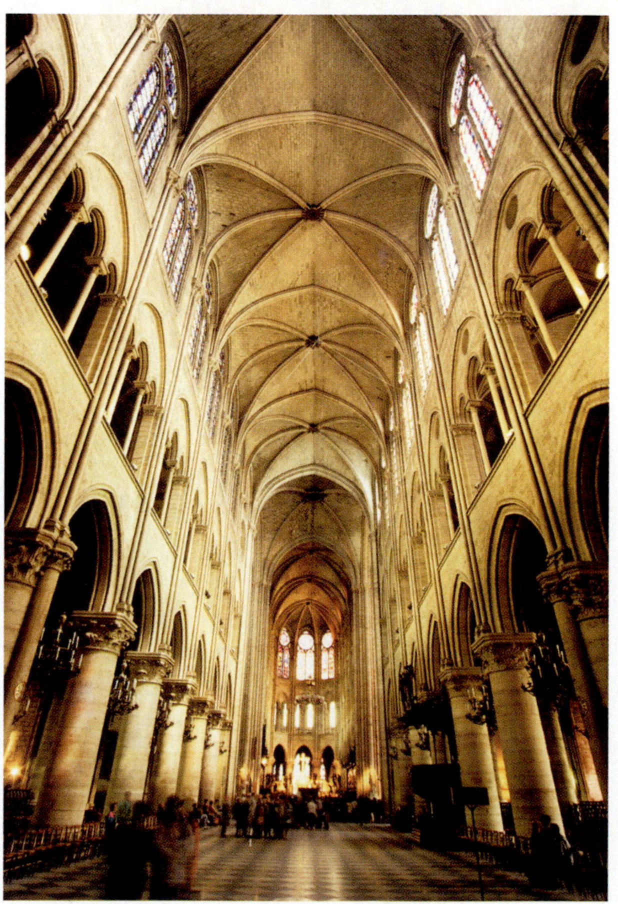

1-15 Looking up into the nave vaults of Notre Dame Cathedral, Paris, begun 1163, modified 1225–1250.

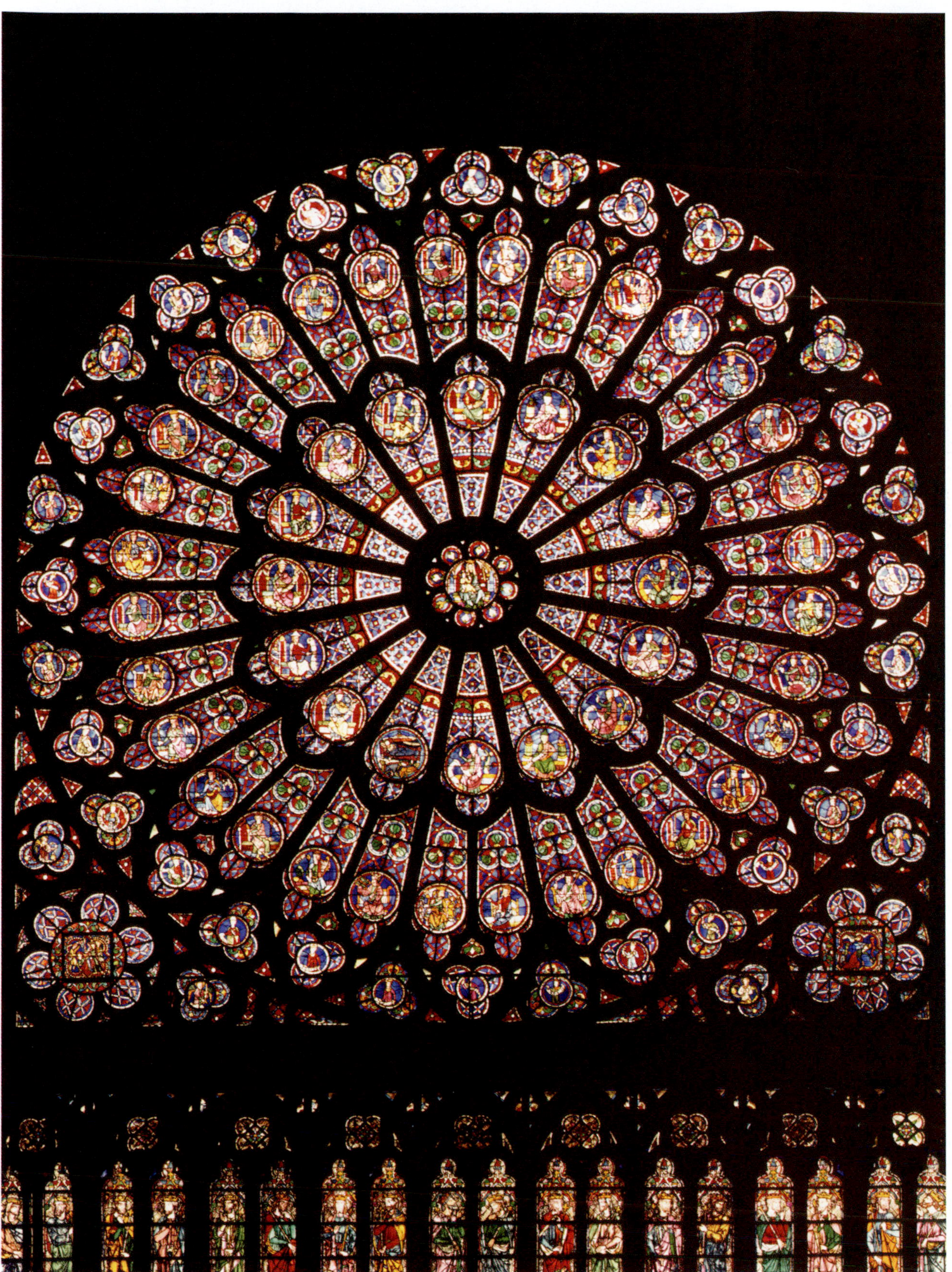

1-16 Jean de Chelles, rose window of the north transept, Notre Dame Cathedral, Paris, 1240–1250. Stained glass, iron, and lead stone-bar tracery, diameter 43′.

as dense and heavy as stone into a structure of such grace, the cathedral becomes a visual representation of the Christian belief in a spiritual existence beyond and above the limitations of physical reality. This heavenly realm is visually symbolized as the viewer's eye is drawn up the soaring lines of the gothic arches to the very top of the pointed vaults and into a space bathed in colored light. Within *Notre Dame* cathedral, we can experience the power of art to transform the physical act of viewing into the spiritual act of worshipping.

ART REPRESENTS IDEALS

Statues of gods and goddesses also have the power to express the ideals of a particular culture in physical form. The art of classical Greece, for example, expresses the Greeks' cultural ideals of physical beauty and athletic strength, as in the statue *Hermes with the Infant Dionysus* by the great sculptor Praxiteles (**1-17**). For the Greeks, a strong and healthy body was extremely important, because physical development was considered equally as important as mental and spiritual growth. They sought a perfect balance between body and mind, a natural harmony between muscular prowess, grace, mental vigor, and physical beauty.

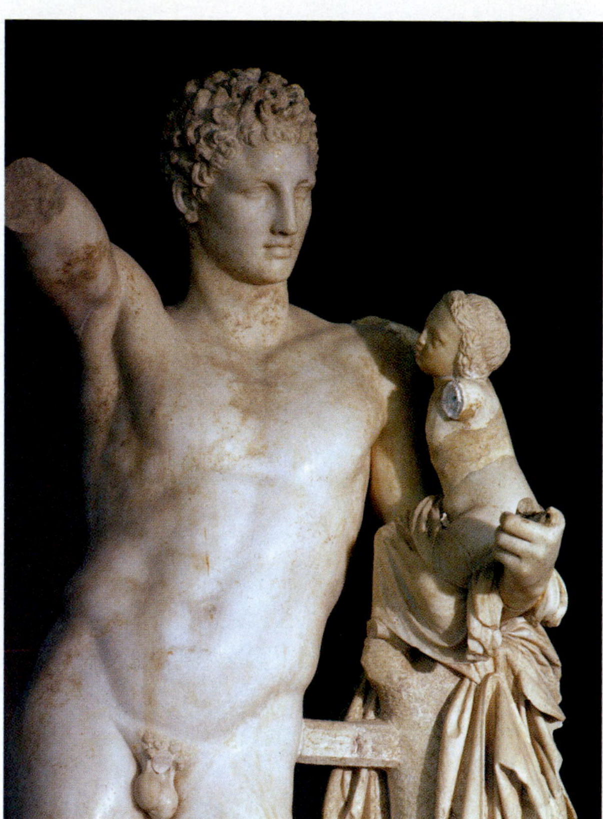

1-17 Roman copy of Praxiteles, *Hermes with the Infant Dionysus* (detail), from Olympia, c. 340 BCE. (?). Marble, approximately 7′ high. Archeological Museum, Olympia.

Greek art also aspired to another balance—between realism and idealism. Greek statues are immediately recognizable as lifelike, accurate representations of the human form. Yet, as in the figure of *Hermes* illustrated here, they idealize the human body, making it more graceful and perfect than any real person could be. Greek sculptures are not portraits of individuals but ideal types. The Western conception of great art as a fusion of the real, or truthful, with the ideal, or beautiful, is descended from the aesthetics of ancient Greece. This philosophy was expressed succinctly by the English Romantic poet John Keats in these famous lines from *Ode on a Grecian Urn*:

> Beauty is truth, truth beauty—that is all
> Ye know on earth, and all ye need to know.

Art as a Declaration of Power

Besides expressing spiritual beliefs or cultural ideals, art from the earliest times has been used to declare the power of rulers. The pharaohs of Egypt erected huge structures to declare their strength; Roman emperors constructed triumphal arches in conquered territories. For thousands of years, artists served kings and queens. During the Renaissance, royal images were not just stylized versions of majesty (as seen in Egypt) but true portraits. One of the finest of the Renaissance court painters was Hans Holbein the Younger, and our image of *Henry VIII* (**1-18**) is forever that of an enormous, insatiable powerhouse because of Holbein's portraits. His *Henry VIII* stands before us seeming larger than life, almost bursting the edges of the picture frame. He is dressed in stunning garments, made of the finest materials sewn with golden embroidery and jewels. Another Holbein portrait (now lost) hung over the king's throne and according to visitors "abashed and annihilated" them when they stood before it. That was the purpose of all the king's portraits—to glorify a man who had supreme power.

Renato Bertelli's *Head of Mussolini* (**1-19**) is a modern approach to paying tribute to a ruler—in this case, Benito Mussolini, the Fascist dictator who led Italy during World War II. Bertelli's sculpture is infused with the spirit of *Futurism,* a movement that celebrated progress and called on Italians to embrace

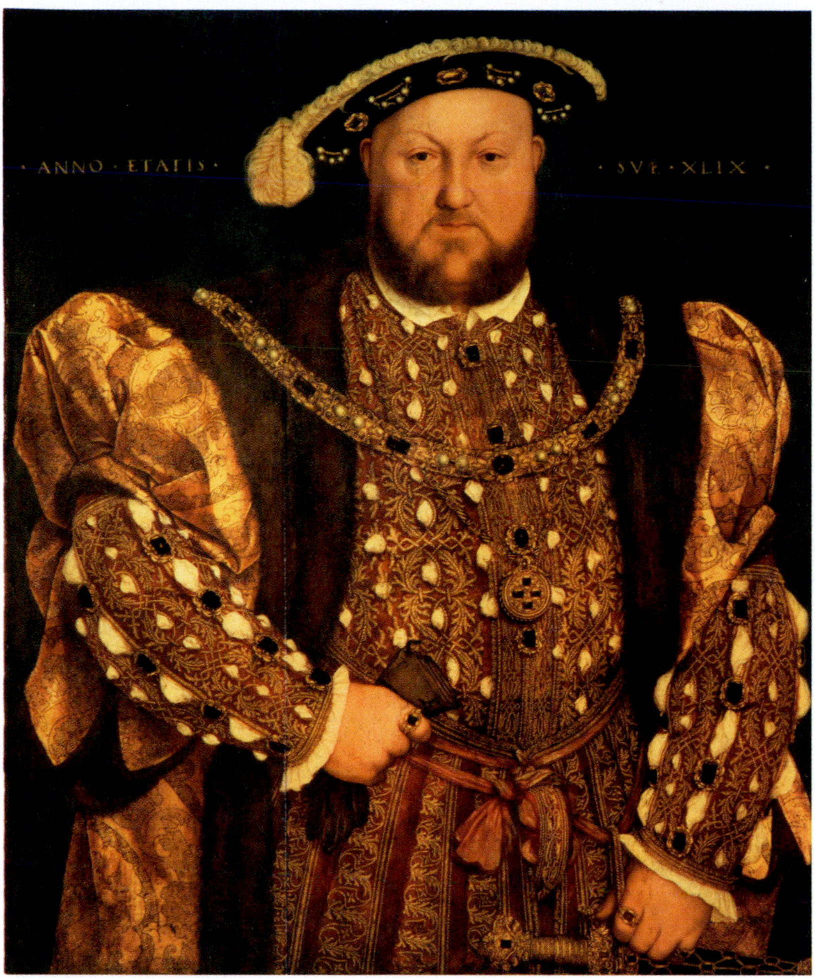

1-18 Hans Holbein the Younger, *Henry VIII,* 1540. Oil on panel, 32½″ × 12½″. Galleria Nazionale d'Arte Antica, Rome.

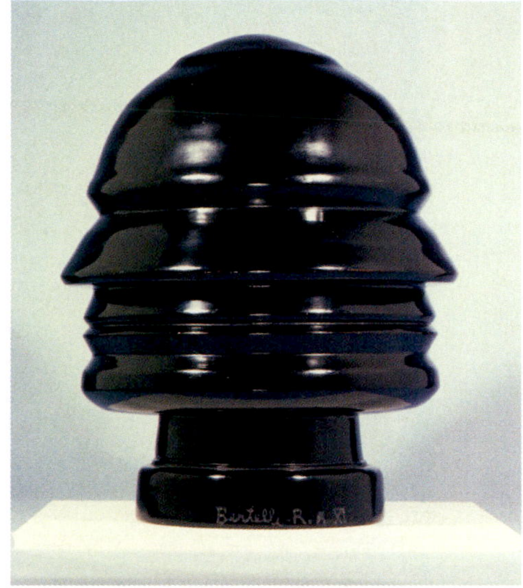

1-19 Renato Bertelli, *Head of Mussolini* (Continuous Profile), 1933. Painted terracotta, 19″ tall. Imperial War Museum, London.

a fresh approach to art, unencumbered by the past. The Futurists called for art "enriched by a new beauty: the beauty of speed" (see Chapter 18). By rotating Mussolini's profile in 360 degrees, Bertelli's "continuous profile" is meant to show the dynamism and modernity of *Il Duce*—"the Leader."

Mussolini's rise to power in the 1920s was greeted with joy by Bertelli and his fellow Futurists. In return, the Italian dictator embraced Futurism's ideals and made it the official style of his regime. This sculpture was approved by the dictator, who ordered its mass production and distribution.

The Power to Convey Immortality

Unlike Henry VIII or Mussolini, Jahangir, the emperor of India who ruled during the height of the Mughal dynasty in the 1600s, directed his artists to portray him as honestly as they could. Yet Jahangir did not totally renounce flattery. While the faces are naturalistic in the painting *Jahangir Preferring a Sufi Shaikh to Kings* (**1-20**), the setting and events are not. The Emperor Jahangir is the source of a brilliant light, too bright even for one of the cupids. Great men have come to pay homage to Jahangir: a wise old saint (who the emperor places above all other admirers), the Sultan of the Ottoman Empire, King James I of England, and the artist Bichitr himself.

The Emperor Jahangir sits on a throne supported by an hourglass whose sand has almost run out. Yet, on the glass, cupids are painting a prayer that he might live for a thousand years. What could resolve this contradiction? It must be the act of painting itself, one of the great passions of the cultured emperor. There were many signs of Jahangir's special love during his reign. One of the greatest royal patrons of arts in history, he provided studios in the palace for his court artists and gave them the finest and most expensive materials to work with. The artists rewarded him with immortality.

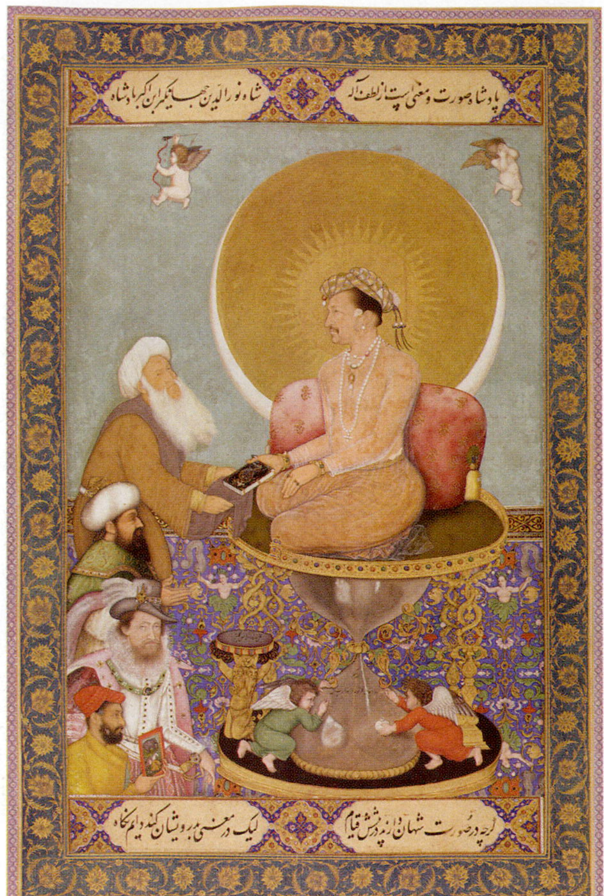

1-20 Bichitr, *Jahangir Preferring a Sufi Shaikh to Kings,* from the Leningrad Album, Mughal, India, early seventeenth century. Color and gold on paper, 10⅞″ high. Freer Gallery of Art, Smithsonian Institution, Washington, D.C. F1942.15a.

The Power to Change Our Beliefs

Art also has the power to change the way we think, the way we understand the world around us. Many contemporary artists use their work to express political viewpoints, to lead their viewers to a moral lesson. In *The Liberation of Aunt Jemima* (**1-21**), Betye Saar comments on the stereotyping of African-American women in advertising and the media. Saar creates her work by incorporating so-called **found objects,** like the mammy doll and cutout pictures of Aunt Jemima from pancake packages. These are arranged inside a box as if the artist were creating a diorama; the doll holds a broom in one hand, and a small print of another happy mammy holding a wailing white baby is propped up in front of her. But the familiarity and friendliness of these images is radicalized by the incorporation of a black power fist in the foreground of the box, as well as a rifle and pistol. Here Aunt Jemima seems to express some of the anger Saar felt, but never expressed, when she experienced discrimination as a young black woman growing up in California. (For instance, Saar won several prizes for her designs for floats in the Tournament of Roses parade before the judges realized she was an African-American. After her race was disclosed, she was given only honorable mentions.) By using real mementos of contemporary culture like the advertising imagery of Aunt Jemima, Saar creates a visual satire that shows how photographic reproductions tend to reinforce racial stereotypes in our society.

The Power to Shock

Related to art's power to change our point of view is its power to shock us. In the early twentieth century, many artists wanted to create works that would wake viewers up and shake them out of their preconceptions about art. One such artist was Marcel

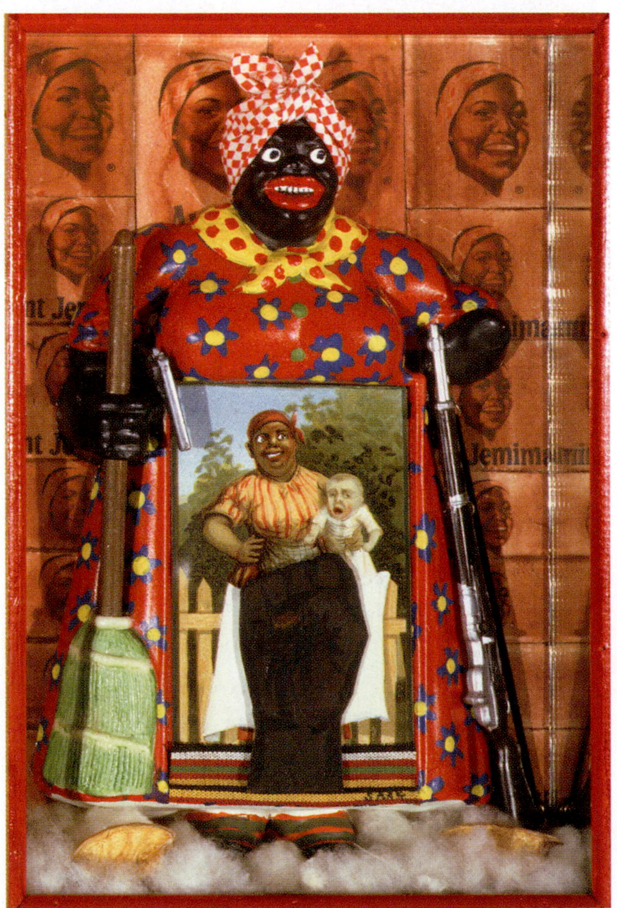

1-21 Betye Saar, *The Liberation of Aunt Jemima,* 1972. Mixed media, 11¾″ × 2¾″. University Art Museum, University of California at Berkeley (purchased with funds from the National Endowment for the Arts). Photograph courtesy of Michael Rosenfeld Gallery, LLC, New York, NY. Photograph by Joshua Nefsky.

Duchamp, and one of his most disturbing pictures was *L.H.O.O.Q.* (**1-22**), a satire of Leonardo da Vinci's *Mona Lisa*. Duchamp chose to make fun of the *Mona Lisa,* especially because it was so beloved and had become almost like a sacred image to people who cared about art. What he did was take a postcard reproduction of the painting, added a moustache, beard, and dark pupils in pencil, and then printed a few initials at the bottom. When pronounced in French, these initials sound out the vulgar phrase, "she has a hot ass."

Duchamp's parody was upsetting on several levels. First, he was making light of Leonardo's great masterpiece. Because the *Mona Lisa* had come to symbolize the best in Western art, he was symbolically rejecting centuries of tradition. Second, Duchamp was taking a reproduction of a painting by another artist, changing it slightly, and claiming that it was a new work of art that belonged to him—that is, he seemed to be stealing someone else's creative work and then (figuratively) spitting on it. A beautiful image was made ugly, even silly. A picture that had come to symbolize the mystery and ideal nature of all women was turned into a joke. Worst of all, he was suggesting that the *Mona Lisa* was "hot stuff."

The creation of artworks *meant* to upset the viewing public is a recent development in the history of art. In earlier times, the purpose of art was to please the person who commissioned and paid for it—the patron.

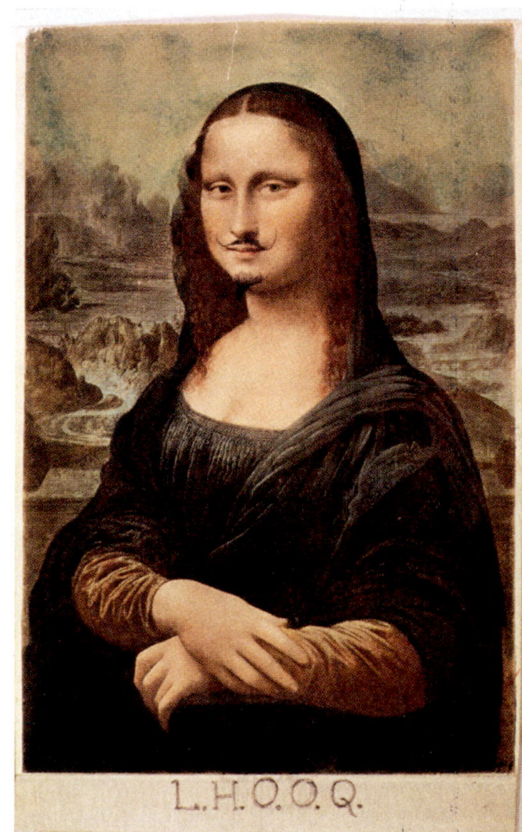

1-22 Marcel Duchamp, *L.H.O.O.Q.*, 1919. Pencil on print, 7¾" × 4¾". Private collection.

The Power to Touch Our Emotions

Art can also profoundly touch the emotions of the viewer. The *Vietnam Veterans Memorial* (**1-23**) in Washington, D.C., was designed especially to reach out to the American people and assist in healing the wounds left by the Vietnam War. The architecture student who designed it, Maya Ying Lin, called her concept "a visual poem." When asked what effect the memorial would have on the public, she thought to herself, "They'll cry" (although she didn't say this out loud until after the project was finished). And visitors do cry at the wall, even those who did not personally know any of the soldiers whose names are listed among the dead and missing in action. No one can doubt that the *Vietnam Veterans Memorial* is the most moving monument on the mall in Washington, D.C., and perhaps the most moving war memorial ever built. What makes it so effective?

The memorial interacts with the site in a unique and powerful way. Instead of building a structure on top of the land, Maya Lin cut into it and edged the slice with a V-shaped black granite wall—one arm pointing toward the Washington Monument, the other toward the Lincoln Memorial. Into this wall more than fifty-five thousand names of all Americans who died during the Vietnam War or remain missing are incised in date order, as if on a mass gravestone. The black granite is polished to reflect its surroundings: the sky, clouds, trees, and land, as well as each person who has come to remember (see box).

The Vietnam memorial is the most popular site on the Mall in Washington, with nearly four million visitors visiting it each year. Many are looking for the names of specific loved ones; others are there simply to pay tribute to all of those who lost their lives. From the first, visitors have interacted with the memorial in unique ways. People reach up to touch the names and make rubbings to carry home as souvenirs. Others leave flowers, photographs, letters, and memorabilia. The memorial is a place for surviving veterans to be reunited with friends, for friends to remember the classmates who never returned, for family members to "meet" the dead father, brother, sister, or cousin who they do not remember, or perhaps never met. Lin's memorial seems to allow

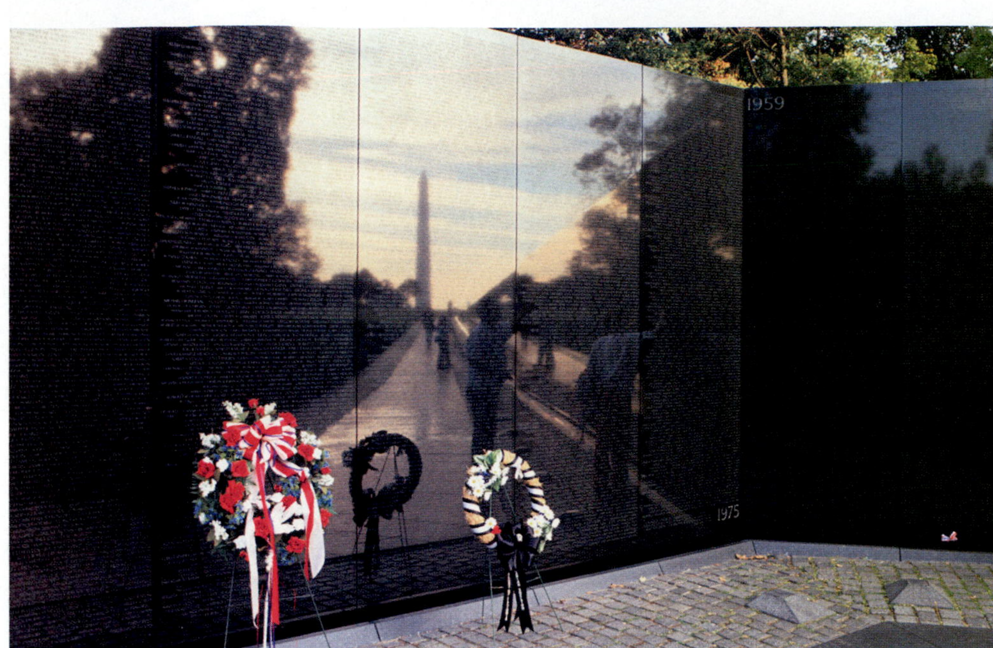

1-23 Maya Ying Lin, *Vietnam Veterans Memorial,* Washington, D.C., 1981–1983. Marble, each wing 246' long.

ART NEWS

Controversy Over the Vietnam Memorial

The *Vietnam Veterans Memorial* was commissioned in the 1980s by the Vietnam Veterans Memorial Fund (VVMF), founded by an independent group of Vietnam veterans. Because money was raised by donations from people throughout the country, and the site on the mall in Washington, D.C., was contributed by the government of the United States, the patrons for this monument included all Vietnam veterans and in some sense all the citizens of the country. The choice of the design was given to a jury of prominent artists, who looked at more than fourteen hundred entries (all reviewed anonymously, so the judges would not be influenced by the name or reputation of the artist). Surprisingly, their unanimous choice was the submission of a young architecture student, Maya Ying Lin.

Although the selection generated little negative comment at first, problems began to develop as the ground-breaking ceremony neared. Many Americans expected a realistic monument like ones seen in parks and town greens around the United States and were shocked by a design that was highly abstract. Some veterans and prominent contributors united to mount a political campaign against the monument, which was described as a "black gash of shame." A lively, and even bitter, debate developed in the press and the halls of Congress. The official patrons—the VVMF—began to fear that the memorial would never be built at all. In the end, the detractors of Lin's winning entry managed to block government approval for a building permit unless the memorial included a realistic statue (**1-24**) and a flag.

Maya Lin was disillusioned by the pressure for these additions, which she felt would ruin the simplicity of her design and compromise the purity of the site. However, although she was the artist, because the patrons had purchased her design, she had no further control over it. Interestingly, Lin compared the addition of a traditional statue to her monument with the disrespectful way Duchamp treated

(continued on next page)

ART NEWS

the *Mona Lisa* in *L.H.O.O.Q.*: "I can't see how anyone of integrity can go around drawing mustaches on other people's portraits," she said. To her, to place a realistic statue in the center of the wall would be a mustache, a desecration of her work. She described the statue as "trite." Frederick Hart, the sculptor of the realistic statue, showed as little respect for her memorial design, comparing it to a "blank canvas," claiming that it was "intentionally not meaningful" and "contemptuous of life."

Eventually a compromise was reached; the statue was erected in an entrance plaza a little distance away from the wall, not in front of it. For her design, Maya Lin had won $20,000 and national fame; she had also experienced criticism, rejection, and a loss of control over her own work. Frederick Hart, a professional sculptor, was paid ten times as much for his statue.

The erection of Hart's statue did not end the controversy over "The Wall's" abstract nature, however. Since then other veterans groups have lobbied for representation at the site. In 1993, a statue honoring the service of women in the Vietnam War was added. It depicts three women in uniform, one a nurse caring for a wounded soldier. Recently, after another long battle, plans were approved for a large underground Vietnam Wall Memorial Center, designed to provide pictures and films to put the war in historical context.

Despite the continuing public debate, the memorial has become one of the most popular attractions in the nation's capital. In the process, it has more than satisfied the original goals of its patrons, which were to list the name of every soldier lost in Vietnam, to honor those who fought there, to make no political statement for or against the war, and to promote reconciliation.

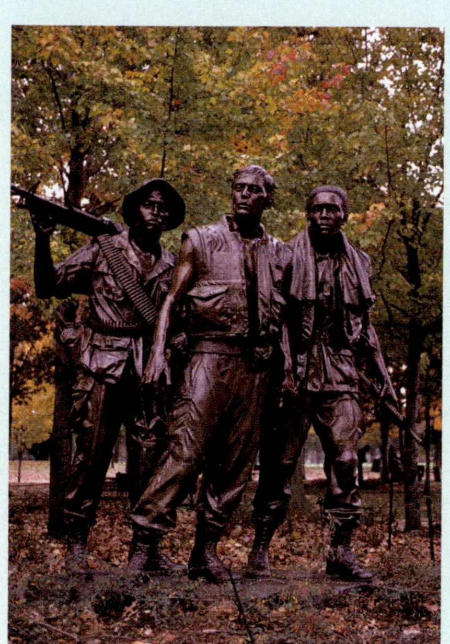

1-24 Frederick Hart, *Statue for Vietnam Veterans Memorial,* Washington, D.C., 1984. Bronze, life-size.

people to experience their loss, while comforting them at the same time. The *Vietnam Veterans Memorial* is a superb example of the power of art (even when very abstract) to reach out to the public.

The Power to Awaken Our Senses

Contemporary life is lived at a fast pace, and it is easy to miss what is going on around us, to have our senses dulled by overstimulation, and to literally lose focus. The great Russian writer Leo Tolstoy warned us of this danger, when he wrote "In the name of God, stop a moment, cease your work, look around you." Art has the power to awaken us to realities that we may not have recognized before, to truly open our eyes. In the modern world, the art of photography has become a medium for this kind of artistic revelation—to slow us down, to make us stop and really look.

Ansel Adams hoped his pictures would reveal eternal truths. His majestic landscape *Clearing Winter Storm* (**1-25**) is a superb example of the images that speak to the richness of nature or what Adams called "an austere and blazing poetry of the real." Adams was born in San Francisco and experienced

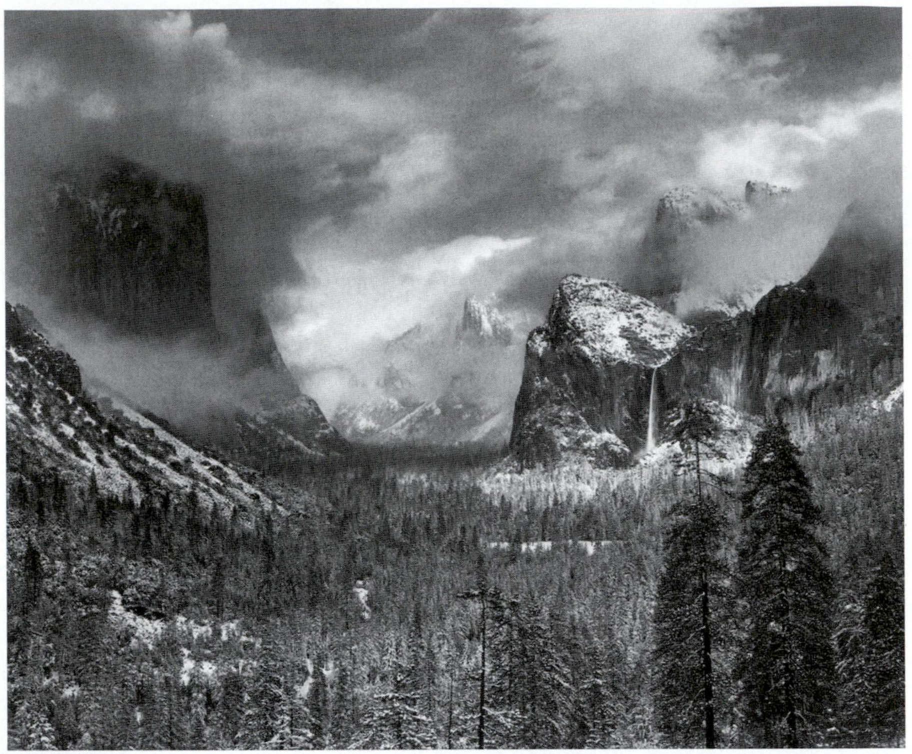

1-25 Ansel Adams, *Clearing Winter Storm,* Yosemite National Park, 1944. Photograph.

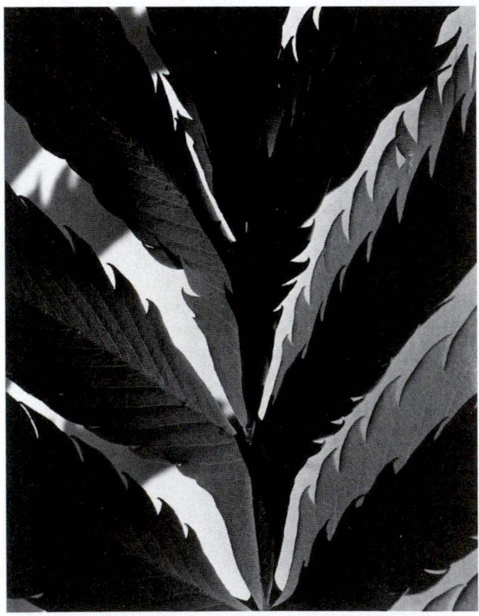

1-26 Imogen Cunningham, *Leaf Pattern,* before 1929. Gelatin silver print. © 1978 The Imogen Cunningham Trust.

its famous and terrible earthquake in the early 1900s. A weak student, he found meaning in his life when he first began hiking in Yosemite as a teenager, carrying one of the early Kodak cameras. He would explore that wilderness into his eighties and become its foremost photographer. Throughout his life, he was not only an artist, but also an important spokesperson for the environment and a leader of the Sierra Club. His images of Yosemite were meant to not only open our eyes, but also to convince us of the importance of preserving the wilderness in this great park. The rich range of tones and textures in *Clearing Winter Storm* testify to his technical mastery (he was the author of ten books on photography techniques). But his skills in the darkroom were always in the service of his vision—the spirituality, beauty, and grandeur of the natural world.

Photographic art also has the power to concentrate our vision, to focus on reality in a new way. Imogen Cunningham was a photographer who spent much of her career exploring the abstract patterns created by natural forms such as plants. Where Adams is interested in immortalizing an entire scene, Cunningham focuses on a close-up detail of her subject (**1-26**). By presenting just a leaf or a flower in sharp focus, her pictures almost seem to increase our vision, to enable us to see their subjects with a kind of superrealism. In this way, her pictures appear to stop time, reminding us of these lines by the English poet William Blake:

> To see a World in a Grain of Sand
> And a Heaven in a Wild Flower;
> Hold Infinity in the palm of your hand
> And Eternity in an hour.

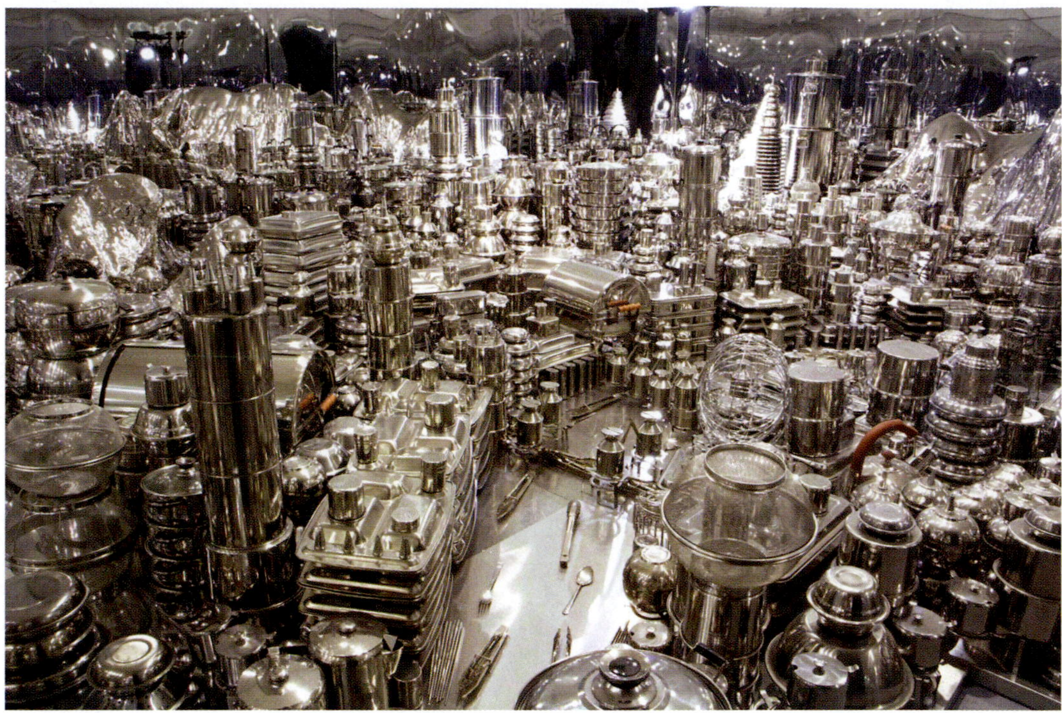

1-27 Zhan Wang, *Urban Landscape,* 2003. Stainless steel, garden rocks, pots, pans, eating utensils, and mirror. Hayward Gallery, © the artist 2006. Photo by Stephen White, Pekin Fine Arts Co. Ltd.

Cunningham's photographs act as powerful reminders that the smallest aspect of nature reflects an infinity of possibilities; there are wonders worth studying all around us.

The Power to Transform the Ordinary

One pleasure of looking at art is enjoying a feeling of amazement that an artist has magically transformed ordinary materials into a marvelous work of imagination. When one enters the room that houses the contemporary Chinese artist Zhan Wang's *Urban Landscape* (**1-27**), one is first struck by the sheer beauty of a shining, fabulous city. Viewers tower above it, as if seeing the glittering metropolis from a low-flying jet. But once our eyes adjust to the glare, we can see that the city was not built with brick, glass, or mortar. It was constructed with highly polished equipment from a restaurant's kitchen—the skyscrapers are stacked colanders, stainless steel pots and pans, and the boats in the river are forks, knives, and spoons.

Ultimately, Zhan hopes the viewers of his city will move beyond its visual brilliance. The artist, who was trained in traditional techniques at an academy, wants us to think about the impact that urbanization has had on Chinese culture. The sparkling, commercial environment of the modern Chinese city is also cold and mechanical, disconnected from age-old customs and nature. Even the mountains that surround *Urban Landscape* are made of stainless steel, like much of modern architecture. The rapid Westernization of cities, like Zhan's native Beijing, has had spectacular results but also has meant much has been lost.

Loss and urbanization were also themes in Rachel Whiteread's *House* (**1-28**), which transformed the most ordinary of materials—empty space—into sculpture.

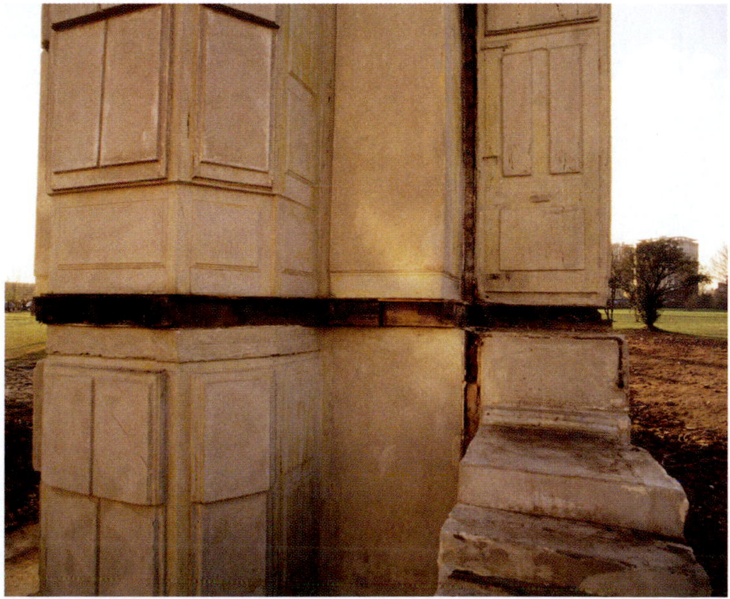

1-28 Rachel Whiteread, *House,* 1993. Commissioned by Artangel Trust and Beck's (corner of Grove Road and Roman Road, London E3, destroyed 1994). Sign placed saying "We still live here."

In the 1990s, as part of an urban renewal project, a group of townhouses were slated for demolition in East London. Whiteread asked for permission to make a cast of the spaces in the very last house before it was torn down. Unlike traditional bronze sculptures that honor heroes in a public park, Whiteread commemorated the lost homes of ordinary people. The sculpture was begun immediately after the last remaining resident left. Wet concrete was sprayed into each room. When dry, the private spaces that were once lived in, walked through, dined in, and slept in became rock-hard. Then the exterior walls were removed to reveal the huge cast sculpture. Unfortunately, *House* existed for less than three months. In order to gain permission to complete the work, the arts organization that sponsored it had to agree that it would be only temporary. Today, the site is a green lawn with no sign of either the homes or the sculpture that commemorated them. It lives, like the buildings it honored, only in memory.

Like Rachel Whiteread, the artists Christo and Jeanne-Claude had to address the concerns of local government agencies to gain permission to make their vision concrete, but their process took much longer. *The Gates* (**1-29**) in New York City's Central Park was first proposed in 1979. Municipal office after municipal office, mayor after mayor, turned them down until the project was finally approved, after four decades of proposals, in 2003. The final contract was forty-three pages long. Christo and Jeanne-Claude are veteran navigators of the formalities and red tape of government bureaucracies and, in fact, consider it part of their art process in all of their work (see Chapter 20). Their projects are not financed by art organizations or corporate sponsors but entirely by themselves. Preparatory drawings that are part of the proposal and early works of the 1950's and 1960's are sold to gather the funds. (The final cost for this project, according to the artists, was $21 million.)

In February 2005, *The Gates* were finally installed and open to the public (**1-30**). That month was chosen by Christo and Jeanne-Claude because in February, the trees are leafless and it allowed the work of art and the buildings surrounding Central Park to be seen. Few tourists venture into the normally popular park on cold winter days. Typically the park's vegetation is dreary and lifeless, with patches of dirty snow on the grass and grimy salt on the paths. But the unveiling of the outdoor artwork transformed the chilly scene into a pageant. The dull hills and fields

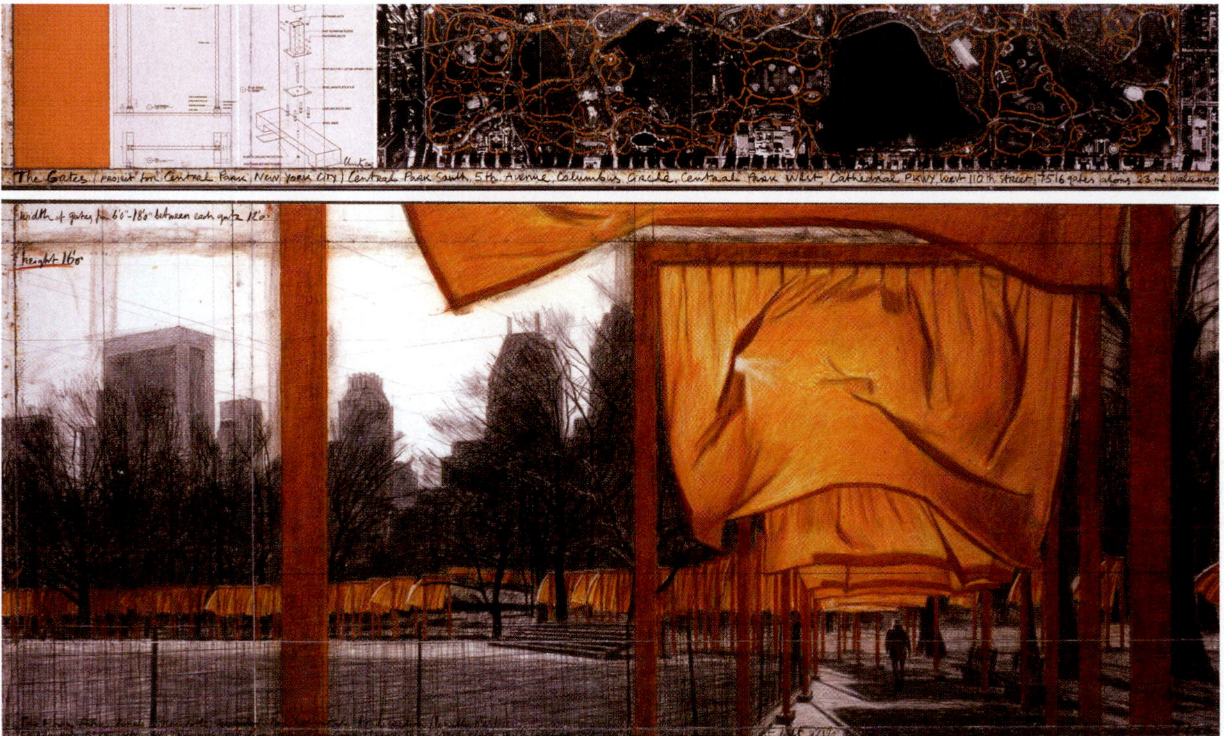

1-29 Christo, *The Gates,* Project for Central Park, New York City. Drawing in two parts, 2003. Pencil, charcoal, pastel, wax crayon,technical data, fabric sample, aerial photograph, and tape on paper; 15″ × 96″ and 42″ × 96″. Photograph: Wolfgang Volz. © Christo and Jeanne-Claude 2003.

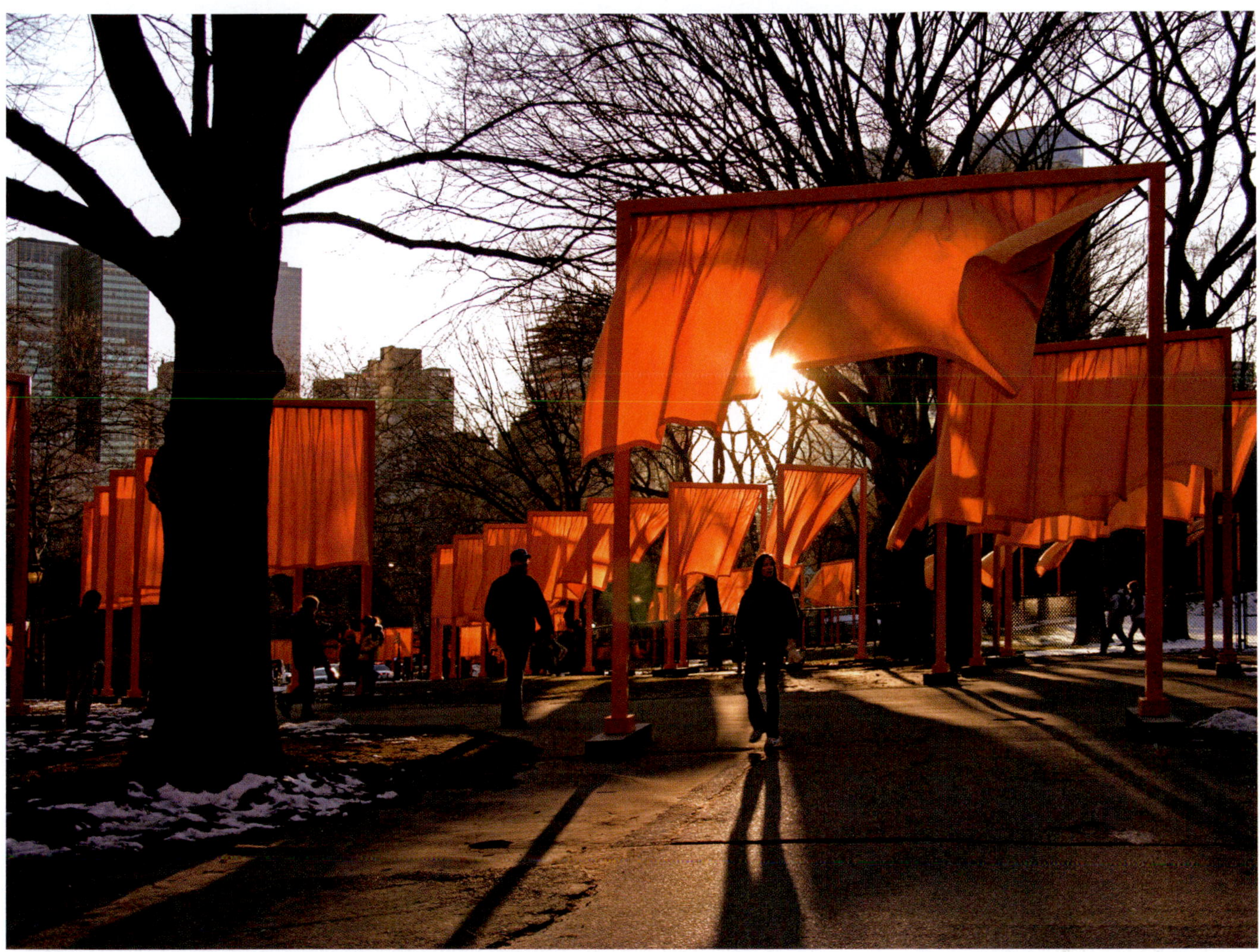

1-30 Christo and Jeanne-Claude, *The Gates*. 2005 Installation, Central Park, New York.
The Gates, Central Park, New York City, 1979-2005. Photo: Wolfgang Volz. ©Christo and Jeanne-Claude 2005

came alive with 7,503 bright saffron sails hanging from sixteen-foot gates that covered twenty-three miles of pathways. *The Gates* became an international event. Tourists and residents, families, friends, and couples were drawn to the park, and smiles could be seen everywhere as people gazed up at the saffron fabric blowing in the wind. Many veteran New Yorkers walked in parts of the park they had never visited before or noticed elements of the original landscape architects' design for the first time.

Three weeks after the installation first began, on a gray day with snow in the forecast, teams hired by Christo and Jeanne-Claude started removing all of the gates (every one of its parts later recycled). By March, Central Park was returned to its typical late winter form, but more than four million people had memories of a lovely February visit.

THE POWER OF ART FOR THE ARTIST

Without the vision and extraordinary persistence of Christo and Jeanne-Claude, there would have been no *Gates*. Of course, without artists, there wouldn't be any art. While we have been exploring the many powerful ways that art can affect and benefit us, we have yet to consider why someone would choose to make art. While a cynical observer might say artists make art to make money, those knowledgeable about art know (despite the headlines about the high prices being paid for certain artworks) that few of the millions of artists at work today will ever make a living strictly from sales of their art. The satisfactions of such a difficult and often painful occupation, then, must be more substantial than dreams of wealth.

Self-Expression

One of the most obvious and important reasons that artists make art is to satisfy the need for self-expression. Through their art, painters, sculptors, architects, photographers, printmakers, designers, and craftspeople are all able to express their personal visions. Mexican painter Frida Kahlo used self-portraits in the style of native folk art to express her own suffering. As a teenager, she suffered a terrible injury when the bus she was riding in was smashed by a trolley. Her spine and pelvis were shattered, and she spent the rest of her life in constant pain, despite thirty-five operations. In her self-portrait, *The Little Deer* (**1-31**), the many insults to her body are displayed in fantastic imagery, yet there is great strength in her face. Kahlo's willingness to use art to reveal her inner life gives her work great impact. For Kahlo, the act of creating such a picture must have had a cathartic, healing power.

The Artist at Play

Visual art has often been used to record personal and artistic suffering, yet it can be an equally effective record of the artist's joy, such as the simple joy of being creative. A sense of spontaneous playfulness, amusement, and imagination were trademarks of the German twentieth-century artist Paul Klee. Both the title of the watercolor *Dance You Monster to My Soft Song!* (inscribed in ink as part of the picture itself; **1-32**) and the way Klee drew his picture are whimsical. The gigantic monster, shaped rather like a bird cage with a bulbous red nose but tiny arms and legs, hovers precariously above the ground, while a strange piano-machine plays on. With legs akimbo and a nervous, cross-eyed look, the monster seems to fear that when the music ends he will crash to earth once more. Like many of Klee's works, the drawing has the quality of a doodle. We sense that Klee

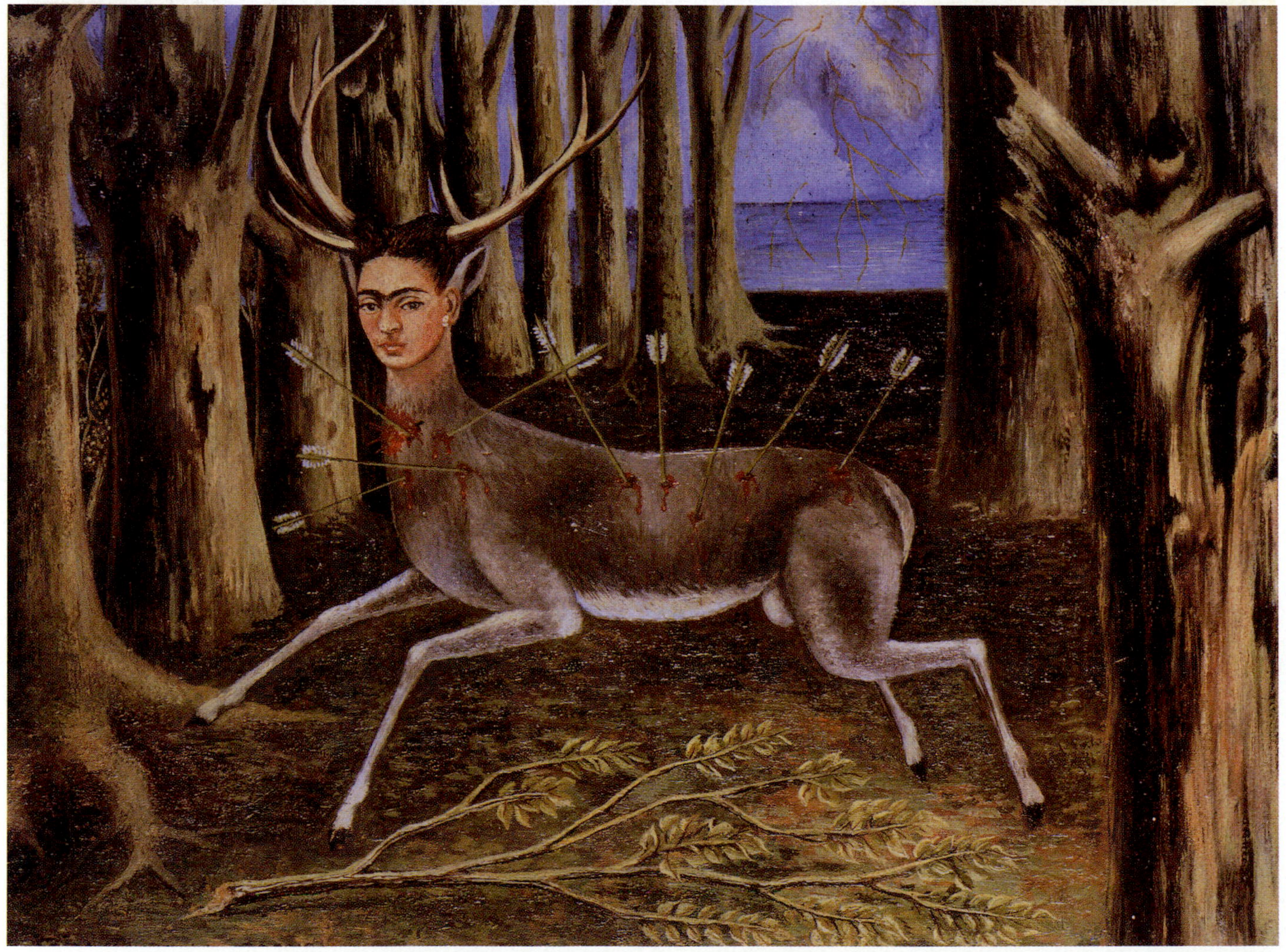

1-31 Frida Kahlo, *The Little Deer,* 1946. Oil on canvas, 8¾″ × 11¾″. Collection of Carolyn Farb, Houston.

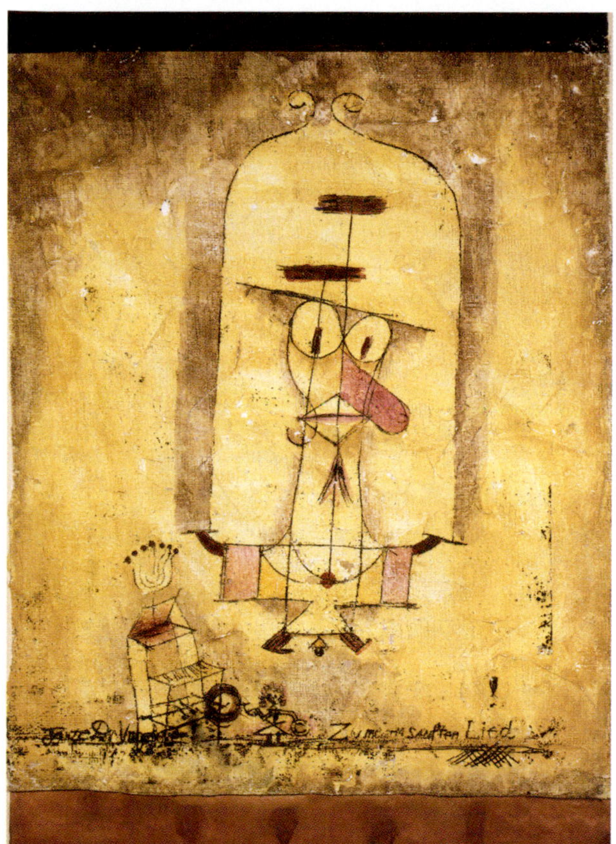

1-32 Paul Klee, *Dance You Monster to My Soft Song! (Tanze Du Ungeheuer zu meinem sanften Lied),* 1922. Watercolor and oil transfer drawing on plaster-primed gauze bordered with watercolor on the paper mount, 17¾″ × 12⅞″. Solomon R. Guggenheim Museum, New York, Gift, Solomon R. Guggenheim, 1938. Accession #38.508.

enjoyed the activity of creating this image, of using lines and colors to build these make-believe figures that could never exist in the real world.

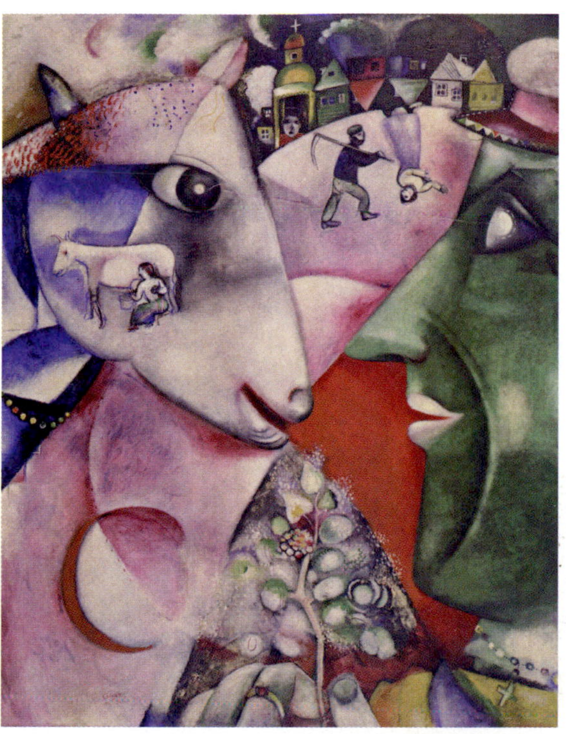

1-33 Marc Chagall, *I and the Village,* 1911. Oil on canvas, 6′ 3⅝″ × 59⅝″. Mrs. Simon Guggenheim Fund. (146.1945) The Museum of Modern Art, New York, NY, U.S.A.

The Artist's Memory

Visual art can also provide a vehicle for memory, a means of recording past experiences. One of the best-known artists to use art as a way of reliving the past was the Russian-born painter Marc Chagall. Chagall was influenced by the most advanced art movements of the twentieth century. As an impoverished young art student, he traveled to Paris and met daring artists like Pablo Picasso, who were experimenting with new ideas. Refusing to be bound by the limits of visual reality, artists at this time wanted to reach beyond what they saw to paint to what they felt, and beyond that to what they dreamed. Yet, even though his style is modern, the work of Chagall is filled with a love for the rural scenes of his childhood in Russia.

In his pictures, time and gravity have no power; people and animals whirl through the heavens regardless of the rules of nature. Looking at *I and the Village* (**1-33**), we see a friendly cow and a man holding a flowering twig in his fingers, looking face to face, united visually by a red disc. The huge cow seems benign and almost as if it is about to speak to the green man, or kiss him. Smaller figures also appear: a young woman milking, a man with a scythe walking to the harvest, a woman placed upside down who seems to be gesturing him forward, a child's face peeking over the edge of a hill behind which the tiny buildings of the village appear both right-side up and upside down.

Throughout his long career (he lived to be ninety-six), Chagall used art to create a magical land of love and wonder—remarkable for a man whose life encompassed two world wars, the Russian Revolution, and the Holocaust (in the 1940s, Chagall, who was Jewish, was forced to flee from his home in France to the United States). In this sense, Chagall's work is a tribute to the power of art to transcend political realities and allow the artist to regain a lost world with memory and imagination.

DEFINING ART

The source of the term art is the Latin word *ars,* which meant "skill." Although this is the oldest meaning of **art,** it is no longer the most common meaning. For us, the realm of the arts suggests *creative* endeavors and includes an entire range of activities classified as *cultural*. These creative arts are often subdivided into the broad categories of the *performing arts* (such as theatre, music, and dance), the *literary arts* (such as poetry, essays, and novels), and the *visual arts.*

In everyday conversation, however, most people assume art means visual art, art that we experience primarily through our sense of sight. Saying that someone is an artist usually suggests that he or she draws, paints, sculpts, or designs. This is the meaning of art that this book will be using. We define the visual arts to include the artistic media of painting, sculpture, and architecture, as well as outstanding examples of drawing, printmaking, photography, design, digital art, decorative arts, and crafts. They are usually subdivided into the **fine arts** (such as painting, printmaking and sculpture) and the **applied arts** (such as architecture and design). For centuries, in Western art, paintings and sculptures have usually been seen as a higher form of artistic production than *applied* (or useful) arts, such as book illustration or wallpaper. However, for the last one hundred years or so, this distinction has not been as important. In Eastern art, there has never been such a division. For example, in the Chinese master Han Kan's *Night Shining White* from the eighth century (**1-34**), the calligraphy on the scroll was considered just as expressive and as much pure art as the painting of the horse.

A work of fine art is usually an original, or one of a kind, creation. Each work of art is the result of the artist's personal effort, the touch of his or her hands, the fresh invention of the artist's mind, spirit,

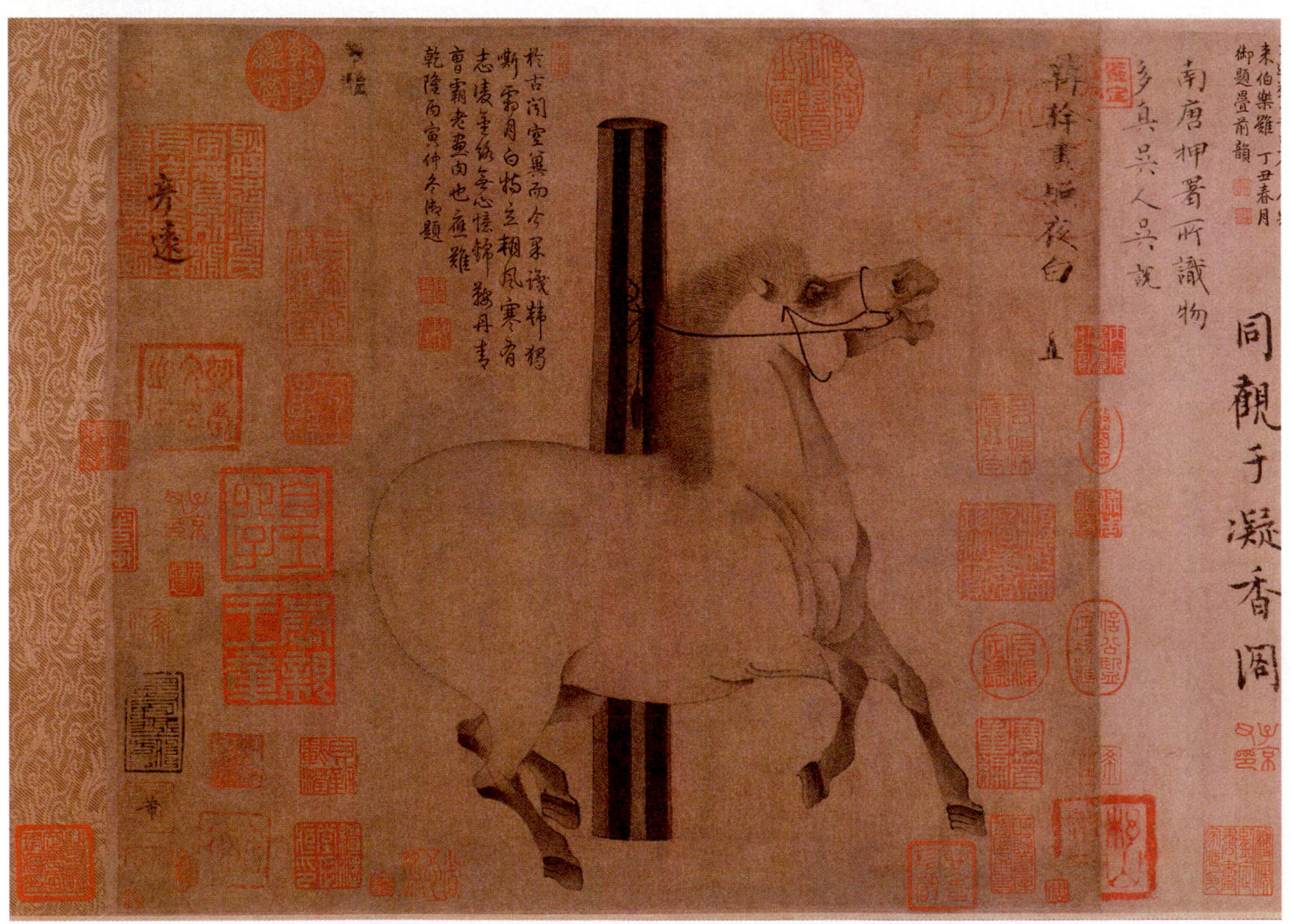

1-34 *Night Shining White,* attributed to Han Kan, 740–756. Album leaf, ink on paper, 11¾″ high. Metropolitan Museum of Art, New York.

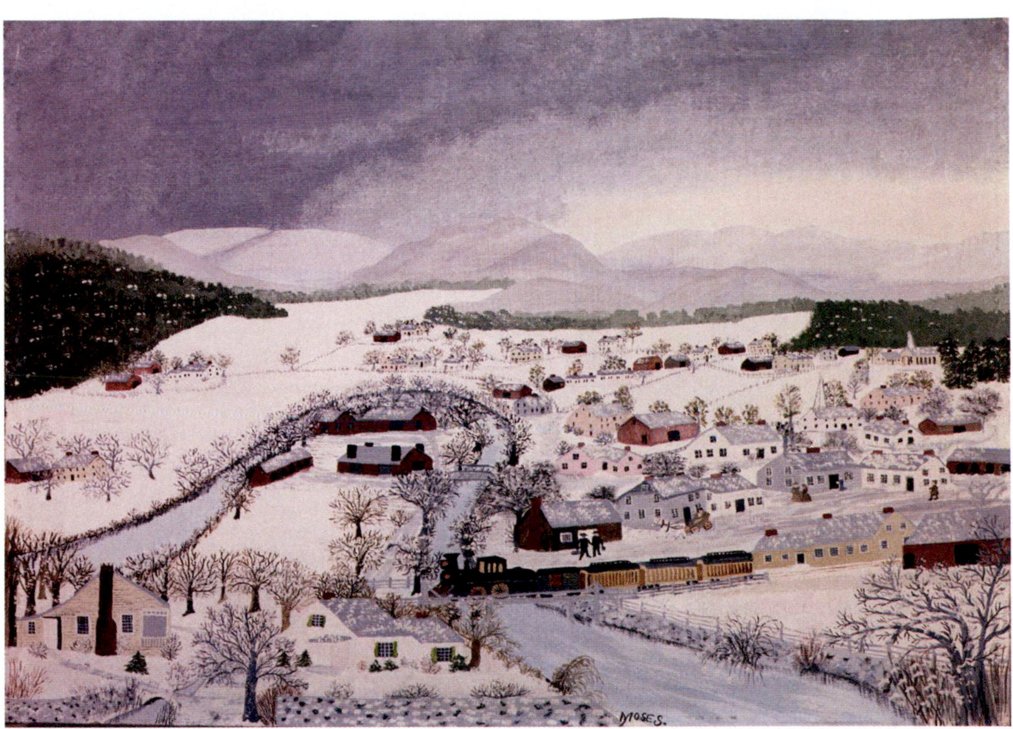

1-35 Grandma Moses, *Hoosick Falls, N.Y. in winter 1944.* Oil on masonite, 19¾″ × 23¾″. Acquired 1949, The Phillips Collection, Washington, D.C. © 1973 (renewed 2001) Grandma Moses Properties Co., New York.

and talent. There are exceptions to this rule. Prints, whether traditional or digital, for instance, are produced in a series from an original "plate" or digital image designed by the artist. Photographs, which were once thought of as mere mechanical reproductions of reality, have also been elevated to the status of fine art. Although their artistic merit has been recognized, however, prints and photographs are usually less valued (and less expensive) than drawings, paintings, or sculptures by the same artists. This reflects the fact that the work is not unique; it has been duplicated. A black-and-white print by a great photographer, however, is far more valuable than the painting of a mediocre artist.

Folk Art

Art is generally considered to be **folk art** rather than fine art when it is the work of untrained artists working in rural areas. Folk art includes painting, sculpture, and all the decorative arts, but where a fine art chest may be made of ebony inlaid with ivory, the folk chest will be a simple wood box painted in bright colors. American folk art has become very popular in recent years and commands high prices in antique stores and galleries; whole museums and galleries are devoted to folk art collections.

A good example of a folk (sometimes called "naive") artist is Grandma Moses, who was born on a farm in New York State in 1860 but did not really begin painting until the 1930s, when she was almost eighty. Although she had no formal training, her pictures (**1-35**) became so popular that by the time she died in 1961, she was a household word in the United States, and her scenes were reproduced on everything from greeting cards to kitchen curtains. Although she is not as well known today as she was at the height of her popularity in the 1950s, Grandma Moses's talent transformed an elderly farm widow, suffering from arthritis, into a nationally famous personality.

The power of her art lies in its freshness and vitality. Through her pictures, Anna Mary Robertson Moses had the chance not only to recreate and in a sense relive her own past but also to share that world with her viewers. Her most popular subjects included maple sugaring, winter sleighing, scenes of old-fashioned farm life, celebrations of holidays, and the seasons. As she concludes in her autobiography:

> In my childhood days life was different, in many ways, we were slower, still we had a good and happy life, I think, people enjoyed life more in their way, at least they seemed to be happier, they don't take the time to be happy nowadays.

Craft and Decorative Art

When artists create useful or functional objects, such as ceramic pots, glass vases, silver bowls, woven rugs, and even wooden chairs, these are typically put in the category of *crafts* or *decorative arts.*

A good example is a Navaho "eye-dazzler" rug (**1-36**). Woven and designed by Native American women in the late nineteenth century, these blankets have a strong visual impact because of their bold use of color and simple geometric designs. These weavings were named "eye-dazzlers" because of their use of new, brighter yarn that became available to the American Indians during this period. Although purists and collectors tended to prefer blankets made with native vegetable dyes, the weavers embraced the new colors. It is not surprising that modern artists in search of a purely visual art have been inspired by these blankets and other decorative arts, such as quilts. The decoration of useful objects has been a source of visual pleasure for viewers in many ages and cultures.

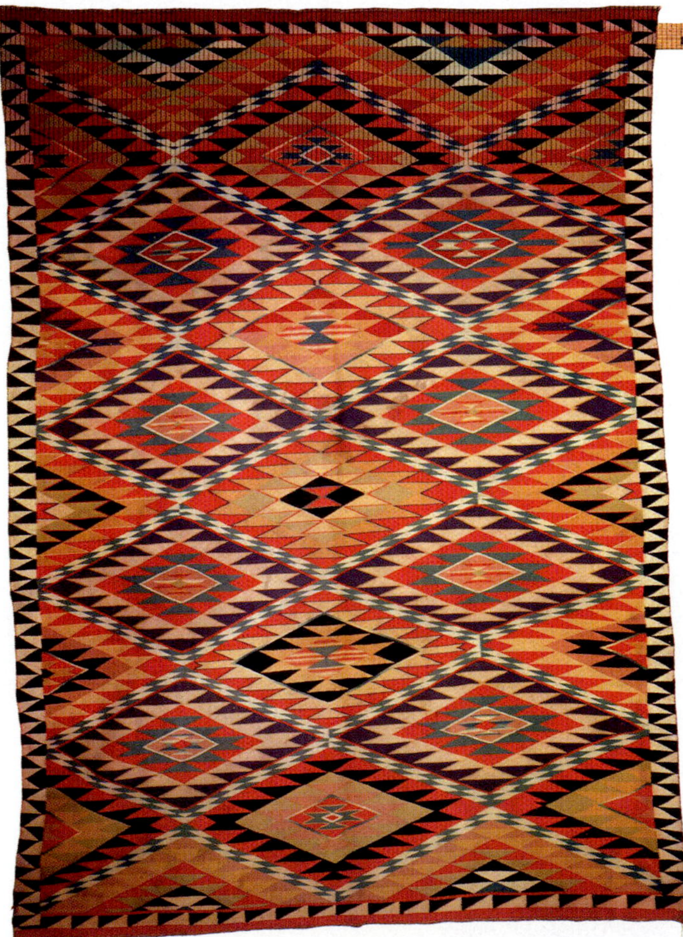

1-36 Germantown "eye-dazzler" rug, Navajo, 1880–1890. Split wool yarn, 2, 3, and 4 ply, 72″ × 50″. Museum of Northern Arizona, Flagstaff.

The term *crafts* is also often used to describe contemporary objects that are handmade. Craft art is perhaps the most popular way of appreciating and practicing art in our society. Many people who would be afraid to invest in an original sculpture are perfectly comfortable buying a hand-thrown pot, while individuals who insist that they "can't draw a straight line" enjoy classes on weaving or wood carving. While some art historians and critics still think that such things as jewelry should not be considered art at all, attitudes are changing. Imaginative metal, fiber, and woodwork are now generally included in international surveys of design.

Design

What about functional items that are mass produced? Are they part of the world of visual arts? A broad definition of art would certainly include manufactured objects that are well designed—in fact, the Museum of Modern Art in New York devotes an entire section to outstanding examples of such objects as telephones, typewriters, and even helicopters. This field of art is known as **industrial design.**

An industrial designer must understand both art and engineering. Industrial design is the aesthetic refinement of products, making functional engineering solutions easy to use and understand, and attractive. The phrase "user-friendly" neatly conveys the goal of all industrial designers. One of the most successful containers ever designed is the Coca-Cola bottle (**1-37**), recognized around the world and used with only modest modification for nearly a century. The bottle not only must hold soda but also dispense it easily and only on demand. The narrow opening provides a continuous but not choking flow. The wide bottom makes sure it rests easily on a table without spilling. The bottle's curvaceous shape allows it to fit comfortably in one hand, the pattern of ribs ensuring that a cold, wet piece of glass does not slip and cheat us of our refreshment.

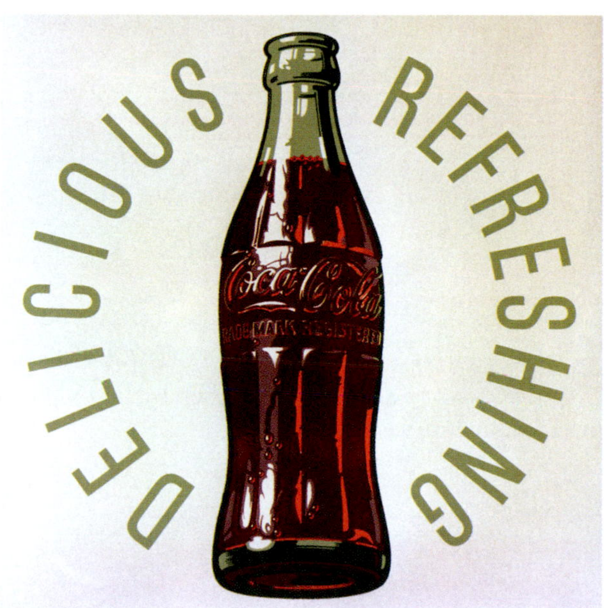

1-37 Alex Samuelson and T. Clyde Edwards, Coca-Cola 6.5-ounce glass bottle. The Coca-Cola Company.

The name "Coca-Cola" is, of course, featured prominently on the bottle. In fact, the ribs on the bottle subtly lead our eyes to the smooth center where it is displayed. This *logo* or trademark was the work of a *graphic designer.* **Graphic design,** sometimes called *commercial art,* includes two-dimensional designs that are mass-produced, such as logos, magazine layouts, decorative posters, and the cover of this book. Much thought and effort goes into every aspect of a logo, since it represents the company. The script Coca-Cola logo implies a product that has been tested by time, but the more modern typefaces that surround it make sure we know it is meant for young and old alike.

While representing a company is certainly important, graphic designers who design currency have the challenge of representing an entire nation and its people. For the arrival of a new millennium in 2000, a team of designers in New Zealand were given the task of designing a special commemorative $10 bill (**1-38**). Their mission was to represent the country's past and future and to capture the "kiwi spirit." In

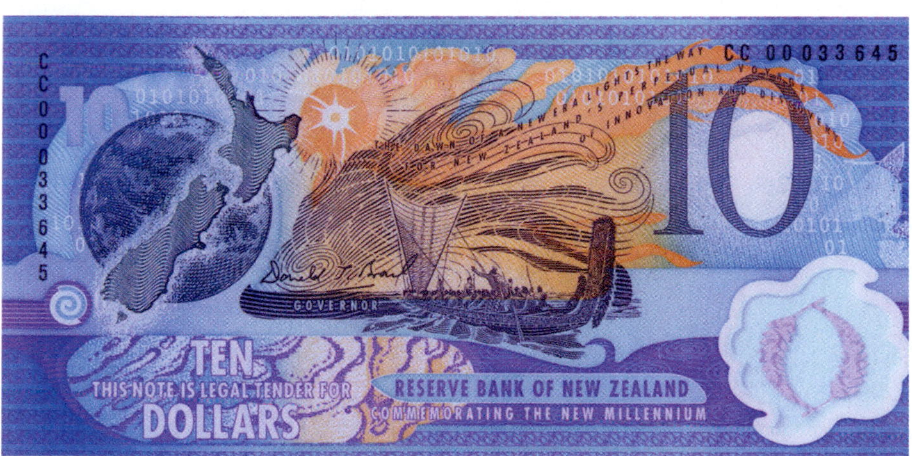

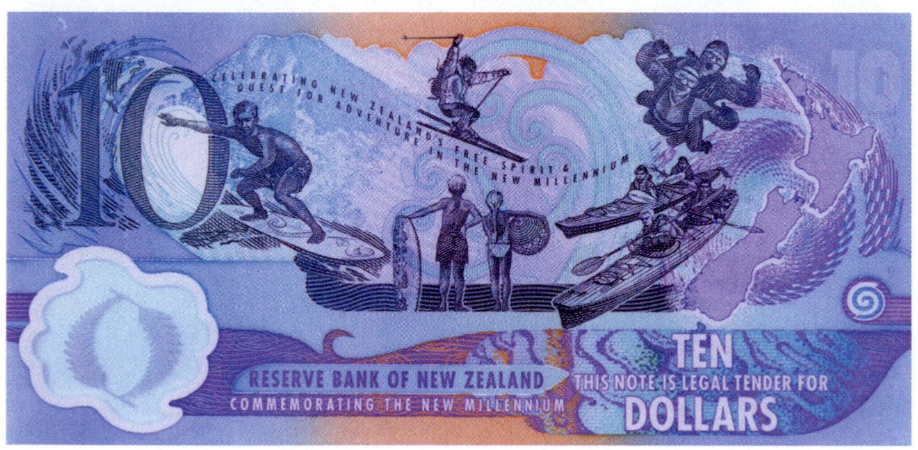

1-38 New Zealand $10 bill, front and reverse.

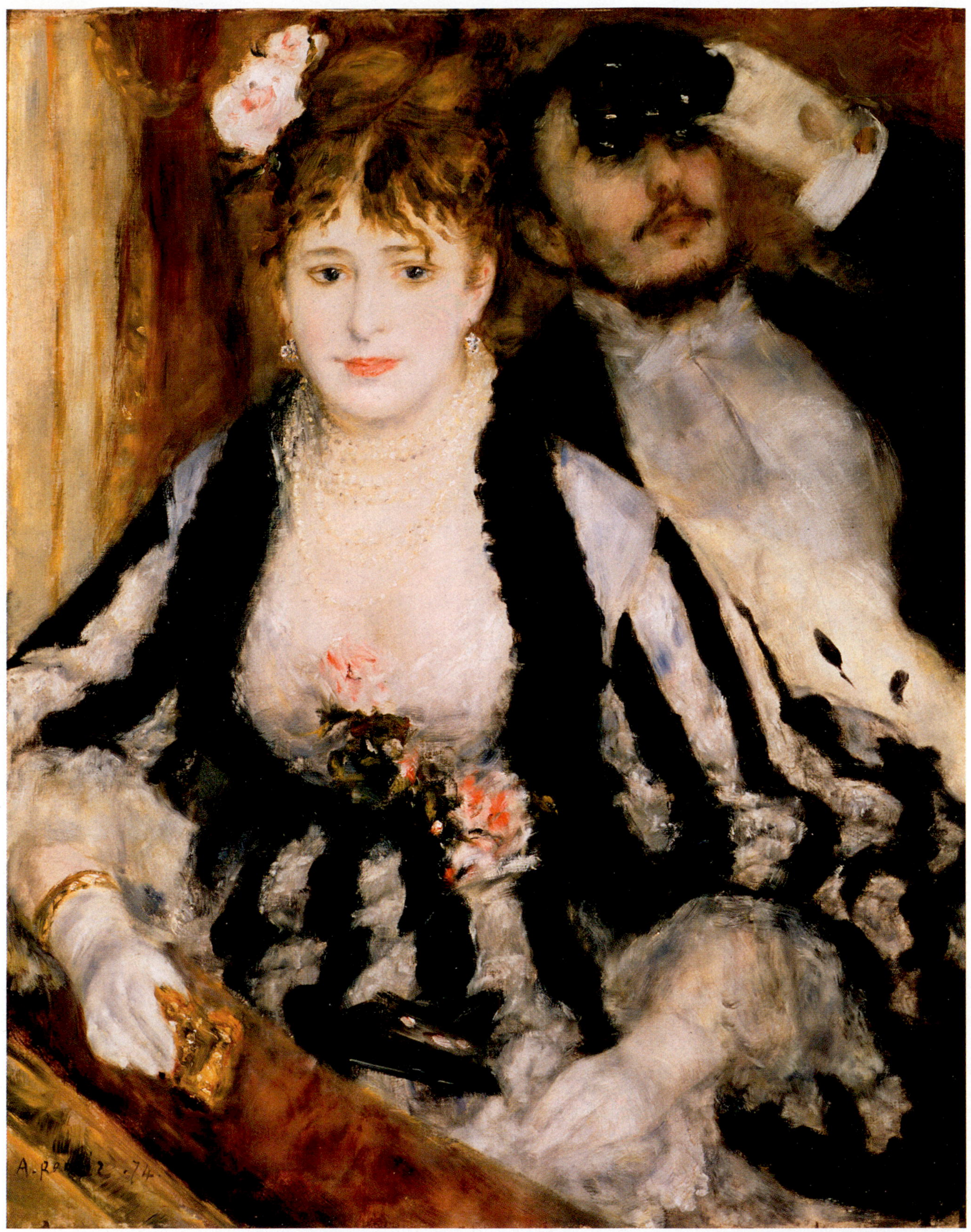

1-39 Pierre-Auguste Renoir, *La Loge,* 1874. Oil on canvas, 31″ × 25″. Courtauld Institute Galleries, London (Courtauld Collection).

addition, they needed to integrate security measures that are essential elements in contemporary banknotes. Naturally, the bill also needed to be clear, attractive, and functional.

The designers succeeded brilliantly and in a fashion quite unlike the stale approach of many other nations. While patterns are used in almost all currency to make counterfeiting difficult, the flowing decorations on the front of the bill are attractive and significant. They are a mix of traditional Maori art, Pacific shell patterns, and digital numbers symbolizing new technologies. At the center, a Maori war canoe plunges toward us—the boat that brought the first settlers to New Zealand. At the right, a satellite dish represents the latest communication media. The reverse of the bill is meant to symbolize the Kiwi spirit of adventure. Surfers, skiers, kayakers, and sky divers surround children at the center. The bill is made of polymer and incorporates the most advanced security features available. As in all aspects of the millennium note's design, this function is joined seamlessly with meaning and aesthetics. The silver ferns in the transparent window at the corner reflect rainbow light when shifted. Within the "0" of the number 10 is a watermark of a sacred Maori head that symbolizes ancestral figures and heaven.

Art Is Beauty

Many people think art must be beautiful to qualify as great art. For them, the primary power of visual art is its ability to delight the eye. Art that is visually pleasing seems to justify itself and needs no other reason to exist. "A feast for the eyes" is one way to describe this type of artwork. This *was* the chief criteria for fine art over several centuries but is no longer accepted as the only or even a vital issue today. As we begin our study of art, it is also important to keep in mind that standards of beauty are not universal. Aesthetic taste can vary with different cultures and time periods.

For example, when the **Impressionists** first exhibited their work in late nineteenth-century Paris, it was rejected as hideously ugly. In fact, one critic accused them of "making war on beauty!" To the ordinary viewer of 1874, pictures like Pierre-Auguste Renoir's *La Loge* (**1-39**) seemed unfinished and crude. Today people flock to see the same work, which looks to the modern eye not only beautiful but also impossibly sweet, romantically ideal.

Although many people assume that visual art should be beautiful, or at least realistic (and preferably both), you will find many artworks in museums that do not fit this mold. Some great works of art get their power from the depiction of "ugly" subjects or the distortion of forms. The subjects are not beautiful or realistically portrayed. Willem de Kooning's *Woman and Bicycle* (**1-40**) is a good example of the kind of painting that upsets some people today as much as the work of the Impressionists did a hundred years ago. "My child (or dog) could do a better job" is not an uncommon reaction to this type of artwork. Viewers are often upset by what they consider the gratuitous ugliness of such modern art.

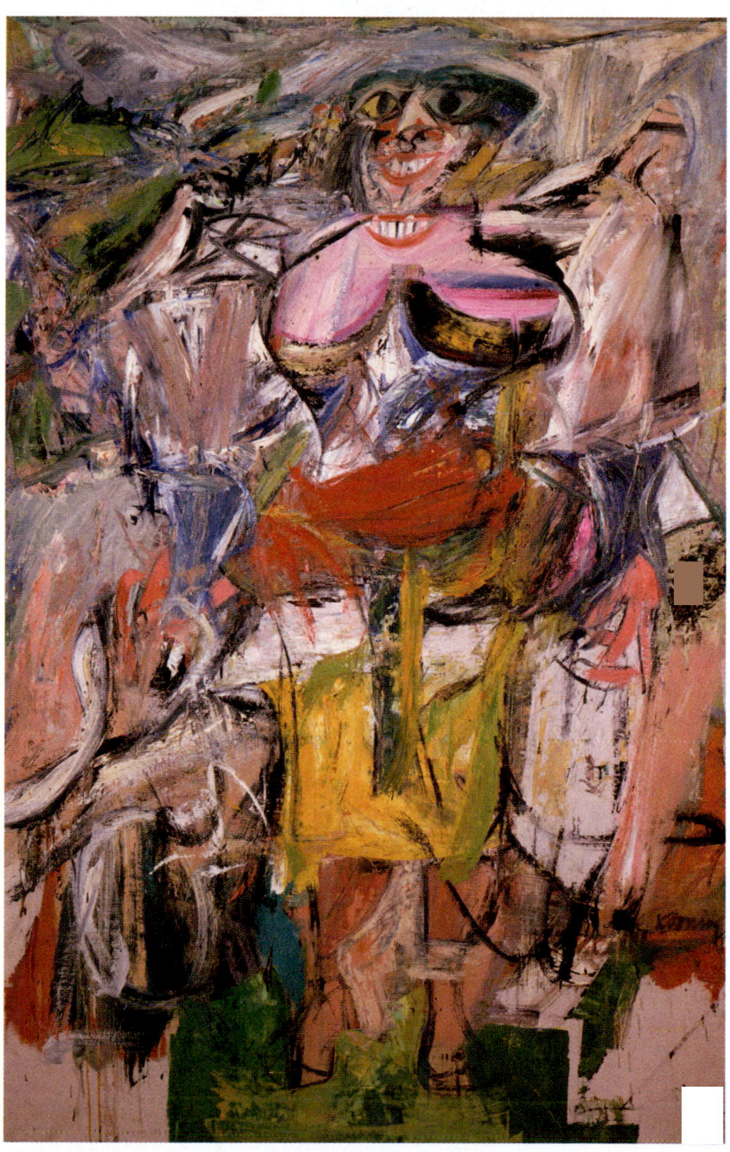

1-40 Willem de Kooning, *Woman and Bicycle,* 1952–1953. Oil on canvas, 6′ 4½″ × 4′ 1″. Collection of the Whitney Museum of American Art, New York (purchase 55.35).

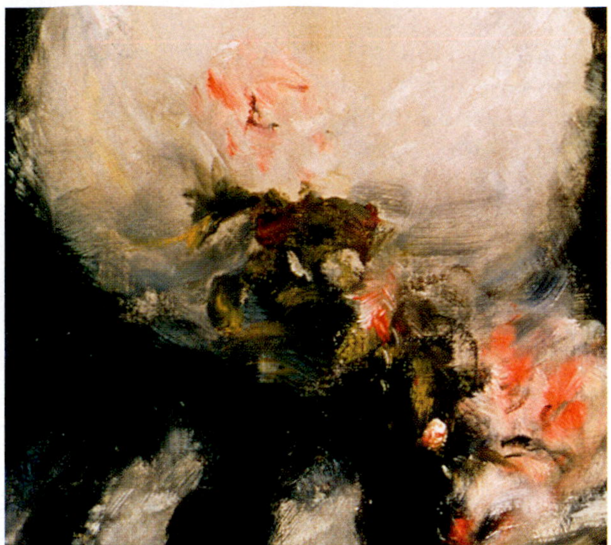

1-41 Detail of figure 1-39.

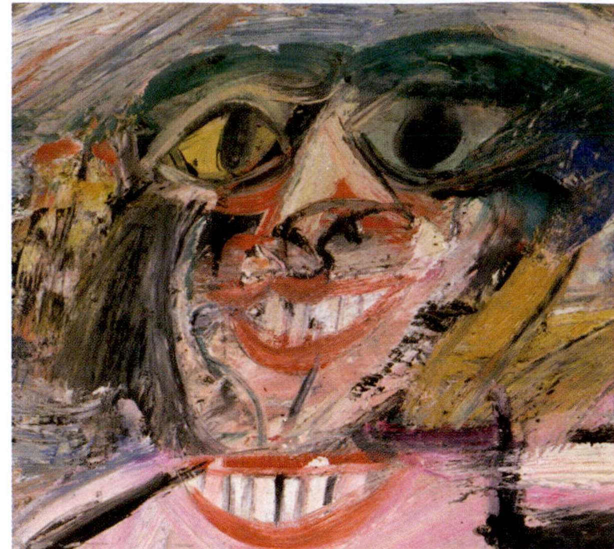

1-42 Detail of figure 1-40.

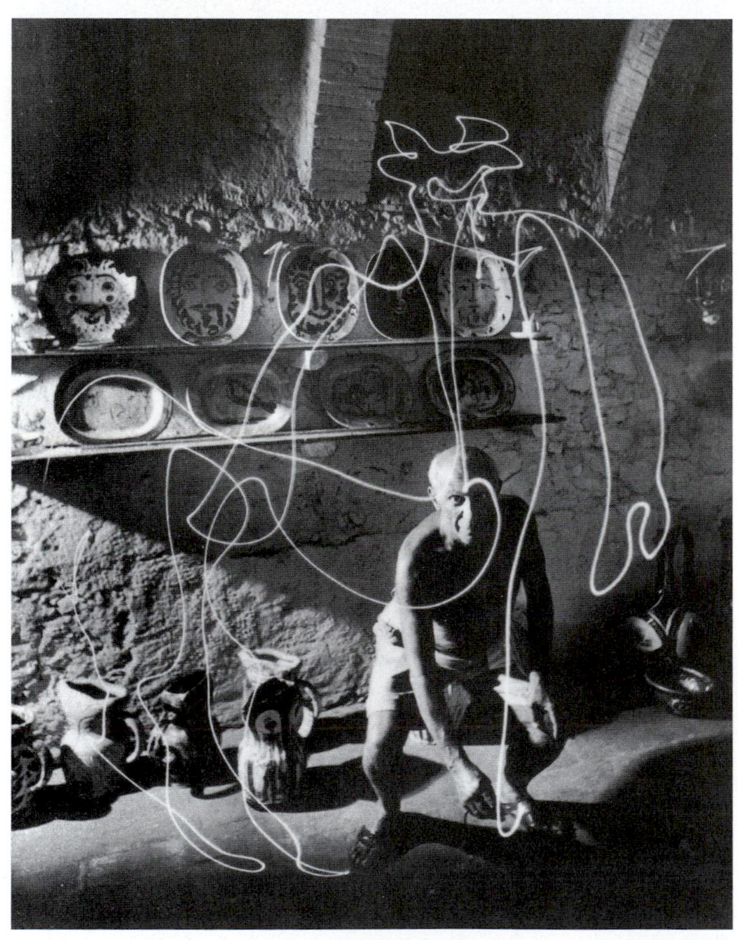

1-43 Gjon Mili, Pablo Picasso drawing a centaur with light, 1950.

As different as they appear at first glance, upon reflection Renoir's and de Kooning's pictures of women do share certain attitudes about art. Both are committed to loose, expressive brushstrokes (see details, **1-41**, **1-42**). Neither artist feels it is necessary to be absolutely precise and descriptive; they feel that art can hint rather than be dogmatic. Both believe in the use of colors to communicate emotion. Even though they are painting eighty years apart, the artists share a philosophy of art that stresses expressiveness. De Kooning's paintings can be seen as a more radical development of the ideas that made Renoir's approach seem unique in the nineteenth century.

Art Is Originality and Creativity

The pictures of Renoir and de Kooning share not only a belief in expressiveness but also a belief in the value of originality. It is often said that the one thing that sets great art apart is its originality. The accepted idea is that a work of art should be a unique creation, the expression of the individuality of the artist. Those artists whom we consider greatest, like Pablo Picasso (**1-43**), kept developing from one successful style to another, always searching for a new mode of visual expression. The photograph (page 32) shows him experimenting with drawing with light, something only possible to see in a photograph. He is in his pottery studio, ceramics being only one of the many media he explored. This constant striving for newness and originality sets him apart from the artists of the cave paintings and the Ancient Egyptians, who repeated a similar style for centuries according to a strict set of rules, or artistic formulas.

Generally, since the beginning of the twentieth century, the word *imitation* is usually associated with unoriginality rather than superior art. But in the last fifty years, even the idea of originality has been challenged by contemporary artists. As aware residents in a world of mass production, mass consumption, and mass media, some artists have created a kind of mass-produced art. Andy Warhol, for instance, became famous for his multiplication of images, as in *30 Are Better Than One (Mona Lisa)* (**1-44**). Using a stenciling technique, Warhol appropriated someone else's design—in this case Leonardo's *Mona Lisa*—and repeated it to create a new work of art. He created similar pictures using such popular images as Campbell's soup cans and identical photographs of Marilyn Monroe. It is rather amusing to see art collectors today attempting to sort out the "genuine" Warhols from the work of his followers and fakes. This is especially difficult since Warhol's work was done in his studio, known as "The Factory," where assistants often made art while Warhol acted out his role as a famous artist, going to parties and talking to the press.

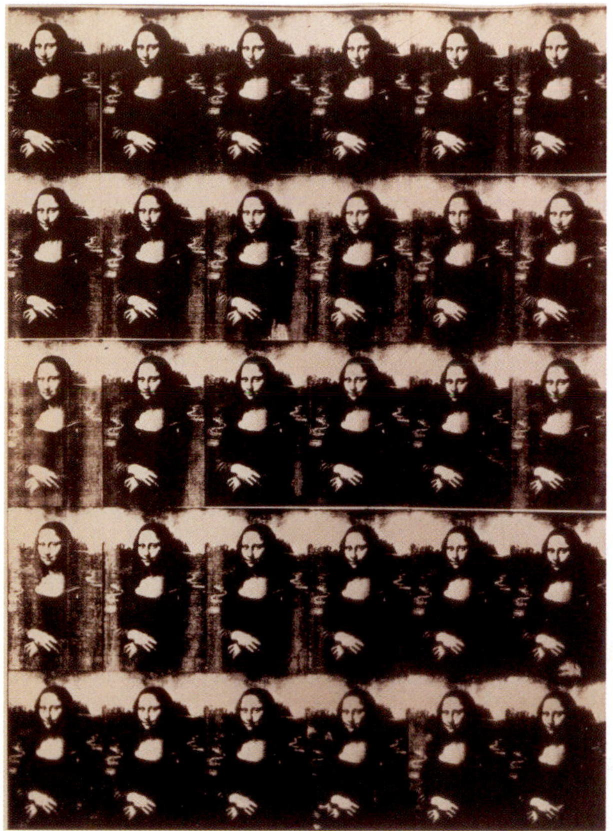

1-44 Andy Warhol, *30 Are Better Than One (Mona Lisa),* 1963. Silkscreen ink on synthetic polymer paint on canvas, 9′ 2″ × 7′ 10½″. © 1993 The Andy Warhol Foundation for the Visual Arts, Inc.

Ways to Understand Art

If our goal is to achieve a fuller knowledge and appreciation of art, we should avoid utilizing only one theory and excluding much of what might be relevant to a work of art. We have already seen that art has a variety of purposes and aspects. No single theory has yet been able to encompass them all in a useful way. To try to fence art in for the sake of any theory seems senseless. No one can determine in advance which questions or information might increase our understanding of a particular work of art. To understand art, our primary question should be, *Why does it look this way?*

The viewer begins with the object itself. The main function of any work of art is to provoke aesthetic interest. But art should also be intelligible to the viewer. Integral to its success are formal concerns: its design and composition. In Chapters 2 and 3, we will study the elements of art and design to understand the structural language of art objects. Examination of the work of art should yield a sense of the artist's mastery of design principles like harmony, balance, rhythm, and pattern. No one element is essential, but if one is missing, its neglect must be justified by a special reason. For example, a chaotic effect might be explained by the artist's desire to reflect the frenzy of modern life. Or it could simply be a lack of the skill necessary to organize the subject matter. In Chapters 4 through 11, the materials and techniques used by artists will be studied. One generally expects an artist to control the necessary means to reach his or her goal. However, skillful handling of materials is what a philosopher would call "a necessary but not sufficient condition." In other words, the presence of technical skills does not necessarily create a work of art, but its absence would require an explanation, like "I am rejecting traditional concepts of skill, which I associate with a dead tradition." As we will see, it is common in the Western art of the last 150 years for artists to invent new techniques rather than follow past practices.

The Artist and the Art

This textbook accepts the notion (not universal, but generally accepted) that the more we know about the conditions under which an artwork was produced, the better we will see it. This includes exploring aspects of an artist's biography that might be relevant. When was the artwork made? What were the artist's previous works? Can we see a progression? What ideas were current then? Was it left unfinished, or can we assume that it was meant to be seen this way? Can we determine the artist's intentions? What did the artist believe in? Even personal questions like, "Who were the artist's friends?" could have an impact on a particular work if some of an artwork's conception was influenced by discussion with a group of artists.

Few artists have been as generous in providing their influences as the nineteenth-century painter Gustave Courbet was in his huge painting *Studio of a Painter: A Real Allegory Summarizing My Seven Years of Life as an Artist* (**1-45**). Courbet called himself a Realist painter, setting himself against the popular movements of his time in France, Neo-Classicism and Romanticism (see Chapters 16 and 17). He rejected grand historical subjects or religious images and once said, "Show me an angel and I'll paint one!" The artist believed that his work was and should be a product of his own experiences, not imagined myths or scenes from the past that he never witnessed. In his studio, we can see the artist at the center, painting a landscape of the woods near his home, with two admirers—a small boy and a nude model (perhaps his son and mistress). At either side are friends (among them well-known philosophers and writers) and local townspeople. Courbet came from a farming family, and he often depicted working-class people from all walks of life in his paintings. This upset viewers, because in his time, people from the lower classes were considered not suitable for high art. Nor was an honest depiction of a nude woman. Nudes were generally given names from mythology, like Venus or Aphrodite, to justify their appearance. When his painting was rejected by an official jury, Courbet took the unusual step of exhibiting the nineteen-foot-wide picture at a

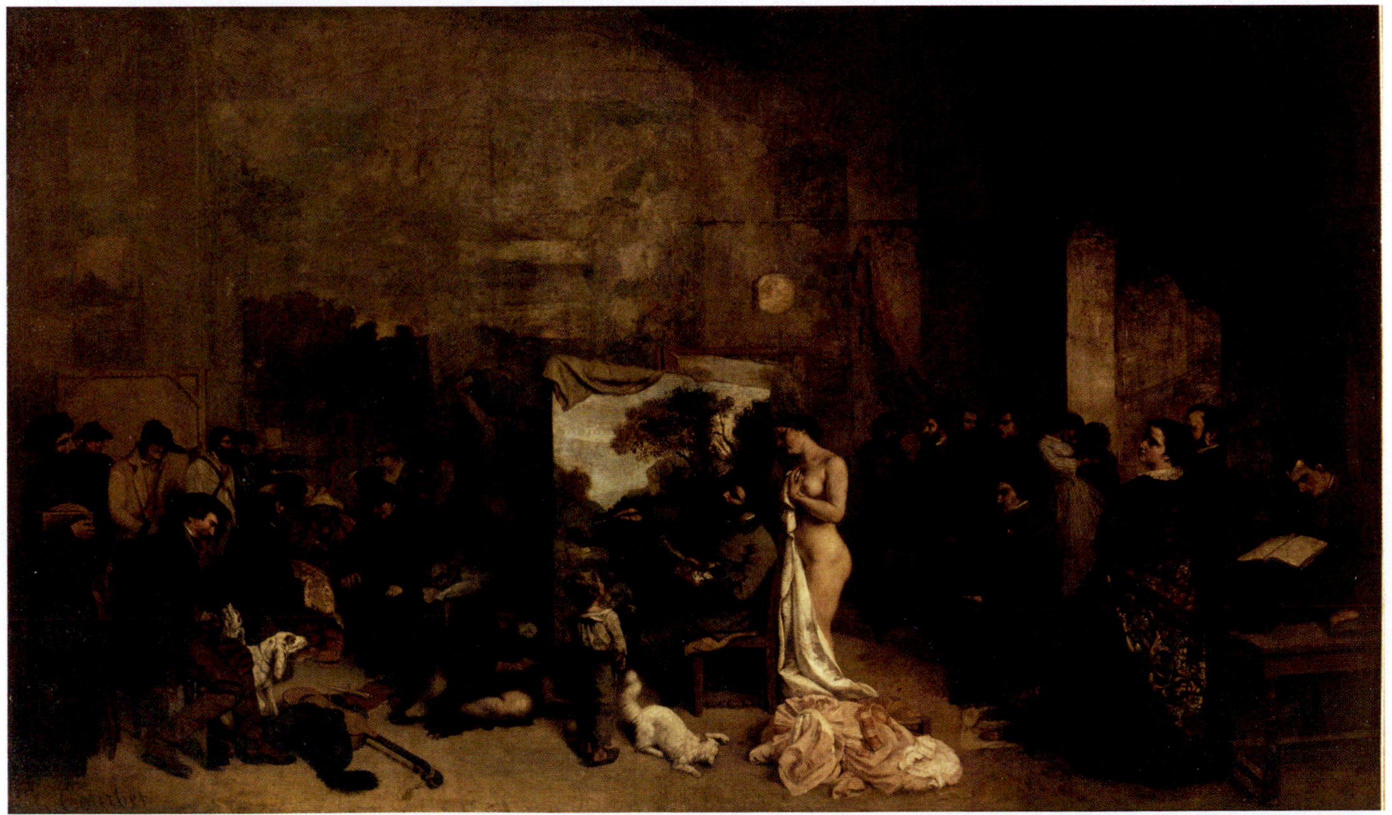

1-45 Gustave Courbet, *Studio of a Painter: A Real Allegory Summarizing My Seven Years of Life as an Artist,* 1854–1855. Oil on canvas, 11′ 10″ × 19′ 7″. Musee d'Orsay, Paris.

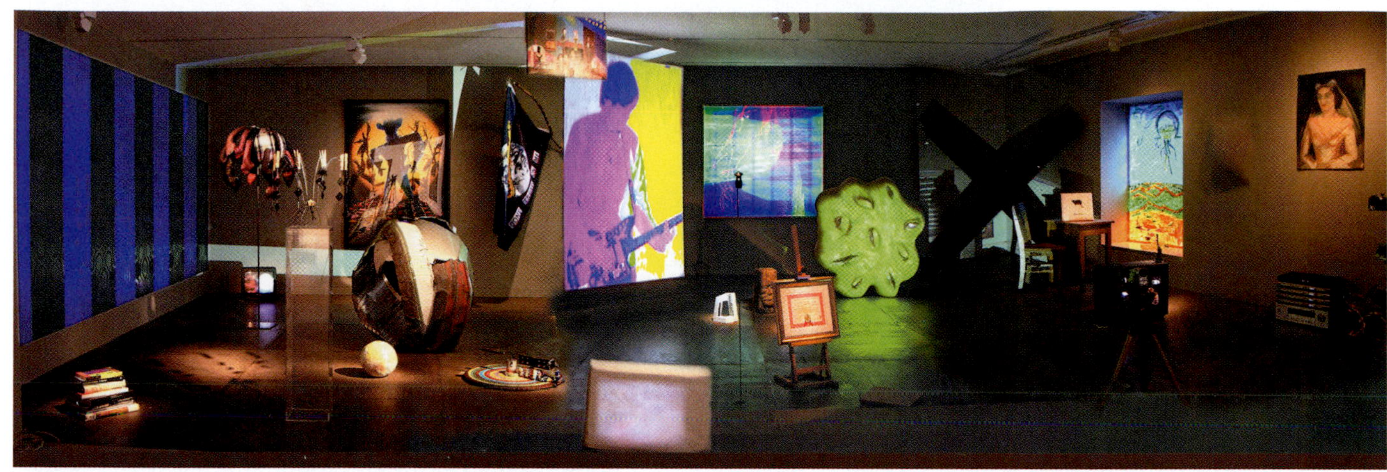

1-46 Tony Oursler, *Studio: Seven Months of my Aesthetic Education (and then some),* 2005. Mixed media installation.

pavilion he paid for himself at the Paris World's Fair of 1855.

The message of *Studio* seems to be that Courbet's approach to art cannot be fully understood without considering where he grew up and who his friends and acquaintances were. Yet Courbet's *Studio,* while designed to be a work of its time, is not only a product of his past but also the past of art history. It was clearly affected in style and subject by a past master who Courbet admired—the Spanish Baroque painter Diego Velazquez's painting of his studio in the royal palace, *Las Meninas* (see 15-17).

Art and Art History

The relationship of an artwork to art history can be a significant matter in determining whether an artwork is significant or inconsequential. Even an artist's rejection of tradition requires an understanding of the tradition—since the artist is still conducting a dialog with it. This is why an artist is often described as "naive" if he or she is unaware of art history. Like all of us, the artist is conditioned and affected by the past. This is no weakness or sign of lack of originality. If there could ever be an entirely original artistic genius, this individual would most likely be a sad genius indeed. The art theorist R. G. Collingwood has written eloquently on Modern Art's love of novelty:

> If an artist may say nothing, except what he has invented with his own sole efforts, it stands to reason he will be poor in ideas.... If he could take what he wants wherever he could find it, as Euripides and Dante and Michelangelo and Shakespeare and Bach were free, his larder will always be full and his cookery . . . be worth tasting. . . . Let all artists . . . plagiarize each other's works like men . . . modern artists should treat each other as Greek dramatists or Renaissance painters or Elizabethan poets did. If anyone thinks that the law of copyright has fostered better art than those barbarian times could produce, I will not try to convert them.

Today, the once revolutionary Courbet's *Studio* is firmly part of the tradition of artist's portraying their studios and has influenced many artists who came after him. Obviously, the title of Tony Oursler's multimedia installation *Studio: Seven Months of my Aesthetic Education (and then some)* (**1-46**) tells us that he designed his installation as a response to the earlier painting. While it is certainly a unique and imaginative work, one of the pleasures of studying it is comparing it mentally with Courbet's nineteenth-century masterpiece. In fact, they were once exhibited next to each other in Paris. But the twenty-first-century artist Oursler created a three-dimensional environment, so the viewer can walk into the studio and experience it in a new way. In addition to housing a collection of his own projects (see 9-25), he invited other artists, musicians, and directors with whom he had collaborated in the past to place examples of their own work. They were also people who he felt were important influences on him. For Oursler, a studio depicts more than an artist's place of work but "a model of the artist's mind, process and world view."

WHEN WE KNOW MORE, WE SEE MORE

This chapter presents ways to better understand and judge art. It is important to remember that an artwork need not be perfect; even a great work of art can fail in some ways and still be a masterpiece. Understanding art is similar to understanding people; the process is never finished but continually deepens as more is discovered. This is part of the power of art. The serious viewer studies the background of a work, which is far more than the white walls and polished wood floor of a gallery. The background can include the artist's biography, inner psychology, and the traditions and society that influenced the artist. All of these elements can tell us why the artist chose to make the artwork look the way it does. No background is absolutely necessary (just as we can appreciate people without knowing everything about them), but the appreciation of a work of art is certainly increased by awareness of the context in which it was produced. It helps us see more than we could before.

Beginning the Journey

As you begin your study of art, think of it as you would a trip to another country. Dedicate yourself to expanding your horizons and remaining open to the many things you will be introduced to in this course. This kind of openness may be difficult to maintain when you are confronted with a work of modern art for the first time. For many viewers who are not familiar with contemporary art, their negative response is probably based on an immediate gut reaction. Nothing is wrong with having a strong, personal reaction to visual art—in fact, modern artists hope to create such reactions; most would rather have people hate their work than be bored by it. But viewers who take a quick look and react to art,

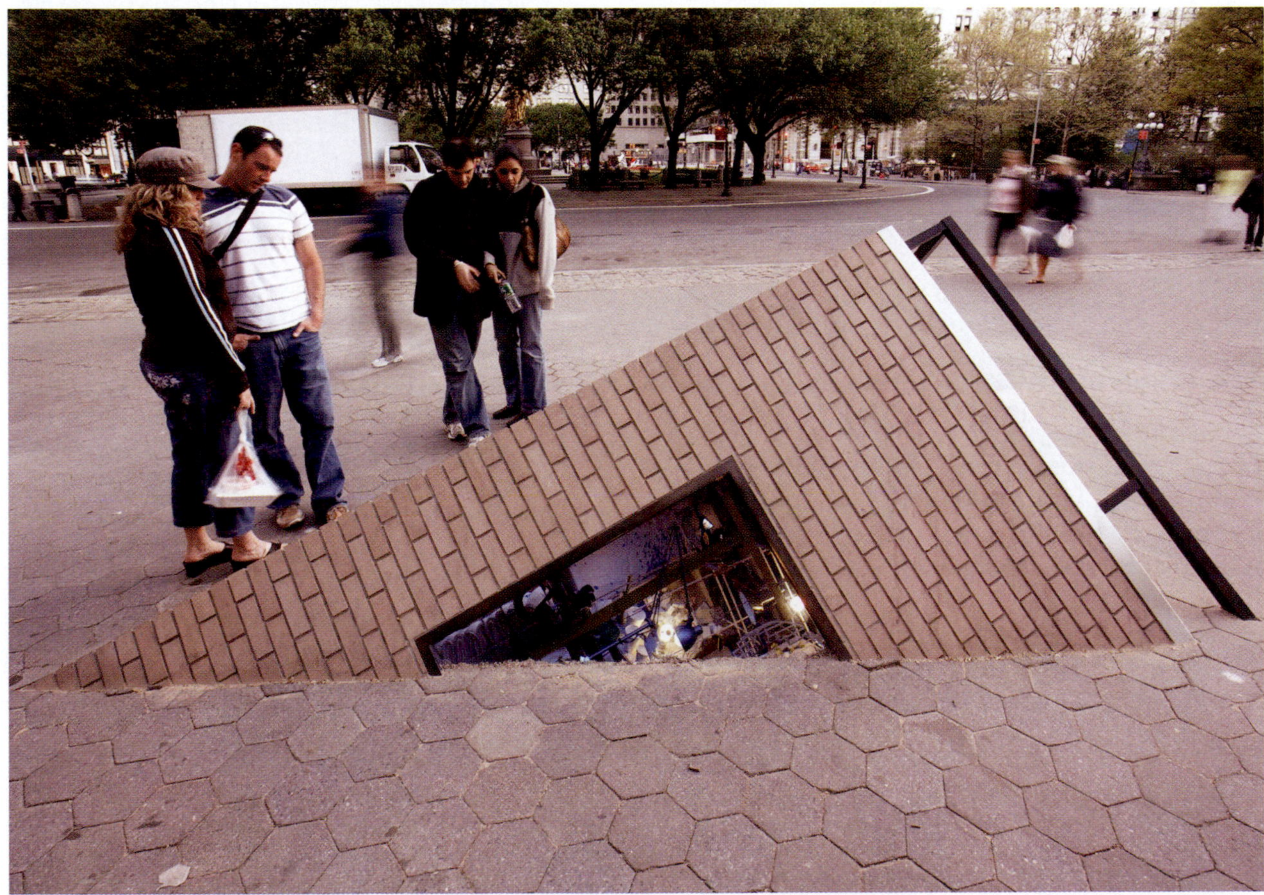

1-47 Sarah Sze, *Corner Plot,* 2006. Outdoor mixed media installation, New York. Courtesy Marianne Boesky Gallery, New York

without really trying to understand it, are missing a rich world of visual experience. All one needs to do is invest some time and thought.

For example, in 2006, pedestrians walking by a corner in midtown Manhattan were amazed to see what appeared to be a piece of a typical city building that had either fallen to the ground or had begun emerging from underneath the pavement (**1-47**). Many New Yorkers simply passed it by, but those who took the time to peek into it were rewarded with a view of an interior of an artist's studio, although one that looked as if it had been hit by an earthquake. Extending below street level was an arrangement of many ordinary items, such as a drafting table, lamps, stacks of paper towels, an iPod, pencils, and a miniature spiral staircase. Those who looked up and around noticed that the strange entity (actually a temporary installation by the artist Sarah Sze) was modeled on a building across the street. According to Sze, her goal for *Corner Plot* was that it would be "a surprise . . . a point of discovery," and so it was for people who stopped to look.

During this course, you will wander around the globe and discover art from many countries and continents. Time will be no barrier as we move across the centuries. We will explore many ways of looking at and understanding art. At our journey's end, when you finish this course, you will be in a better position to say whether you think the *Mona Lisa*'s reputation is deserved, whether de Kooning had any talent, or whether Duchamp should be considered an artist. And your decision will be based on knowledge rather than prejudice or gut feelings.

After the course is over, keep in mind that you have begun a lifelong journey, one in which you will never be alone. As the French novelist Marcel Proust wrote:

> Only through art can we get outside of ourselves and know another's view of the universe which is not the same as ours and see landscapes which would otherwise have remained unknown to us like the landscapes of the moon. Thanks to art, instead of seeing a single world, our own, we see it multiply until we have before us as many worlds as there are original artists. . . .

That is the power of art.

CHAPTER 2

The Primary Elements

For many viewers, one of the most frustrating aspects of art is trying to describe what they see. It is as if they were trying to explain something in a foreign language. This chapter introduces the vocabulary of the language of art, which revolves around the basic visual elements that all artists use: space, line, shape, light, texture, and color. With these elements, artists are able to create incredibly diverse images, from Egyptian pyramids to the *Mona Lisa*. The fundamentals of art and design provide a way to describe the various forms of art; they are the basis of the language in which all art is discussed.

SPACE

In the Old Testament we are told, "In the beginning . . . the earth was without form and void." Empty space is the most fundamental of the elements of art and design. Each artist has a profound sense of the void as he or she stares at the piece of paper, the canvas, the block of marble, or the empty site before beginning work. Space is the field of action on which all artists do battle. Many artists feel as Rembrandt seems to in *The Artist in His Studio* (**2-1**), a little overwhelmed as they begin. Artists work within two kinds of space. **Two-dimensional space** is flat and can only be viewed from one side. Anything that exists in this space, like the space itself, will have height and width but no real depth. However, two-dimensional art forms such as drawings or paintings often create the *illusion* of depth. **Three-dimensional space** contains objects that can be viewed from all sides, objects that have height, width, and depth. This is the kind of space we actually live in. Sculpture and architecture are examples of three-dimensional art forms.

Defining space and controlling it with the other visual elements is what making art is all about. The process begins with the artist choosing from the range of elements. In many cases, the first choice is the simplest of elements—the line.

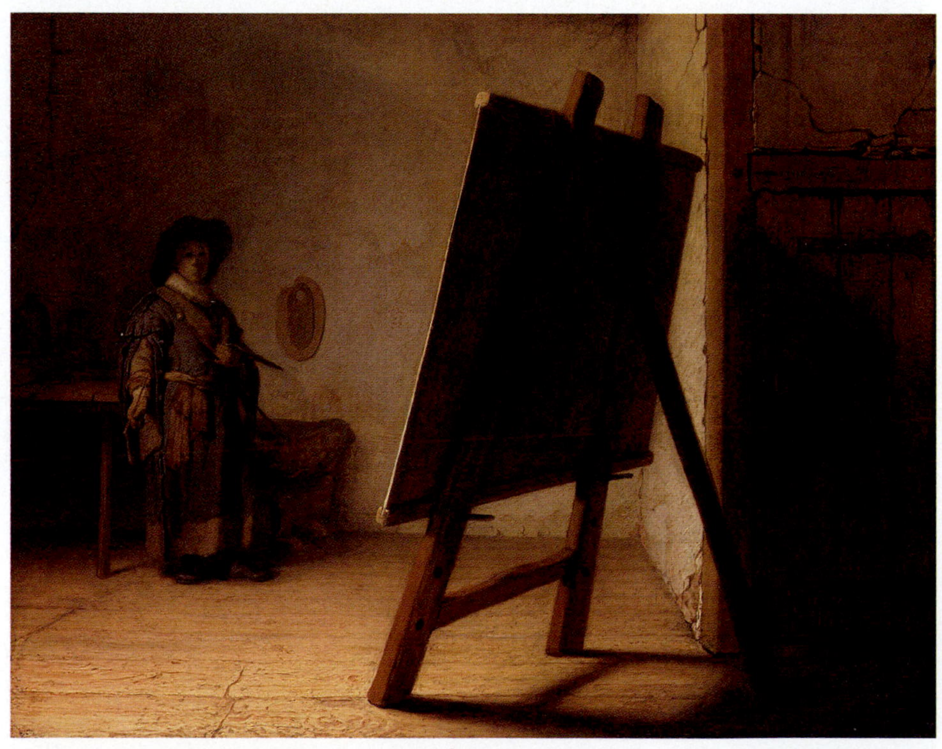

2-1 Rembrandt van Rijn, *The Artist in His Studio,* c. 1628. Oil on panel, 9¾" x 12½". Museum of Fine Arts, Boston. (Zoe Oliver Sherman Collection, given in memory of Lillie Oliver Poor). 38.1838. Photograph © 2008 Museum of Fine Arts, Boston.

LINE

To a mathematician, a line is the shortest distance between two points. To an artist, a line is much more than that. It is an element of infinite potential, capable of conveying a wide variety of emotions and meanings. Vincent van Gogh's drawing *Fishing Boats at Sea* (**2-2**) shows the versatility of a line. By varying length and width, or by choosing various types of lines (straight, curved, or angular), the artist creates a seascape of great complexity, reflecting the many forms of nature.

All lines are the result of an artist's movement. When they particularly reveal the action of drawing, the motion of the hand and arm, they are described as *gestural*. Van Gogh's gestures are what make his drawing exciting. Notice how different kinds of lines convey different moods. Horizontal lines seem calm, verticals inspiring, and diagonals and curves energizing. A line's texture, whether it is scratchy or smooth, for example, can imply feelings as well. The many and various lines in van Gogh's drawing almost "sound" different. One can imagine the crash of the swirling lines in the foreground as opposed to the calm, bold lines of the sea. We can hear the sails pulling taut in a stiff breeze because of the tight geometry of their lines.

By varying a line's width (or *weight*) as it is drawn, an artist can make a line seem to twist and turn as if it were moving in space. The viewer sees the line as if it has depth, as if it were curling. Artists also use this technique to create the illusion of a solid form.

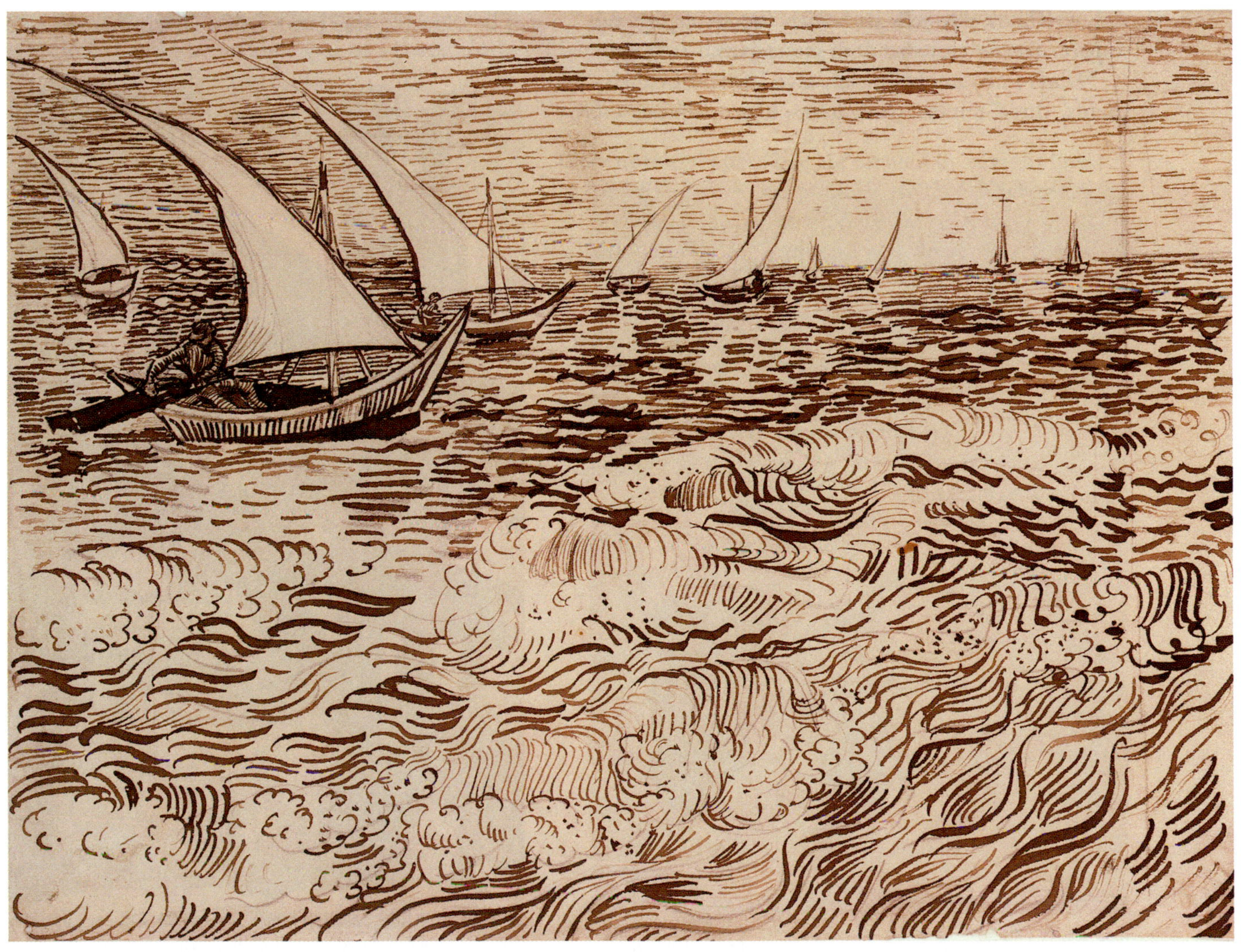

2-2 Vincent van Gogh, *Fishing Boats at Sea,* 1889. Pencil, reed pen, and ink on wove paper, 9½″ × 12⅝″. Kupferstichkabinett, Staatliche Museum zu Berlin, Berlin, Germany.

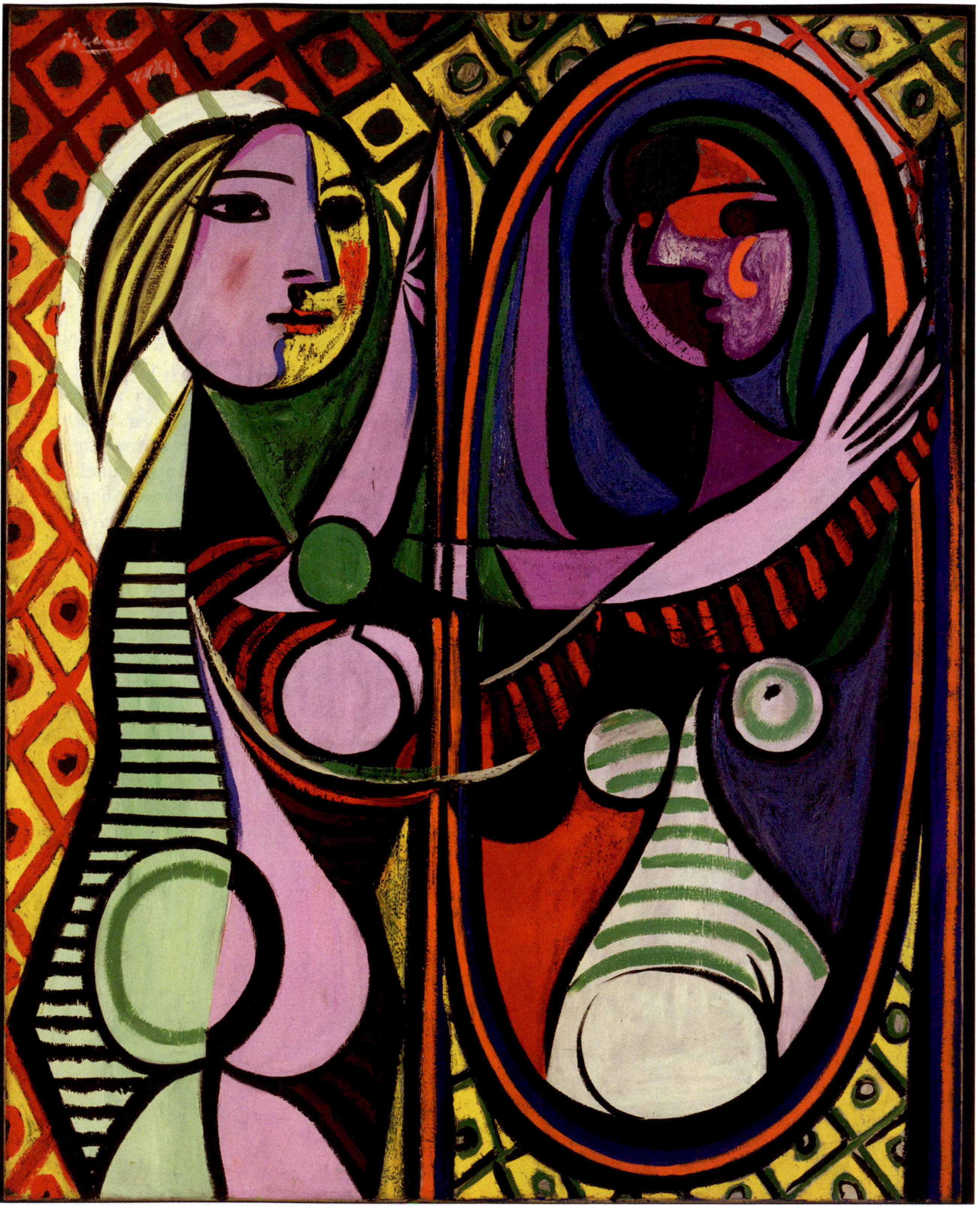

2-8 Pablo Picasso, *Girl before a Mirror*, 1932. Oil on canvas, 63¾″ × 51¼″. The Museum of Modern Art, New York (gift of Mrs. Simon Guggenheim).

Abstract shapes are representational shapes that have been simplified. Even when they have been reduced to their basic underlying forms, distorted or exaggerated, the original sources of the shapes will remain recognizable. Abstract shapes can be either organic or geometric.

Nonrepresentational shapes are those that are not meant to refer to anything we can see in the real world. They are sometimes called *nonobjective* or *totally abstract.* These shapes can also have either organic (*soft-edged*) or geometric (*hard-edged*) qualities.

In *Girl before a Mirror* (**2-8**), Picasso creatively employs all types of shapes and even shows how one shape may share the qualities of two different kinds. The young woman's face, for example, is recognizable but is missing many of the details. Because it has been simplified, we say it has been *abstracted.* It has also become more geometric. The curve of her belly has also become an abstract form because it has been simplified and exaggerated. Still, it remains a naturalistic abstract shape. Behind her are nonobjective shapes (perhaps wallpaper) that form a colorful pattern in the background. We do not have to identify them to enjoy their rhythm and bright colors.

THE SPIRIT OF THE FORMS

All geometric forms, whether two- or three-dimensional, suggest order, mathematics, and reason. Buckminster Fuller's *United States Pavilion, EXPO 67* (**2-9**) reflects these qualities of geometry. His building seems perfect and ideal. The absolutely consistent repetition of one basic element gives it unity and coherence. Yet it is not without a sense of movement. Most curved geometric forms, like circles and spheres, convey a feeling of motion. On the other hand, "squared-off" geometric shapes, like a square or a cube, generally imply perfect calm and stability. This is why most architects prefer them for their buildings.

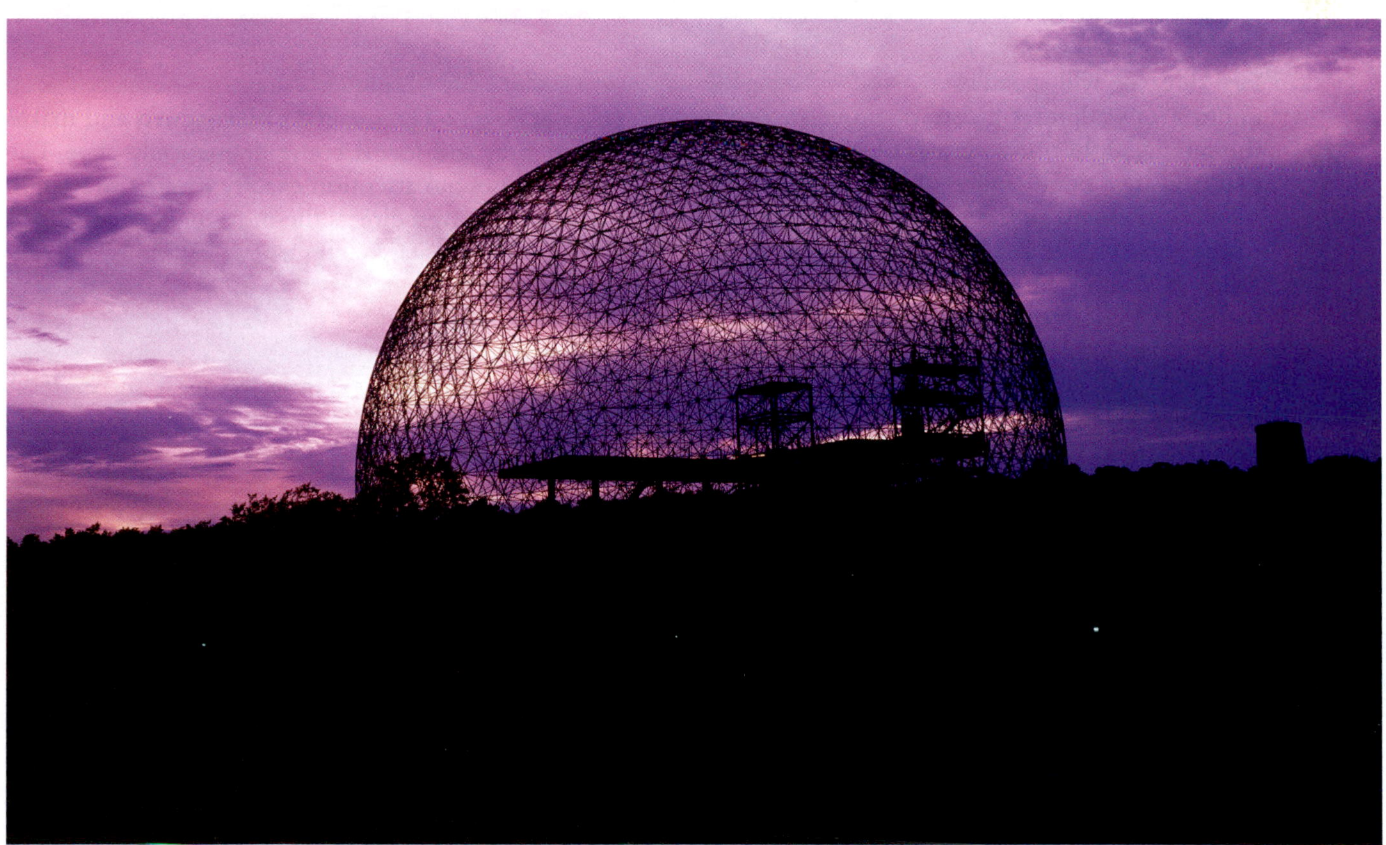

2-9 Buckminister Fuller, *United States Pavilion, EXPO 67,* Montreal, 1967. Steel and Plexiglas geodesic dome, shown under construction, 137′ high, 250′ diameter.

the back wall. As one comes closer to the painting, it grows more luminous. If you have the courage to try to touch the mysterious painting, you are in for a surprise. Your hand will pass through it into a deep, empty space. There is no painting. The rectangle is made of light. You can even stick your head into it and gaze around. Inside you experience a seemingly infinite blue space—a place with no edges or shadows, an extraordinarily peaceful, pure experience of light.

TEXTURE

Turrell's work depends not just on light, but that a powerful human instinct will be stronger than our fear of security guards. Our fingers are used from birth to understand our environment. When we "cannot believe our eyes," we will use touch to confirm or deny what our eyes have told us. We will touch something to see if it is warm or cold, soft or hard. Many textures can be pleasurable; for example, soft velvet, smooth marble, and silky water are three very different pleasing textures. Sculptors find deep satisfaction in plunging their hands into wet clay and manipulating it. Some textures are disturbing, even painful, like the coarseness of sandpaper or the jagged edge of broken glass.

Artists who work in three dimensions create *tactile* textures, textures that can actually be felt. Like Turrell, most sculptors actually intend their art to be understood both visually and tactilely, and sometimes not just by people. Visitors to the estate where the sculptor Henry Moore lived for the last forty years of his life are expected to walk the grounds and to run their hands along the huge sculptures. He always thought that the barriers between art and viewers were arrogant and pretentious. At Perry Green, viewers can get a sense of works like *Sheep Piece*'s (**2-14**) metal surface when they touch it, its substantial weight when they lean against it, and its great size when they put their arms around it. However, when Henry Moore designed *Sheep Piece,* he wasn't thinking of people. It was inspired by and made for the sheep that graze the meadows around his home. The large metal sculpture's opening at the bottom is at a height that not only provides shelter for the sheep but is also comfortable for them to scratch their backs. The overall abstract design represents a ewe and a lamb, a kind of mother and child, where the large form protects the smaller one. Moore drew sheep often and described them as "rather shapeless balls of wool with a head and four legs," but he was always aware that "underneath all that wool was a body."

One does not need to touch all art objects to appreciate their textures. The African craftsman who made the *Oath-Taking Figure* (**2-15**) provided a visual feast of textures. The ritual figure mixes smooth wood, hard metal nails, soft animal hide, and a shiny mirror. While it may not be inviting, this strange (to Western eyes) combination of materials provides contrasts that are visually and tactilely interesting.

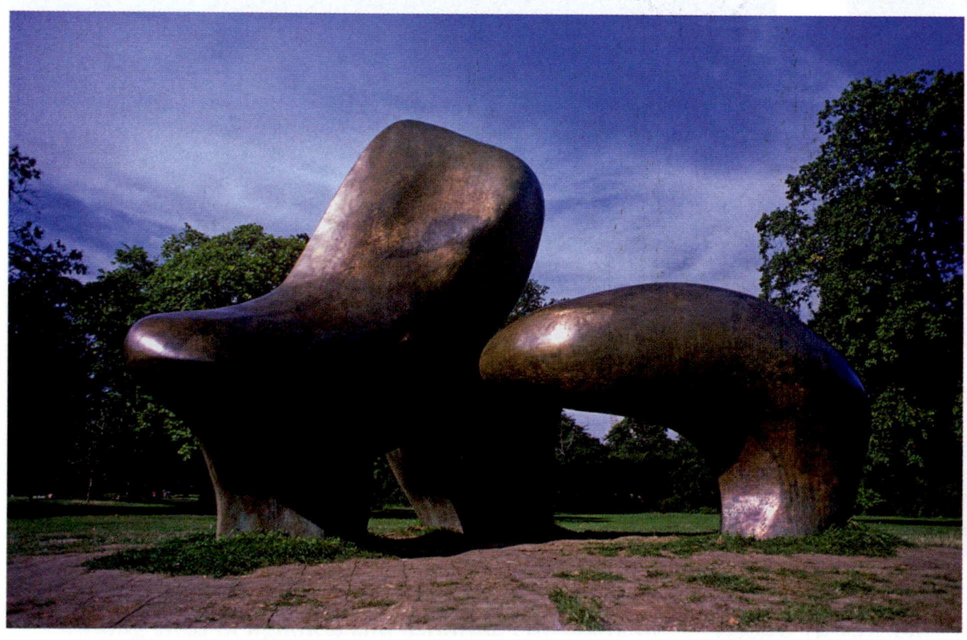

2-14 Henry Moore, *Sheep Piece,* 1971–1972. Bronze, 19′ tall. Hoglands, Hertfordshire, England. [SHEEP PIECE one of several Henry Moore sculptures forming an open exhibition by The Serpentine in Kensington Gardens Summer of 1978 permanently installed at Perry Green in Hertfordshire] The Henry Moore Foundation.

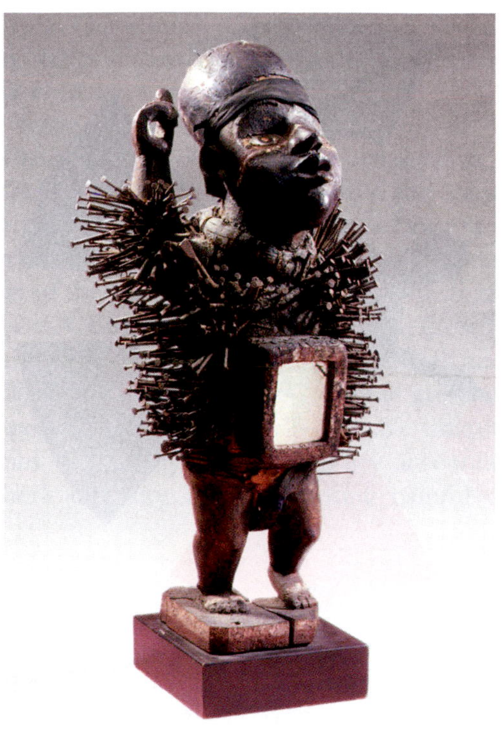

2-15 *Oath-Taking Figure,* Congo, 1880–1920. Wood, nails, cloth, glass, paint.

Creating the illusion of texture has been an interest of two-dimensional artists for centuries. For a Northern Renaissance artist like Jan van Eyck, it bordered almost on obsession. In his desire to recreate visual reality and demonstrate his accomplishments, he would crowd his pictures like *The Virgin with the Canon van der Paele* (**2-16**) with all sorts of textures. With the use of delicate brush strokes, which are difficult to detect, and smooth transitions of light and dark, van Eyck shows us soft skin, curly hair, translucent glass, shiny armor made of many metals, smooth marble tile floors, an ornately carved stone throne, and fabrics of all kinds, including elaborate rugs. Van Eyck's dedication to visual truth, as seen in the lavish simulation of surfaces, shows not only his skill but also his religious devotion. He worked many hours to surround the Madonna and her child with a gorgeous and sumptuous setting.

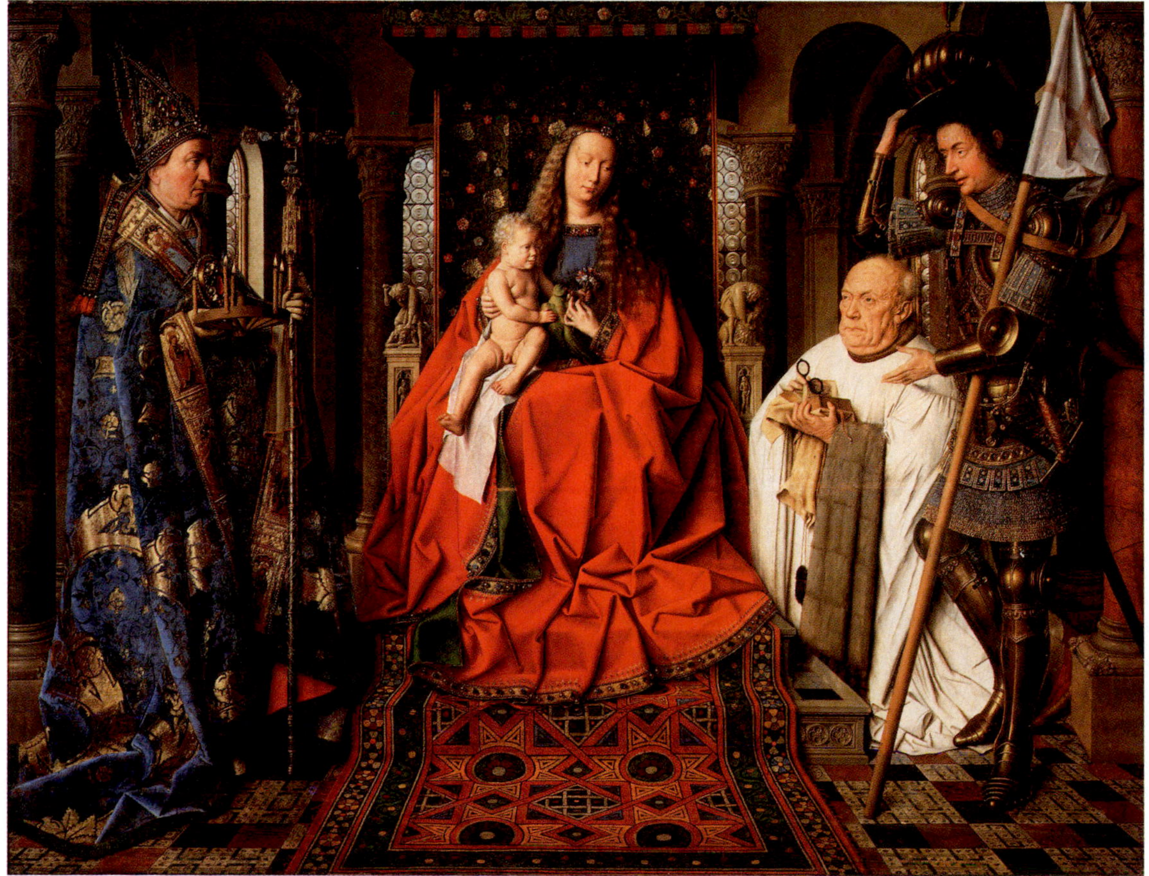

2-16 Jan van Eyck, *The Virgin with the Canon van der Paele,* 1436. Tempera and oil on wood, approximately 48″ × 62″. Groeningemuseum, Bruges, Belgium.

An analysis of Kees van Dongen's *Modjesko, Soprano Singer* (**2-25**) will give us an opportunity to use our new vocabulary of color. The painting combines warm and cool colors, but the warm colors dominate and make the strain of singing seem intense. That is because warm colors tend to excite, while cool colors relax the viewer. This is particularly noticeable in the singer's face—as the bright yellow changes to red, we feel the blood rush to her face as she reaches for a high soprano note. Warm colors tend to advance toward the viewer, while cool ones recede. Van Dongen takes advantage of these special properties. The singer's intensely yellow chest seems to expand against the pale blue dress, as does her throat, constricted by the cool ribbon around her neck.

In the background, around the figure, van Dongen uses red at its highest intensity. Shades of red become progressively lighter in value as they move away from the figure. Her hair, eyebrows, and eyes are painted in a dark tint of blue, so dark that at times they approach black. The painting's three-dimensional forms are created not by shading, as you would find in a drawing, but by changes in color value and intensity. For example, the face is shaped by shades of orange and red, with more intense colors reserved for the areas in deepest shadow. This combination of intense and pale, warm and cool colors creates the emotional, dramatic flavor of a singing performance.

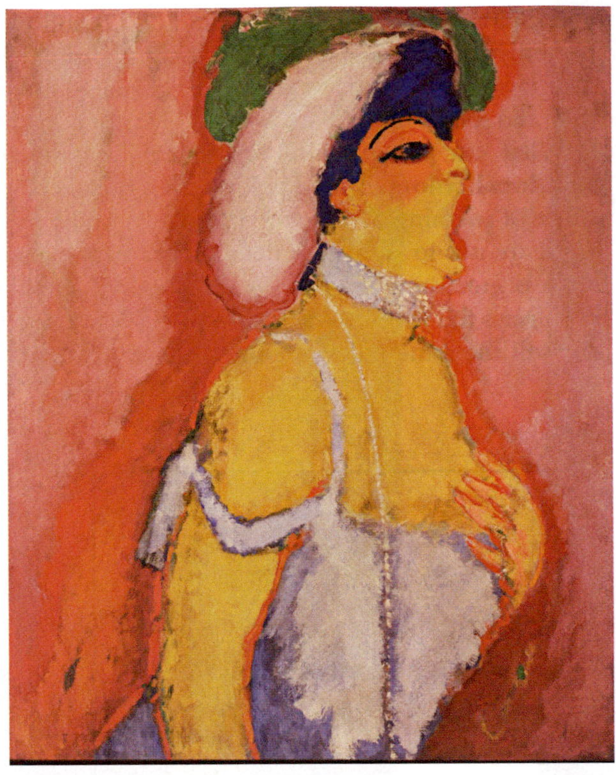

2-25 Kees van Dongen, *Modjesko, Soprano Singer,* 1908. Oil on canvas, 39⅜" × 32". The Museum of Modern Art, New York (gift of Mr. and Mrs. Peter A. Rubel).

Naturalistic versus Arbitrary Color

Modjesko, Soprano Singer is an example of the deliberate use of **arbitrary colors.** The subject's skin, hair, and costume are not painted in realistic colors; these colors are the invention of the artist. Invented colors can accentuate the meaning of a picture and give it an emotional content. Arbitrary colors were also used in Picasso's *Girl before a Mirror* (2-8).

For many centuries, however, European artists rarely used arbitrary colors. From the end of the medieval period to the late 1800s, artists preferred to use colors that imitated those in the real world, or **naturalistic colors.** John Constable's *The Glebe Farm* (**2-26**) is, as the artist described it, "very rich in color, and fresh and bright." Although he limited his palette to realistic hues, the painting also uses many of the properties of color we discussed in van Dongen's picture. The warmth of the earth with its reddish browns helps bring the path toward us. The cool blue sky is far away and gives the picture great depth; the hints of red in the lower clouds bring the sky just above the trees forward. As they move back in the distance, the trees have more blue mixed into the greens so they seem to recede.

Colors can help direct the viewer's attention. Notice how the red coat of a traveler draws us to the center of the picture. While Constable uses colors imaginatively, all of them—whether the white and brown markings of a dog or the pale yellow-green of a lawn—remain naturalistic. Throughout the history of art, one of color's most important uses has been to help the viewer identify subjects by use of their naturalistic colors. John Constable, like many artists before him and many since, follows that tradition.

Emotional Resonance

In the twentieth century, many artists have explored more directly the ability of color to affect our emotions. Some modern artists have felt that if used without reference to specific objects in the real world, color could create its own visual language of emotion, an art of pure feeling, like music.

Vasily Kandinsky's *Pink Accent* (**2-27**) experiments with the expressive potential of the visual weight of different colors.

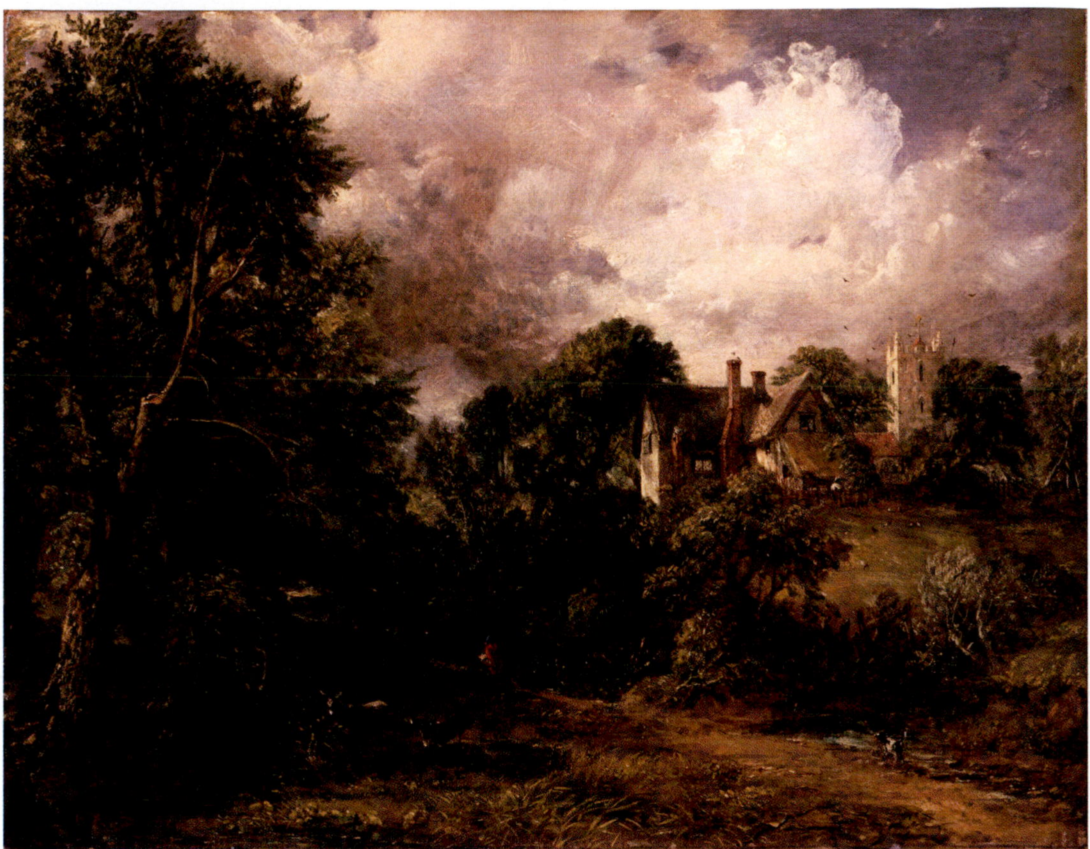

2-26 John Constable, *The Glebe Farm,* 1827. Oil on canvas, 18″ × 23⅝″. © The Detroit Institute of Arts (gift of Mrs. Joseph B. Schlotman).

This picture has its own inner life; the feelings we receive from it come from colors and shapes that do not need to refer to things we recognize in the ordinary world. Kandinsky created his own totally abstract characters, with what he called

> these unique beings we call colors—each alive in and for itself, independent, endowed with all the necessary qualities for further independent life and ready and willing at every moment to submit to new combinations, to mix among themselves and create endless series of new worlds.

Vasily Kandinsky, when he described colors mixing among themselves and creating endless series of new worlds, could also have been describing any of the other elements of art. Kandinsky thought of his elements as if they were living creatures, expressing a belief that many artists share: that in a successful work of art every point, every line, every element should be a living thing.

Kandinsky also wrote, "in art, as in nature, the wealth of forms is limitless." The challenge for an artist is to select and organize the many possible elements into a **design** that most suits the artist's intentions and is also visually satisfying. The next chapter will explain the principles behind successful designs. There are just as many possible approaches as there are elements.

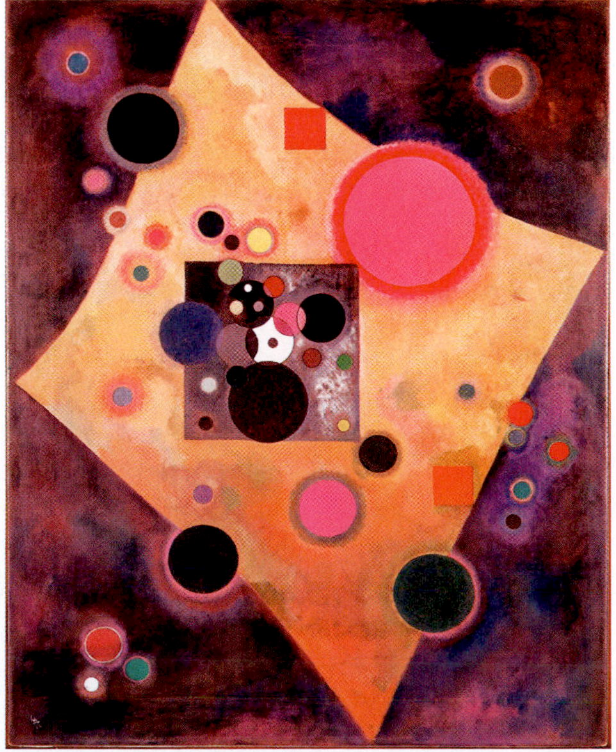

2-27 Vasily Kandinsky, *Pink Accent.* Collection Nina Kandinsky, Neuilly sur Seine, France.

CHAPTER 3

The Principles of Design

Human beings have a limited tolerance for disorganization; we are made uncomfortable by chaos and prefer order. Organization provides a sense of security; it is part of our desire to control our environment. We are not alone in the animal kingdom in our desire for regular meals, regular sleep, or regular hours, as anyone who owns a pet knows.

The artist reflects these basic instincts when he or she controls or **designs** the environment of a work of art. There are many possible strategies for a successful design, but almost all incorporate at least some of what can be called the *principles of design*. These have proven over time to be capable of organizing a coherent work of art from the wide range of ingredients at an artist's disposal.

As discussed in the last chapter, all artists deal first with empty space. In nature, while large open spaces that seem endless are beautiful, most humans do not choose to make their homes in the midst of them. We like to limit an area and then populate it with buildings. For the two-dimensional artist, the first important design decision is also how to limit space and define its borders. The boundaries demarcate what is known as the **picture plane,** the playing field of the art elements. Its frame establishes a separate arena for artistic activity from the whole world that surrounds it. Its proportions will determine the effect of whatever is within its borders.

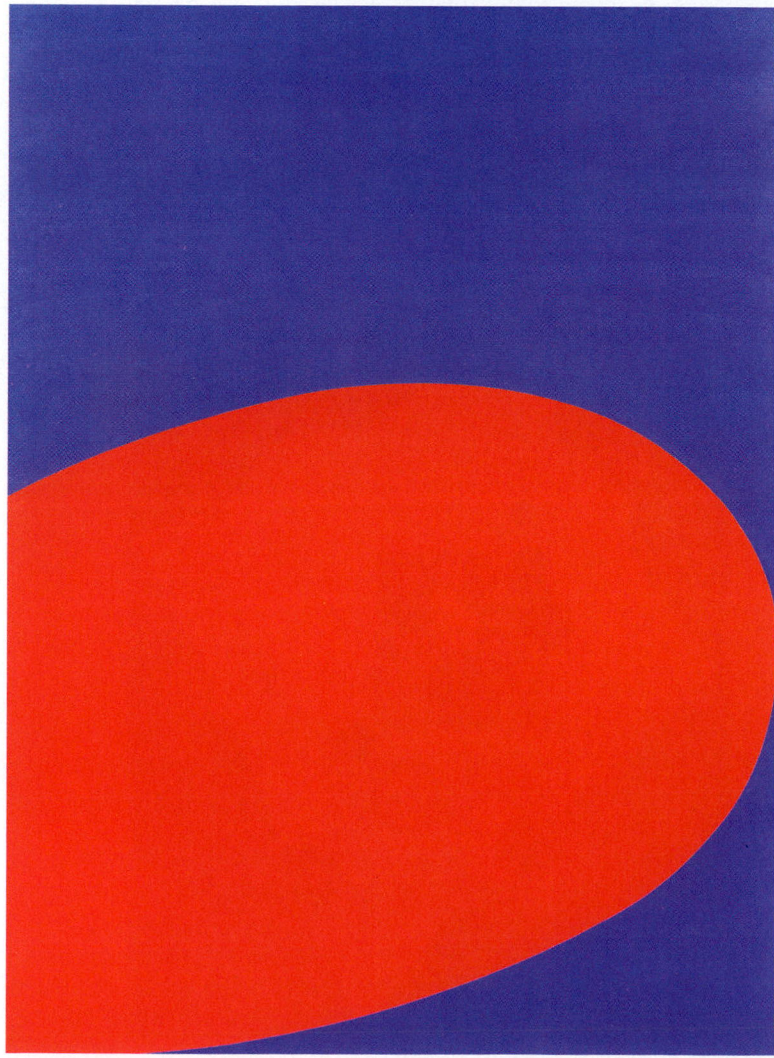

3-1 Ellsworth Kelly, *Red/Blue.* Oil on canvas, 90″ × 66″ (228.6 cm × 167.6 cm). Whitney Museum of American Art, New York. Purchase 96.53.4a-b ©Ellsworth Kelly.

PLACEMENT

The first element put inside the picture plane has a profound effect. Now the field is no longer neutral; it is actively involved in a dialogue with what has entered it. The arrival of the first element actually produces two shapes in a picture plane. The empty space around the element becomes an important shape, too, and must be consciously dealt with. The element is called the **positive form,** and the altered space is the **negative form** or **negative space.** They are also called the **figure** and the **ground.**

Artists are particularly aware of the effect each element has on negative space. To an artist, space is never really empty; it is more like space in physics, as described by Albert Einstein, an invisible solid. By placing different elements within it, the artist manipulates space. To summarize, the arrangement of elements in the picture plane is not only a design of lines and shapes but also a design of the spaces between them—the negative spaces. The artist must control both the subjects and the spaces around them to create a successful artwork.

Ellsworth Kelly's painting *Red/Blue* (**3-1**) may appear at first glance to be very simple, but the placement of the orange shape on the blue ground was carefully thought out. By having that shape just touch the right border, Kelly creates two new shapes from the blue ground, one large, one small. Because the orange form sits toward the bottom of the picture plane, it conveys a sense of weight. Placed higher it would appear light like a balloon. Tilting the form upward adds a bit of liveliness to the picture. If you hold up your hand and block your view of the blue shape at the bottom, you can see what the picture would be like if the orange shape had filled the bottom half. Would it be more or less dynamic? Artists often block parts of their pictures in this way to consider changes to a composition and to see possible effects.

While most people think of photography as a way to capture reality, James Welling used it to create totally abstract designs of positive and negative spaces. His series of *photograms* (**3-2**) called "New Abstractions" were produced by combining darkroom and computer techniques to make multiple reversals of photographic negatives and positives. A photogram is a photograph made without a camera. It is made by placing objects on sheets of light-sensitive paper and then exposing them to light (see Man Ray's *Rayograph,* 7-13). In Welling's approach, strips of thin board were laid on photographic paper. After it was exposed and processed, the paper became black where the light had hit and white where cardboard blocked the light. Then Welling scanned the paper and used his computer to make a high-contrast negative. The negative was taken back to the darkroom to make the final photographic print. The resulting image is filled with positive and negative spaces of great variety. At times black seems to be the figure, but at other times it is white. Because of the mix of thin and thick flat shapes, it also has parts that seem to be three-dimensional.

Designing space is a more complex task for an artist actually working in three dimensions. Part of the experience of viewing a building or most sculptures is moving around them freely. A three-dimensional form should provide a new encounter every time we shift our position. Therefore, a three-dimensional artist has to consider spatial issues from every possible vantage point. This includes not just the sculpture itself but also the many negative spaces that are being carved out by the positive forms. Planning for all of those different points of view is difficult with only

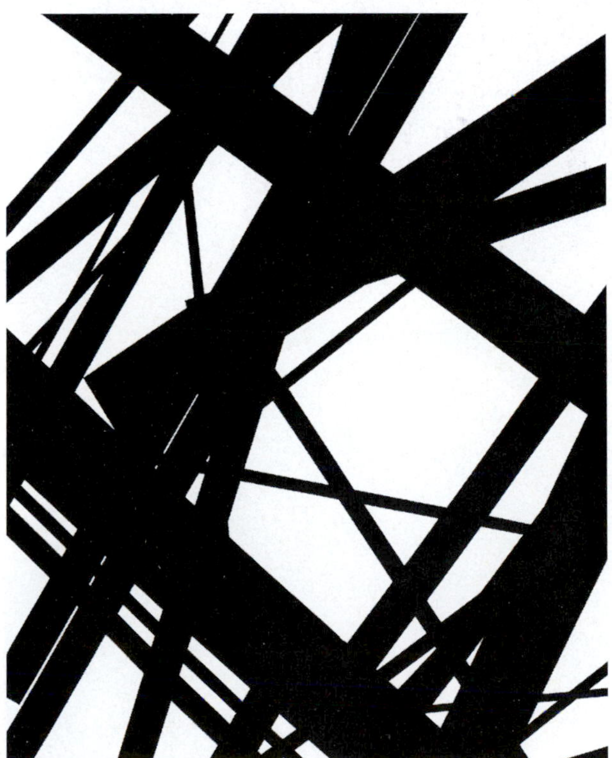

3-2 James Welling, Untitled, no. 25 (New Abstraction), 1998. Silver gelatin print, 52 ⅛″ × 38 ⅛″. Donald Young Gallery, Chicago.

flat drawings, so many sculptors build small studies out of simple materials like paper, styrofoam (**3-3**), or clay, as in the 1958 photograph of the modern sculptor, Alberto Giacometti (see also 3-14).

Architects also must define negative spaces, like the windows or doorways of their buildings. By decorating the portal (**3-4**) with a carving of a giant's face, the architect of the Palazetto Zuccari provides an animated but rather forbidding entrance to his palace. One is forced to walk through the large mouth of a monster if one wants the privilege of entering.

Inside the "gullet" or entrance hall, one would encounter another kind of space that three-dimensional artists must design, a *confined space*. Architects must control both the exterior and interiors of their buildings. A good architect will make every room and every corridor into an aesthetic experience, even taking into account the experience of progressing from room to room (see 3-11).

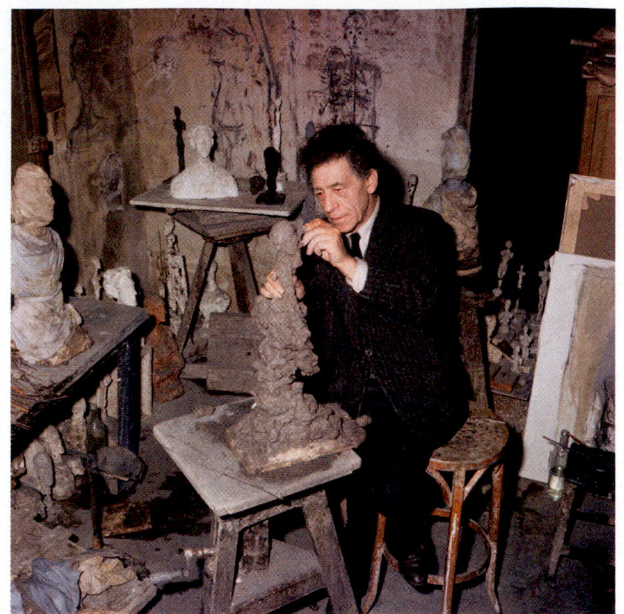

3-3 The artist Alberto Giacometti at work on a sculpture in his studio, 1958.

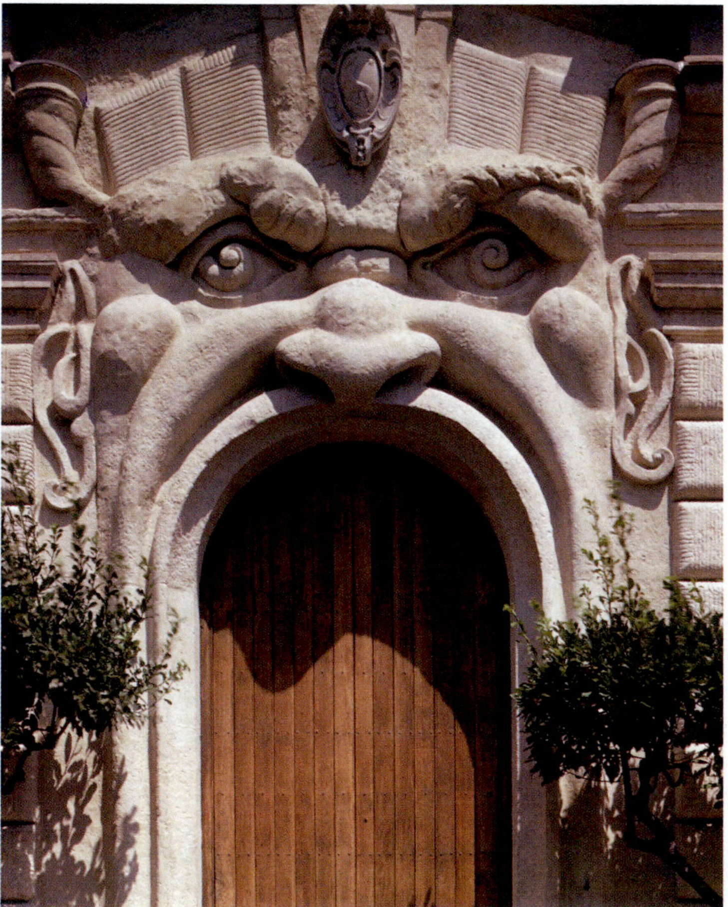

3-4 Portal of Palazetto Zuccari, Rome.

Balance

Balance is a natural human desire. We admire people who are well-balanced and tend to avoid those who are not. A loss of our ability to balance is disturbing, as anyone who has had an inner ear infection will know. Without it, we lose our state of well-being. Visually, we also find that achieving balance is an essential property in a satisfying work of art. The oriental symbol for *yin and yang* (**3-5**) is an example of perfect balance. It is also a good example of **figure-ground ambiguity,** where it is unclear which part should be called *figure* and which should be called *ground*. As in a checkerboard pattern, one can see either black

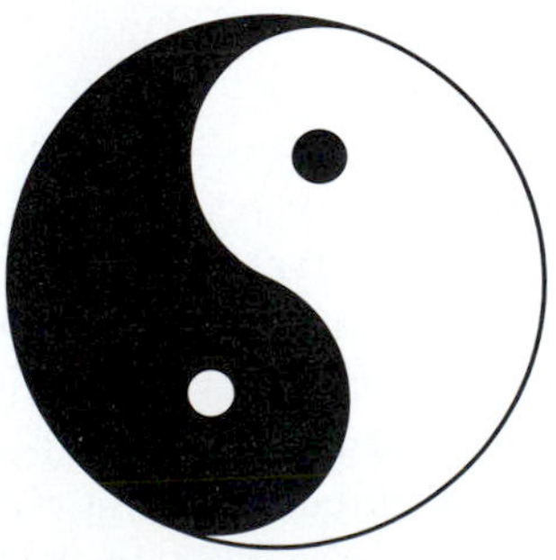

3-5 Yin/Yang Symbol.

or white as the subject. For someone from the Eastern world, however, this is not simply an interesting illusion but a meaningful symbol of the correct way of living. The perfect balance portrayed is the balance of the life forces of yin and yang, the resolution of opposites. It is a symbol of an ideal world where night and day, work and play, emotions and logic, male and female, hot and cold, activity and rest all exist together in equivalence. One's life is out of balance when any of these things is stressed more than its opposite.

During the design process, balance is constantly changing. A mark as simple as a dot can affect the whole *equilibrium* or balance of a work of art. For example, imagine shifting one of the dots in the yin/yang symbol. It would unsettle the balance, thereby requiring a change of position or another element to be added in the field to create equilibrium. When the element enters, a new balance will need to be struck. Depending on its placement, the new shape could dominate its neighbor, be its equal, or seem overwhelmed by it.

The importance or **visual weight** of each element in a picture plane is always relative; it competes with its neighbors and is affected by the arrival of any new form. The visual weight also varies as its own position, color, size, shape, or texture changes. As the number of elements increase, the relationships become more and more complex, and maintaining equilibrium in the design is a greater challenge.

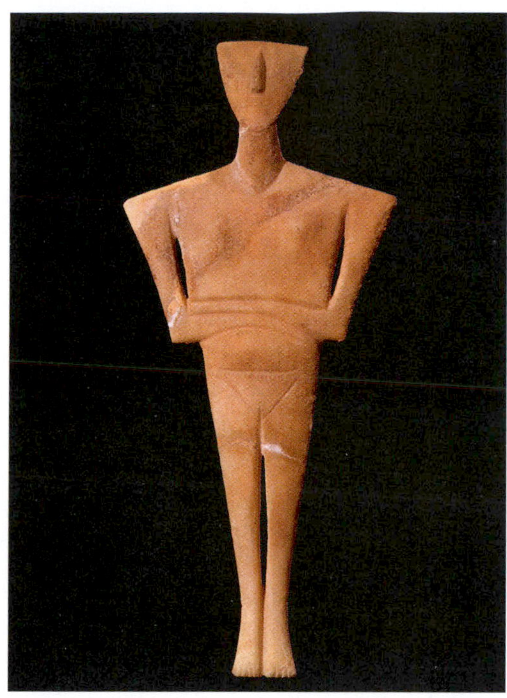

3-6 Cycladic idol, Syros, c. 2500–2000 BCE. Marble, 8 ½″ high. National Archaeological Museum, Athens.

Symmetry and Asymmetry

Art has taken many forms throughout its history, but the basic solutions to the problem of composition have remained surprisingly stable. Three basic methods of maintaining balance—symmetrical balance, radial balance, and asymmetrical balance—have proven effective. In **symmetrical balance** (sometimes known as *bilateral symmetry*), there is a general equivalence of shape and position on opposite sides of a central axis; if folded in half, the forms would match. With minor exceptions like the position of our hearts, all humans are designed to be bilaterally symmetrical. Ancient Cycladic idols (**3-6**) illustrate the special qualities of symmetrical balance. Their smooth, simplified forms and perfect symmetry provide a sense of calm and order—qualities appropriate to images of the "mother goddess."

When all elements revolve around a central point, **radial balance** is created. The whole world seems to pivot around the center in *Shamsa* (**3-7**) or "sunburst," which draws our attention irresistibly.

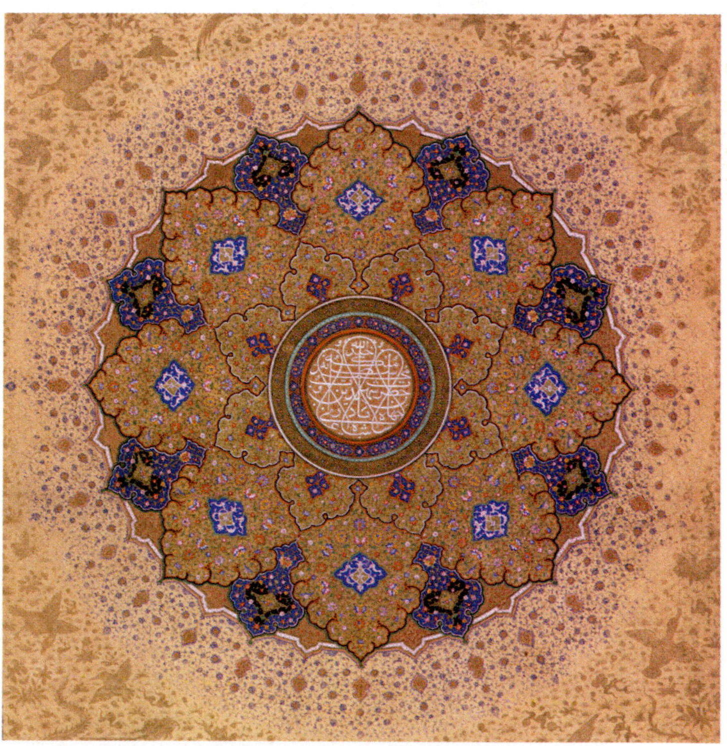

3-7 Ex Libris page from an album *Shamsa* ("sunburst" inscribed with the titles of Shah Jahan), c. 1640, colors and gilt on paper, 15 3⁄16″ × 10 7⁄16″. The Metropolitan Museum of Art, New York (purchase with Rogers Fund and The Kevorkian Foundation Gift, 1955).

The elaborate and beautiful details combined with the sumptuous use of gold paint creates a heavenly image, similar to the **mandalas** that Buddhists use for meditation. The titles of the Indian shah who sponsored this work (and built the Taj Mahal) are inscribed in the calligraphy at the center, along with the words, "May God make his kingdom last forever!"

In many cultures the circle is considered a perfect form. The Renaissance architect Donato Bramante's *Tempietto* (**3-8**) is based on a series of pure circular elements sharing the same center. From the stairs to the cylindrical columns to the dome and its cupola at top, circular forms of countless kinds are arranged with extraordinary imagination. By utilizing radial balance to organize his building, he created a sense of order and rationality. Meant to be admired as a representation of ideal forms and divine balance, the *Tempietto* is more a symbolic building than a functional one. Conducting a church service inside is practically impossible, because the interior is actually only fifteen feet wide.

Unlike symmetrical or radial, **asymmetrical balance** is much more dependent on an intuitive balancing of visual weights. The parts do not revolve around a center or form a mirror image around an axis but can be positioned anywhere and be any size. Unlike symmetry, which is basically fixed and static, asymmetry is active. So, while it is more challenging to balance an asymmetrical artwork, when achieved, the equilibrium will be much more dynamic than in symmetrical or radial compositions. The twisting and turning forms in Pieter Paul Rubens's (and Frans Snyders's) *Prometheus Bound* (**3-9**) create a sense of violent movement. This is a portrayal of the Greek mythological hero who stole fire from heaven and gave it to mankind. As a punishment, Zeus chained him to a mountaintop where he was endlessly tortured.

EMPHASIS

Emphasis in a work of art is essential for its success; if every part is of equal value, either confusion or monotony will numb the viewer. *Prometheus Bound* provides a good study of ways to create emphasis: *relative size, lines of force, focal point,* and *contrast.*

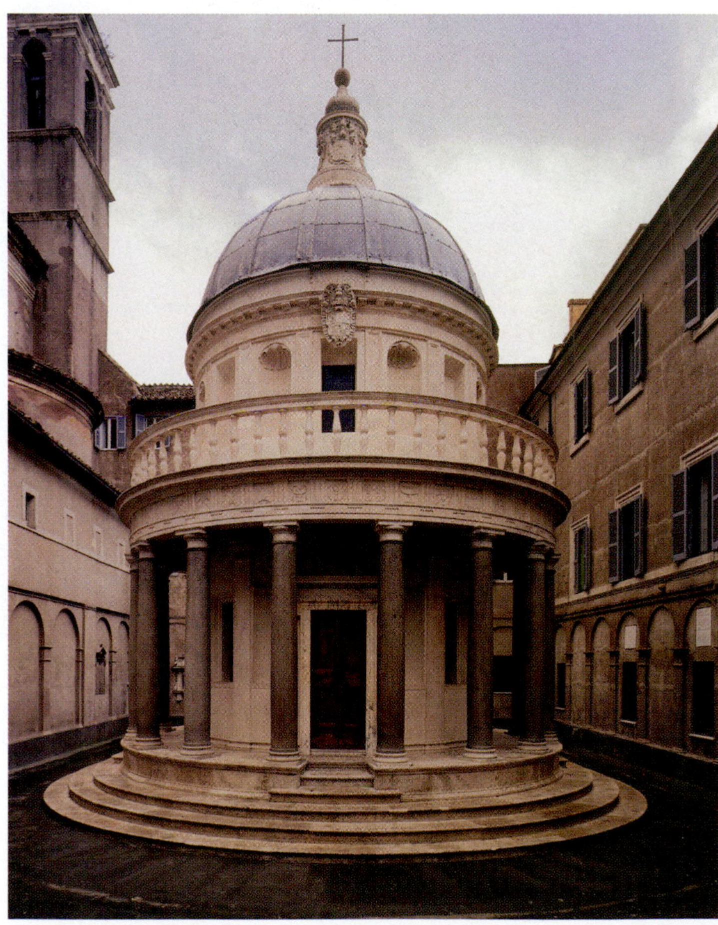

3-8 Donato Bramante, *Tempietto*, 1504 (?). San Pietro in Montorio, Rome.

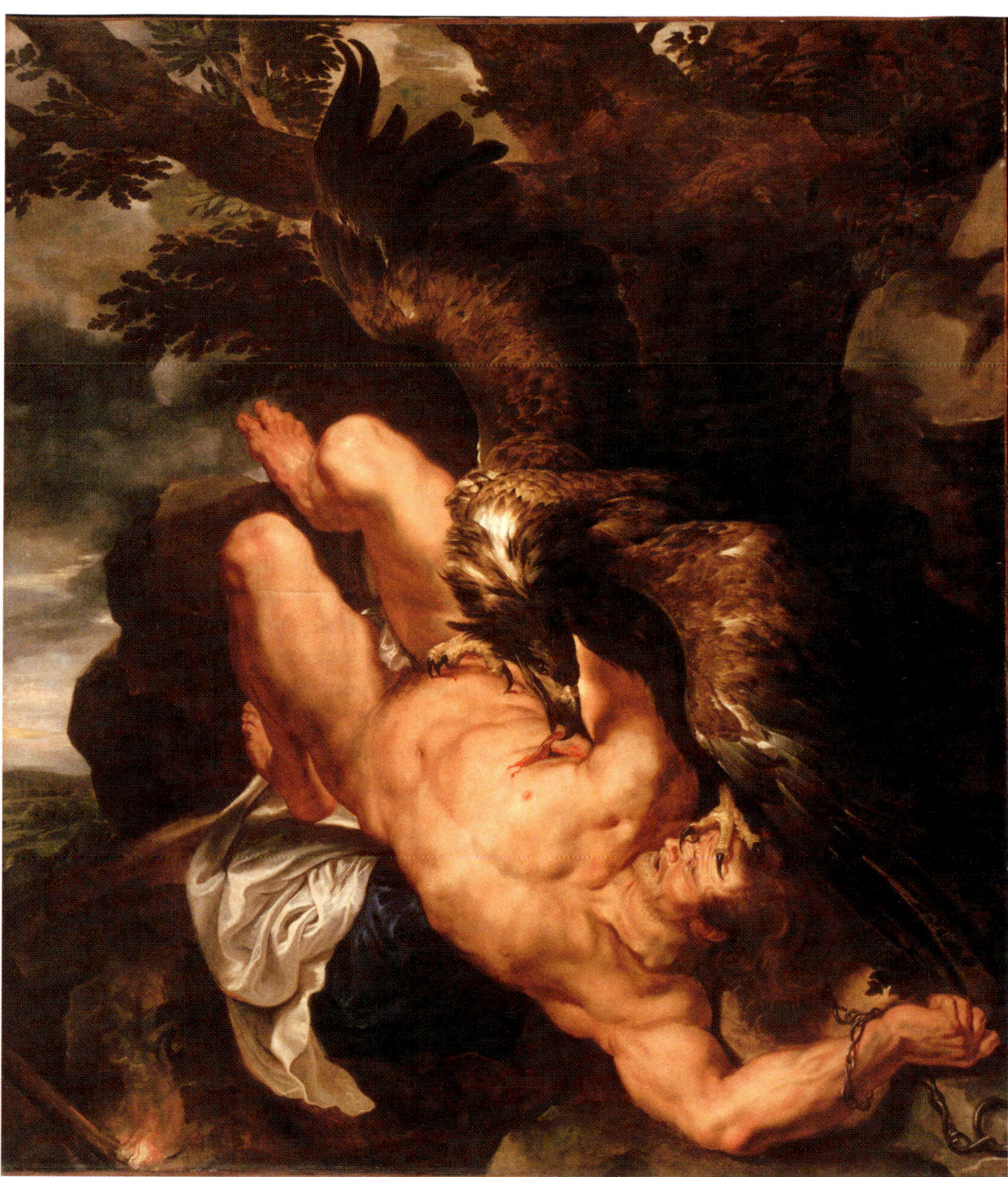

3-9 Pieter Paul Rubens (and Frans Snyders), *Prometheus Bound,* 1611–1612. Oil on canvas, 95⅞″ × 82½″. The Philadelphia Museum of Art (W. P. Wilstach Collection).

While the picture was a collaboration, the brilliant design of the composition was by Rubens (see Chapter 15). Snyders, an expert on animal subjects, painted the magnificent eagle. The eagle and Prometheus are obviously the main characters because of their great *relative* size compared to all of the other elements. The main thrust or *line of force* in the picture is the diagonal body of Prometheus, which is falling toward the viewer. The eagle that swoops down from the right creates an opposing diagonal that crosses Prometheus at his bloody liver, which is torn out every day. The crossing lines of force *emphasize* the cruel act, making it the *focal point* of the picture. Lines that converge on one location are a powerful artist's tool. They irresistibly draw the eye of a viewer. In a picture of this complexity, it is especially important for the artist to control the viewer's gaze, to choose which parts dominate. To make doubly sure that the main subject is the center of our attention, Rubens also bathes it in a bright light that *contrasts* with the general darkness.

The quest for ideal proportions has been pursued for centuries. Many societies have believed that these proportions would be a window into divine order. The Roman architect Vitruvius believed that the proportions of human beings were such a window and that all buildings should be built with those proportions in mind. He came to this conclusion after observing that a man with his arms and hands extended would fit into the two most perfect geometrical shapes—the circle and the square. Leonardo da Vinci shared Vitruvius's belief and also believed that scientific study of the functions of our bodies would ultimately reveal the workings of the whole universe. He wrote, "Man is the model of the world." In one of his notebooks, he drew the famous image of *Vitruvian Man* (**3-13**), which updated Vitruvius's theory. Unlike the Roman architect, da Vinci had actually done measurements of human beings and learned that the square and circle would not be able to share the same center. Notice how da Vinci shifts the square down from the circle's center.

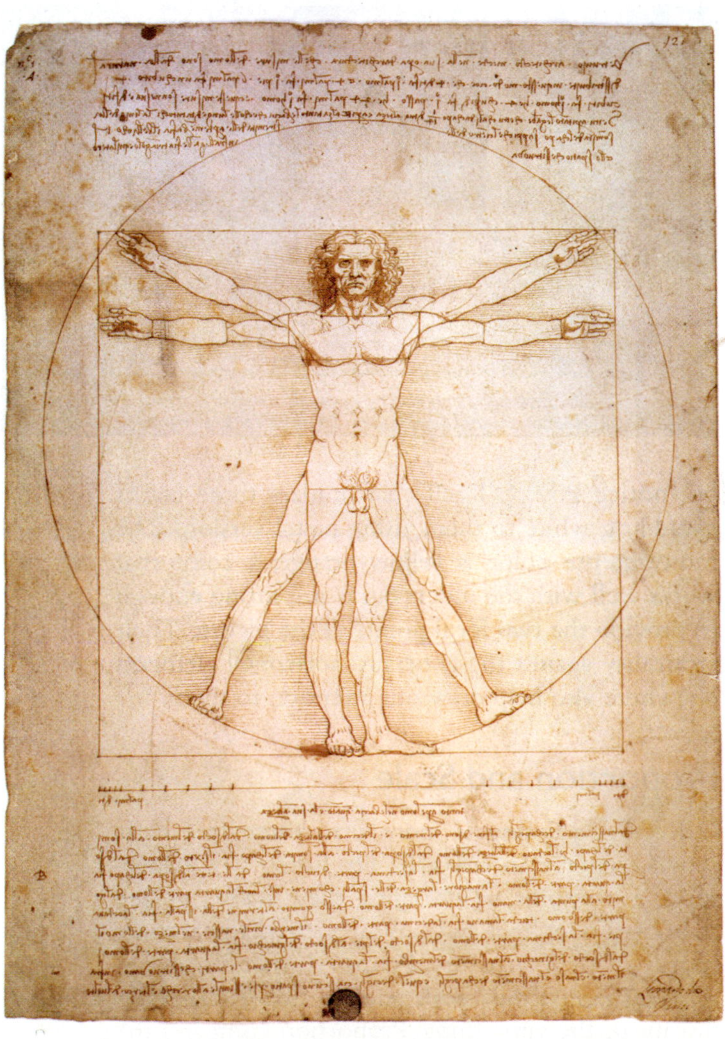

3-13 Leonardo da Vinci, *Vitruvian Man,* c. 1490. Ink and watercolor on paper, 13½″ × 9⅝″. Gallerie dell' Accademia, Venice.

Vitruvius was preceded in the search for ideal proportions by the Ancient Greeks. Their concept of the *Golden Mean* (sometimes called the *Golden Proportion, Ratio,* or *Section*) was the guiding principle for the designs of their greatest buildings like the Parthenon in Athens. By tradition, Pythagoras is credited with the discovery of the ratio. Some believe this ideal preceded the Greeks and that one can see the ratio in the Pyramids of the Ancient Egyptians. Others have claimed it was used in Ancient India.

This Golden Ratio can be determined in several ways, the simplest being to place a small rectangle and square together, thereby forming one big rectangle. When the proportions of the smaller rectangle equal that of the big overall rectangle, then it is the Golden Mean. The mathematical formula is $a/b = b/(a+b)$ or numerically 1:1.618. The Greeks simply referred to it by using the letter phi. As complicated as the formula may seem, admiration for buildings built with it has been nearly universal. Renaissance architects based their buildings on the Golden Mean. Even contemporary surveys have found that people prefer designs based on the Golden Mean compared to any other system of proportions.

For artists, however, proportions do not always have to be ideal. The impact and meaning of Alberto Giacometti's *Walking Man II* (**3-14**) is based not on perfect proportions but in its difference from the normal proportions of man. It is part of a series that occupied the sculptor for decades. His figures are so thin that they hardly exist at all. They are faceless. Moving along without grace, it seems to take all the effort their skin and bones can muster to drag along on large heavy feet, almost rooted to the earth. Through their unique proportions, therefore, they speak about the fate of modern man—anonymous, exhausted, and feeble, soon to be buried in the ground.

As with proportions, changes in scale are meaningful in art. The Ancient Egyptians used hierarchical scale in their works to show the relative importance of the individuals portrayed. In *Chest of Tutankhamen with Hunting and War Scenes* (**3-15**), a painted chest found in his tomb, the famous pharaoh is hunting both lions and his enemies. Behind him are the other members of the hunting party, but their heights are no more than one-third of his because of their lower status. The targets of his arrows—the lions and his enemies—seem even more insignificant in compari-

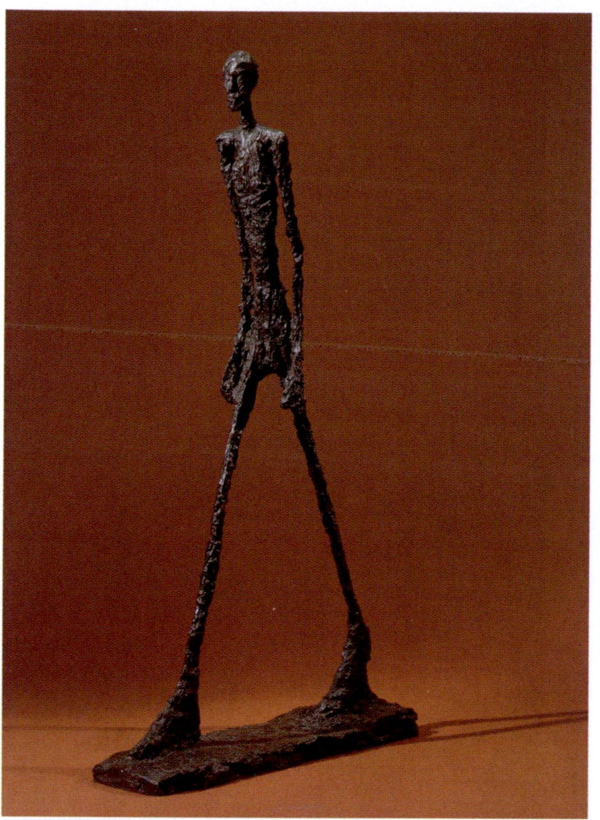

3-14 Alberto Giacometti, *Walking Man II*, 1960. Bronze, 188.5 cm × 27.9 cm × 110.7 cm (74¼″ × 11″ × 43⅝″). Gift of Enid A. Haupt. 1977.47.7. Image © 2007 Board of Trustees, National Gallery of Art, Washington, DC.

son to Tutankhamen. The use of hierarchical scaling is not unique to the Ancient Egyptians and has been used in cultures around the world. Examples can be found in Medieval, Assyrian, and Benin relief sculptures (13-26, 9-2, 9-3), as well as Renaissance altarpieces.

"Larger than life" is a common expression that means something is larger than an average person or *large scale*. Anything that large tends to attract our attention (see box). Religious buildings and shrines are often built on a majestic scale, either to impress a god with the people's devotion or to impress a people with the greatness of their god. Gothic cathedrals, Greek temples, and Islamic mosques all follow this idea of the power of enormous buildings, but few temples and statues (it is both) can compare to the forty-five-foot-tall *Colossal Buddha* of China (**3-16**), which was carved out of solid rock. Believers go inside the Buddha to worship at elaborate shrines at human scale, but the exterior's scale explains why viewers come away with a sense of an all-seeing and powerful god. If this statue were only three inches tall, the effect would be entirely different.

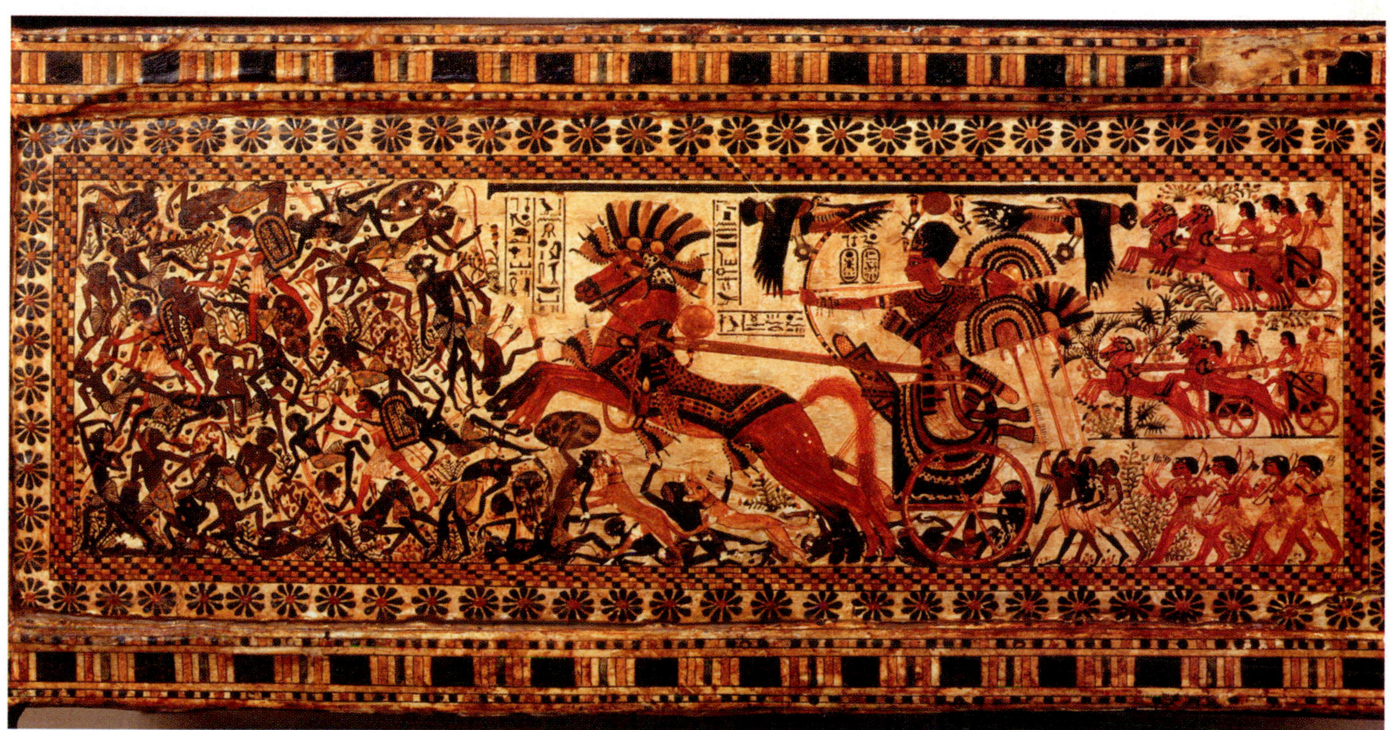

3-15 *Chest of Tutankhamen with Hunting and War Scenes* (side), c. 1323 BCE. Egyptian Museum, Cairo.

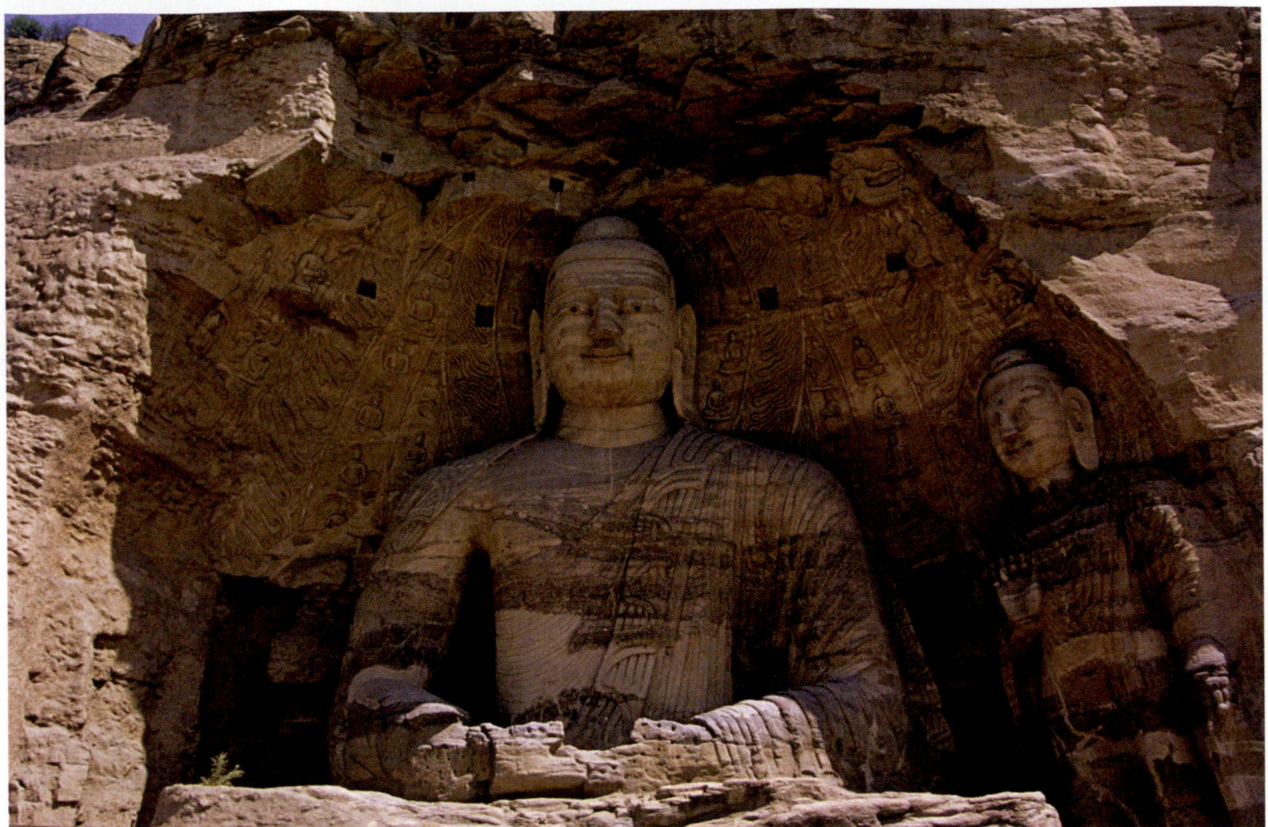

3-16 *Colossal Buddha,* Cave XX, Yungang, Shansi, China 450–500. Stone, 45′ high.

Pipilotti Rist's video installation, *Selfless in the Bath of Lava* (**3-17**), explores just that possibility. Her work is easy to miss in a gallery or museum because *Selfless* is just a few inches in size and is not hung on a wall. The sound of a woman's faint but desperate cries causes viewers to pause and search for its source. The hunt leads downward. The cries come from a small, jagged hole in the floorboards. Just beneath the hole is a three-inch video of a nude woman (the artist) that can only be seen by squatting down. She is trapped in glowing, fiery lava. Pale and white-haired, the damned woman reaches up and screams. Pleading, she yells in several languages, "You would have done everything better. Help me. Excuse me." The scale of the video changes each viewer, making him or her a giant, all-powerful being with the fate of this poor woman placed in their hands.

Quite the opposite effect is created by the scale of Robert Therrien's *Under the Table* (**3-18**). While the sculpture depicts a completely ordinary subject—a wooden table and chairs—their huge size takes the ordinary into the realm of fantasy. Scale, as stated earlier, is based on a frame of reference, often the size of a human being. Without the people in the illustration, we would assume it was a photograph of a dining room set taken from a low point of view. In fact, the idea for this sculpture came while Therrien was taking photographs of his own furniture. Because we can see the people, we understand that the table is gigantic, nearly ten feet tall. When visitors walk under the table, the effect is like being transported back in time—to a point-of-view we had when we were babies.

A more disturbing vision of infancy can be seen in David Siquieros's *Echo of a Scream* (**3-20** on page 70). Here scale and relative size is used to intensify this vision of the effect of poverty on the young. The enormous duplicate of the baby's head amplifies the power of the scream. The baby's body, however, seems weak and helpless because of its relation to the mass of surrounding garbage. Shapes in the foreground in another context might remind us of bent paperclips, but compared to the baby, they are twisted, broken pipes.

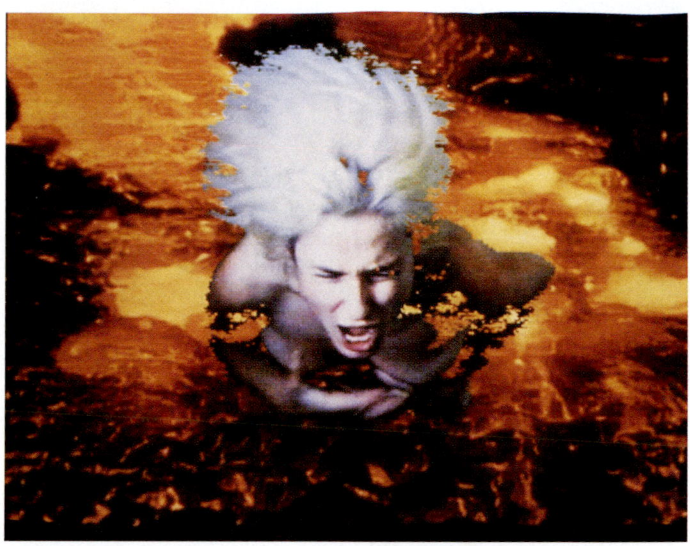

3-17 Pipilotti Rist, *Selbstlos im Lavabad (Selfless in the Bath of Lava)*, 1994; audio video installation by Pipilotti Rist (video still). Courtesy the artist and Hauser & Wirth, Zurich/London.

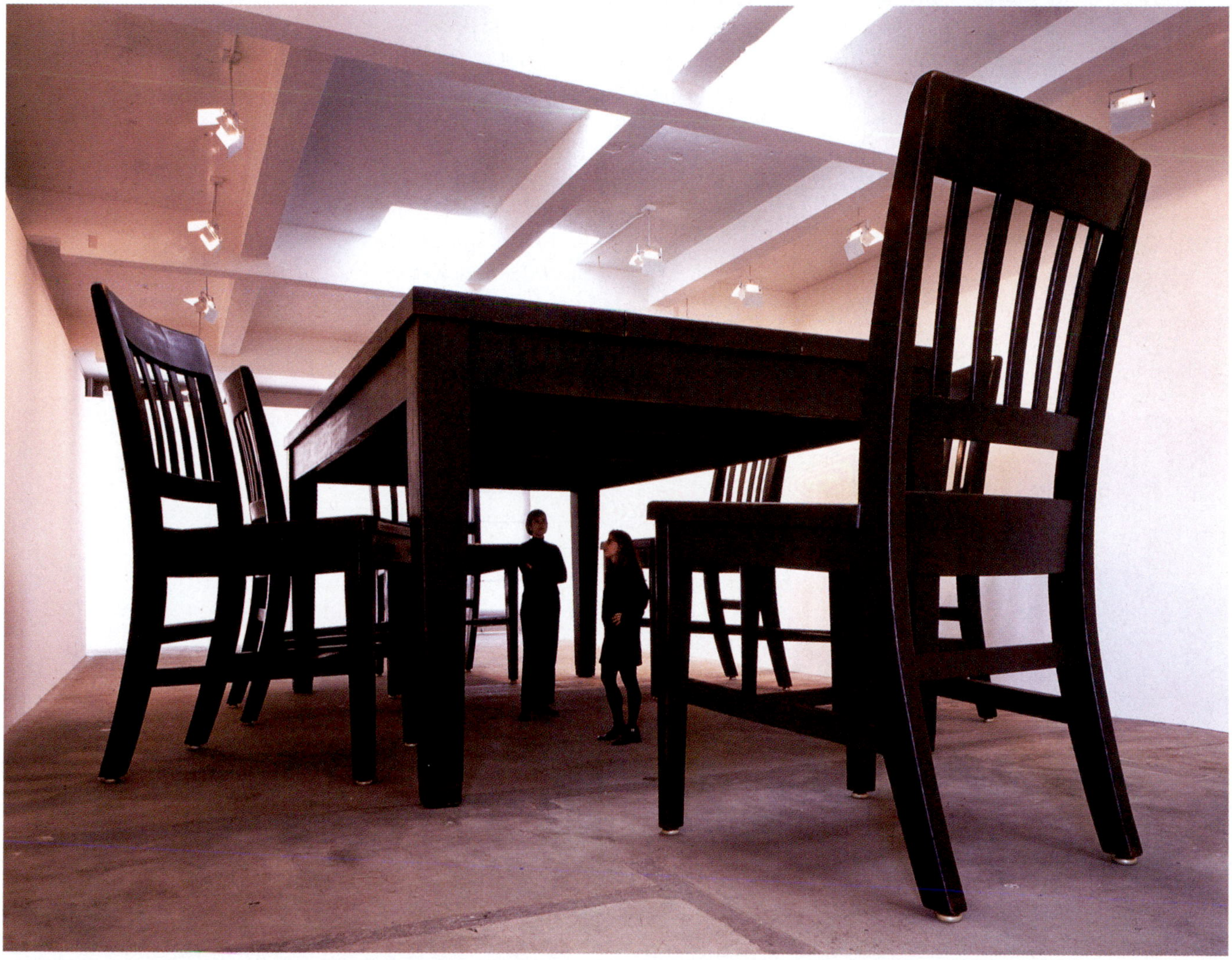

3-18 Robert Therrien, *Under the Table,* 1994. Wood and metal, 117″ × 312″ × 216″ overall. The Broad Art Foundation, Santa Monica, California. Photography: Douglas M. Parker Studio, Los Angeles.

ART NEWS

Scale on Trial: The Tilted Arc Controversy

In the 1980s, a sculpture in which no one could find any sexual, political, or even representational content became controversial just because of its scale and placement. The ultimate fate of Richard Serra's *Tilted Arc* (**3-19**), an outdoor sculpture commissioned by the federal government, would take nine years of bitter debate and court battles to resolve. During that time, it became a lightning rod for discussion about government-supported art and the rights of artists versus the public.

In 1979, Richard Serra, a Minimalist sculptor, was chosen by a panel of experts to design a sculpture for a plaza in front of a federal building complex in New York City. Serra is a well-known and critically acclaimed sculptor who had already designed sculpture for plazas in Berlin, St. Louis, Barcelona, and Paris. Serra's New York commission was part of the "Art in Architecture" program supervised by the General Services Administration (GSA) of the federal government. This program sets aside one-half of 1 percent of the monies allocated for new federal buildings toward the purchase of public art designed for the site. At the time of the commission, the federal buildings were already completed. The semicircular plaza in front of them already had a fountain at its center and was regularly traversed by thousands of federal employees.

After many consultations with engineers and the design review board of the GSA, the chief administrator of GSA in Washington, D.C. gave Serra the go-ahead for his design. It was completed and installed in 1981 and greeted with immediate hostility. *Tilted Arc* was both tall and menacing, graceful and impressive. Constructed of Cor-Ten steel (which is used for bridges) 12 feet tall and 120 feet long, it swept across almost the entire plaza between the fountain and the entrance. The sculpture formed a very gradual arc that crossed and balanced the opposing curves of the circular paving stones of the plaza. The wall of steel also tilted at a slight angle toward the central building.

Serra had decided not to embellish the fountain and buildings but to alter the whole experience of the plaza. "After the piece is created," Serra said, "the space will be understood primarily as a function of the sculpture." In other words, he wanted to make his sculpture the focus of the entire area. He succeeded in fulfilling his intention, but with a reaction he never imagined. Workers dubbed the new sculpture "the Berlin Wall of Foley Square." Instead of walking directly across the plaza as they had in the past, they were forced to walk around the sculpture. Rather than confronting and contemplating the artwork as Serra hoped they would, the workers were simply irritated by its placement. While it made a strong abstract composition when seen from the building's windows at ground level, it also blocked their view of the fountain. Angry letters flooded local newspapers and magazines, and thirteen hundred employees at the federal complex signed a petition demanding its removal.

In 1985, the head of the GSA's New York office organized three days of public hearings on the *Tilted Arc*. Testimony was heard from office workers who described the sculpture as "garbage," "an irritation," "rusted junk," and "hideous" and demanded its removal. It was clear that no one had considered consulting the occupants of the Federal Plaza, even though they would have to live with the sculpture every day. Museum curators, art scholars, critics, and artists testified in favor of the work. It was

ART NEWS

suggested that the GSA put some effort in "building public understanding" of the art it had commissioned. Serra attempted to explain his sculpture to the public:

> *Tilted Arc* was constructed to engage the public in dialogue. . . . The sculpture involved the viewer rationally and emotionally. . . . The viewer becomes aware of himself and his movement through the plaza. As he moves, the sculpture changes. Contraction and expansion of the sculpture results from the viewer's movement. Step by step, perception of not only the sculpture but the entire environment changes.

The judgment of the panel was that the sculpture should be removed. Shocked at first, Serra responded with a $30 million lawsuit, charging that the GSA had deprived him of his constitutionally protected rights of free speech and due process of law, along with breaching his contract. Serra argued that his contract called for a permanent sculpture. He had designed it specifically for the site, so it would not work in the same way in any other location. Its removal would destroy it. A judge ruled in 1987 that since the GSA had purchased the sculpture from Serra, he had no further rights connected with it. It was up to the government whether to keep it in the plaza, move it, or destroy it.

In March 1989, in the middle of the night, construction workers used jackhammers and cranes to disassemble the *Tilted Arc*. Broken into three pieces, the remains of the sculpture were taken to a city parking area and stacked while the GSA said it was looking for another site. Serra publicly announced that he would never cooperate with the government in its search. *Tilted Arc* was never seen again.

Because of the controversies surrounding his work, Richard Serra would likely agree that artists can no longer trust the commitment that the government makes for permanent displays of art. If an artist must fear immediate public outrage, isn't it likely that he or she will use safe, conventional approaches to commissions rather than ambitious ones? Will caution decorate our public places instead of imagination? The judge's ruling was particularly unsettling to artists. Can the government destroy any of its thousands of artworks?

On the positive side, awareness of the need to involve the general public in decisions on public art has increased. The GSA has instituted new policies that reflect the need for social responsibility in the designs it chooses. Artists are not given commissions after sites are finished but work with the architects during the planning stages. Concerned citizens are also invited into the planning process. Education of the community is considered an integral part of any plan to bring art to civic places.

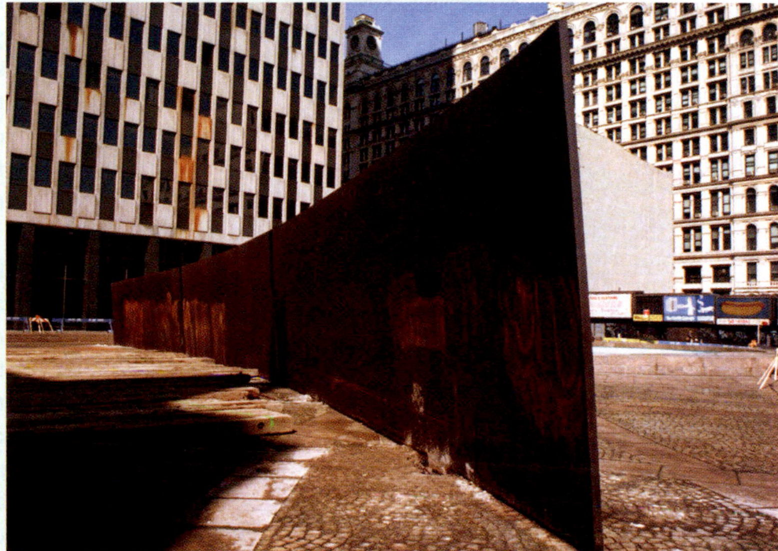

3-19 Richard Serra, *Tilted Arc,* 1981. Hot-rolled steel, 120′ long. Federal Plaza, New York.

CHAPTER 4 Drawing

A good craftsperson knows what materials and tools are appropriate to the job ahead, and this is also true for any artist. In fact, many of the materials and tools used by artists are also used by carpenters and construction workers. Artists use paper, paint, steel, and fabric; chisels, hammers, cameras, and welding torches. Artists' materials, like oil paint or clay, are referred to as **media.** Each **medium** has its own unique characteristics, demanding the knowledge of special techniques and requiring specific tools. The tools and materials artists use can influence the creation of an artwork just as much as historical and social factors. By learning about them, we will discover another way to understand art.

For most of us, drawing is the way we first experienced making art. From the first scribbles of a child to the sophisticated rendering of an adult, drawing is also the most common measure of artistic talent. In many people's minds, the wildest, most abstract artworks cannot be viewed seriously without first knowing whether an artist can draw. For them, drawing means the capability of recreating objects in the visible world accurately with a pencil. While this is a limited use of the word, many artists have shared this view. Many have also believed that drawing is the foundation for all art. For example, the great nineteenth-century draftsman, Jean-Auguste-Dominique Ingres, told the young artist Edgar Degas (see Chapter 17), "Draw lines, lots of lines, and you will become a good artist."

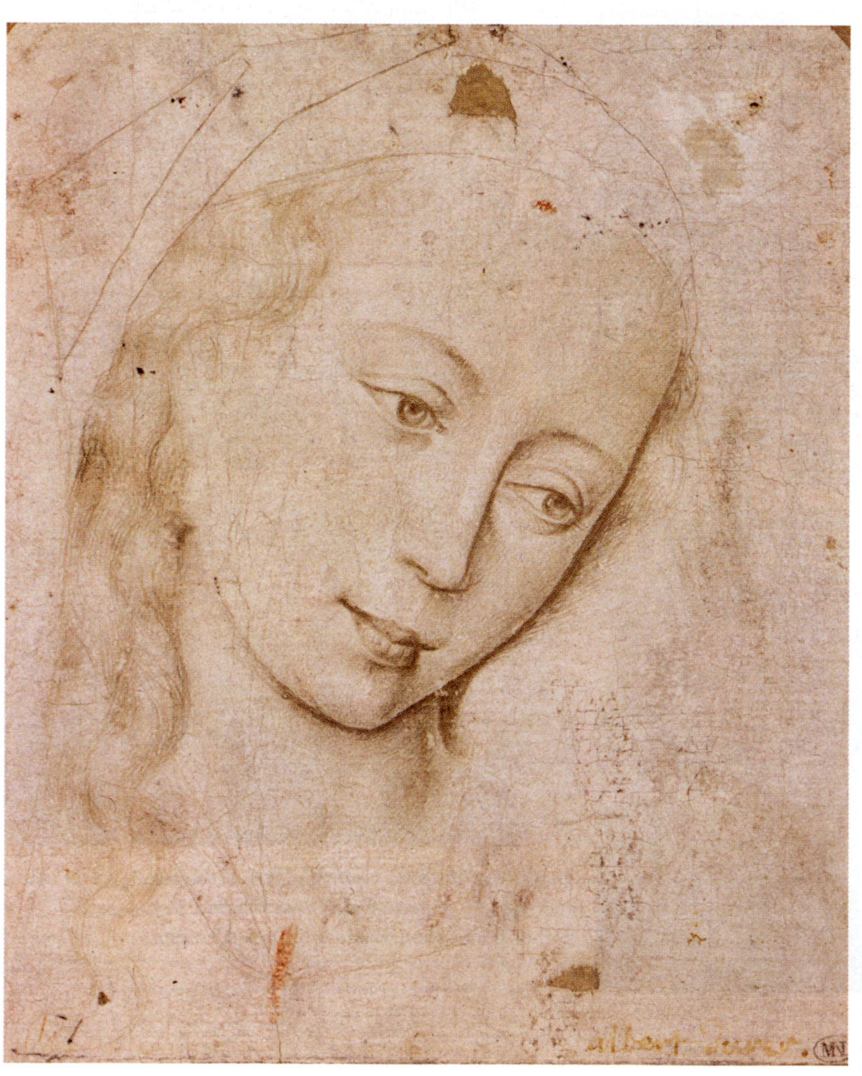

4-1 Rogier van der Weyden, *Head of the Virgin*, c. 1455. Silver nib on prepared paper with light applications of red to the lips and cheeks, 5 ¼″ × 4 ½″. Louvre, Paris.

Drawing *is* important for just about every artist. Whether a painter, sculptor, printmaker, designer, or architect, every artist draws. Many artists cannot imagine a day passing without drawing even under the worst of circumstances (see box). A drawing can be a way to plan a work in another media, or simply a way to play with ideas. Sketches range from studies of forms in nature to copies of another artist's work, but a drawing can also be a finished picture by itself. Drawing is not limited to using ordinary pencils on white paper. A variety of tools and materials fall under the category of drawing.

GRAPHITE

The most common instrument for drawing is a *graphite,* often inaccurately called "lead," pencil. The term "lead pencil" persists as a reminder of the drawing tool graphite replaced in the late sixteenth century. For the previous two hundred years, artists who were interested in pure, precise lines had used **metalpoint,** which was actually a thin metal wire in a holder. While silver was the preferred metal, other metals including lead were also used. Rogier van der Weyden's *Head of the Virgin* (**4-1**) is an example of the delicate beauty of metalpoint drawings. Because it is made with the scrapes of light-colored metal on pale paper, a vision of the Virgin Mary appears to have materialized rather than to have been drawn.

Graphite sticks became a favored drawing tool after 1560, when the finest graphite in Europe was discovered in a mine in Cumberland, England. More and more artists were attracted to the advantages of the new material. While metalpoint produces delicate lines that are fairly light, graphite is able to make similar lines *and* bold, dark, dramatic ones. It is also more conducive to creativity, because metalpoint lines are nearly impossible to remove, but graphite lines are easily erased. Graphite permitted a less methodical and more experimental kind of drawing.

Graphite *pencils* were first created when the splendid English graphite was in short supply on the European continent during a war in the 1750s (in fact, it was considered so valuable there was concern about an invasion of graphite-deprived French artists). An inferior grade of graphite was ground into a powder and compressed into rods. The rods were slipped into wood cylinders, usually cedar. Even though the graphite deposit was mined out in the 1800s, graphite sticks continue to be used today. However, the less messy pencils have become the most popular drawing tool of artists and art students.

Few, if any, artists have ever displayed greater mastery of graphite than the nineteenth-century Frenchman Jean-Auguste-Dominique Ingres. His stunning portrait of his wife, Madame Delphine Ingres (**4-2**), shows in its delicacy the influence of metalpoint drawings by the great masters he so admired. But the variety of tones and widths in Ingres's lines are unique to graphite. Notice how one line will change its weight, beginning thin and almost invisible, gradually thickening, then thinning again. These subtle changes require tremendous skill and produce a convincing illusion of three-dimensional form within one line. In addition to superbly crafted lines, Ingres also creates soft tones that add to the illusion of solidity.

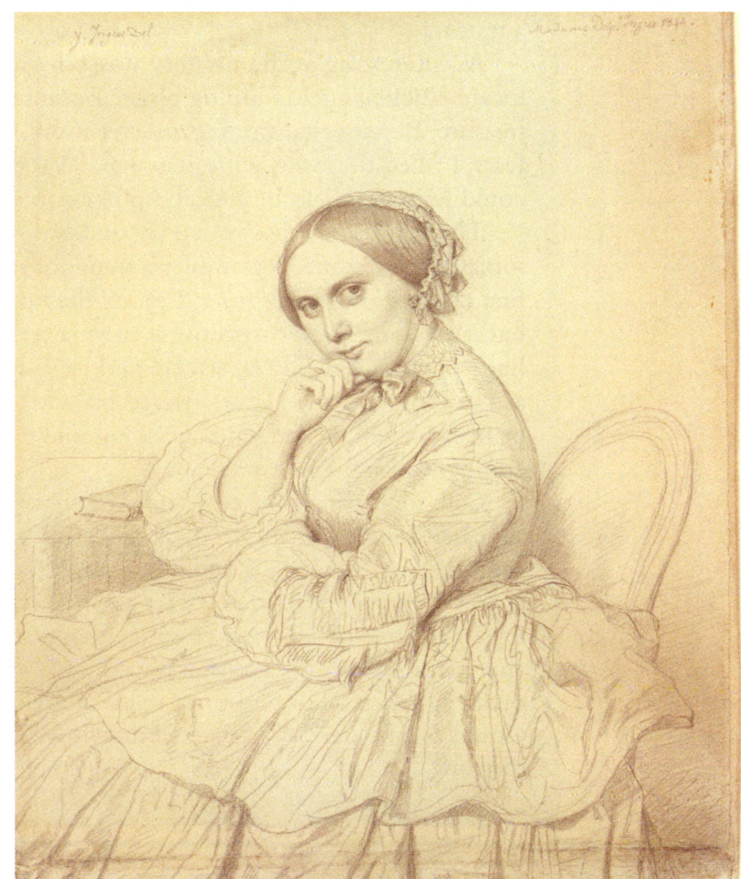

4-2 J. A. D. Ingres, *Portrait of Madame Ingres,* 1855. Graphite on white wove paper, 13¾″ × 10¾″. Courtesy of the Fogg Art Museum, Harvard University Art Museums (gift of Charles E. Dunlap).

CHAPTER 5

Painting

When most people think of art, they think of painting. This seems to be true of both the layperson and the connoisseur. Our museums devote more space to painting than any other art form. During the Renaissance, there was a great deal of discussion about whether painting was the highest of the arts. Leonardo da Vinci thought it was, placing it above sculpture and poetry. He wrote:

> if the painter wishes to see enchanting beauties, he has the power to produce them. If he wishes to see monstrosities, . . . he has the power and authority to create them . . . if in the hot season he wants cool and shady places, or in the cold season warm places, he can make them. . . . Indeed whatever exists in the universe, whether in essence, in act, or in the imagination, the painter has first in his mind and then in his hands.

There was even a questionnaire on this issue distributed to many of the important artists of the time. A painter, Pontormo, responded that the complexities of his medium were much more challenging than the others. He wrote:

> there are the various modes of working—fresco, oil, tempera . . . all of which require great practice in handling so many different pigments, to know their various results when mixed various ways, to render lights, darks, shadows, high-lights, reflections, and many other effects beyond number.

The painting media are certainly more complicated than the drawing media discussed in the last chapter. Many formulas for paint have been used over the centuries, and some artists have almost become chemists in their desire to create the perfect paint. However, all paints share a general formula that is not difficult to remember: They are a combination of powdery pigments combined with a liquid *binder,* also called a *medium.* This glue-like substance holds the paint together and attaches it to the surface (called the **ground**). What differentiates the painting media from each other, and gives each one its special qualities, is the type of medium used.

ENCAUSTIC

Encaustic is a painting medium that is at least seven thousand years old. It is created by mixing colored pigments with hot beeswax and then painting the mixture on a surface before it cools. After it hardens, the wax surface is remarkably permanent, and the painted colors can retain their brilliance for thousands of years.

We are not sure when this method was first used, but Homer describes in *The Iliad* how the ancient Greeks waterproofed and decorated the hulls of their ships with hot, colored wax. The realistic portraits on Egyptian mummy cases from the first century BCE are some of the earliest surviving examples of encaustic painting. The colors painted on ancient Greek and Roman marble statuary were usually in encaustic (probably because it also waterproofed

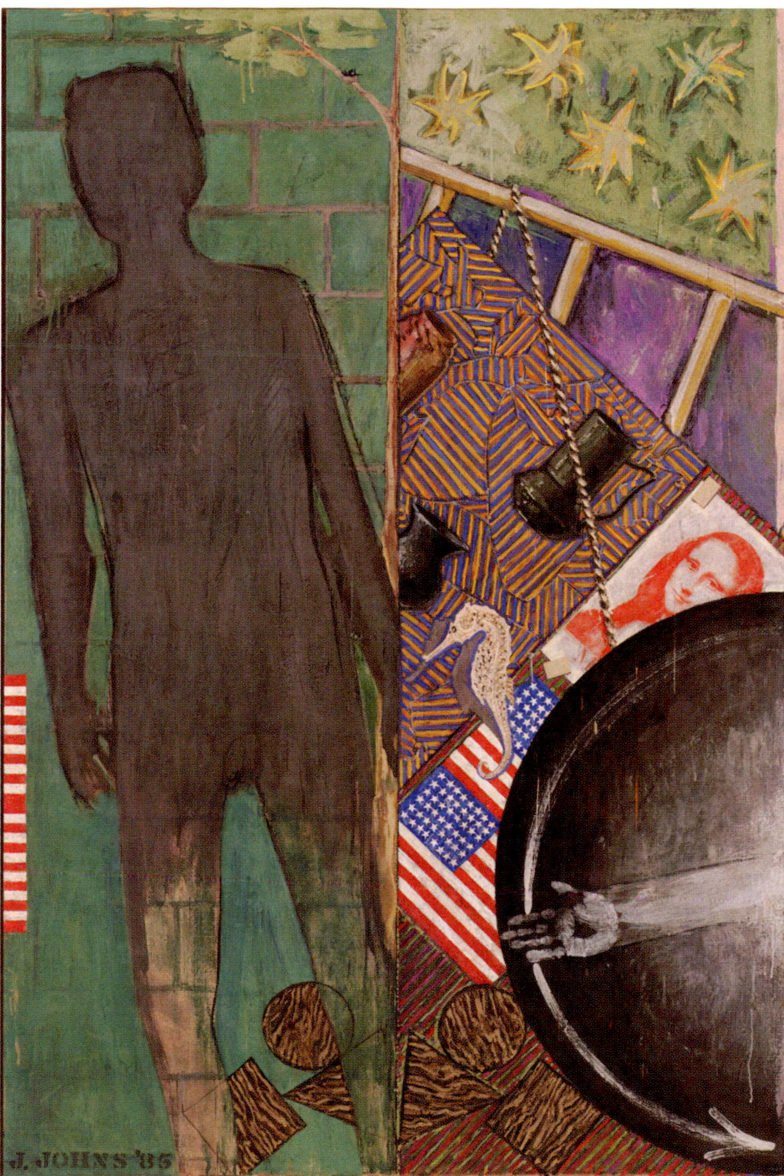

5-1 Jasper Johns, *The Seasons: Summer,* 1985. Encaustic on canvas, 75″ × 50″. Gift of Philip Johnson, Museum of Modern Art, NY. Art © Jasper Johns/Licensed by VAGA, New York, NY

them). In the past fifty years, this ancient painting medium has experienced a revival among contemporary artists.

Jasper Johns has been one of the leaders of the encaustic renaissance. His series of encaustics, *Seasons*, from the 1980s, were done when the artist was in his late fifties and contemplating moving. By increasing the amount of wax in encaustic paint, it becomes more transparent. Johns uses this property when painting his silhouette, a projected shadow that appears in all four of these autobiographical paintings.

Encaustic also allows an artist to build up many layers of textured paint. The complexity of Johns' pictures comes from the many layers and the amount of subject matter he includes. Surrounding his silhouette are many objects that have personal meaning for the artist. In *The Seasons: Summer* (**5-1**), bits of his earlier works, like his early American flag series (see Chapter 20), can be seen, all held up by a rope, strung across a ladder. There are references to the discoveries of his young adult years, like the art of da Vinci, as well as a love of pottery. At the bottom are outlines of building blocks, as if to say these were the building blocks of my career. In *Fall,* the ladder snaps, the rope comes loose, and different pictures tumble down. Greens have turned to brown and the arm swings lower like a clock. By *Winter,* the hand is straight down and the scene is gray and covered with snow.

CHAPTER 6

Printmaking

During the Renaissance, so many important changes took place in the Western world that it seems impossible to select the most significant development. However, the invention of the printing press in the 1450s is certainly among the greatest innovations of this period. To use just one example, Martin Luther's Protestant **Reformation** would probably never have occurred if thousands of copies of his ninety-five criticisms of the church ("95 Theses"), supplemented with printed cartoons for the illiterate, had not been circulated all over Europe. No wonder Luther said, "Print is the best of God's inventions."

In art, printing's effect was perhaps not quite as dramatic, but its contribution has been very significant. The book you hold in your hands is a product of the print revolution. The modern concept of art appreciation would not be possible without printing presses. Because of art reproductions, art—once the exclusive domain of the very wealthy and powerful—is today available to virtually everyone.

The term *print,* however, has a special meaning to the fine artist. It does not mean photographic reproductions like those in this book, but reproductions or *multiples* made directly from a block, plate, stone, or screen that an artist created. The number of prints is limited by an artist and is called the **edition.** Once the last print of an edition is "pulled," the block, plate, or other source is destroyed. Usually an artist will sign each print and also number it. For example, "23/100" means the print was the twenty-third out of an edition of one hundred. Even though an edition can number in the hundreds, each individual print is still considered an original work of art. Even before printmaking, there were other precedents for this understanding of what is an "original"—for example, limited sets of bronze casts made from a clay sculpture.

One of the most important effects of printmaking has been making fine art originals available to more people. Because they are multiples, prints are generally less expensive than other art forms. Many artists chose to be printmakers because printmaking seemed less elitist, more democratic than the other media.

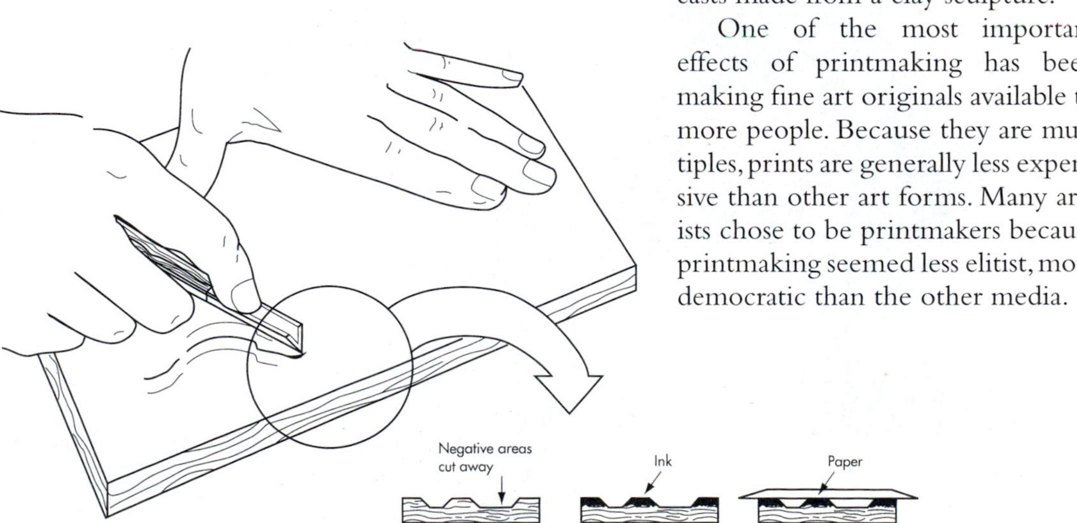

6-1 Woodcut relief process.

RELIEF PRINTMAKING

Woodcut

In the past five hundred years, many forms of printmaking have evolved. The first in the West was the **woodcut** print, adapated from an Asian technique for printing cloth. When illuminated (handpainted) manuscripts were replaced by printed books, a way to print illustrations was also needed. Woodcut blocks were found to be the most appropriate because they fit easily into the printing press along with the type. Woodcuts are among the simplest of the print media (**6-1**). They are made by carving directly into a smooth piece of wood and removing any areas of the surface that are not part of the future image. In essence, the negative spaces of a design are cut away, leaving the positive areas raised up, ready to be printed. Usually a drawing is made directly on the wood, and then the background is cut out around it. The carved block is inked with a roller; the uncarved wood remaining on the surface will receive the ink and make an impression on the paper. Because the print's marks are made from inking what is left in "relief" on the block, woodcuts fall into the category of **relief printmaking.** Linoleum cuts and rubber stamps also fall into this category.

For example, in Albrecht Dürer's *The Four Horsemen* (**6-2**), all of the white areas had to be carved out of the block so the thin black lines in the print could appear. To make the actual print, a piece of paper is placed on top of the inked woodblock and either

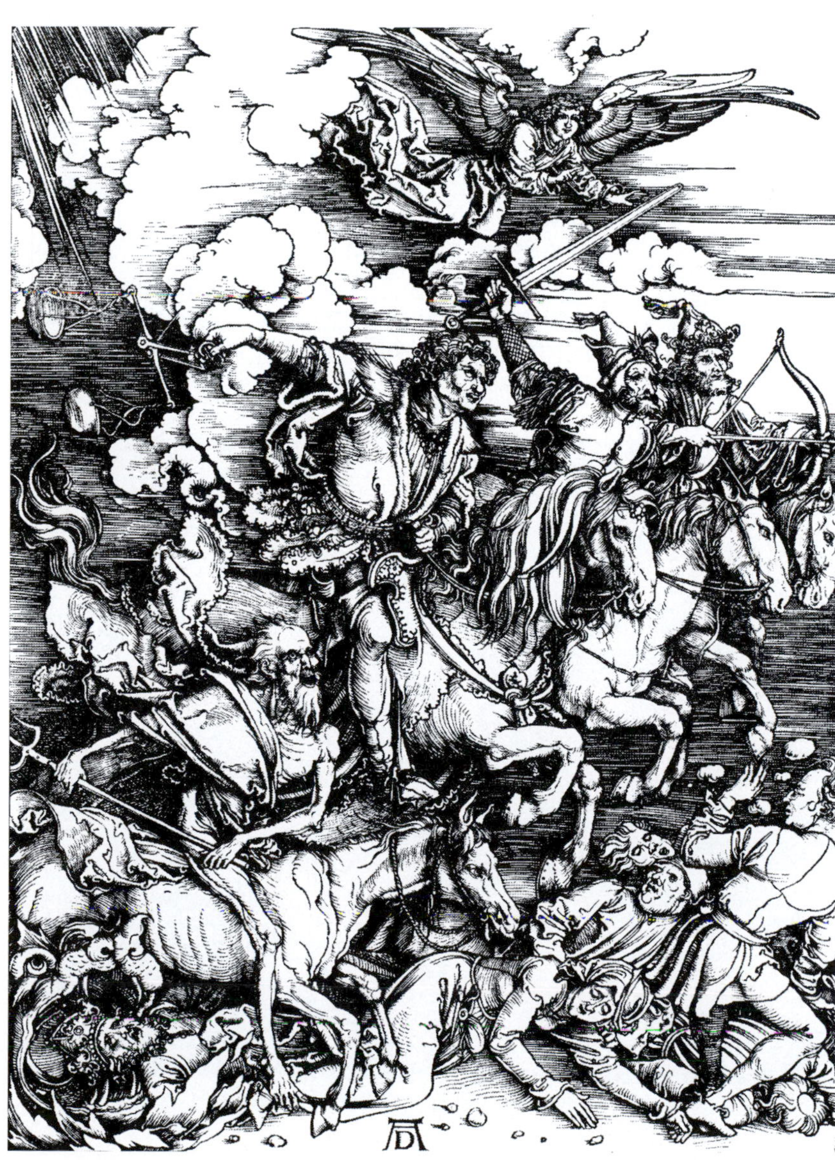

6-2 Albrecht Dürer, *The Four Horsemen,* from the Apocalypse series, c. 1498. Woodcut, 15 ½″ × 11″. British Museum, London, Great Britain.

rubbed on the back by hand or passed through a printing press to transfer the image to the paper.

The first woodcut prints in Europe were decorated with crude, simple images. Purchased by ordinary people, most were either playing cards or devotional images, like saints or charms for warding off evil. Albrecht Dürer was the first Renaissance artist to show that prints could be the equal of painting or any of the other fine arts. At the time he created *The Four Horsemen,* Dürer had just returned from Italy, where he had seen the works of the great Renaissance masters for the first time. He wanted his woodcuts to have the vital force and imaginative compositions that he admired in Italian painting. The fine details in this print, the result of elaborate carving, had never been seen by Europeans in a woodcut. By recreating drawing's parallel hatching on his woodblock, he was able to model his forms and provide a sense of movement and excitement. The subject of the print is taken from Chapter 6 of the Book of Revelation and known as the four horsemen of the Apocalypse (or end of the world). The first horseman on the right holds a bow and symbolizes conquest; the second holds a sword, symbolizing war; the third a pair of scales, symbolizing famine; and the horseman at the front left of the image is Death riding a pale horse. In the lower lefthand corner is Hades, the mouth of hell:

> And behold, a pale horse, and its rider's name was death, and Hades followed him; and they were given power over a fourth of the earth, to kill with sword and with famine and with pestilence and by wild beasts of the earth.

Dürer's print brings this fantastic scene to life, with the skeletal figure of death creating a vivid, unforgettable image of horror.

Woodcuts with fine details and elaborate design were familiar in Asia centuries before Dürer's landmark work. Paper, a necessary material for traditional printmaking, was invented in China approximately one thousand years before it first appeared in the West. So it is not surprising that the first woodblock prints also appeared earlier in the orient, around AD 800. Buddhist scrolls printed in China found their way to Japan, which eventually produced some of the greatest prints ever made. Even Dürer's superb woodcut seems rather crude next to Kuniyoshi Utagawa's *Various Stages of Making a Color Print* (**6-3**).

As seen in this print, the Japanese woodcut printing process was very different than the one Dürer followed. Dürer designed and carved his blocks himself. In Japan, a color print was the work of several artisans, each with a specialized role. Utagawa was the designer of the print, making the drawing and planning the color scheme. Cutters would then carve the block, while printers would ink and print

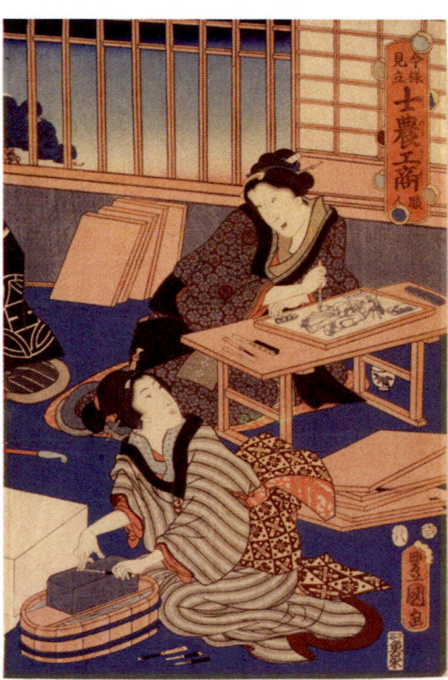
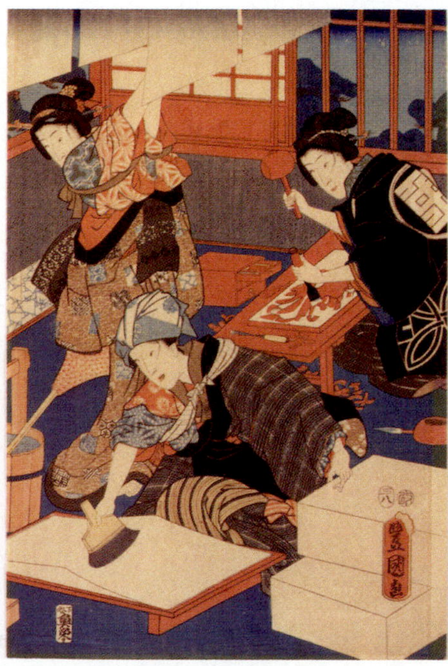
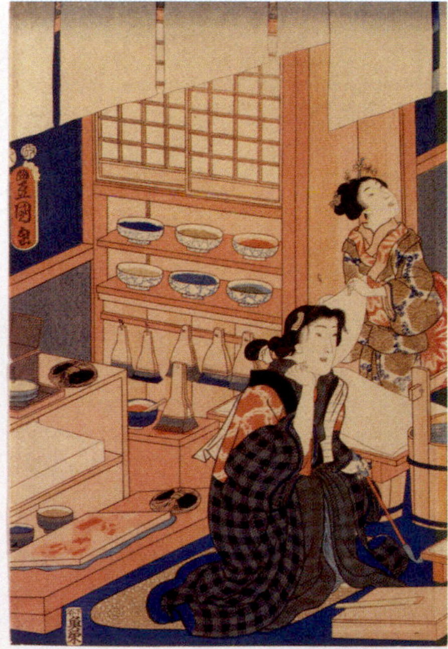

6-3 Kuniyoshi Utagawa, *Various Stages of Making a Color Print,* 1857. Color woodcut, 9¾″ × 14½″. Victoria & Albert Museum, London.

it. They worked as a team, with no member considered more important than another. The Japanese did not share the Western idea that the artist's unique concept is the most valuable part of an artwork. The Japanese characters at the sides of the print are the marks of the various workers, much like the credits at the end of a film.

In a color print like this one, each separate color is the product of a different carved wooden block. As in all color prints, each color must line up correctly with the previously inked color images as it is added to the print (known as proper **registration**), or the print will be ruined—blurred or mismatched. This registration requires skill and planning by both artist and printer. We will see later in this chapter and in Chapter 17 that Japanese print design was extremely influential in the development of both modern printmaking and Modern Art.

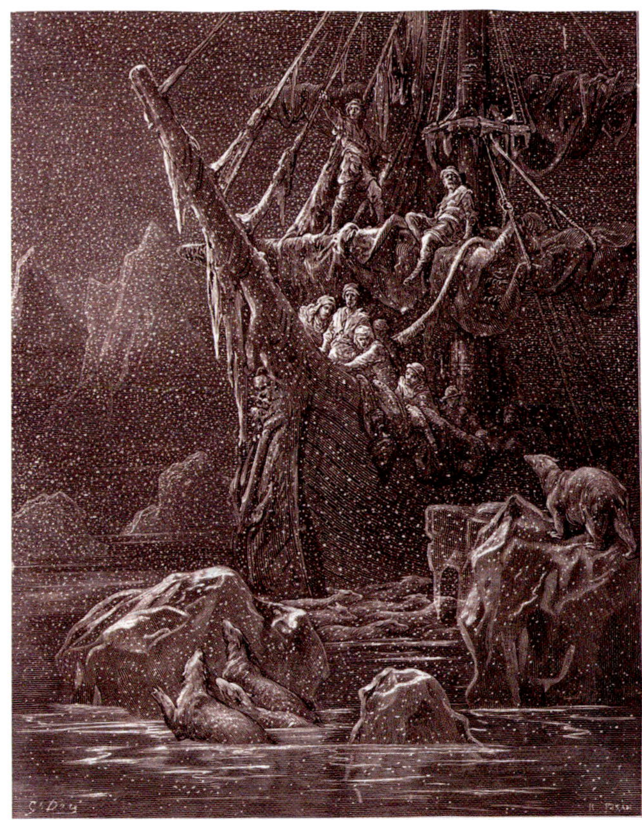

6-4 Gustave Doré, illustration from Samuel Taylor Coleridge's *The Rime of the Ancient Mariner,* 1878. Woodcut, 9¼″ × 12″. Published by Harper & Brothers Publishers, New York, 1878.

Wood Engraving

Another relief process is **wood engraving,** first used in the 1800s. It is similar to woodcut but uses the endgrain on blocks of very hard wood, and because the endgrain is so hard, tools designed to cut metal are needed. The wood's density permits very fine, precise lines to be created, and, compared to woodcuts, many more prints can be made before the block begins to deteriorate. These two properties made wood engraving particularly useful for book illustration.

Gustave Doré was the preeminent French illustrator of the mid-1800s. It was his aim to illustrate all of the great books in Western literature. Figure **6-4** shows one page from his illustrated edition of the English Romantic poet Samuel Coleridge's famous poem *The Rime of the Ancient Mariner.* Doré would work on several blocks at once, first drawing directly on each block and then moving around his studio making careful cuts on one, then another, until they were all finished. The section of the poem illustrated by this engraving tells of a sailing ship sent off-course by a storm and reads:

> And now there came both mist and snow, And it grew wondrous cold:
> And ice, mast-high, came floating by, As green as emerald.

Notice how Doré was able to engrave delicate, almost perfect, parallel lines throughout his print. By varying their width, three-dimensional forms emerge, like the icebergs in the distance. He contrasts the precision of his lines with the natural effect of falling snow made freely with short stabs into the wood. Remember that the white lines, shapes, and spots represent cuts in the wood's surface; the black areas represent the surface of the wood that was left uncut.

INTAGLIO PRINTMAKING

Intaglio printmaking is the opposite of relief printing; here what is removed ends up being printed (**6-5**). Lines are cut into the surface of metal plates using either sharp tools or acids. The cut lines act as little channels that retain the ink after the plate has been inked by a roller and its surface wiped off. Then a piece of moistened paper is placed over the plate. Finally, the paper and plate are run through a press, the heavy pressure of which forces the damp paper into the ink-filled grooves and thereby transfers the image. Like the letters in an engraved invitation, the lines of an intaglio print are raised, because each line on the paper was formed by being pushed into a depression in a metal plate.

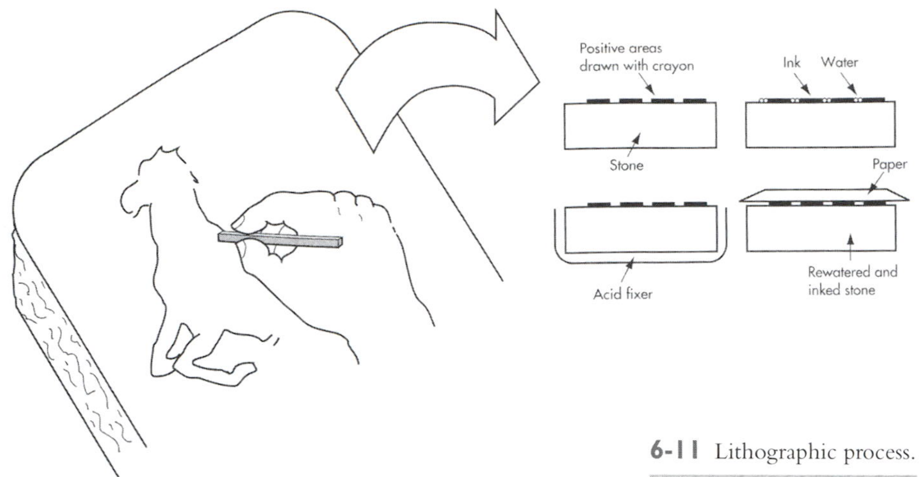

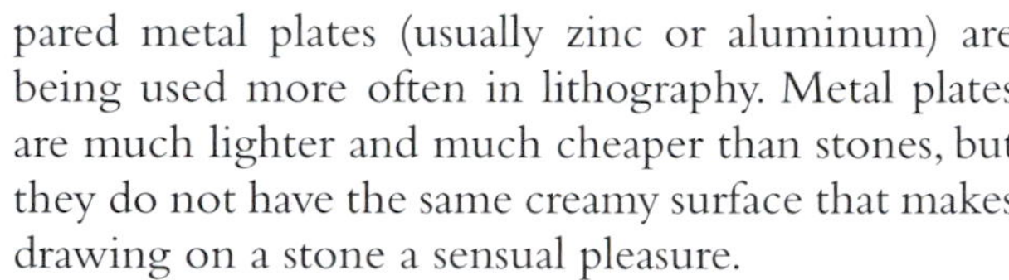

6-11 Lithographic process.

rare. Printers around the world consider them their most valuable possessions; dropping and cracking a Bavarian stone is considered a tragedy. Because of the difficulty in obtaining such stones, specially prepared metal plates (usually zinc or aluminum) are being used more often in lithography. Metal plates are much lighter and much cheaper than stones, but they do not have the same creamy surface that makes drawing on a stone a sensual pleasure.

Many nineteenth-century artists designed lithographs, but Henri de Toulouse-Lautrec raised colored lithography to the status of fine art. *Miss Loie Fuller* (**6-12**) is a print designed to capture the essence of the American performer who took Paris by storm in the early 1890s. A dancer who did not dance, Fuller used huge billows of fabric and theatrical lights to create an impression of fluid motion. Here Lautrec shows Fuller suspended against a dark background, with only her small head and two tiny feet projecting beyond the exuberant, moth-like wings of her costume. You can see the curved corners of the stone block that the print was drawn on, as well as sinuous outlines of the figure drawn in tusche, and spatters of ink as well as areas of shadow created by a greasy crayon. After this drawing was made, Lautrec experimented with different color combinations as he printed. In this version, the colors of the costume blend into each other, reproducing the effect of the colored electric lights Fuller used during her performances. Lautrec published an edition (or series) of these prints, but each one is slightly different.

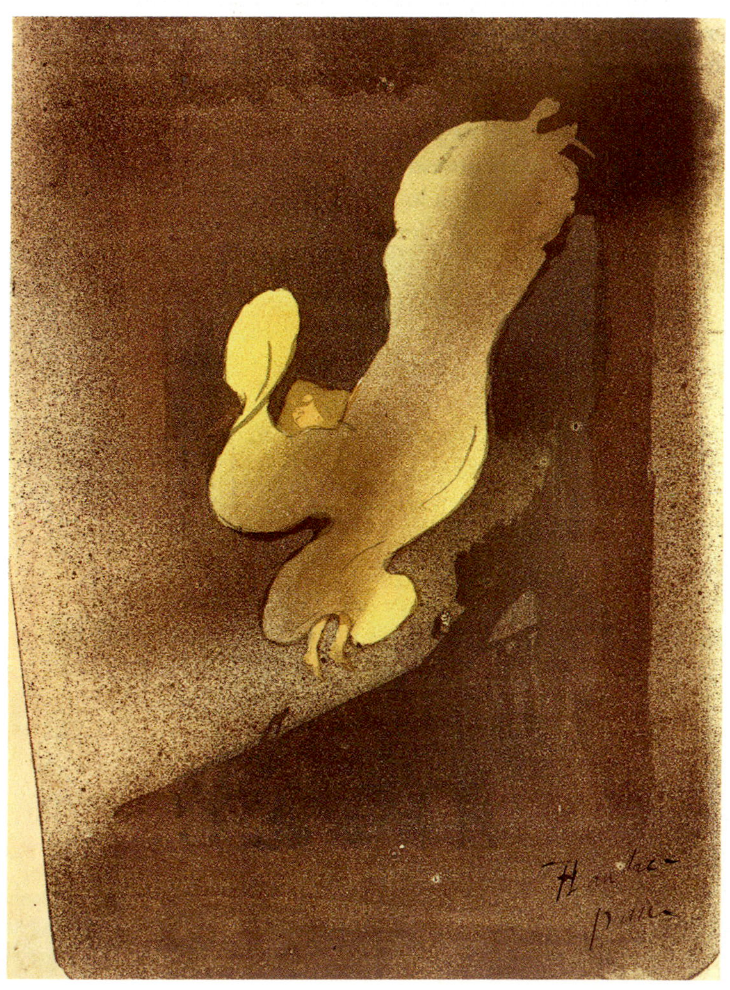

6-12 Henri de Toulouse-Lautrec, *Miss Loie Fuller,* 1893, lithograph, printed in color, 14½″ × 10 9/16″ (36.8 cm × 26.8 cm). British Museum, London.

ART ISSUES

What's the Difference between a Print and a Poster?

Do you know the difference between a fine art print and a poster? Both are printed duplicates, both are two-dimensional works of art that can be in black-and-white or color, and both can be used to decorate one's home. Both can show works by famous or unknown artists. Usually, both are printed on paper. So what's the difference?

In general, artists' prints are limited editions in which each individual print is considered an original work of art. These types of prints are usually printed or supervised by the artist, carefully numbered, and sold to galleries, museums, or collectors. Posters are reproduced mechanically in huge print runs, and can be sold by the millions in bookstores, museums, on the street, even over the World Wide Web. There was no dramatic difference between prints and posters until the nineteenth century. Most print runs were fairly small and the presses were operated by hand. In the 1800s, however, the industrial revolution also created a revolution in printing. Now images for a general public could be mass-produced in factories.

To understand the difference between prints and posters better, consider the work of Toulouse-Lautrec. We have already seen his print of *Miss Loie Fuller* (6-12), which appeared in a limited edition for collectors in 1893. Around the same time, Lautrec was also designing posters for events in Paris—posters to be plastered on walls around the city. Instead of being paid by art lovers and collectors, Lautrec was working for businesses—usually theatrical shows—that wanted to advertise their products and services.

In addition to Loie Fuller, turn-of-the-century Paris went wild for a series of female entertainers. One of the most famous was dancer Jane Avril, also a close friend of Toulouse-Lautrec. The artist featured her in several posters, including this one for *Divan Japonais,* a popular cabaret (**6-13**). Pictured behind Avril is a well-known music critic, and performing on stage (though with her

6-13 Henri de Toulouse-Lautrec, *Divan Japonais,* 1893, lithographic poster, printed in color, 31 13⁄16″ × 23 15⁄16″ (80.8 cm × 60.8 cm). The Museum of Modern Art, New York, Abby Aldrich Rockefeller Fund, 1949.

(continued on next page)

ART ISSUES

head cut off by the edge of the paper) is another female celebrity, the singer Yvette Guilbert.

Although it was created as a poster, Lautrec's color lithograph has the same brilliant design as his prints and paintings (see Chapter 17). The treatment of Avril's black dress and hat with their flat, bold shapes is a result of a fascination with Japanese prints that he shared with Mary Cassatt and other Post-Impressionists (see box on Japonisme, Chapter 17). But Japanese prints had been made with small, light blocks of wood. The colors in this lithographic print are a tribute to the dedication and imagination of Lautrec, because each color had to be printed separately using a different stone. Since Lautrec had to use several heavy stones to complete *Divan Japonais* (one black, one yellow, one green, one orange), exact registration was a challenge, yet all of the edges meet crisply. Because he was a great artist, Lautrec's posters have become valued prints over the years. This striking advertisement, once made as one of a storm of competing posters, is now in the collection of the Museum of Modern Art.

Most students purchase posters to decorate their walls, from reproductions of paintings to advertisements for movies, concerts, and rock groups. Such mass-produced decorative images, like Lautrec's posters, can increase in value over time, some even attaining a kind of cult status. This might be said of posters made for rock concerts in the 1960s. With their curving lines and pulsating electric colors, these images reflect the interchange between the counter-culture of the era and commercial mass culture. "Go with the Flow," a catchphrase of the Sixties, might be a fitting subtitle for this poster designed by Bonnie Maclean in 1967 for a concert at the Fillmore starring The Yardbirds and The Doors (**6-14**). The type and colored, peacock-tail pattern seem to flow down the surface of the poster, creating a message that is challenging to read, yet intriguing to decipher. Interestingly, this poster—like Lautrec's—is in the collection of the Museum of Modern Art, but as part of their design collection. Chapter 11, "Crafts and Design," will further explore the place of design in the visual arts.

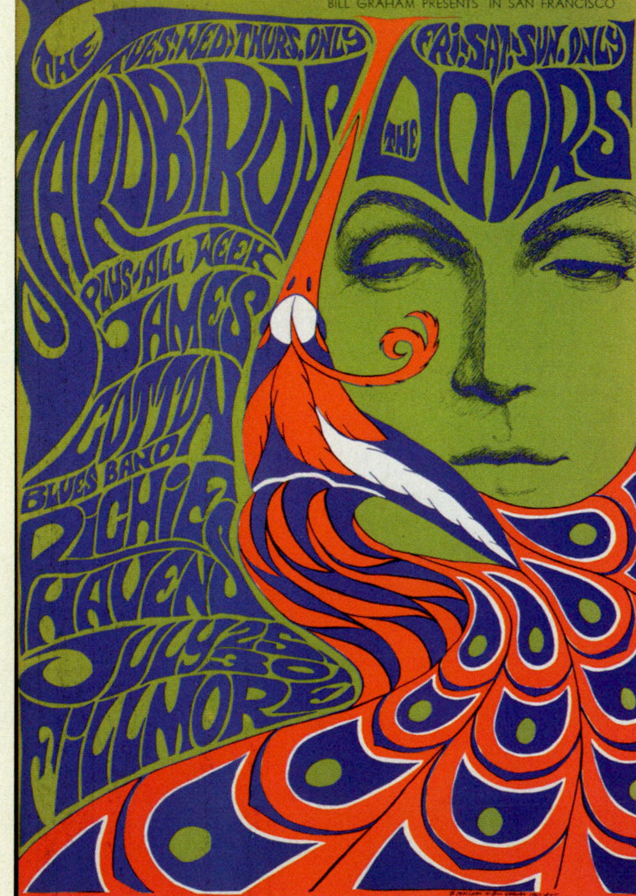

6-14 Bonnie Maclean, *The Yardbirds, The Doors,* 1967, offset lithograph, 21 ¼″ × 14″ (54 cm × 35.5 cm). Private Collection.

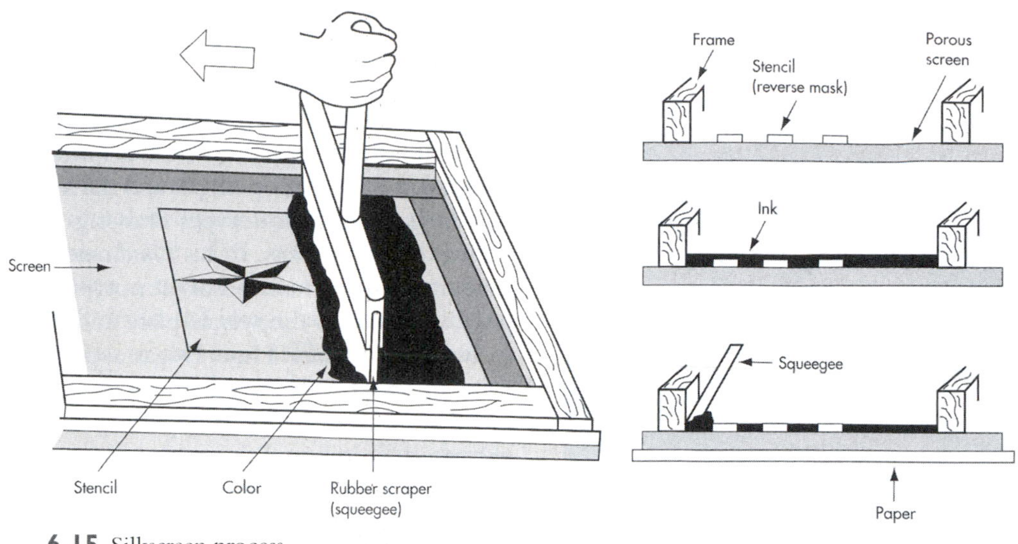

6-15 Silkscreen process.

SILKSCREEN

Silkscreen printing (or *serigraphy*) is one of the newer printmaking media, developed originally for industrial printing of patterns on fabrics. It is an inexpensive method of producing very large editions of prints and is often used for posters and T-shirts. Silkscreen is based on the ancient technique of stenciling. A stencil is attached to a screen of silk that has been tightly stretched over a wooden frame (**6-15**). After a piece of paper is placed underneath the screen, ink is spread across the screen with a rubber blade or squeegee. The open areas of silk (those not covered with a stencil) let the ink come through and print onto the paper. As in woodcut prints, no press is necessary.

A silkscreen stencil can be created with anything that will block the ink. Heavy paper stencils produce shapes that will print with crisp edges, or glue can be painted directly onto the silk for looser effects. With the use of photosensitive chemicals, it is also possible to create stencils from photographic sources, as in Barbara Kruger's *Untitled (We don't need another hero)* (**6-16**). Here, Kruger combined two kinds of subjects: photographs and written words. She utilized a photo-stencil to borrow (or **appropriate**) imagery from another source—an illustration from the 1950s. Her statement "We don't need another hero" is a strong condemnation of the "macho" tendencies in men that the era glorified.

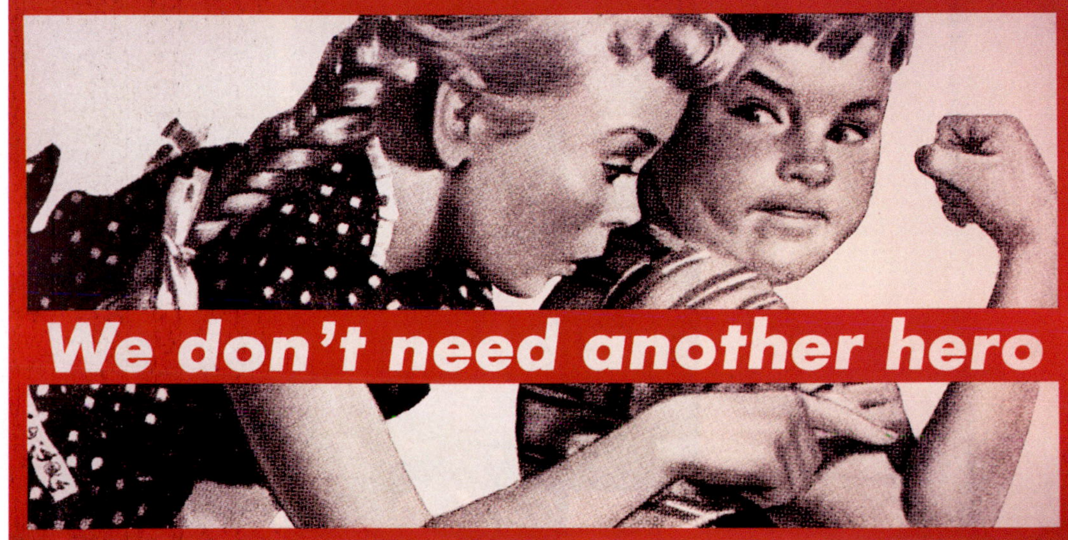

6-16 Barbara Kruger, *Untitled (We don't need another hero),* 1987. Photograph silkscreen and vinyl, 109″ × 210″. Collection of Emily Fisher Landau, New York. Mary Boone Gallery, NY

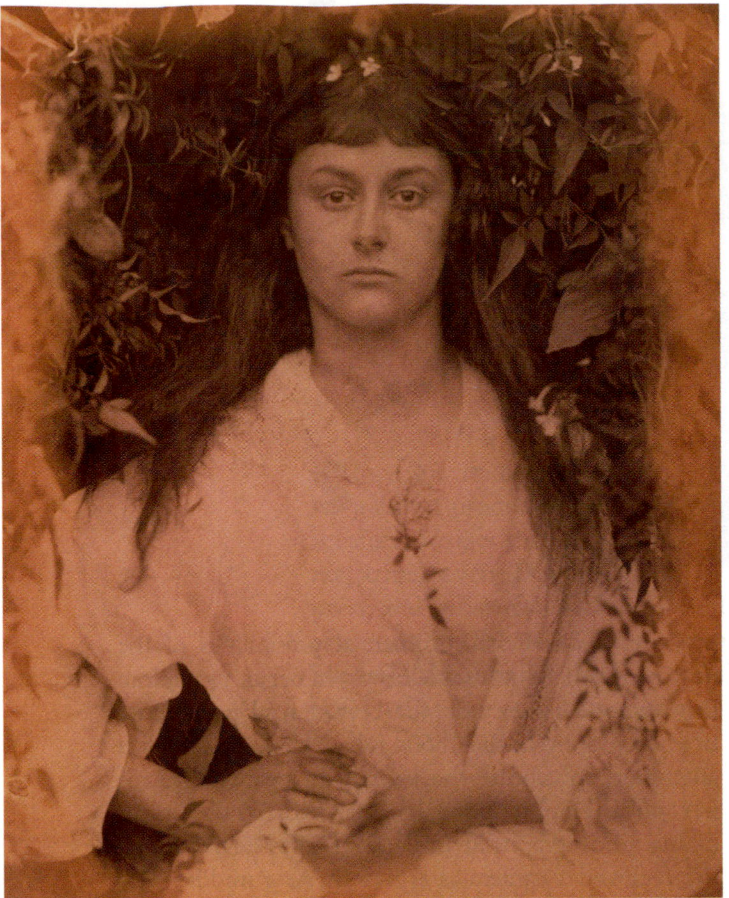

7-4 Julia Margaret Cameron, *Pomona,* 1872. Private Collection.

Cameron's close-up images of her friends and family have a monumental, mythological quality, each face representing both an individual and a perfect type of beauty. In *Pomona* (**7-4**), Cameron presented her young sitter, Alice Liddel, as the goddess of fruit trees, dressed in an ethereal white gown and surrounded by lush vegetation. Yet the subject's face radiates intelligence and assertiveness, suggesting that our view of the ideal Victorian woman as self-effacing and demure may be inaccurate. As a child, Alice had also modeled for a true amateur photographer—Lewis Carroll. In fact, she is the Alice who was the inspiration and model for his famous children's books, *Alice's Adventures in Wonderland* and *Through the Looking-Glass.*

As the nineteenth century progressed, scientists in Europe and the United States continued working on technical improvements. By 1880, film that needed to be exposed for only 1/1000 of a second was available. The daguerreotype had long since been eclipsed, replaced by a series of photographic media.

THE CAMERA

All cameras share five basic parts (**7-5**): a *light-tight box,* which forms the structure of the camera and prevents any unwanted light from hitting the film; a **lens,** which focuses the light onto the film; a **shutter,** which is triggered by the photographer and controls the time of the exposure; an **aperture** (or diaphragm), an adjustable opening that controls the amount of light entering the camera; and the *viewfinder,* which permits the photographer to see what the camera sees.

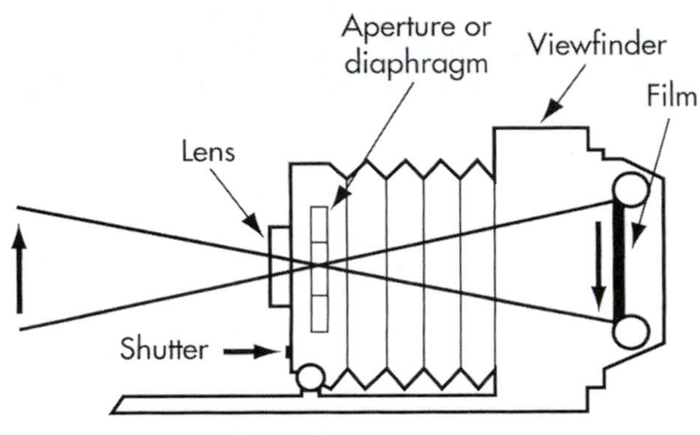

7-5 The basic parts of a camera.

In the earlier years of photography, camera equipment was rather cumbersome and expensive, but in 1887, an American named George Eastman introduced a simple box camera called the *Kodak.* This camera would soon make taking a photograph as common as taking a train ride. Eastman's slogan was "you press the button, we do the rest." After shooting a roll of one hundred exposures on the Kodak (which reportedly got its name from the sound the shutter made), the photographer would send the entire camera to the factory in Rochester, New York. At the factory, the film would be removed and developed, and a new roll would be loaded into the camera. Within twenty years of the first Kodak camera, George Eastman was in charge of the world's largest photographic manufacturing company. In the years since then, Kodak and other companies have introduced new precision lenses, electronic flashes, 35mm film, color film, instant photography, digital photography, and many other advances that make up modern photography.

STYLES OF PHOTOGRAPHY

Straight Photography

One way the new invention called photography (literally, "drawing with light") was first used was to make images of distant, exotic lands available to the public. Expeditionary photography, the precursor to *landscape photography,* was a field for adventurous artists. Timothy O'Sullivan, one of the pioneers of this medium, began his career as a Civil War photographer. After the war he traveled with geological survey groups throughout the Western United States. O'Sullivan had to bring his camera, chemicals, and plates with him, all of which were very heavy. He also brought along a portable darkroom in an ambulance pulled by mules. Despite these handicaps and the newness of the medium, his photographs of the Canyon de Chelly in Arizona (**7-6**) are among the most beautiful landscape photographs ever made. The immense scale of the canyon is made apparent by seemingly tiny ruins of buildings (just one of the many clearly depicted details). Opposed to the overall feeling of great height are the many tilting horizontal parallel lines, which provide variety and help unify the whole composition.

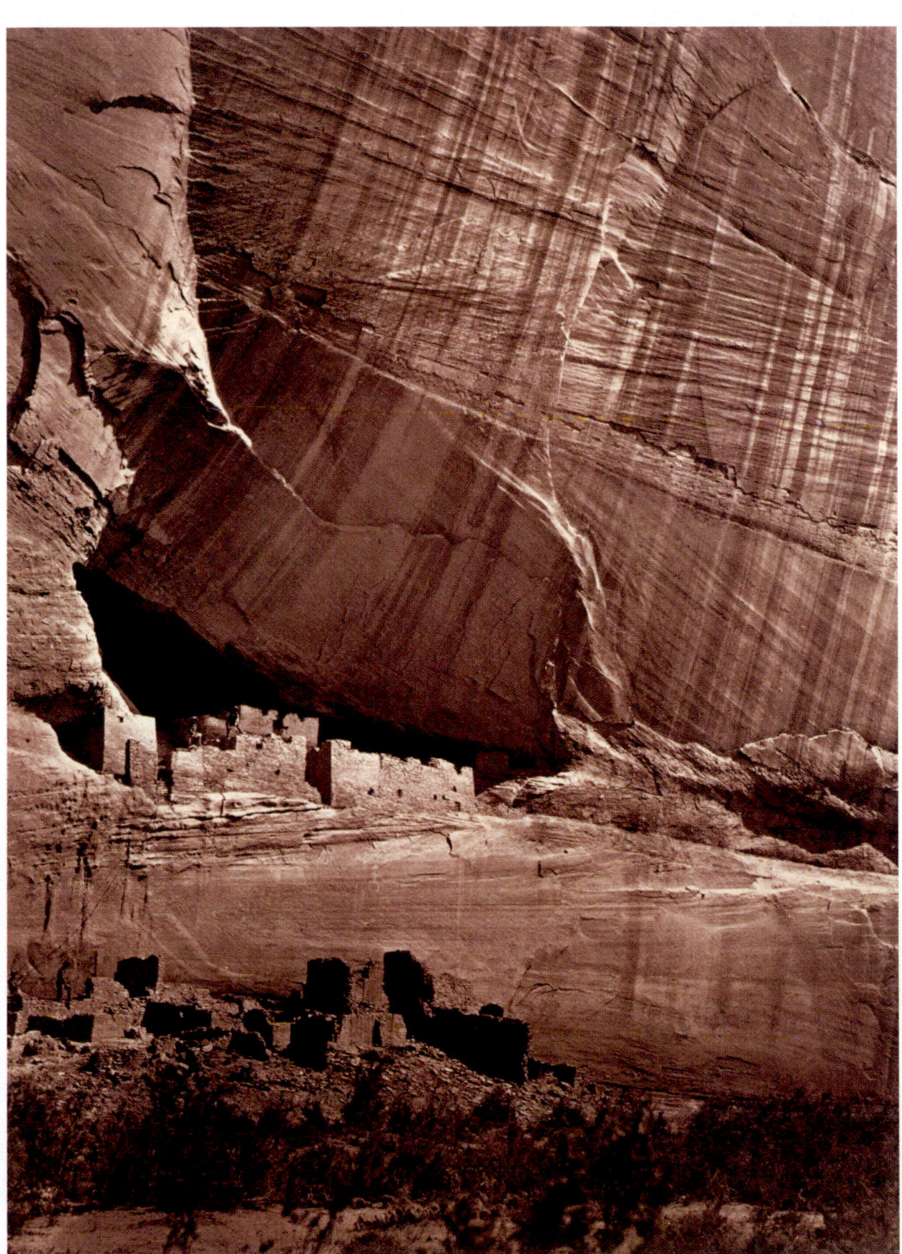

7-6 Timothy O'Sullivan, *Ancient Ruins in the Cañon de Chelle, N.M., in a Niche 50 Feet above the Present Cañon Bed* (now Canyon de Chelly National Monument, Arizona), 1873. Albumen Print.

The huge camera that O'Sullivan carried out West was similar to one used by many large-format fine art photographers today. However, the smaller-format 35mm camera—lightweight and with lenses capable of taking pictures with very fast exposures—overwhelmingly became the camera of choice for twentieth-century photographers. Its portability opened up many subjects for the photographic eye, from the top of Mount Everest to the depths of the sea.

As cameras became lighter and more portable, photographers were able to take pictures that recorded the moments of everyday life and even motion. One such photographer was Jacques-Henri Lartigue, who received his first camera when he was just seven years old. He used it to record and hold onto the joys of upper-middle-class life in France before World War I. The spoiled darling of a well-off family, his life as photographed seems to have been made up of all play and no work—silly pet tricks, backyard amusements, gymnastics and sports, fashionable ladies showing off their costumes and walking their dogs, dances, fun parks, theatrical performances, and trips to the beach and the races. As a young man of the early twentieth century, Lartigue was particularly fascinated by airplanes and fast cars, and he photographed these subjects many times.

In *Delage automobile, A.C.F. Grand Prix* (**7-7**), Lartigue conveys the speed of the automobile age through the elliptical whirling wheel that seems to run across the print, the streaks of the roadbed, and the backward slant of figures in the background, as if left behind by the sharply focused driver on the right-hand side of the picture. Beyond his technical innovations, however, Lartigue's great strength as a photographer was his outstanding eye for a strong composition, enabling him—even as a youth—to create visually memorable images.

Another French photographer, Henri Cartier-Bresson, utilized the 35mm camera's speed to capture what he called "the decisive moment," an instant that reveals the truth. His *Behind the Gare Saint-Lazare, Paris* (**7-8**) shows the unique ability of photographs to freeze a single moment in time. Forever poised above the puddle that reflects his image, a silhouetted figure is caught mid-jump as he leaves the station. Cartier-Bresson is categorized as a *straight photographer,* one who does not tamper with the negative or image in any way once it has been taken. Straight photographers value honesty above artistry, yet here artistry results as well from the almost-abstract design created by the visual elements unexpectedly framed by Bresson's camera.

A type of straight photography that became increasingly important in the twentieth century was

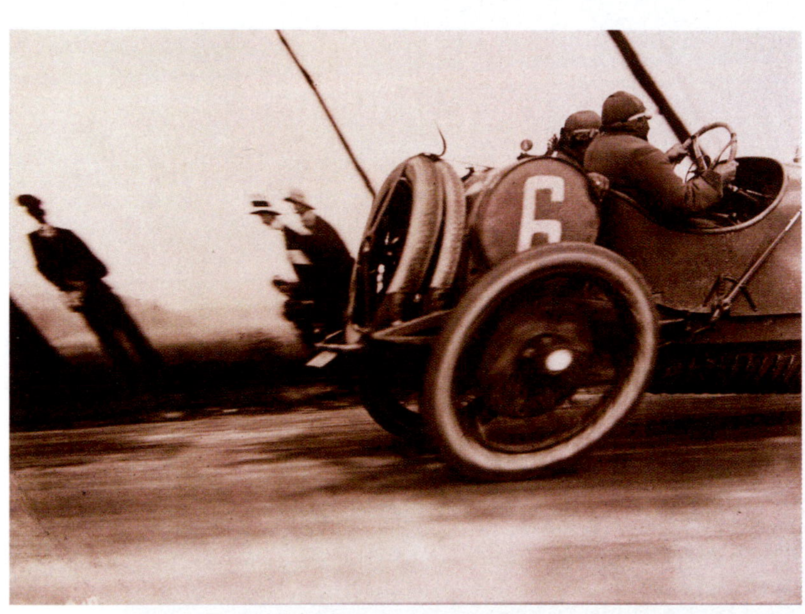

7-7 Jacques Henri Lartigue, *Delage automobile, A.C.F. Grand Prix.* Dieppe circuit, June 26, 1912. The Minneapolis Institute of Arts. The Kate and Hall J. Peterson Fund.

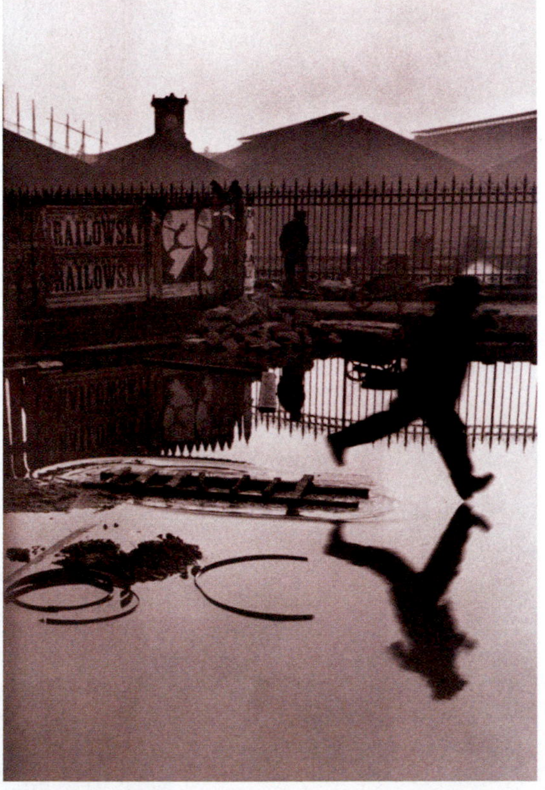

7-8 Henri Cartier-Bresson, *Behind the Gare Saint-Lazare, Paris,* 1932. Gelatin silver print, 20″ × 16″.

documentary photography—authentic, unretouched photographs that record important social conditions and political events. One of the great strengths of photography has been its evident truthfulness, the idea that a photograph cannot lie. Many photographers have valued the medium as a tool for social reform as much as a means of artistic expression. These goals are not mutually exclusive. Although we have seen their haunting images many times in textbooks, we may not think of these pictures as art. Yet these individuals saw themselves as social realist artists in the service of humanity.

During the Great Depression, the U.S. government hired photographers like Dorothea Lange to provide pictures illustrating the miserable living conditions of Americans who were suffering from hard times. Working for the Farm Security Administration (FSA), Lange and other professional photographers traveled the country in search of evidence to support the New Deal programs. In her famous image of a migrant mother and her children (**7-9**), the composition draws our attention to the mother's face, ensuring that we become conscious of her worry and pain. Two of her younger children press against her, hiding their faces in her sides, while she holds a baby in her lap. Lange also provided reports on her subjects. Her notes for this photograph read, in part:

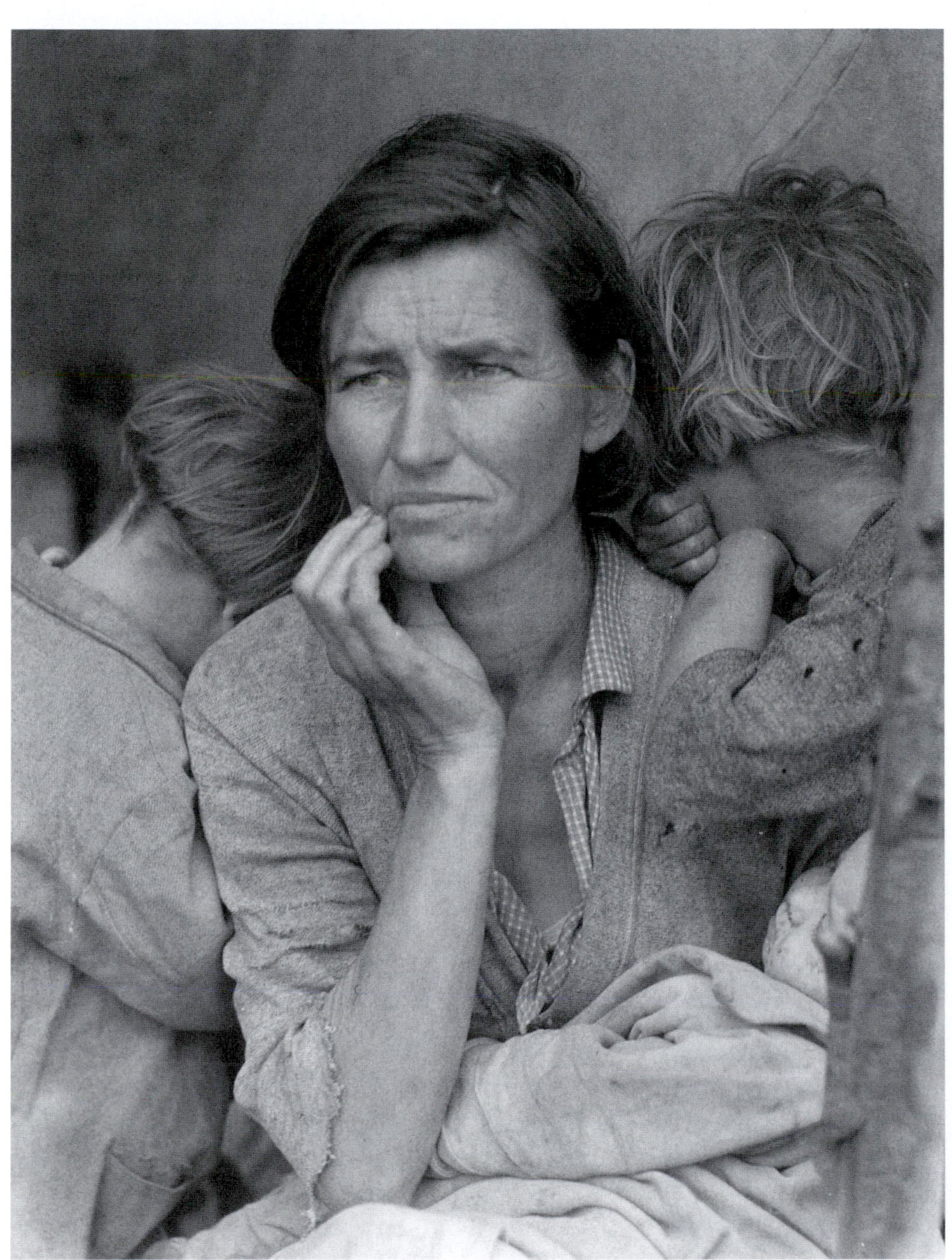

7-9 Dorothea Lange, *Migrant Mother, Nipomo Valley,* 1936. Gelatin silver print. Library of Congress, Prints and Photographs Collection.

Camped on the edge of a pea field where the crop had failed in a freeze. The tires had just been sold from the car to buy food. She was thirty-two years old with seven children.

This single image has become a symbol of the dispossessed families of Depression-era America, like those described by John Steinbeck in *The Grapes of Wrath*. Often reproduced without Lange's descriptive information, the image still conveys a heartbreaking story and retains its ability to move us more than seventy years after it was taken.

Beyond Reproduction: Fine Art Photography

Although Europeans like Julia Margaret Cameron had experimented with the artistic potential of photography for decades, it wasn't until Alfred Stieglitz founded the *Photo-Secession* group in 1902 that American photography began to be accepted as a fine art medium. Stieglitz was a man of great energy and vision. He edited the magazine *Camera Work* to promote photography. In its first issue, he promised to show "only examples of such work as gives evidence of individuality and artistic worth, regardless of school." His 291 Gallery in New York City exhibited photography alongside painting, prints, and sculpture and was one of the most advanced galleries in America. The first in this country to show Modern Artists like Matisse and Picasso, the 291 Gallery became a gathering place for young artists. Stieglitz believed that the eye of the photographer was more important than the sophistication of his or her equipment. His own photographs, like *The Steerage* (**7-10**), which he called a "picture of shapes," reveal his ability to find design and life in unposed images. His patience was legendary; he would stand for hours, no matter what the weather, waiting for the right moment.

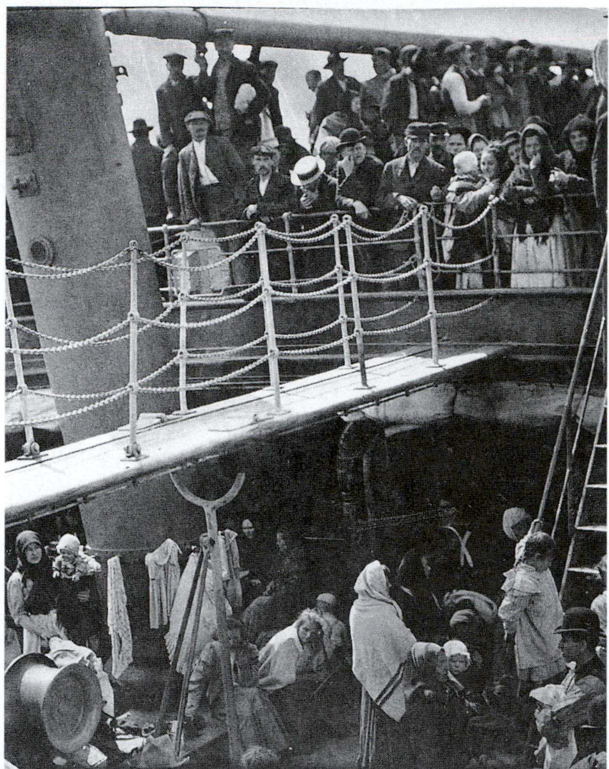

7-10 Alfred Stieglitz, *The Steerage,* 1907.

His own eye for the work of other photographers was also of the highest quality. *Camera Work* introduced the finest and most advanced photographers to the public. One was Edward Steichen, whose long and varied career in photography began as Stieglitz's assistant. Like his mentor, Steichen believed photographers should be free to manipulate their images. His portrait of the French sculptor Rodin (**7-11**) pondering his famous *Thinker* (see Chapter 14) is actually the combination of two separate images

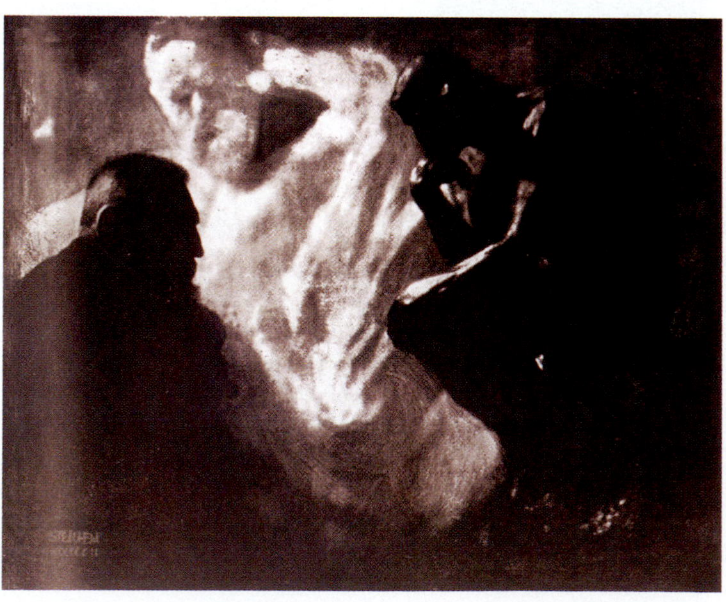

7-11 Edward Steichen, *Le Penseur,* 1902. Gum print.

taken in the sculptor's studios. Steichen played with the chemistry of photography to achieve more painterly effects.

By the 1930s, artists had begun to approach photography as a purely artistic media. In a completely different approach to photography-as-art, the experimental artist Man Ray grasped that the supposedly realistic medium of photography was actually much more subjective than most people realized. Its images could be very deceptive. By varying position and lighting, a photographer could present a subject in many different ways and produce contradictory truths. Ray also realized that photography had the power to show worlds that were not even part of ordinary visual reality. Experimenting with the medium as a purely artistic form, Man Ray invented a new kind of photograph that did not require a camera. He called it a "rayograph," made by placing objects on photographic paper in a darkroom and then exposing the paper to light. In *Le Souffle* (**7-12**), mysterious waves seem to penetrate a transparent machine. The image is bizarre and otherworldly, using effects not possible in any other medium.

While Ray explored photographic innovations, Edward Weston transformed ordinary objects into abstract compositions. In *Pepper 30* (**7-13**), he focused on a single pepper, lighting it as if it were a precious work of art. Seen in this way, the pepper loses its normal identity as something to eat, and becomes instead a voluptuous series of curving lines and undulating shapes. There is something *anthropomorphic* (human-like) in its twisted form and sensuous flesh.

Photomontage

The widespread reproduction of photographs has given artists new materials for collages, providing an enormous palette of realistic images. The imaginative combination of photographic images is called **photomontage.** With this medium, artists can create impossible pictures that still seem connected to the real world.

Between the world wars, the German photomontage artist Hannah Höch used found images from publications like newspapers and magazines—what has been described as the debris of modern life. By connecting heads, bodies, and machines, Höch's photomontages showed how people were becoming dehumanized cogs in the industrial process. In *Cut with the Kitchen Knife* (**7-14**), machinery overwhelms the characters, creating confusion. Who is responsible for this world? In the upper-right corner, we see

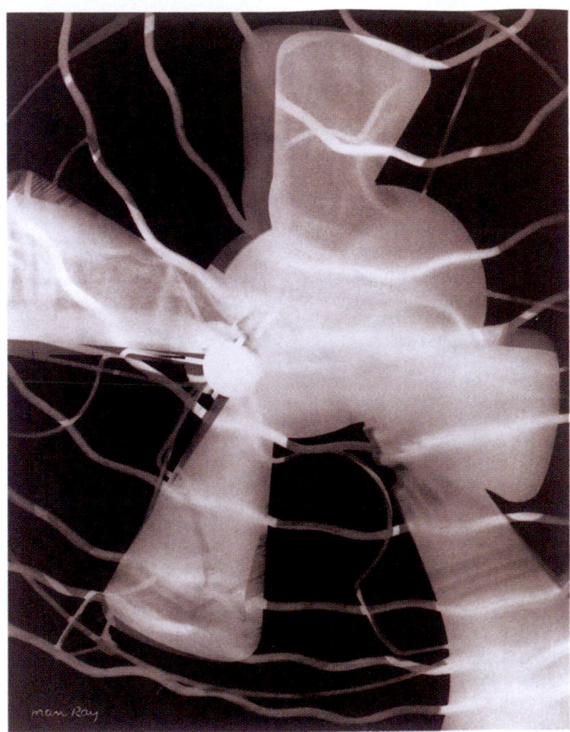

7-12 Man Ray, *Le Souffle* (from the portfolio *Electricité*), 1931. Rayograph. The Museum of Modern Art, New York, NY.

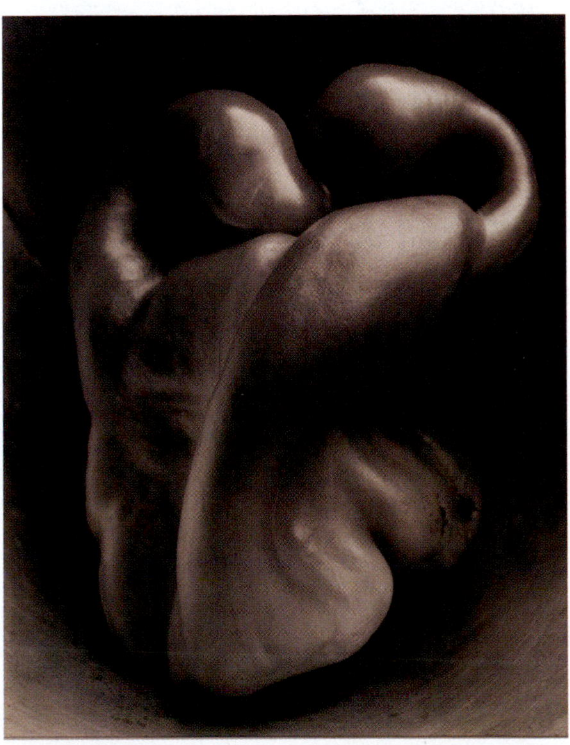

7-13 Edward Weston, *Pepper 30,* 1930. Gelatin silver print. The Museum of Modern Art, New York, NY.

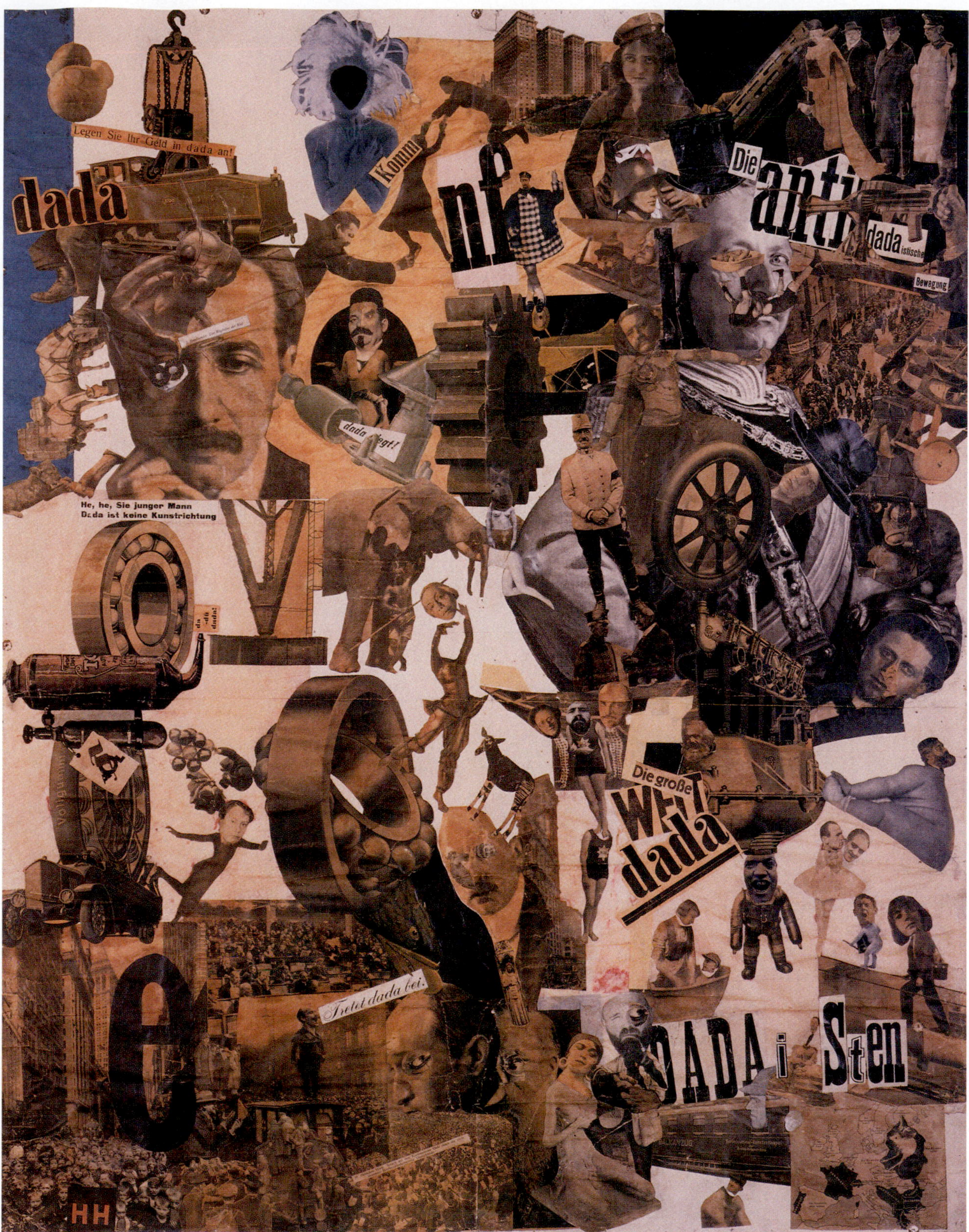

7-14 Hannah Höch, *Schnitt mit dem Küchenmesser Dada durch die erste Weimarer Bierbauchkulturepoche Deutchlands (Cut with the Kitchen Knife through the Last Weimar Beer Belly Cultural Epoch),* 1919. Staatliche Museen Preussbischer Kulturbesitz, Nationalgalerie, Berlin.

ART ISSUES

Can Art Be Obscene?

The questions of what is obscene and whether art should be banned if it is obscene have haunted modern artists for more than a century. Many important works of art that were once condemned as obscene in the past—for example, Manet's *Le Dèjeuner sur l'herbe* (17-4)—are now considered masterpieces. Even in the twentieth century, art was put on trial because of sexual content. In literature, the bannings of James Joyce's *Ulysses* and D. H. Lawrence's *Lady Chatterly's Lover* were battled in the courts and ultimately overturned. The verdicts were seen as important victories for individual civil liberties and artistic freedom. Today, the books are considered modern classics and are traditional parts of college and university curricula.

More recently, the photographs of Robert Mapplethorpe brought national attention to the conflict between artistic freedom and what community standards call obscene. Although relatively few Americans had seen his pictures, Mapplethorpe's name became a notorious household word in 1990. Mapplethorpe was brought up in a middle-class Catholic home in suburban New York. Early in his art career, he was already exploring the limits of conventional morality by collaging sexually explicit photographs into sculptural frames that he made. As he developed as an artist, he became a successful commercial photographer. Few have questioned his marvelous technical skills. His prints brought an almost glamorous quality to whatever he portrayed, whether nudes or flowers. It is his photographs' erotic atmosphere that has disturbed many viewers.

In *Ken Moody and Robert Sherman* (**7-15**), Mapplethorpe idealizes his subjects; they are living men but seem like statues. Their flesh looks as if it is carved out of the purest black and white marble. The directional lighting envelops them in a soft, glowing light. The geometric composition is uncomplicated and dramatic, a formal progression of simple forms from white to gray to black. The image has a timeless, Classical quality.

A man and a woman, or two women posed in the same manner by Mapplethorpe, would probably have not been controversial. But Mapplethorpe shows two men who appear to be naked and who are from different races as well. Despite the serene beauty of the photograph, the sexual feeling and interracial nature of the image has aroused a great deal of hostility. Many people cannot accept a male artist's loving attitude toward other men. Even more controversial were photographs of male sadomasochistic lovers and an innocent child in a park who seems unaware that anyone cares that she wears no underwear.

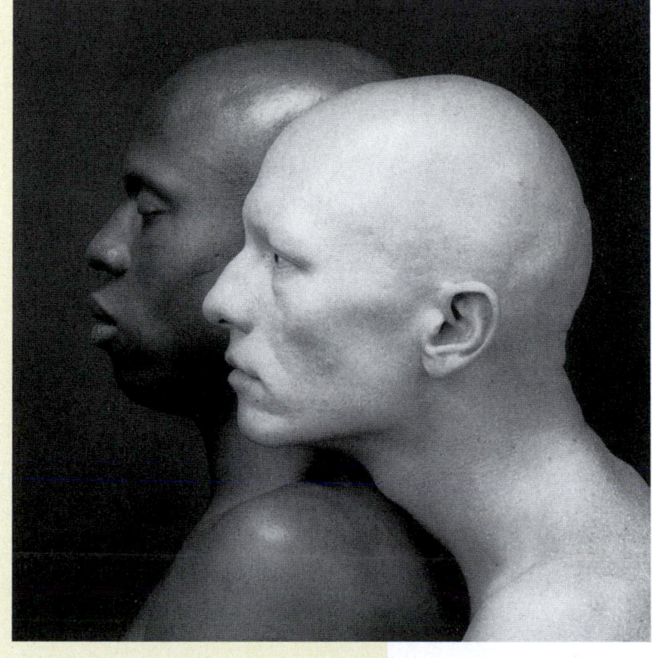

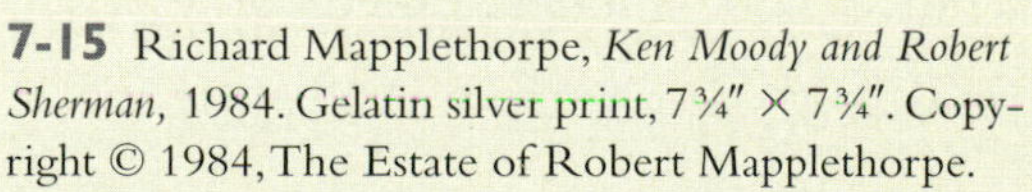

7-15 Richard Mapplethorpe, *Ken Moody and Robert Sherman,* 1984. Gelatin silver print, 7¾″ × 7¾″. Copyright © 1984, The Estate of Robert Mapplethorpe.

(continued on next page)

ART ISSUES

Mapplethorpe's pictures challenge the morality of his viewers. He brought the same glamorous and artful approach to whatever he portrayed, including graphic sexual acts and "kinky" paraphernalia. What many expect to remain hidden, the photographer openly exhibited as beauty, without apparent shame. One question for viewers is whether Mapplethorpe transformed his subject matter into art, or is this subject matter so taboo that it is not possible art material? What is the line between an artist's rights to explore and exhibit his or her interests and the need to protect society from what is obscene?

The controversial nature of Mapplethorpe's images became a national issue when a retrospective of his work was organized with funds from the National Endowment for the Arts (NEA). The exhibition traveled through many cities in the United States and became the subject of intense public scrutiny. A museum director was put on trial for allowing the exhibition to be shown in Cincinnati, Ohio. Even though the museum director was ultimately acquitted, the Mapplethorpe retrospective controversy raised important new questions: Should public funds support artists who make works that some consider obscene? Should morality enter into funding decisions? What is the proper role for taxpayer dollars in the support of the arts? After the trial ended in Cincinnati, the NEA became the next battleground over artists' rights and responsibilities.

The NEA was established by Congress in 1965 to encourage and support national progress in the arts. In the more than forty years since its founding, the NEA has become the largest single supporter of the arts in the United States. In the visual arts, it has distributed grants to museums, arts organizations, and individual artists in cities and small towns across America. It also supports dance, music, film, video, and public broadcasting. Its founding legislation prohibited any interference with the content of art it supports. In light of the controversy over the Mapplethorpe exhibition and others, congressional amendments were proposed to change the charter's goal of noninterference by establishing limits to the content of the art the NEA could support. Many in Congress felt they had the responsibility to determine what art taxpayers' dollars supported. They said that not giving grants to controversial art was not the same as censorship. Artists would remain free to do what they wanted, just not at public expense.

In the arts community, there was widespread fear of a chilling effect on artists and art organizations similar to the McCarthy era in the 1950s. Would artists be less daring than before? Would museums show only "safe" art? Which was more dangerous, someone being offended or censoring freedom of expression? Ultimately, in the summer of 1990, the Senate and the House reached a compromise when both agreed to cut $45,000 from the NEA budget, the amount used to fund the Mapplethorpe and another controversial exhibition, and to, in effect, punish the organization for its decision to fund these exhibits (it also killed an amendment with much graver cuts). The NEA (capitulating to pressure or returning to common sense, depending on your point of view) changed its procedures, requiring anyone who was awarded a grant to sign an oath stating their work would not be obscene:

> Including, but not limited to, depictions of sadomasochism, homoeroticism, the exploitation of children, or individuals engaged in sex acts.

top-hatted figures of respectability along with an old general, symbolizing bankrupt authority. The artist pokes fun at this type of authority figure toward the center of the image by setting the head of a proper bourgeois gentleman on top of the body of a belly dancer. Hoch's photomontages are satirical, even funny, but her political message was quite serious.

CONTEMPORARY APPROACHES

Contemporary photographers continue to work in all of the styles discussed in this chapter. One who pursues the documentary tradition is Brazilian artist Sebastião Salgado, who has produced several epic series of photographs recording the plight of the poor and refugees at the turn of the twenty-first century. For instance, his series "Workers" took him to twenty-six countries over four years, from 1986 to 1992, while his recent series "Exodus" exposes the plight of migrants around the world. Unlike Lange, however, Salgado's work is not underwritten by the government. Instead, Salgado is a successful commercial photographer, selling pictures through Amazonas Images, the photo agency he created with his wife Leila, and exhibiting his prints in museums and galleries.

Salgado's images often have a cinematic quality, as with *Gold Mine, Serra Pelada, State of Para, Brazil* (**7-16**). Hundreds of miners appear like a cast of thousands in a blockbuster film. Sadly, however, these are real workers, some of the fifty thousand who slave under brutal conditions in these mines for pitiful wages.

While Salgado uses his art to record devastating realities, other contemporary photographers, like Sandy Skoglund, take advantage of the commonly held faith in the truthfulness of photographs to confuse the viewer's sense of reality. Her *Radioactive*

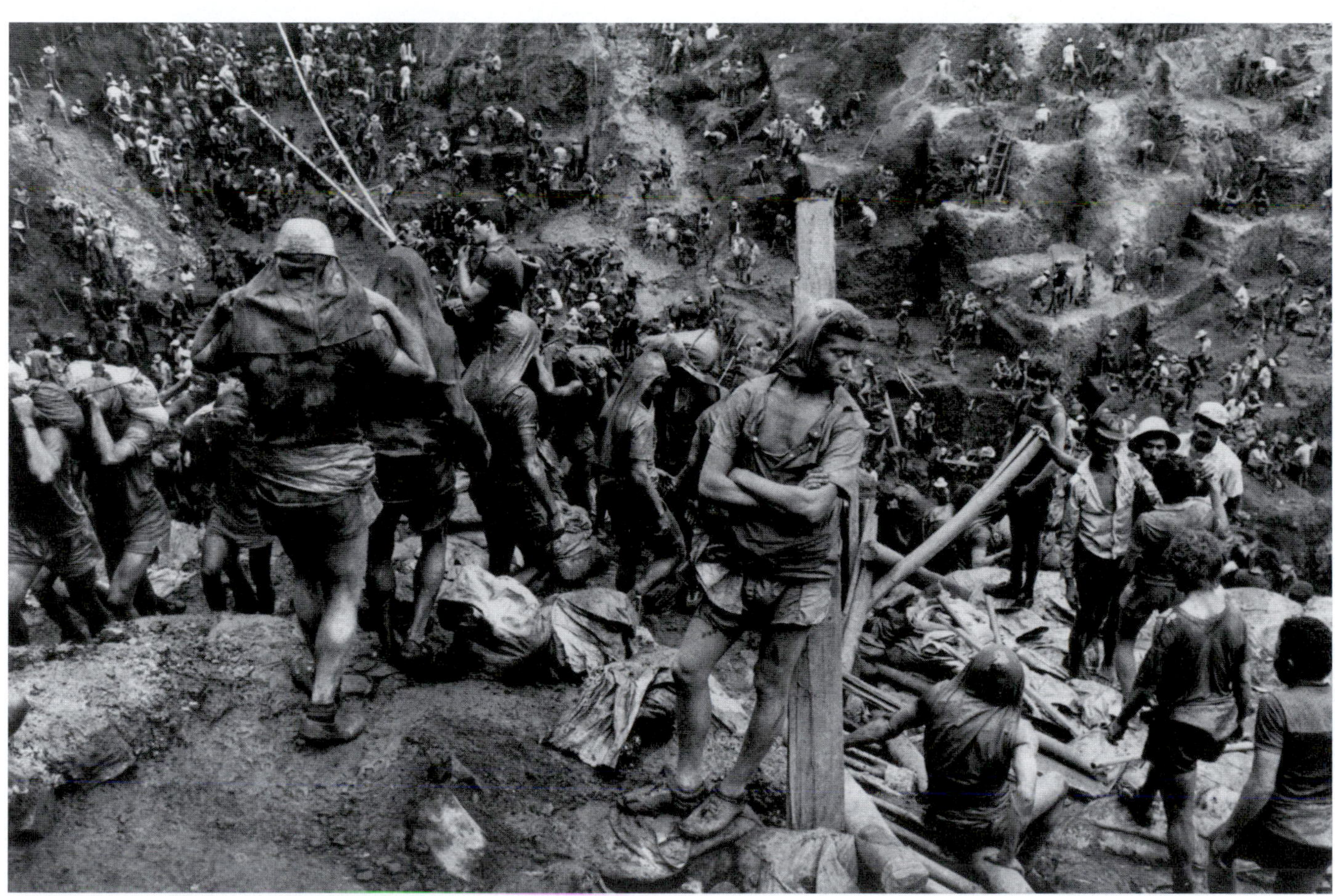

7-16 Sebastião Salgado, *Gold Mine, Serra Pelada, State of Para, Brazil,* 1986. Iris Print, 24″ × 20″.

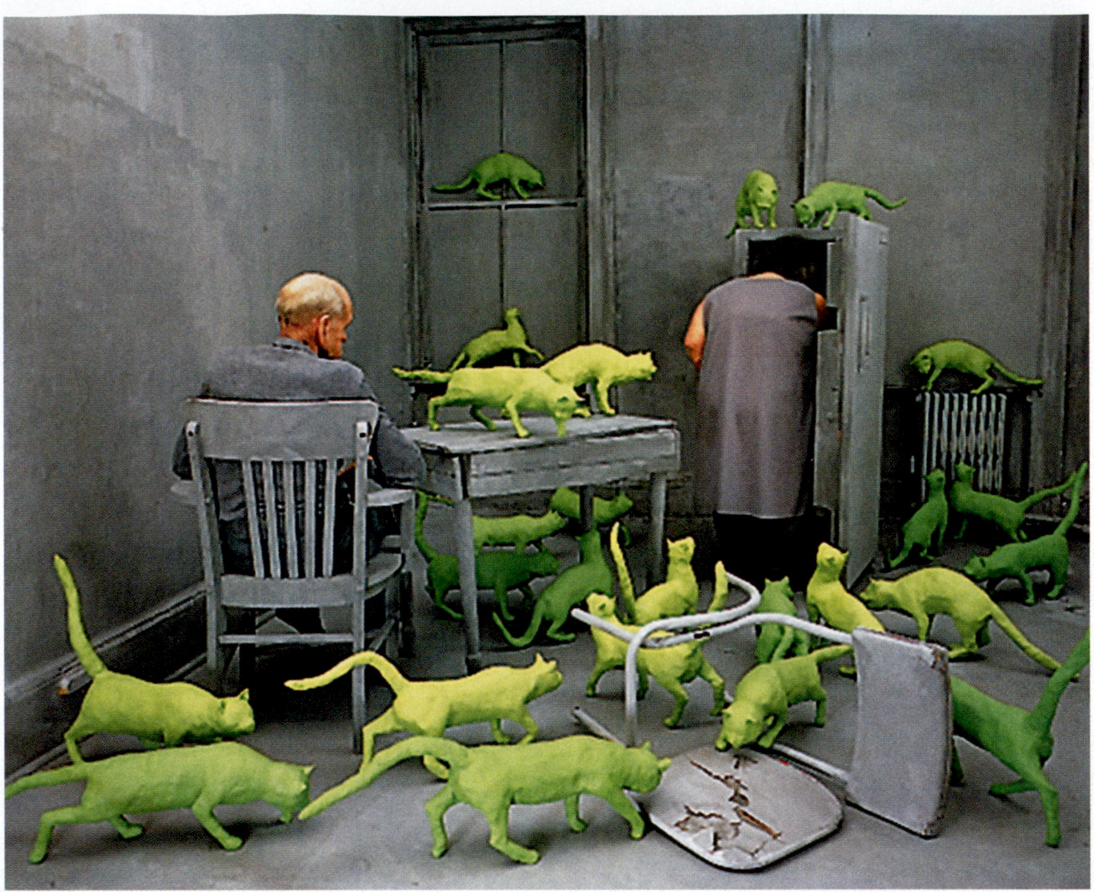

7-17 Sandy Skoglund, *Radioactive Cats,* 1980. Cibachrome, 30″ × 40″. © 1980 Sandy Skoglund.

Cats (**7-17**) is anything but a straight photograph. Every part of what we see has been carefully planned and arranged. Yet, this scene did exist and was photographed. Part of the artistic process Skoglund follows is the construction of her subject, including posing and costuming her models and applying fluorescent colors to ceramic cats she created. Following the lead of pioneer artistic photographers like Man Ray, Skoglund does not respect or believe in the neutrality of photography. Instead, she uses its power of deception for creative purposes. The result is a vivid fantasy of what the world might be like after a nuclear war.

The ambitious and theatrical photographs of Cindy Sherman are such elaborate productions that they almost constitute performances. For them, Sherman stars in an endless assortment of roles, from innocent hippie to tired housewife, young girl at her first ballet recital to an autistic patient in an asylum.

Many critics have seen her pictures as studies of women's roles in the popular media. But as her pictures have become more complex visually, they have also shown less stereotypical women and situations. *Untitled* (**7-18**) shows Sherman as an apparent murder victim on what appears to be an isolated forest floor. Her throat is cut, her clothing soaked and stained. Flecks of dirt on her head and neck imply a struggle took place. Insects are hovering over her bruised face. The viewer is drawn magnetically toward the brightly lit blond-wigged head with glazed blue eyes. Notice how her head is set at the crossing point of the diagonals made by her body and the line of green moss. To produce such a carefully composed and complex image, Sherman had to become a special-effects wizard, controlling lighting, sets, makeup, and costumes. Her most successful images evoke setting and subject without making us aware of how they were constructed. In other words, while totally artificial, they seem natural.

Unlike Skogland's or Sherman's photographs based on carefully planned sets, Jerry Uelsmann's

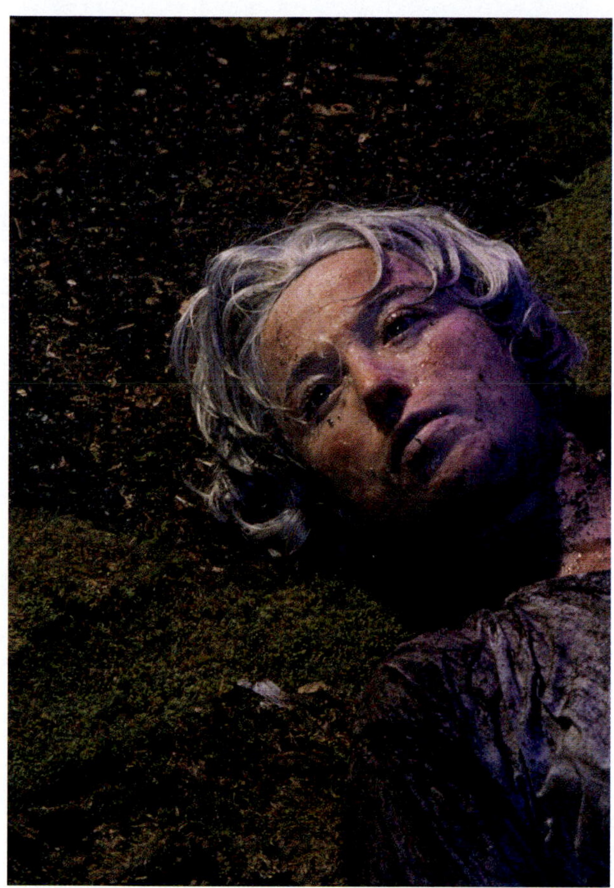

7-18 Cindy Sherman, *Untitled # 153,* 1985. Color photograph, 67 ¼″ × 49 ½″. Courtesy of the Artist and Metro Pictures.

otherworldly environments are constructed imaginatively in the darkroom. Photographs like *Meditation Mystery* (**7-19**) mix images of natural elements to create enigmatic worlds that appear dreamlike and mythic. Uelsmann works in a darkroom with eight enlargers, each holding a negative with just one of the elements for the final image. He blends the images by moving a sheet of photographic paper from enlarger to enlarger and exposing only part of the paper at each station. For Uelsmann, the "decisive moment" described by Henri Cartier-Bresson occurs in the darkroom—"a certain moment when things just come together." His goal is simply "to amaze myself" with scenes that are "emotional, irrational, intellectual, and psychological."

Today, most viewers assume when they see a Uelsmann photograph that it was made on a computer, but his multiple-image scenes continue to be made with the same traditional photographic techniques he has used for forty years. He is not opposed, however, to computers or image-editing software and acknowledges their value to many photographers.

Photography, which revolutionized image-making at the beginning of the twentieth century, is now in the midst of its own revolution. The invention and acceptance of digital photography is turning out to be more momentous than even the use of computers and imaging software. Digital cameras have become so popular that traditional cameras, and the photographic methods that went with them, may soon seem as old-fashioned as the daguerreotype. Famous camera-makers like Nikon and Kodak are abandoning traditional cameras for their digital counterparts. There are few remaining manufacturers of black-and-white papers for the darkroom. Although film and darkrooms may still be used by artists interested in historic techniques, the digital arts described in the next chapter are quickly moving to the forefront of photographic innovation. But the impact of the computer on art is much broader. It is even changing the nature of the art world itself.

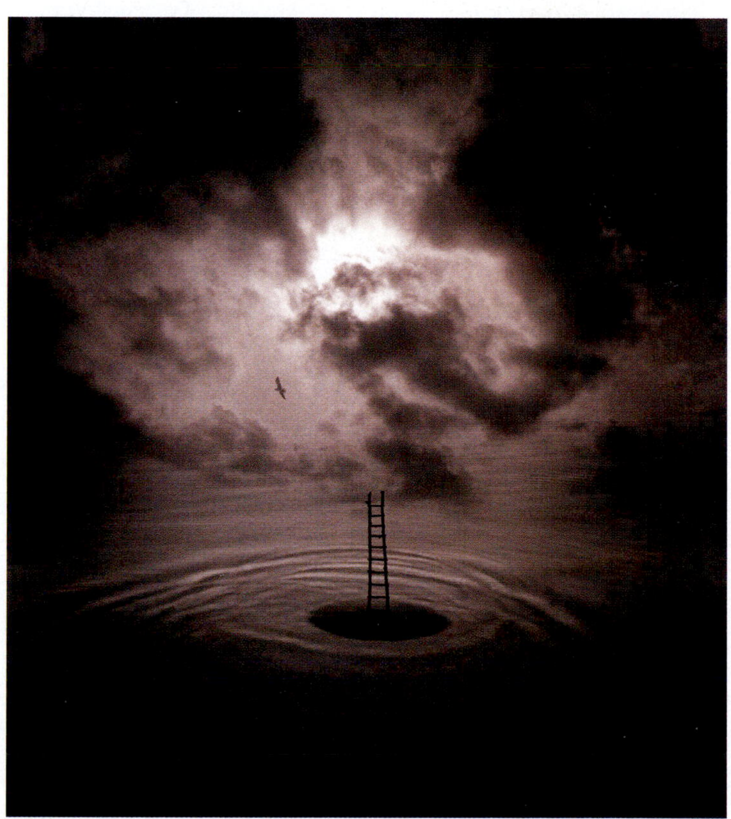

7-19 Jerry Uelsmann, *Meditation Mystery,* 2001.

CHAPTER **8**

New Media: Time and Digital Arts

The story of art was transformed in the past century by new media developed from new visual technologies. As we have seen in the last chapter, artists seized on photography as a new medium of expression from the moment it was invented. The marvels of motion pictures, video, and most recently, computer technologies were also embraced by artists as new paths for exploration. While art critics, gallery owners, and museum curators were busy debating whether these new technologies could be used to create art, artists simply plunged ahead. In the twenty-first century, this pattern has continued, and if anything the pace has quickened.

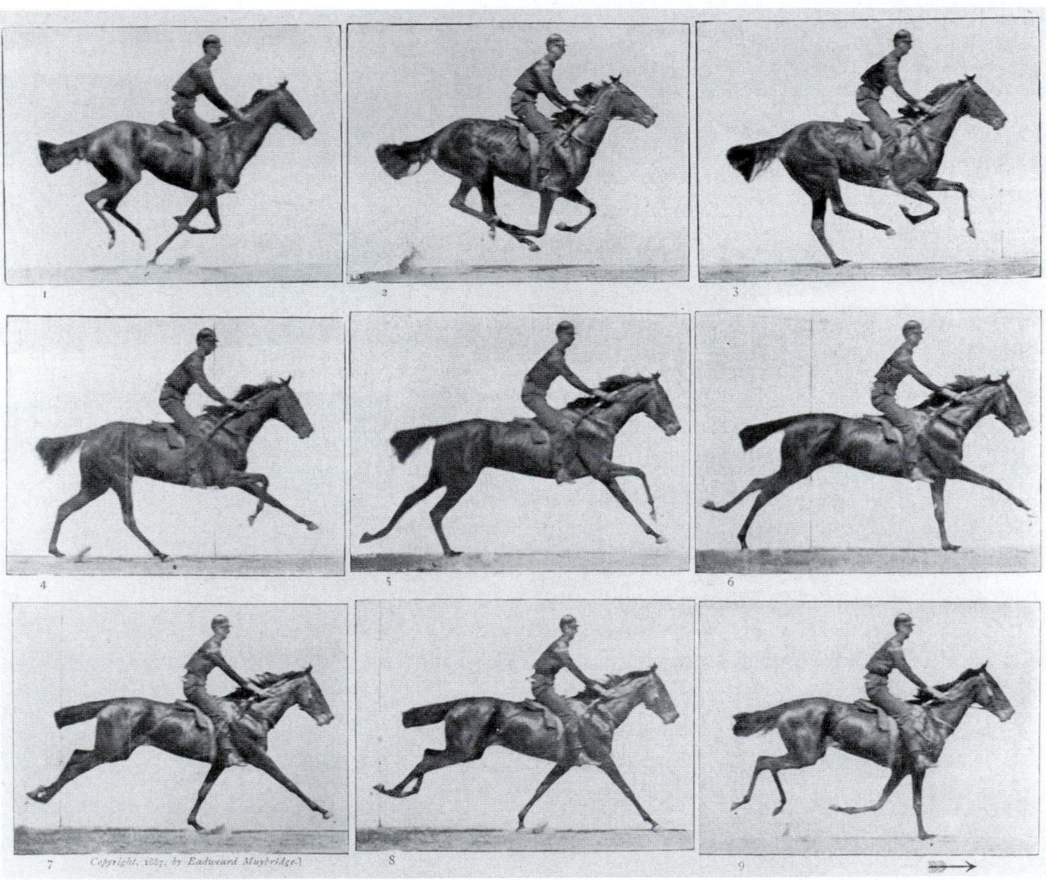

8-1 Eadweard Muybridge, *Galloping Horse,* 1878.

TIME AS AN ARTIST'S MEDIUM

A revolution in transportation and communication began in the early nineteenth century. Stagecoaches were replaced by railroads on land and sails by steam on the seas. The new speed of travel made distant places more accessible and started an age of tourism not only for the rich, but also for the newly arrived merchant class. Messages that once took months to be delivered became nearly instantaneous with the inventions of the telegraph and telephone and the laying of the transatlantic cable. Speed had become a mark of the age, and artists tried to portray it.

But how can you portray speed in a single image? In the early days of photography, critics celebrated the photograph as a way to defeat time. But some artists, like Eadweard Muybridge, used photography as a way to include time in their works. Muybridge was a professional photographer whose fame rests on his exhaustive studies of figures and animals in motion.

His best-known series from the 1870s studied a horse galloping. Financed by a millionaire sportsman, it provided an answer to a question that had been debated by artists and the racing world for centuries: when a horse runs, is there any moment when all of his legs are off the ground? Most artists believed that such a moment was not possible, because the horse would fall to the ground. Muybridge's photographs (**8-1**) proved conclusively that there were such moments, and his images were printed on the cover of *Scientific American* and in European scientific journals. One journalist wrote, "Mr. Muybridge has completely exposed the fallacy of all previous ideas on the subject."

Muybridge's photographs were collected in a series of books on locomotion. An encyclopedia of movement, they include women walking down stairs, men lifting heavy stones, babies toddling, and all sorts of animals in action. When these images were made available in print, artists poured over them. For example, Edgar Degas (see Chapter 17) used the famous horse photographs as the basis of his many paintings of racetracks. The modern enthusiasm for science also damaged the reputation of some older artists. The most famous and popular horse painter of the era, the Realist Rosa Bonheur (see Chapter 16), was ridiculed for the inaccuracies of her depictions after Muybridge's photographs were published. Muybridge's volumes on locomotion remain standard reference books for artists and animators even today.

The new age of transportation proceeded nonstop with the start of the twentieth century. The arrivals of the automobile and the airplane were greeted with particular enthusiasm by the Futurist artists in Italy (see Chapter 18). Feeling the heavy burden of trying to create new art surrounded by the grandeur of Roman, Renaissance, and Baroque art, the Futurists saw the new age as an opportunity to shake off this great weight and "free Italy from her numberless museums" and "useless admiration of the past." F. T. Marinetti wrote in *The Futurist Manifesto* that "the splendor of the world has been enriched with a new form of beauty, the beauty of speed."

To depict speed and movement, Futurists like Giacomo Balla looked to the motion studies of photographers like Muybridge. Balla's *Dynamism of a Dog on a Leash* (**8-2**) depicts an everyday sight in the city—a woman walking a dog—in a new way. As in a multiple exposure, we can see the frenetic actions of the small dachshund trying to keep up with its master. The chain-link leash vibrates almost musically. The range of motion of boots, paws, tail, and ears form blurred arcs of dynamic action. Although this type of view is familiar—if still amusing—today, when first painted it personified the thrill the Futurists felt for life in the new, vital modern city. It celebrated a new way of seeing and a new era for art.

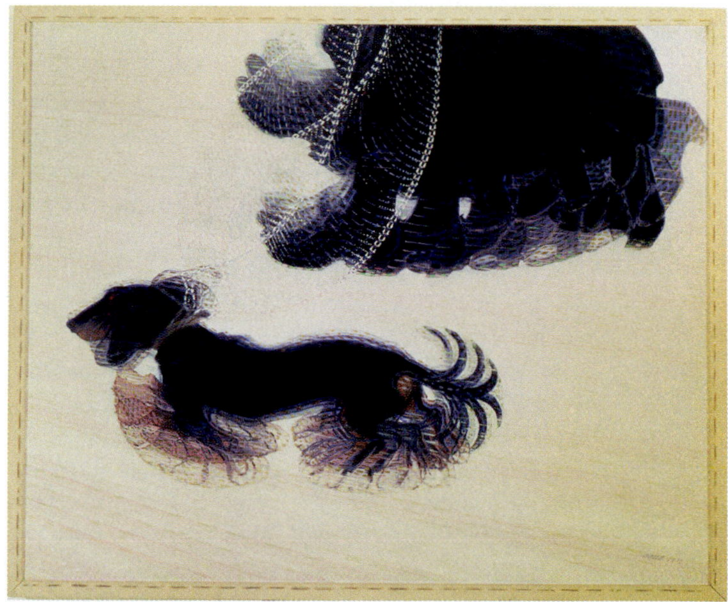

8-2 Giacomo Balla, *Dynamism of a Dog on a Leash,* 1912.

Moving Pictures

The invention of motion pictures offered a much more direct way to represent motion. In 1888, the famous American inventor Thomas Edison met with Muybridge to discuss a revolutionary idea. Edison thought that by combining the cylinders of his phonograph with Muybridge's multiple-image photographs, he might be able to make a system that would show moving pictures. Edison eventually succeeded when he abandoned the idea of using cylinders and switched to film in long bands. In 1893, he unveiled his first motion picture camera, the *kinetoscope.* One of his first films that year showed blacksmiths at work, based on a similar series by Muybridge.

But Edison's first films could only be seen by one person at a time. In 1895, the Lumière brothers in Paris developed a projection system. Their first films were simply scenes of ordinary events—workers leaving a factory, a train coming into a station. The fact that the pictures moved was thrilling enough for audiences.

By the early 1900s, however, audiences were enjoying comedies, fantasies, and dramatic stories on film. France was the leading film producer in the world up until World War I, when the United States took over the role that it continues to have to this day.

In most new media, early practitioners tend to utilize the conventions of a previous medium. For example, the first photographic artists tried to recreate the look of traditional painting to make their work appear more serious. It was only later that photographers understood and respected the unique qualities of photography.

So it is not surprising that in the early days of film, directors shot their movies to resemble theater productions. Audiences were accustomed to the traditions of the stage. When directors began to try new techniques, the results initially shocked audiences. It has been reported that when the legendary American director D. W. Griffith first showed a close-up of an actor's head, the audience screamed. They thought that the actor had been beheaded.

By 1928, when the Surrealists Luis Buñuel and Salvador Dalí (see Chapter 18) made their short film *Un Chien Andalou (The Andalusian Dog,* **8-3**) in Paris, the conventions of film techniques were well understood by audiences. But the artists had no interest in making a conventional film. Their goal was to shock and repulse their audience.

Surrealist artists believed in an art that depicted dreams and the repressed passions of the unconscious mind. Buñuel and Dalí saw film as an ideal artistic medium to construct the irrational world of a dream. In a film, like a dream, whatever you see appears real at the time. According to the artists, the script was constructed from two of their dreams. They described their collaboration as "magical rapport." While *Un Chien Andalou* (a title that is meaningless) begins with "once upon a time," the film is no fairy tale and contains some of the most awful scenes in the history of cinema. It is a Surrealist love story where repressed passions form an illogical nightmare.

The film begins with one of the most disturbing and unforgettable scenes in cinema history. Puffing on a cigarette, Buñuel sharpens a razor, with cheerful tango music in the background. He then calmly slices the heroine's eye with a razor as a cloud passes through the moon. In the next scene, she is unhurt. The male lead stares in fascination at his hand, drawing the interest of the woman (who he loves). The camera slowly focuses on the hand and the audience sees that it has a deep hole in the palm and ants are crawling out of it. The same man later moves his hand across his mouth and, when he's done, his mouth is gone. He wipes again and it is covered with the armpit hair from the woman. Outside, another young woman stands in traffic pushing an amputated hand with a stick. When she is killed by a car, it arouses the man's passions and he begins chasing his girlfriend around her room. To attract her admiration, the man drags two grand pianos into the room with great effort, each with a bleeding horse's head on top and a priest tied to it (one is Dalí).

In *Un Chien Andalou,* time is confused. Characters die and return in the next scene. Toward the end of the film, a title reads "16 years before" but appears to be on the same day. It ends with a beach scene where the film's two lovers are dead and buried in

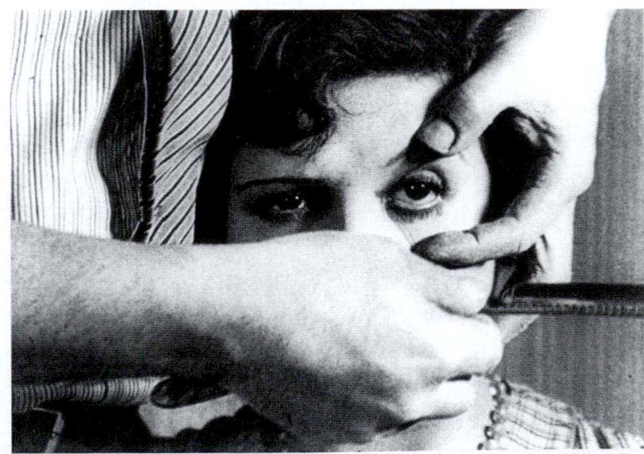

8-3 Luis Buñuel and Salvador Dalí, still from *Un Chien Andalou,* 1928.

the sand up to their chests. Because of the disturbing way the artists utilized film conventions to sabotage reality (along with its capacity to shock an audience many decades later), *Un Chien Andalou* remains a landmark in film and art history.

Video Art

The same year that Buñuel and Dalí completed their short movie in Paris, a new technology was tested in New York City that would eventually surpass the popularity of movies. In an RCA studio, an image of a Felix the Cat doll on a rotating record turntable was sent over the airwaves. Through the 1930s, regular broadcasts of what were originally called "radio movies" began on the first networks. However, the audience remained very small. Even by 1945, only seven thousand homes in the United States had television sets. It wasn't until the 1950s that television took its place as the center of American cultural life.

Like photography and movies before it, artists seized upon the newly popular medium and transformed it into an art medium. Known as **video art,** it is one of the oldest of the electronic media, but can still be said to be in its formative years. As the Korean-American artist Nam June Paik (who originated this art form) reminded his audiences, it was a long time after the invention of the printing press before there was a Shakespeare.

Paik was born in Korea in 1932, but his family was forced to leave in 1949 during the Korean War. At this time, Paik was a talented young music student. He later lived in Hong Kong, Tokyo, Germany, and the United States. In 1963, Paik's love affair with television began. For his first solo exhibition, called "Exposition of Music—Electronic Television," he filled a German gallery with thirteen used television sets, along with pianos covered with found materials like doll's heads and photographs. A fellow artist, Joseph Beuys (see Chapter 9), entered the gallery and demolished a piano with an axe. Intentionally or not, that act signified the conversion of Paik from musician to electronic artist.

Paik became television's playful poet, an artist constantly expanding video art's vocabulary. Working with electronic engineers, he was always interested in being at the cutting edge, developing equipment to create increasingly more complex video imagery. In the 1960s, he already experimented with the color synthesizers and editors that are now in regular use by conventional broadcast television.

Conceptually, some of Paik's most thought-provoking (and humorous) work concerns the relationship of television imagery to reality. In *TV Buddha* (**8-4**), a traditional sculpture of the Buddha appears to be watching his own "live" image intently on a monitor. The Buddha contemplates his electronic self, apparently mesmerized by television like any child in America. Oddly, the effect is not only comical but also peaceful; the empty setting and unchanging nature of the image is reminiscent of the Zen Buddhist goal of attaining nonbeing.

Television is rarely thought of as a spiritual medium, but like the videos of Paik, Bill Viola's art can seem mystical. While Paik's work often combines sculptural installation and video, Bill Viola's

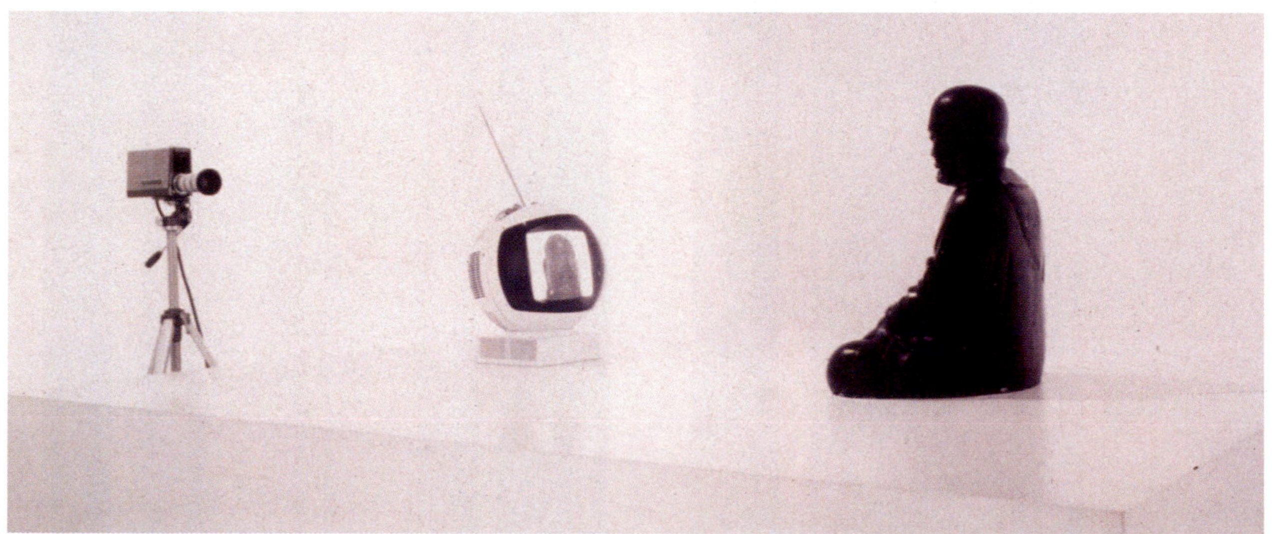

8-4 Nam June Paik, *TV Buddha*, 1974–1982. Mixed media, 55″ × 115″ × 36″. The Museum of Modern Art, New York.

are usually presented in a purer atmosphere. To see *The Crossing* (**8-5, 8-6**), you leave the bright white walls and lights of the gallery and enter a large dark room with black walls. Two screens hang from the ceiling, each showing a man who emerges out of the darkness. In one, he stops and stands unhurt in a mounting fire, and in the other rain begins to fall on him. Because both videos are run in a repeating loop, depending on when you enter the room, the videos can be dark and nearly silent, or bright and loud. Ultimately, the man is engulfed in an inferno of bright yellow and orange flames, which roar around him. On the other screen, the slow drip of water turns into a deafening downpour of rain covering his body in blue and white. The figure doesn't appear to suffer, but instead seems to be transformed.

Viewers of *The Crossing* are transported into visions that relate to our experience but become intensified beyond reality. Critics have compared Viola's videos to ancient myths and biblical visions, and he has not rejected their analyses. Viola has said, "The search for something deeper than this world is a common aspect of all religions." He doesn't believe that answers can be meaningful "without connection to a process of transformation." For him, "video is a medium that deals with movement, change, and transformation."

Those qualities can certainly be found in *Sip My Ocean* (**8-7**), a video by the Swiss artist Pipilotti Rist, but the mood is quite different. Viewers plunge into an underwater paradise. The camera explores a world filled with rich, saturated colors and light. Traveling with us as we look at the plants and sea life is a frolicking young woman in a bikini. The soundtrack is Rist singing.

Apparently all is not well in paradise; the song is Chris Isaak's "Wicked Game," a tale of a lover's betrayal. Household objects float down from above, polluting paradise with plates and cups, records, and children's toys. The tone of Rist's voice changes from sweet singing to shrieking the lyrics ("No, I don't want to fall in love"). But unlike the work of Bill Viola, Rist's video never becomes dark or frightening. Because everything is floating in luminous light and brilliant colors, there is a buoyant and dreamy mood. The young swimmer remains playful and never seems worried or concerned. We, too, remain enchanted, perhaps because the clear, blue ocean is bigger than any domestic issues.

Rist (who combined her name, Charlotte, with that of her childhood heroine, Pippi Longstocking) studied in Vienna, Austria, and Basel, Switzerland. After school, she directed music videos for European bands and sang in a female rock group. She continues to compose music for her own works, which are often compared to music videos. Water and travel are recurring themes in Rist's work. Like other video artists, she is enthusiastic about the arrival of digital video technologies. In the past, she had to supervise editors and technicians to get the results she wanted. Today, she can work directly on her videos, allowing

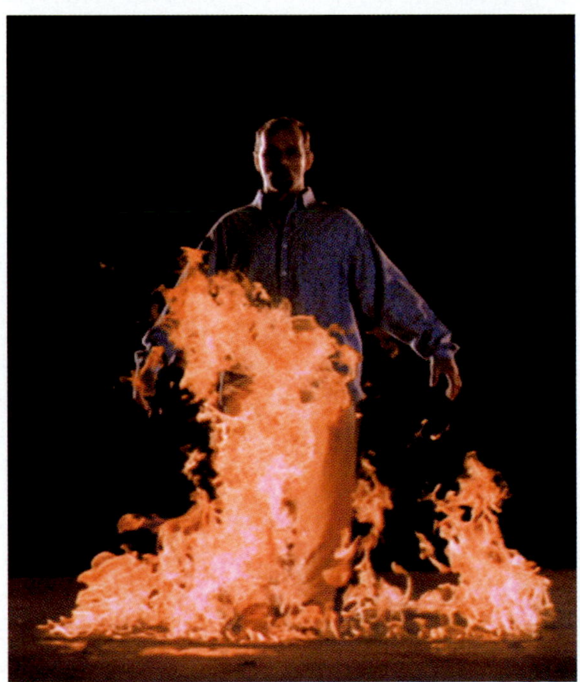

8-5 Bill Viola, still from *The Crossing,* 1996. Photo: Kira Perov

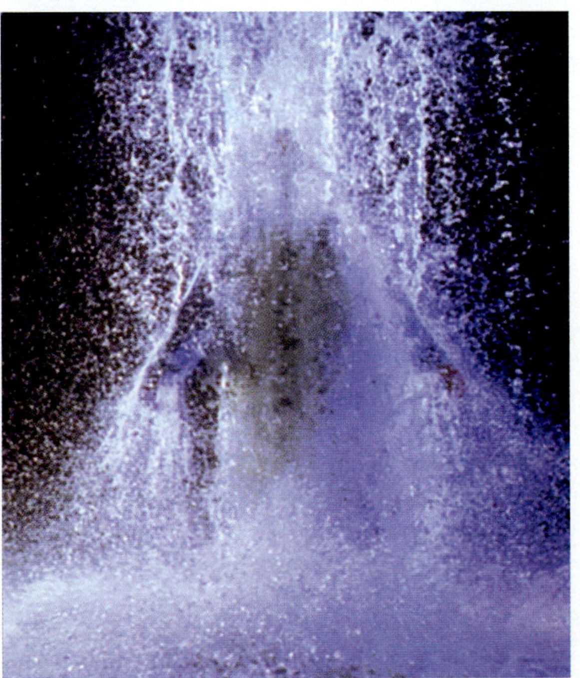

8-6 Bill Viola, still from *The Crossing,* 1996. Photo: Kira Perov

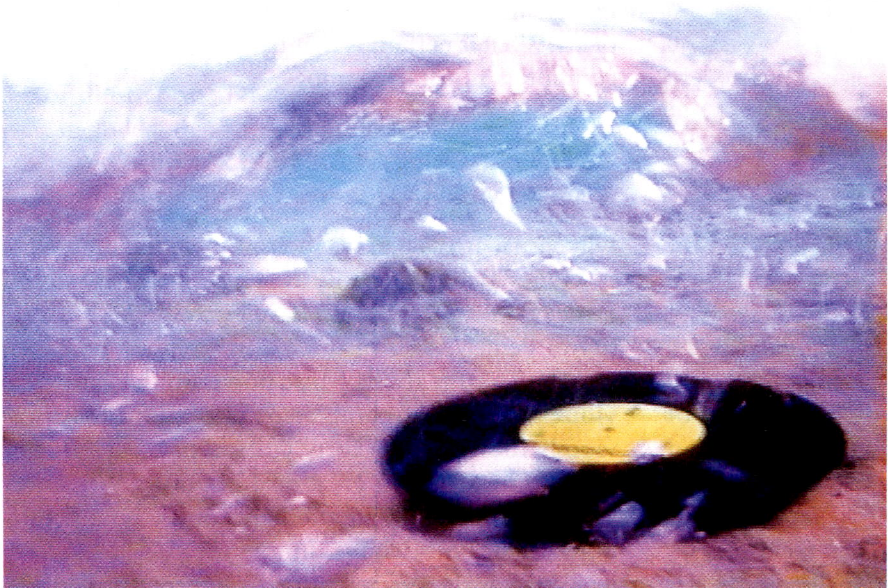

8-7 Pipilotti Rist, *Sip My Ocean* (Schlürfe meinen Ozean), 1996, audio video installation by Pipilotti Rist (video still). Courtesy the artist and Hauser & Wirth, Zürich/London

her work to have not only more complex effects, but more important, a more "experimental quality." Like Rist, artists all over the world are discovering new ways of working in the new digital era.

THE ARTIST AND THE COMPUTER

The Computer Age has transformed so much in our world; it is not surprising that it has changed the art world as well. The arrival of the *digital arts* (or *digital media*), the art forms created with the aid of computer technology, is affecting just about every one of the traditional art media. Although the history of art is filled with examples of new media transforming the way artists work, it is unprecedented for artists to be given so many new techniques in so short a period and for their impact to be so pervasive. Certainly, many of the new media can be understood as digital versions of traditional tools, but some have even changed the nature of the artist's process itself.

A particularly revolutionary tool is one that seems simple—the greatest eraser in the history of art—the "undo" command. In the past, artists have had to live with the fear that any simple action (adding a new color, a chipping movement by a sculptor, or erasing a line) could in the end be a disaster and ruin a day's worth of work or even the whole work. To be a successful creative artist, one had to manage that fear and move on. Today, however, digital artists "work with a net" because they can "undo." And most digital media software allows one to undo not just the last action but five, ten, or even a hundred previous steps. Some contain a "history palette," where all changes are recorded and a mere click can bring a picture back to a previous state from hours earlier. History can even be used as a drawing tool. By drawing with a history eraser, you can bring back a past version wherever you erase.

When an artist or designer can undo any experimental action instantly, or even move back and forth in time, he or she can work without fear of disaster and feel free to try just about anything. This is an extraordinarily liberating experience. Compare today's digital painter to a Renaissance fresco artist (see Chapter 5), who had to complete all of his or her painting before the wall dried and sealed the picture forever.

It is not just that artists have been given more tools. In an age of computers and high-speed global communication, the art world is in the process of being transformed. Because of the World Wide Web, new avenues for collaboration among artists and promoting artist's work have opened up. The gallery and museum system can even be bypassed entirely if artists choose to distribute their art around the globe via the World Wide Web.

Nevertheless, while the new digital media break new ground, they remain fundamentally connected to traditional media. This is most obvious when software is named *Illustrator* or *Painter,* but even within uniquely titled software packages, many of the most important tools bear the name of their analog parents. When a digital artist "cuts and pastes," the name

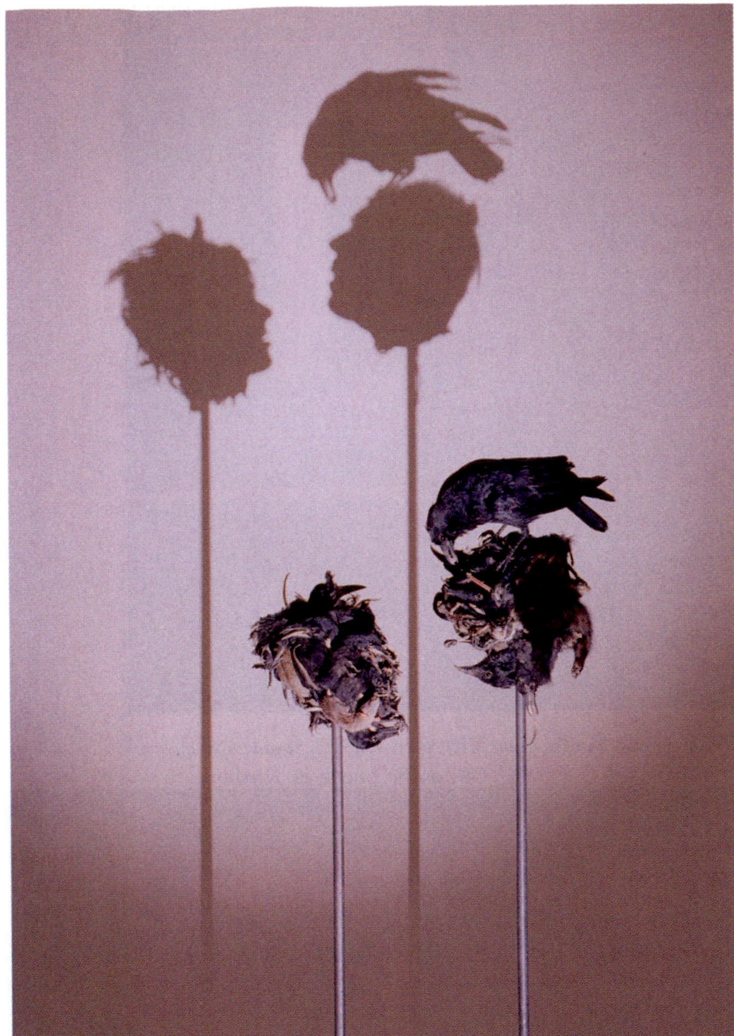

9-23 Tim Noble and Sue Webster, *Kiss of Death,* 2003. Taxidermic animals (carrion crows, jackdaws, rooks, minks, and brown rats), various bones, light projector, and metal stand; overall: 70⅞″ × 31½″ × 19 11/16″. Solomon R. Guggenheim Museum, New York. Purchased by exchange, with funds contributed by Dakis Joannou and with a special International Director's Council fund in honor of Dakis Joannou, 2003. Accession #2003.79. Photograph by David Heald ©The Solomon R. Guggenheim Foundation, New York

paint pulls everything together. The use of black also enhanced Nevelson's lighting; she compared herself to "an architect that's building through shadow and light and dark," creating a mysterious new world.

CONTEMPORARY APPROACHES

We have seen in this chapter that sculpture is a dynamic field, retaining methods used in the Ice Age but also developing new media and approaches. It is not hard to be swept up in the excitement over the possibilities for contemporary artists. Unexpected materials abound as artists mix media, blur the line between freestanding sculpture and earth art, art and craft, sculpture and architecture. Some works, like *Kiss of Death* (**9-23**), even combine elements of two- and three-dimensional media.

Mixed Media

As discussed in Chapter 5, mixed media, not surprisingly, refers to art that combines more than one of the media. It is most often used in reference to art that combines both two- and three-dimensional media. *Kiss of Death* is an unconventional mixed-media project created by the British team Tim Noble and Sue Webster. The sculptors shaped two constructions out of taxidermic birds and rodents: carrion crows, jackdaws, rooks, minks, and rats, combined with bones. These rather gruesome—though strangely fascinating—assemblages were set on poles, then lighted so that they cast silhouette portraits of the artists. The shadow portrait of Noble seems to show a crow pecking out one of his eyes. The entire effect is rather bizarre, horrible, yet humorous.

Tony Oursler's art combines sculpture, video projection, and installation. The sculpture *Woo* (**9-24**) from 2003 is a simple biomorphic shape made of painted white fiberglass, but it comes to life when a disturbing

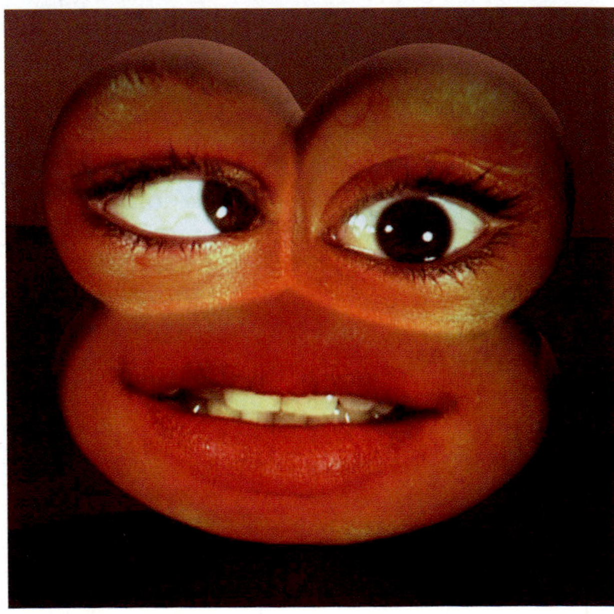

9-24 Tony Oursler, *Woo,* 2003. Fiberglass sculpture, Sony VPL CS5 projector, DVD, DVD player, 33″ × 35″ × 16″. Courtesy of the Artist and Metro Pictures.

video of bulbous eyes and a mouth in constant motion is projected onto the form. The result is a strange combination of the familiar and the alien. The face mutters, sometimes seductively. When Oursler first exhibited these sculptures, he set up a room full of creatures varying in form, color, and human characteristics. One was clownlike, one wept constantly, while another had four eyes. Each was named like a character in a science fiction novel—Cyc, Sug, and Coo. Their eyes seemed to be seeking out the visitors. One said, "dreamy, dreamy, come here." Although these forms are three-dimensional, their combination with two-dimensional video images and sound brings them to life.

Contemporary artists are also exploring the boundaries between installation and Earth Art, using natural materials to build site-specific pieces that last only for a limited time. Patrick Dougherty is a master of this approach. He designs a unique construction for each site, using natural, local materials such as tree saplings and sticks. For his *A Cappella* (**9-25**), built at the Montalvo Arts Center in California, Dougherty created a "private sanctuary":

> I could see a baroque folly in the wild wood made from branches and serving as a kind of forest confessional where the lore of trees might unfold. It could be an elegantly domed nest with an arched doorway that beckoned to morning walkers.

In fact, viewers are welcome to enter Dougherty's constructions, passing in and out of the sculpted space, truly experiencing both the inside and outside of this magical sculpture in the round. Depending on where one stands, one's experience of both the space and the texture of the walls is ever-changing. In some ways, his works are more like architecture, while their temporary life span and natural materials and settings tie them to installations and Earth Art. Once built, they are meant to last only a few seasons until they collapse, disintegrate, and ultimately disappear back into the earth (though many, like this one, are eventually dismantled). Dougherty was delighted by the reaction to his "pantheistic hideaway," as he heard comments like: "Honey, we could live here. No, honestly, we could."

As we have seen with each of the media explored so far, contemporary approaches have led to a blurring of the lines between all of the media, much like the current blurring of the lines between journalism, history, and fiction in literature; documentary and fantasy in film; or reality and performance on television. In the next chapter we will explore the ways in which architecture is a distinct three-dimensional medium, and again how contemporary architects are breaking through barriers to create innovative and exciting art forms.

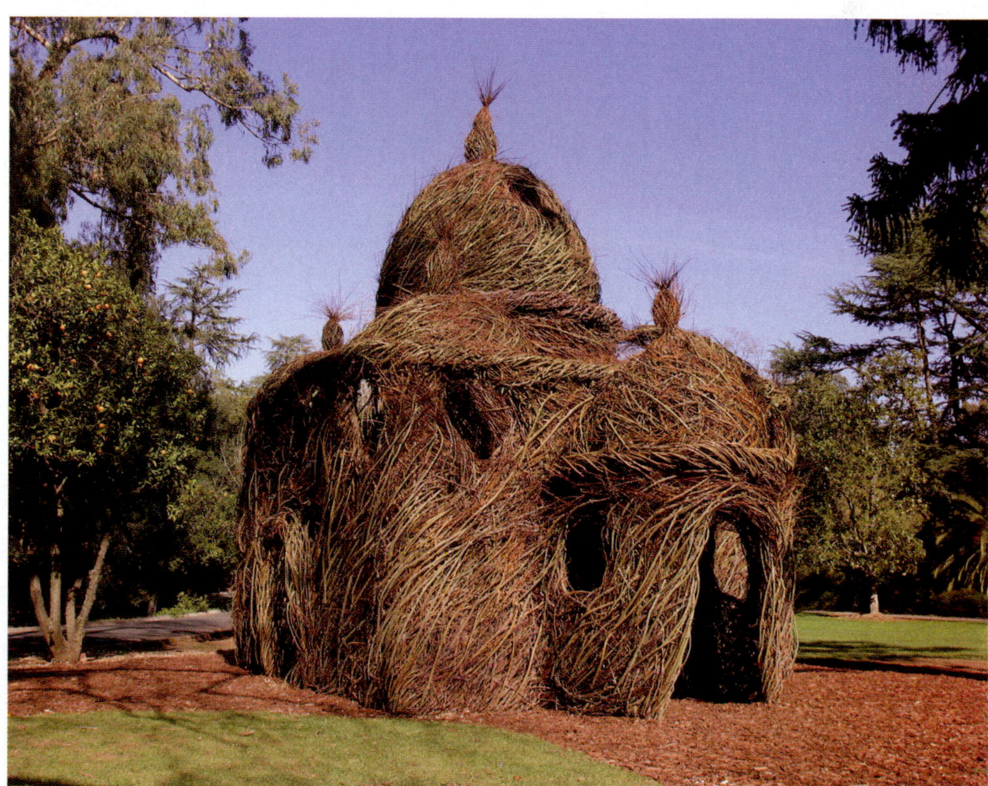

9-25 Patrick Dougherty, *A Cappella*, 2003–2005. Willow and bay laurel saplings, 35′ × 25′ × 25′. Photo: Rod Johnson.

CHAPTER 10

Architecture

THE ART OF ARCHITECTURE

Architecture has been called both the greatest and the least of the arts. The architect Walter Gropius called it "the most public of arts." Because important buildings often incorporate sculpture, paintings, murals, frescos, or mosaics, as well as decorative objects, architecture is also known as the "Queen of the Arts," uniting and ruling over a kingdom of different media. Architecture is also simply the largest art form, with pyramids, fortresses, and skyscrapers rivaling the drama of mountains and other natural wonders. A city like New York, Tokyo, Paris, or Rome—a collection of structures designed and built by humans—is as much a "wonder of the world" as the Grand Canyon.

Yet architecture is sometimes considered less "pure" than the arts of painting and sculpture because, like the decorative arts and design, it is meant to be *useful*. We do not put buildings or bridges on pedestals or hang them on gallery walls; we live in them, we move through them, and often we do not see them as art at all. But architecture is the most omnipresent form of art. Because it is experienced by nearly everyone on our planet, architecture can be said to be a universal art form. Instead of needing to search it out, all we need to do is open our eyes, because architecture of some kind surrounds us wherever we live.

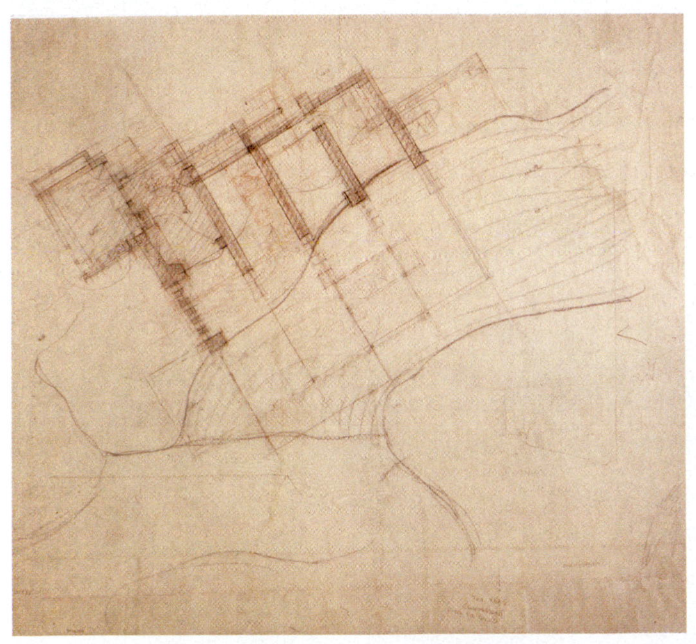

10-1 Frank Lloyd Wright, Kaufman House (Fallingwater), Bear Run, Pennsylvania, 1936–1939. Preliminary study of the floor plans; different levels are drawn in different colors.

Like sculpture, architecture is a three-dimensional art form; it cannot be comprehended in a single glance or understood by standing in only one spot. Yet architecture seems to exist in more than three dimensions. Because most structures are designed to have both an outside and an inside, to really appreciate a work of architecture, we must walk not only around it but also *through* it. As we relate interior to exterior views in our minds, structures exist in memory as well as space and therefore acquire the fourth dimension of *time*.

The Architect as Artist and Engineer: Planning

The architect must be a cross between a pure artist and an engineer, because a building is not meant only to be seen—it must be functional. Buildings have to match the purpose for which they are constructed. A train station must funnel thousands of people in and

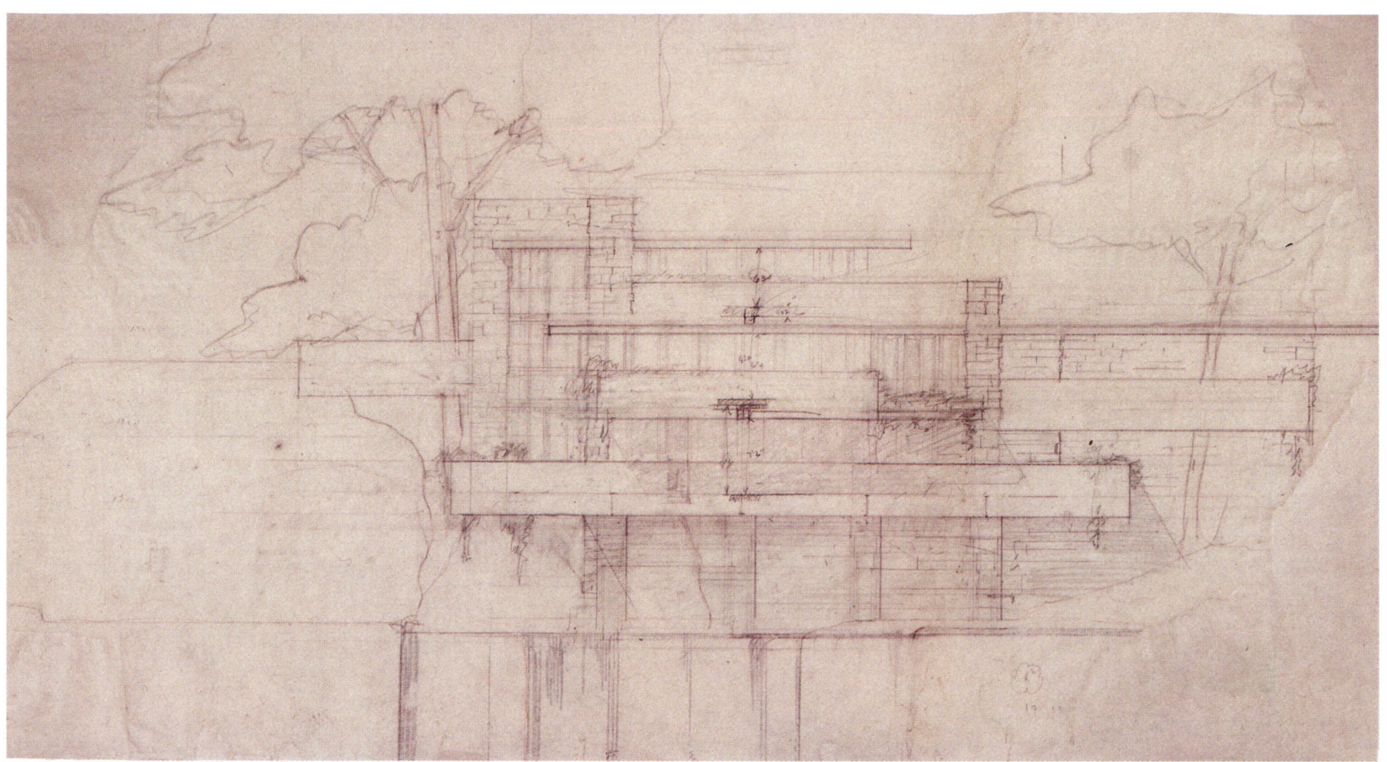

10-2 Frank Lloyd Wright, Kaufman House (Fallingwater), Bear Run, Pennsylvania, 1936–1939. Preliminary sketch of the south elevation.

out; a home should be comfortable and hospitable. Floors must support each other; walls should not fall in or out. Skyscrapers should be able to stand in high winds and even earthquakes. In modern buildings, the architect must also plan for services such as heating, cooling, electricity, and air circulation. Besides aesthetics and engineering, there is also a business side to architecture. As in all commissioned art, the architect must consider the needs of the patron and the cost of materials in any design decision.

As part of their design process, architects make drawings and models. Some architectural drawings, like Frank Lloyd Wright's, are as beautiful as the final buildings. In 1936, the great American architect made a preliminary visit to a site for a client's new home in the woods of Bear Run, Pennsylvania. After seeing a mountain stream with a waterfall, he came up with the inspired idea of placing the house over the cliff and letting the water pass underneath it. He made *floor plans* or flat views from above (**10-1**); **elevations** or views from the sides (**10-2**); and **perspectives,** views that give a three-dimensional impression of the new building in its setting (**10-3**). These were shown to the client and, with minor modifications, became a modern masterpiece, the Kaufman House (Fallingwater). By comparing the drawings to a photograph of the finished building (**10-4**), you can see how close it is to Wright's original conception.

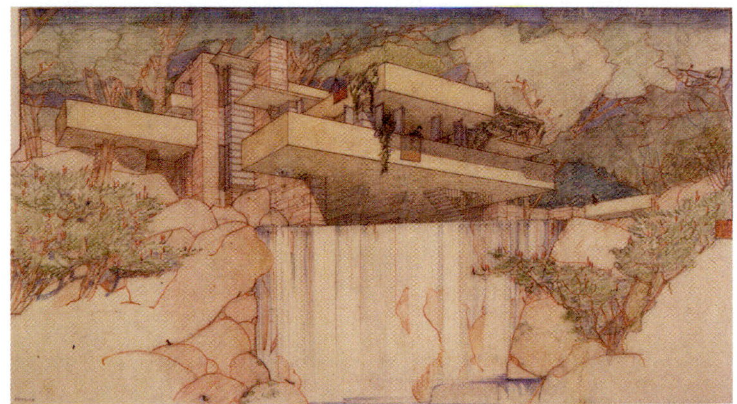

10-3 Frank Lloyd Wright, Kaufman House (Fallingwater), Bear Run, Pennsylvania, 1936–1939. Presentation drawing.

Over the years, however, Fallingwater has developed structural problems. Completed in 1939, it was donated by the Kaufman family to a conservancy, and opened to the public in 1964. Its brilliant design is famous throughout the world, and in

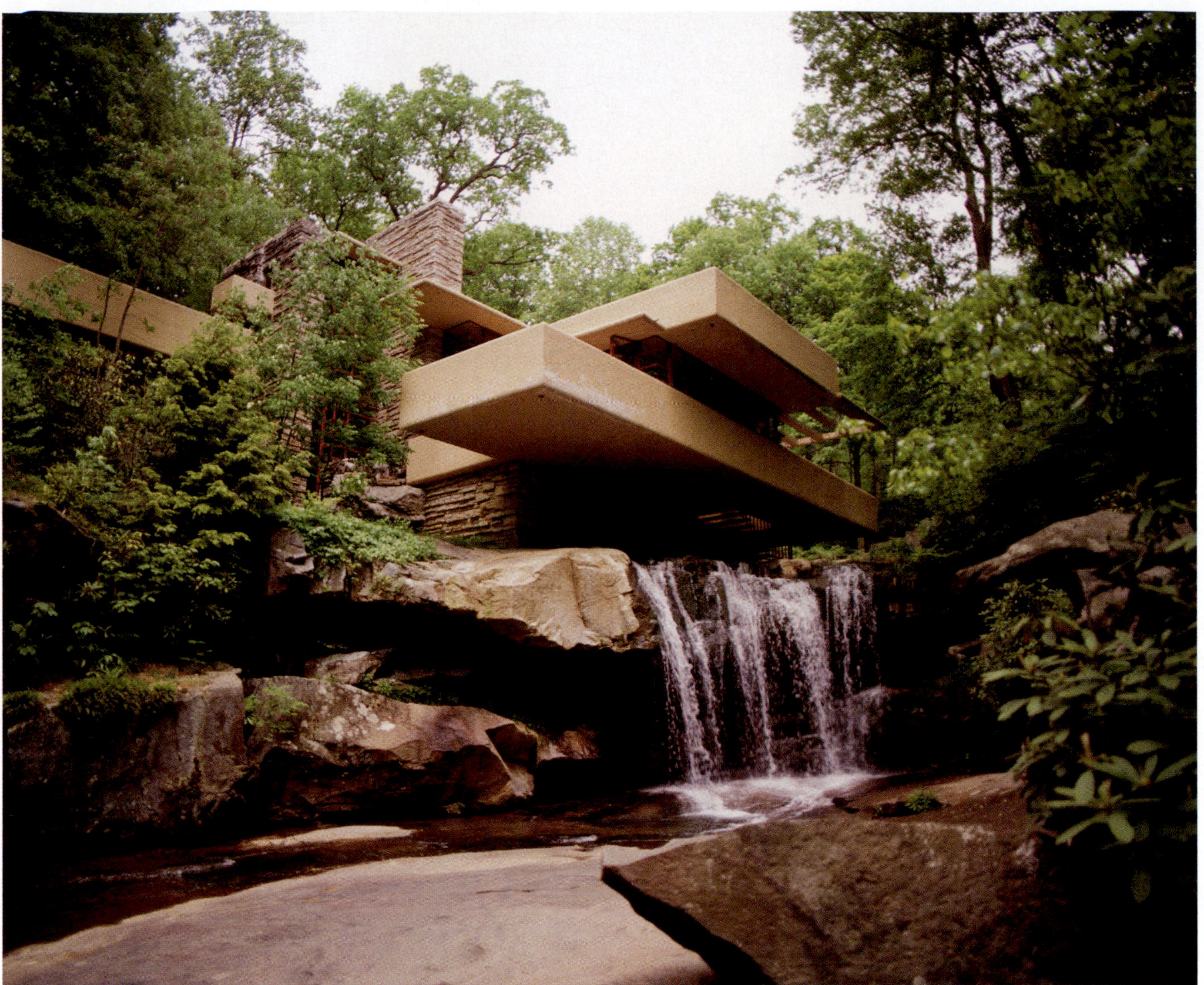

10-4 Frank Lloyd Wright, Kaufman House (Fallingwater), Bear Run, Pennsylvania, 1936–1939.

1991, the American Institute of Architects voted it the "best all-time work of American architecture." But because of fears that it would collapse, the structure is now resting on temporary steel supports. It appears that Wright should have reinforced his concrete slabs with steel rods, but refused to do so. Since the late 1990s, the conservancy has been working to stabilize—and then restore—the structure.

Harmony of Exterior and Interior Design

Unlike other art forms, architecture has both an outside and an inside to be experienced, and the design of both aspects should be in harmony. Such harmony can be seen in the façade (the outward face of a building) and interior of the majestic *Dome of the Rock* (**10-5**) in Jerusalem. This early mosque was built in the seventh century—only a little more than fifty years after the death of the Prophet Muhammad—to commemorate the victory of Islam in capturing Jerusalem from the Byzantine Empire (see Chapter 13 for the history of Islam). The setting is the Temple Mount, a sacred space to three religions. It is believed to be the location where God tested Abraham by asking for the sacrifice of his son Isaac (Judaism), as well as the place from which Muhammad was taken to view both heaven and hell (Islam). The Temple Mount is also located next to the shrine of the Holy Sepulcher, where Jesus was thought to

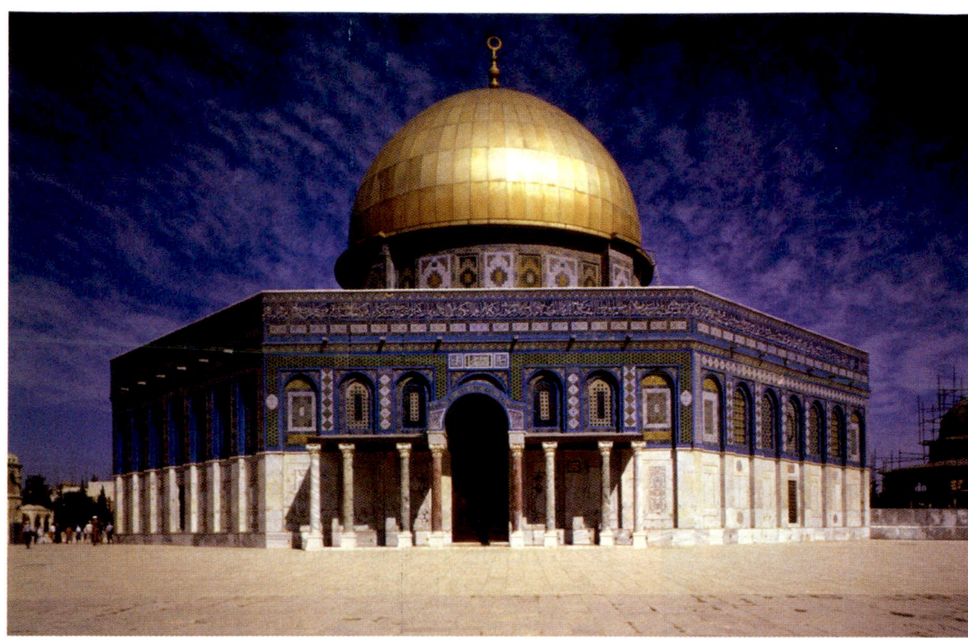

10-5 Dome of the Rock, Jerusalem, 687–692.

have been buried (Christianity). Because it is set on a hill, the *Dome* is visible throughout the city.

The octagonal shape of the mosque was probably inspired by early Christian sites in Jerusalem, similar to St.Vitale in Ravenna (see Chapter 13), but here the wooden dome is much larger and more imposing than Roman and Byzantine domes. The combination of white and turquoise tiles and gold sparkles in the Middle Eastern sun, and is typical of many Islamic shrines. Inside the Dome of the Rock (**10-6**), the original mosaics (those on the outside were later replaced by tiles) glow with a golden light and impress us with their elaborate patterns of vines. Because the early Moslem religion rejected any attempt at realistic images as idolatrous, artists created decorative patterns to enrich the space that Christian houses of worship would fill with bible stories. Both inside and outside, the lowest level of the mosque is made of beautiful marble pillars (taken from older Roman monuments), the upper levels with bands of mosaic or tile designs. At the center of the interior space is the sacred rock from which Muhammad rose to heaven, encircled by a low decorative wall.

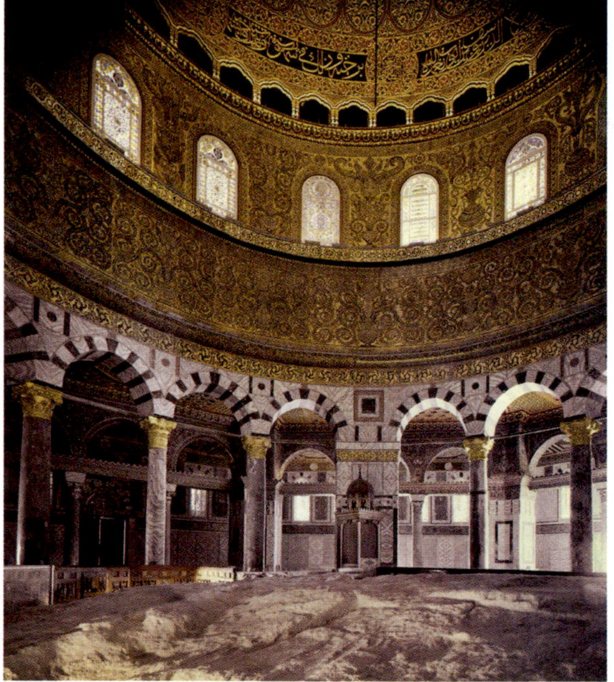

10-6 Interior, Dome of the Rock, Jerusalem.

Harmony with Natural Setting

The natural setting of each building also has an effect on its appearance and often influences the way it is designed. As in Wright's Fallingwater, to plan a successful building, an architect must consider local climate, available building materials, the building site, and its surroundings. The architect must also consider how to orient a building to take advantage of natural light, attractive views, and prevailing wind patterns. In certain climates, the design of exterior spaces such as patios, courtyards, and **arcades** (covered walkways) can be just as important as that of the

A GLOBAL VIEW

in 1972 had completed restoration by 1983. Estimated to have been constructed around 800 AD, Borobudur is a Buddhist site, about four hundred feet long on each side and almost one hundred feet tall, including hundreds of life-size statues of the Buddha and more than a thousand relief sculptures. Built on top of a hill, Borobudur is a stupa (see 12-13 and discussion of The Great Stupa), a place of worship that is not entered, but *circumambulated* (walked around). Here, one is meant to start at the lowest level and follow the walkways until one reaches the highest, circular level and a final stupa at the pinnacle of the hill. Along the way are relief sculptures showing the previous lives of Buddha, then scenes from Buddha's life, and visions of heaven toward the top. If these reliefs were laid out in a row, they would be ten miles long!

Another successful restoration campaign took place in the Angkor Archeological Park of Cambodia, between 1993 and 2004. The most famous site in this area is the Hindu temple complex of Angkor Wat (**10-10**). Built by Suryavarman II, a King of the Khmer Empire, in the twelfth century, the temple had been overrun by vegetation—not surprising, since the Angkor Park is in the middle of a jungle. Angkor Wat is constructed in the shape of the symbolic "world mountain," with five peaks rising higher and higher toward the center. Originally, it was surrounded by a moat of four thousand by five thousand feet, fed by a huge irrigation system. As at Borobudur, the stone walls are covered with beautiful relief sculptures—in this case representing either the King or the Hindu God Vishnu in his various forms.

It would take hundreds of pictures to explore the glories of Borobudur and Angkor Wat, now preserved for humanity through the efforts of the United Nations. Other cultural wonders on the World Heritage list include Machu Picchu in Peru, the entire city of Venice, Italy, and the pyramids at Giza—the only original remaining wonder of the ancient world.

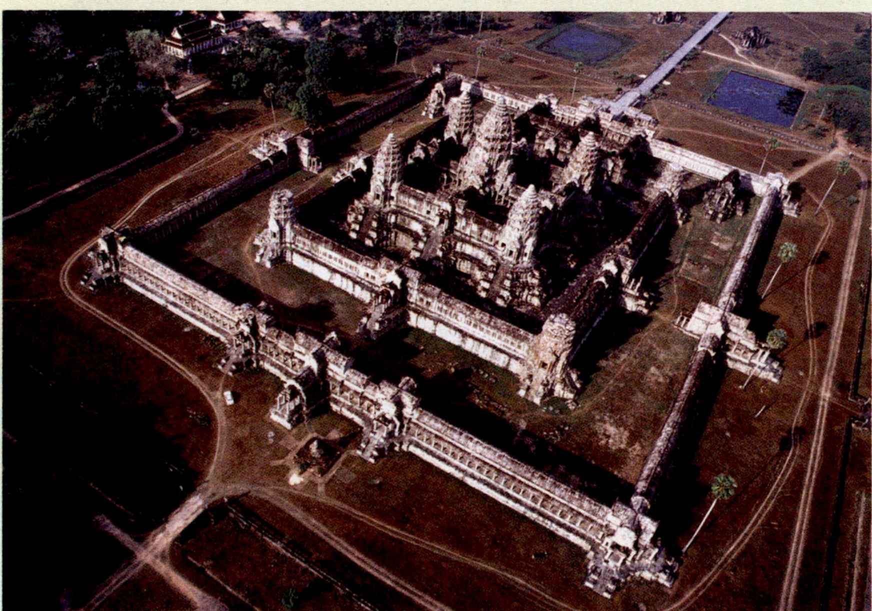

10-10 Angkor Wat, Ankor, Cambodia, first half of twelfth century.

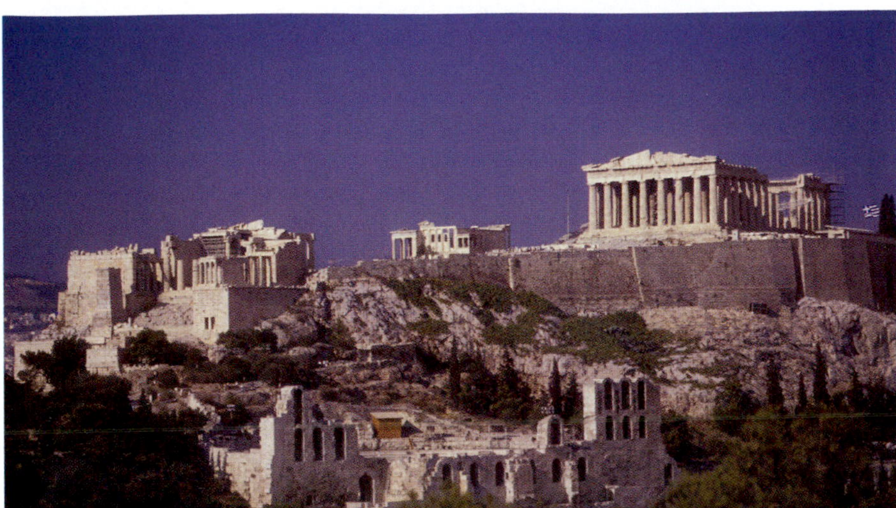

10-11 Acropolis, Athens, Greece.

The Parthenon

When historians look back to the beginnings of architecture as an art, they usually think of the magnificent structures of the great civilizations of the past. In the ancient world, temples, palaces, monuments, and tombs were the most important art forms. Also, because they are the most visible and lasting remnants of their era, their importance has actually been magnified by the passage of time. No examples of Greek mural painting remain; many statues of the golden age of Greece exist only in later Roman copies. But the architecture of the Athenian *Acropolis* (**10-11**) lives on as a symbol of Greek culture, equivalent to the *Iliad* and the *Odyssey*—the works of the great Greek dramatists and philosophers. The Greeks built edifices that speak of human intellect separate and above earthly concerns.

The word *acropolis* means simply "high place," and the Greeks chose such a hill in Athens as a setting for their most important religious center. In 480 BC, during the Persian Wars, the original buildings and statues were destroyed, but the Athenians decided to rebuild the temples to be even more magnificent. The centerpiece of the new design was the famous *Parthenon* (seen at the top of 10-11, and **10-12**), a temple devoted to Athena, the patron goddess of the city. Its marble exterior enclosed a magnificent forty-foot statue of the goddess in ivory and gold created by Phidias, the most famous sculptor of the day. The fame of the temple's architects has lasted, too. Almost twenty-five hundred years later, we still know their names—Iktinos and Kallikrates.

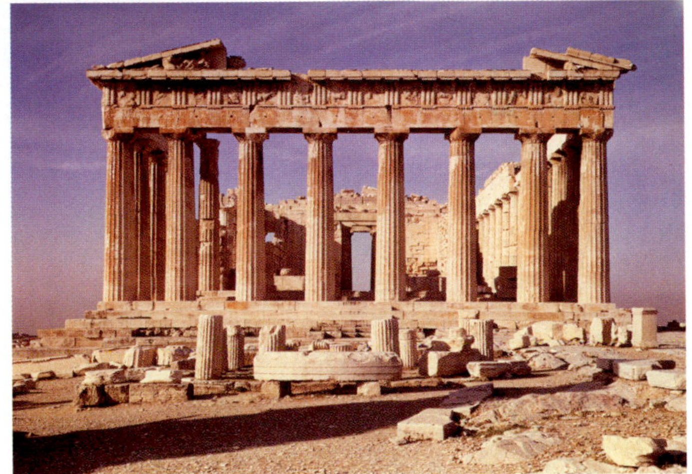

10-12 Iktinos and Kallikrates, rear view of the Parthenon, Acropolis, Athens, Greece, 448–432 BCE.

Like any building with a long history, the Parthenon has had many different occupants and functions over the centuries. It became a Christian church during the era of the Holy Roman Empire and an Islamic mosque in later centuries. For two thousand years, it remained largely intact, not the ruin we see today. Then, in 1687, while being used by the Ottoman Turks to store gunpowder, it suffered a direct rocket hit from the forces of the warring Venetians, and much of the interior was blown up. In 1801, a British aristocrat found many of the priceless marble statues lying about in a state of disrepair. According to one's viewpoint, Lord Elgin either saved or stole these statues by shipping them off to England, where they remain, known as "The Elgin Marbles" in the British Museum (see Chapter 12). Despite all its troubles, the Parthenon is probably the most famous, and most studied, human-made structure in the world.

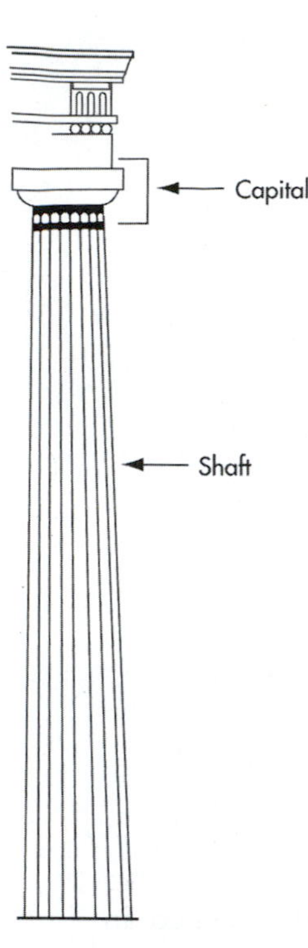

10-13 Doric

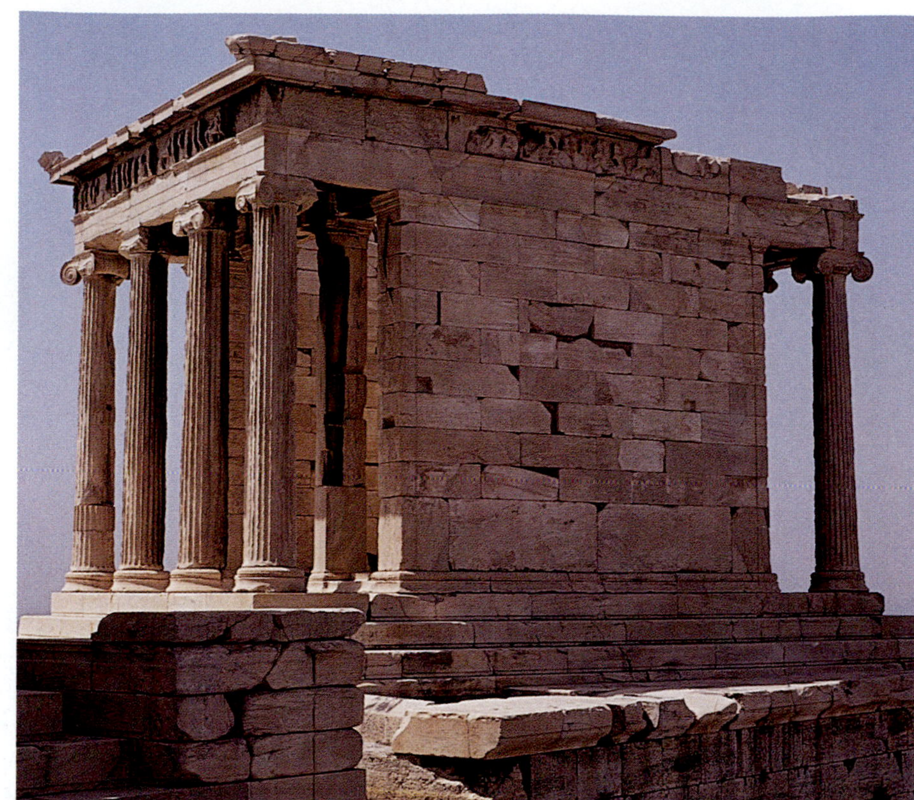
10-14 Kallikrates, the Temple of Athena Nike, Acropolis, Athens, Greece, 427–424 BCE.

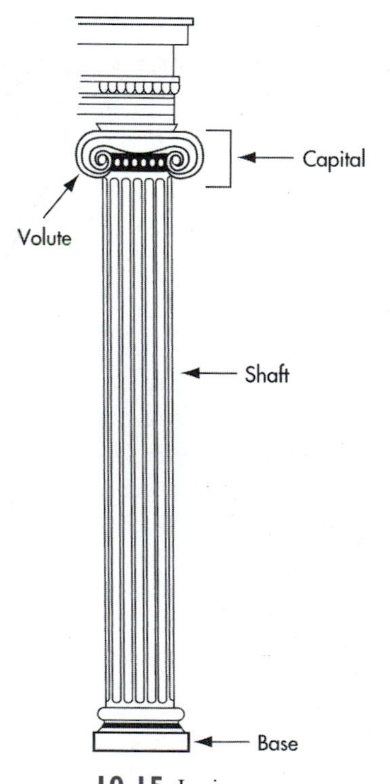

10-15 Ionic

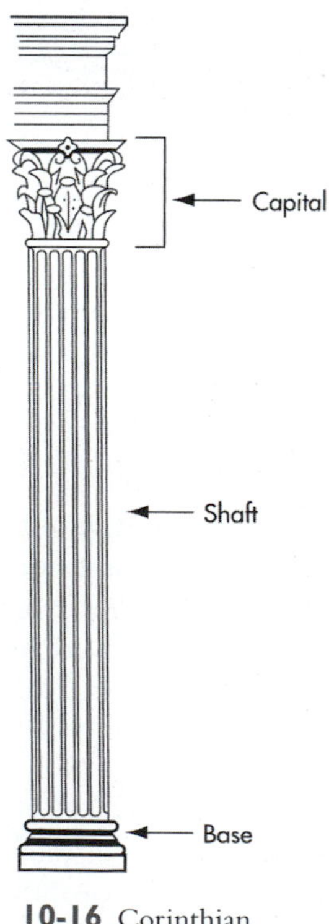

10-16 Corinthian

The Greek Orders

The *Doric* column used in the design of the Parthenon (**10-13**) was the earliest and simplest of the *Greek orders* (column style). Doric columns were unornamented, almost severe in their plainness. This purity was characteristic of early Greek art. For the Greeks, beauty was to be found in perfection of line, shape, and proportion, not excess decoration. This simplicity, this harmony and repose, gives the Parthenon its universal appeal. Because of the abstract geometric beauty of their designs, Greek temples have been compared to works of sculpture by many art historians. This is certainly demonstrated by the exquisite design of the *Temple of Athena Nike* (**10-14**), also on the Acropolis. In this little temple, slim *Ionic* columns (**10-15**), their **capitals** (tops) adorned with graceful **volutes** (spirals), harmonize with the delicate proportions of the structure. A more decorative order, the *Corinthian* column (**10-16**), was rarely used by the Greeks. It was more consistent with later Roman tastes; the famous *Pantheon* (12-27) uses Corinthian columns both outside and inside.

MATERIALS AND METHODS

Architectural structures have been categorized and described in many different ways. Just as two- and three-dimensional art forms can be discussed in terms of both their materials (or media) and techniques, so various types of architecture can be organized by building matter—such as stone, wood, clay, brick, glass, and steel—and their method of construction. Each material has different visual, tactile, and tensile qualities; each produces a different impression; and each is capable of being used to construct structures of different sizes and shapes.

Earth, Clay, and Brick

One way to build is simply to pile up dirt, mud, or clay to form walls. **Adobe** is a kind of sun-dried brick, made of clay mixed with straw, which was used by Native American tribes in the Southwest to build their settlements. In Taos, New Mexico, traditional adobe *pueblos* (**10-17**), first constructed about five hundred years ago, are still in use and utilize the **bearing wall** method, where the walls support the weight of the roof and floors above. The sun-dried mud bricks are stacked to form thick walls, which are stuck together with a mortar of wet mud. Each building is topped with logs that protrude from the outer wall. Branches and grass are laid over these logs to form a roof, which is then covered with another thick layer of mud. Finally, the outlines of the bricks are hidden by a hand-smoothed coating of mud, or adobe plaster, which can be refreshed every year.

In adobe construction, the window openings must necessarily be small, since the walls are what hold these structures up. This is actually an advantage in a desert climate, where it is beneficial to keep light, and heat, out of the buildings. The massive mud walls act as natural temperature regulators, providing shade and coolness during the heat of the day as the walls absorb the sun's energy. At night, as the environment cools, these same walls release their heat slowly and keep interior temperatures relatively stable and comfortable. The same process keeps the clay buildings in a Dogon village (10-8) relatively cool even in the heat of Mali, Africa. Long before air-conditioning, and with optimal energy efficiency, these peoples on opposite sides of the world used natural materials to construct attractive and comfortable dwellings.

Bricks are blocks made of clay, usually hardened by being baked in ovens or kilns. Kiln-fired bricks can be glazed in different colors and arranged in interesting patterns. During the early years of the American republic, or what is called the *Federal period* in architecture, many attractive American mansions such as Thomas Jefferson's *Monticello* (see 10-38) were constructed of brick.

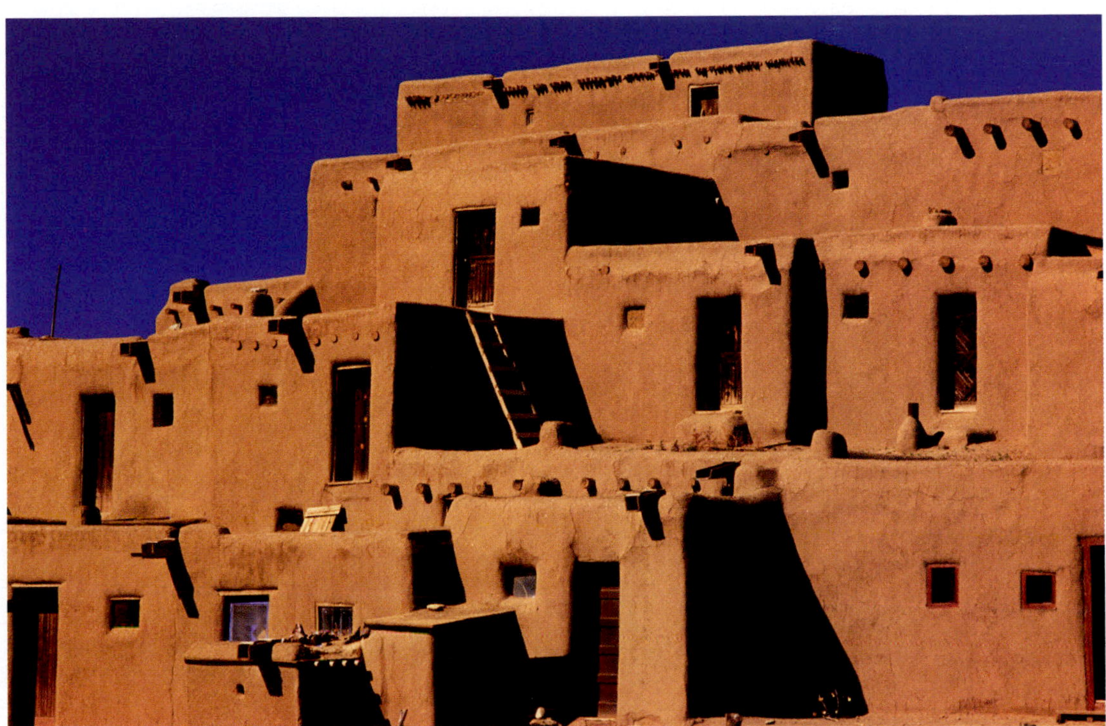

10-17 Taos Pueblo, Taos, New Mexico.

Stone

Buildings made of brick are sometimes referred to as being constructed of *masonry,* but that term is more commonly used when talking about structures built of blocks of stone, such as marble or granite. Stone or masonry construction has historically been associated with strength. Castles, fortresses, and the protective walls around settlements were typically built out of stone. Masonry construction was preferred for buildings that were meant to last.

The history of stone buildings is also a story of efforts to open wider and wider areas on the exterior and inside them. The Greeks perfected a form of construction called **post-and-lintel** (**10-18**), where posts or columns support horizontal lintels or cross beams. The Parthenon (10-12) provides a clear example of this method. The heavy weight of stone lintels keeps the columns steady. This method permits more open buildings than those constructed by bearing-wall methods and is just as permanent. Temples built of stone thousands of years ago, like those on the Acropolis, are still standing.

A later development in stone construction was the **round arch** (**10-19**), used extensively for the first time during the Roman Empire. The arch allowed far wider spaces between columns than post-and-lintel construction. The huge entrances into the Colosseum in Rome (Chapter 12) are rounded arches. Triumphal arches like the *Arch of Constantine* (**10-20**) are excellent examples of the huge openings permitted by arches.

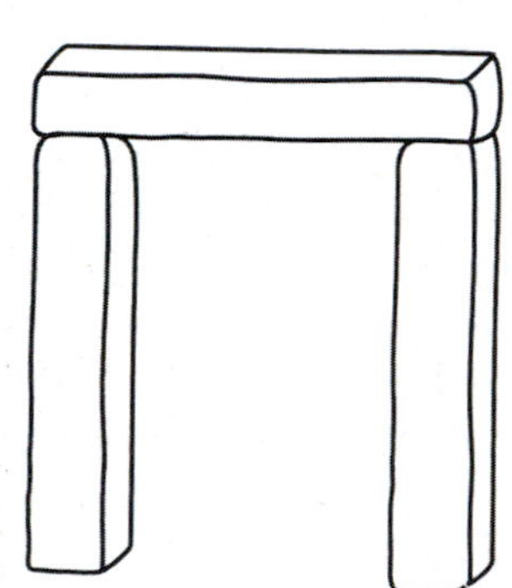

10-18 Post-and-Lintel

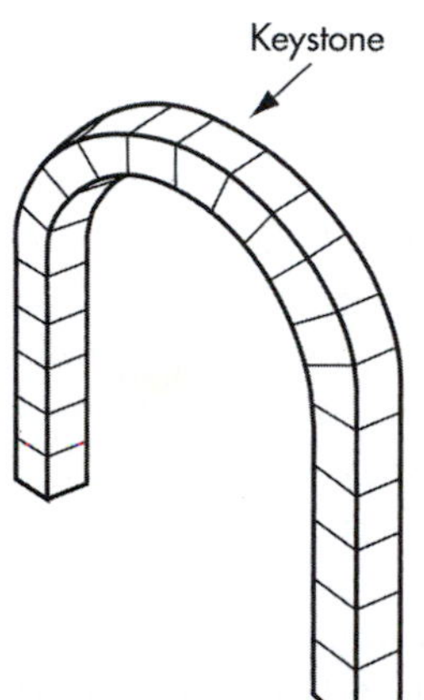

10-19 Round Arch

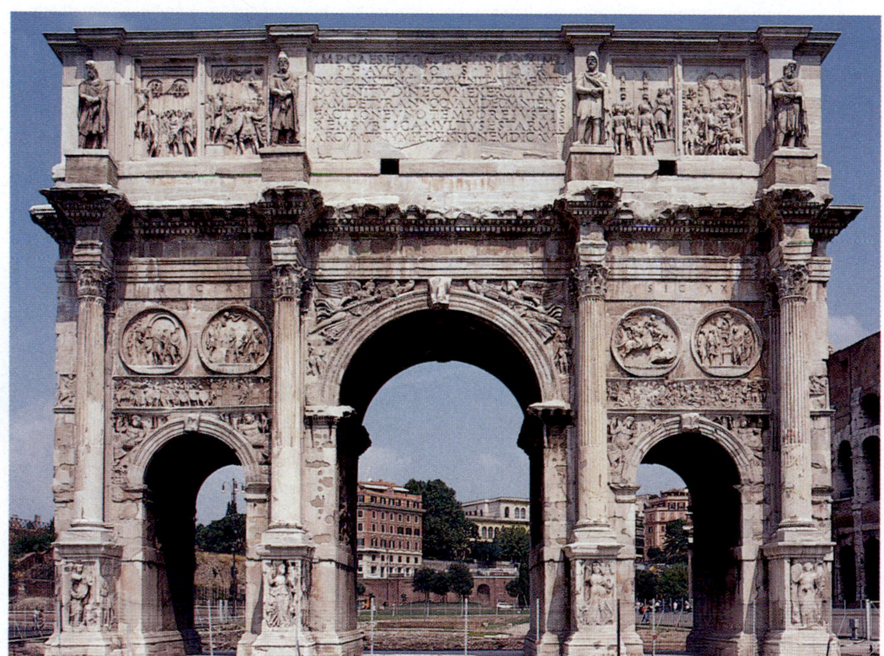

Index/Artphoto

10-20 Arch of Constantine, Rome, Italy, 312–315.

Such triumphal arches were constructed by the Romans throughout the Mediterranean world, symbols of victory to mark their territory and reminders of their governing authority. Carved into the arches were relief sculptures illustrating military scenes and inscriptions that hailed the conquering heroes. The great size of the arches was necessary because of their part in one of the most popular Roman events—the triumphal march. In these parades, trumpets would announce the arrival of their victorious generals on chariot, followed by Roman legions, slaves, conquered treasures, and humiliated enemies.

The use of the arch was expanded during the Middle Ages. **Barrel vaults** (**10-21**), as seen in the nave of the *Church of Sainte-Madeleine* at Vézelay in France (**10-22**), opened up large and long public spaces in stone buildings, particularly cathedrals. **Groin vaults** (10-21) are made by crossing two barrel vaults at right angles. Buildings made with barrel and groin vaults were, however, limited in height by the width of each arch. Only small windows were possible without weakening the stability of the arches. The awe-inspiring impression of Gothic cathedrals,

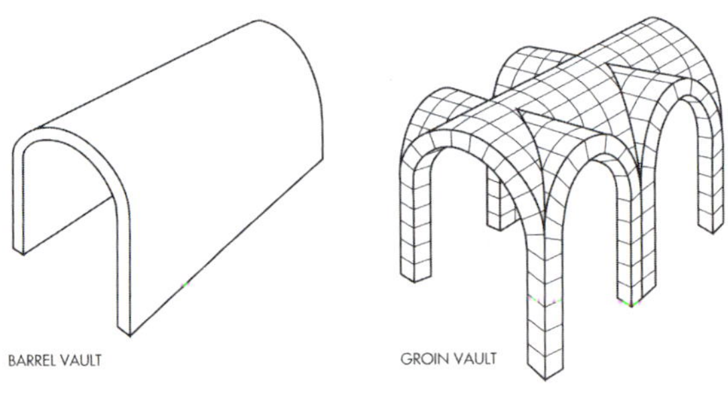

10-21 Barrel Vault and Groin Vault

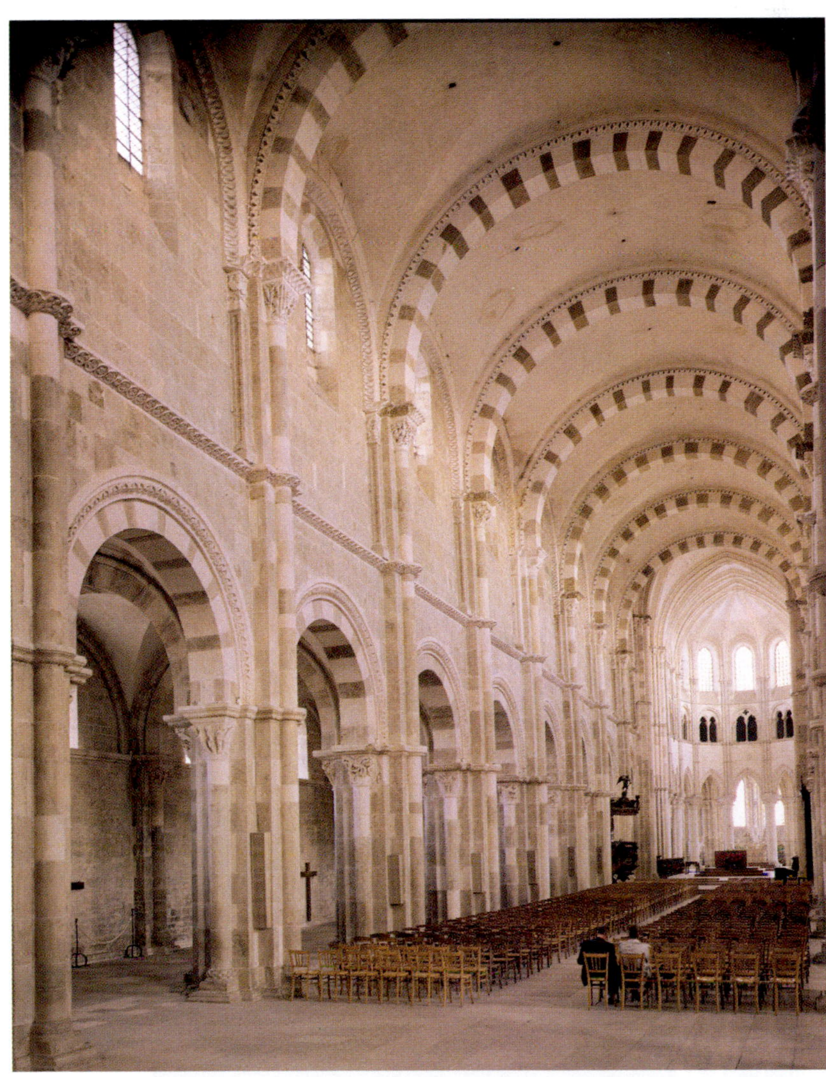

10-22 Nave of Sainte-Madeleine, Vézelay, France, twelfth century.

Iron and Glass

Until the nineteenth century, almost all buildings were made of clay, brick, stone, or wood. The industrial revolution created new techniques that made innovative building materials available. With the advent of coal furnaces and mass production, iron became one of the important new materials of the industrial age. This modern building material was often preferred for new types of buildings, such as factories, warehouses, railroad sheds, and large exhibition halls. Because iron was stronger than wood and lighter than stone, the pillars could be thinner and spaced farther apart than wood or stone posts. Cast-iron columns were combined with large panels of glass to make dramatic, airy exhibition halls, such as the famous *Crystal Palace,* built for the Great Exhibition of 1851 in London. The most famous and dramatic structure ever built of iron is the *Eiffel Tower* in Paris (**10-28**). At the time it was built, and for more than twenty-five years afterward, the Eiffel Tower was the tallest building in the world—one thousand feet high. The tower was built not by an architect but by an engineer and builder of bridges, Gustave Eiffel, who had previously designed the metal skeleton for the Statue of Liberty. Eiffel's tower was constructed as the focal point for the Paris Exhibition of 1889, one of the many popular international trade exhibits of the second half of the nineteenth century.

The Eiffel Tower was largely an experiment for the potential of iron as a building material. In fact, it was built over the objections of many of the successful artists and writers of the time, who considered its design to be hideously ugly. Later, however, modern artists became fascinated by the tower as a symbol of advanced technology, the machine age, and modern life.

Steel and Glass

Despite its advantages, cast iron enjoyed a relatively brief period of popularity. Although it had been touted as fireproof, the dramatic Chicago fire of 1871 (and, ultimately, the burning of the Crystal Palace in 1936) proved otherwise. Iron actually melted at high temperatures, totally destroying the building it was meant to support. Yet something like iron was needed to hold up the new, taller buildings being constructed in large American cities.

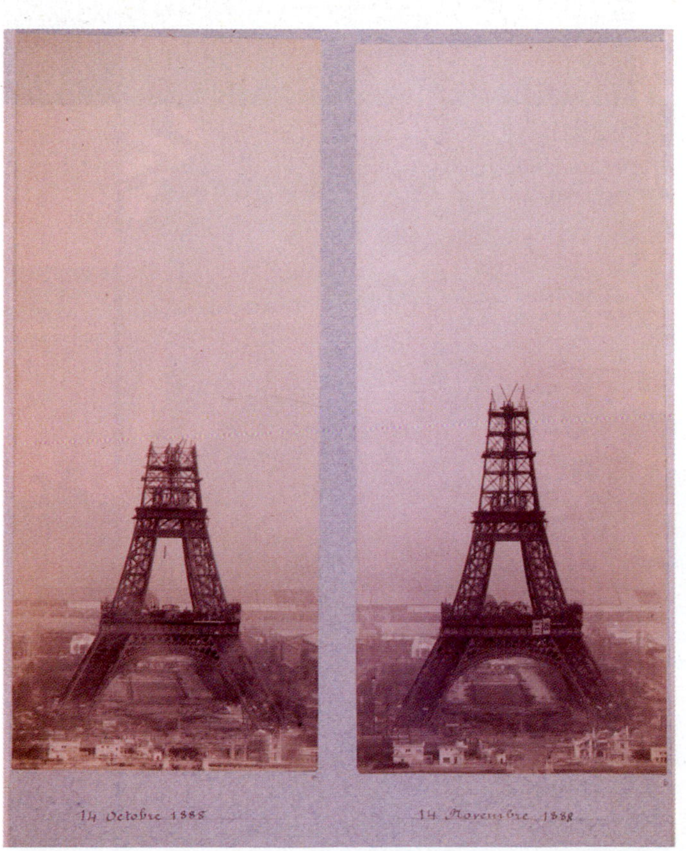

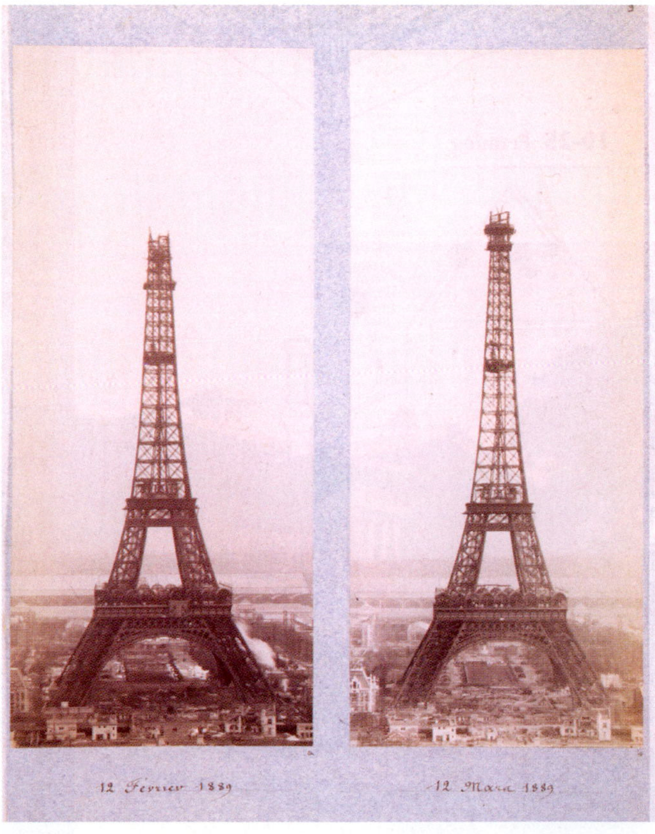

10-28 Construction of the Eiffel Tower, 1888–1889. Musée d'Orsay, Paris (Eiffel Tower Collection).

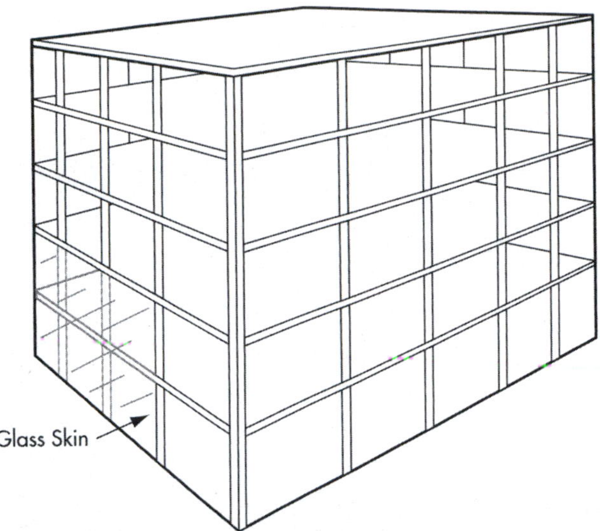

10-29 Steel-frame Construction

Luckily, a better material was available for the support of the new tall buildings—*steel*. Steel is both stronger and lighter than iron, and with the development of the steel industry in the 1890s, it became affordable for builders. With a new kind of construction, **steel frame** or **cage** (**10-29**), which employs an interior skeleton for the structure, neither stone walls nor wooden beams are needed for support. Therefore, what we see as the exterior "walls" of a steel frame building are often simply a "skin" of glass. This dramatic innovation in structural design is reputed to have been invented when an architect noticed his bird cage could support a heavy stack of books.

With a better material and a new building method, the way was cleared for an American invention—the *skyscraper*. The best of these tall steel-and-glass towers, or skyscrapers, convey a strong impression of lightness, refinement, and elegance. Such buildings were often used as giant symbols of corporate money, power, efficiency, and modernity during their heyday in the mid-twentieth century. Companies vied with each other as they commissioned new headquarters by the foremost architects of the period, attempting to outdo their neighbors in sheer size. One of the most notable, and well-designed, commercial structures was the *Seagram Building* (**10-30**) in New York by architects Ludwig Mies van der Rohe and Philip Johnson. Built from 1954 to 1958, its exterior is made of amber-colored glass with bronze frames, or *mullions*. Because of this sensitive and unusual combination of materials, the building at night has been described as a giant "golden crystal."

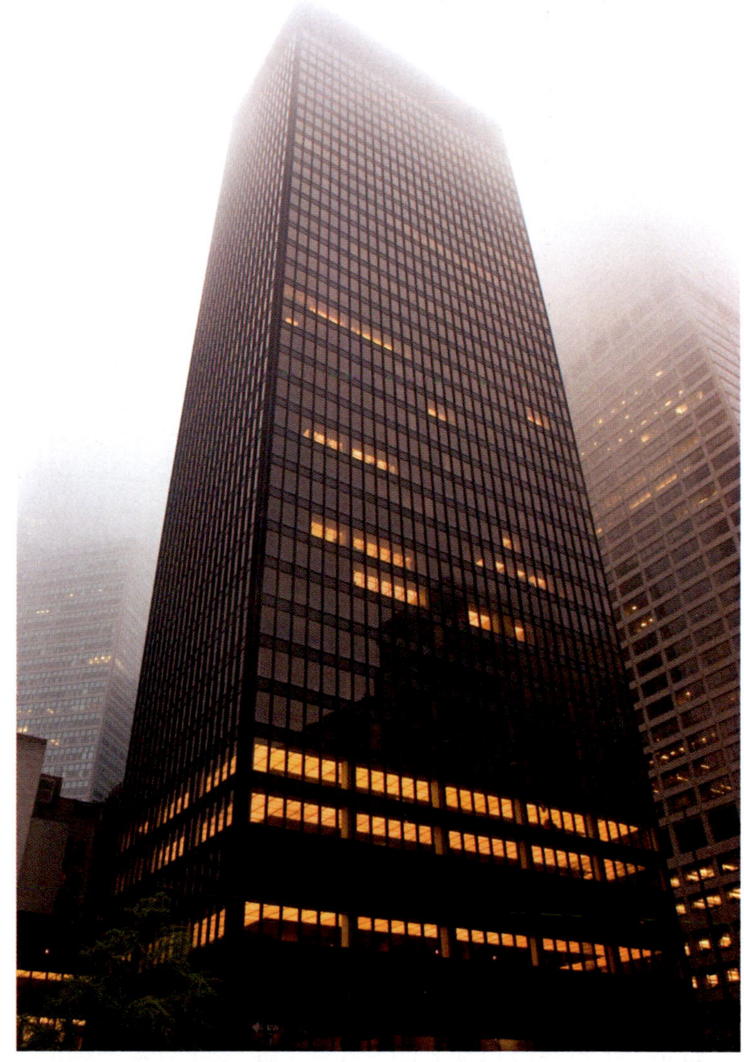

10-30 Ludwig Mies van der Rohe and Philip Johnson, Seagram Building, New York City, 1956–1958.

Reinforced Concrete

Reinforced concrete (or **ferroconcrete**) became another exciting new building material in the twentieth century. Although concrete (a mixture of cement, sand, and gravel) was a favorite material of the ancient Romans, reinforcing that material with small iron rods enabled architects to make structures that were not only strong but also shaped in dramatic new ways. Most buildings in the past were designed of intersecting geometric forms, such as boxes, cubes, and half-spheres. Buildings of reinforced concrete can be shaped organically as well as geometrically, with walls and roofs like swelling waves instead of straight lines. The *Trans World Airlines (TWA) Terminal* at Kennedy Airport in New York (**10-31, 10-32**),

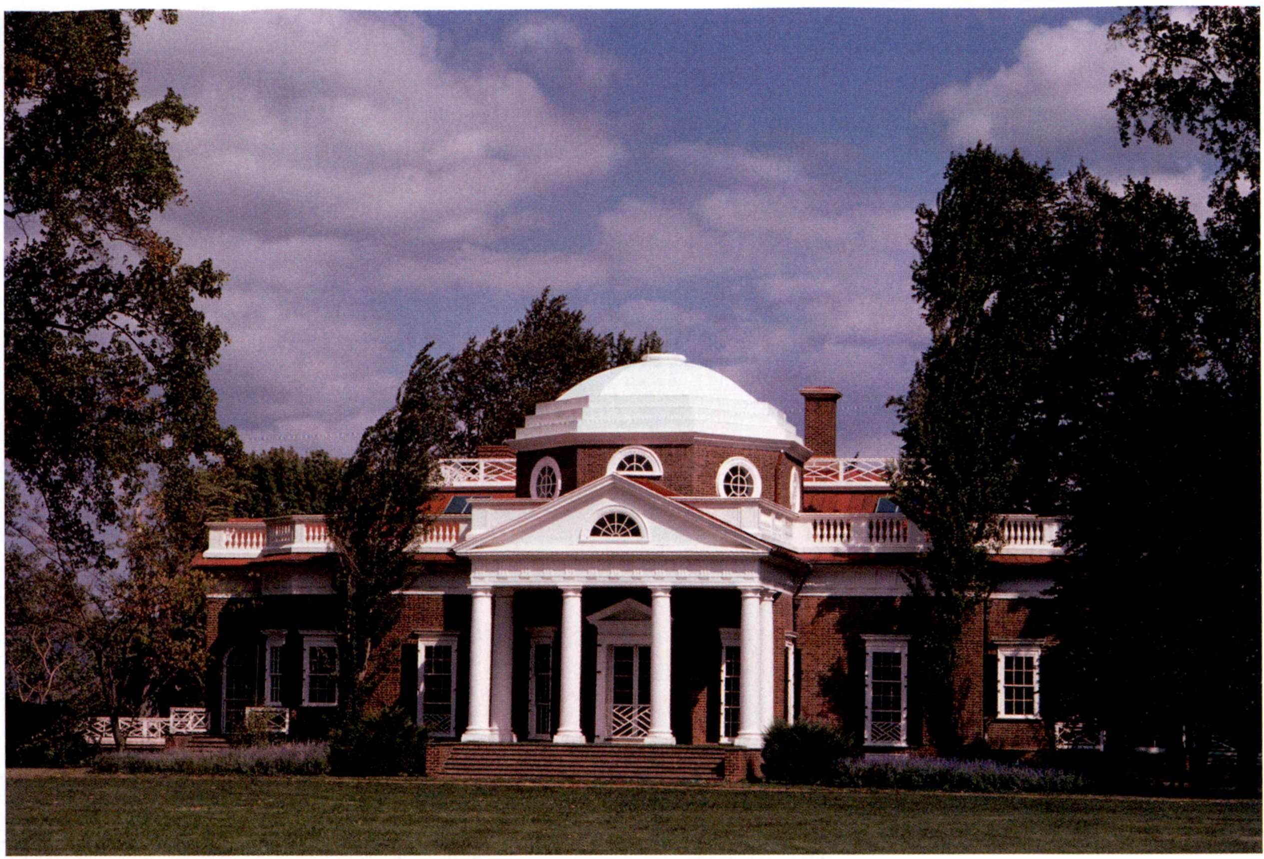

10-38 Thomas Jefferson, Monticello, Charlottesville, Virginia, 1770–1806.

Monticello

Thomas Jefferson was a man of diverse talents and interests—a farmer, statesman, and scholar as well as an inventor and architect. Heir to a comfortable Virginia estate, he can be described as a gentleman-amateur architect, a type common in the eighteenth century. While serving as the American ambassador to France, he had visited Italy and had seen the ancient ruins. But even before visiting Europe, Jefferson had studied classical architecture through English books. Jefferson was attracted to Greek and Roman architecture because of its historical associations of good government, as well as its style and simplicity. Now that America was independent, he was eager to replace the British-influenced colonial style.

In *Monticello* (**10-38**), Jefferson had the chance to design his own dream house. The home took more than thirty years to complete to his satisfaction. Set on top of a mountain (unlike other Southern plantation manors of the period), Monticello reveals an eighteenth-century taste for combining classical architectural elements, like columns, domes, and simple geometric shapes, with a natural, romantic setting. As a classical scholar, Jefferson was particularly fond of Roman poets, who described the delights of country life in a villa, and he himself wrote about the view from his home:

> Where has nature spread so rich a mantel under the eye? mountains, forests, rocks, rivers. With what majesty do we there ride above the storms! How sublime to look down into the house of nature, to see her clouds, hail, snow, rain, thunder, all fabricated at our feet! and the glorious sun, when rising as if out of a distant water, just gilding the tops of the mountains, and giving life to all nature!

Stripped of excess ornament and conveying a sense of purity, Monticello is harmonious and calm. Its beauty can be appreciated at first glance; carefully designed in human scale, the building does not overwhelm or awe the visitor. Monticello looks like what it is—a building meant to encourage a mood of speculation and intellectual pursuits, as well as gracious family living. The simple, empty room under the dome is particularly lovely, like a material representation of the human intellect, or Jefferson's extraordinary mind (**10-39**).

But Jefferson's pursuit of ideal beauty and idyllic lifestyle had a darker side. Both the money and labor he used to create his dream house and the life he lived there were produced by slave labor. (Of course, this was also true of the Greek and Roman civilizations that he admired, although their slavery was not based on race.) Jefferson's *Monticello* reflects the ideals of individualism and respect for private property embraced by the founding fathers of the United States.

The powerful expression of ideals in architecture can influence building for decades, even centuries to come. Monticello, itself a reflection of the endurance of classical Greek and Roman architectural ideals, had a profound and powerful effect on American architecture. Saint Peter's has also influenced countless buildings throughout the Western world. The style of our own *United States Capitol* building (**10-40**) owes as much to Michelangelo's dome as to Jefferson's promotion of neoclassicism for the government buildings of the new republic. It is just one example of the power of architecture to both express and transmit cultural values.

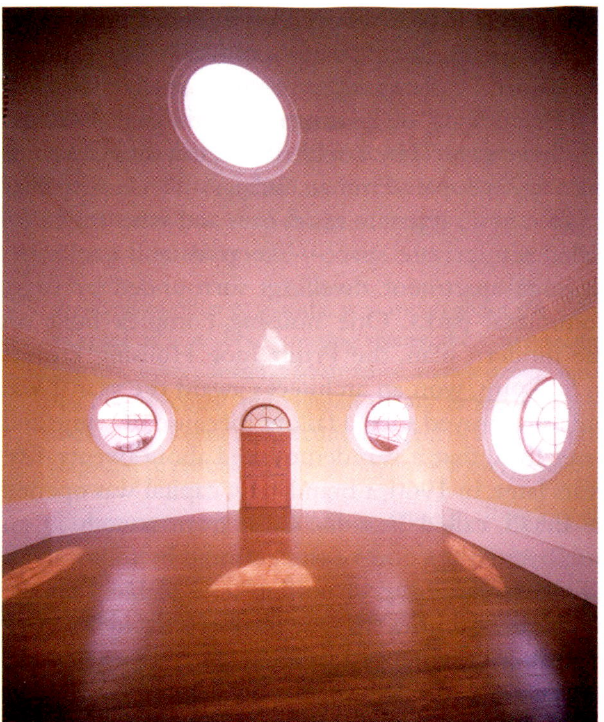

10-39 Thomas Jefferson, interior of dome at Monticello.

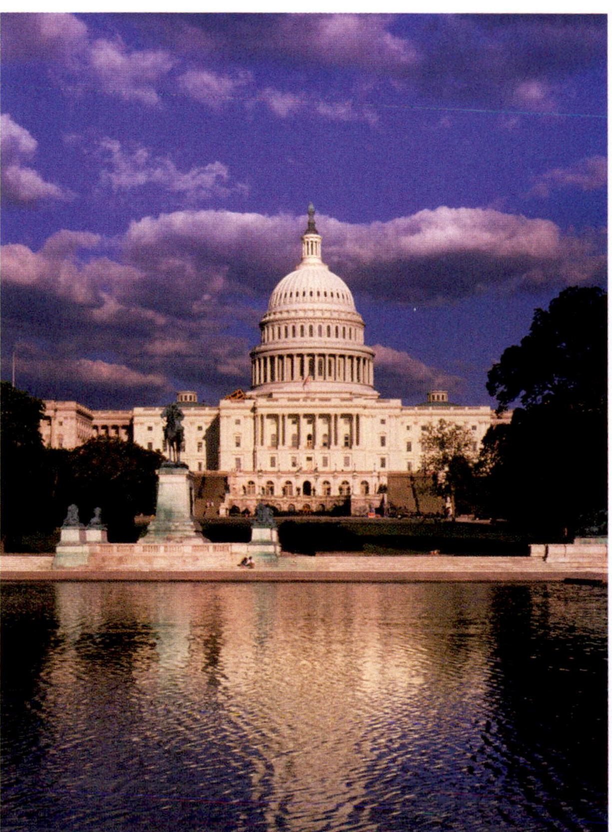

10-40 Benjamin Latrobe, United States Capitol, Washington, D.C., designed c. 1815.

URBAN PLANNING

Beyond the design of individual buildings and their settings, contemporary architects are also concerned with *urban design* or *planning*. The question of how a city of the future should look is a fascinating one that has been answered in many ways during the past fifty years. This question has taken on special importance because many people find today's cities—with their crowding, traffic, crime, pollution, and lack of greenery—an unlivable nightmare.

When the Modern movement in architecture was at its height in the mid-twentieth century, a standard kind of plan was devised to reform the design of cities. One of the major innovators and creators of the new urban planning was Le Corbusier (**10-41**), a Swiss-born Frenchman who worked around the world. Le Corbusier designed any number of new neighborhoods and housing projects for cities from Paris to Pakistan; most were never built, but some were, and the ideas behind them became quite influential. The idea of these plans was to house people in highrise apartment complexes, surrounded by parks and recreational areas. It was hoped that such developments would allow for both living and leisure.

the faithful wife of the hero Odysseus, spent the ten years of his absence weaving. Cloth can be woven out of fibers, such as wool, cotton, flax, and silk, into many different patterns, textures, and strengths. Most weaving is done on a **loom,** where one set of parallel threads, the **warp,** is held in a tense position. To make fabric, another set of parallel threads, the **weft** or *woof,* is arranged at right angles to the warp. The fabric is filled in by bringing these weft threads in and out, moving them back and forth, interlacing them with the warp. By using threads of different colors and textures, elaborate designs can be created. Although most cloth is used for making clothing, weaving can also provide decorative items such as carpets and wall hangings.

The most famous carpets in the world have come from the Middle East, where the geometric and organic patterns of Islamic art—also seen in tiles, calligraphy, and architectural decoration—have been translated into elaborate floor coverings. In this example, *The Ardabil Carpet* from Iran (**11-10**), a central sunburst motif is echoed at each of the four corners, while delicate blossoms connected by scrolling lines seem to float on a dark blue background. The pattern was created by hand-knotting wool in ten colors onto a silk warp and weft—304 knots per each square inch, over the entire surface of more than thirty-four by seventeen feet! The style is typical of carpets produced in the sixteenth-century Iranian Safavid kingdom, where the art of designing Persian carpets reached its height. This particular carpet is "the world's oldest dated carpet, and one of the largest, most beautiful, and historically important in the world," according to the Victoria & Albert Museum, where it now hangs as the highlight of a new Islamic gallery.

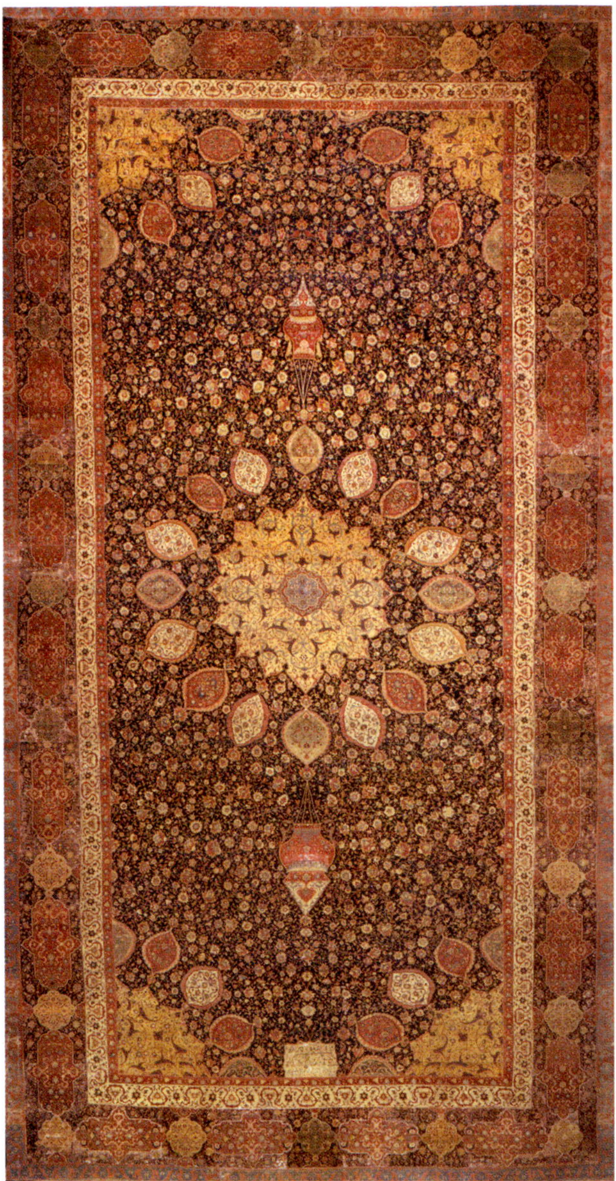

11-10 *The Ardabil Carpet,* Iran, c. 1539–1540. Hand-knotted woolen pile, on silk warp and weft; 304 knots per sq. in. 34′ 6″ × 17′ 7″. Victoria & Albert Museum, London.

In the West, quilting and embroidery have historically been done by women who did not have the freedom to become professional artists. The feminine "needle arts" provided an opportunity for women to express themselves creatively, painting their designs in thread and fabric. Such designs have ranged from pictorial and narrative, as in embroidered samplers showing people and places, to completely nonrepresentational, as in geometrically patterned quilts.

Some women have consciously used fabric and thread to make pictures that tell stories. This was the case with Harriet Powers (**11-11**), a former slave who designed several quilts based on biblical themes. Her method for making these quilts is one called **appliqué,** in which fabric silhouettes are cut out and stitched onto the background of another fabric. Such an appliqué technique is common in West Africa and may have been passed on to Powers by her forebears. What she did with this medium, however, was quite unusual. Instead of making attractive patterns, Powers used the squares of her quilts to vividly illustrate stories from the Bible. In this quilt she told the stories of Jonah and the whale, Adam and Eve, and the Day of Judgment, among others. While her silhouettes are simple, their arrangements demonstrate her sophisticated sense of design. Each panel is both a clear and visually interesting picture.

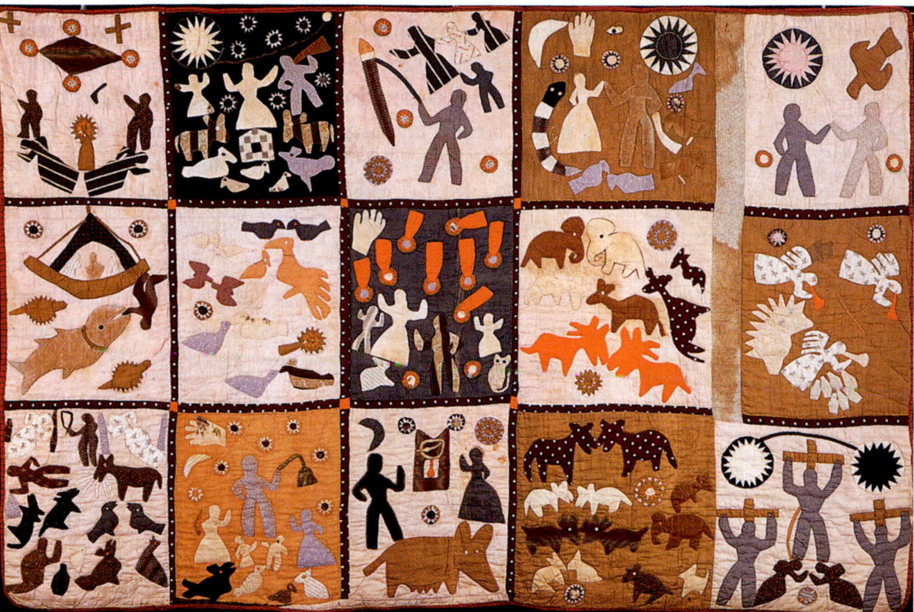

11-11 Harriet Powers, *Bible Quilt: The Creation of the Animals,* Athens, Georgia, c. 1895–1898. Pieced, appliquéd, and printed cotton embroidered with cotton and metallic yarns, 69″ × 105″. Museum of Fine Arts, Boston (bequest of Maxim Karolik).

Wood

Wood has been used over millennia for many objects: simple containers, tableware, utensils, and furniture. Handcrafted wooden objects and furniture were common to the most modest homes in colonial America. Most of us have seen sturdy old wooden chests and tables in antique shops that have lasted more than a hundred years. Just being handmade, however, does not automatically make an object artistic or beautiful. The craftsperson must be sensitive in shaping materials, and in creating a design that is visually pleasing. Like other materials, wood can be used to create objects that are plain or extremely ornate.

The Aesthetic Movement, an arts-and-crafts movement in the last decades of the nineteenth century, established a deliberate goal of making the useful beautiful. In a reaction to poorly designed, mass-produced furniture, artists and critics in Britain and the United States began to call for more artistic and tasteful design. The elaborately detailed wood cabinet shown here (**11-12**) is a superb example of furniture in the aesthetic style—meant to be beautiful, but not overwhelming or aristocratic. Designed for upper-middle-class homes and lifestyles, such pieces include carving and metalwork that suggest a Gothic inspiration, because the medieval period had come to be associated with fine craftsmanship. This particular cabinet, thought to have been designed by architect Frank Furness, was executed in the late 1870s by Daniel Pabst, a Philadelphia cabinetmaker.

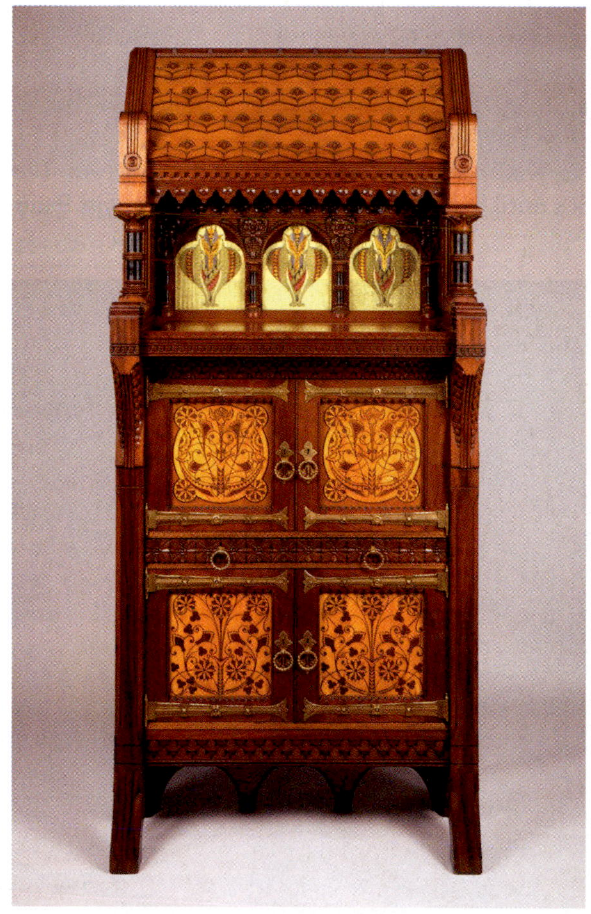

11-12 Daniel Pabst, *Cabinet*, c. 1877–1880. Walnut, maple, white pine, glass, 96″ × 42″ × 20″. Friends of the American Wing Fund, 1985. The Metropolitan Museum of Art, New York.

today. Breuer began as a student at the Bauhaus, but after graduation ran its carpentry workshop. This particular chair, the first to use tubular bent steel, is known as the "Wassily" because it was designed for painter Wassily Kandinsky, another member of the Bauhaus faculty. Breuer's chair is easily manufactured because of its simplicity. The chromed steel tubes slip into one another, so no screws and bolts are required. Even though the chair is made of hard metal and rugged fabric (designed by textile students at the Bauhaus), it is very comfortable because it flexes with the weight of the person sitting.

One might say that the Bauhaus created the modern field of industrial design, fabricating products that were aesthetically pleasing and capable of being mass produced. **Industrial design** is the aesthetic refinement of products, making functional engineering solutions easy to use and attractive. An industrial designer must understand both art and engineering. Marianne Brandt, like Marcel Breuer, was a student at the Bauhaus who later headed a workshop. Her simple *Table Clock* (**11-27**) of 1930, hardly looks designed at all, yet this one is in the collection of the Museum of Modern Art. With its straight hands, the hours indicated only by short lines (no numbers), plus its total lack of ornamentation, this clock looks familiar to us but was revolutionary at the time. If you study it closely, you will see that Brandt also paid careful attention to proportion, readability, and style, rounding the edges of the square and setting the clock on a sleek chrome base. Other Brandt designs (or their descendants), like her bedside lamps, desk lights, and ceiling globes, are in homes throughout the world. Clocks like this one are still available, for example, although the central hole that would have been used to insert a wind-up key is now gone, since today's clocks are electric.

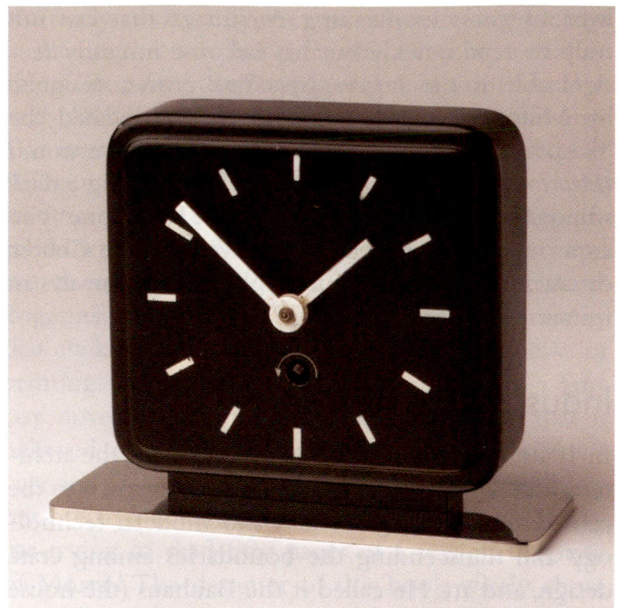

11-27 Marianne Brandt, *Table Clock,* c. 1930. Painted and chrome-plated metal, 5¾″ × 6⅞″ × 2¾″. The Museum of Modern Art, New York.

Interior Design

We tend to think of *interior design* as decorating: deciding on how to color and fill a room that has already been shaped. But interior design is also an integral aspect of architecture. When an architect designs any building, he or she is thinking as much of the interior as the exterior. The shape of the structure will determine the size and shape of the rooms. Some architects are careful to design every aspect of the buildings they create, including staircases, windows, light fixtures, and even furniture, curtains, and rugs. The Greene brothers (**11-28**) specialized in harmonizing their interior design with their architecture (see 10-27). Their *Gamble House* in Pasadena,

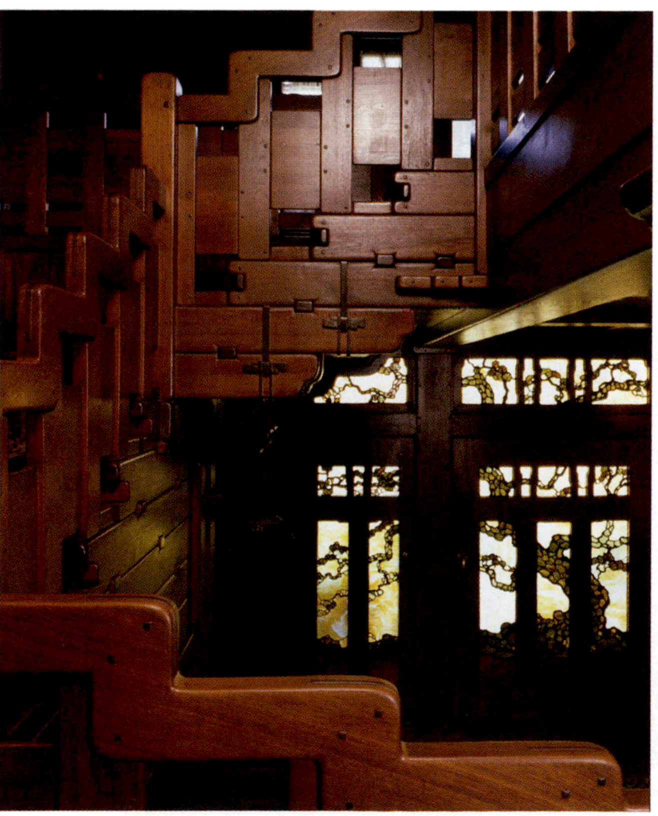

11-28 Greene Brothers, *Gamble House,* staircase, 1908–1909, Pasadena, California.

California, is decorated with built-in wooden cabinets, closets, and mantels, all with a beautiful hand-rubbed finish, highlighting rather than hiding the natural color and grain of the wood. Like a flowing river, the wooden banister is designed in a series of steps echoing the steps below.

The Art Nouveau interiors of Victor Horta were also inspired by nature, but European design of this period was more elegant and elaborate than that of the California Arts and Crafts movement of which the Greene brothers were part. Covered with flowing swirls and branchlike shapes, Horta's staircase for his own home in Brussels, Belgium (**11-29**), features wrought-iron handrails, walls painted with stylized white blossoms growing out of vertical white stems, and an airy glass dome to flood the interior with light. While the *Gamble House* staircase seems as massive as a tree trunk, Horta's is as light as a vine, reaching up to the sun.

The modern taste of the mid-twentieth century is revealed in the furniture showroom displayed by Knoll International in San Francisco in 1957 (**11-30**). Designed by Florence Knoll, this brightly colored interior appears far more pared down and functional than either the Greene Brothers or the Horta interiors. The sharp lines, simple shapes, clear colors, and subtle textures reflect the influence of modern style on items as diverse as pillows and ashtrays. Compare this room to a painting by Mondrian (see Chapter 16), and the relationship between decorative and fine arts will become evident. Not only is the furniture functional (with a clear Bauhaus influence), but the space is open, the colors bold, and the arrangement carefully designed for comfort and traffic flow.

Florence Schust had studied with Eero Saarinen, then worked for Walter Gropius and Marcel Breuer briefly before meeting visionary entrepreneur Hans Knoll during World War II. They began working together, formed Knoll Associates, Inc., and were married in 1946. The Knolls imagined a revolution in interior design to coordinate with modern architecture. Hans was the salesman while Florence (known as Shu) became the brains behind the Knoll Planning Unit, working to collaborate the designers hired by the company with the manufacturing plant in order to produce "well designed 'equipment for living' within the reach of a large consumer market," according to *Arts and Architecture*. She became an innovator in efficient office design, and created the showrooms that sold their ideas—and products—to the public. After her husband's death in an auto accident in 1957, everything from the furniture to the showrooms to the letterhead and business cards was controlled by Mrs. Knoll, according to one of their designers.

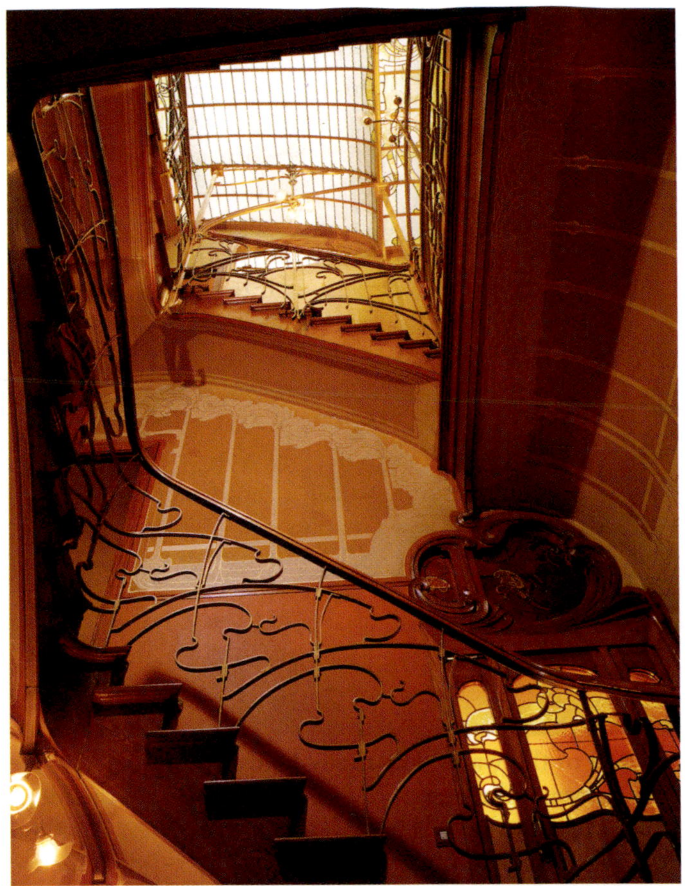

11-29 Victor Horta, *Horta House,* staircase, Brussels, Belgium, 1898.

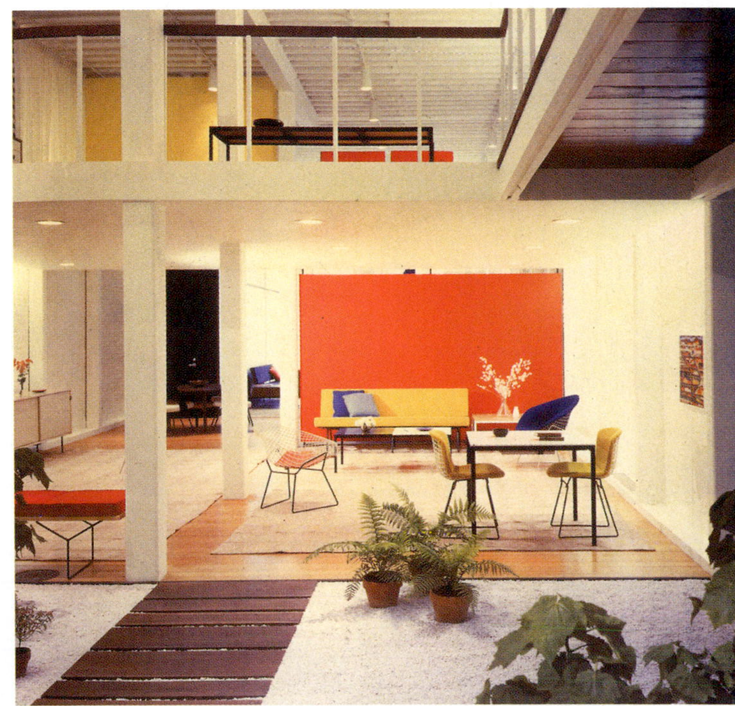

11-30 Florence Knoll showroom in San Francisco, 1957.

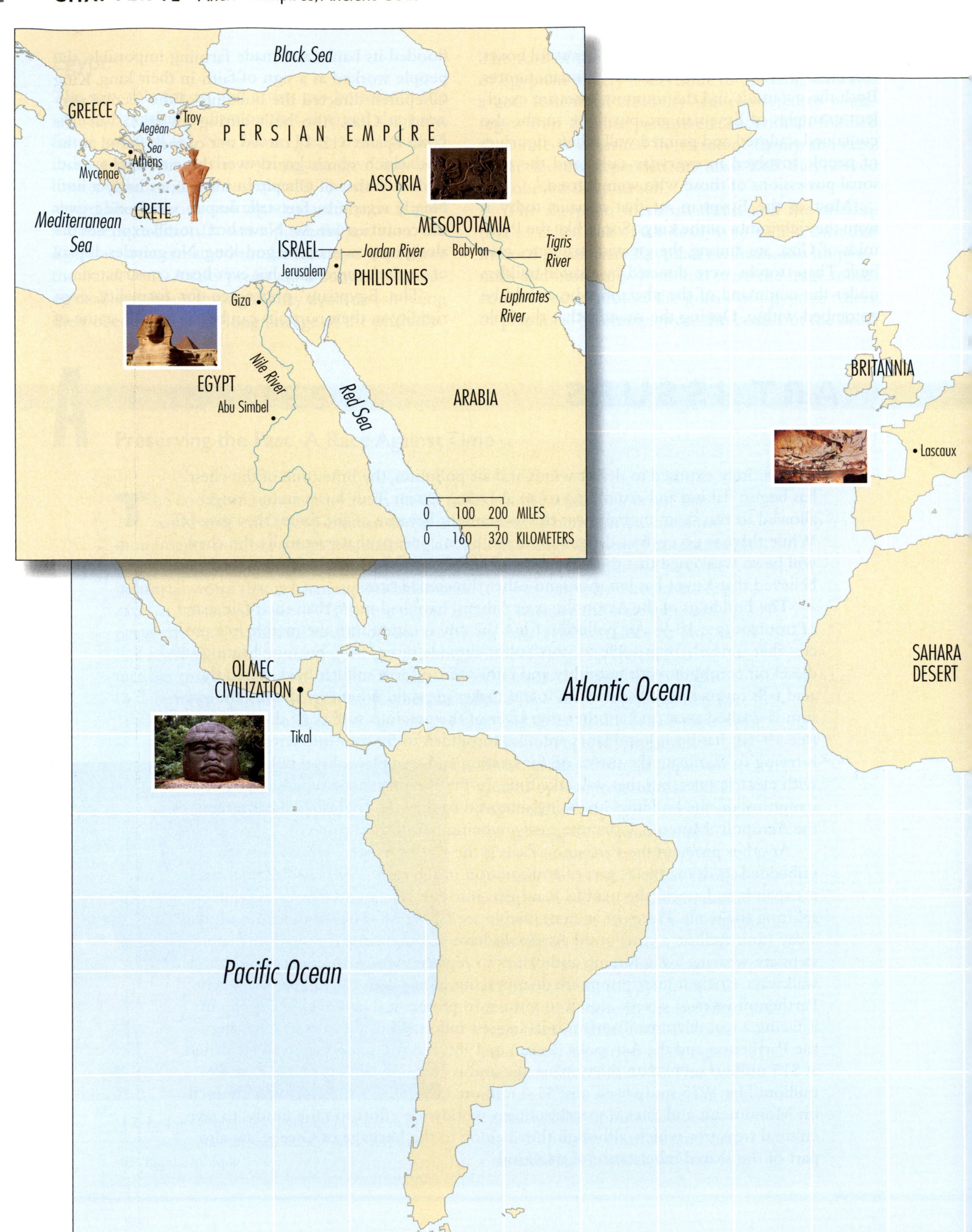
Black Sea
GREECE
Troy
Aegean Sea
PERSIAN EMPIRE
Athens
Mycenae
ASSYRIA
CRETE
Mediterranean Sea
MESOPOTAMIA
ISRAEL
Jordan River
Babylon
Tigris River
Jerusalem
PHILISTINES
Giza
Euphrates River
Nile River
EGYPT
Abu Simbel
Red Sea
ARABIA
0 100 200 MILES
0 160 320 KILOMETERS
BRITANNIA
Lascaux
SAHARA DESERT
Atlantic Ocean
OLMEC CIVILIZATION
Tikal
Pacific Ocean

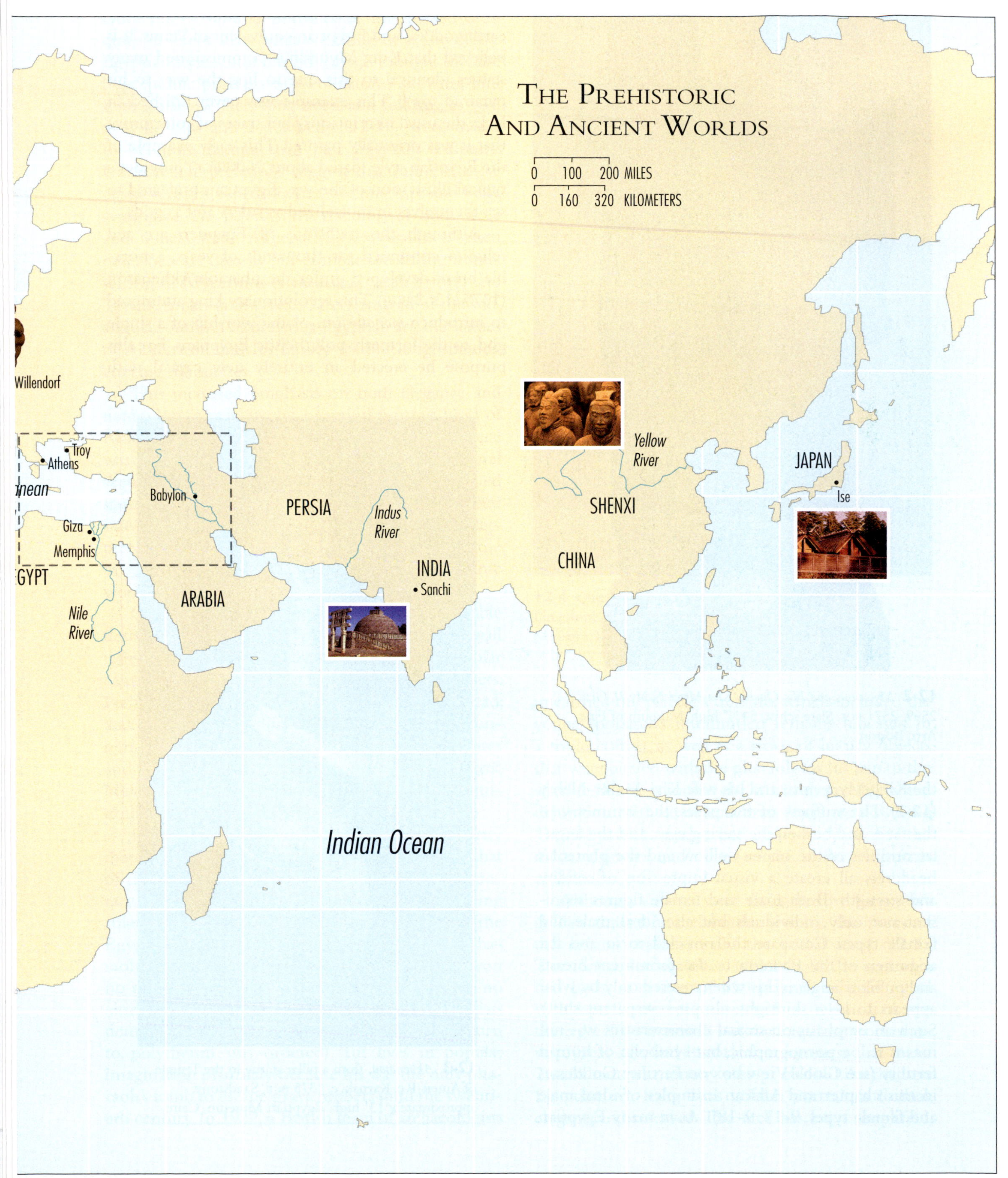
THE PREHISTORIC AND ANCIENT WORLDS
0 100 200 MILES
0 160 320 KILOMETERS
Willendorf
Troy
Athens
nean
Babylon
Giza
Memphis
EGYPT
Nile River
ARABIA
PERSIA
Indus River
INDIA
Sanchi
Yellow River
SHENXI
CHINA
JAPAN
Ise
Indian Ocean

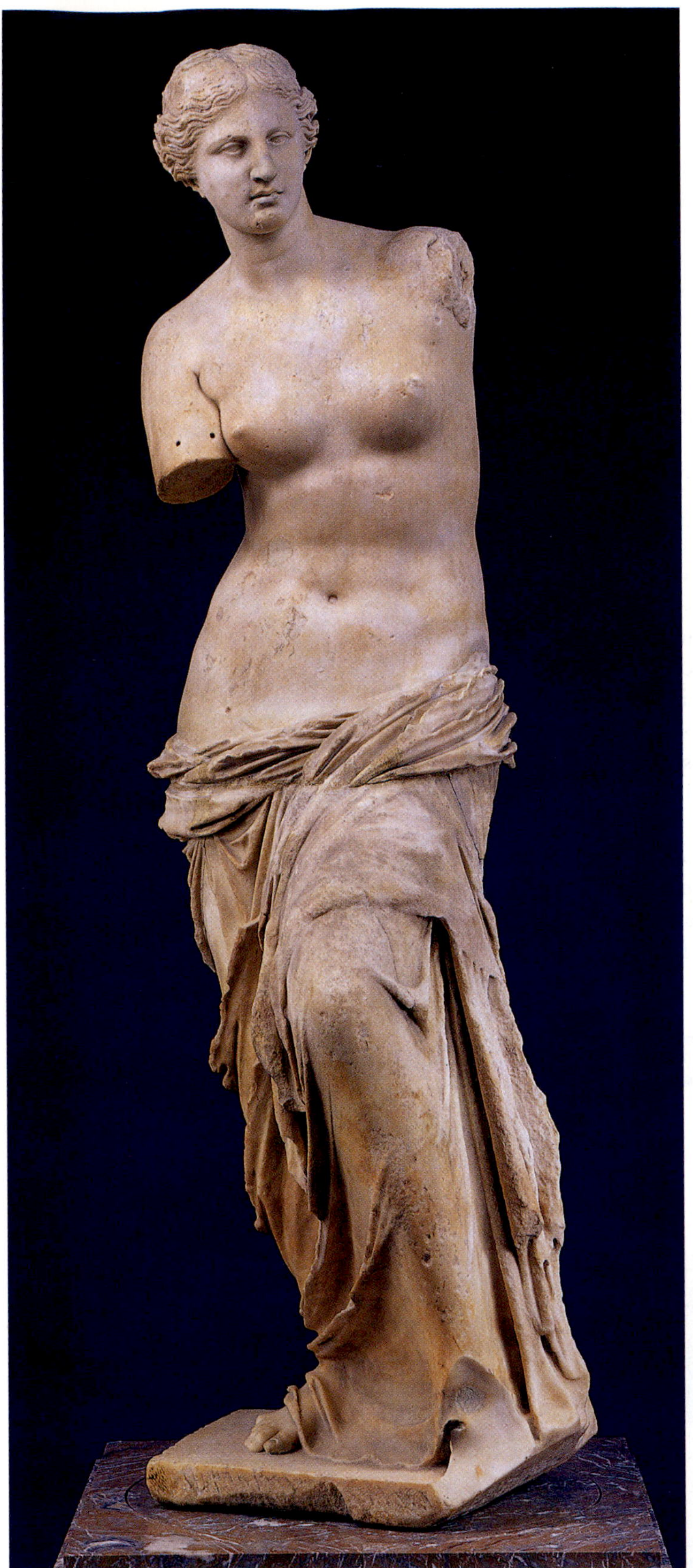

12-19 *Aphrodite of Melos*, c. 150–100 BCE. Marble, approximately 6′ 10″ high. Louvre, Paris, France.

by the artist—the pause between the athlete's upward and downward motion.

Another statue of this period that had a great influence on later Western art is the *Doryphoros*, or Spear Carrier (**12-17**). Again, what remains is a much later Roman copy of a bronze original cast by the famous artist Polykleitos. The statue has not only lost its spear, but supports have been added in the form of a tree trunk and a brace between the thigh and the wrist. Nevertheless, we can recognize some essential qualities of Greek sculpture: the nude, athletic male; the graceful, natural stance; the well-defined muscles and understanding of human anatomy. Despite its pose of relaxed movement, the figure is shown as balanced and unified.

This statue is particularly important because it was known as the *canon,* which means measure or model. It exemplified, according to the Greeks, the most perfect and pleasing proportions for representing the human figure. Polykleitos was one of the most famous Greek sculptors; after his death, his name even came to mean "sculptor." Artists who followed him studied his ideas and abided by his perfect proportions.

Hellenistic Greece

After the classical period, Greek history and art entered what is called the Hellenistic Age. This period began with the age of Alexander the Great (356–323 BCE), when not only all of the Greek city-states were conquered and unified, but also an attempt was made to conquer the rest of the known world. Alexander, the student of Aristotle, reached as far as India, and although his empire was divided after his death, cultural connections between the subcontinent and the classical world began to flourish.

Greek sculpture became more naturalistic, more illusionistic, and more human during this period. The work of Praxiteles (1-17) and the *Aphrodite of Melos* (known commonly as the *Venus de Milo*, **12-19**) illustrate how Greek sculptors made marble resemble flesh. Although she is missing her arms, the life-size *Venus de Milo* still illustrates the voluptuous charms of the Greek goddess. Not only are her breasts bare, but also her hips and abdomen. We can imagine this Venus breathing, moving, like a real person. These sculptures appeal less to the rational mind and more to the senses than the restrained works of the classical period. Also, during the Hellenistic Age, a more elaborate style of column gained popularity—the *Corinthian* order (see Chapter 10), which was topped with a capital of sprouting leaves.

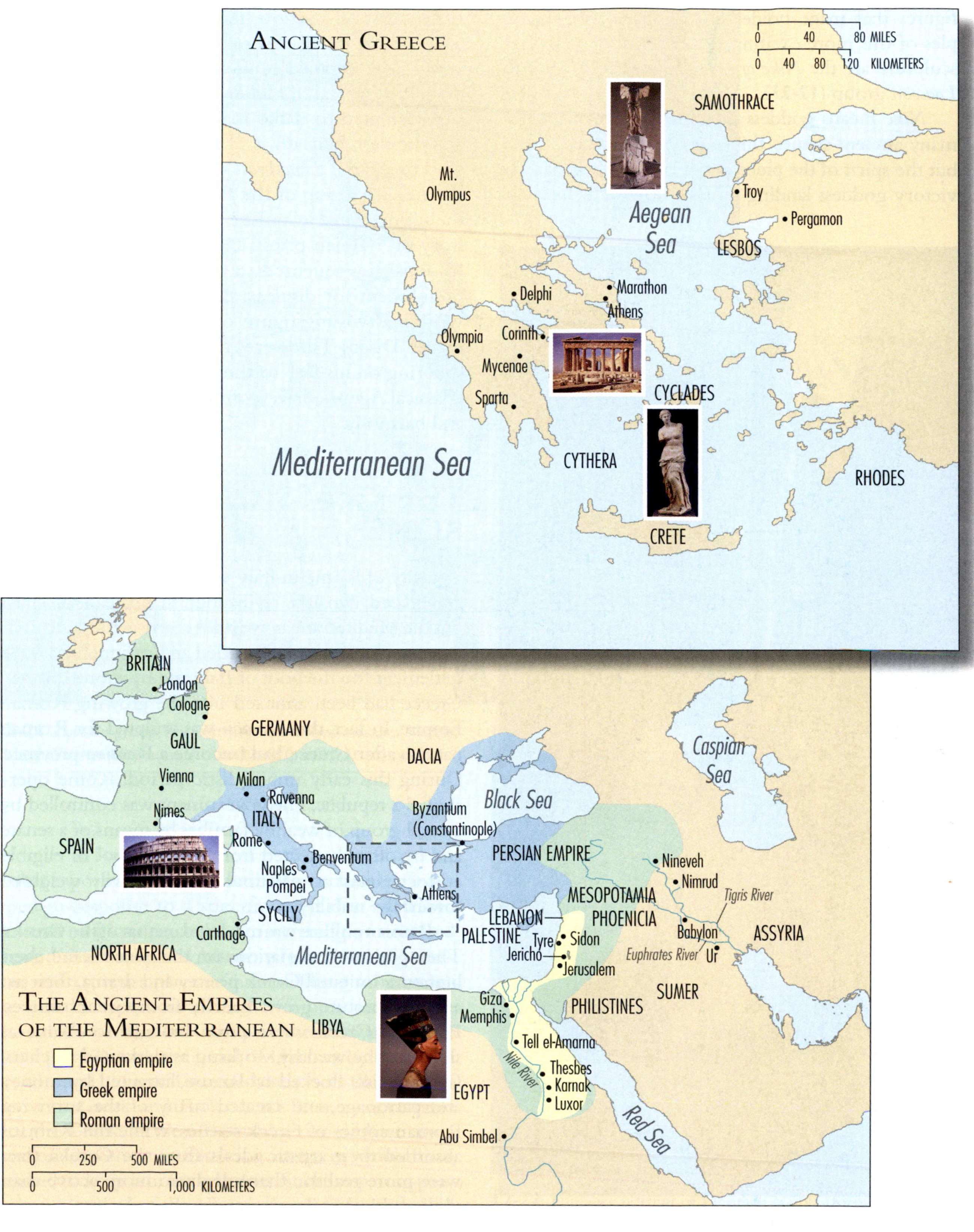
Ancient Greece
0 40 80 MILES
0 40 80 120 KILOMETERS
SAMOTHRACE
Mt. Olympus
Troy
Aegean Sea
Pergamon
LESBOS
Delphi
Marathon
Athens
Olympia
Corinth
Mycenae
Sparta
CYCLADES
Mediterranean Sea
CYTHERA
RHODES
CRETE
BRITAIN
London
Cologne
GAUL
GERMANY
DACIA
Vienna
Milan
Ravenna
Nimes
ITALY
Byzantium (Constantinople)
Black Sea
Caspian Sea
SPAIN
Rome
PERSIAN EMPIRE
Naples
Benventum
Pompei
Athens
Nineveh
Nimrud
MESOPOTAMIA
Tigris River
SYCILY
LEBANON
PHOENICIA
Carthage
PALESTINE
Tyre
Sidon
Babylon
ASSYRIA
NORTH AFRICA
Mediterranean Sea
Jericho
Jerusalem
Euphrates River
Ur
SUMER
Giza
Memphis
PHILISTINES
The Ancient Empires of the Mediterranean
LIBYA
Egyptian empire
Greek empire
Roman empire
Tell el-Amarna
Nile River
Thesbes
Karnak
Luxor
EGYPT
Red Sea
Abu Simbel
0 250 500 MILES
0 500 1,000 KILOMETERS

THE EARLY MIDDLE AGES

The Germanic tribes who looted Rome and swept across Europe in the fourth and fifth centuries did not bring with them a culture with elaborate sculpture and architecture, well-established literature, or even a written language. Some of their names, like Goths and Vandals, remain even today associated with barbarians and thieves. The values they stressed were the characteristics needed to win in combat: courage and ruthlessness. There was no concept of loyalty to the state or nation, which did not exist. Instead, warriors (the aristocracy) gave their loyalty to individual warlords who had proven their valor in battle.

After a period of destruction—the looting of cities, burning of libraries—some of these tribes from the borders of the old empire began to settle in distinct areas. A tribe called the Franks settled in Gaul, which would become present-day France. The Angles, Saxons, and Jutes settled in Britain; the language of the Angles developed into English and gave us the name England. The art of these Germanic tribes was dramatically different from that of the Greeks, Romans, and Byzantines. These were migratory people organized in warlike bands, not wealthy aristocrats living in cities. Instead of temples to the gods, the Germanic princes built large wooden halls where they could feast and drink with their comrades. When the Angles and Saxons saw the ruins of great stone buildings left by the Romans in Britain, they imagined they were the work of a race of giants.

The art of the Angles and Saxons, like other Germanic tribes, did not depict the human figure at all. It was a decorative art of small, intricately patterned golden and jeweled objects. The Germans were great metalworkers and wonderful weapons makers; they also used their skills to create elaborate jewelry. For the warrior-aristocracy, such treasure was both symbolic of their special status and prized for its own sake. The great Anglo-Saxon epic, *Beowulf*, tells us of their love for bright colors and precious metals, materials that gleamed and glowed. Such treasure had an almost magical fascination for them. Heroes like Beowulf wore rich golden buckles on their costumes and were buried with these ornaments as part of a pagan ritual. In the 1930s, the remains of an entire seventh-century Anglo-Saxon warship was found buried in England at a place called Sutton Hoo. The treasures unearthed there included an elaborate golden buckle (**13-9**) about five inches long, whose intricate patterning seems incongruous with its barbarian source. Three plain golden circles are interlaced with a fine web of serpents. The interwoven pattern and the theme of interlocking animals, especially serpents, is typical of the Germanic style.

Although Rome had ceased to be the center of the empire, it remained the center of the Christian church in the West. In 597, missionaries were sent by the pope to England to convert the heathen Anglo-Saxons. The conversion of the English to Christianity began a rich period of artistic production, especially the illustration of manuscripts. Book illustration had not been a very important artistic medium in the Roman world, but because the Christian New Testament was so central to the new faith, the decoration of the Gospels became worthy of the greatest effort. Elaborately decorated manuscripts were prepared in monasteries where monks devoted their lives to the glorification of God.

Lindisfarne (or "Holy Island"), on the English coast, was one of the earliest sites of an especially fruitful mingling of the earlier Irish or Celtic tradi-

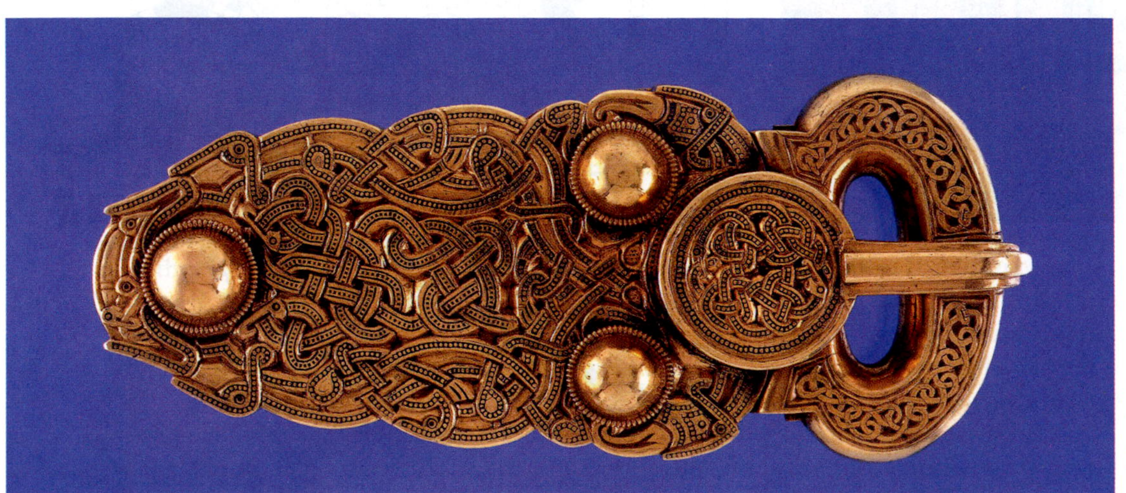

13-9 *The Golden Buckle of Sutton Hoo.* Anglo Saxon, seventh century. Gold and enamel, 5 ¼″ long. British Museum, London.

tions, the Anglo-Saxon artistic style, and the Roman-Byzantine. Two pages from the same book of Gospels, the *Book of Lindisfarne* of about 700, illustrate the dramatically different artistic styles being practiced at this time on the edge of what had once been the Roman world. In the page with an ornamental cross (**13-10**), we can immediately recognize the same interlaced decorative pattern of lines that the Anglo-Saxons used in their metalwork, in this case twisted dog-headed serpents and wild birds. Here, however, the formerly pagan design is superimposed with the shape of a cross—the most powerful symbolic shape in Christian art. Without sacrificing the amazing richness and complexity of the northern style, the artist-monk has brought order out of chaos by using the shape of the cross to organize the overall page.

The original of this artwork is only a little larger than nine by twelve inches. Think how different this is from the human scale of Greek art or the superhuman scale of Roman architecture! For centuries, people have been amazed by the delicacy, the imagination, and the fantastic detail of Irish and English manuscripts of this period. Some even thought the work must have been done by angels. For the artist, producing the illumination was probably a kind of religious discipline, like fasting. To paint with such patience demonstrated an almost obsessive devotion and love of God.

In the same book, however, we find pictures of another type. These are portraits of the four Evangelists, or authors of the four Gospels. While the border surrounding *Saint Matthew* (**13-11**) matches the style of the cross page, the rest is typical of a surprisingly different style. It shows the figure of the saint sitting on a bench, writing his gospel about the life of Christ; above him is an angel. Since the northern tribes had no tradition of human portraiture, what was the source of this image?

Historians suspect that visiting monks from the Mediterranean world brought to Lindisfarne a gospel book or books in the Byzantine style. Notice the similarities between the figure of Saint Matthew and the mosaics of Justinian and Theodora. Although the mediums and sizes are completely different, the sharp lines of the drapery and the long, thin bodies certainly resemble each other. Still, Saint Matthew is not exactly like a figure in a true Byzantine manuscript or mosaic.

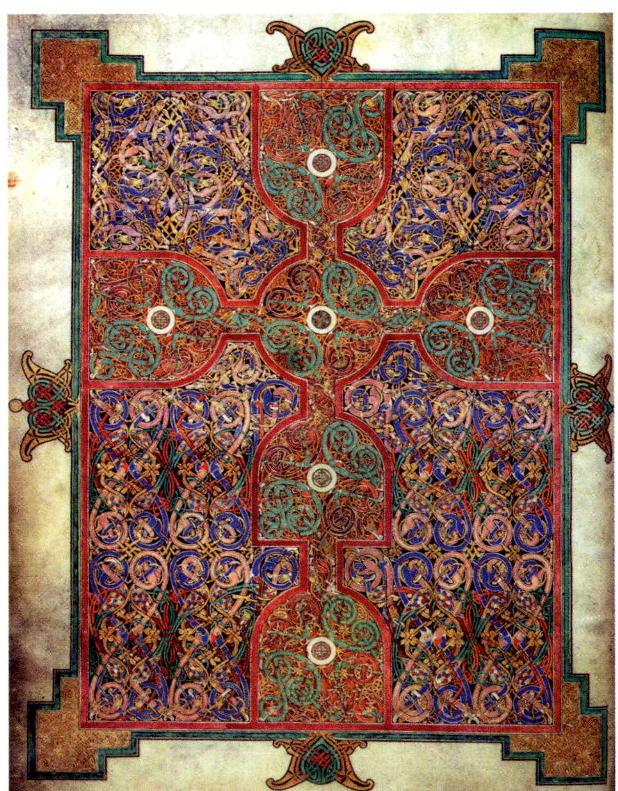

13-10 Ornamental page from the *Book of Lindisfarne* (Cotton MS Nero D IV f 26v), from Northumberland, England, late seventh century. Illumination, approximately 13″ × 10″. British Library, London.

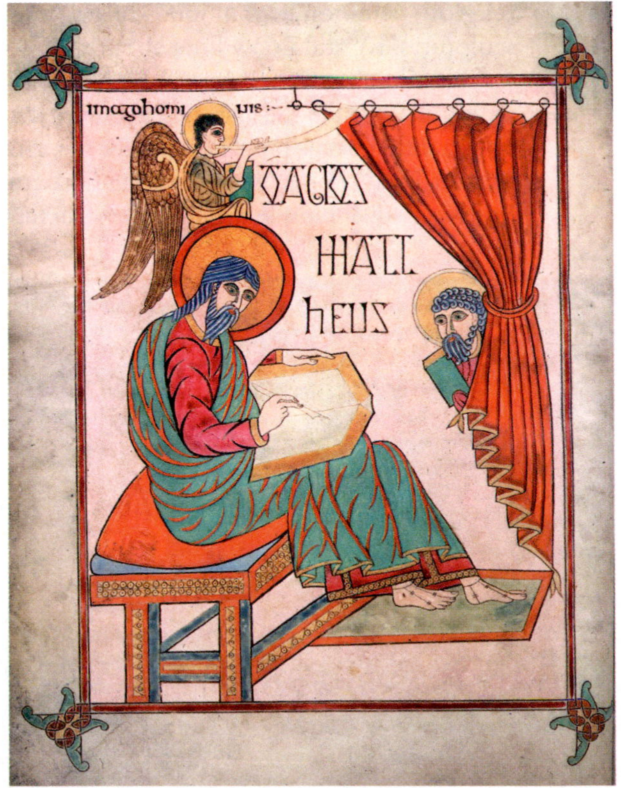

13-11 Saint Matthew, from the *Book of Lindisfarne* (Cotton MS Nero D IV f 25v), from Northumberland, England, late seventh century. Illumination, approximately 11″ × 9″. British Library, London.

Originally built by Justinian in the early sixth century, about the same time as San Vitale, the Hagia Sophia was the most famous and dramatic church in the capital of the eastern Roman Empire. Influenced by Roman architecture, the church was topped with a huge dome. To change the magnificent structure from a church to a mosque, the new rulers of Constantinople (which they renamed Istanbul) simply removed all of the Christian mosaics and added four delicate minarets—slender towers with balconies from which believers are called to daily prayer—at the building's corners. This combined style of a central dome flanked by minarets then became a new model for Islamic architecture.

Buddhism

As described in Chapter 12, Buddhism was founded by Siddhartha Gautama, a prince from Nepal who lived in the sixth century BCE. In his search for the meaning of life and the reason for human suffering, the Buddha experimented with a number of paths to enlightenment and experienced many adventures and temptations. Through the revelation that all life is an illusion, and the only way to escape pain is to renounce all desires, the Buddha was able to escape what Hindus believed was the endless cycle of life, death, and rebirth and attain **nirvana,** a state of endless bliss.

One of the classic representations of the Buddha is the sculptural depiction of *Seated Buddha Preaching the First Sermon* (**13-19**) from the fifth century. Every element is symbolic. The Buddha is seated like a yogi, or Indian holy man. A beautifully carved halo is behind his head. The position of his hands is known as the teaching gesture, also called "turning the wheel of the law." Around him are the symbols we saw in the Lion Capital, the wheel of the law behind and stylized lions on either side. Certain features, such as the elongated earlobes from heavy earrings and the stylized arrangement of the hair, show that the Buddha was once a noble Indian prince. The statue balances such finely carved details against smooth, undecorated expanses of stone. The quiet, harmony, and idealization of the figure contribute to a sense of repose, as do the downturned eyelids and calm smile.

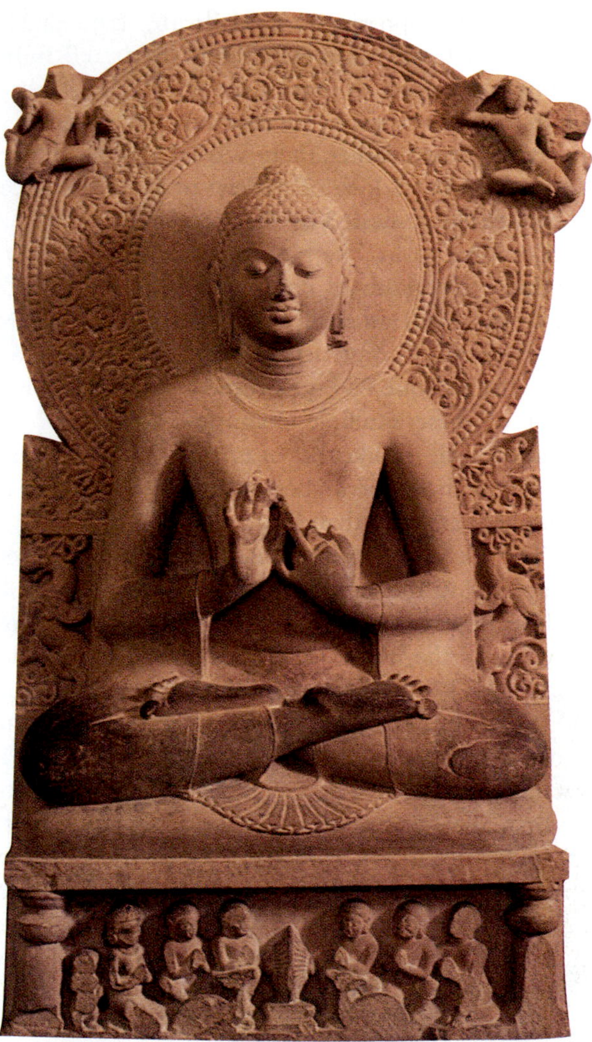

13-19 *Seated Buddha Preaching the First Sermon,* from Sarnath, India, fifth century. Stele, sandstone, 63″ high. Archeological Museum, Sarnath, India.

The classic figure of this Indian Buddha underwent many transformations as the religion spread throughout Asia. For instance, the dramatically different *Colossal Buddha* from China (3-18) was hewn out of rock at about the same time as the Indian statue. The Japanese *Amida Buddha* (1-6) is more elegant and aristocratic. Buddhism traveled not only east to China and Japan but also into Southeast Asia. The *Walking Buddha* of Thailand (**13-20**) was done about a thousand years after the Indian Buddha from Sarnath. This figure represents the Buddha in his role as missionary—a fitting role, considering the vast spread of Buddhism from its original base. The bronze sculpture is more than life-size. Its utterly smooth surface and sinuous curves are typical of Thai art (compare him to Rodin's *Walking Man*, 9-15), and its ideal beauty is described by Thai Buddhists as "arms like the hanging trunk of an elephant." In a way utterly unlike Western art, particularly religious art, the essence of both sexes is reflected in this image of divinity.

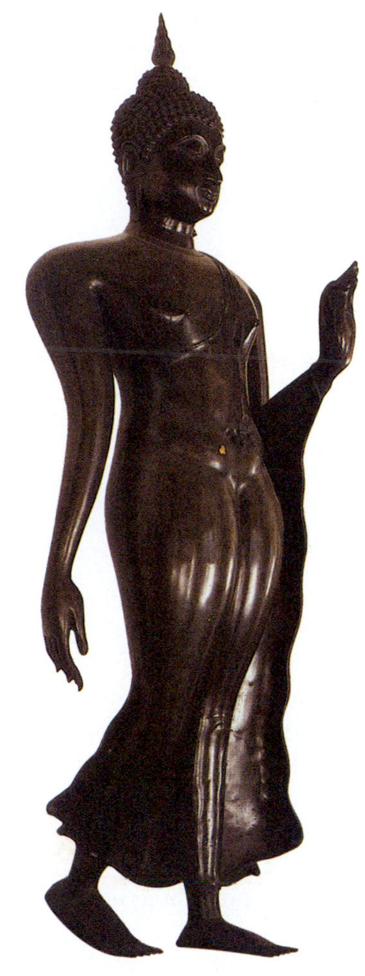

13-20 *Walking Buddha,* fourteenth century. Bronze, 88″ height. Monastery of the Fifth King, Bangkok, Thailand.

Hinduism

Like Judaism, Christianity, and Islam, Buddhism and Hinduism are also related religions. Hinduism is an earlier system of beliefs, an ancient religion native to India. Hindus believe that humans are fated to experience an unending cycle of birth, life, death, and rebirth, known as reincarnation. The final goal of this cycle is oneness with the absolute, or the Supreme Being, who is present in the world in innumerable forms. The concept of *karma* determines one's fate: the deeds of one lifetime influence one's status in the next. This idea is reflected in a rigid caste system, where one's social status is absolutely determined by birth into one of five castes, or classes: priestly, warrior, producer, menial, and untouchable.

Hinduism is polytheistic, incorporating many major and minor deities. However, the most important god is a threefold divinity: Brahma, the Creator; Vishnu, the Preserver; and Shiva, the Destroyer. This god includes within itself several opposing concepts: light and dark, birth and death, beauty and ugliness, good and evil, male and female. Because the idea of destruction carries within it the seeds of its opposite, rebirth and reproduction, the god Shiva has many faces, from fierce destroyer to calm and caring preserver. His most famous role is that of *Shiva Nataraja, Lord of the Dance* (**13-21**). The dance of Shiva symbolizes the most powerful forces in the universe, the rhythm of creation, conservation, destruction, and liberation. In this incarnation he is shown surrounded by a halo of fire that represents the universe; his long hair streams out like wings on either side of his head as he dances. This fine bronze sculpture was made in the eleventh century and demonstrates that Indian artists excelled in metalwork as well as stone carving. The figure appears both strong and graceful, dynamic and balanced, reflecting the contrasting forces typical of Hindu beliefs.

Hindu religious architecture is not so much constructed as carved, and the temples are often said to

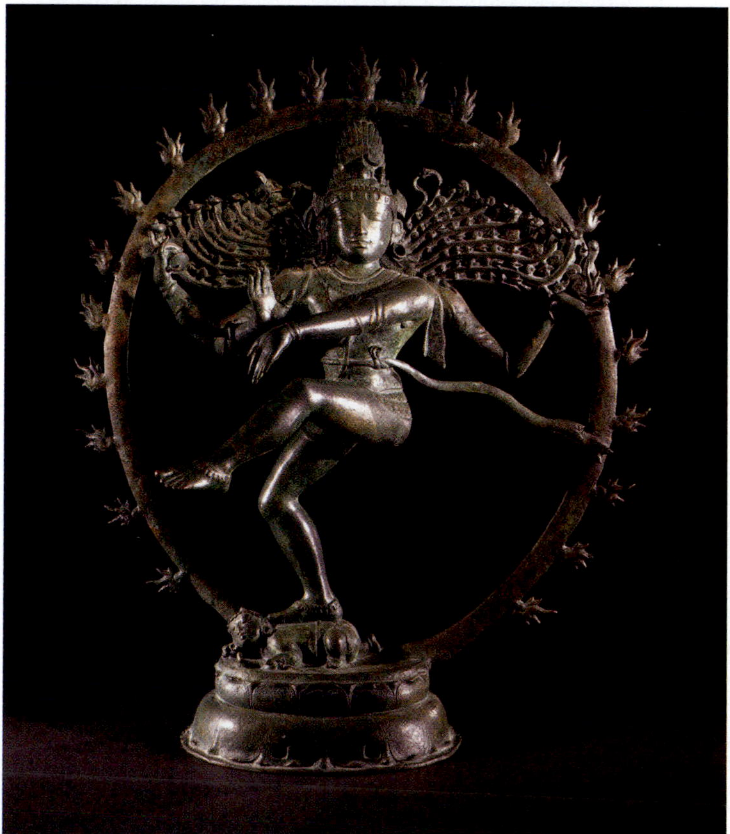

13-21 *Shiva Nataraja, Lord of the Dance,* India, c. 1100. British Museum, London.

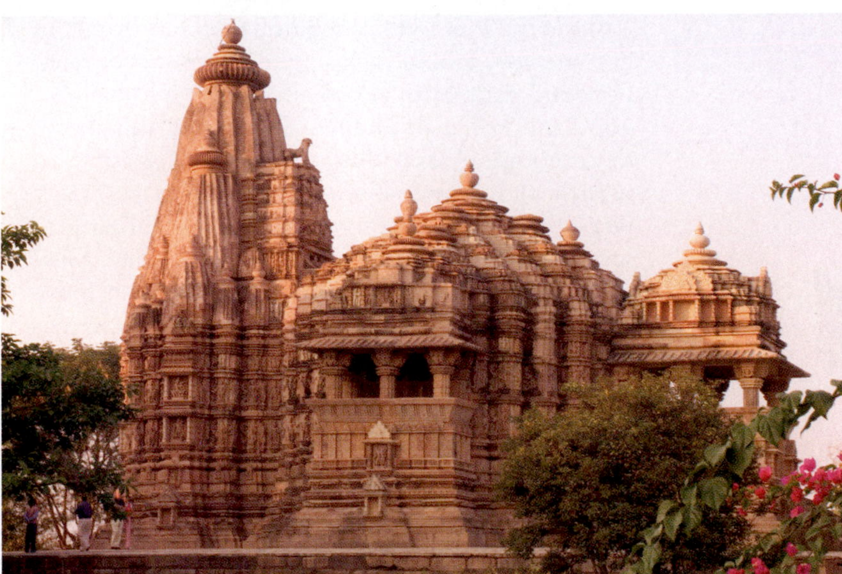

13-22 The Jagadambi Temple, Khajuraho, India, c. 950–1050.

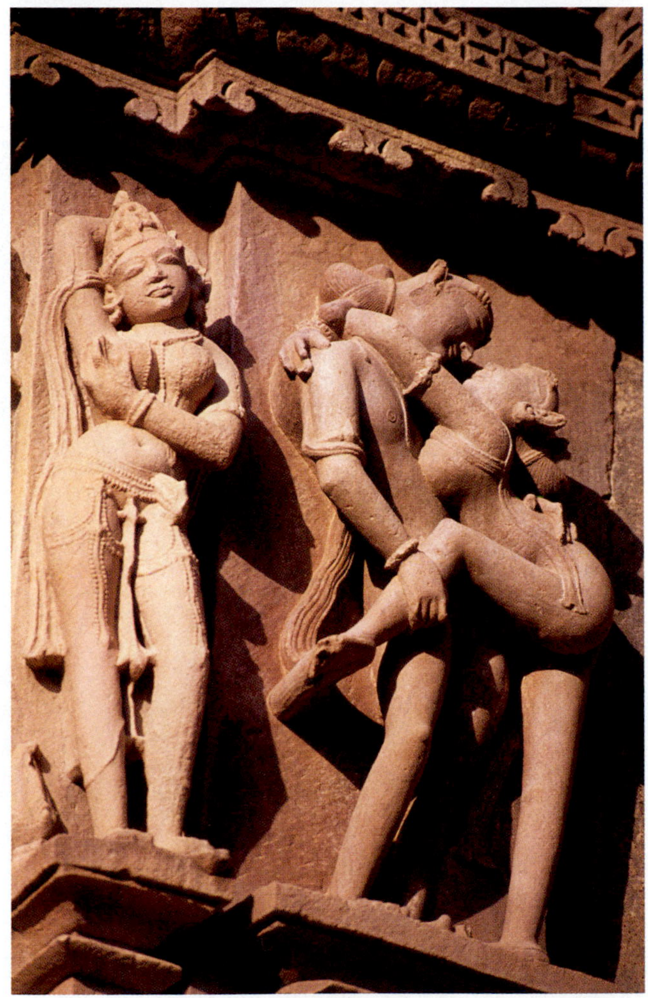

13-23 Celestial deities, Jagadambi Temple, Khajuraho, India, c. 1000.

be more like huge, complex sculptures than architecture. One dramatic example is the temple at Ellora, which is completely carved out of a mountain (see 9-14). Other Hindu shrines, such as those in Khajuraho, India, were built to resemble mountains. The *Jagadambi Temple* (**13-22**) is one of what were once more than eighty temples built around the year 1000 by the Chandela dynasty. Later hidden in the jungle and lost for hundreds of years, this magnificent complex was rediscovered in the twentieth century and now includes the remaining twenty-two structures. The Western group, including the Jagadambi, were named a World Heritage Site by UNESCO in 1986. The Khajuraho temples are considered to be the finest example of the northern Indian style of architecture, and sculpture, for the medieval period. Constructed on platforms, these temples rise vertically, but in a series of horizontal layers, with towers echoing the foothills and higher peaks of the Himalayas.

Perhaps the most startling aspect of Hindu art to Christian (or Moslem) eyes is the incorporation of the theme of sexual pleasure into places of worship. We have already seen the voluptuous Yakshi who adorned the Buddhist stupa at Sanchi (12-19); her image was related to native Indian fertility rites. However, the exterior carvings on the Jagadambi Temple (**13-23**) go beyond the realm of the voluptuous and into that of the erotic. Rather than rejecting the body and sensual delights, Hinduism incorporates the worship of the youthful human body. Sexual pleasure becomes a symbol of the union of the human with the divine, not a source of guilt or shame.

THE MIDDLE AGES

How different was the attitude toward the human body and sexuality during the early Middle Ages in the West! The art of the early Middle Ages appears almost obsessed with the ideas of death and sin. The years between 850 and 1000 were a dark period for the arts in most of Europe. The second wave of invasions disrupted cultural and economic recovery. People found little comfort on earth and concentrated on the prospect of their heavenly reward—or the fear of eternal damnation. One work of art that seems symbolic of this period is a panel from the magnificent bronze doors of the church of Saint Michael's in Hildesheim, Germany, *Adam and Eve Reproached by the Lord* (**13-24**). This illustrates the Old Testament story in which God discovers that Adam and Eve have disobeyed him and eaten from the Tree of Knowledge, committing humanity's "original sin." God, on the left, seems to convict Adam with the pointed finger of condemnation. The cowering Adam passes the blame on to Eve, who tries to hide her nakedness and point to the serpent at the same time.

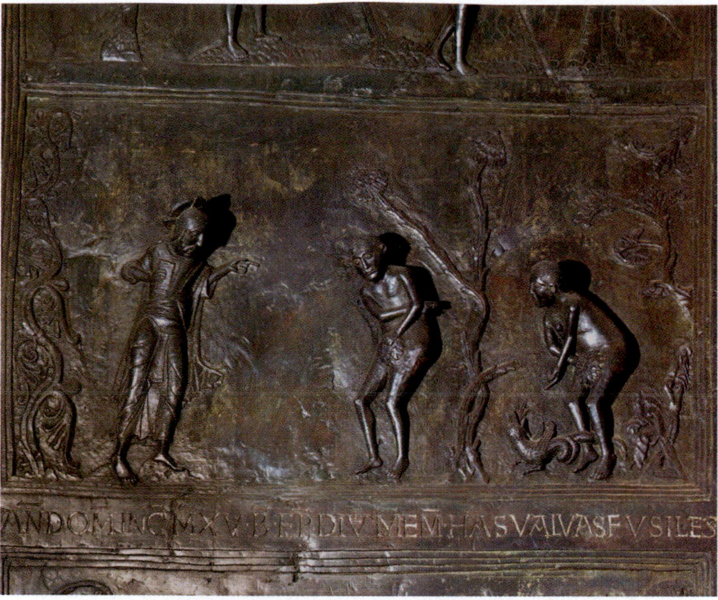

13-24 *Adam and Eve Reproached by the Lord,* from the bronze doors commissioned by Bishop Bernward for Saint Michael's at Hildesheim, Germany, 1015. Bronze, 23″ × 43″.

A comparison of Adam and Eve to any Greek or Roman nude statue immediately illuminates the change from classical to medieval artistic styles and cultural values. In the Hildesheim doors, cast in 1015, humans attempt to hide their spindly, naked bodies before God. They are ashamed to be nude. These bodies show none of the ideal beauty or athletic grace of Greek and Roman statues, and certainly none of the sensual delight of Indian carvings. This is not simply because the medieval artist is unskilled—on the contrary, the crafting of these great bronze doors was a complex project that took tremendous artistic talent. But the message of the art is anguish and guilt rather than pride and confidence, and thus calls for a new style.

The Romanesque Style

By the time the great doors at Hildesheim were made, northern Europe had begun to recover from the period of invasions. The Crusades to the Holy Land were beginning to turn the militancy of warriors away from their European neighbors. Travel within Europe became safer and easier. Pilgrims streamed across Europe from shrine to shrine, on foot, in search of salvation. In the eleventh century, a vast building program seems to have begun almost spontaneously, with monasteries erecting magnificent new churches to attract and accommodate pilgrims. One of the important stops on the pilgrimage route through southern France was the church of Saint Pierre at Moissac.

The most famous sculpture at Moissac is the figure of a prophet (**13-25**), done around 1115, or about one hundred years after the Hildesheim doors. Carved into the **trumeau** (the central pillar of the main doorway) of the church is the emaciated, elongated, and extremely expressive figure of an Old Testament prophet. The body of this holy man seems to have been stretched vertically and twisted horizontally to fit it into the space of the column. It is almost as if the prophet were eternally, awkwardly trapped in a prison of stone. He is not only a man of God, but the victim of a kind of divine energy. His gentle face and long, flowing beard, his bony feet and writhing body all give the impression of a person who has left physical concerns and material comforts far behind.

Around the year 1000, the theme of the end of the world, or the final day of judgment, became common in medieval art. Many believed this time was near. A vision of the Apocalypse, or end of time, from the New Testament Book of Revelations, was carved into the entrance of the Cathedral at Autun. Completed just a few years after the prophet from Moissac, we see the *Last Judgment* (**13-26**) described in grisly detail. The moment pictured is one where four angels blow their trumpets, and the dead are resurrected to

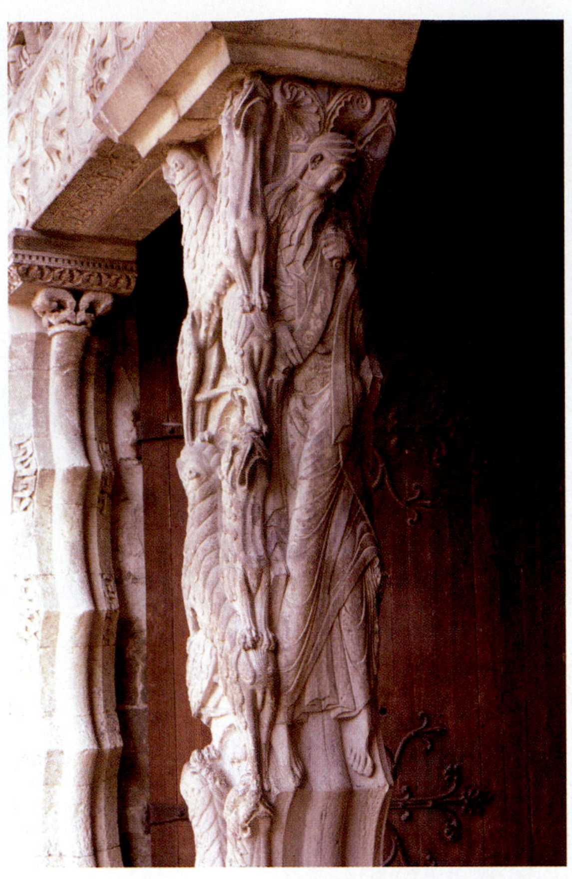

13-25 *The Prophet Jeremiah (Isaiah?),* from the trumeau of the south portal of Saint Pierre, Moissac, France, c. 1115–1135. Stone, life-size.

be judged. The angels appear with long, curved horns in the corners of the work. The huge figure of Christ in the center dominates the composition, completely out of scale with the other figures. On the left side, the saved are allowed to enter heaven and worship God. On the right, horrible monsters join the Archangel Michael in the task of weighing souls (**13-27**). Under the semicircular tympanum, on the horizontal lintel of the doorway, we see the figures of the dead—on the left prepared for heaven, on the right pushed off toward hell. Beneath the earth the damned wait in terror for their punishment; one is in the process of being plucked up by a set of disembodied hands. As in the trumeau at Moissac, angular figures seem to be cramped into the space

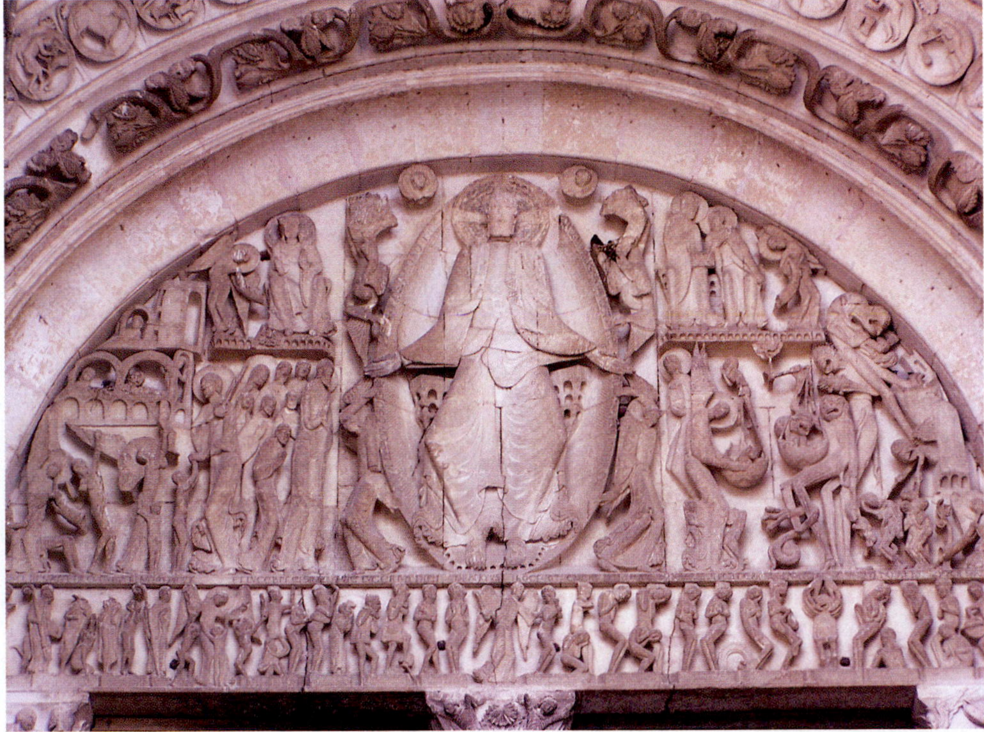

13-26 Gislebertus, *Last Judgment,* from the west tympanum of Saint Lazare, Autun, France, c. 1130. 11′ 4″ high, 21′ wide at base.

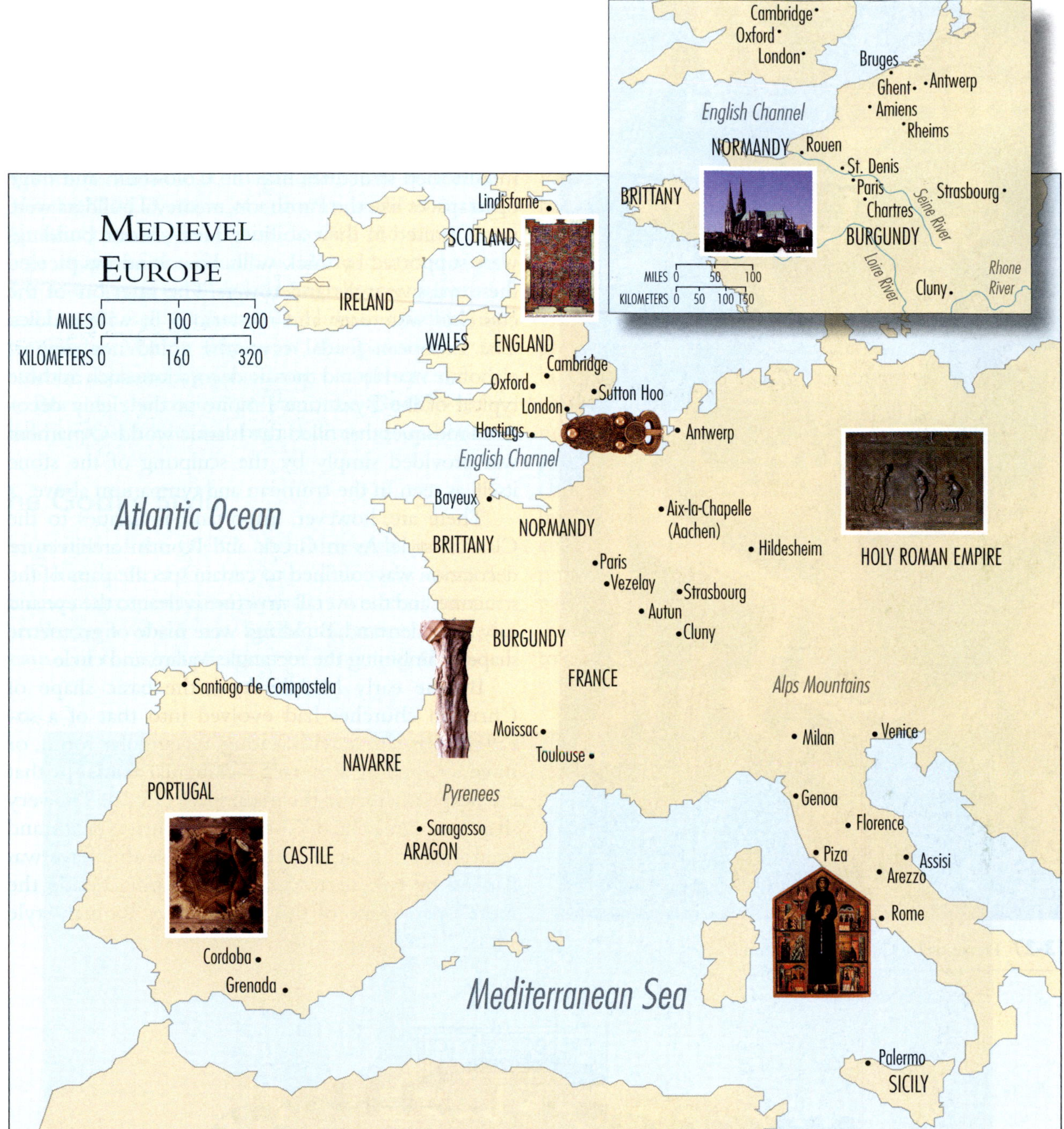

they inhabit. Classical balance and repose are totally lacking, replaced by energy and tension. As before, nude bodies are objects of shame. The overall message is truly horrifying.

Although fairly typical of the *Romanesque style,* Autun is unusual because most of the sculpture was done by a single artist and one who has left us his name, Gislebertus. The entire sculptural program of the church is the result of his very personal vision and imagination. This is not a case of the artist copying from past models (as in the *Book of Lindisfarne*) but of an artist who is reinterpreting a story in a fresh and immediate way. The work at Autun is proof that by 1100, some medieval artists were allowed to express their individuality.

Individuality and self-expression were not, however, typical of most art done during the eleventh and early twelfth centuries. As befitted the warlike times, architecture tended to be massive, solid, and strong. This was true not only of castles and fortresses, but

CHAPTER 14

The Renaissance

In the Italian town of Padua around the year 1300, a simple chapel was built alongside a palace. Because an ancient Roman amphitheater had once occupied that site, the chapel became known as the Arena Chapel. Its plain, unassuming exterior seems to make it an unlikely site for one of the most important achievements of Western civilization. But an extraordinary experience awaits those who enter the chapel because the flat, unadorned walls were transformed between the years 1305 and 1310 by one of the pivotal figures in the history of art, an artist named Giotto.

	PERIOD	HISTORICAL EVENTS	
1300–1400	First signs of the Renaissance in Italy Gothic Period in Northern Europe Moorish rule in Spanish Granada Yuan Dynasty of the Mongols overthrown by Ming in China Aztec empire established in Mexico	Dante's Divine Comedy c. 1310 Papal court moves to Avignon 1309 The Black Death in Europe 1348	
1400–1492	Early Renaissance in Europe Inca civilization in Peru Golden Age of Venetian Empire Print revolution in Europe	Joan of Arc burned at the stake 1431 The Medici rule of Florence begins 1434 Ottoman Empire conquers Constantinople renamed as Istanbul 1453 The Gutenberg Bible 1455	Portuguese mariners round tip of Africa 1487 Columbus sails to the Americas 1492
1492–1560	High Renaissance in Italy The Renaissance continues in the rest of Europe European Age of Exploration and Discovery African slaves transported to Americas Mughal dynasty in India Height of Ottoman Empire	The Protestant Reformation begins 1517 Machiavelli's *The Prince* 1517 Cortez conquers the Aztecs 1519–1521 Magellan's voyage circumnavigates the globe 1519–1522 Henry VIII becomes Head of the Church of England 1531	Copernicus declares the planets revolve around the sun 1543

Initiating a return to visual realism, Giotto almost singlehandedly created the Renaissance style of painting. In *Lamentation* (**14-1**), one of the frescos in the Arena Chapel, we can see a sculptural solidity that had not been seen for more than one thousand years. There is weight to the figures, bulk, and flesh; they are rooted to the ground by gravity. They are solid people on a solid earth. If we compare this fresco to Berlinghieri's *Saint Francis Altarpiece* (13-37) done eighty years earlier, the change becomes very apparent. No longer are sacred stories being arranged to make a design. Giotto has a new way of telling stories; rather than multiple scenes in one panel, he chooses one significant moment. He tries to imagine how the holy scene might have really looked. The spaces between the figures seem natural. Figures are in true proportion to each other. They are placed in a natural setting.

More importantly, Giotto tries to imagine how his characters felt. Real human emotion is being displayed as the Virgin Mary and Christ's followers mourn over the dead body of Jesus. The viewer can empathize with each person and understand what he or she is feeling because Giotto has created a unique pose and facial expression for each one of them. Even the ethereal angels experience human emotions of grief and anguish, each in their own way. Giotto's characters are not generic people copied from a pattern book or people pictured by symbols of their roles in society. Now each is an individual first, a unique person. Giotto literally brought religious art down to earth.

Giotto was revolutionary in another way—he was a *famous* artist. For the past fifteen hundred years, since the Greeks, an artist was thought of as just another craftsperson, like a carpenter or a barrel-maker (Gislebertus being a rare exception). But Giotto's genius was recognized almost immediately; his services were in great demand by the most powerful leaders of fourteenth-century Italy. Dante Alighieri, his contemporary and friend, mentions Giotto's dominance of the art world in the *Divine Comedy,* writing "now the hue and cry is for Giotto." Beginning with Giotto and the Renaissance, the history of art is the history of great and famous artists.

ART

Giotto, *Lamentation* 1305

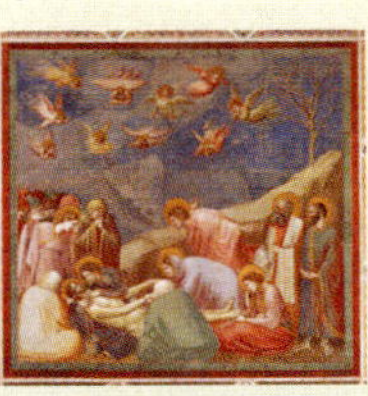

Wu Chen, *Bamboo in the Wind* early fourteenth century

Schwedagon Pagoda fourteenth century

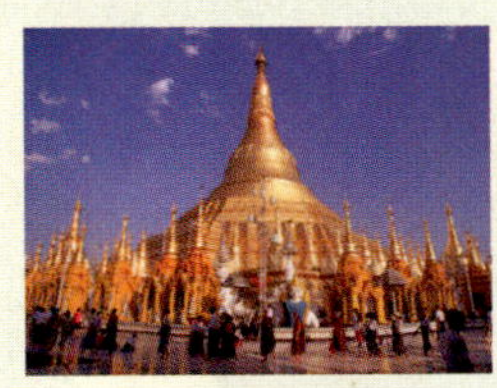

Court of the Lions, the Alhambra 1354–1391

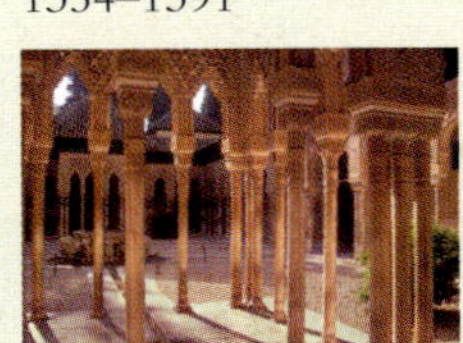

Sluter, *The Well of Moses* 1395–1406

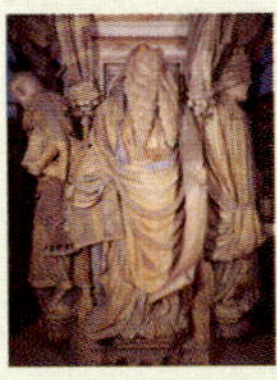

Brunelleschi, Dome of Florence Cathedral 1420–1436

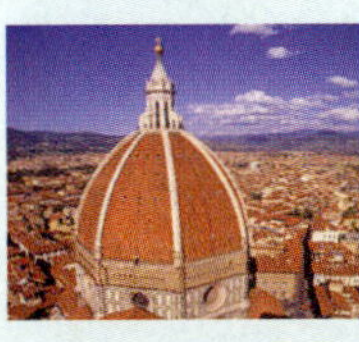

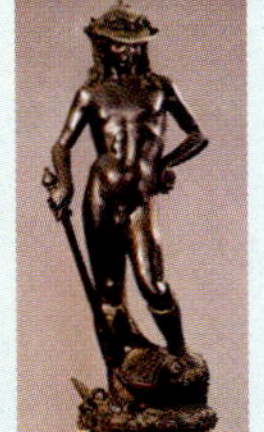

Donatello, *David* c. 1428–1432

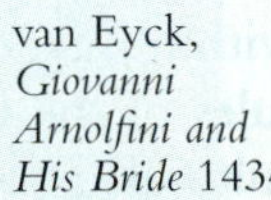

van Eyck, *Giovanni Arnolfini and His Bride* 1434

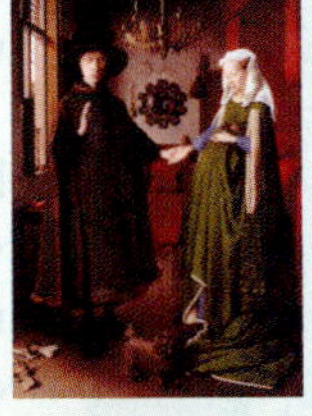

Aztec calendar 1479

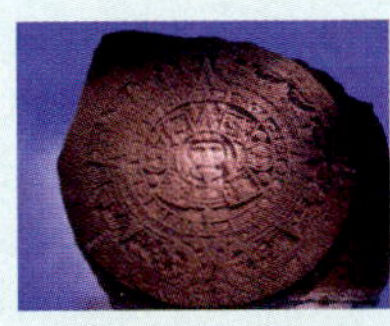

Botticelli, *The Birth of Venus* c. 1482

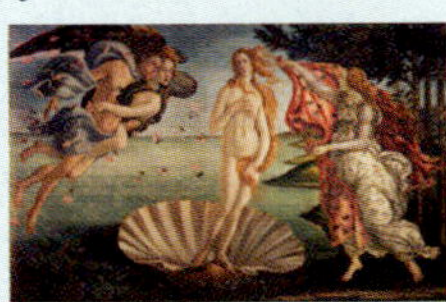

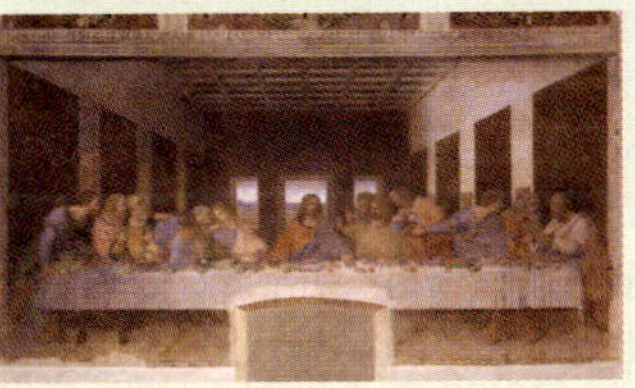

da Vinci, *The Last Supper* 1495–1498

Michelangelo, *David* 1501–1504

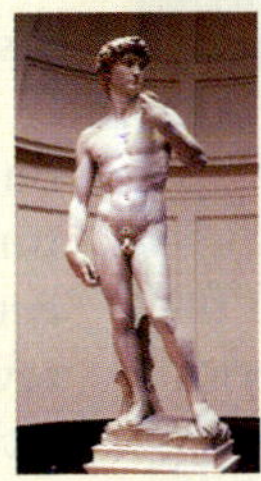

Raphael, *Madonna della Sedia* 1510–1512

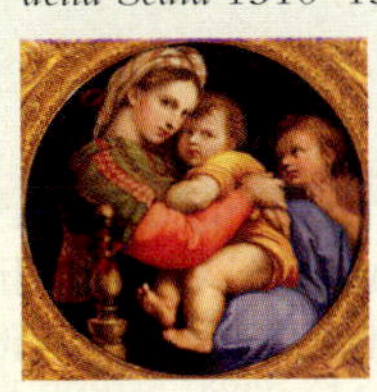

Ryoanji Zen Temple c. 1525

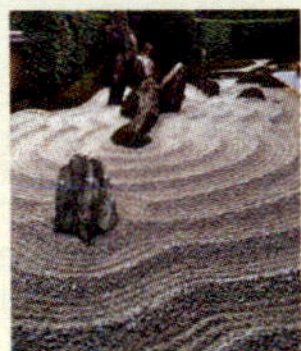

tures down. In fact, his figures float—they hardly touch the ground. Learning from the ancients was mixed with a graceful line and rhythm.

Botticelli's *The Birth of Venus* (**14-9**) is popular today because of its sweetness and the innocent quality of Venus as she floats in a fantasy world. Yet it is also a work of serious study, demonstrating that the artist was a scholar of ancient myths. The tale of Venus's birth is found in Hesiod's *Theogony.* When Cronus (the god of time) castrated his father Uranus (the sky god), he tossed his father's genitals to earth, which fell into the sea. From the foam of the splash, Venus was born. Botticelli's painting shows Zephyr, the god of the wind, blowing her to shore. In his arms is his wife Chloris, the goddess of spring, who blows flowers toward the newborn goddess. The symbolic meaning of the picture is that love triumphs inevitably over brutality, because out of the most brutal of acts, the goddess of love was born.

In the centuries since the fifteenth century, Botticelli's Venus has continued to symbolize ideal beauty. Yet if we look closely at her, we will see that she is not in perfect proportion. Her neck is quite long with a steep incline along the shoulder. Her left arm is also exceedingly long. But these distortions are intentional; they do not make for a deformed goddess of love. In fact, they help create a more graceful image than any realistic picture could. Distortion can sometimes create greater beauty.

Leonardo da Vinci

During the Renaissance, artists joined scholars in a search for the fundamental cosmic truths of proportion, order, and harmony. At the beginning of the era, the medieval tradition of looking to the authors of the past for these truths remained (see Arts News box on "Modern Anatomy"). Ancient masters like Aristotle were considered to have almost sacred authority, second only to the Old and New Testaments. Leonardo da Vinci was familiar with the old texts but questioned them, too. Unlike most of his

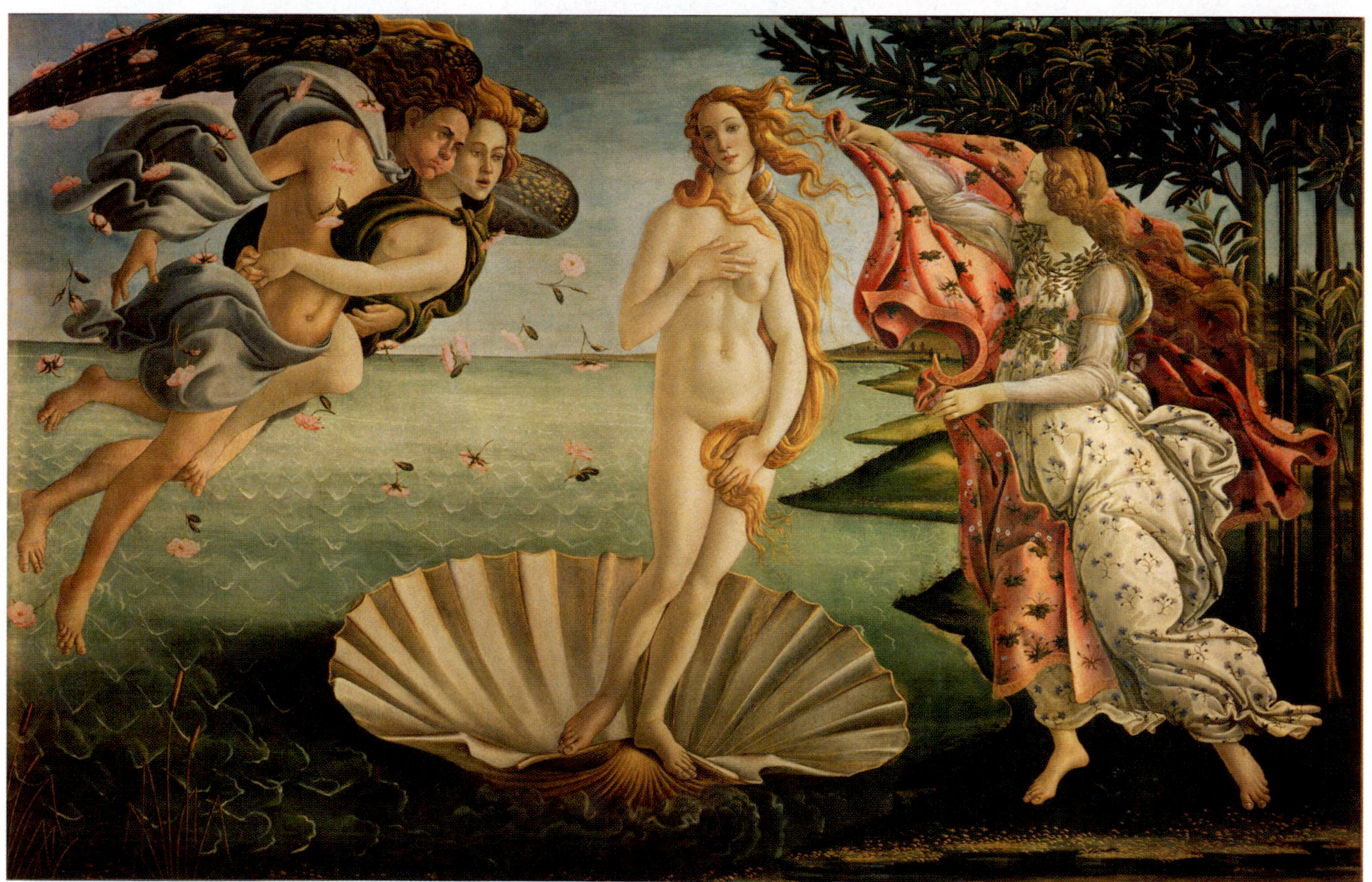

14-9 Sandro Botticelli, *The Birth of Venus,* c. 1482. Tempera on canvas, approximately 5′ 8″ × 9′ 1″. Galleria degli Uffizi, Florence.

contemporaries, he wanted to find out things for himself. If he came across a problem, he would not look solely for the answer in books, he would devise experiments to solve it. Leonardo was a leader on a new path—to nature and imagination, and a scientific approach to knowledge. He believed in observation and analysis. For example, to learn about flying, he would watch birds, not just read books. His famous drawing of *Vitruvian Man* (3-13) is a good example of his approach. He corrects the ancient architect's theory of ideal proportions to fit the actual ones of human beings. The method Leonardo used is called **inductive reasoning,** where one observes phenomena directly and then uses information gathered to develop general rules. The medieval method is known as **deductive reasoning,** where already accepted general rules determine how you explain natural phenomena.

ART NEWS

The Birth of Modern Anatomy

The medieval schematic of the muscle system (**14-10**) dates from the same period in which Giotto was painting. It is one of the earliest attempts to show the inner structure of the human body. Surprisingly, it is based solely on the work of Greek physicians. The art of Greece had beautiful representations of the human form, but it was truly a superficial understanding, because they did not know what lay beneath the skin. Dissections were forbidden in ancient and medieval times, so there were not many opportunities to learn the details of the human inner structure. Inner organs were revealed only after terrible accidents or wounds, which were probably not the best moments to make detailed studies.

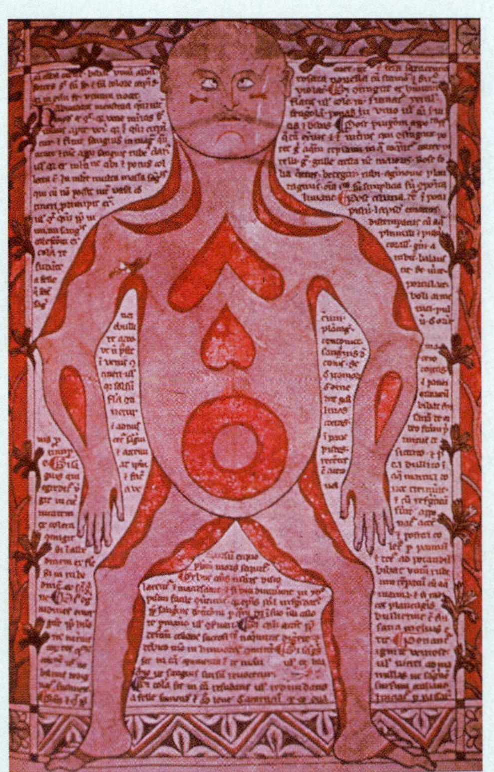

14-10 Medieval schematic of the muscle system, *Ashmolean Codex 399, folio 22R,* early 1300s. Bodleian Library, Oxford.

However, in the early Renaissance, lawyers had an important role in increasing the knowledge of the human body, because they began requesting autopsies for their cases. By the end of the 1400s, dissections of cadavers were permitted and anatomy was an officially recognized part of the university curriculum. Still, the study of anatomy made little progress because professors would never actually touch a cadaver. Their knowledge was not based on any actual study but rather on readings of ancient medical texts. In their anatomy classes, they would sit on a throne and lecture in Latin (the traditional language of the universities). Assistants (usually a local butcher) would do the carving. Another assistant would point with a stick to the area the professor was describing; however, he knew little about anatomy and usually did not understand Latin.

(continued on next page)

ART NEWS

It was an artist who made the first serious study of anatomy: Leonardo da Vinci (**14-11**) turned his incredible curiosity to the exploration of the unknown territory of the body. Obsessed by detail, he believed that detail revealed God's design. He did many anatomical studies, dissecting more than thirty cadavers before Pope Leo X barred him from sneaking into the mortuaries at night. By then, da Vinci had described the circulation of the blood (one hundred years before its official discovery). He was also the first person to study the reproductive system of women.

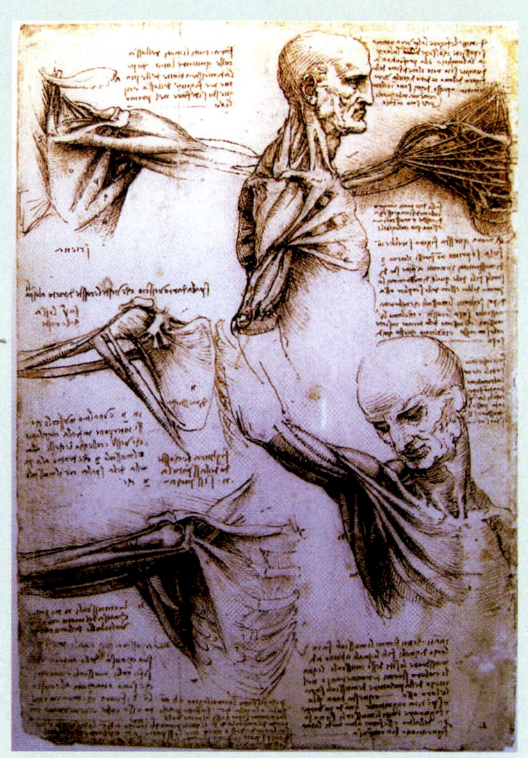

14-11 Leonardo da Vinci, anatomical muscle studies, late fifteenth or early sixteenth century.

However, Leonardo's notebooks were the private records of an artist. Vesalius was the first scholar to publish detailed studies of the human body (**14-12**). Vesalius was a zealous scientist (obtaining cadavers from graveyards, mortuaries, and the gallows), and his illustrations are works of art. When he became a professor at the University of Padua (the day after he earned his medical degree there), he disregarded the old traditions and did the dissections himself. His drawings are very accurate despite the serious handicaps he faced. Because the corpses he worked on were not preserved in formaldehyde, he had to work fast and have a photographic memory for details. Vesalius was a very popular lecturer and traveled to universities all over Italy to demonstrate dissections. At the University of Pisa, the outdoor theatre collapsed during one of his lectures from the weight of the huge crowds—a tragedy, but also evidence of the universal love of learning in Renaissance Italy.

Vesalius's and Leonardo's research avoided a pitfall of the unconditional admiration in the Renaissance of the ancient Greeks and Romans. Modern anatomy could only be born when the old texts were abandoned and self-reliant scientists conducted truly scientific research on their own.

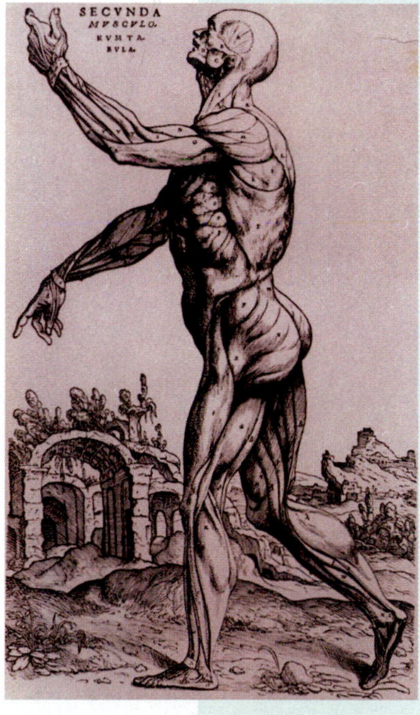

14-12 Vesalius, "The Muscle System," from *De Humani Corporis Fabrica Libri Septem,* 1543. Fratelli Fabbri, Milan, Italy.

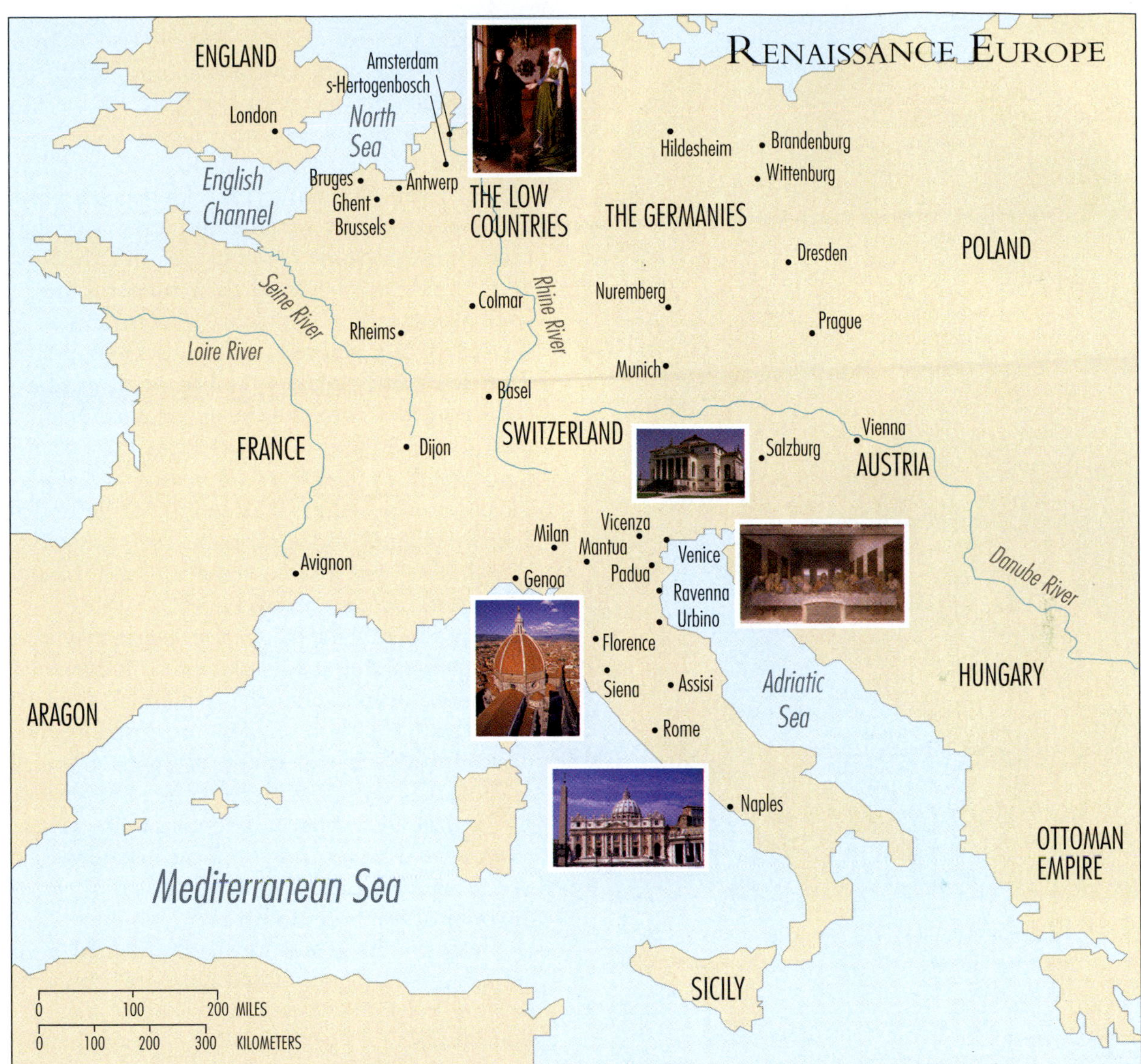

DaVinci is the embodiment of the term "Renaissance man" because he worked in so many fields: anatomy, aeronautics, hydraulics, military engineering, and urban planning (see pages from his sketchbooks in figures 1-5, 14-11). During his long lifetime, he invented helicopters, armored vehicles, air conditioning, brakes, and transmissions. Among his many discoveries are how water flows, how birds fly, and that the heart pumps blood. Yet Leonardo never thought of himself as a scientist; he was first and foremost an artist. He believed that observation and investigation of the laws of nature were necessary for an artist to have a true understanding in order to produce works of art. But, of course, it was more than that. As revealed in his notebooks full of detailed drawings, Leonardo, like many of his contemporaries, was in love with the act of seeing. He epitomized the Renaissance's enthusiastic rediscovery of the natural world.

THE HIGH RENAISSANCE

Leonardo's *The Virgin of the Rocks* (**14-13**) marks a new period in art—the *High Renaissance.* Compare it to a work of thirty years earlier, Mantegna's *The Dead Christ.* Mantegna's picture seems stiff. Its cold clarity seems impoverished when contrasted

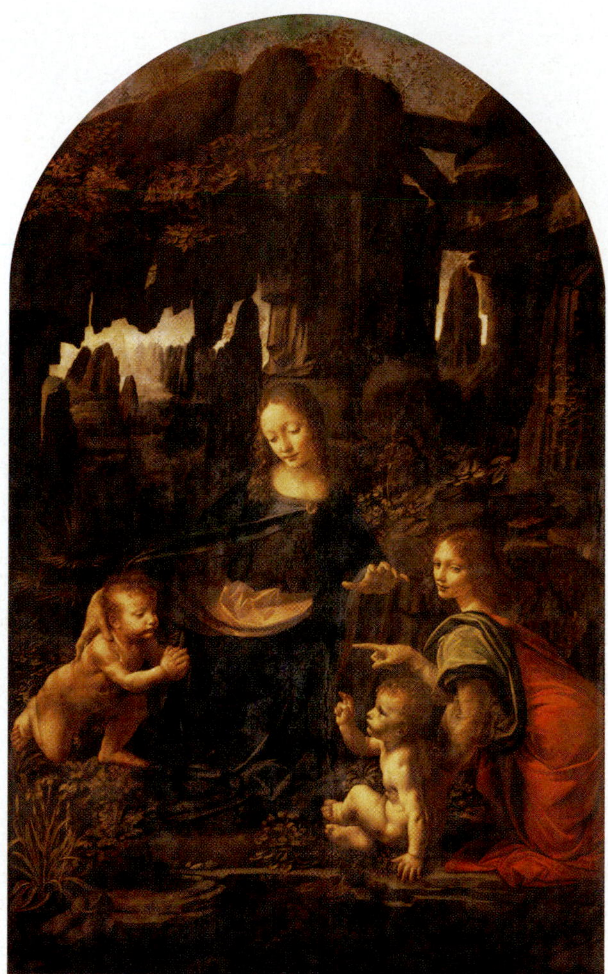

14-13 Leonardo da Vinci, *The Virgin of the Rocks,* c. 1485. Oil on wood (transferred to canvas), approximately 6′ 3″ × 3′ 7″. Louvre, Paris.

with the liquid atmosphere and subtle muted light of Leonardo's picture. In this painting, hard edges are nonexistent. While it looks real, it is more like a dream, a vision. The figures of the Virgin Mary, the infant Jesus, his cousin John the Baptist, and the angel are not entirely of our world, nor should they be.

The *Virgin of the Rocks* shows the perfect ease and accomplishment, the effortlessness—the *grazia*—that Renaissance artists were looking for. But underlying the softness is a new structural innovation, a geometric underpinning, which will be used throughout the Renaissance—the **figure triangle.** Leonardo also used a new medium that had been developed in northern Europe—oil painting. The smooth and subtle transitions between light and dark are made possible by this revolutionary medium (see Chapter 5). As seen in Chapter 1, Leonardo also revolutionized portraiture. His *Mona Lisa* has movement and life beyond any seen before.

For the dining hall of a monastery in Milan, Leonardo painted *The Last Supper* (**14-14**). To make the event vivid to the Dominican brothers, he placed Christ's table in line with the tables of the monks. All of the figures are life-size. The moment he chose to portray is when Christ discloses to his followers: "One of you will betray me." The apostles react to the announcement in different ways, according to their character. Some recoil in horror. Others discuss who could have betrayed their master. One gentle soul asks Jesus if it could have been himself. Judas, the only figure whose face is in darkness, pulls back from Jesus and clutches his bag of silver. *The Last Supper* shows a masterful use of perspective and symmetry. Leonardo used Christ's head as the vanishing point, so all parallel lines on ceiling and walls lead directly to the center of attention. While no halo is actually painted above Christ's head, the pediment above creates one, and the light from the center window creates an aura around him.

Unfortunately, the masterpiece began to deteriorate almost immediately. Leonardo, incessant experimenter that he was, had altered the traditional chemistry of fresco (see Chapter 5) to allow more opportunities to make changes. The experiment was not a success. Even in Leonardo's own time, pieces of the paint began to fall off the wall. Today, after a time-consuming restoration to preserve what remains, some art historians estimate that the restored picture is no more than 20 percent of the original (see Issues in Art box).

Because of his genius, Leonardo, the child of a peasant, was given a high social position and became familiar with kings and queens. The king of France even threw his own mother out of her château so Leonardo could stay there. But toward the end of his life, Leonardo, acknowledged as the great artist of his time, felt the challenge of a younger man, one who would become the predominant artist of the High Renaissance.

Michelangelo

Giorgio Vasari, a painter, is best known for his *Lives of the Artists,* a contemporary biography of the important Renaissance artists (many of whom he knew). He introduced his chapter on Michelangelo Buonarroti with a description that seems more like the birth of a god than a man. After noting the achievements of Giotto and his followers, Vasari says:

> the great Ruler of Heaven looked down and, seeing these vain and fruitless efforts and the presumptuous opinion of man more removed from truth than light from darkness resolved, in order to rid him of these errors, sent to earth

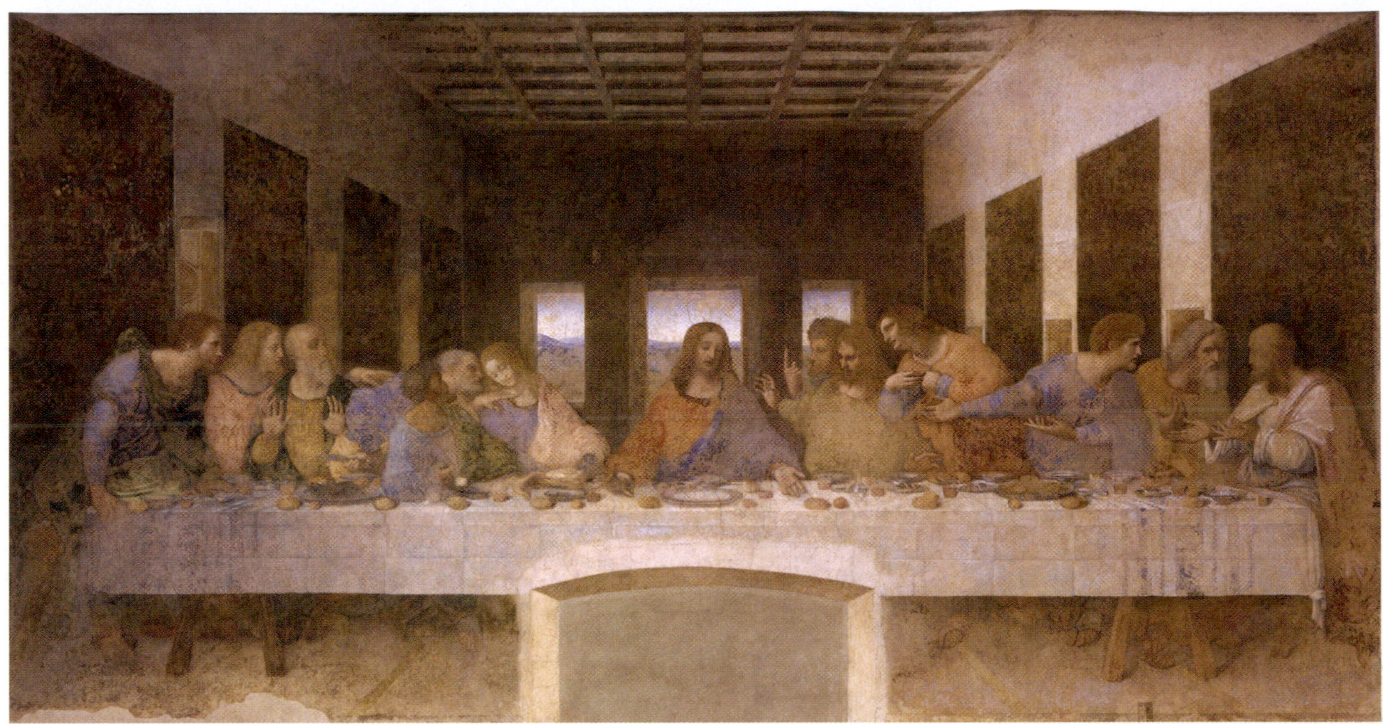

14-14 Leonardo da Vinci, *The Last Supper,* c. 1495–1498. Fresco (oil and tempera on plaster). Refectory, Santa Maria delle Grazie, Milan.

> a genius universal in each art, to show single-handed the perfection of line and shadow, and who should give relief to his painting, show a sound judgment in sculpture, and in architecture. . . . He further endowed him with true moral philosophy and a sweet poetic spirit, so that the world should marvel at the singular eminence of his life and works and all his actions, seeming rather divine than earthly.

Michelangelo was a child prodigy. As a young man, it was said that no pose was too difficult for him to draw (see 4-1). Despite his great talent, his family (who believed they had noble roots) considered his vocation an embarrassment, and he was regularly beaten by his father and brothers. Apprenticed around the age of thirteen, he attracted the attention of the ruler of Florence, Lorenzo de' Medici, who arranged for Michelangelo to study sculpture in the private academy on the grounds of the Medici Palace. When he was only twenty-three years old, he was hired by a cardinal to sculpt the *Pietà* (**14-15**) for a church in Rome. The marvelous but melancholy Pietà shows the dead body of Christ after having been removed

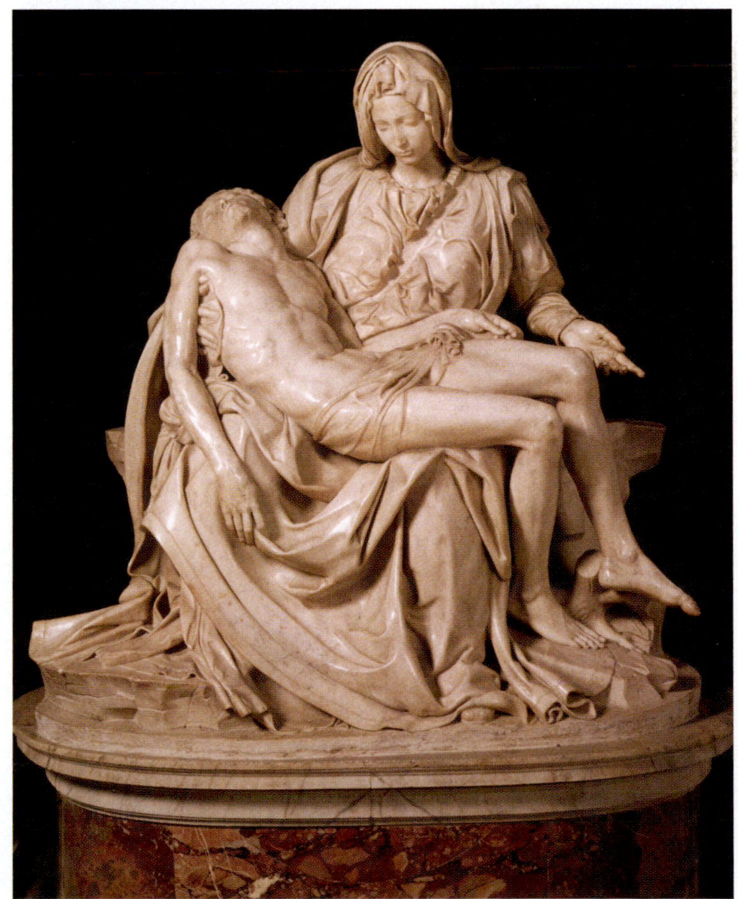

14-15 Michelangelo Buonarroti, *Pietà,* 1499. Carrara Marble, 69″ high. Saint Peter's, Rome.

from the cross, lying across his mother's lap. Mary is sad but dignified, the gesture of her left hand signifying acceptance. The unusual proportions (he is smaller than she) remind us that no matter what the age of Jesus at his death, we are looking at a mother whose child has died. As in Botticelli's *The Birth of Venus,* imaginative distortion increases his art's power.

After his success in Rome, Michelangelo returned home to Florence to work on an eighteen-foot block of marble that had been prepared for Donatello but left unused for decades. When Michelangelo transformed the enormous stone into the finished statue of *David* (**14-16**), the city fathers decided to put it in the Piazza Vecchio, the main square, as the symbol of Florence. The statue shows David before he killed Goliath. David is tense but confident, sling across his shoulder, his right hand loosely fingering the stone. His eyes stare intensely as if he is choosing the right moment for his attack. Unlike Donatello's version (14-6), this David is not a child but a powerful young man, a worthy symbol of the youthful vitality of Florence.

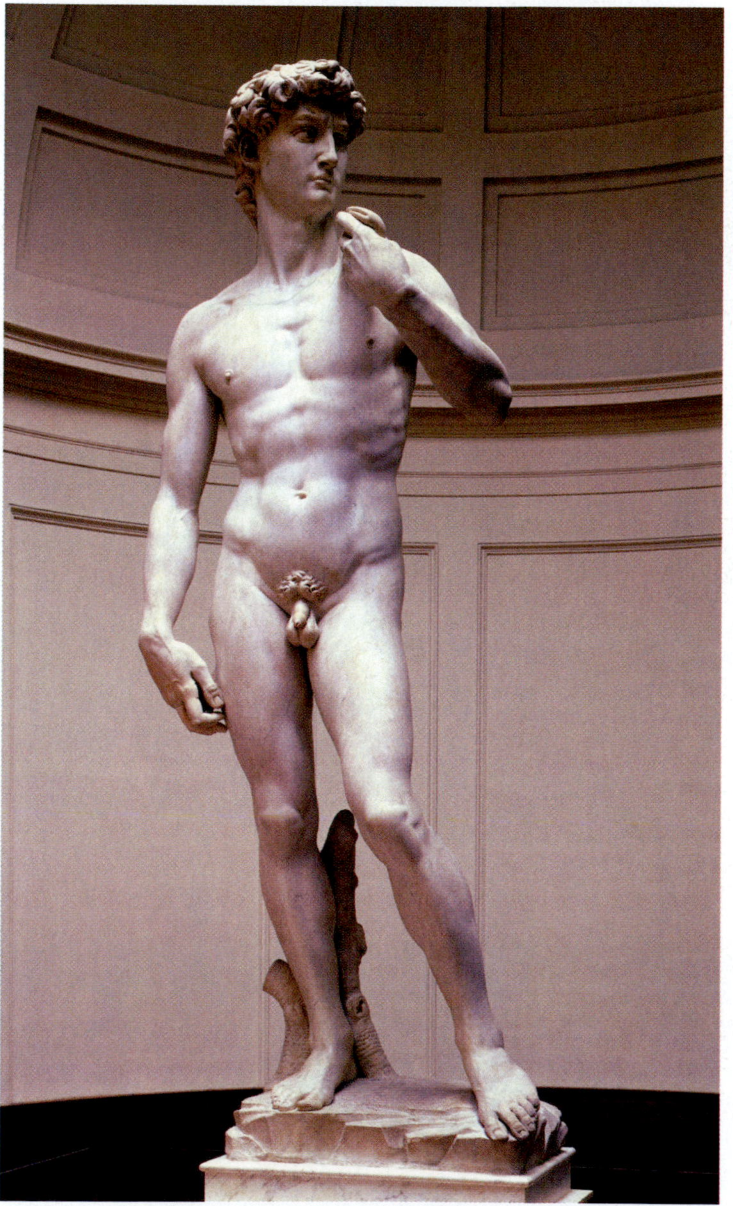

14-16 Michelangelo Buonarroti, *David,* 1501–1504. Marble, approximately 13′ 5″ high. Galleria dell'Accademia, Florence.

When Michelangelo was thirty years old, Pope Julius II summoned him to Rome for his first papal commission: sculpting the pope's tomb. With youthful enthusiasm, Michelangelo drew up a design for an enormous tomb with forty bigger-than-life statues. He left Florence for the marble quarries of Carrera. He spent several months picking out the marble because of his singular vision of the sculptural process. Michelangelo believed that if chosen properly, his sculpture was already alive in the block of stone. He needed only remove the excess to release the figure within.

Michelangelo returned from his months in the quarries and filled half of Saint Peter's square with his stones. However, the pope was no longer interested in the tomb. He did not tell Michelangelo, but he had decided to tear down the old Saint Peter's, the most venerated building in the Christian world, and replace it with a new one, a massive undertaking (see Chapter 10). Michelangelo was furious and told Julius II (known as "the terrible pope" for his temper) he was leaving Rome, and he would never have any dealings with him again. Rather than hunting down Michelangelo and executing him, as might have been expected, emissaries of the pope began negotiations through the leaders of Florence for Michelangelo to return to Rome. The pope had a new commission for Michelangelo—to cover the ceiling of a tremendous chapel adjoining Saint Peter's (the old ceiling had developed cracks). It was 5,800 square feet, blue covered with gold stars.

Michelangelo was not interested in this new commission. First, he wanted to complete the project for the tomb he had spent so much time planning, and second, he told the pope, he was a sculptor not a painter. This was not an overstatement. The artist had only completed one painting since his apprenticeship. He finally agreed to paint the ceiling after many heated discussions because the pope promised he could finish the tomb afterward. What this "sculptor" created was the world-famous masterpiece, the ceiling of the *Sistine Chapel* (**14-17**).

Working on scaffolding seventy feet from the floor, it took Michelangelo about four years to complete this project. At first, eager to finish quickly and begin again on the tomb, he planned to paint only the corner spaces, making portraits of the twelve apostles in each of them. However, the word "ambitious" is hardly sufficient to describe what became his ultimate plan. Michelangelo decided to represent the history of the world before Moses, from the first event in Genesis—the separation of light from darkness—to the story of Noah. Surrounding the main scenes are prophets who predicted the coming of Christ. Supporting every subject and scene are realistically painted architectural elements and nude figures who react to the scenes they frame. The Sistine ceiling contains more than three hundred figures, all in an incredible variety of poses and actions and all depicted as fully rounded three-dimensional forms, as one would expect from the hand of a sculptor. Pope Julius II, while reputed to be impatient, cooperated with just about all of Michelangelo's requests. Special scaffolding was built to his specifications, pigments he required were imported from Turkey, and it is believed that he hired thirteen assistants. No one else was permitted in the chapel while Michelangelo was at work (see Art Issues box on "The Cost of Restoration").

While it is filled with philosophical and religious references, generally, the story Michelangelo tells over the length of the ceiling is the movement to pure spirit from the physical. He began painting in reverse chronological order. The first important scene shows Noah, his spirit numbed by alcohol, naked before his children and ridiculed by them. The next scene is *The Flood,* the torrents of rain and water sweeping the earth. Michelangelo realized after this scene that he had underestimated the effect of the height of the ceiling and began painting larger figures, starting with the *Expulsion from Eden.* After that comes *The Creation of Adam* (**14-18**), the most famous of the scenes, where a powerful and compassionate God (who resembles the ancient god Zeus) brings a still-weak Adam the spark of life. *The Creation of Eve* shows her pulled from the side of a sleeping Adam by a simple gesture of God.

Moving back farther in time, we are shown God racing back and forth across the heavens in *Creating the Sun, Moon, and Planets* and *Congregating the Waters.* The climax of the ceiling is the first moment of creation—the *Separation of Light and Darkness.* With *Jonah and the Whale* (symbolizing Christ's resurrection) just over the altar, they announce the inevitable triumph of the spirit over the physical world.

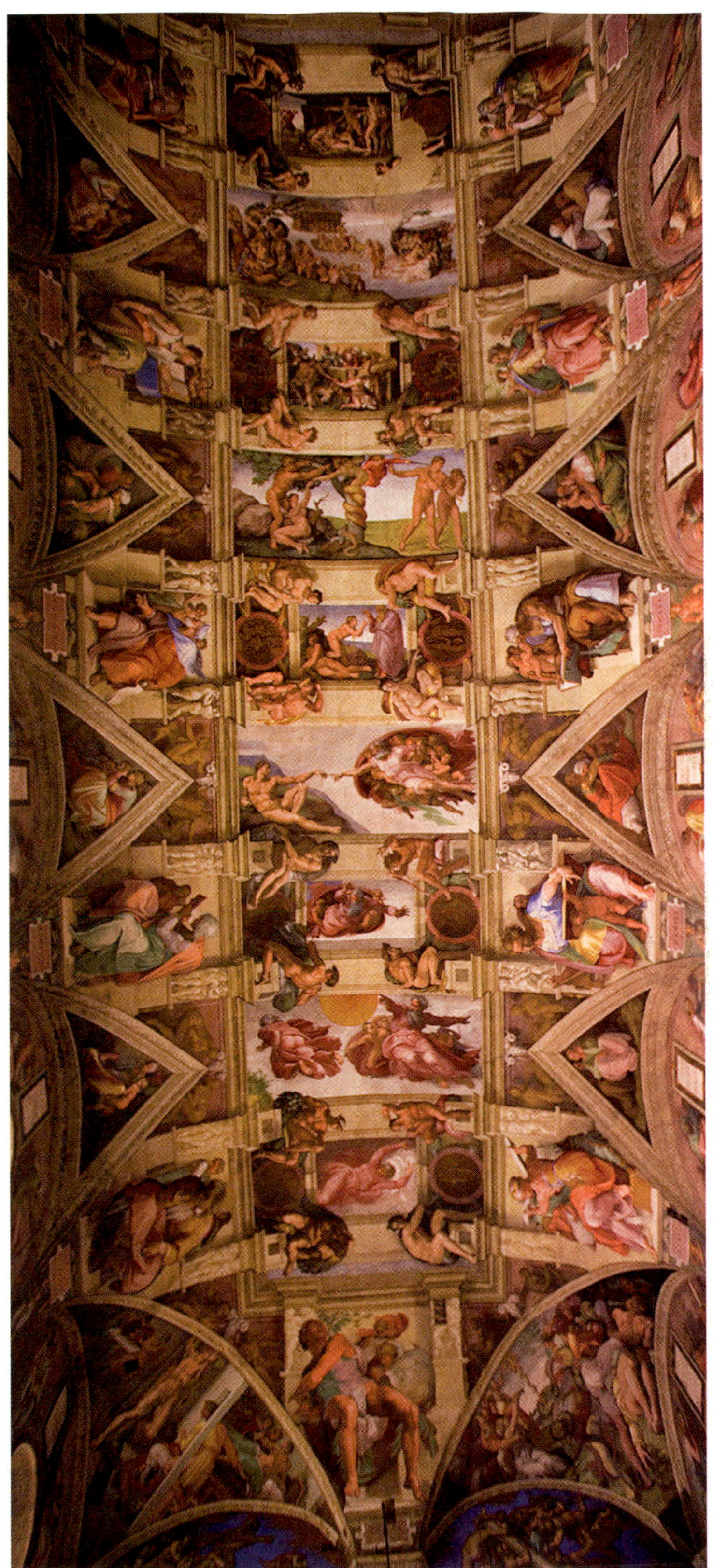

14-17 Michelangelo Buonarroti, the ceiling of the Sistine Chapel, Rome, 1508–1512. Fresco.

ART ISSUES

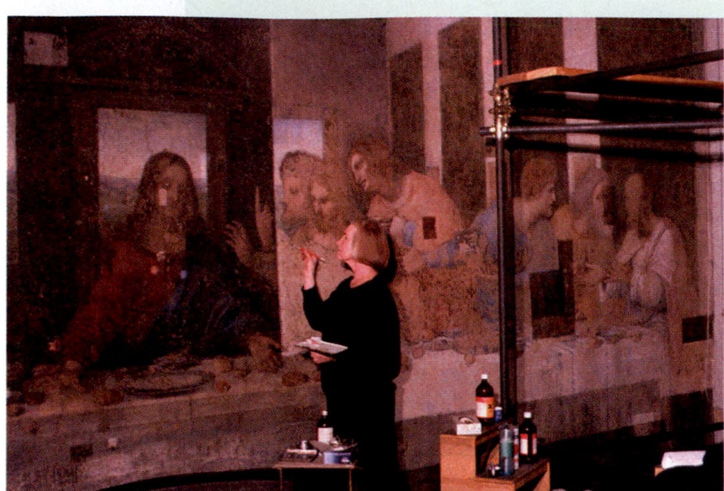

14-20 Restoration of Leonardo da Vinci's *The Last Supper.*

restorations flaked off, each flake took some of Leonardo's original paint with it. Subsequent restorers decided to repaint the picture rather than restore it, some changing the artist's original vision. Their over-painting also damaged the chemicals in Leonardo's paint. Twentieth-century restorers did better work, but during World War II an Allied bombardment hit the refectory, shaking the painting and caving in the roof. The *Last Supper* was covered for years while the building awaited repairs. Mildew grew on its surface during that time.

The primary goals of the most recent restoration were to remove all previous restorations and to reattach only the remaining original parts of the masterpiece. Pinin Brambilla Barcilon devoted two decades of tedious labor to the project. Now a woman in her seventies with weakened eyesight and chronic pain, she said, "Centimeter by centimeter I worked with a knife and microscope for 20 years to remove what five centuries of restoration and dirt had left behind." A day's work might only complete an area the size of a postage stamp. The most advanced technologies available were used. Infrared and chemical analyses were used to determine which paint was original. Small borings into its surface were made and miniature cameras inserted to examine the structural integrity of the wall. Today, the painting is protected by being exhibited only to small groups by appointment and in a completely climate-controlled environment.

Like the restoration of the Sistine Chapel, this restoration has been controversial in the art world. The decision to retain only Leonardo's original paint meant that Brambilla and her team removed much that had been familiar for centuries. For example, Christ's red beard was eliminated because it was determined to be a later addition. Many areas were left empty because they no longer had any of the original paint. While the colors in many parts are once again bright and luminous, the painting clearly reflects its substantial damage over the past five hundred years.

The restorations of the Sistine Chapel and *The Last Supper* cost many millions of dollars. Many millions of dollars will be needed to restore the Acropolis in Athens, and millions more on the damaged medieval stained glass in France (see the Art News box in Chapter 13). The costly and time-consuming restoration of paintings, sculptures, quilts, pottery, and buildings occupies tens of thousands of people around the world. How can such expenditures be justified in a world with so many problems, where children go to sleep hungry and families have no homes? It must be that people believe that, just as we have a responsibility to preserve our natural environment for the sake of future generations, we must preserve our cultural environment, the harvest of the best efforts of centuries of men and women.

Raphael

As you can imagine, this masterpiece had a profound effect on the artists of the Renaissance. Perhaps the biggest effect was on the younger Raffaello Santi, the artist we call Raphael. In 1508, the pope called on Raphael, then twenty-five years old, to decorate his private library in the Vatican, now known as the "Stanza della Segnatura." Because this was his first great commission, Raphael chose a great humanistic subject. Raphael decided to sum up all learning; each of the four walls would represent one discipline: theology, law, literature, and philosophy.

While decorating these walls, he managed to see Michelangelo's unfinished work on the Sistine ceiling. Legend tells us that he bribed the guards to let him see the ceiling while Michelangelo was away. He slipped into the chapel, climbed up the scaffolding, and was stunned by the masterpiece. Raphael immediately realized that his pictures in the library seemed backward compared to Michelangelo's and quickly redesigned and repainted all of his pictures.

The School of Athens (**14-21**) is the most famous wall of the Stanza. It is a picture of a heavenly world of knowledge, the Elysian (or "delightful") Fields spoken of by the Greek poets. We see the greatest philosophers of the classical period in discussion, thinking, teaching, and arguing. In the center is Plato, pointing upward to the ideal, and Aristotle, pointing downward to reality. On the lower left, Pythagorus, a Greek philosopher and mathematician, is writing; at right, Euclid, the Greek founder of geometry, is surrounded by many students.

The connection felt between those ancient times and the Renaissance of Raphael is given visual form by the artist's choice of models for the philosophers. Plato is also a portrait of Leonardo da Vinci, for example. Euclid is the architect Bramante who designed the new Saint Peter's and whose ceilings and archways can be seen overhead. In the foreground, alone and moody, is Michelangelo as Heraclitus, known as the "weeping philosopher." At the farthest right, a sign of his modesty, is Raphael himself, posing as a student of Euclid.

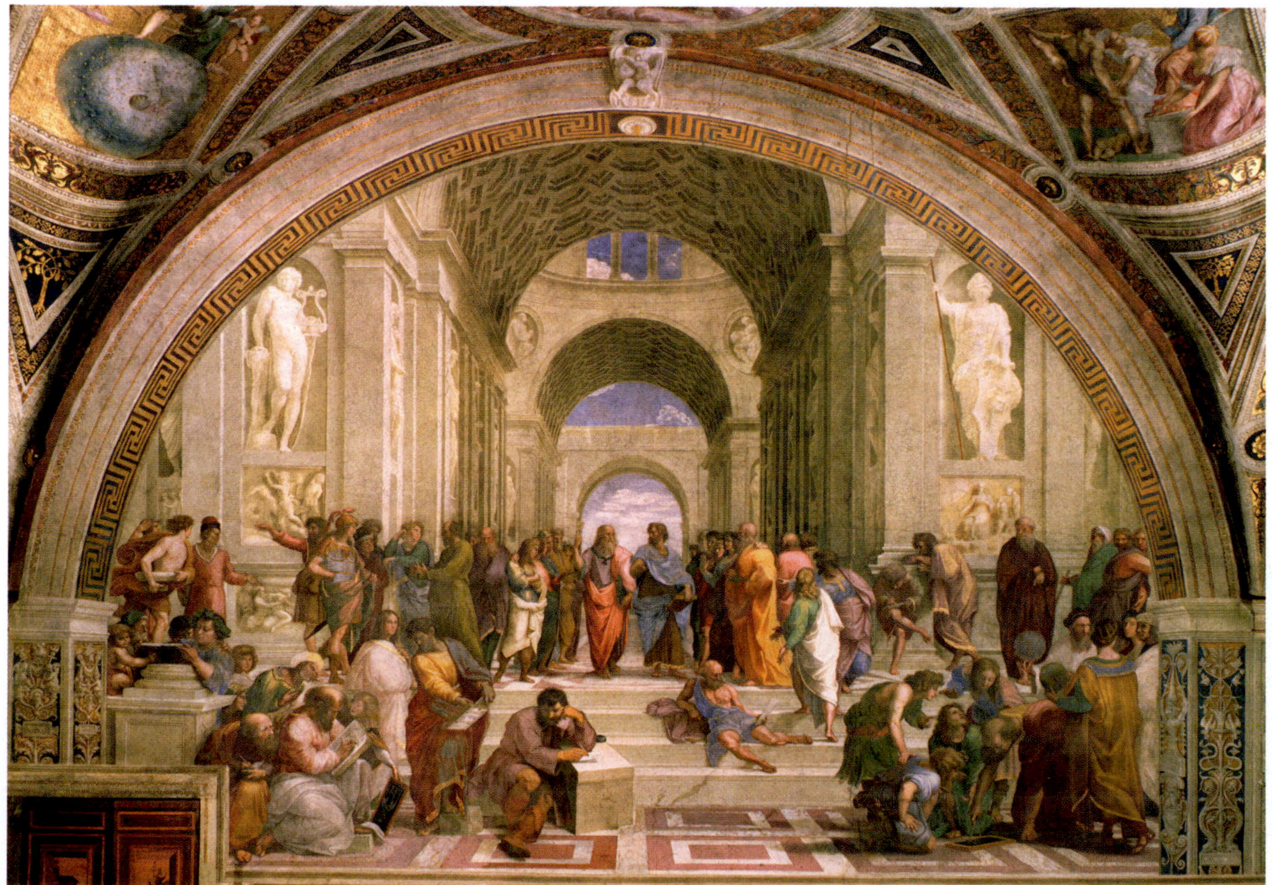

14-21 Raphael, *The School of Athens,* 1509–1511. Fresco, Stanza della Segnatura, Vatican Palace, Rome.

Preparatory sketches were always important for Raphael, but he never made more than he did for this project. *The School of Athens* is known for its perfect composition and perspective. Unity is achieved by the repetition of arched (elliptical) shapes throughout. Even the figures form a large ellipse. As in Leonardo's *The Last Supper,* the vanishing point is placed at the center of attention—Plato and Aristotle. Notice how the seemingly casual form of the reclining Diogenes on the steps also points at the central figures. Even though it is more complicated than Leonardo's picture, *The School of Athens* remains a vision of order and dignity. Raphael achieves a harmonious composition of freely moving figures, something artists have admired in his work throughout the centuries.

The School of Athens shows Raphael's formal, mathematical side, but his *Madonna della Sedia* (**14-22**) shows his sweet and loving side. The sheer, ideal beauty of his pictures of the Madonna and Christ child made Raphael famous. Over the centuries, Raphael's *Madonna della Sedia* has been seen as artistic perfection. As a modern critic said, this picture would be recognized as a masterpiece even if it were found dusty and unlabeled in an attic. It is in a circular format called a *tondo,* which means in Italian "simple," yet it is probably the most difficult form for a painting compositionally because of a tendency to seem unbalanced and rolling. Raphael secured the scene by providing the strong vertical of the chair post. But that is merely a technical issue. The picture's lasting fame depends on the warmth, softness, and pride of Mary as she cuddles with the wriggling infant Jesus. One cannot imagine a sweeter expression of the love of a mother for her child.

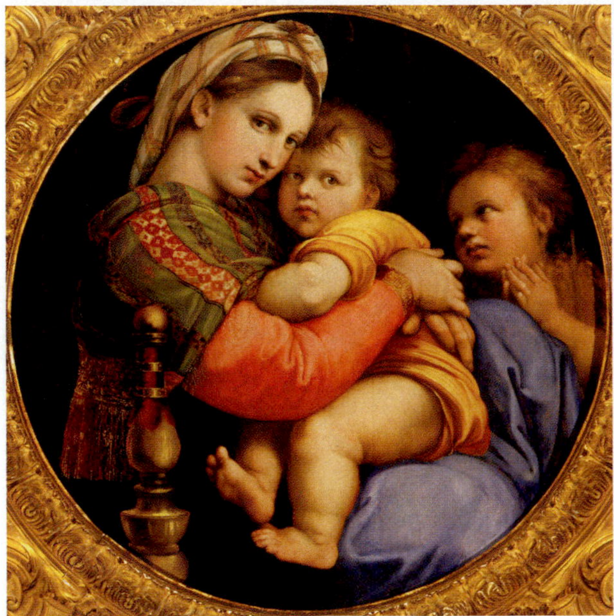

14-22 Raphael, *Madonna della Sedia,* 1510–1512. Panel painting, tondo, 28″ diameter. Pitti Gallery, Florence.

Those who lived at the peak of the Renaissance believed the power of the mind made anything possible. The world seemed good and understandable. Raphael, one of the greatest masters of the Renaissance, managed to achieve its highest goals: *beauty, proportion, grace,* and a *sense of human virtue.*

THE RENAISSANCE IN VENICE

In the medieval period, bright colors were used for decorative and symbolic purposes; artists were not concerned with reproducing actual colors or even realistic forms. Partly in reaction to that art, the Florentines of the Renaissance were most interested in drawing issues, such as the realistic depiction of forms. Perspective and composition were the things that fascinated them: color was a secondary interest.

However, color was not a mere adornment for the artists of Venice but central to their work, giving energy and movement to their pictures. The greatest colorist and painter of the Venetian Renaissance was Tiziano Vecellio, or Titian. Unlike the geniuses of Florence and Rome, Titian's sole interest was painting; he was not an architect or a scientist. He mastered the medium with a single-mindedness that was unique for his time. He developed new techniques—for example, **impasto,** where thick layers of paint are built up for added richness (see Chapter 5). Titian would vary the texture of the paint itself, sometimes scratching into it with his fingers. His surfaces are full of energy.

Sensuality became a hallmark of Venetian painting, and the *Venus of Urbino* (**14-23**) probably epitomizes the Venetian love of sensual delight better than any other work. Here is Titian's ideal beauty, and she is very different from Raphael's or Leonardo's. She is an openly sexual woman, lying on cool sheets on a hot day. The purpose of this picture is not to give moral or religious instruction but to give pleasure. Notice how Titian uses color as a compositional element. The large red pillow (the hue is known as either Venetian or Titian red today) in the foreground is balanced by the red skirt in the background. The white shapes of the pillow and arm form triangles that lead back into the background. Titian had cre-

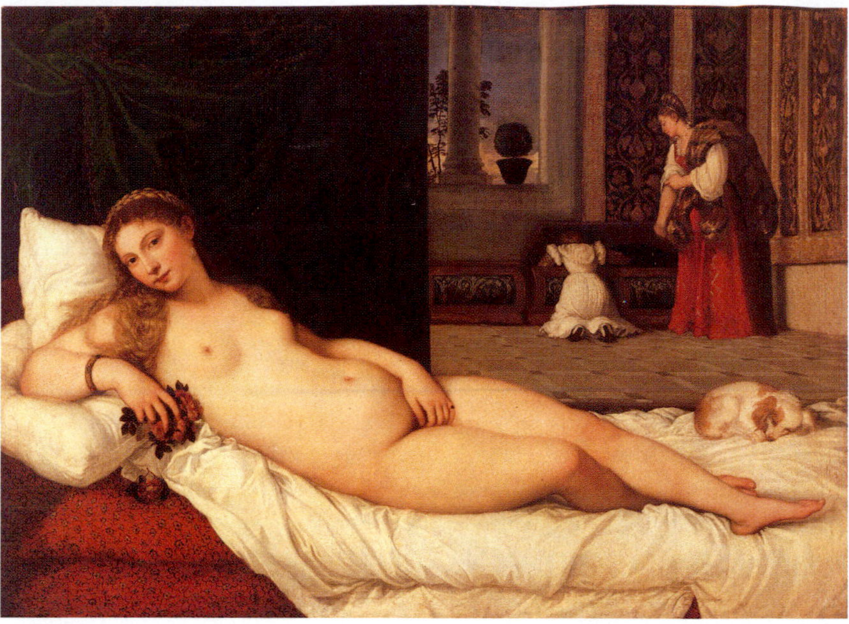

14-23 Titian, *Venus of Urbino,*1538. Oil on canvas, approximately 48″ × 66″. Galleria degli Uffizi, Florence.

ated a new type of image, one that would be borrowed by artists for centuries. Romantics, Classicists, Realists, and Impressionists would all choose to continue the *tradition of the reclining nude.*

Palladio and Architecture

While Leonardo, Michelangelo, and Raphael engaged in architectural projects, architecture never was a primary interest for them. The quintessential Renaissance architect was Andrea Palladio. His most influential building, the *Villa Rotonda* (**14-24**), has been a model for architects in every century since it was built, in the mid-1500s. It is the essence of calm and harmony, a study of the purest geometric forms. The building is perfectly symmetrical, with four identical façades designed like a Roman temple on each side. A circular hall topped by a dome is the center of the building, making Palladio's design a circle within a square. This private retreat of a wealthy landowner rests on a hillside outside the city of Vicenza and provides four different views of the countryside from each of the entrances. Many classical-style statues on the pediments and stairways share the lovely views, which the occupants could choose from, depending on time of day, weather, or whim.

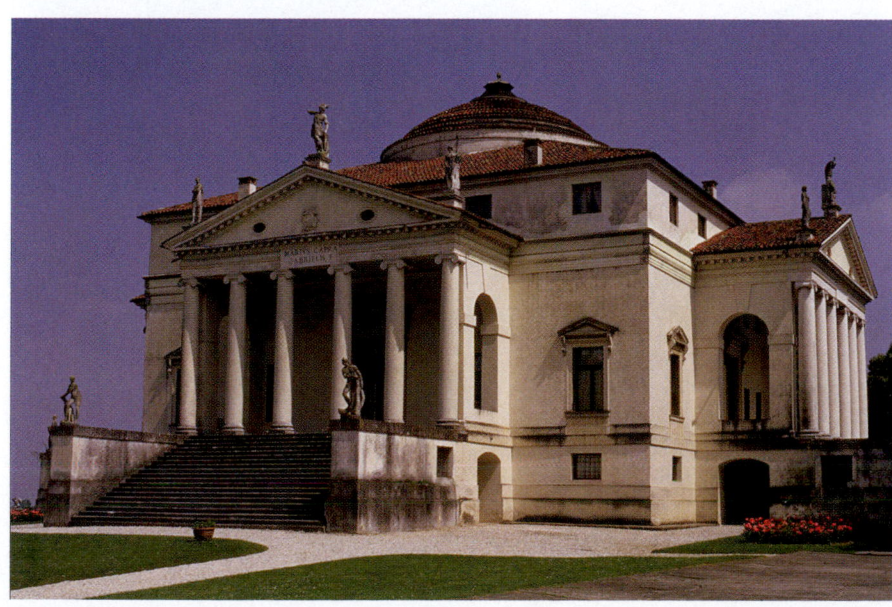

14-24 Andrea Palladio, *Villa Rotonda* (formerly Villa Capra), near Vicenza, Italy, c. 1566–1570.

Palladio was a scholar of ancient architecture and, like his predecessor, Brunelleschi, made many trips to Rome to study the ruins there. His influential treatise, *The Four Books of Architecture,* was written to encourage the construction of buildings that would bring the world into an ideal state. With floorplans and drawings, the book systematically explained classical architecture. Palladio also included the designs for his buildings, thereby putting his own work on the same level as the greatest architecture of the past. His treatise became the primary source of information on the buildings of the Greeks and Romans and was widely circulated. The familiarity of the Palladian style of architecture testifies to his treatise's acceptance as the authoritative guide to ideal architecture. Among many others, he would influence architects of the early American republic like Thomas Jefferson (see Chapter 10).

THE END OF THE HIGH RENAISSANCE IN ITALY

Unlike Raphael, who was only thirty-seven when he died, Michelangelo had a long, full life (living until the age of eighty-nine). Despite his immense talent, Michelangelo ended his life as a frustrated and angry old man. Many of the projects he began (like the tomb of Pope Julius II) were left unfinished. By the 1530s, he could see the age of the High Renaissance was ending, never to return.

In 1534, Michelangelo returned to the Sistine Chapel to paint an enormous fresco on the wall behind the altar. Thirty years had passed since he had completed the ceiling of the chapel. Since then, his beloved Italy had become a battleground, the victim of many invasions from the north. Even Rome had been sacked in 1527, leaving it in

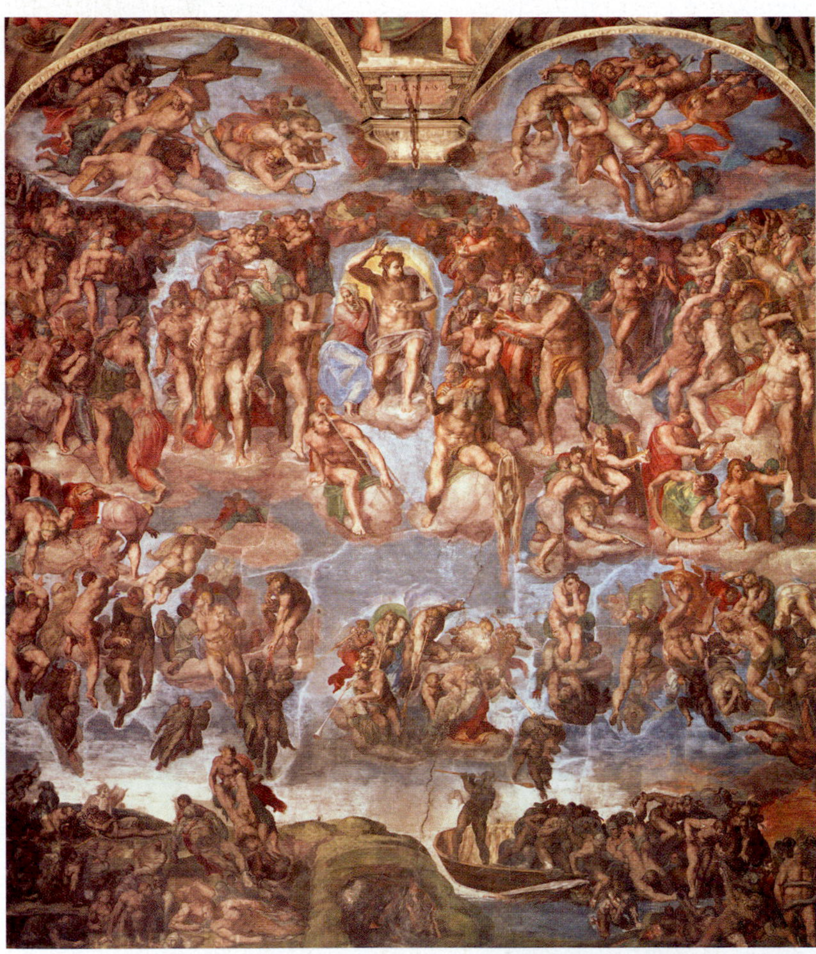

14-25 Michelangelo Buonarroti, *The Last Judgment,* fresco on the altar wall of the Sistine Chapel, 1534–1541.

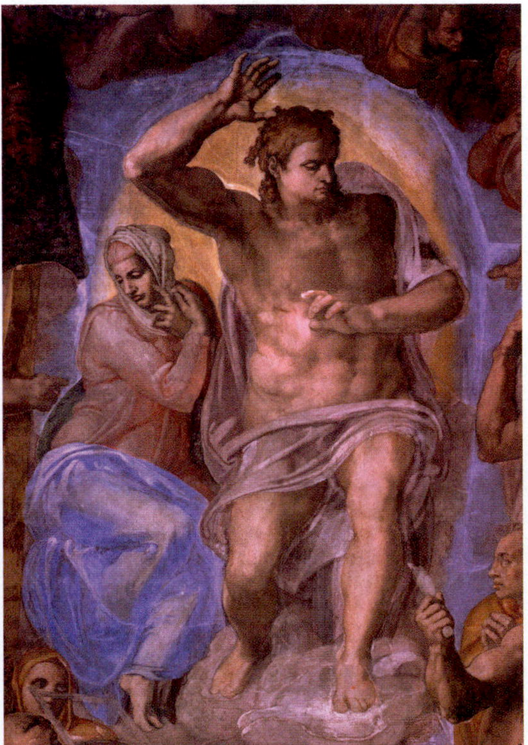

14-26 Detail of figure 14-25.

disarray. In Florence, the Medicis, once his patrons, had become tyrants who were propped up by the Spanish king. All across Europe, there was change. The Protestant Reformation (see following section) had split Christianity. Michelangelo became deeply concerned about the fate of humanity. He felt the world had gone mad, and he worried about the fate of his own soul.

Even though they share the same room and were done by the same artist, *The Last Judgment* (**14-25**) has a very different mood from that of the Sistine ceiling. On a dark and turbulent Judgment Day, Christ has come, but his arm is lifted in damnation as if he is destroying the world (**14-26**). Mary, his mother, turns her head away; she cannot bear to see his judgment. The heavens are in chaos. Ideal beauty and perfection no longer have a place in Michelangelo's painting. At the end of his life, using ugliness and terror for their expressive power, the greatest artist of the High Renaissance moved beyond its ideals.

THE BEGINNING OF THE NORTHERN RENAISSANCE

The Renaissance did not take place only in Italy. In the early 1400s, a century after Giotto but long before the birth of Michelangelo, it had also begun in northern Europe. As in the Italian Peninsula, growing cities made more powerful by trade altered the structure of society. The new wealthy courts in the Netherlands, Germany, France, and England became centers for art. Unlike Italy, however, the cultures of northern Europe had flowered during the Middle Ages. The Medieval Era, for example, was the era of the great Gothic churches and stained-glass windows in France. Therefore, the difference between medieval art and that of the Early Renaissance in the north is not as clear-cut as it was in Italy. However, during the fifteenth and sixteenth centuries, with commerce on the rise between Northern and Southern Europe, the ideas of the Italian Renaissance began to be gradually assimilated in the north.

Art in the Courts of the Duke of Burgundy

Based in both Dijon, France, and Flanders (now Belgium), the courts of the duke of Burgundy were two of the most significant artistic centers in the north by the end of the fourteenth century. This French duke had inherited the Netherlands, one of the most prosperous lands in northern Europe, from his father, the king. By the end of the Renaissance, the Netherlands would replace Florence as the center of European finance.

The French felt that the artists of the Netherlands were the best in Europe. Therefore, it is not surprising that in 1395, Philip the Bold, the duke of Burgundy, sent for the Flemish artist Claus Sluter to design a huge crucifixion for a church in his capital of Dijon. Originally twenty-five feet tall, the statue's base is all that remains intact. Today it is called *The Well of Moses* (**14-27**), because it was originally placed over a fountain. It is an extraordinarily naturalistic sculpture, with life-size portraits of individuals who seem only to be leaning against the backgrounds temporarily. The Old Testament prophets Moses, David,

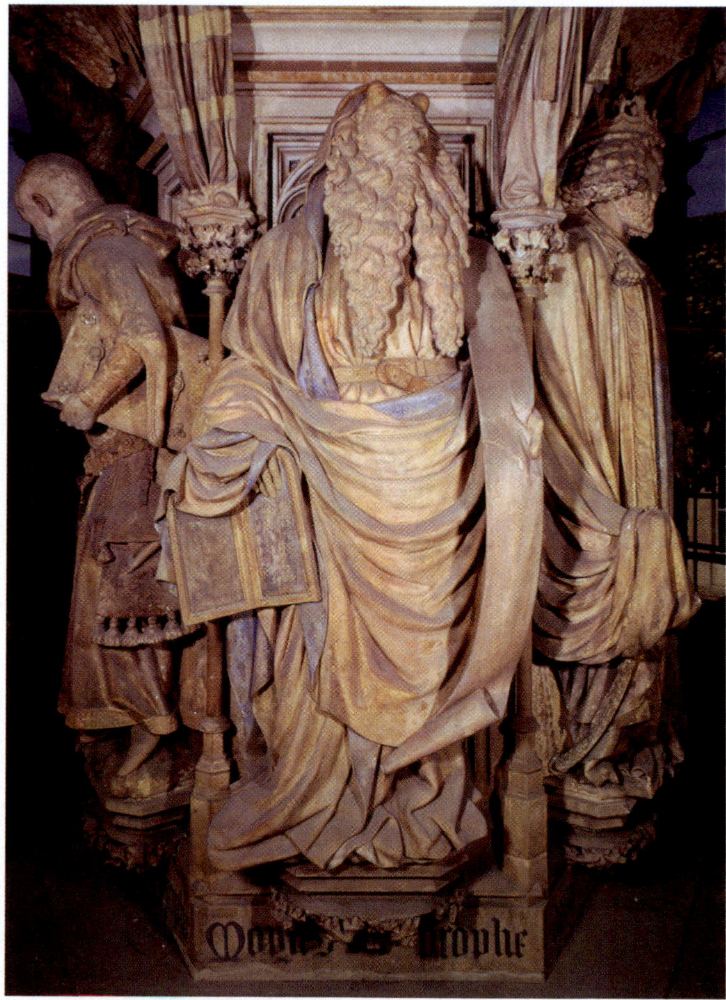

14-27 Claus Sluter, *The Well of Moses,* 1395–1406. Figures approximately 6′ high. Chartreuse de Champmol, Dijon, France.

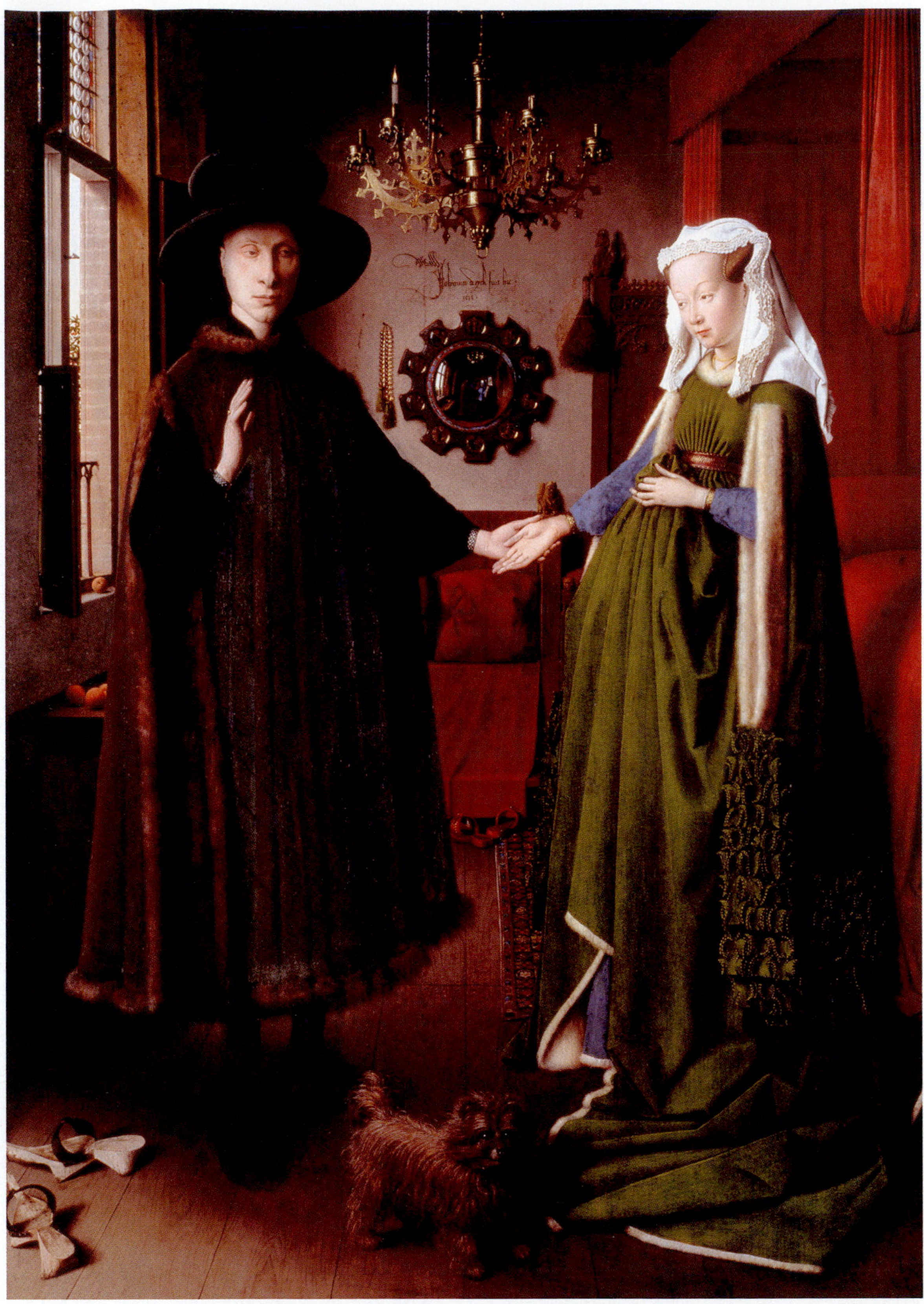

14-28 Jan van Eyck, *Giovanni Arnolfini and His Bride,* 1434. Tempera and oil on wood, approximately 32″ × 23½″. National Gallery, London.

Jeremiah, Zechariah, Daniel, and Isaiah look as if they are about to leave the fountain, walk into the congregation, and begin to preach. Each is a unique character, and every part has been sculpted by Sluter with careful attention to realistic detail. Notice how the heavy cloth of Moses's robes is held to his waist by a precisely delineated belt. As realistic as the statues seem today, originally they were even more so, because they were not bare stone but painted. Moses wore a blue robe with golden lining. Jeremiah even had on a pair of metal spectacles.

Jan van Eyck

Another Flemish artist, Jan van Eyck, was the favorite artist of a later duke of Burgundy, Philip the Good. Although we do not know much about this artist's life, his sober, realistic style was most likely influenced by Sluter's. Like Sluter, he lived in Brussels but also traveled widely as a diplomat of the duke.

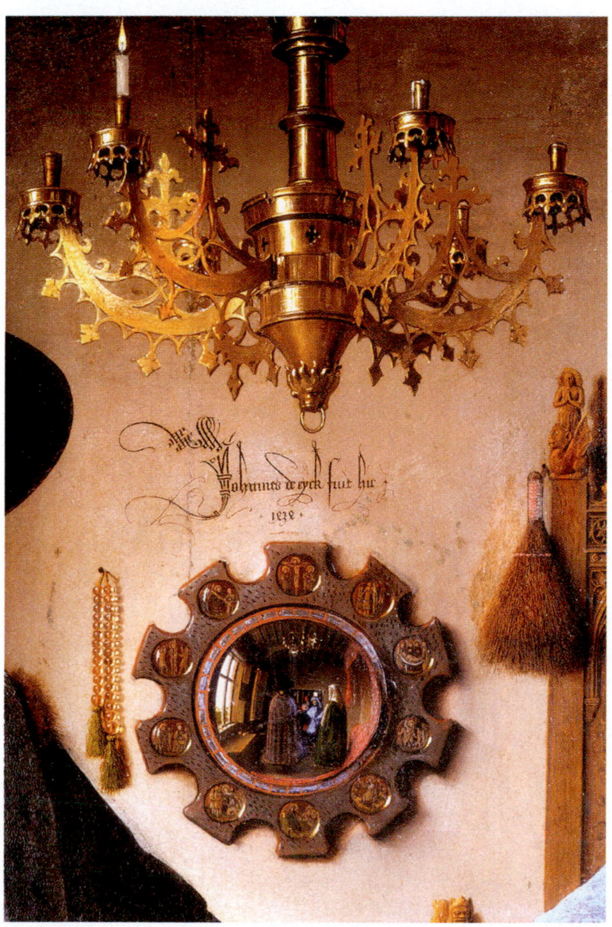

14-29 Detail of figure 14-28.

While the Italian Renaissance artists like Leonardo da Vinci were pursuing naturalism with the technique of *sfumato* light, van Eyck used a different approach to reach a similar goal. As seen in his *Virgin with the Canon van der Paele* (2-16), van Eyck used detail upon detail to carefully recreate nature. This obsession with detail is common in northern Renaissance painting and one of the clearest ways to differentiate it from the art of the south. If the painting is concerned with the beautiful surface of things, then it is most likely from the north.

Giovanni Arnolfini and His Bride (**14-28**, 5-5) is van Eyck's most famous work and is evidence of the growing trade between Northern and Southern Europe. It depicts the marriage ceremony between an extremely wealthy Florentine banker who lived in Flanders and the daughter of a rich Flemish family. At this time, civil marriages (versus church ceremonies) were permitted as long as they were witnessed by a government official. Since the painter was an appointed official of the duke, the painting served as both portrait and official document. On the back wall, between the bride and groom, is his elaborate signature—"Jan van Eyck was here 1434."

Van Eyck's painting is a good example of **secondary symbolism.** Medieval artists loved to make symbolic puzzles out of pictures, and van Eyck continues the practice. It was part of a desire to give realism even greater meaning by making each detail meaningful. The dog, for example, symbolizes Fidelity (Fido). Peaches ripening on the desk and windowsill suggest fertility. The chandelier has only one candle—the nuptial candle, carried during the ceremony and by tradition blown out right before going to bed on the wedding night. The ceremony is not totally secular. The main participants have removed their shoes because it is sacred ground. The mirror (with tiny scenes of the Stations of the Cross around its edge) probably represents the eye of God witnessing the ceremony (**14-29**). In it we can see the backs of the couple as well as van Eyck and his assistant. A rosary hangs to its side. The entire scene, while very naturalistic, symbolizes the holy sacrament of marriage.

Albrecht Dürer

Van Eyck mastered detail, color, texture, and realistic portraiture, but knowledge of mathematical perspective had not yet come from Italy. Like his fellow northern Renaissance artists, he accepted what he saw but did not search for underlying universal laws.

One man took it upon himself to bring the ideas of the High Renaissance to northern Europe—the German artist, Albrecht Dürer, who became known as the "Leonardo of the North" because of the variety of his interests: writing treatises on painting, perspective, human proportions, fortifications, and many other topics. Like Leonardo, he did many sketches from nature, studying its most delicate details.

Dürer is probably the first artist to paint pictures devoted solely to a self-portrait. His *Self-Portrait* (**14-30**) in 1500 shows him at the age of twenty-eight, after his return from Italy, where he studied the great works of the Italian Renaissance and became determined to bring this knowledge north. While the careful detailing of his fur collar is very typical of the northern style, his interest in High Renaissance composition is revealed by the pyramid construction of the picture. If you look closely, you will discover, in fact, that the composition contains several triangles. The portrait's striking resemblance to European images of Christ is conscious but not blasphemous; Dürer is saying he is a creator, too (note his hand's position).

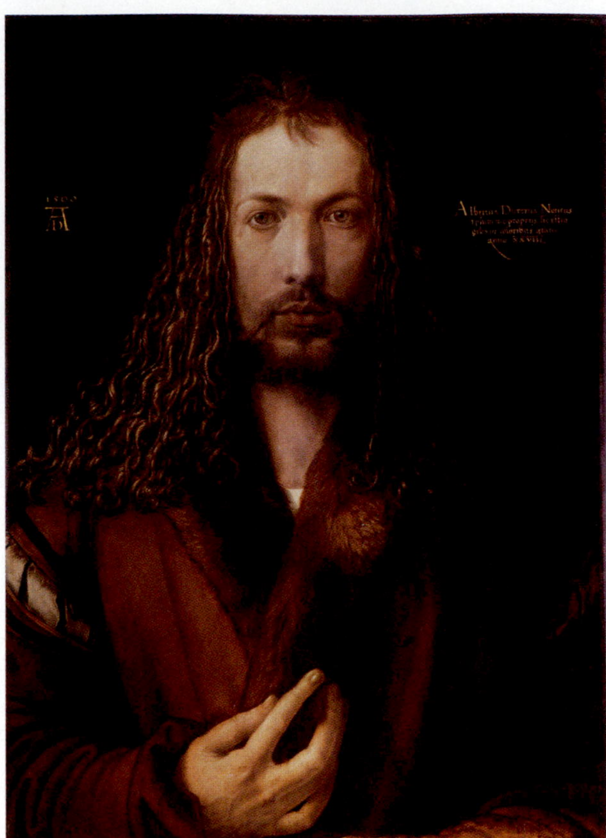

14-30 Albrecht Dürer, *Self-Portrait,* 1500. Panel, 26½″ × 19¼″. Alte Pinakothek, Munich.

Despite the exceptional skill demonstrated in his self-portrait, Dürer's greatest talent was not as a painter but as a printmaker. His graphic work, such as the *Four Horsemen* from his *Apocalypse* series (5-2), made him rich and famous in his time and maintains his reputation even today. Dürer's technical skill and inventive mind are equally demonstrated in his metal engravings. He inherited his skill from his father, a goldsmith, who trained him (see Global View box on "Gold of the New World"). His technical mastery was combined with a marvelous eye for detail and the patience to render detail upon detail. *The Knight, Death, and the Devil* (**14-31**) contains an incredible variety of textures and shading. In it a Christian knight rides without fear through the Valley of Death with his faithful dog. Death, riding a horse, attempts to distract the hero with an hourglass, pointing out the shortness of life. He and the Devil—whose head is a grotesque collage of beasts—are ignored as the knight moves by on his way to glory and salvation.

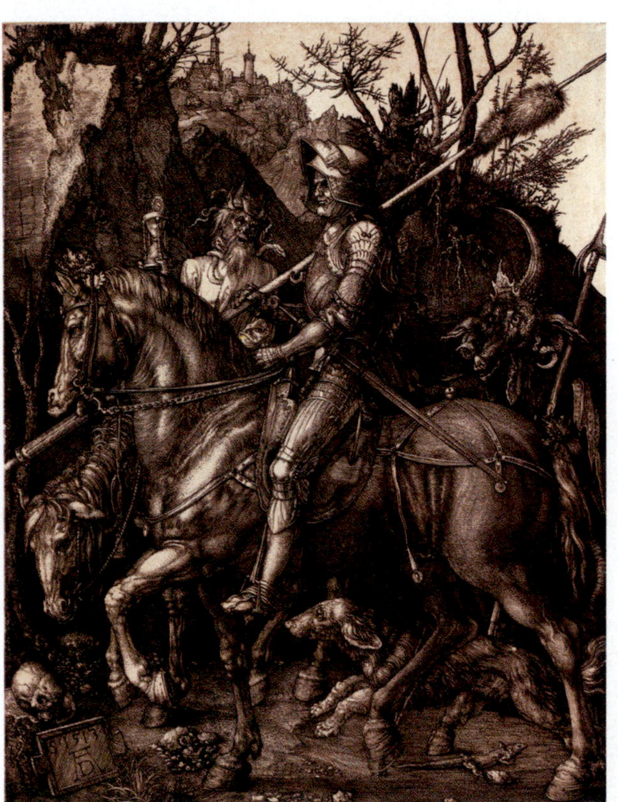

14-31 Albrecht Dürer, *The Knight, Death, and the Devil,* 1513. Engraving on paper, 9¾″ × 7½″. British Museum, London.

Dürer demonstrated that effects once thought possible only in paint could be accomplished by a master printmaker and helped make the print the equal of any other fine art form. He was recognized as being among the greatest masters even in his own time. In a discussion with the Holy Roman Emperor Charles V, Michelangelo said of Dürer: "I esteem him so much that if I were not Michelangelo, I should prefer to be Albrecht Dürer than Emperor Charles V."

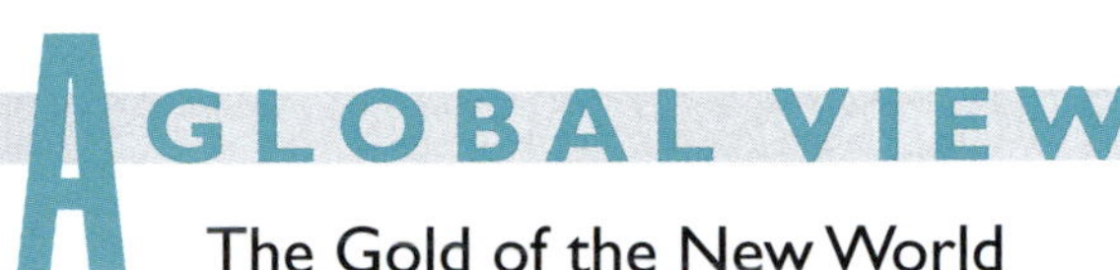

The Gold of the New World

In 1520, during a visit to the court of the Holy Roman Emperor Charles V in Brussels, the artist Albrecht Dürer saw objects from another culture that took his breath away. He wrote in his journal:

> Then I saw the things which were brought to the King from the new Land of Gold [Mexico]: an entire golden sun a full fathom wide, and likewise an entire silver moon equally as large, likewise two rooms full of armor of the people there, all kinds of wondrous weapons; most strange clothing, bedding and all sorts of marvelous objects for human use which are much more beautiful to behold than things spoken of in fairy tales.
>
> These things were all so precious that they were valued at 100,000 florins. In all the days of my life I have seen nothing which so filled my heart with joy as these things. For I saw among them wondrous works of art, and I marveled over the subtle genius of those men in strange countries. Truly, I cannot tell enough of the things which I saw there before me.

Dürer was writing about some of the first objects brought from the New World to Europe by the Spanish Conquistador Hernán Cortés, presents from the Aztec leader Montezuma. Only a year earlier, the Spanish ships had arrived on the shore of Mexico. Montezuma believed at first that they were mountains that divine beings sailed on the seas. Cortés, his body covered in gleaming metal, was thought to be a legendary god returning—Quetzalcoatl, one of the gods who created the world. Montezuma was wrong about the ships but terribly right in his belief that the arrival of these divinities would mean the destruction of his empire. The riches that Cortés presented to Charles V were given to the conquistador in a futile effort to convince this divine being to spare Montezuma's people. Hundreds of messengers were sent back and forth to deliver huge objects of gold and silver to Cortés. Among the gifts were the treasures that the Aztecs had revered as belonging to Quetzalcoatl.

During the European Renaissance, the royal families and the Catholic Church first began building great collections of art. Charles V, who ruled an empire that stretched from Spain to Austria, was not the only collector of what has since become known as *Pre-Columbian* art. The Medicis of Italy and the Popes also added the treasures of the Americas to their collections. But, unfortunately, the primary goal for Cortés's patrons was not a love of art but simply of wealth. Cortés was sent to the Americas for silver, precious stones, and especially gold. By the mid-1500s, each year more gold was shipped to Europe from the New World than was mined in all of Europe.

Precious few of the golden artworks of the Aztecs like the ones that amazed Albrecht Dürer remain. A rare survivor depicts a great warrior (**14-32**). Beautifully crafted with intricate details, he wears ear, nose, and lip jewelry, which were common

(continued on next page)

A GLOBAL VIEW

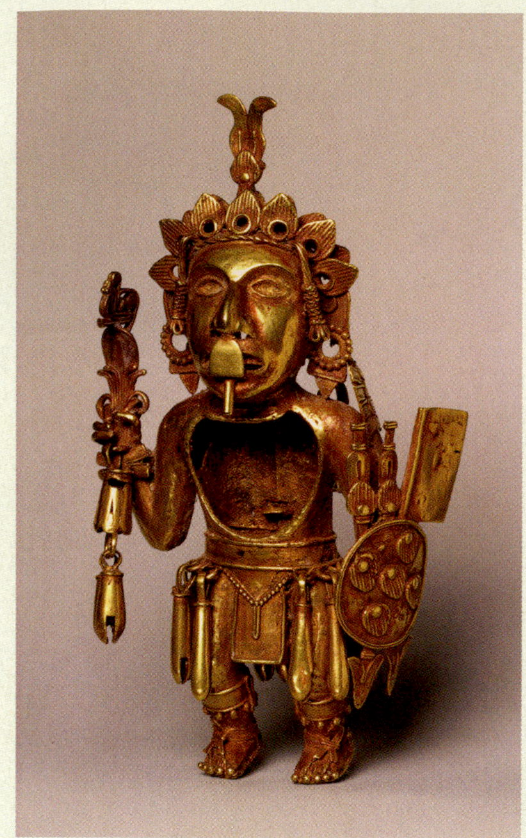

14-32 *Figure of a Warrior,* fourteenth to sixteenth century, Central Mexico, Aztec. Cast gold-silver-copper alloy, 11.2 cm × 6.1 cm. Cleveland Museum of Art.

among high-born Aztecs. He carries a spear with a serpent's head in one hand and a shield and darts in the other. At the time of Cortés's arrival, the Aztec capital in Tenochtitlan had a population of 200,000, but the civilization was doomed. Its Great Temple, the center of its rituals and the empire, was destroyed and buried beneath the ground. A new Mexico City was soon built on its ruins and the land renamed New Spain.

Two hundred feet tall, The Great Temple of the Aztecs remained lost and buried for centuries. It was discovered by accident in 1978 during the excavations for a new subway line in Mexico City. In 1987, the Templo Mayor (Great Temple) Museum opened and exhibited many of the artifacts found at the site. One of its saddest objects is in its last room. It tells the tale of what happened to almost all of the golden statues and jewelry of the Aztecs. It is a foot-long bar of gold—one of thousands made by the Spanish from melted cultural treasures.

Hans Holbein and the Protestant Reformation

In one of his many treatises, Dürer included among a painter's most important responsibilities "to preserve the appearance of men after their death." A younger German, Hans Holbein, made that goal his main occupation and became one of the greatest portraitists who ever lived. He came from a family of painters and began his career after Dürer's mission to spread the influence of the Italian Renaissance had taken hold. Like Dürer, Holbein traveled to see the great Italian masterpieces firsthand, and by the time he was thirty years old, he had assimilated the learning of the Renaissance. Settling in Switzerland, he painted beautiful altarpieces and was on his way to becoming the leading painter of the German-speaking world when that world, and Europe, suddenly changed profoundly.

The Protestant **Reformation** led by Martin Luther turned Europe upside down and had deep and pervasive effects on the art world, too. The rebellion against the Roman Church was sparked by the church's practices, like the sale of indulgences (which Pope Julius II had zealously promoted to pay for his new Saint Peter's). Northern Europeans were outraged by the idea that Christians could buy their way into heaven. Luther and his followers preached that Christians needed only faith and knowledge of the Bible to reach salvation, but the rise of the Protestant

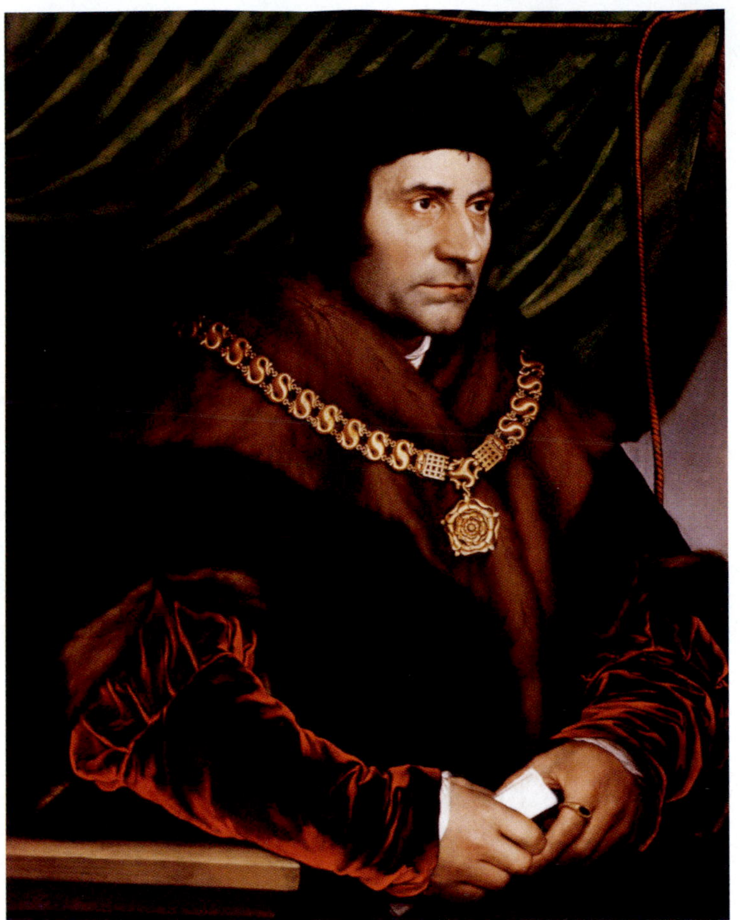

14-33 Hans Holbein the Younger, *Portrait of Sir Thomas More,* 1527. Panel, 29 ½″ × 23 ¾″.

Reformation came with a terrible cost for art and artists. There was a wave of *iconoclasm*—the destruction of religious imagery (Luther, a close friend of a painter, was horrified by this development). Many Protestants associated imagery not only with the Roman Church but, like the early Christians, with idolatry. All over northern Europe, Protestant mobs swept into churches destroying altarpieces, decapitating statues, and burning crucifixes. The lack of decoration in most Protestant churches today is a result of this darker side of the Reformation.

While most of his religious paintings were being destroyed, Holbein desperately looked for a safe haven where he could continue his career. He sailed to England and was given refuge by Sir Thomas More, a world-famous writer, scholar, and political leader. His *Portrait of Sir Thomas More* (**14-33**) was painted soon after Holbein's arrival when More was Speaker to the House of Commons. With meticulous detail, it shows an intelligent, dignified, and successful man wearing the symbol of his high office. The picture provides sensual pleasures as well. Holbein masterfully reproduces a variety of textures: More's soft hands, the stubble of his beard, red velvet, black satin, gleaming gold, and fur. Underlying all of Holbein's work is his marvelous drawing ability. We believe every detail without question; we are convinced this is how Sir Thomas More looked.

When the Reformation came to England, even powerful friends like More could not prevent the end of Holbein's career as a painter of religious art, but More helped Holbein become Henry VIII's court portraitist (see his portrait of the king in Chapter 1). He was a prolific painter, so even though he died of the plague at the relatively young age of forty-six, we have an almost firsthand acquaintance with the many members of the Tudor court.

If we compare Holbein's portrait of Sir Thomas More to Leonardo da Vinci's *Mona Lisa* (1-1, painted less than twenty-five years earlier), we can see some of the characteristic differences between northern and Italian Renaissance painting. Northern artists accentuated detail and crispness of edges, while in the south, a soft diffuse light—*sfumato*—eliminated definite edges. Interest in delineating fabrics, textures, and patterns precisely was the common feature in northern Renaissance art.

NORTHERN RENAISSANCE: THE DARKER SIDE

There are other differences between the two European Renaissances. For example, nobility of gesture, perfect proportion, and harmony are notably absent from Matthias Grünewald's *Isenheim Altarpiece* (**14-34**), a set of paintings that would have horrified an artist like Raphael. But the Northern artist's goals were quite different. Because it was designed for a hospital, Grünewald painted a crucified Christ that the suffering patients could identify with and pray to, a figure who seemed to express all possible human torments in his sickly-colored flesh and broken body. No matter what physical tortures the patients may have felt, this cruel masterpiece seems to say that Christ had already suffered the same. His body hangs heavily on the cross and his feet twist painfully; his expressive hands reach up in anguish. Grünewald portrays a massive crown of thorns upon Jesus's head and dried blood running down his sore-covered body.

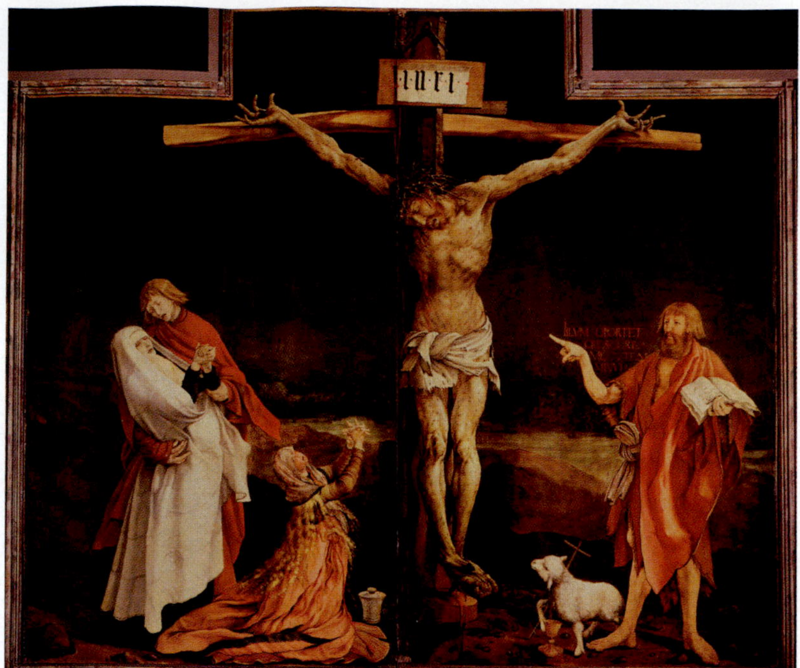

14-34 Matthias Grünewald, *The Isenheim Altarpiece* (closed), Crucifixion (center panel), c. 1510–1515. Oil on wood, center panel 9′ 9½″ × 10′ 9″. Colmar, France.

Yet the crucifixion scene is only part of the altarpiece, which was made to unfold and open to reveal a series of images. Inside the picture of suffering and death is one of rebirth and resurrection (**14-35**). Here, Christ's body—now glowing white rather than sickly green—rises dramatically out of the grave. He holds out his hands with their **stigmata** (bloody signs of the nails that held Christ to the cross), as if proving that he is ultimately unhurt by his ordeal. These wounds are no longer sources of pain but now sources of light. All of the torture of the first scene has been replaced with triumph. Christ's face glows like a rising sun. Here, in Grünewald's *Isenheim Altarpiece,* you have the essence of the Christian doctrine of God's suffering and rebirth, the victory of good over evil. For the hospital's patients, this altarpiece was meant to replace fear of illness and death with a vision that inspired faith and hope.

During this period, there lived another northern artist whose pictures are among the most fantastic, weird, bizarre, and visionary of any age—Heironymus Bosch. We know little of his life, except it was quite unlike the experiences of the educated city dwellers Dürer and Holbein. His was the world of northern villages before the Reformation, where alchemy was an accepted practice, superstitions were unquestioned, and the Roman Church had its hands full trying to control the widespread use of magic. Preachers used pornographic images to make their points, and prostitutes could be seen at work in the churches.

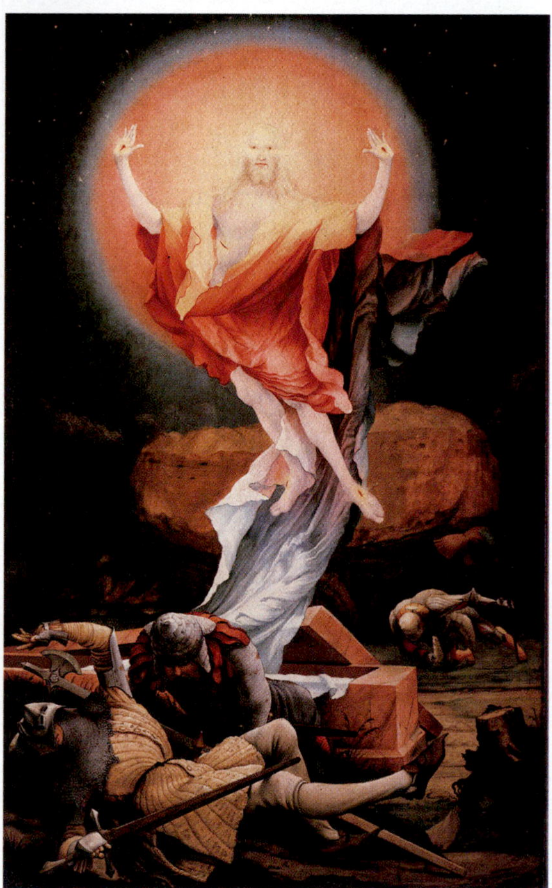

14-35 Matthias Grünewald, *Resurrection,* detail of the inner right panel of the first opening of *The Isenheim Altarpiece.* Approximately 8′ 8⅜″ × 4′ 6¾″.

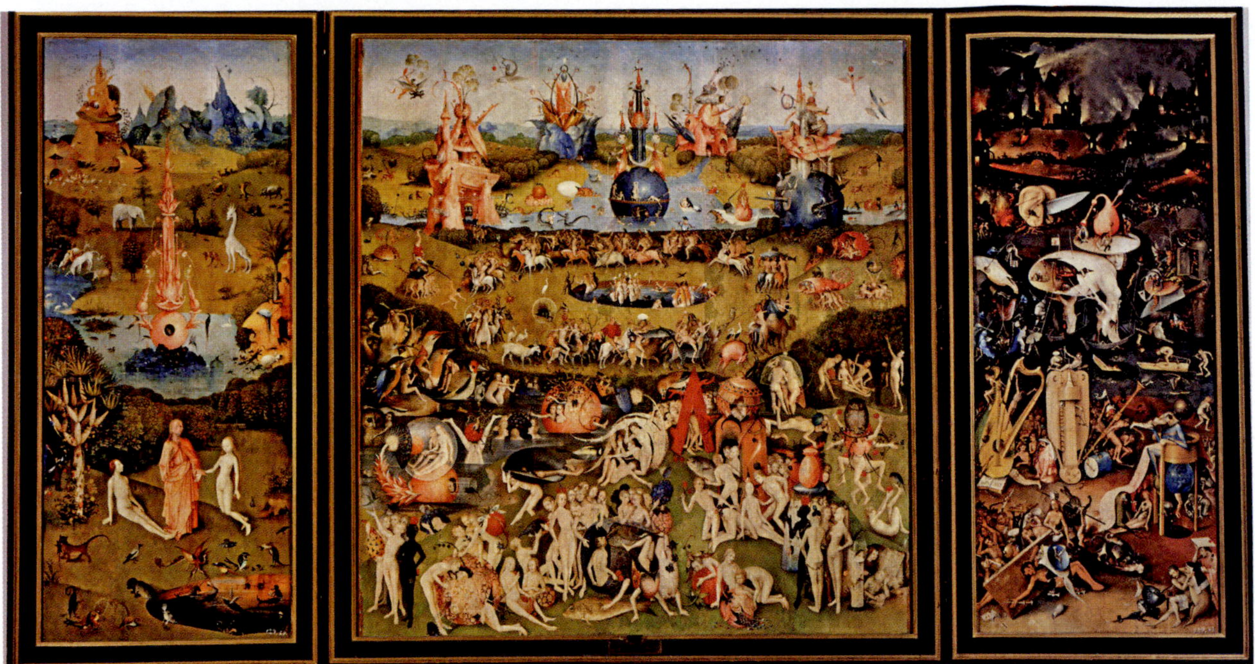

14-36 Hieronymus Bosch, triptych of *The Garden of Earthly Delights, Creation of Eve* (left wing), *The Garden of Earthly Delights* (center panel), *Hell* (right wing), 1505–1510. Oil on wood, center panel 86⅝″ × 76¾″. Museo de Prado, Madrid.

Bosch cared little for the new ideals of Renaissance painting. He was interested in creating visions that taught moral lessons and used the achievements of the Renaissance only to help make his visions look more real. Most of Bosch's pictures are very symbolic and difficult to decipher. *The Garden of Earthly Delights* (**14-36**) is his greatest and most famous painting, but scholars are still trying to understand it. The left panel shows Christ introducing Adam and Eve in the garden of Eden before the Fall. The central panel (**14-37**) gives the triptych its name, showing the world after the Fall and symbolizing Bosch's era. The setting seems to be a park where nude men and women are indulging in pleasure, enjoying free and open sexuality. But Bosch is not celebrating this scene. What he wants to show is a false paradise. Bizarre acts are rampant, as revelers engage in acts restricted only by the limits of Bosch's fertile imagination.

After an orgy of false pleasures comes the right panel—Hell (**14-38**), a nightmare from which sinners can never wake. There is torture of all the senses and emotions. Buildings explode into flame in the background. In the foreground, a rabbit carries a victim on a pole, and blood spurts out of the victim's belly. A proud lady is forced to admire her reflection on the backside of a demon. Victims are crucified on a harp or stuck to a lute. A man tries to balance

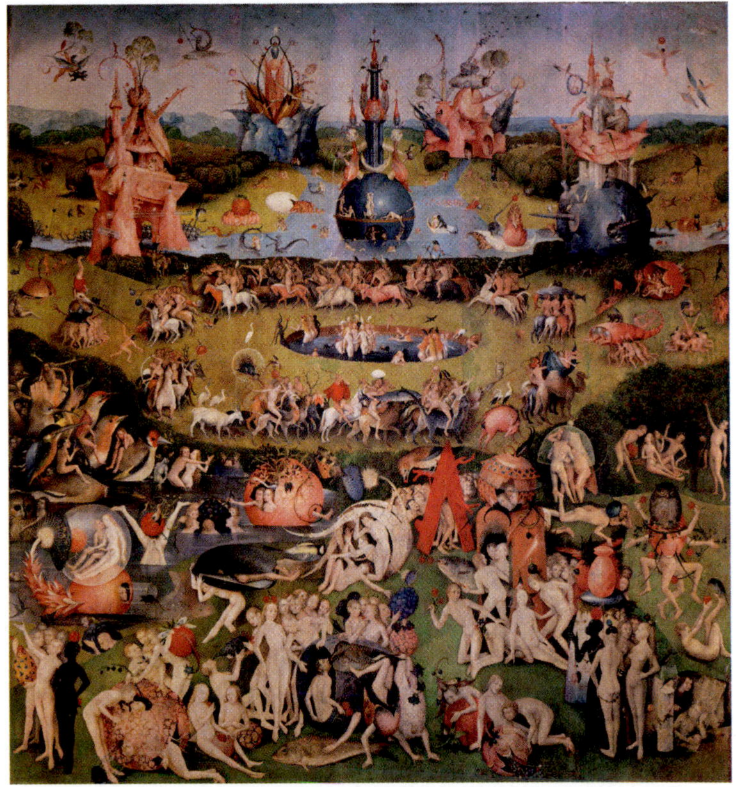

14-37 Central Panel of figure 14-36, *The Garden of Earthly Delights.*

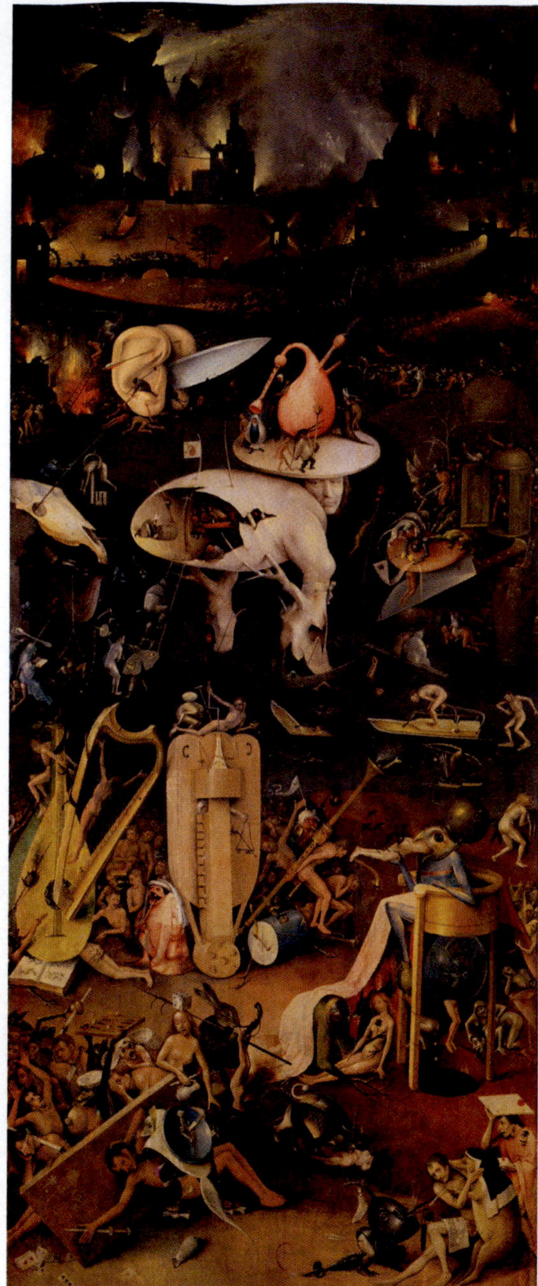

14-38 Right panel of figure 14-36, *Hell.*

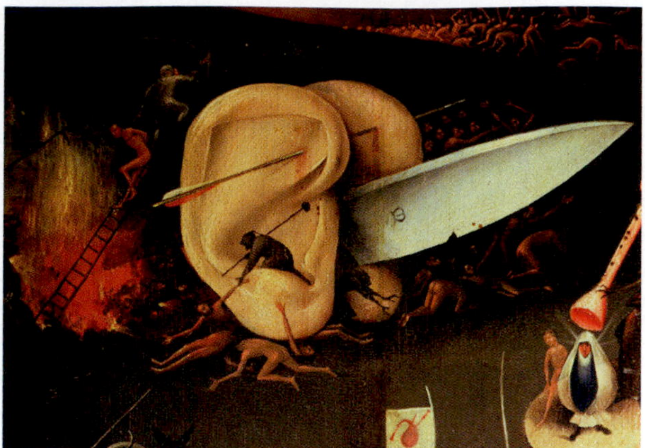

14-39 Detail of figure 14-38.

on a giant skate and heads straight for a hole in the ice. A pair of ears with a giant knife proceeds like a tank, slicing up the damned (**14-39**). The dreamlike reality of the scene is most apparent in the Treeman, who has sinners in his hollow chest and arms rooted in the foundation of Hell. Is he Hell's monarch or another victim?

Surprisingly, the *Garden of Earthly Delights* was an altarpiece for a church. It was a kind of Last Judgment in an age when the Apocalypse was thought to be near. Bosch showed the results of humanity lost to sin and warned that if people continued to live as they did, no one would be saved. Yet one can see little hope for humanity; lost in temporary pleasures, the people in the *Garden of Earthly Delights* give no thought to consequences or repentance. Michelangelo had a similar pessimistic vision thirty years later in his *Last Judgment* (14-26).

GENRE: SCENES FROM ORDINARY LIFE

Although Pieter Bruegel began his career with Bosch-inspired work, he eventually developed his own unique subject matter. Bruegel is best known for his paintings of country life. His *Landscape with the Fall of Icarus* (**14-40**) is an unusual retelling of the ancient Greek myth in a sixteenth-century Flemish setting. Icarus was the son of Daedalus, a clever artisan imprisoned by King Minos of Crete in a fabulous labyrinth (or maze) Daedalus had designed himself. To escape, the father fashioned wings of wax and feathers for his son and himself. He warned his son not to fly too close to the sun, but Icarus ignored him. When his wax wings melted, Icarus fell into the sea and was killed. Usually understood as a cautionary tale about blindly confident youth and reckless ambition, Bruegel presents the myth quite differently. Almost the entire picture is devoted to a scene of a typical day in the fields of Netherlands alongside the sea. The central figure is busy plowing; the plow is shown actually cutting and turning the heavy earth. This is far from the classically inspired mythological paintings of the Italian Renaissance, such as Botticelli's *The Birth of Venus* (14-9) or Raphael's *The School of Athens* (14-21). Imagine how an Italian artist would have portrayed the myth—a marvelous-looking boy filling the can-

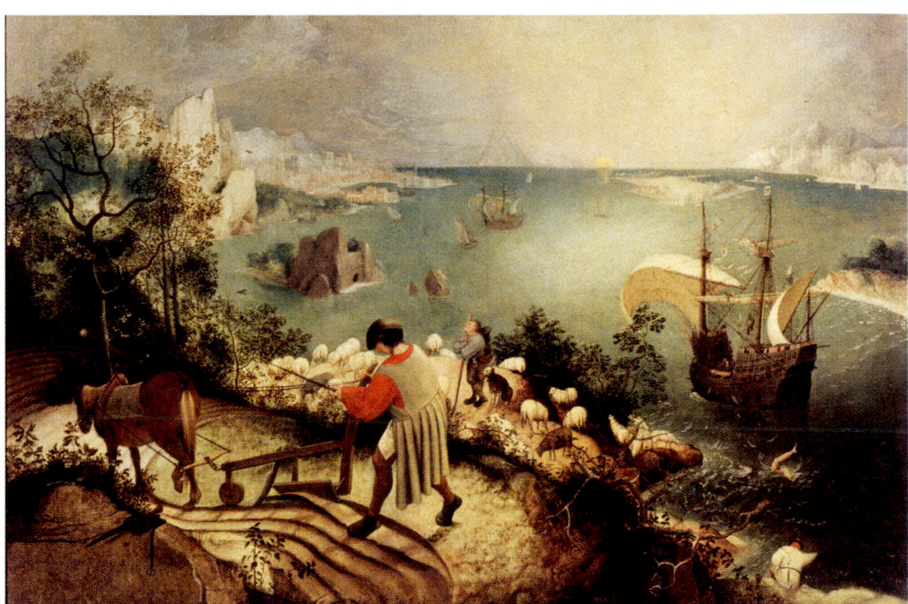

14-40 Pieter Bruegel the Elder, *Landscape with the Fall of Icarus,* c. 1554–1555. Oil transferred from wood to canvas, 29″ × 44 ⅛″. Musées royaux des Beaux-Arts de Belgique, Brussels (photo Speltdoorn).

vas as he tumbles through glorious sun-drenched skies. But here the plunge of Icarus to his death in the sea seems almost incidental to the picture. All we see of Icarus is two tiny legs making a small splash in the water. No one seems to notice the cosmic event. One man looks up, but in the wrong direction; the rest are just busy living their lives.

Bruegel's work is one of the first to use **genre** (ordinary and commonplace) subject matter. His approach to his subject is a statement that not only is our world worth portraying, but it is much more significant than an ancient myth. For most people, cosmic events have less importance than their own everyday concerns.

In *Hunters in the Snow* (**14-41**), a variety of typical winter activities is depicted: hunting with dogs, cooking on outdoor fires, and skating on the frozen pond. Bruegel's painting exhibits an almost perfect balance between the depiction of a subject—in this case, winter as experienced by Flemish peasants—and the formal arrangement of lines, shapes, and colors into a totally satisfying visual experience. The dark silhouettes against the pale snow of hunters, dogs, and trees create a wonderful rhythmic pattern; the icy blue and white of the landscape contrast with the glowing red fire. The line of the trees and the birds leads the viewer's eye irresistibly past the tired hunters and down the hill to the town below. We are able to share the temperature and tones of a winter day from four centuries ago because of Bruegel's mastery. He has allowed us to connect to the lives of people long gone and reminds us that we are all in a cycle of life. We feel that our experiences, like trudging along in the snow, were experienced by past generations and will be for generations to come.

Although it is very different from Leonardo's or Michelangelo's masterpieces, *Hunters in the Snow* is not too distant from the work of Giotto that began the Renaissance. More than two hundred fifty years later, as the Renaissance comes to an end in Europe, Bruegel's pictures bring to a profound realization the humanistic advances of the old Italian master. It would be difficult to find finer examples of realistic space, true emotion, and above all, honestly portrayed human beings.

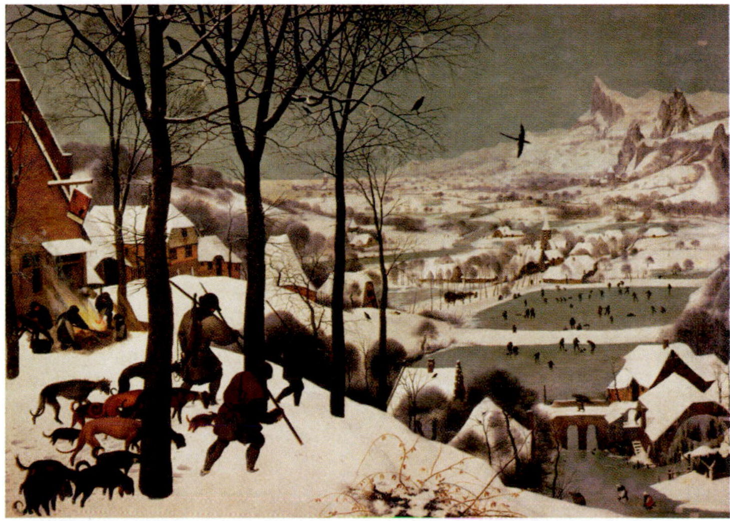

14-41 Pieter Bruegel the Elder, *Hunters in the Snow,* 1565. Oil on wood, approximately 46″ × 64″. Kunsthistorisches Museum, Vienna.

CHAPTER 15

Drama and Light: Mannerism, the Baroque, and Rococo

By the 1530s, with Raphael dead and Michelangelo returning to Florence, Rome was in the hands of a new generation of talented young artists. Yet it was a difficult time for them. The goals of the High Renaissance, already accomplished by Raphael and Michelangelo, did not seem to leave much room for other artists to become outstanding. The young men realized they could not repeat what had already been done, and even if they did, they would find it almost impossible to compete with those great masters. Italy was in a period of serious economic decline. Italian society had been disrupted by repeated invasions from northern Europe. Raphael's achievement of beauty, proportion, grace, and a sense of human virtue no longer seemed appropriate to the troubled times. The young artists decided to abandon the old goals and go beyond nature.

	PERIOD	HISTORICAL EVENTS	
1530–1600	End of the Renaissance Italian Mannerism The Counter Reformation The Scientific Revolution Court of Benin Mughal period in India	Council of Trent begins the Counter Reformation 1545–1563 Vasari publishes *Lives of the Artists* 1550 Mercator publishes map of the world for navigators 1569 Ottoman Turks win Cyprus from Venice 1573	Buried Roman city of Pompeii discovered 1592
1600–1715	First English settlements in North America The Baroque The Enlightenment in Europe Classicism	Shakespeare's *Hamlet* 1600 Tokugawa period begins in Japan 1603 African slaves brought to Virginia 1619 Galileo condemned by Inquisition 1633	Descartes, "I think therefore I am" 1637 Reign of Louis XIV 1643–1715 Isaac Newton presents the law of gravitation in *Principia* 1687 Parthenon damaged during Venetian attack 1687
1750–1790	Rococo Neoclassicism	J.S. Bach, *The Brandenburg Concertos* 1721 Handel's *Messiah* 1741 The American Revolution 1776–1783 The French Revolution begins 1787	

MANNERISM

In Parmigianino's *Self-Portrait in a Convex Mirror* (**15-1**), the young artist is clearly fascinated with the distortions of a mirror. Still, even if the results include a bizarrely oversized hand, the picture appears to be an objective recreation much as Leonardo might have done. But in Parmigianino's *Madonna dal Collò Longo* or *Madonna of the Long Neck* (**15-2**), there is a great deal that would have shocked Leonardo. The space is nothing like the realistic and accurate space created by Renaissance artists. Many of the figures are distorted, and true proportion is seemingly abandoned at whim (notice the tiny prophet at the bottom right). An unfinished column supports nothing. Even more disturbing is the image of the Virgin Mary, an aristocratic figure who holds the infant Jesus at a cool distance. Warmth and love, traditional to this theme, are noticeably absent. The smooth-skinned angels seem like servants. The Christ child looks cadaverous and deformed.

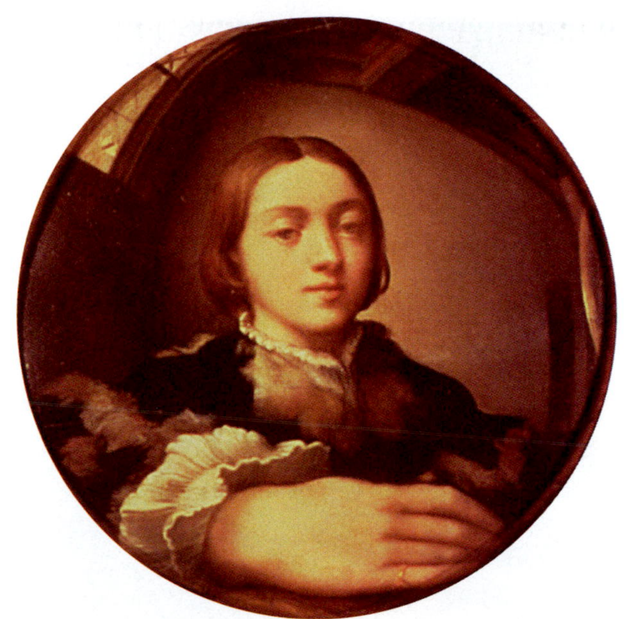

15-1 Parmigianino, *Self-Portrait in a Convex Mirror,* c. 1523. Oil (?) on wood sphere, 15⅜″ diameter. Kunsthistorisches Museum, Vienna, Austria.

ART

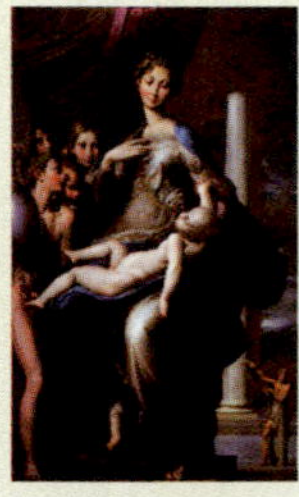

Parmigianno, *Madonna dal Còllo Longo* 1535

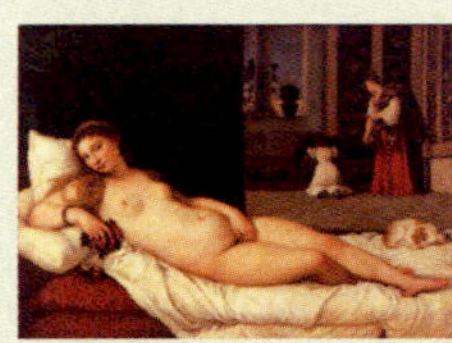

Titian, *Venus of Urbino* 1538

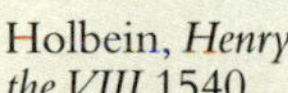

Holbein, *Henry the VIII* 1540

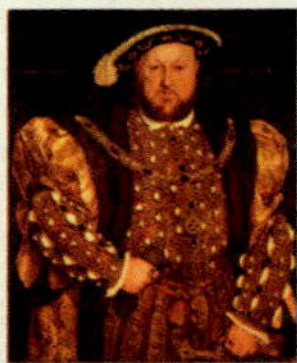

Plaque showing King mounted with attendants, Benin sixteenth century

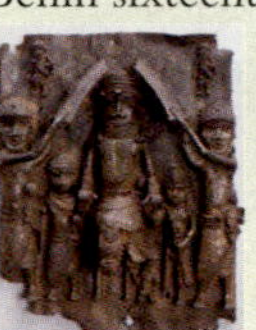

Palladio, Villa Rotonda 1566–1570

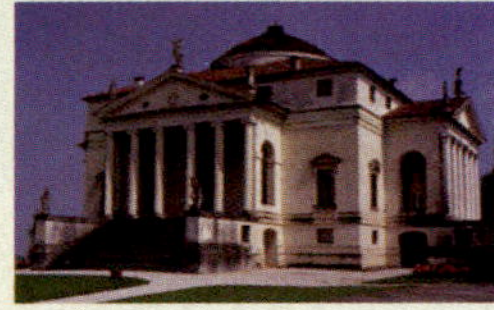

Bernini, *David* 1623

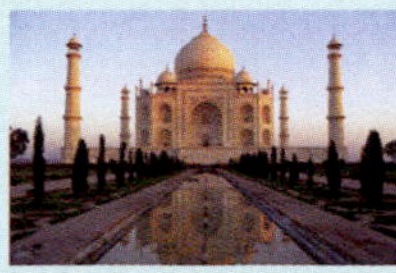

The Taj Mahal 1623–1647

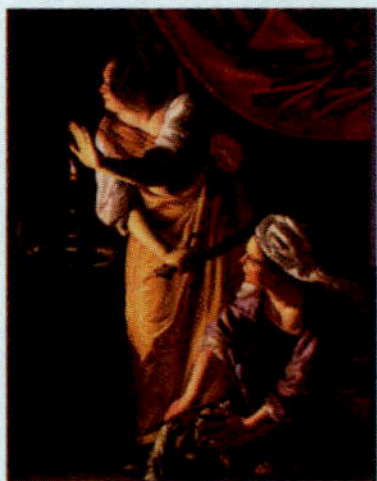

Gentileschi, *Judith and Maidservant with the Head of Holofernes* c. 1625

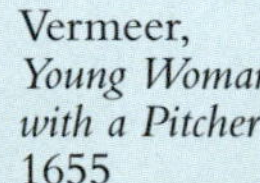

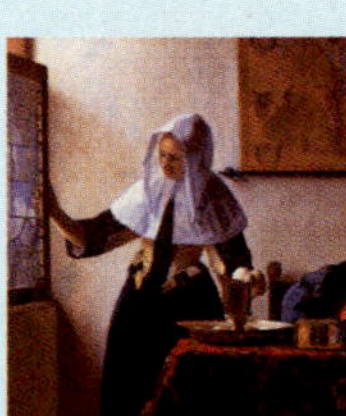

Vermeer, *Young Woman with a Pitcher* 1655

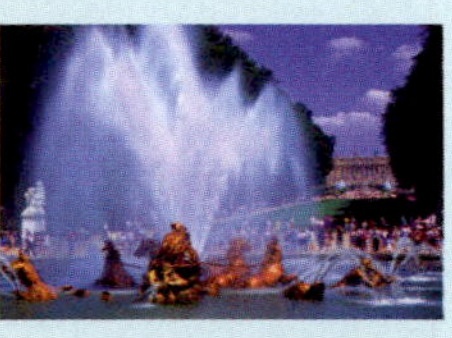

Fountain of Apollo Versailles 1672–1674

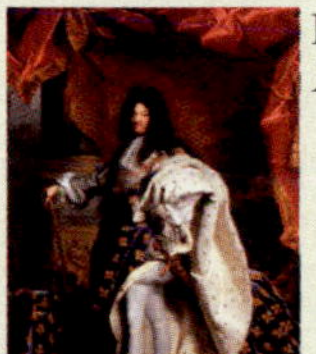

Rigaud, *Louis XIV* 1701

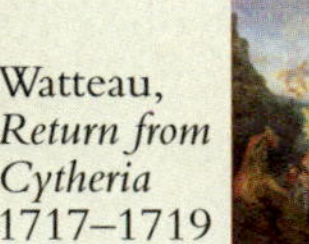

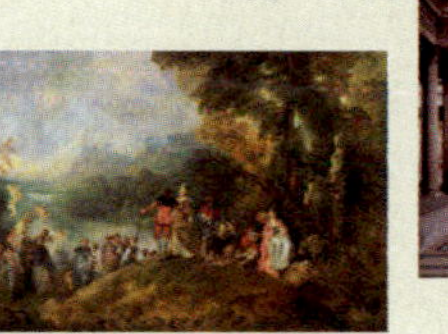

Watteau, *Return from Cytheria* 1717–1719

Soufflot, *Pantheon* 1755–1790

Fragonard, *The Swing* 1766

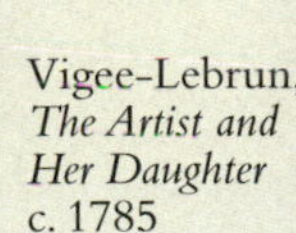

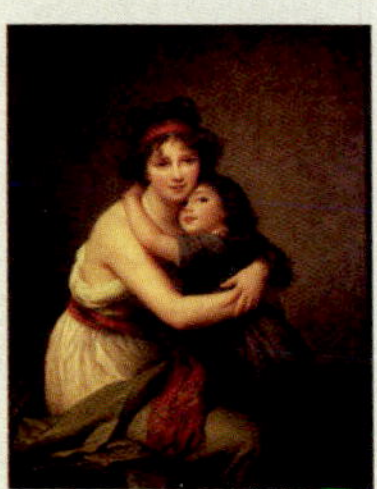

Vigee-Lebrun, *The Artist and Her Daughter* c. 1785

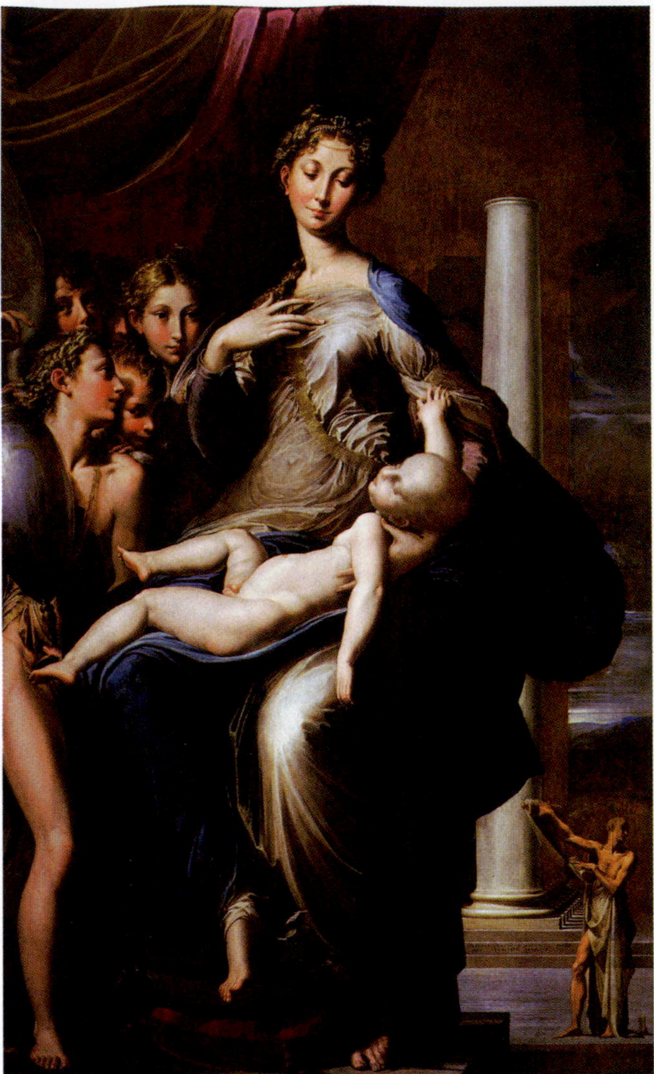

15-2 Parmigianino, *Madonna dal Còllo Longo,* c. 1535. Oil on wood, approximately 7′ 1″ × 4′ 4″. Galleria degli Uffizi, Florence.

Commissioned for a church in Bologna, but never actually presented to his patrons, Parmigianino's strange seven-foot-tall painting is characteristic of a new style called **Mannerism.** Instead of picturing inner and outer realism, Mannerist artists produced demonstrations of their inventiveness and refinement. Their highest goal, which Parmigianino exemplified, was elegance. In Mannerist works, the subject is rarely important and functions only as an excuse for a painting or sculpture. Emotions are ignored for the sake of elegance and what was called "style." The perfect balance of High Renaissance painting had been exchanged for unique, strange compositions, a kind of artful choreography.

One artist of the time wrote:

> in all your works you should introduce at least one figure that is all distorted, ambiguous and difficult, so that you shall thereby be noticed as outstanding by those who understand the finer points of art.

The Mannerists believed the body was most elegant when posed so the limbs and torso resembled the letter *S.* They called this pose the **serpentinata,** or the twisting of a live snake in motion. Many of the distortions in the *Madonna dal Collò Longo* are caused by the characters being forced to conform to S-like shapes.

Federico Zuccaro's portal of the *Palazetto Zuccari* in Rome (3-4) is an example of the Mannerist spirit in architecture. The wild conception of an entrance as a giant mouth leading into a long gullet of a hallway was the kind of idea that intellectuals of the time would call "the modern way."

THE COUNTER-REFORMATION AND TINTORETTO

The Mannerist period was relatively brief. It disappeared at the start of the **Counter-Reformation,** the Roman Catholic Church's attempt to combat the Protestant Reformation that had swept through much of Europe during the early sixteenth century. In 1545, Pope Paul III convened the *Council of Trent* to recommend changes in church policy and new initiatives. Abuses of the past, such as the sale of indulgences, were eliminated. Because the arts were considered one of the most important arenas for fighting against Protestantism, the Catholic Church encouraged a new vitality in Christian art and decoration. It proclaimed the need for art that would entertain and electrify the faithful.

Pictures like the *Madonna dal Collò Longo,* not surprisingly, were considered offensive and decadent by religious leaders who were concerned with the revival of Catholic values. Still, while short-lived, Mannerism served as an important link between the Renaissance and the next great period of art—the **Baroque.** The Venetian artist Jacopo Robusti, known as *Tintoretto,* also bridges this gap and reflects the dynamic spirit of the Counter-Reformation. Elegance and beauty were not enough for this painter; he wanted his pictures to be exciting, to make the biblical stories live. His goal was to combine Titian's rich color with the vigorous drawing and design of Michelangelo.

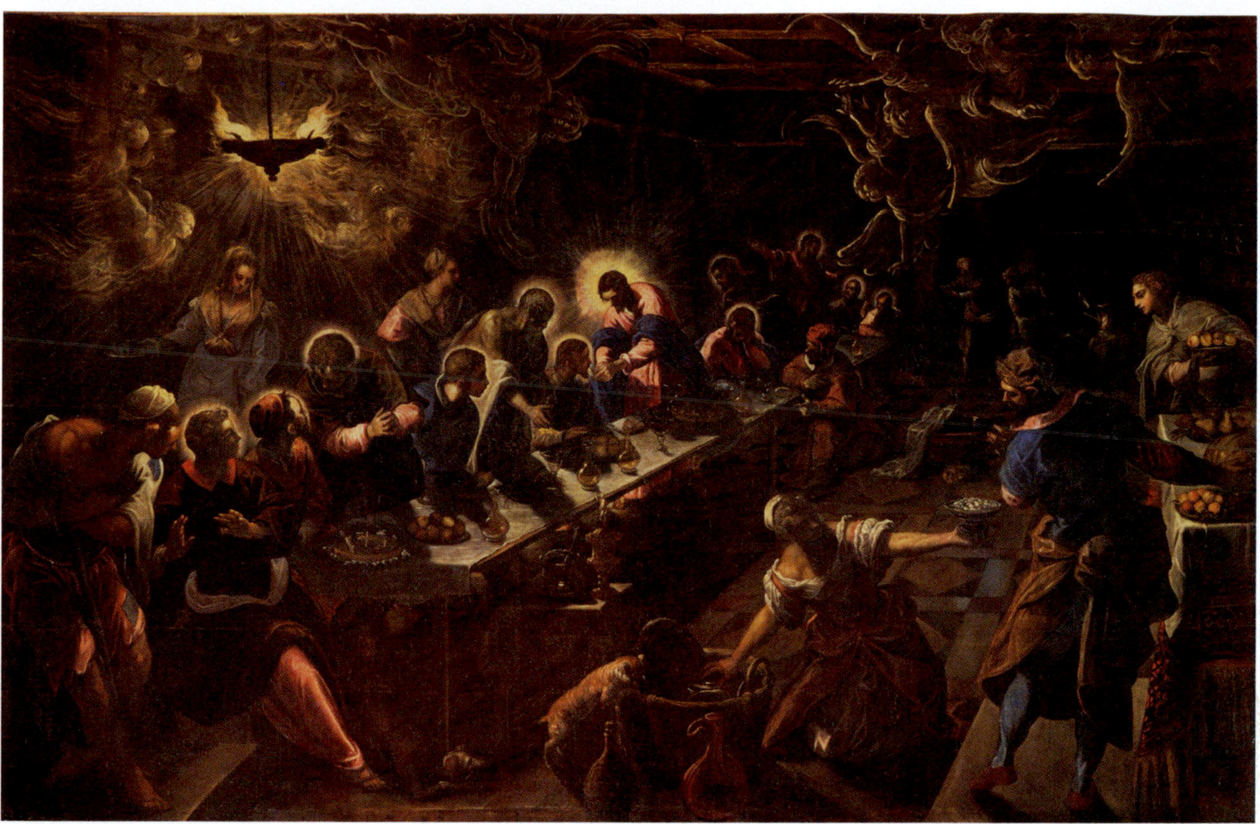

15-3 Tintoretto, *The Last Supper,* 1594. Oil on canvas, 12′ × 18′ 8″. Chancel, San Giorgio Maggiore, Venice.

Tintoretto's pictures *are* dramatic. His *The Last Supper* (**15-3**) is far from a mannerist composition like the *Madonna dal Collò Longo,* with effete, elongated figures arranged in limp poses. Instead, it is full of energy, opposing motions, and swirling lines. Tintoretto was known as *il furioso* for his speed as a painter; this nickname is appropriate to the spirit of his works, too. If we compare Tintoretto's *Last Supper* to Leonardo's (14-16), we will see clearly the difference between an early Baroque and a Renaissance interpretation of the same subject. Leonardo's fresco, painted almost one hundred years before, is harmonious and balanced. The light is natural. The geometry of the room is stressed, and the composition arranged so Christ is at its perfect center. The table on which the story of the last supper is being acted out is a simple horizontal band; the focus of the picture is on the poses of the characters, which seem frozen in time. Leonardo chose to illustrate the human side of the story, the moment when Christ predicts his betrayal by one of his apostles.

Tintoretto's version is totally different. The first visual element we notice is the energetic diagonal of the table, plunging back into space. Christ is not a static, stationary figure, nor is he the clear center of the composition. He stands about halfway down the table, handing out bread. We can distinguish him because his halo bursts forth from his head like a sun (Leonardo's Christ has no painted halo). The heads of disciples also glow against the rich, smoky darkness of the room. The only natural, rather than supernatural, light source is a hanging lamp that emits twisted tongues of flame and coils of smoke. This smoke is transformed into angels, outlined only in white paint, as if drawn on a chalkboard. In the foreground of the picture, Tintoretto has added everyday events, like the servants clearing away food and a cat looking into a basket. This normal scene makes the rest of the picture seem even more miraculous by contrast.

In his painting, Tintoretto has chosen to focus not on the human drama of the betrayal of Judas but on the supernatural meaning of the Last Supper. As he passed out the bread at his last meal with the disciples, Jesus said: "This is my body which is given for you; do this in remembrance of me." This theme was particularly important at the time of the Reformation, because the Protestants claimed that during the Mass (communion service), bread and wine only symbolized Christ's body and blood and were not miraculously changed into his actual body and blood, as the Catholic Church taught.

We can see in the work of Tintoretto many of the attributes that were new to the Baroque movement: its dramatic use of light and dark, its preference for dynamic movement and theatrical effects, and the inclusion of elements of ordinary life in religious scenes.

THE BAROQUE PERIOD

The period of the Baroque (generally defined as spanning the years 1575 to 1750) was one of great confusion. Everything from the place of the earth in the universe to the place of the individual in society was being reconsidered. People questioned authority in religion, in government, in science, and in thought. One of the great thinkers of the time was the Frenchman René Descartes, who began his philosophical inquiry by doubting the existence of anything, including himself. The scientist Galileo used a telescope to study the heavens and declared in 1632 that the earth was not the center of the universe. The Catholic Church was so upset by his discoveries, which appeared to contradict the wisdom of the ages and the Bible itself, that he was forced to renounce them on pain of possible torture and death. England, a Protestant country, was more open to scientific discoveries. There, Sir Isaac Newton began a new era in science when he published his *Principia* in 1687, which announced, among other important physical laws, his discovery of the laws of gravity.

The great age of European exploration and discovery was coming to a close, but an active period of colonization and world trade followed. Borders were changing. Great conflicts were taking place in Europe: bloody wars, rebellions, intense religious disputes, and persecutions.

El Greco

When Domenikos Theotokopoulos, known as *El Greco,* arrived in Spain around 1576, the Spanish Empire was at its very height as a great military and colonial power, but its art was backward and provincial. There had been no great Spanish artists during the Renaissance. Born on the Greek island of Crete, this young man had been trained as an apprentice to make icons, or religious images, in the centuries-old Byzantine style. At the age of twenty, Domenikos Theotokopoulos went to Venice, where he absorbed the lessons of the great Venetian masters Titian and

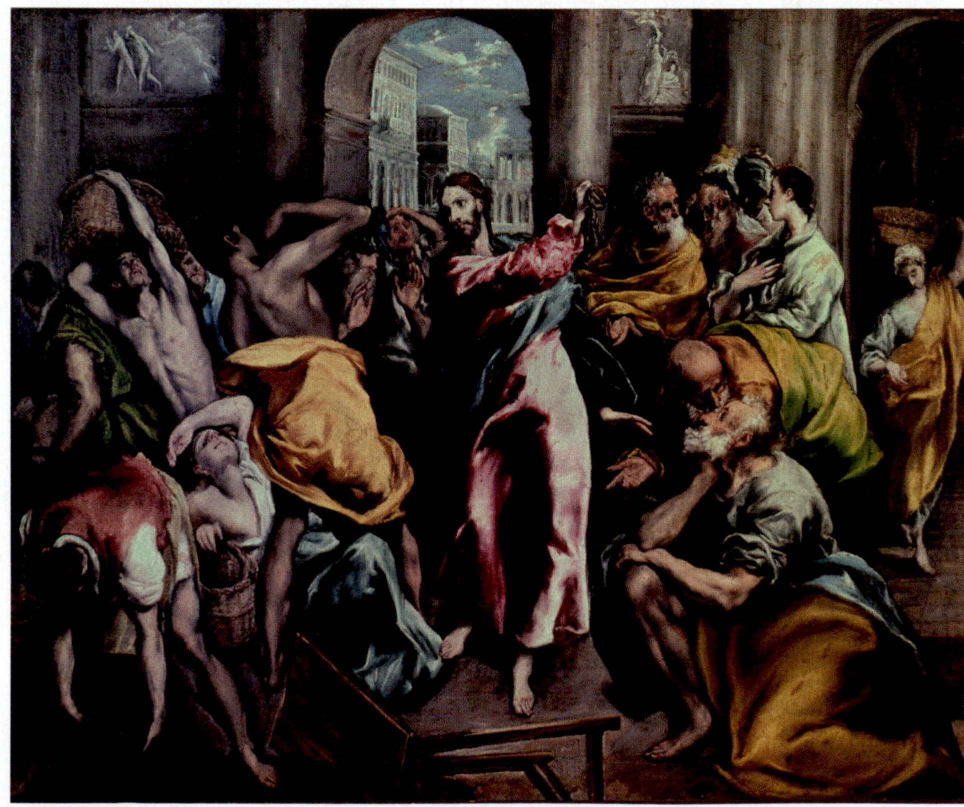

15-4 El Greco, *Purification of the Temple,* 1600. Oil on panel, 3′ 6″ × 4′ 3″. National Gallery, London.

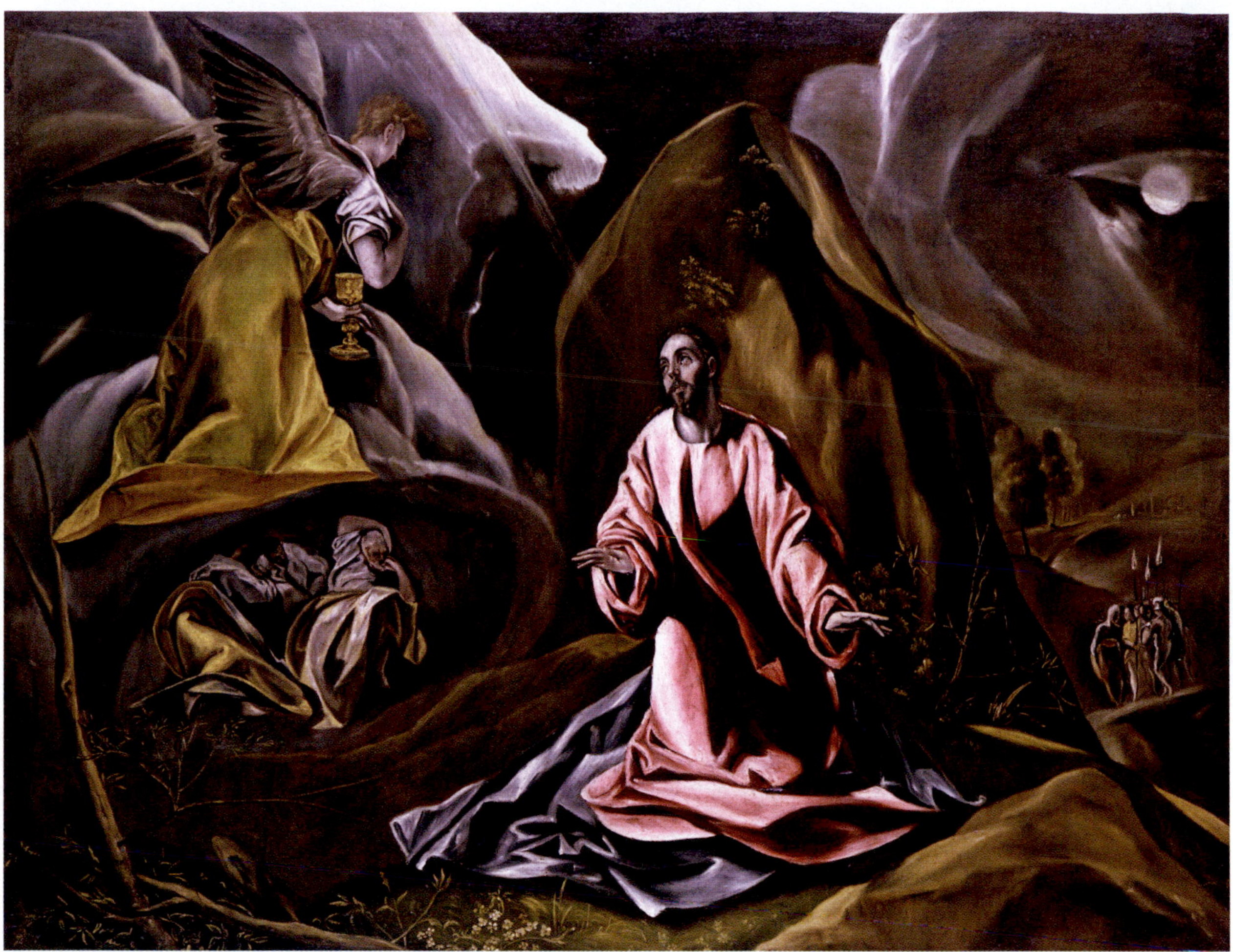

15-5 El Greco, *The Agony in the Garden,* c. 1590–1595. Oil on canvas, 40 ¼″ × 44 ¾″. National Gallery, London.

Tintoretto: their light, color, and energy. He then visited Rome and fell under the influence of Mannerism, especially its elongated, distorted figures. Like Tintoretto, El Greco is sometimes categorized as a Mannerist and, like Parmigianino, he had certainly learned to use the tool of distortion. But his work is not cool and refined; it is intensely emotional and wholeheartedly committed to the goals of the Counter-Reformation.

The *Purification of the Temple* (**15-4**) is a good example of El Greco's mature style. Christ comes thundering in to purify the temple in Jerusalem. The figures on either side pull away and are distorted, as if by the shock waves of Christ's anger. On the left are the lower-class peddlers who react physically to Christ, cringing and trying to protect themselves. Their limbs are arranged in sharp angles; they take strange and twisted poses. On the right are the Jewish elders who react mentally rather than physically, intensely discussing Jesus's actions. The entire picture stresses dynamic diagonal lines rather than the calmer verticals and horizontals favored by Renaissance artists. Even the folds of the costume's drapery are angular and sharp. El Greco's brushstrokes are bolder than those of his contemporaries, giving his paintings a rough, active—rather than smooth and calm—surface.

In some of El Greco's paintings, reality is almost completely ignored in favor of creating a spiritual world. These visions appear modern to our eyes, and, in fact, El Greco became more famous and popular in the twentieth century than he was in any of the intervening centuries since his own time. In *The Agony in the Garden* (**15-5**), deep religious feeling seems to heave up the very ground on which Christ kneels. The figures are wrapped in strange, swirling cocoons—rocks, clouds, drapery all resemble each other, framing and isolating Christ, the angel, and the sleeping disciples. El Greco gave up the truth of the eyes for an inner truth. The Renaissance is now far behind us.

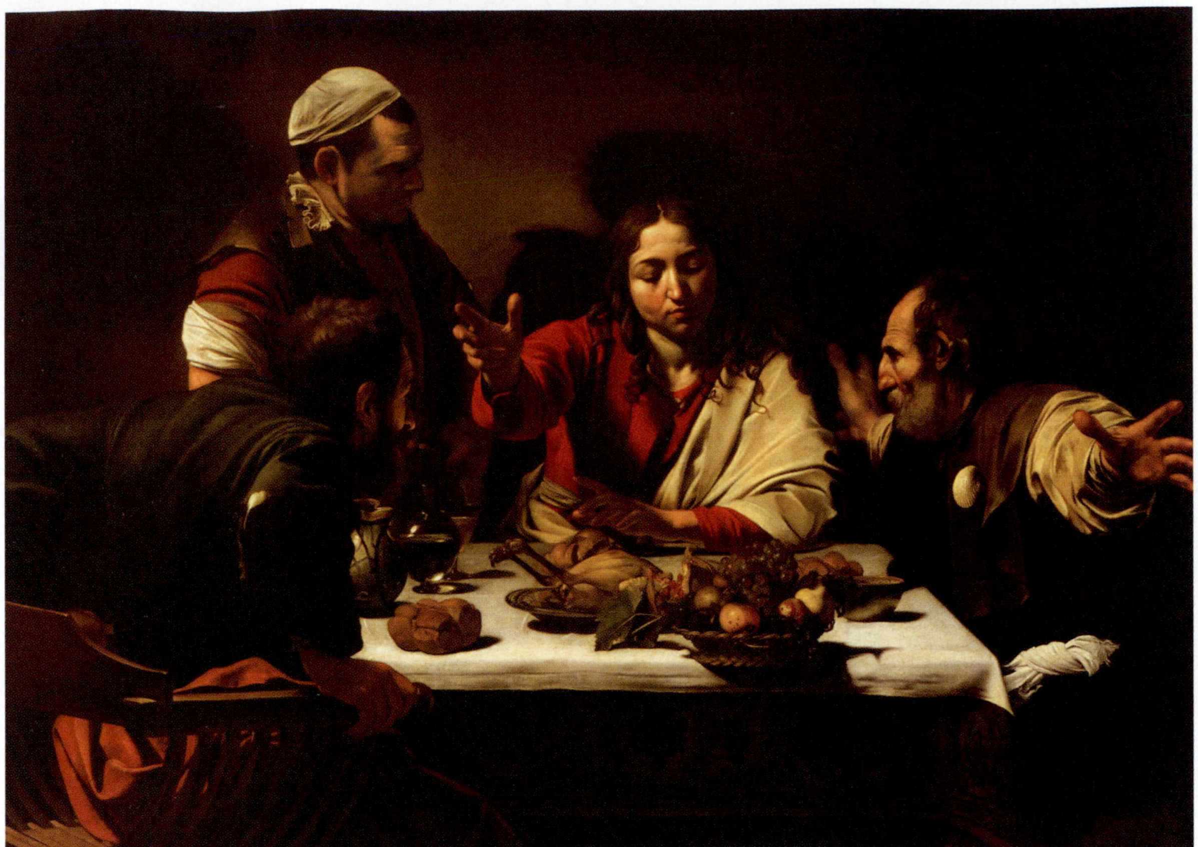

15-6 Caravaggio, *The Supper at Emmaus,* c. 1598. Oil on canvas, 55½″ × 77¼″. National Gallery, London.

Caravaggio and Naturalism

As Mannerism declined in Rome, a new artist emerged who would become a brilliant innovator. This painter had grown up in northern Italy, where painting traditions were less influenced by the Renaissance desire for perfection and harmony, and a style of greater realism prevailed. Michelangelo de Merisi, called *Caravaggio* after the small town where he grew up, became the greatest Italian painter of the seventeenth century and one of the most influential of the entire Baroque period.

Caravaggio was orphaned at the age of eleven and came to Rome when he was seventeen. This exceptionally talented artist was also an outsider and soon considered a violent, unpredictable rebel. In *The Supper at Emmaus* (**15-6**), Christ and his attendants are depicted as real working-class people, with torn clothing and worn faces. This New Testament story takes place after Christ's resurrection, but before his followers realize that he has truly risen from the dead. Two of the disciples were on the road to Emmaus, a small town outside Jerusalem, and were joined by a stranger whom they did not realize was Jesus because "their eyes were kept from recognizing him." Stopping in the village, they urged their fellow traveler to stay with them overnight. As they sat down to eat, Christ "took bread, and blessed it, and broke it, and gave it to them" in a reenactment of the Last Supper. At this point "their eyes were opened, and they knew him." It is this very moment of illumination that Caravaggio chose to illustrate.

The architecture of the room, so important in Renaissance paintings, has been eliminated here in favor of the flat backdrop of a wall. The viewer is quite close to the figures, who make dramatic gestures that almost seem to leap out of the picture into real space. For instance, the man on the left, whom we see from the rear (a favorite visual device of Carravagio's, allowing us the illusion of peeking into a real scene) is about to push his chair backward, and his elbows jut toward us as if they might break through the canvas. On the right, an elderly apostle thrusts out his hand in a dramatic gesture, like an actor on the stage. But the most theatrical effects are provided by the stark lighting—illuminating the face of Jesus, accentuating the wrinkles of the careworn faces, focusing our attention on the most important gestures, and casting dark shadows on the wall behind Christ's head in a "reverse" halo.

Consider how different this painting is from the work that preceded it, even the work of Tintoretto and El Greco. Here, although a miraculous event is taking place, there are no supernatural halos or angels, no distortions, just ordinary people painstakingly observed. Caravaggio shares with Titian and El Greco, however, his taste for dramatic and theatrical effects, a taste that is typically Baroque. In *The Conversion of Saint Paul* (**15-7**), he topples the figure of the saint directly toward the viewer, his head almost touching the bottom edge of the canvas. The dramatic action of the scene seems to be frozen by a flash of light—the horse's hoof is shown in midair.

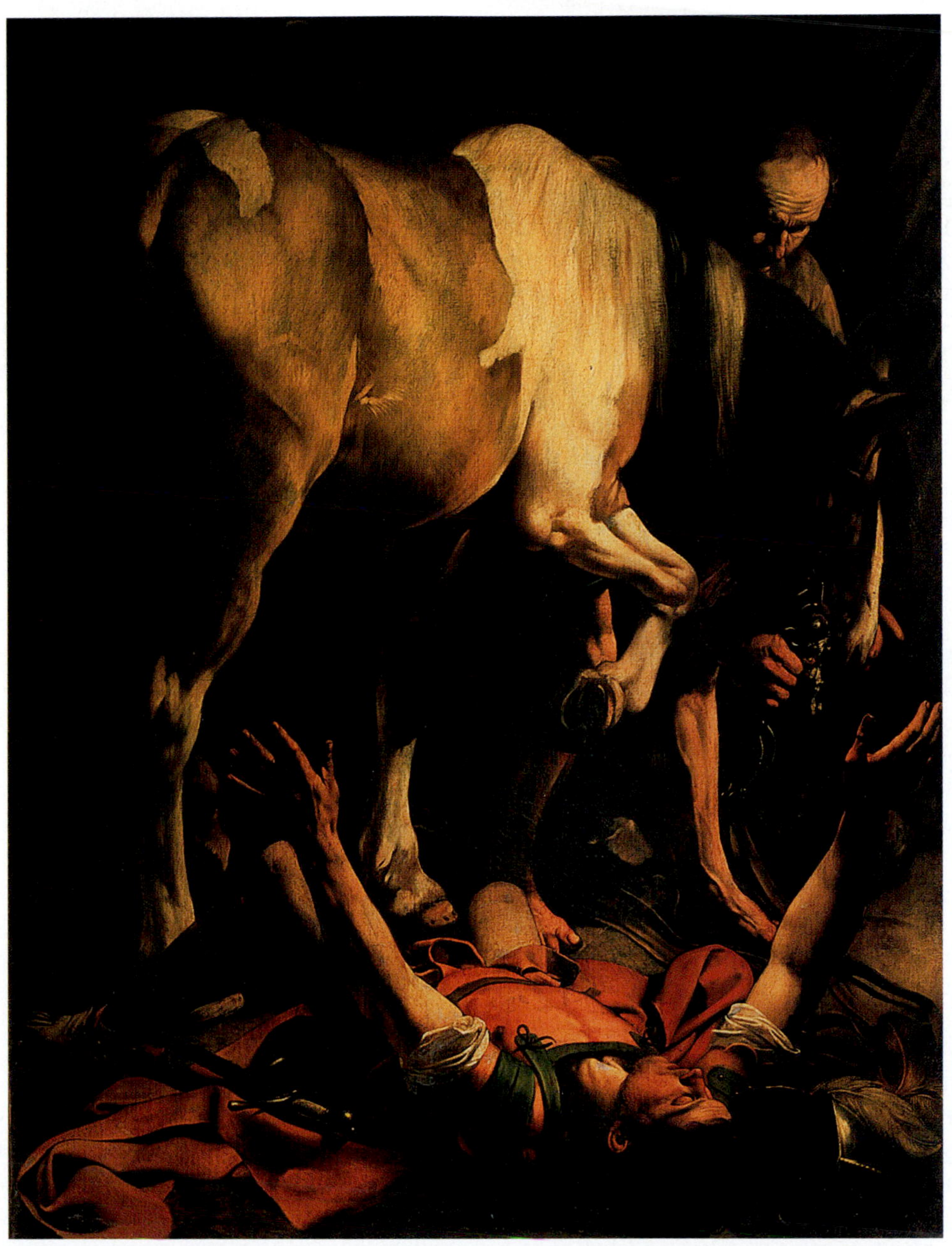

15-7 Caravaggio, *The Conversion of Saint Paul,* c. 1601. Oil on canvas, approximately 7′ 6″ × 5′ 9″. Chapel, Santa Maria del Popolo, Rome.

Saul was a Roman citizen who delighted in persecuting the early Christians. On the road to Damascus—a city in Syria where he was headed to continue his persecutions—he experienced a vision. In his own words: "Suddenly there shown from heaven a great light all about me, and I fell to the ground." Then Saul heard the voice of Jesus asking, "Why do you persecute me?!" and directing him to go to Damascus. Blinded by his experience, Saul had to be led into the city, where he met a devout Christian and was converted and baptized. He took the name of Paul and became the greatest leader, writer, and theologian of the early Christian Church.

Here we see a mystical moment portrayed with high realism. Saul has just hit the hard ground and lies as if in a trance, listening to the voice of Jesus. The New Testament account states that although they saw the light, the men who accompanied Saul could not hear this miraculous voice. True to the story, Caravaggio pictures a horse and servant drawing back in surprise, unsure of what is going on. Miraculous light is a perfect subject for Caravaggio, who, as we saw in *The Supper at Emmaus* and in *The Sacrifice of Isaac* (2-11), had been using the power of light symbolically in his paintings to indicate supernatural happenings. Caravaggio's use of **chiaroscuro,** the dramatic contrast of light and dark, would influence many artists and would be copied throughout Europe.

Caravaggio was condemned by the art critics of his time as a "naturalist," while his religious paintings were condemned by the clergy. Some said that his way of painting meant the end of painting. They felt that his use of working-class people to portray the apostles and Christ himself was offensive, even sacrilegious, despite the fact that Christ and his followers had actually been poor, simple men and women. The controversy over Caravaggio's pictures reflects a difference of opinion about what the correct style for Counter-Reformation painting should be. While some admired his revolutionary honesty and directness, other critics felt that Caravaggio's work did not serve to promote the Catholic faith. The most powerful members of the Roman establishment—the papal court, for example—preferred artists who simply glorified the church and its saints.

Caravaggio lived only thirty-nine years (he died of malaria after being banished from Rome by the pope), but he left behind a great body of work that influenced artists during the entire Baroque period. His revolutionary naturalism and dramatic use of chiaroscuro light would prove to be one of the strongest legacies in the history of art. Among the many great artists who learned from his work were Velázquez in Spain, Rubens in Flanders, and Rembrandt in Holland, but first we will discuss his direct influence on another Italian painter, Artemisia Gentileschi, who also suffered from the prejudices of Roman society, although for different reasons.

Artemisia Gentileschi: The Spread of *Tenebroso*

Most women artists of the Baroque period were the daughters of painters; for example, Tintoretto had a favorite daughter who acted as an assistant on many of his huge canvases. Artemisia Gentileschi's father, Orazio, was a talented follower of Caravaggio and taught her many of his techniques. Most of Gentileschi's pictures show women as biblical or mythological heroines. One reason Gentileschi specialized in the female figure was that she was easily able to find models and to study female anatomy in great detail. It would have been considered improper for her to study the nude male figure; this limitation hampered female artists until the twentieth century.

The Old Testament story of Judith and Holofornes was one that Gentileschi painted several times. Holofornes was an Assyrian general who laid siege to an Israelite city. To save her town from the attacking general, Judith dressed in her most beautiful clothes, then crept with her maid behind enemy lines. They were soon captured and taken to the tent of the general. He was attracted to Judith and invited her to dine. She drank with him until he was unconscious, and when he passed out, she took his sword and, with the help of her maid, chopped his head off. Judith and the maid then escaped, and the next morning displayed the head of Holofornes on the city walls, sending his invading army into panic and retreat.

Some critics speculate that Gentileschi's attraction to this theme of feminine revenge was the result of an unfortunate experience early in her career. When she was a young woman, her father arranged for her to be tutored in perspective by another painter named Tassi, who raped her several times, and then promised to marry her. Her father took this man to court, not only for raping his daughter, but also for stealing some of his pictures (Tassi had already been convicted of arranging the murder of his own wife). During the trial, Artemisia was tortured on the witness stand with thumb screws—a primitive type of lie detector. To add to her humiliation, the rapist was jailed only a few months, and then eventually acquitted. After the trial, Gentileschi married a man from Florence and left Rome for the next ten years. Strangely, because of this episode in her life, throughout history she has had the reputation of a wanton woman.

Other critics dismiss the importance of her early traumatic experience and point out that the subject of Judith and Holofernes was a common one of the period for male and female painters. No one can deny, however, that Gentileschi brought an unusual passion and realism to her versions of the theme (she painted at least six). In an earlier version, Gentileschi chose the gruesome moment of the actual decapitation. In the later picture, considered her masterpiece, *Judith and Maidservant with the Head of Holofernes* (**15-8**), the artist chose instead to imagine the time after the general has been murdered, when Judith and her maid are waiting to escape from the enemy stronghold. It is a huge work, more than six feet tall, so the figures are larger than life-size. Gentileschi has used a single light source—a candle flame—then interrupted it with Judith's raised hand, so it throws weird shadows on her figure. The mood is suspenseful. We glimpse the figures as they pause in the midst of their secret crime, perhaps hearing a sound and fearing discovery. Judith covers the candlelight calmly, holding her sword in readiness, while the maid tries to cover the head.

This is a painting in the **tenebroso,** or dark manner. The followers of Caravaggio who specialized in such night scenes were known at the time as *Caravaggisti*. Gentileschi was not only one of the Caravaggisti, but she also spread the style throughout Italy as she moved from Rome to Florence, back to Rome, and on to Naples, visiting Genoa and Venice as well. Through the influence of Caravaggio and followers like Gentileschi, the Baroque style became truly an international art movement.

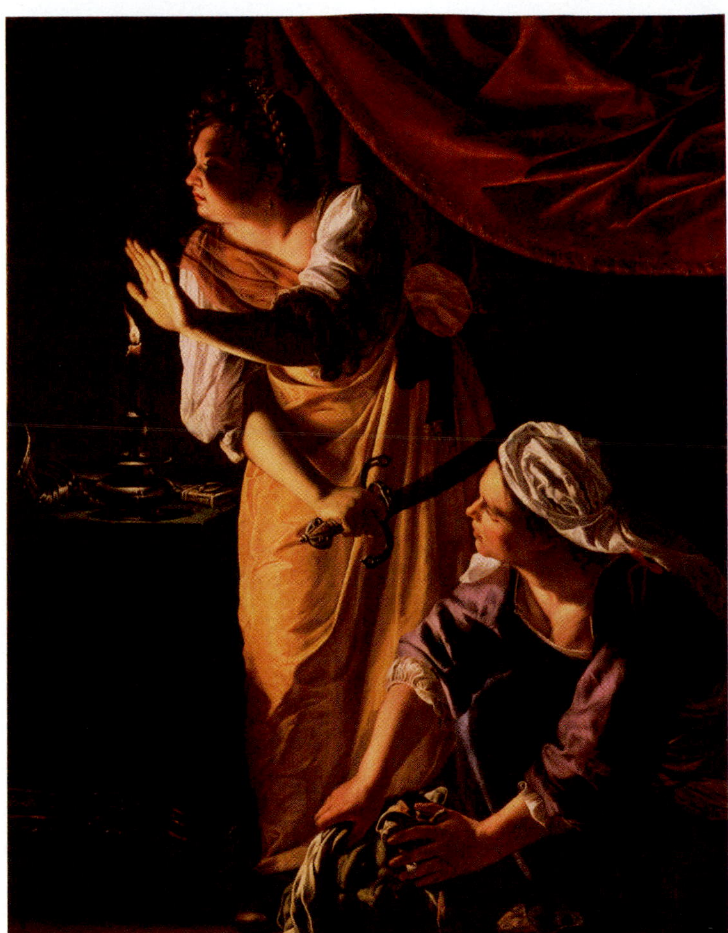

15-8 Artemisia Gentileschi, *Judith and Maidservant with the Head of Holofernes,* c. 1625. Oil on canvas, approximately 6′ × 4′ 8″. Detroit Institute of the Arts (gift of Leslie H. Green).

Bernini

In contrast to the unfortunate Caravaggio, Gianlorenzo Bernini was a highly successful and internationally famous architect and sculptor. Only Michelangelo was ever held in as high esteem by popes, the powerful, wealthy art patrons, and other artists. Like Michelangelo, Bernini was a brilliant sculptor in marble, but he was also a painter, architect, and poet. Unlike Michelangelo, Bernini was known for his great charm and wit; he was fond of people and a good husband and father.

Bernini was only twenty-five or so when he sculpted *David* (**15-9**), one of his masterpieces. Just as the contrast between Tintoretto's *Last Supper* and Leonardo's can be used to illustrate the differences between Renaissance and Baroque painting, one can see the changes in sculpture by comparing Bernini's *David* with Michelangelo's (14-18). Both were tours de force, carved when the artists were in their twenties. Unlike Bernini, Michelangelo strove for harmony and the ideal beauty of a perfect young man. His enormous statue (more than fourteen feet tall) is in elegant proportion; the figure stands motionless, self-contained. But Bernini's *David* is captured at a specific moment—the split second before he releases his slingshot at the giant Goliath. There is great dynamic energy in this figure, the first version of David to show the subject in motion. Bernini's David is a mature man who contorts his less-than-ideal features into a grimace of concentration as he

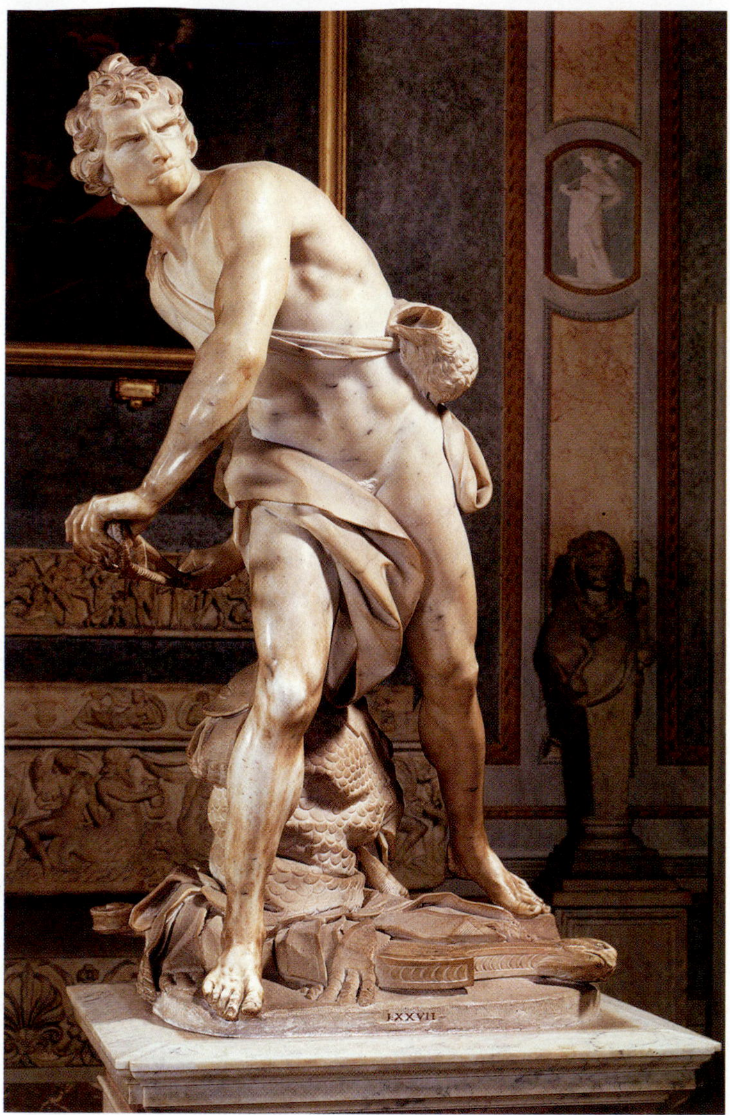

15-9 Gianlorenzo Bernini, *David,* 1623. Marble, life-size. Galleria Borghese, Rome.

puts total effort into his coming shot. The statue's gaze is so intense that the unseen Goliath becomes part of the sculpture. In this way Bernini breaks down the barrier between art and the real world. Realistic details also make the biblical event convincing. As in his *Apollo and Daphne* (9-5), Bernini skillfully creates a variety of textures in stone (flesh, drapery, leaves, and hair), as well as incredibly minute work like the taut rope of the sling. The differences between the two Davids are reminiscent of the contrast between calm and balanced Classical sculpture, such as the *Doryphoros* (12-17), and the writhing motion typical of later Hellenistic sculpture like the *Laocoon* (12-21).

The type of work for which Bernini became most famous was not the sculpting of individual statues, however powerful, but the creation of total artistic environments. *The Ecstasy of Saint Theresa* (**15-10, 15-11**), which combines sculpture with architecture and painting, was designed for a chapel in the small Roman church of Santa Maria della Vittoria. The materials include white marble, colored marble, gilded bronze, stucco, fresco, and stained glass. Here, the effect of the whole is far greater than the sum of the parts. The ceiling of the chapel is decorated with a fresco of angels frolicking on billowing clouds. To the sides, statues of the Cornaro family members observe the scene from boxes, as if at the opera. At center stage is Bernini's marble statue of Saint Theresa in ecstasy.

Saint Theresa of Avila was a sixteenth-century Spanish nun and mystic who lived about the time that El Greco was painting in Spain. Through her widely circulated writings, she became an important

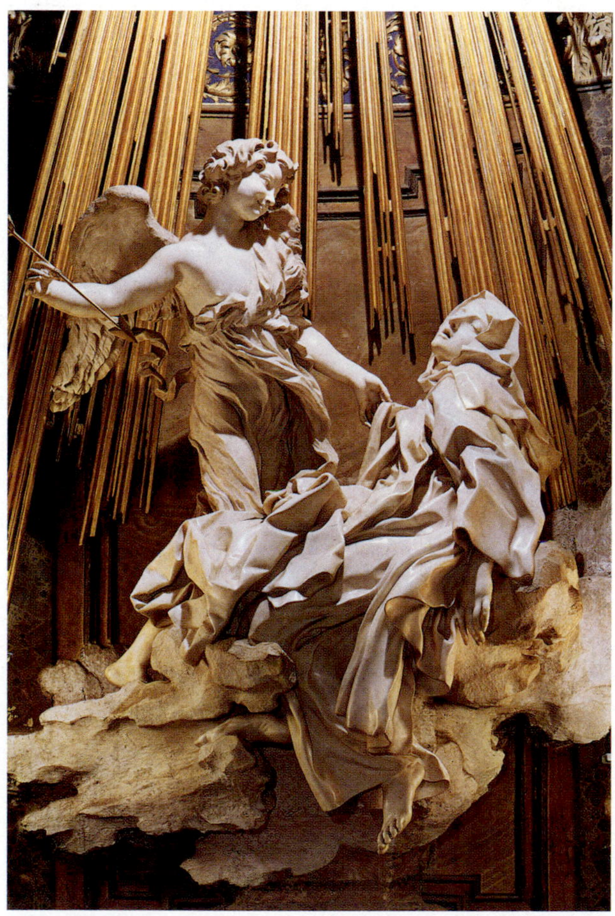

15-10 Gianlorenzo Bernini, *The Ecstasy of Saint Theresa,* 1645–1652. Marble, group 11′ 6″ high. Cornaro Chapel, Santa Maria della Vittoria, Rome.

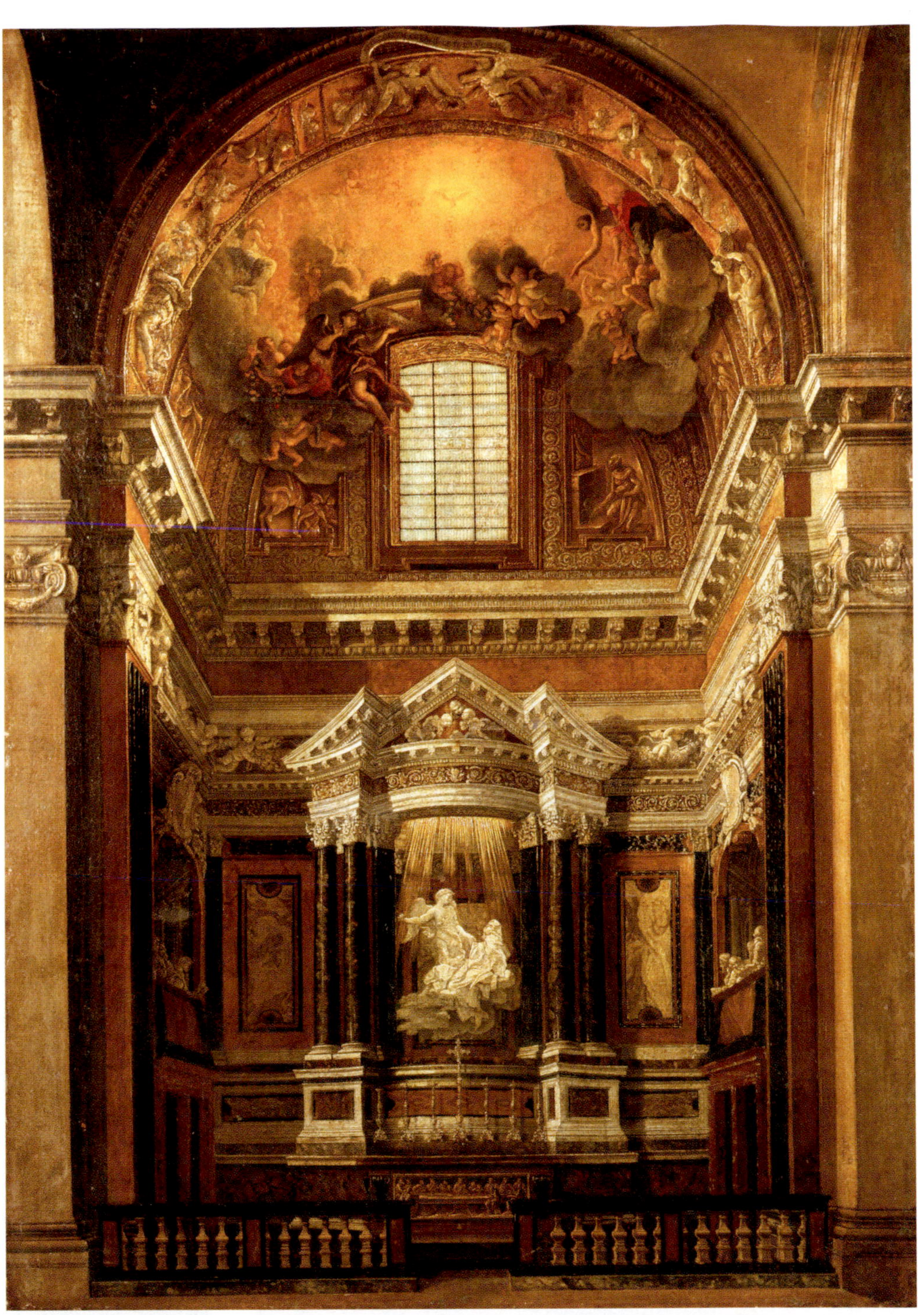

15-11 Gianlorenzo Bernini, interior of the Cornaro Chapel, 1645–1652, Santa Maria della Vittoria, Rome. Eighteenth-century painting, Staatliches Museum, Schwerin, Germany.

saint of the Counter-Reformation. Many of these writings describe her personal, mystic visions. For this chapel, Bernini illustrated a spectacular vision of a visit from an angel, about which Saint Theresa wrote:

> In his hands I saw a great golden spear and at the iron tip there appeared to be a point of fire. This he plunged into my heart . . . again and again and left me utterly consumed by the great love of God. The pain was so acute that I groaned aloud several times; yet the pain was so sweet that no one would wish to have it go away.

Bernini mixes realism and illusion here just as he mixes media. He shows Saint Theresa's spiritual passion as physical: Her head lolls to one side in rapture, her body falls back limp, her bare foot escapes from beneath her voluminous habit. Even her clothing

A GLOBAL VIEW

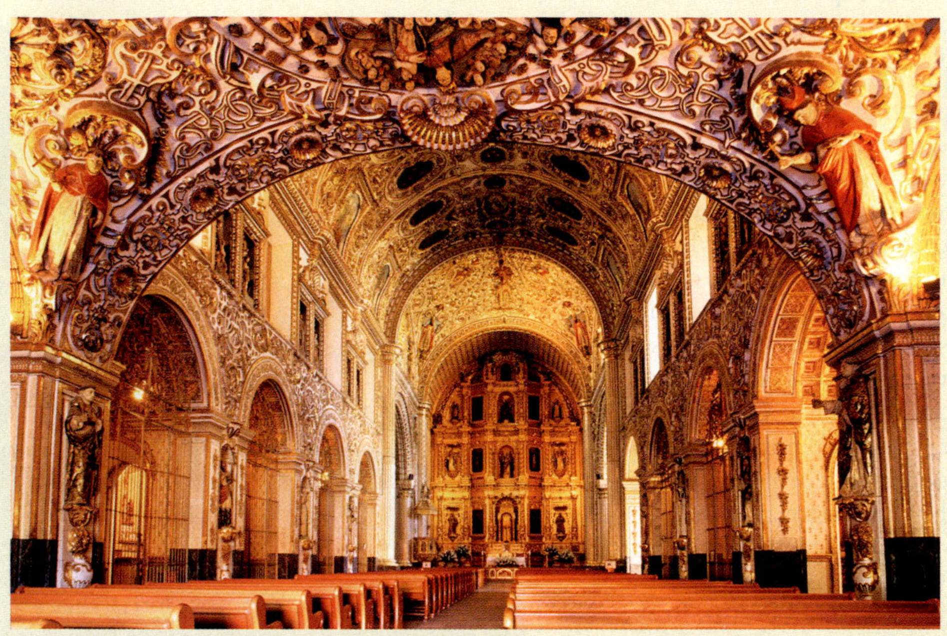

15-15 Interior, Santo Domingo de Guzman, Oaxaca, Mexico.

The church's main altar is covered with more than sixty thousand sheets of gold leaf and devoted to the Virgin of Guadalupe, the patron saint of Mexico. Each sunset, during the late afternoon mass, light pours in through the choir window, so that the entire church glows with a heavenly light and no space seems to remain unadorned. No wonder the British writer Aldous Huxley described it as "one of the most extravagantly gorgeous churches in the world." Here the Baroque reached its furthest extreme.

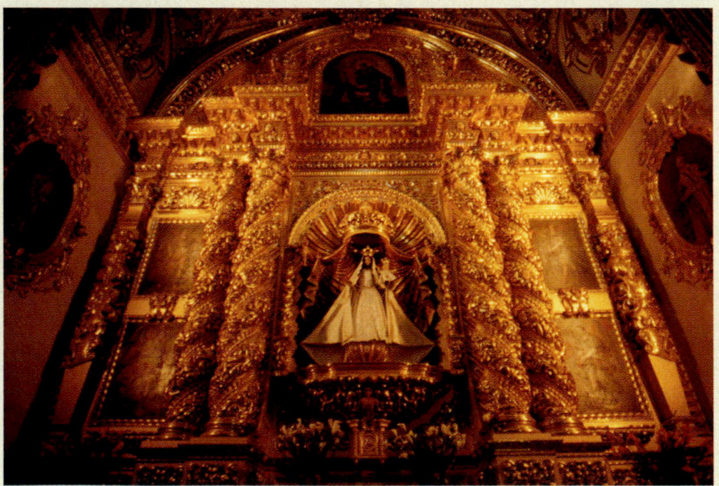

15-16 Chapel of the Rosary, Church of Santo Domingo de Guzman, Oaxaca, Mexico.

Baroque Naturalism in Spain: Velázquez

The greatest master of Spanish painting and one of the greatest painters of the Baroque was Diego Velázquez. Inspired by the simple, realistic paintings of Caravaggio, his approach to art flew in the face of the flamboyant trends popular in his day and went even further in the direction of naturalism. Surprisingly, when he was twenty-four, the honest realist was appointed the court painter to the king. More surprisingly, Velázquez succeeded in his new role without changing his approach. Even though he never flattered the royal family, he was made a court chamberlain and given the rare honor of a home attached to the palace with its own studio. For thirty years, he painted King Philip IV, his family, and members of the court.

Las Meninas (**15-17**) is Velázquez's great masterpiece, a huge work, ten and one-half by nine feet tall. It demonstrates a mastery of realism that has seldom been surpassed. Here he shows a moment in the

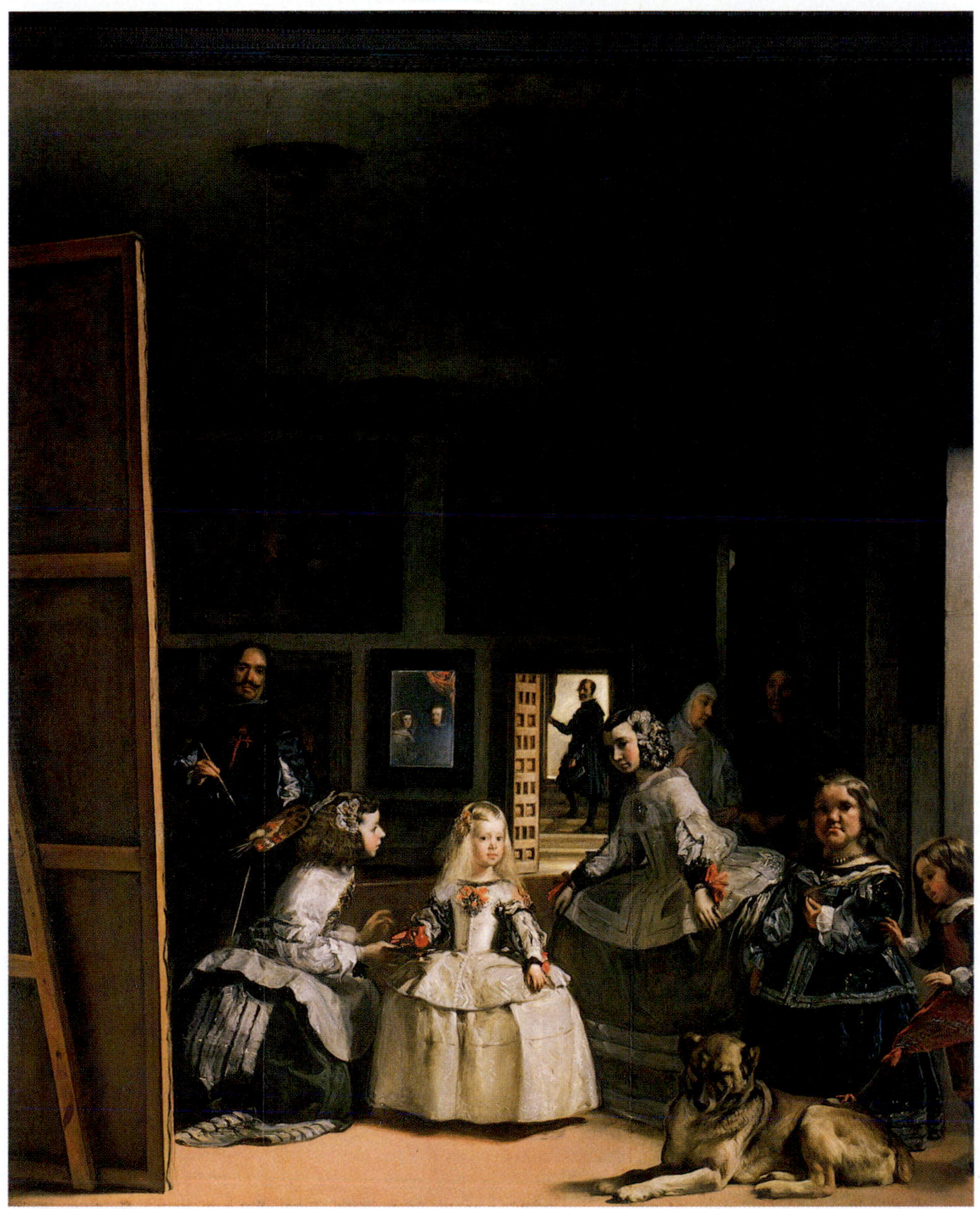

15-17 Diego Velázquez, *Las Meninas,* 1656. Oil on canvas, approximately 10′ 5″ × 9′. Museo del Prado, Madrid.

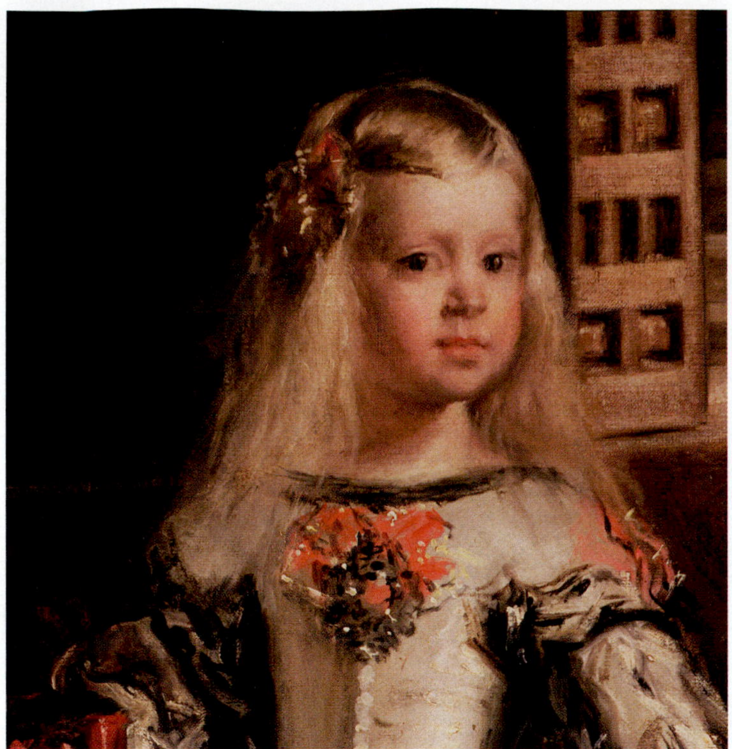

15-18 Detail of figure 15-17.

life of the court. Because Velázquez is an important member of that court, he shows himself painting a picture. But what is he painting? There are two possible answers. It might be a portrait of the princess, who is in the center of the picture (and therefore the painting we are looking at), or it is the king and queen, whose reflections we can see in the mirror at the back of the room. In either case, it is a life-size portrait of the royal family and their attendants. At the center are the Infanta Margarita (detail, **15-18**) with her maids of honor, a dog, a dwarf, and a midget. The Spanish royal family had a tradition of keeping dwarves and midgets around them, almost as toys, for entertainment. Velázquez always portrayed them with sympathy and respect, rather than as victims or clowns. Perhaps he felt that his situation was not so different from their own. In the background, a court official pauses to glance back through the doorway. Notice how the painter honors the viewer by giving us the same viewpoint as the king and queen.

Velázquez, unlike the northern Renaissance artists van Eyck and Holbein, did not attain realism by observing and copying minute details. Instead, he captures the impression of realism through suggestive brushstrokes, a method that would influence not only other Baroque painters but also the Impressionists of the nineteenth century. The hair and corsage of the princess, for instance, are painted in loosely rather than reproduced line by line (15-18). Yet, if one steps back to view the entire scene, it is as if the strokes come together to produce an extremely convincing impression of reality. To use a second example, Velázquez's dog looks much more real than the dog in van Eyck's *Giovanni Arnolfini and His Bride* (14-29), even though the artist has not taken the trouble to paint it hair by hair. He paints what he sees rather than what he knows intellectually is there (we do not see every hair on a dog from across the room). In this way, he can create an illusion of reality that is actually more vivid than an enormously detailed work.

THE BAROQUE PERIOD IN THE NORTH

The fortunes of Spain and its territory, the Netherlands, were linked during the Baroque period. The Netherlands was particularly important to the Spanish Empire because it had many important centers of trade. But the Protestant cities of the Netherlands longed for political independence and religious freedom from their devout Catholic rulers. In the 1620s, the Netherlands was plunged into civil war. The rebellion ultimately succeeded in driving the Spanish from the northern half of the Netherlands, which became the *Dutch Republic,* an independent Protestant state. The south, *Flanders,* whose people were predominantly Roman Catholic, remained a territory of Spain. This division of the Netherlands is approximately the division of Holland and Belgium of today (see map).

Rubens

During this period, an artist from Flanders, Peter Paul Rubens, spent months in the Spanish court as a diplomat and befriended the younger painter Velázquez. They studied the Spanish royal art collection together. Velázquez felt honored to accompany the man he thought of as the model of a learned painter. Besides being the most learned, Rubens was also the most popular, most successful, and most internationally famous artist of the Baroque age.

Like many northern painters, Rubens gloried in the textures of real things and portrayed in fine detail leaves, flesh, and clothing. But he was profoundly influenced by a trip to Italy when he was twenty-three. Remaining eight years, he filled his notebooks, many of which have survived, with studies of the great masters. *The Elevation of the Cross* (**15-19**) was painted soon after Rubens returned to Flanders. We can recognize the rich color of the Venetians and the active, muscular figures of Michelangelo, as well as the dramatic lighting of Caravaggio—a potent combination. As the men strain and pull, they exhibit extraordinary muscular vitality. The strong diagonal of the cross and the many directions of activity are brought to a dynamic equilibrium by the young master.

Rubens completed Albrecht Dürer's mission of a century earlier and created a synthesis of the northern and southern European painting styles. Before Rubens, painters in the north had mostly painted on a small scale. *The Elevation of the Cross,* like much of his work, is enormous, more than fifteen feet tall. Rubens's grand, powerful religious pictures suited the Catholic Church's desire to regain its past strength during the Counter-Reformation.

Rubens's art has a buoyant energy, a love of splendor that also made it perfect for the rich and aristocratic courts of Europe. He received commissions from all of the Catholic monarchs in Europe

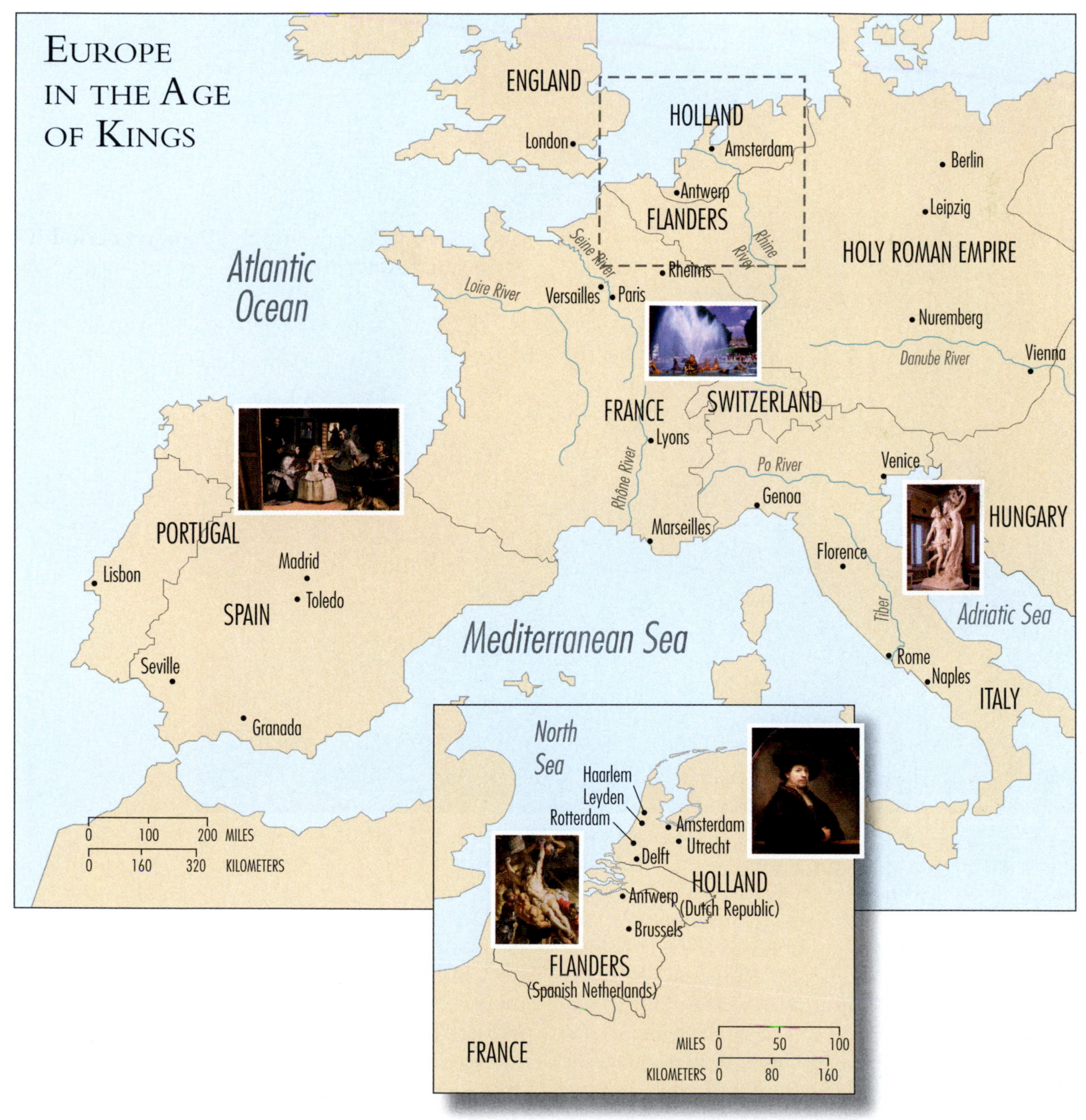

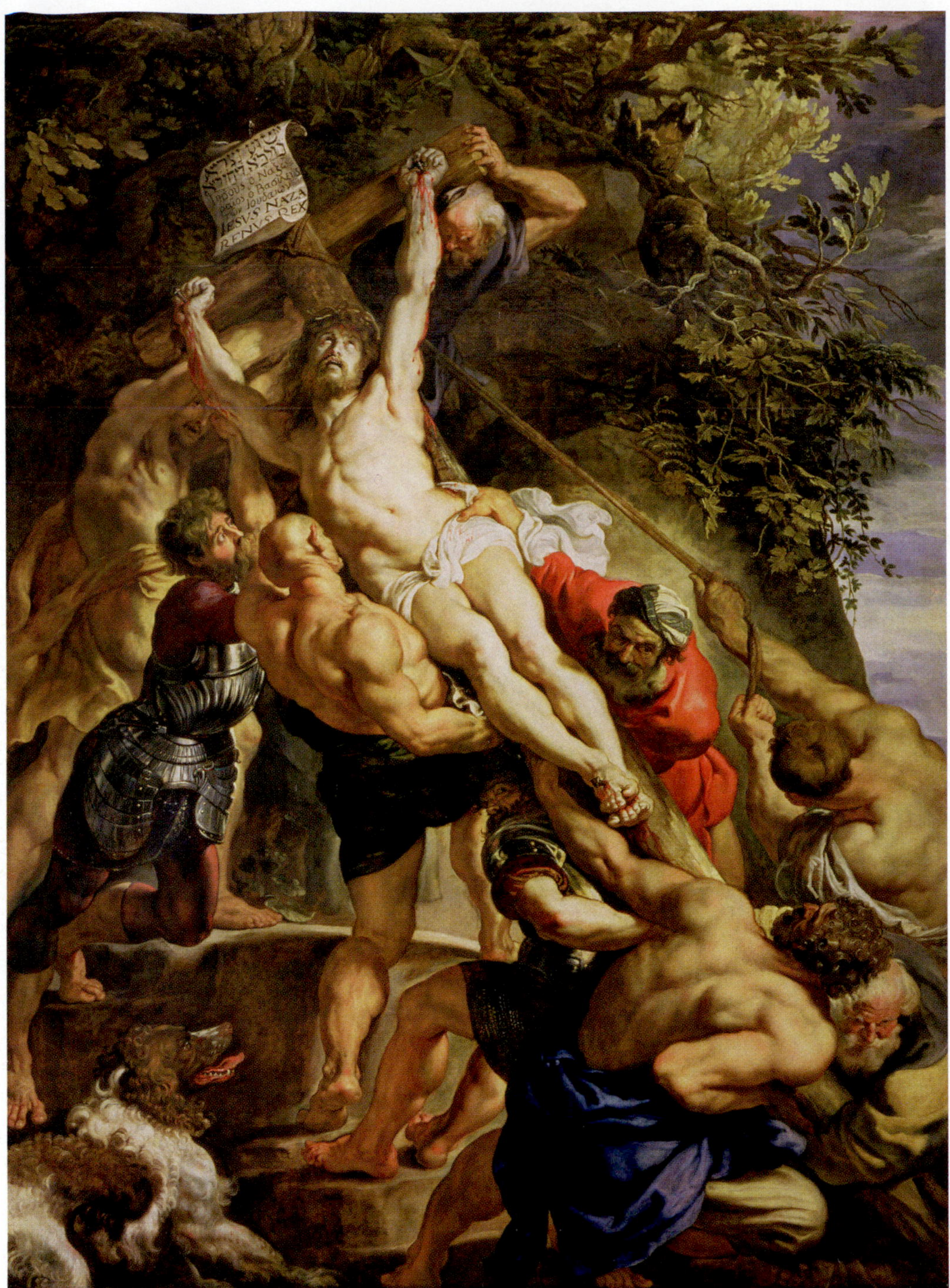

15-19 Peter Paul Rubens, *The Elevation of the Cross,* 1610. Oil on canvas, 15′ 2″ × 11′ 2″. Antwerp Cathedral, Belgium.

and was even knighted in England. The *Arrival of Marie de' Medici at Marseilles* (**15-20**) shows why his work was so popular with the powerful. The arrival of a young Italian princess to marry King Henry IV of France is extravagantly pictured. Rubens makes it a mythic, exciting event. The swirling figures and the decoration give the picture great vitality. There are no Christian symbols, even though it celebrates the union of Henry and the Catholic princess Marie de' Medici. Instead, pagan gods and goddesses surround the scene as if they arranged the union. Fame flies above trumpeting the great news.

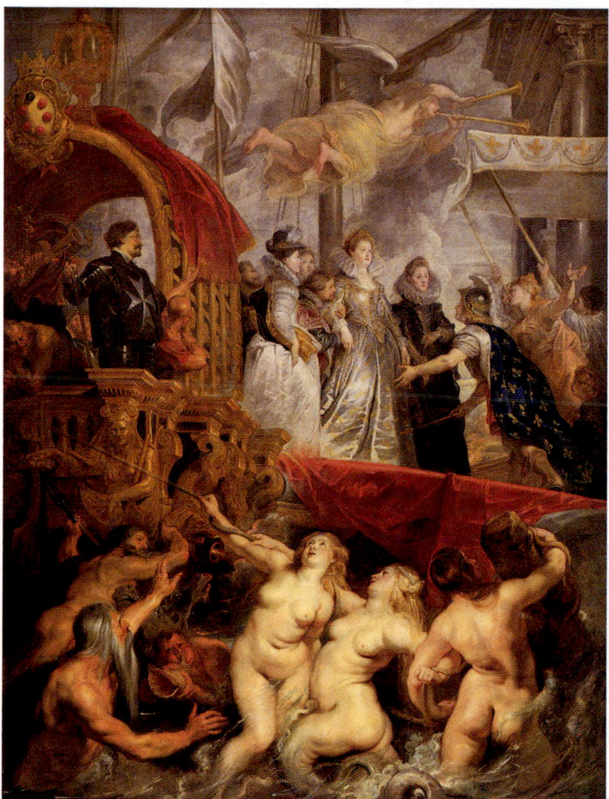

15-20 Peter Paul Rubens, *Arrival of Marie de' Medici at Marseilles,* 1622–1625. Oil on canvas, 61″ × 45⅔″. Louvre, Paris.

Rubens lived like no painter before him. He had an excellent education and spoke many languages fluently. When he traveled from country to country in Catholic Europe, besides painting portraits, he acted as an official diplomat for Flanders and the Spanish king on matters of the highest importance. Respected and successful, he was a very rich and happy man who dominated the Catholic art world. Rubens was also a loving husband and father who recorded his family in many pictures. *Self-Portrait with Isabella Brant* (**15-21**) was painted on the occasion of his wedding. Modest in comparison with the mythic arrival of Marie de' Medici, it portrays a young couple of substantial means whose relationship combines love and mutual pride. Their hands touch gently as they sit surrounded by honeysuckle, whose textures are delicately portrayed.

Rubens was a painter who loved not only the souls of women but also their flesh. In terms of today's standards of athletic slimness, his females may appear unattractively pudgy, but in the world of the seventeenth century, starvation was more to be feared than excess weight. Plumpness was a sign of wealth and upper-class status. For Rubens, it was also a glory of nature. Today, these proportions are often described as *Rubenesque.* In the *Garden of Love* (**15-22**), his pink-cheeked, double-chinned, dimpled females seem to promise all the delights of the flesh to their devoted swains. Some even glance provocatively at the viewer, almost enticing one to enter the world where they recline languorously on the grass or stroll with their arms about each other's waists. There is nothing pornographic or openly erotic in this scene, yet it is clearly a celebration of physical rather than spiritual love. At the time he painted this picture, the widower Rubens (in his fifties) had just married his second wife, a lovely girl of sixteen. You can see them at the left of the picture, where a cupid pushes her into his arms.

Rubens's home in Antwerp (pictured in the *Garden of Love* and still standing) could easily be mistaken

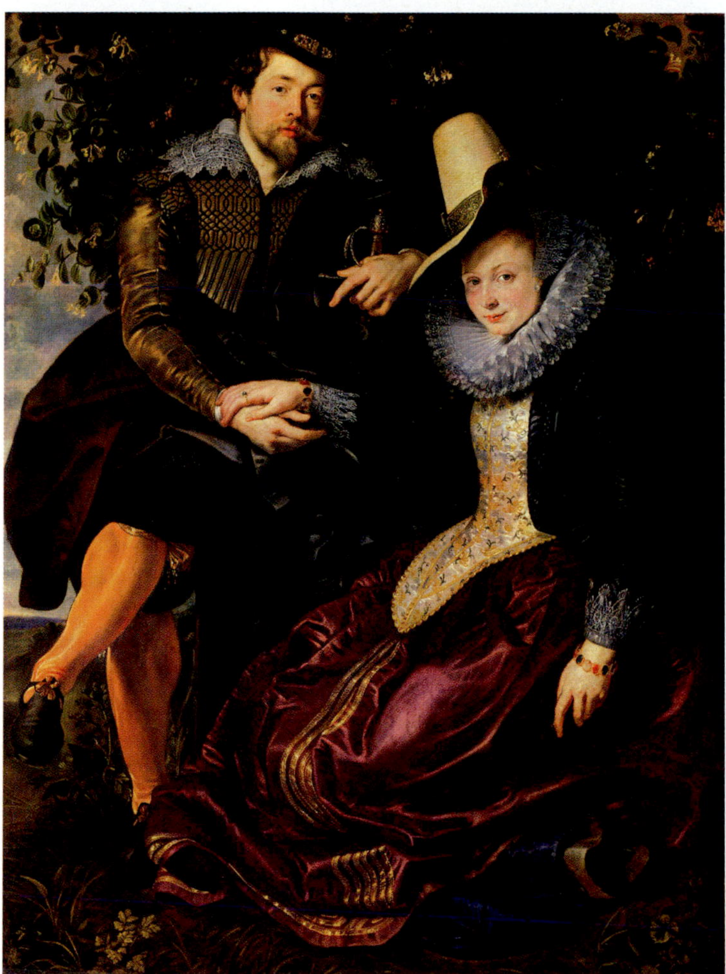

15-21 Peter Paul Rubens, *Self-Portrait with Isabella Brant,* 1609–1610. Oil on canvas, 69″ × 53½″. Alte Pinakothek, Munich.

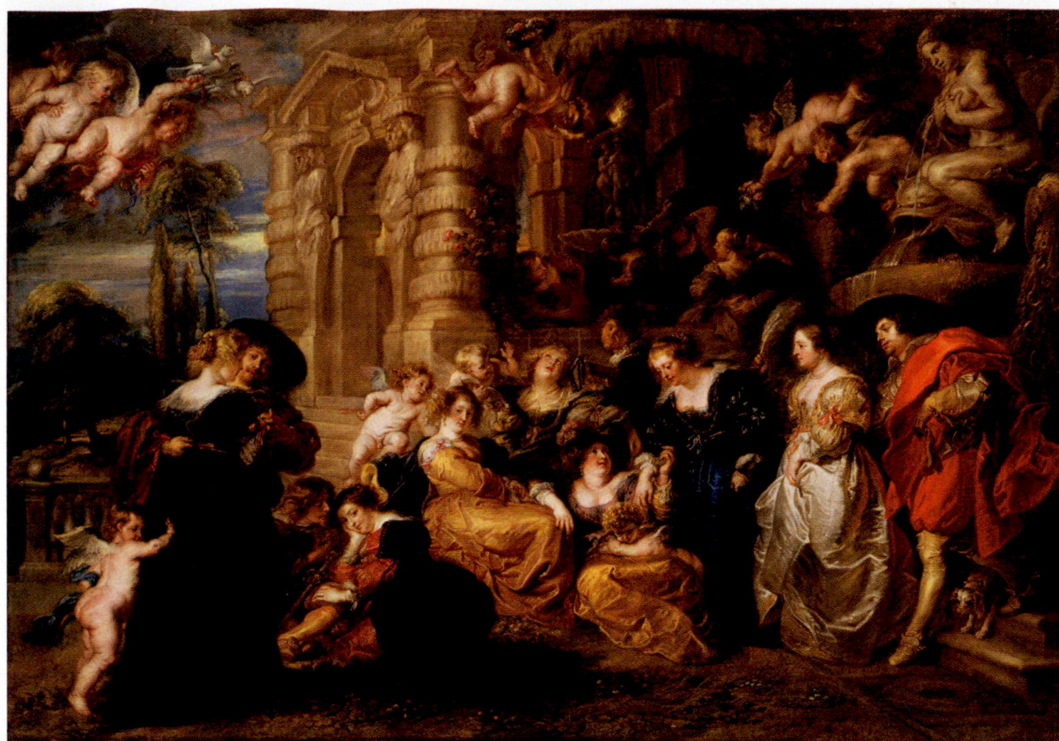

15-22 Peter Paul Rubens, *Garden of Love,* c. 1632–1634. Oil on canvas, 6′ 6″ × 9′ 3½″. Museo del Prado, Madrid.

for a palace. Attached to it was a huge workshop with many assistants, functioning like a painting factory in Rubens's time. He charged clients by the size of each painting and how much he had worked on it. Because the quantity of commissions he was offered could never have been accomplished by a single man in one lifetime (or even three), most of the talented artists of Flanders worked in the Rubens workshop.

The Dutch Republic

The art world of the Dutch Republic was very different from the one Rubens dominated. The art of the Protestants of northern Netherlands was entirely different, as was their art market. The Protestant Church did not patronize artists, and there was no large wealthy aristocracy. Holland was governed by a bourgeois, middle-class society of merchants. In this atmosphere, an art reflecting middle-class life began to flourish. Dutch painting became concerned with the everyday life of the towns, and with portraits. In Holland, the humanistic development of art that began in the fourteenth century with Giotto reached its climax in a profound naturalism. One of the most accomplished masters of the beauty of simple scenes was Jan Vermeer.

In Vermeer's work, as in that of his fellow countryman's, the Renaissance painter Bruegel, we see an everyday event raised to a high artistic plane. *Young Woman with a Water Jug* (**15-23**) is an extraordinary work of art. The subject of a woman standing at a window holding a pitcher in her hand is utterly simple, and one Vermeer used more than once. What is unique about this painting is the combination of vivid realism and idealism. The realism is seen in the artist's ability to depict textures flawlessly. The rug appears thick and shaggy; the design is clearly woven into the fabric rather than drawn on top. The silver of the pitcher and bowl reflect the rug exactly as they would in real life. The woman's plain headdress is absolutely readable as stiff, wrinkled linen. Still, the face and costume of the figure seem to have been simplified. The pale blue light from the window bathes the picture in a beautiful cool radiance. The simple geometric volumes of her head, along with the repeated curves of the bell-shaped collar and skirt, create a quiet, harmonious, almost spiritual, image.

In the Dutch Republic, artists, like other merchants, sold their wares independently, and success was ruled by the marketplace. Many Dutch artists, to be more easily identifiable in the marketplace, specialized in one kind of painting. Vermeer's specialty was interiors. Others specialized in still lifes, animals, or the new, popular subject of landscapes.

Portraits were Frans Hals's specialty. While he was one of the most prominent of the first generation of artists in the new Dutch Republic, we know

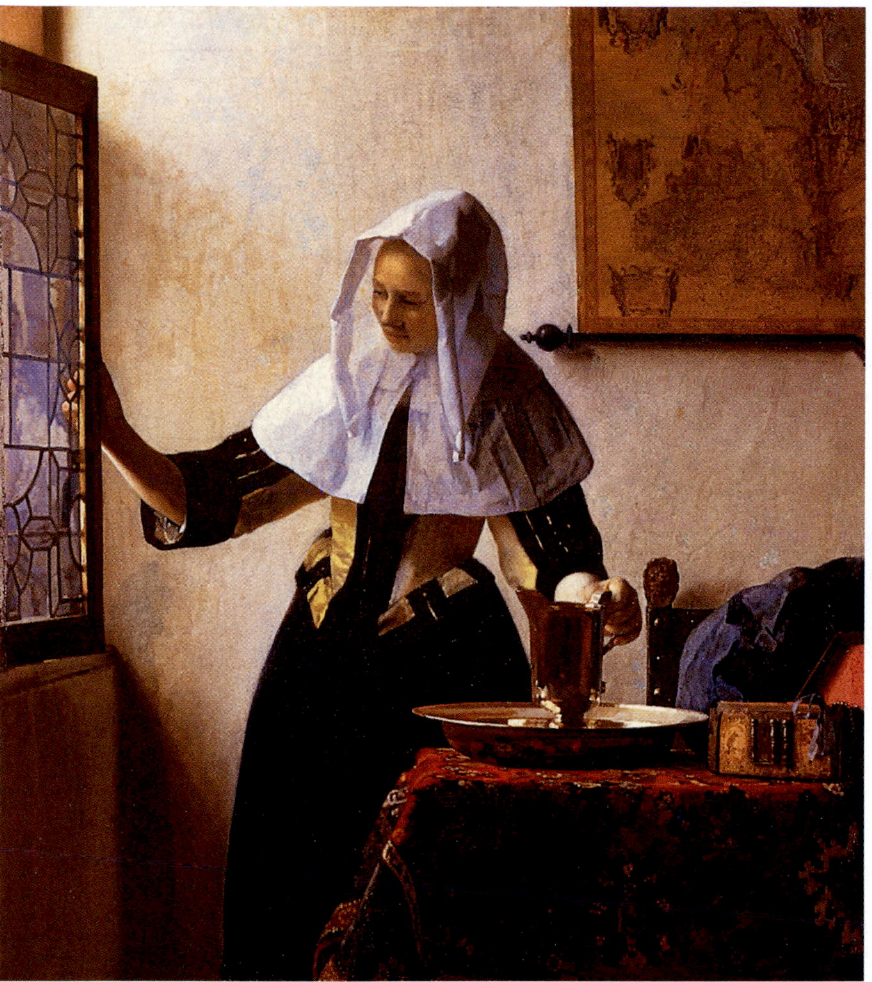

15-23 Jan Vermeer, *Young Woman with a Water Jug,* c. 1655. Oil on canvas, 18″ × 16″. The Metropolitan Museum of Art (gift of Henry G. Marquand, 1889, Marquand Collection).

very little about him. Most of the surviving documents mentioning his name are records of debts and loans to repay debts. He must have been a very careless manager of money because he had an excellent reputation and many commissions. His *The Laughing Cavalier* (**15-24**) engages us as few pictures do. It looks much more casual than most posed portraits. It seems as if the dashing man posed only for an instant and was impatient to move again. The energetic brushstrokes in the hair, in the mustache, and in the collar add to the liveliness of the scene.

Hals was painting in Holland at the same time Rubens was working in Flanders. They share a lively, optimistic approach, but Hals's subjects are very far from the aristocrats and goddesses of Rubens. The ordinary, even lower-class characters he portrayed against simple backgrounds identify Hals as a

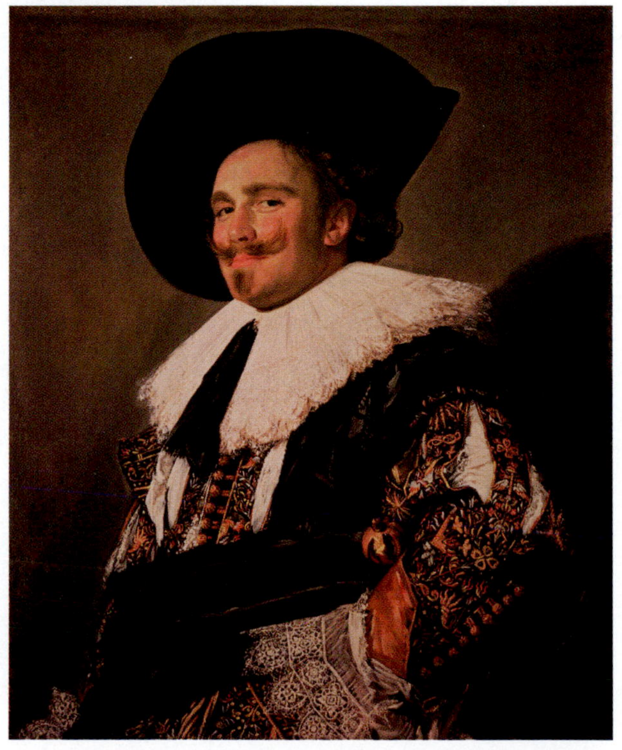

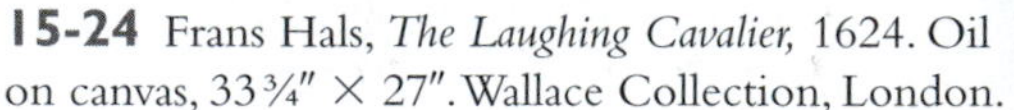

15-24 Frans Hals, *The Laughing Cavalier,* 1624. Oil on canvas, 33¾″ × 27″. Wallace Collection, London.

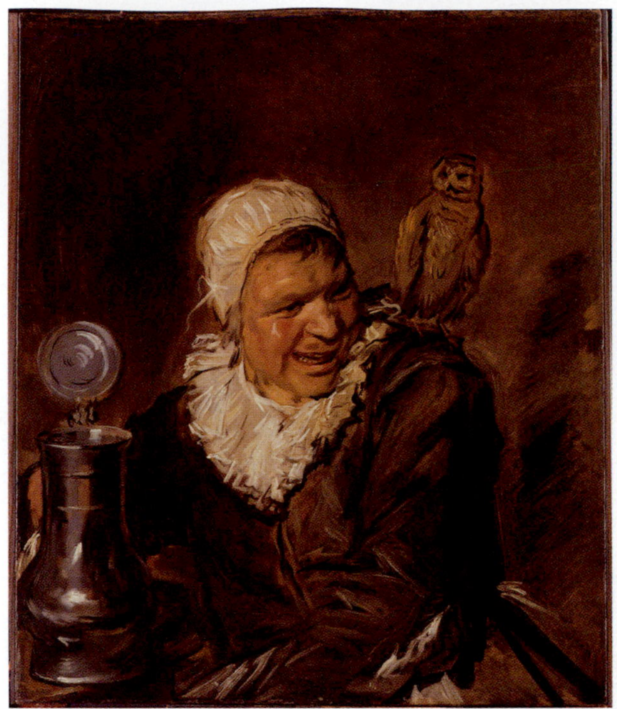

follower of Caravaggio. In a later portrait, *Malle Babbe* (**15-25**), Hals demonstrated an even more spontaneous and looser style. There is more expression in his brushwork, which is filled with feeling and is almost electric. There is also the illusion of great speed, as if Hals could dash off a painting in a few minutes. With a series of rapid spontaneous marks, Hals captures the wild drunkenness of a mad woman, probably an object of ridicule in her town. This style of painting is called **alla prima.** Previously, oil paintings were built up layer by layer over a long period of time with a series of glazes. Instead, Hals's picture is done quickly and at one sitting, *alla prima,* meaning "at the first." This daring and spontaneous way of painting would have a great influence on the Impressionists of the nineteenth century.

15-25 Frans Hals, *Malle Babbe (Mad Babbe),* c. 1650. Approximately 30″ × 25″. Staatliche Museen Preussischer Kulturbesitz, Gemäldegalerie, Berlin.

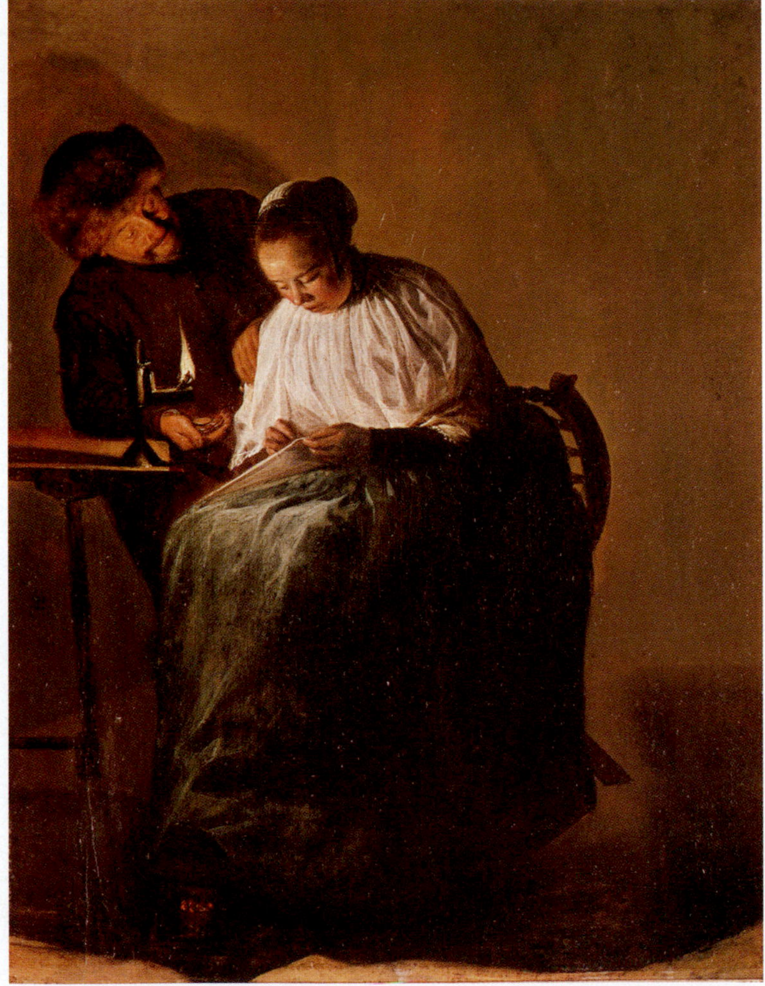

15-26 Judith Leyster, *The Proposition,* 1631. Oil on canvas, 11⅞″ × 9½″. The Mauritshuis, The Hague.

Judith Leyster was a friend of Hals whose pictures were similar in several ways (see the Art News box). But *The Proposition* (**15-26**) has a seriousness and understanding that is noticeably absent in Hals's work. The bold lighting and the lack of glamour in the scene shows the influence of Caravaggio more profoundly. In the painting, a man is hanging over a seated woman and offering her money in an effort to convince her to become a prostitute. The woman seems modest and embarrassed, uninterested in the proposition. She is trying to ignore the leering "gentleman," pretending not to hear, as if she were too absorbed in her sewing to notice.

The theme of a proposition is a common one of the period, but Leyster's picture is untraditional. Generally, when men had portrayed this theme, the woman would be dressed provocatively and smiling in a drunken, lusty way. The woman in *The Proposition* is dressed modestly and is clearly uncomfortable. Leyster counters male fantasies with realism.

ART NEWS

Judith Leyster Rediscovered

For three hundred years, *The Jolly Toper* (**15-27**) was thought to be a masterpiece by Frans Hals. This was not an unreasonable assumption, since the painting does resemble his subject matter and style. Yet when the picture was cleaned by a twentieth-century restorer, an important discovery was made—two initials had been painted over. They were not "F.H." but "J.L." While *The Jolly Toper* may look superficially like the work of Hals, it is actually the work of a woman named Judith Leyster. It is not unusual for a woman artist's work to be attributed to a more famous male artist. Sometimes this has been done unintentionally or out of ignorance, or because of wishful thinking, but often it has been done so pictures could sell for a higher price. In this case, the signature may well have been hidden by a dishonest dealer.

Hals and Leyster shared an interest in portraying happy drunkards, so the confusion might have been natural. Because Leyster was listed as a witness at the baptism of one of Hals's children, we can assume they were friends. If we compare her picture to his *Laughing Cavalier* or *Malle Babbe,* we notice other similarities. The figures are cut off below the chest, there are plain flat backgrounds, and both works share an immediate, snapshot quality. Leyster, however, does not use loose active brushwork. The texture of the paint is not meant to be noticed. What is important to her is creating a clear, honest portrait.

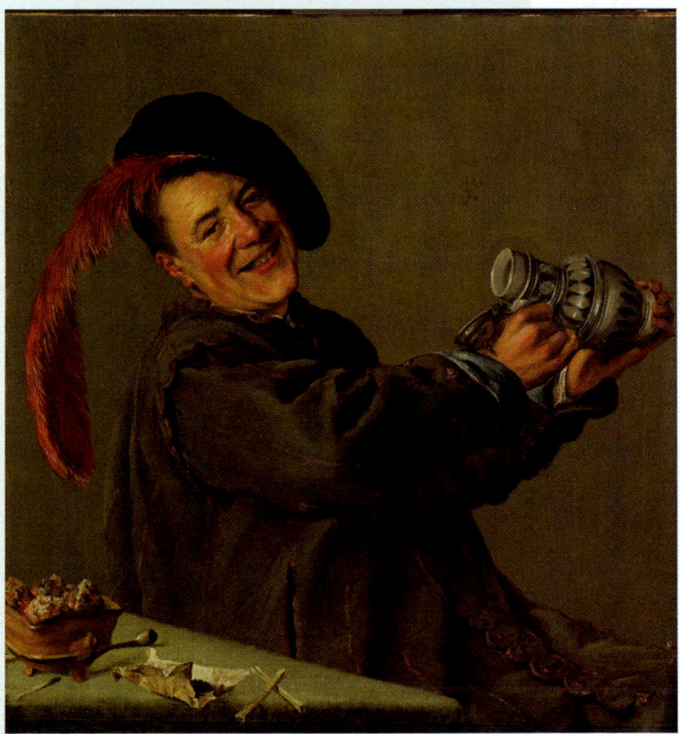

15-27 Judith Leyster, *The Jolly Toper,* 1629. Oil on canvas, 35″ × 33 ½″. Rijksmuseum, Amsterdam.

Rembrandt

While Hals seems to effortlessly capture the personality of the sitter and go no further, Leyster brings depth to her approach. Rembrandt van Rijn also attempted something more profound—to reveal the sitter's soul. The *Self-Portrait as a Young Man* (**15-28**) was done in his thirties. Like the Renaissance painter Albrecht Dürer, Rembrandt did many self-portraits during his lifetime. But Rembrandt never represented himself as Christ (14-31). He portrayed people, even himself, with great honesty and no intent to flatter. Rembrandt's devotion to Caravaggio's naturalism, as well as his understanding of chiaroscuro, is apparent in this early self-portrait. These remained his principal means of expression throughout his career.

Rembrandt, the son of a miller, was born in a small Dutch village. At an early age, he was recognized as an artistic genius. A painting done when he was only twenty-four was said to be "a work that could be compared with anything in Italy and with any of the beauties and marvels that have survived from the remotest antiquity." Underlying his talent was his remarkable skill as a draftsman, which can be seen in both his drawings and prints. His *Woman at a Window* (4-10) is a drawing that captures in only a few strokes a personality and a scene. His *Christ with the Sick around Him* (6-9) is an etching of great complexity and imagination, a masterly orchestration of light and shadow. In contrast to the work of most artists (Picasso is one exception), Rembrandt's drawings and prints are held in the same high regard as his paintings.

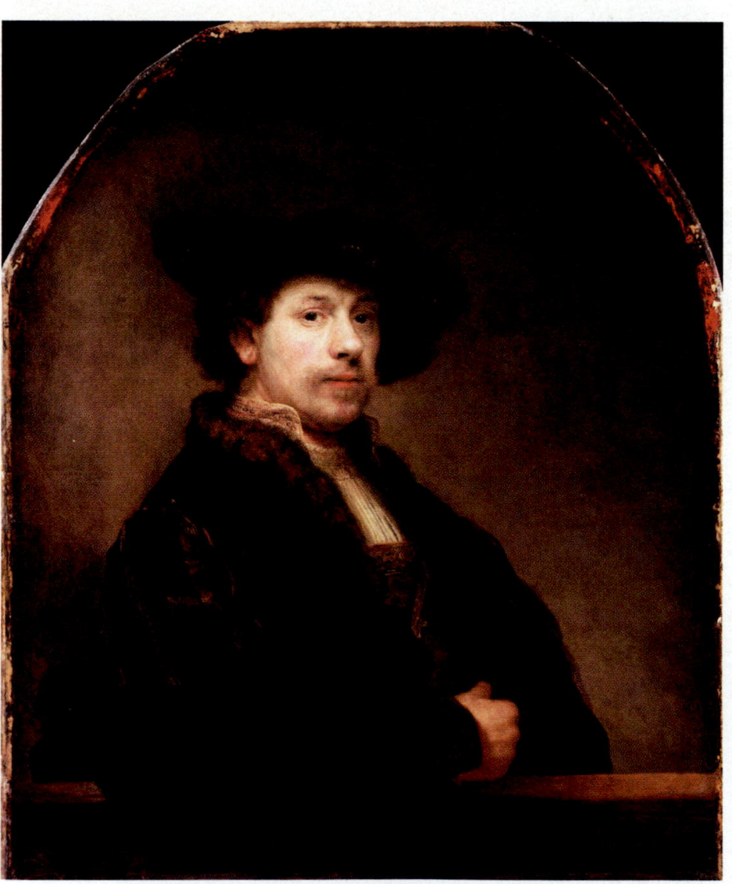

15-28 Rembrandt van Rijn, *Self-Portrait as a Young Man,* 1639. Oil on canvas, 40⅛″ × 31½″. National Gallery, London.

In the 1640s, the ambitious Rembrandt was Holland's most popular portrait painter and had become quite wealthy. Yet his dream was to be a painter, like Rubens, of impressive historical and biblical scenes. The *Sortie of Captain Banning Cocq's Company of the Civic Guard* (**15-29**), known traditionally as the *Night Watch,* marks a turning point in his career. The large painting (it is more than fourteen feet long) was commissioned by a company of officers under the command of Captain Frans Banning Cocq. The artist knew them and had probably watched them leave for patrol many times, because he lived on the same street as their headquarters. Each of the eighteen men depicted paid one hundred guilders and expected, in return, a traditional portrait. Rather than show everyone equally, however, Rembrandt decided to have a more imaginative composition. Some figures, like the captain, are featured, but others are almost hidden. For example, one soldier, at the right, had the bad luck to have his face blocked by an arm pointing to the center. Some individuals are also concealed by heavy shadows because, rather than using a dull, even light, Rembrandt used dramatic chiaroscuro. The final result was impressive, but, not surprisingly, many of his subjects were unhappy. After the portrait was unveiled, Rembrandt's commissions began to decrease.

The year 1642 marked another sad turning point in his fortunes: His beloved wife and model, Saskia, died after giving birth to their son, Titus. In the *Sortie,* she appears as a small ghostly presence just to the left of center. The loss of Saskia also meant the loss of her trust fund, on which he had become dependent despite his success. Unfortunately, Rembrandt had developed a taste for the finer things in life. He also liked to drink and eat well. As his fortunes declined, he found it impossible to restrain his free-spending ways.

Rembrandt's art came under attack in the 1650s. As the Dutch Republic aged, it became richer and more conservative, less concerned with honesty and

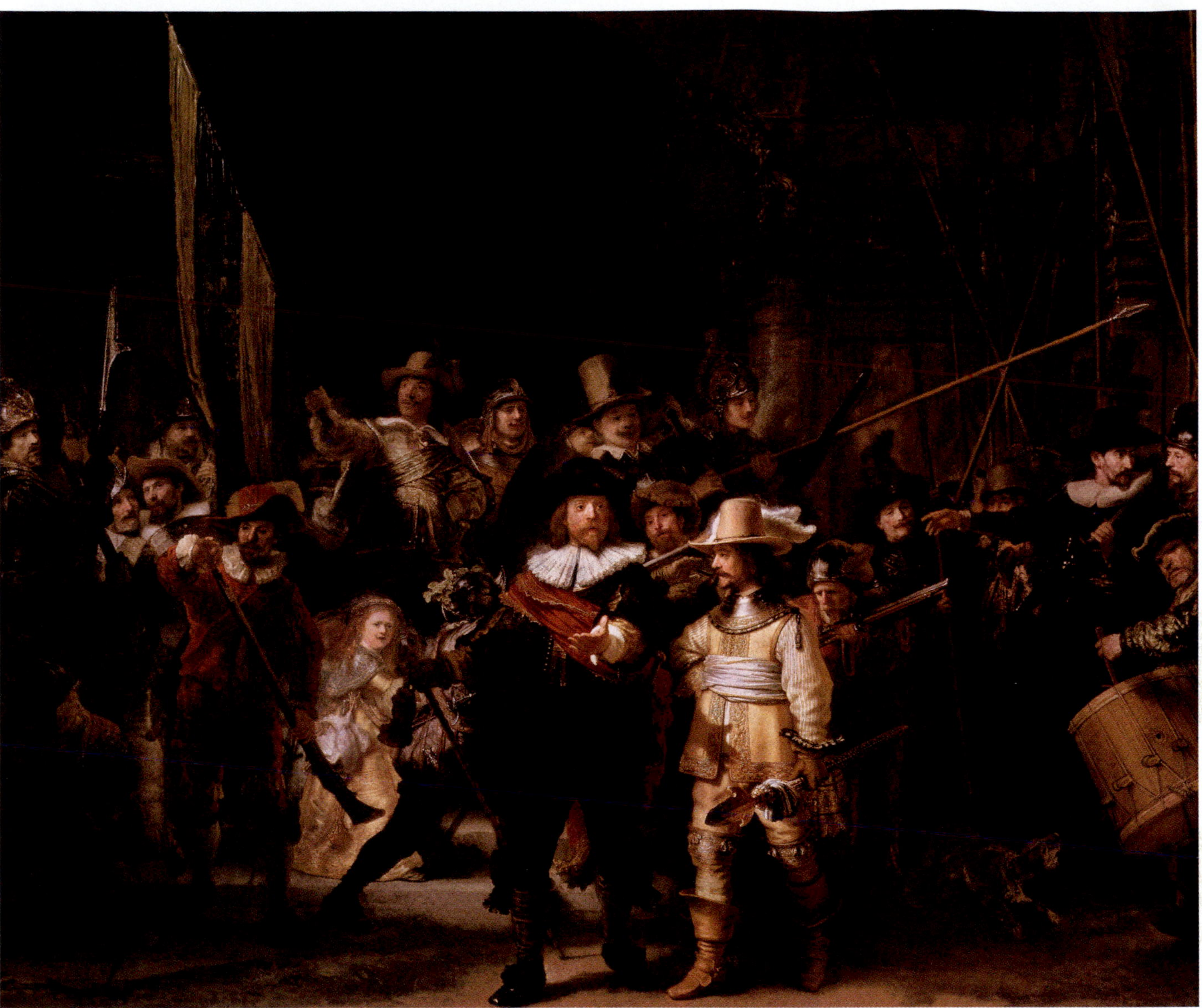

15-29 Rembrandt van Rijn, *Sortie of Captain Banning Cocq's Company of the Civic Guard (Night Watch),* 1642. Oil on canvas, 12′ 2″ × 14′ 7″. Rijksmuseum, Amsterdam.

realism. Patrons wanted a more classical-looking art, reminiscent of Raphael and ancient Greek statues. This new taste was developing, not only in Holland, but also all over Europe. Like Caravaggio before him, Rembrandt was criticized for his naturalism. It was said his pictures were too dark; they contained too many ugly and vulgar types. Rembrandt refused to change.

Even though he was a Protestant in a Protestant country, Rembrandt thought of himself as the natural heir to Rubens, the great painter of the Catholic Baroque in the North. Therefore, unlike Hals, Leyster, and Vermeer, he painted many religious subjects. Yet Rembrandt's approach was more spiritual and personal than the grandiose extravaganzas of Rubens. *Jacob Blessing the Sons of Joseph* (**15-30**) not only illustrates a story from the Old Testament but also is a touching family scene. Encircled by utter darkness, the family of Jacob surrounds the old man in a gentle world of love. Jacob's family is probably not unlike Rembrandt's own, who helped him endure continuing troubles and became his shelter from the storm. He was near financial ruin and harassed by creditors at the time because of his extravagant spending (he owed more than 17,000 guilders—more than most Dutch then could earn in a lifetime).

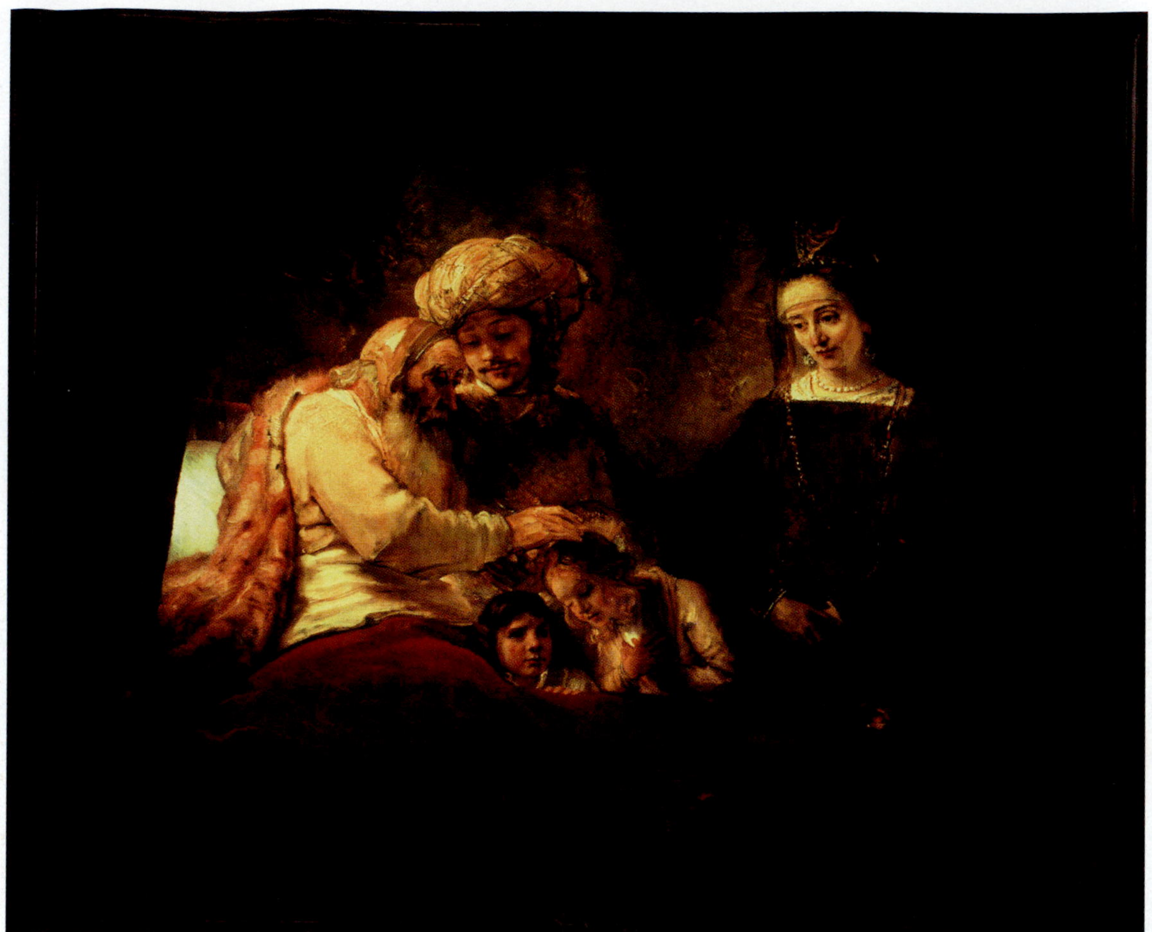

15-30 Rembrandt van Rijn, *Jacob Blessing the Sons of Joseph,* 1656. Oil on canvas, 5′ 8½″ × 6′ 11½″. Gemäldegalerie, Kassel, Germany.

Rembrandt's biography is told in his many self-portraits. The man seen in the self-portrait of 1660 (**15-31**) is much changed from the confident young man of twenty years earlier. In the intervening decades, his self-portraits had shown a tattered but defiant, almost confident Rembrandt. By 1659, he had been forced to declare bankruptcy and sell off his personal art collection. Here we see the artist as a tired, worried old man who seems to see little hope in the future. Although he would live another seven years, before his death he would lose both his son Titus and his beloved mistress Hendrickje, and finally become dependent on their daughter, Cornelia.

Rembrandt's dedication to his principles and resistance to Classicism cost him dearly, but his contribution to art was immense. If the Renaissance can be seen as the beginning of the rise in the importance of the individual, then Rembrandt's work can be seen as an important new development of that idea. In his pictures, *his* own unique impressions and thoughts became even more important than realistic depiction of his subjects. This is the beginning of an important part of the modern approach to art, where the sensibility of the artist is now a crucial element of the subject matter. In other words, not only imitation was to be valued but also expression.

THE BAROQUE IN FRANCE

In Chapter 11, France was discussed as the birthplace of Gothic art, but it would not be an important art center again until the Baroque period. In the seventeenth century, France's power increased rapidly until it became the most powerful nation in Europe and the virtual capital of Western art, a position it would hold for nearly three centuries, until World War II.

Classicism, the same movement that ruined Rembrandt's career, was centered in France. Nicolas

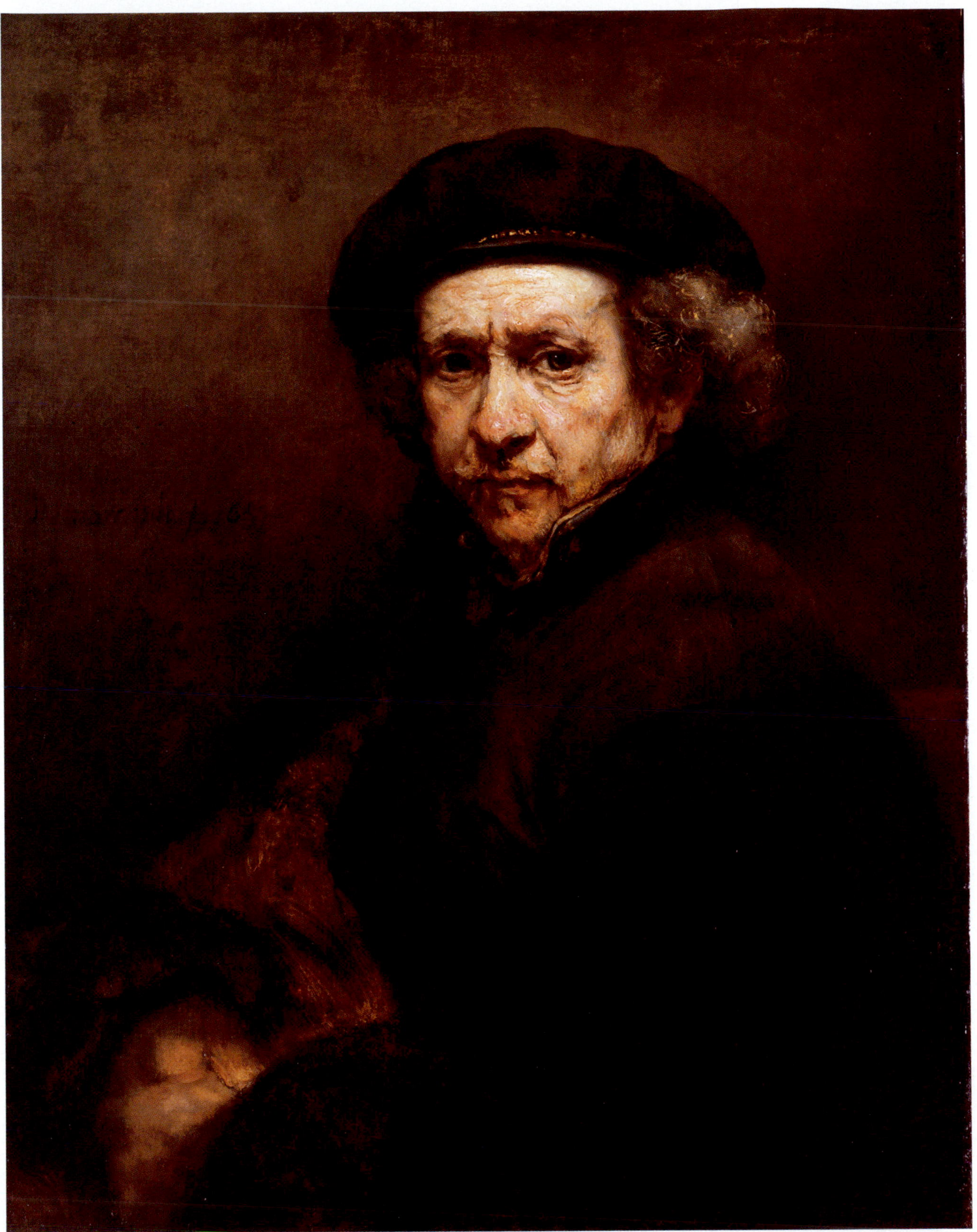

15-31 Rembrandt van Rijn, *Self-Portrait,* 1659. Oil on canvas, 33 ¼″ × 26″. National Gallery of Art, Washington, D.C. (Andrew W. Mellon Collection). 1937.1.72.

Poussin was the emperor of Classicism; his ideas and career helped formulate the basic doctrines of the new international movement. He lived for many years in Rome, the mecca of the Classicists. There he made copies of the works of his heroes, the Renaissance masters, along with drawings of ancient Greek and Roman sculptures. His approach to learning would form the basis of the traditional course of study in the French Royal Academy of Painting and Sculpture founded in the seventeenth century. It became the model for academies of art all over Europe, where students were taught the following doctrines of **Classicism:** (1) reject Naturalism, especially the portrayal of authentic emotions; (2) the highest aim of a work of art is to represent noble and serious thoughts; (3) an artist should make images with logic and order—not as things really are but as they should be; (4) true art should depict great themes and raise viewers up by appealing to their reason, not their base emotions. These doctrines were inscribed in a treatise by Poussin and became the bylaws of the movement, a major force in Western art for centuries.

Poussin's paintings reflect his belief in an art based on ideals, not naturalism. The shepherds in *Et in Arcadia Ego* (**15-32**), for example, are not portrayed as peasants but are closer to the statues of archaic gods. This scene is in fact set in an ideal ancient past, as are all of his works. The light and color are not dramatic but calm, as in the Madonnas of Raphael. The shepherds are reading and reflecting on the words carved into a tomb, "Et in arcadia ego," or "even in Arcadia I am." "Arcadia" was an ancient mythical land, a rustic paradise that symbolizes perfect earthly life. "I" refers to death. The inscription therefore means that even in an ideal pastoral landscape, death rules supreme. The spirit of death is at the right, in the form of a goddess. She calmly puts her hand on one of the shepherds, perhaps announcing the end of his life. All elements of the picture are carefully staged to create a sense of Classical serenity, a dignified world ruled by logic and understanding.

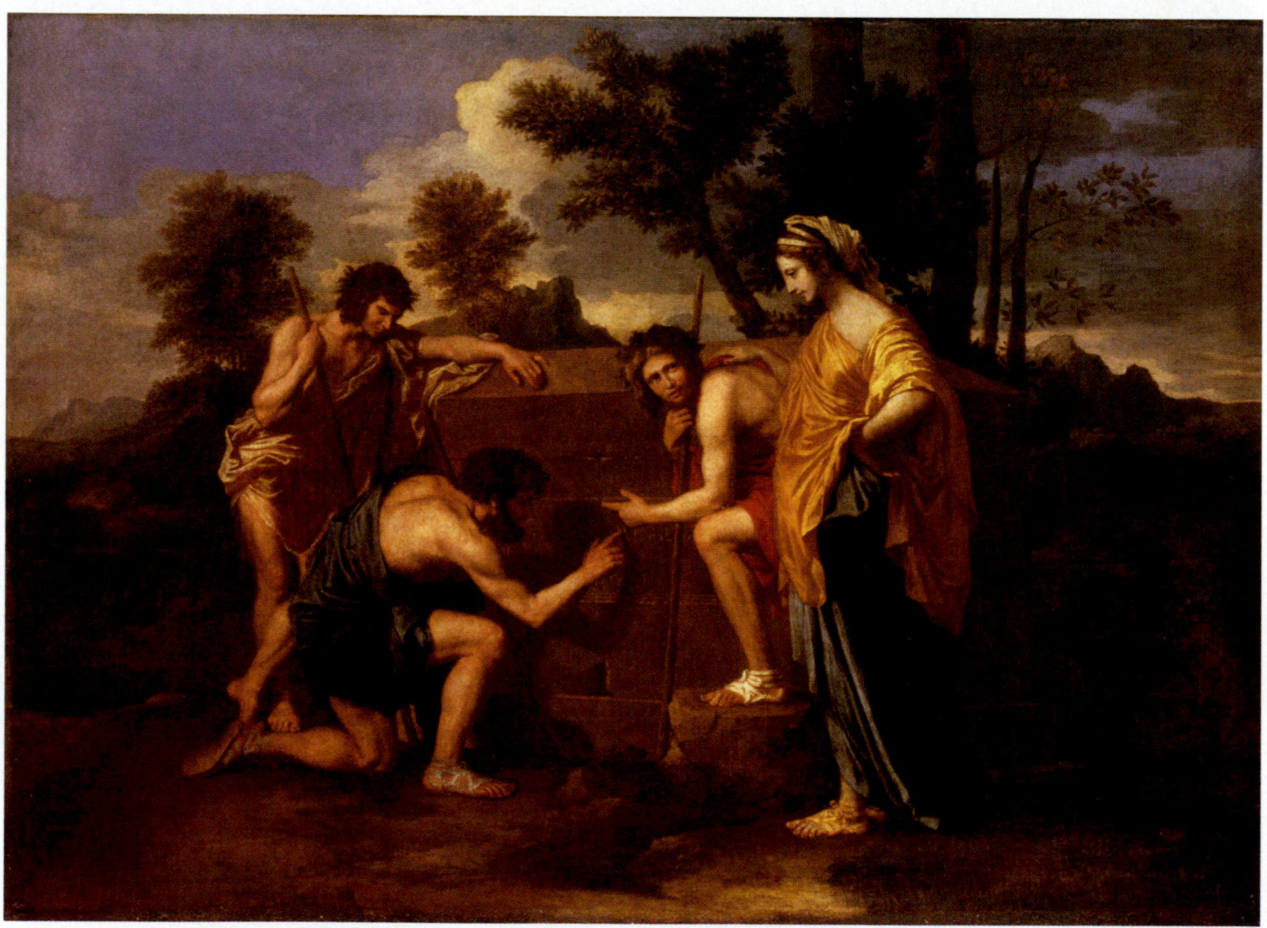

15-32 Nicolas Poussin, *Et in Arcadia Ego,* c. 1655. Oil on canvas, 34″ × 48″. Louvre, Paris.

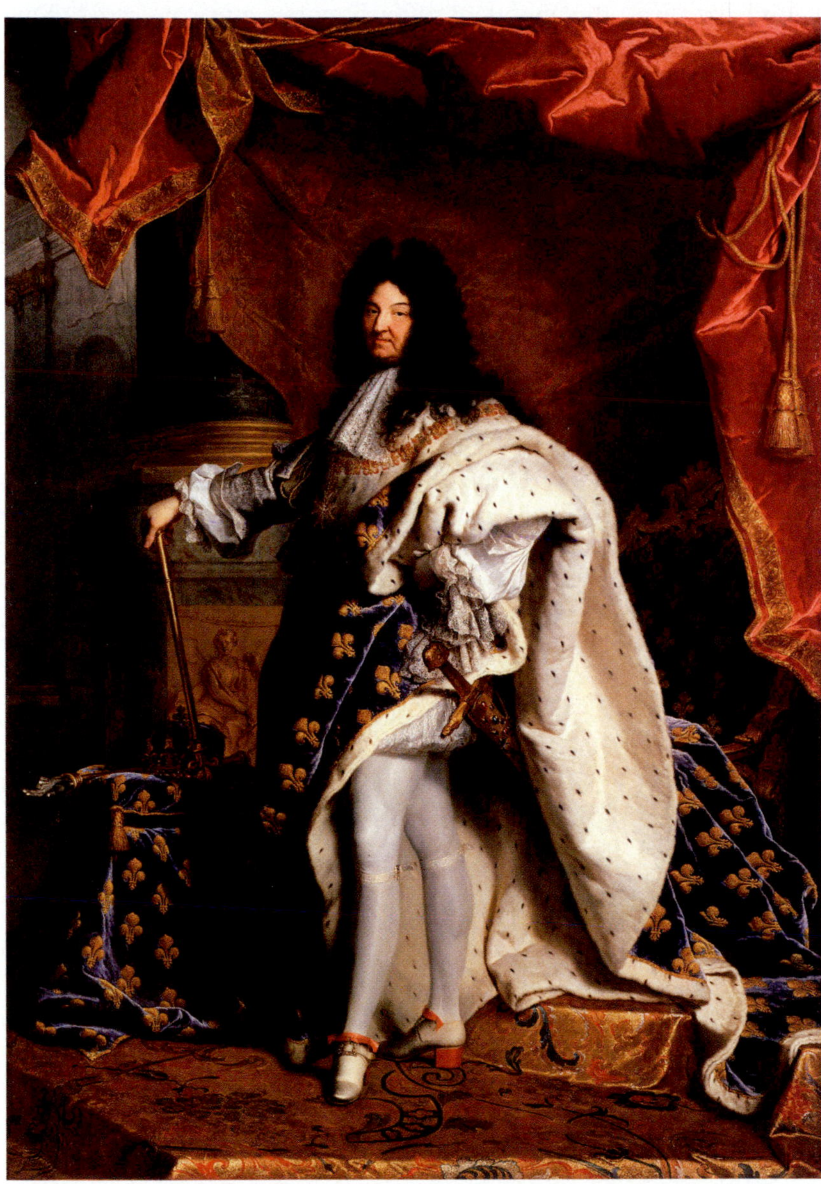

15-33 Hyacinthe Rigaud, *Louis XIV,* 1701. Oil on canvas, 9′ 2″ × 6′ 3″. Louvre, Paris.

Louis XIV and Versailles

The dominance of France during the seventeenth and eighteenth centuries was not just artistic but military and political, too. Its preeminence was due to its king, Louis XIV, the most important figure of the Baroque period. After a childhood made insecure by civil war and factional strife, he created a new kind of nation-state based on his absolute rule, sustained by his claim to divine authority. Louis's most famous quote, "L'etat, c'est moi" ("The state, it is myself"), characterizes perfectly his attitude toward governance. Known as the *Sun King,* he was the most powerful monarch in Europe and ruled for seventy-two years.

In his official portrait by Hyacinthe Rigaud (**15-33**), the sixty-three-year-old Louis is surrounded by sumptuous fabrics and classically inspired architecture. As was characteristic of almost everything associated with Louis XIV, his portrait is gigantic and larger than life, more than nine feet tall. It looms over the viewer and is meant to impress one with its absolute power. The pride with which he reveals his slim legs may seem silly to us today, but simply reflects a change in cultural values—men of this period were as interested in fashion and vain about their personal appearance as women. The large, jeweled sword hilt seen just above his stockings reminds us that he was a man of immense power.

In the mid-1600s, the king grew dissatisfied with his major palace, the Louvre, and decided to make a new one away from the crowds of Paris (whose population had doubled in eighty years), and which reminded him of the political strife of his youth. Hundreds of architects, decorators, sculptors, painters, and landscape designers were sent into the countryside to convert a royal hunting lodge into a palace so grand that it would be capable of glorifying the most powerful ruler in Europe. Because of the astounding size of Louis XIV's *Palace of Versailles,* no one photograph can capture it, even one taken from the air (**15-34**). A city was created, attached to its grounds, to house all of the court and government officials, the military, clergy, and thousands of servants. Under Louis, Versailles became a world all to itself, cut off from the distractions of city life. Its famous gardens literally extend for miles (see Chapter 11, pages 206–207).

The palace is a combination of both Classical and Baroque elements. Among the hundreds of rooms inside, the *King's Bedroom* (**15-35**), decorated in gold-and-silver brocade, was the center of activity in the palace. All roads in Versailles led to it, and most of the important official business was conducted there. The great event of each day was the rising or *levee,* of the Sun. As the sun would appear above the horizon, the Sun King would rise from his bed. Once dressed, he would push open his elaborately carved bedroom door. It opened into the *Hall of Mirrors* (**15-36**), which would reflect bright sunlight around Louis XIV as he progressed down the hall with his courtiers by his side.

The hall extends the entire width of the central wing's second floor, and the windows provide a fine view of the marvelous gardens. In daytime, the seventeen grand mirrors reflect the light of the large windows across from them, making the hall bright without any artificial lights. Besides mirrors, the walls are covered with marble of many colors, and the ceiling tells of the magnificent accomplishments of the king. As beautiful and elaborate as it is today, compared to Louis's time it is rather bare. It was once filled with gold-and-silver chairs and trees covered with jewels. This and other halls were open to the public to impress visitors with the majesty of Louis XIV. Versailles was the center of many festivals that took place in this hall: comedies, balls, music,

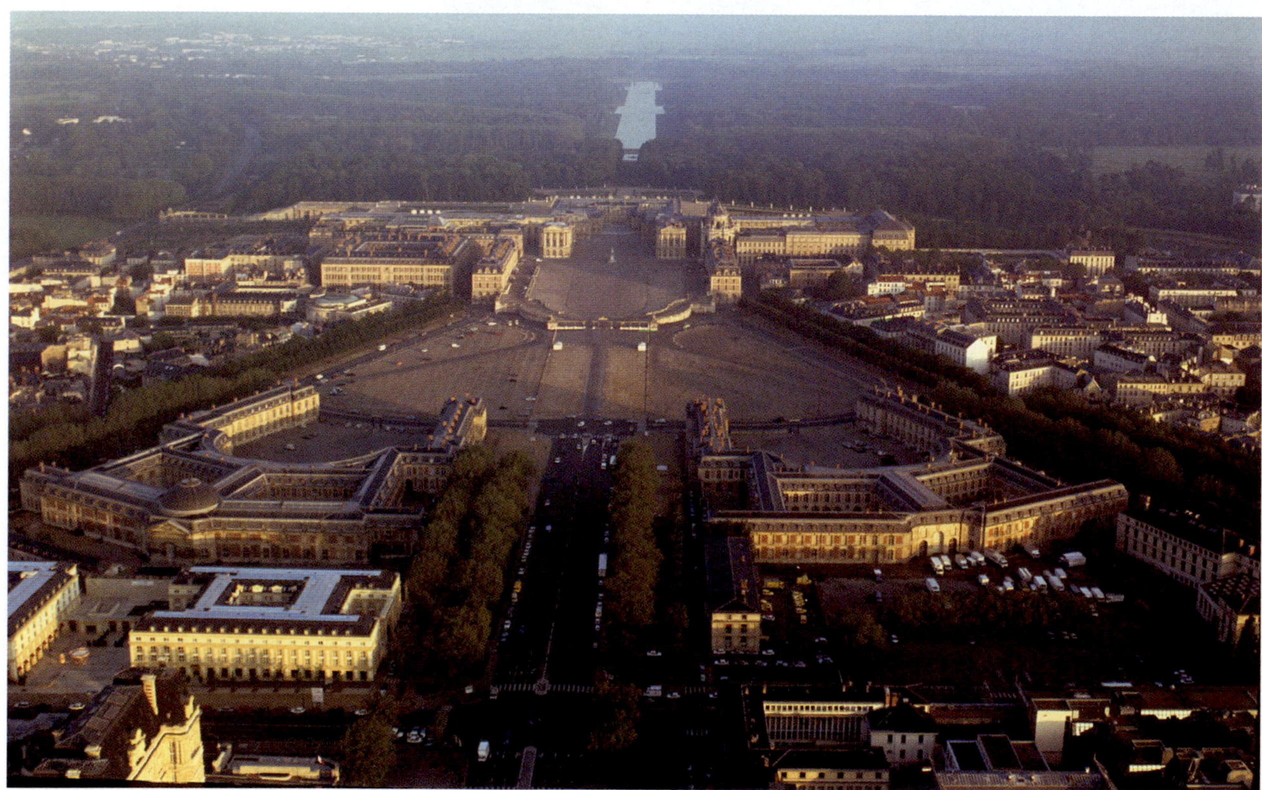

15-34 Aerial view of the Palace of Versailles, France, and the surrounding park, 1669–1685.

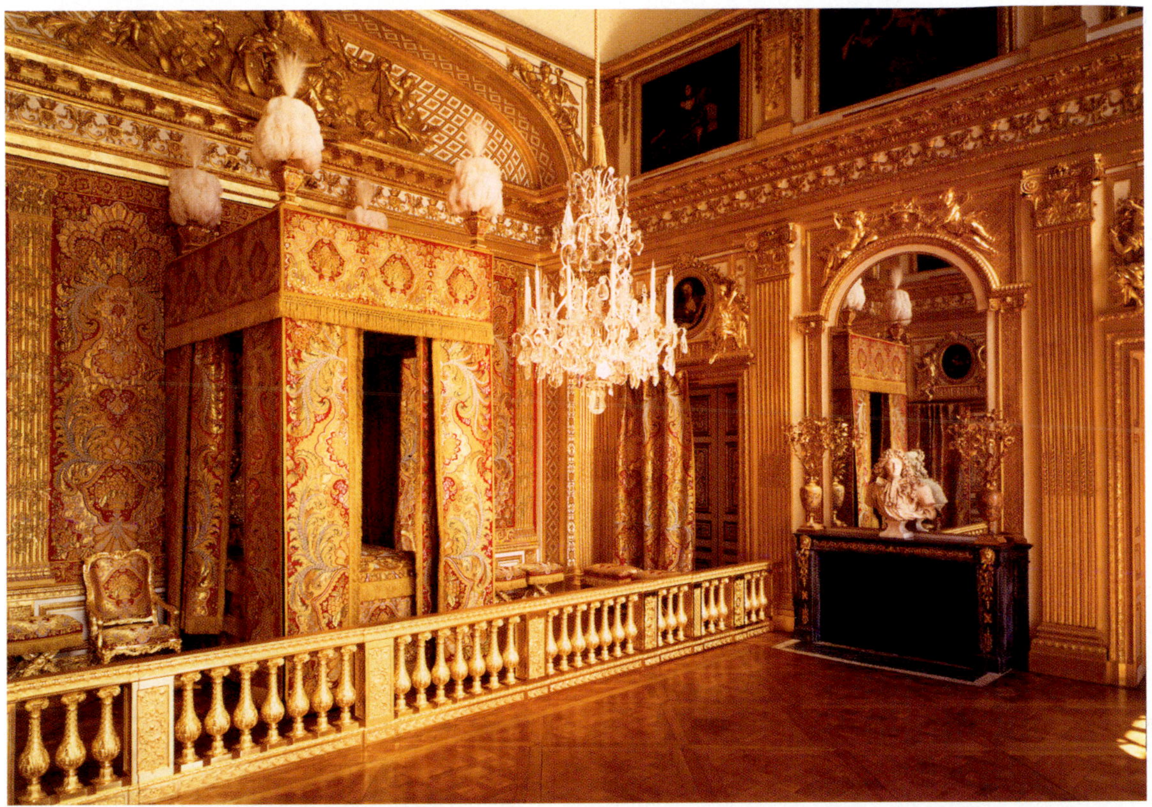

15-35 King's Bedroom, Palace of Versailles, France.

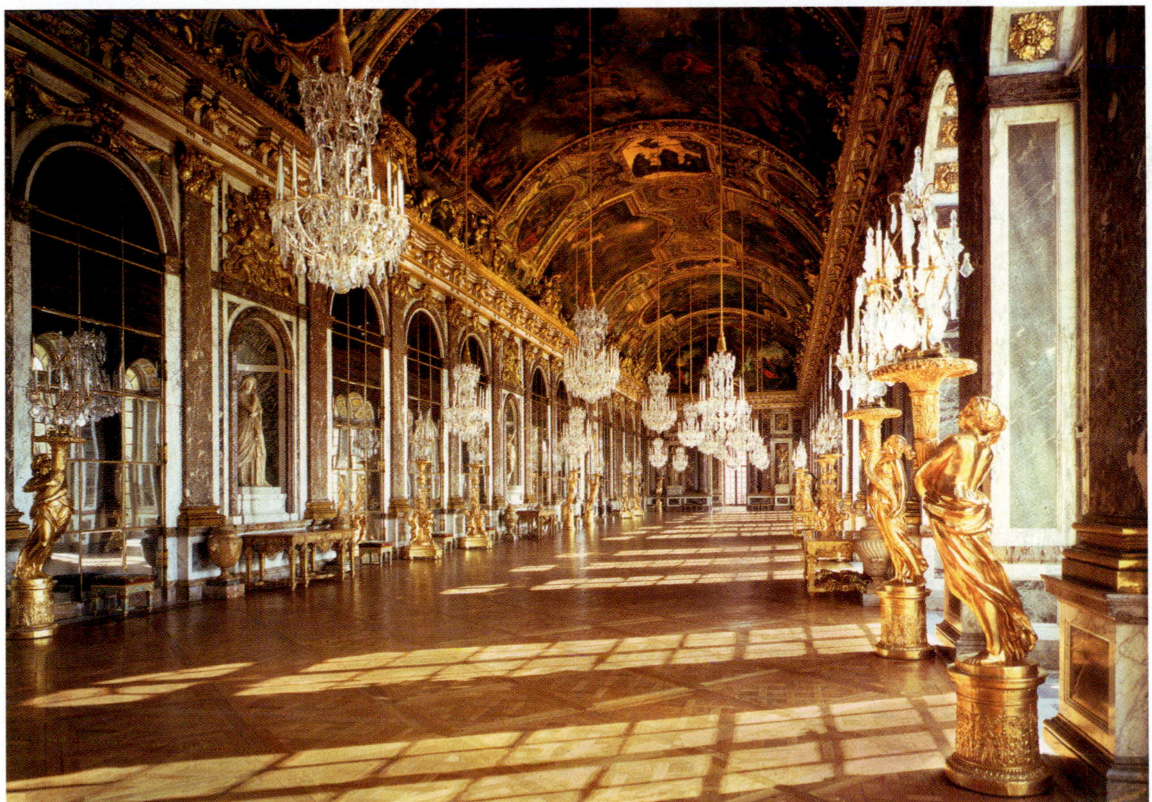

15-36 Jules Hardouin-Mansart, Hall of Mirrors, Palace of Versailles, France, 1680.

fireworks, and suppers by torchlight. The mirrors would reflect and magnify the magnificence of the great *fetes* or parties, some lasting for days.

Louis XIV's era was a bloody one in Europe, and he bears a large responsibility for this. He loved war and owed much of his power to it. Attached at one end of the Hall of Mirrors is the *Salon de la Guerre* (War Room, **15-37**), where he made his plans to crush France's neighbors. The central feature of the room is a marble relief that shows him on horseback trampling his enemies in triumph. Around the room are such pictures as "Germany on her knees" and "Denmark surrendering." At the other end of the hall, his queen built a "Salon de Paix" (Peace Room) to balance her husband's ferocity. Sadly, it never seemed to have its intended effect. Still, Versailles captured the imagination of Europe, and soon there was building everywhere. It was as if every member of the European nobility had to build his own little Versailles.

The Rococo in France: The Aristocracy at Play

Much to the relief of Europe (and France, which was almost bankrupt after more than fifty years of extravagance and wars), Louis XIV finally died in his glorious bedroom in 1715, after ruling for seven decades. When he died, a new period of art began. Its characteristics were not formality and grandeur but lighthearted, playful decoration, as if artists along

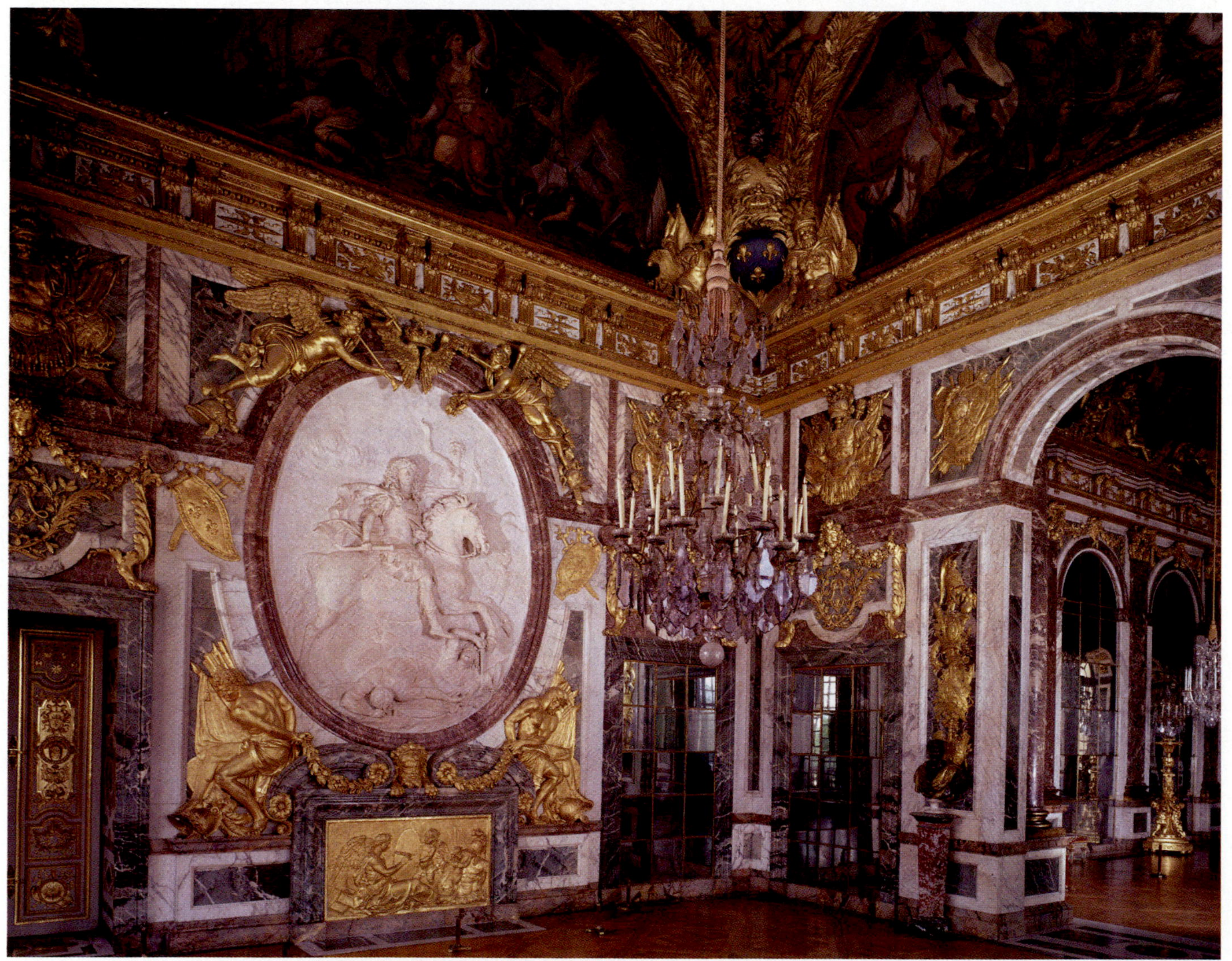

15-37 Salon de la Guerre, Palace of Versailles, France, 1683–1685.

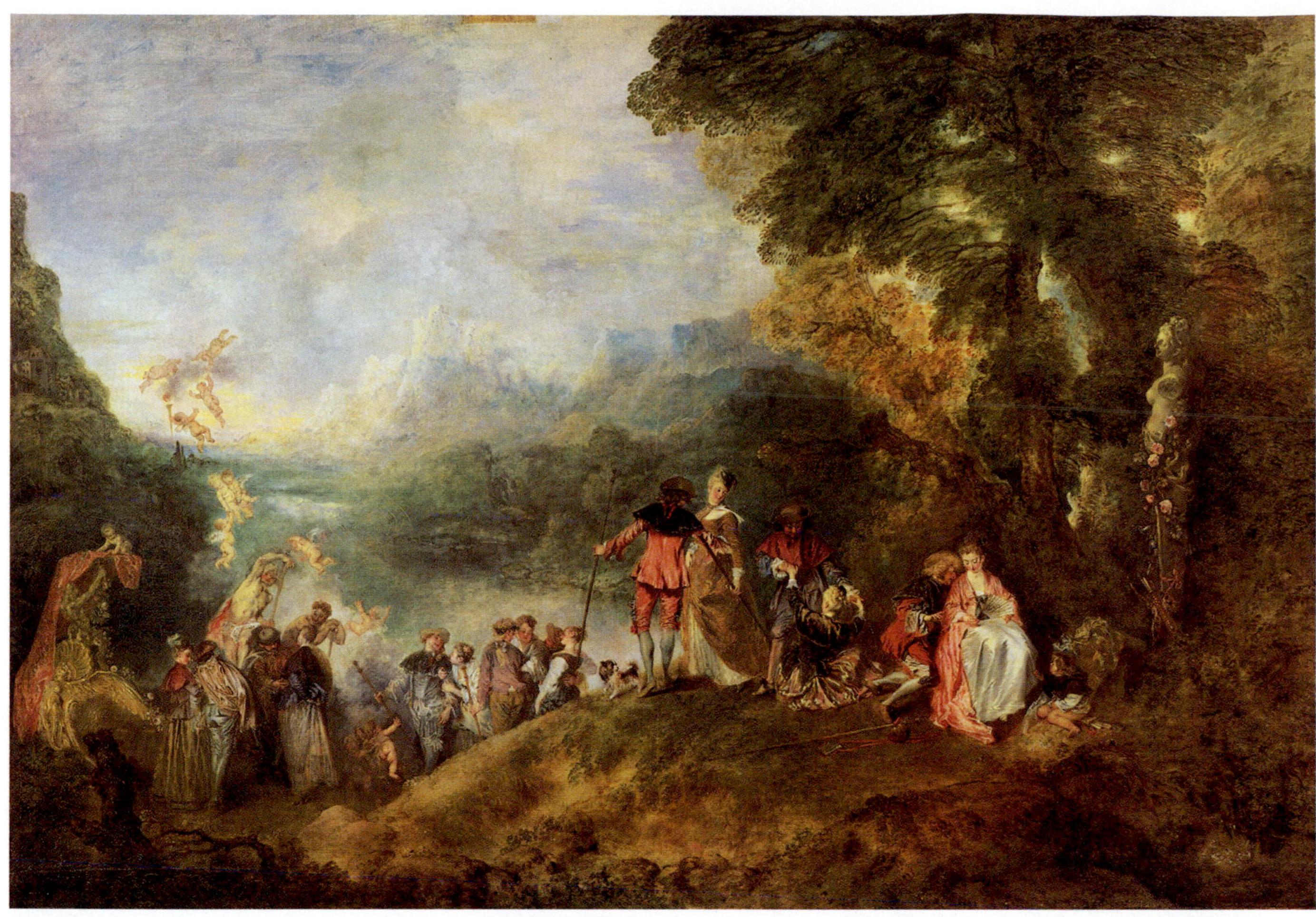

15-38 Antoine Watteau, *Return from Cythera,* 1717–1719. Oil on canvas, 4′ 3″ × 6′ 4″. Louvre, Paris.

with the rest of Europe heaved a deep sigh, relaxed, and began to enjoy themselves.

This new period in art is called the **Rococo,** and Antoine Watteau was its preeminent painter. Born in Flanders (a nation Louis XIV had conquered), he only lived to be thirty-seven, but in his short life he painted many scenes—of parties, picnics, and love—that typify the Rococo spirit. His style was influenced by his countryman, Rubens. Notice the similarities between Rubens's *Garden of Love* and Watteau's masterpiece *Return from Cythera* (**15-38**). Curving *S* shapes and the theme of love reign in both. Each show a variety of actions. The differences, however, illustrate a distinction between the Baroque and the Rococo. Because it is set in the midst of a large landscape, the *Return* seems much more peaceful than the *Garden of Love.* The characters are distant, rather than pushed close to the viewer. The lighting is soft and gentle. Watteau's picture is therefore not nearly as intensely energetic as Rubens's. While Rubens made many paintings on a grand scale, most Rococo pictures are more modest. One of Watteau's largest works, the *Return from Cythera* is a bit more than six feet long; many of Rubens's are twice that.

In Watteau's painting, a group of lovers are about to leave Aphrodite's isle of Cythera, a mythical island where love never dies and one never grows old. We can see that the lovers find it difficult to leave this idyllic island; many look back sadly. Every figure is paired in a couple, some almost swooning in rapture. As in many of Watteau's pictures, a classical sculpture of a bust of Aphrodite, the goddess of love, keeps a watchful eye over lovers, protecting them. Cupid, her son, has left his arrows at its base, because they are unnecessary here. He tugs at one woman's dress, trying to get her attention and tell her that it is time to leave. Swarms of cupids tumbling in the air surround the gondolas at the right, preparing to lead them back to the real world beyond the hazy blue mountains.

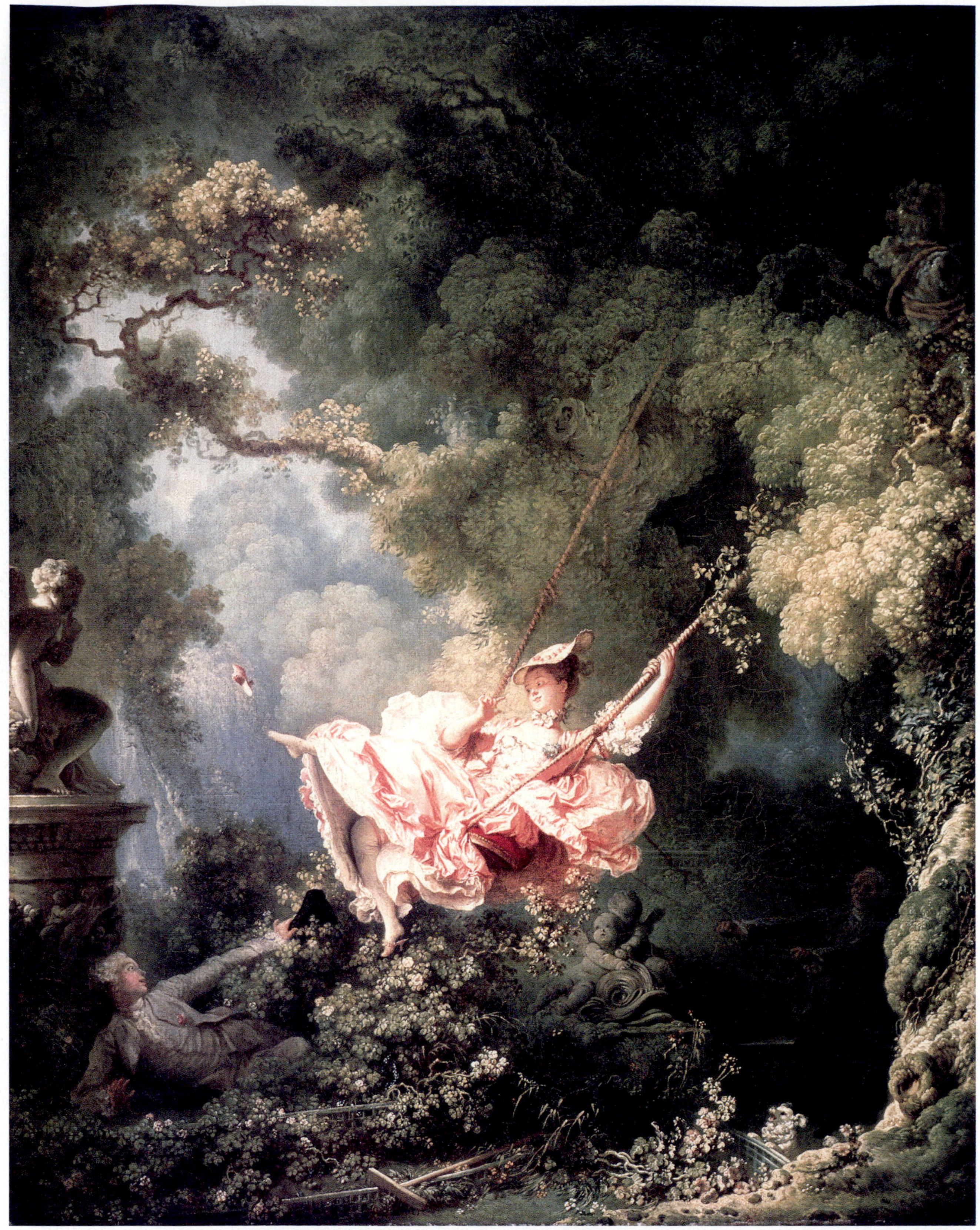

15-39 Jean Honoré Fragonard, *The Swing,* 1766. Oil on canvas, approximately 35″ × 32″. Wallace Collection, London.

As romantic and lovely as it is, there is a sadness in this and many of Watteau's paintings, as if the wonderful days of youth and love are passing too fast. He may have known he was dying of tuberculosis (what was then called consumption) when he painted this picture. Perhaps he is telling us he does not want to leave just yet. Ten years after his death, the Rococo style had swept Europe; even the clothing worn by his characters in the *Return* had become *the* style for the aristocracy.

The visual idea of love in a garden was especially popular in the France of Louis XV, where the court was dominated by the king's mistresses and intellectual life flourished in the salons of famous female hostesses. French aristocrats of the eighteenth century seemed to be bound by no moral scruples; extramarital affairs and illegitimate children were common. Romantic love was the theme of many works of art, especially those painted to decorate the rooms of wealthy ladies. One of the most famous is *The Swing* by Jean-Honoré Fragonard (**15-39**). The mood of this picture is light and playful; love is a game, courtship an art. We see a tastefully dressed young woman swinging above her would-be lover, who is hiding in the bushes. The young man has paid an elderly bishop (seen in the shadows) to bring his beloved to this spot and swing her higher and higher so he can peek up her skirt. The young lady is well aware of her admirer's trick and plays along with it, going so far as to kick off one of her shoes. Even the statues of cupid partake of the intrigue; one holds his fingers to his lips as if to say, "Sssh! It's a secret."

The French aristocracy turned to Fragonard for images to hang in their boudoirs but to Marie Louise Élisabeth Vigée-Lebrun for their portraits. A child prodigy, she supported her widowed mother and brother from the age of fifteen. By the time she was twenty, Vigée-Lebrun commanded the highest portrait prices in France. Her success was enhanced by the patronage of the queen of France, Marie Antoinette, whom she painted more than twenty times. Vigée-Lebrun's *The Artist and Her Daughter* (**15-40**), painted on the eve of the French Revolution, illustrates how the new Classicism even had begun to influence the work of a painter devoted to portraying the aristocracy. In the next chapter, we will see how this style was a factor in the coming upheaval.

The successes of Watteau, Vigée-Lebrun, and Fragonard were due in part to the desire of the aristocracy to be cut off from the cares of everyday life and ordinary people. Their pictures, devoted to the elegant lifestyles of upper-class pleasure, simply ignore the existence of any other classes. As the eighteenth century came to an end, however, social and political changes would make it impossible for the aristocracy to ignore the outside world. Because of her close association with the royal family, Vigée-Lebrun was forced to flee during the French Revolution and spent her most productive years visiting the capitals of Europe, a figure of international stature patronized by the crowned heads of Europe. As for Fragonard, he stayed in France. After the Revolution, grace and charm were no longer considered admirable qualities, and his career would sink along with his clients, the nobility.

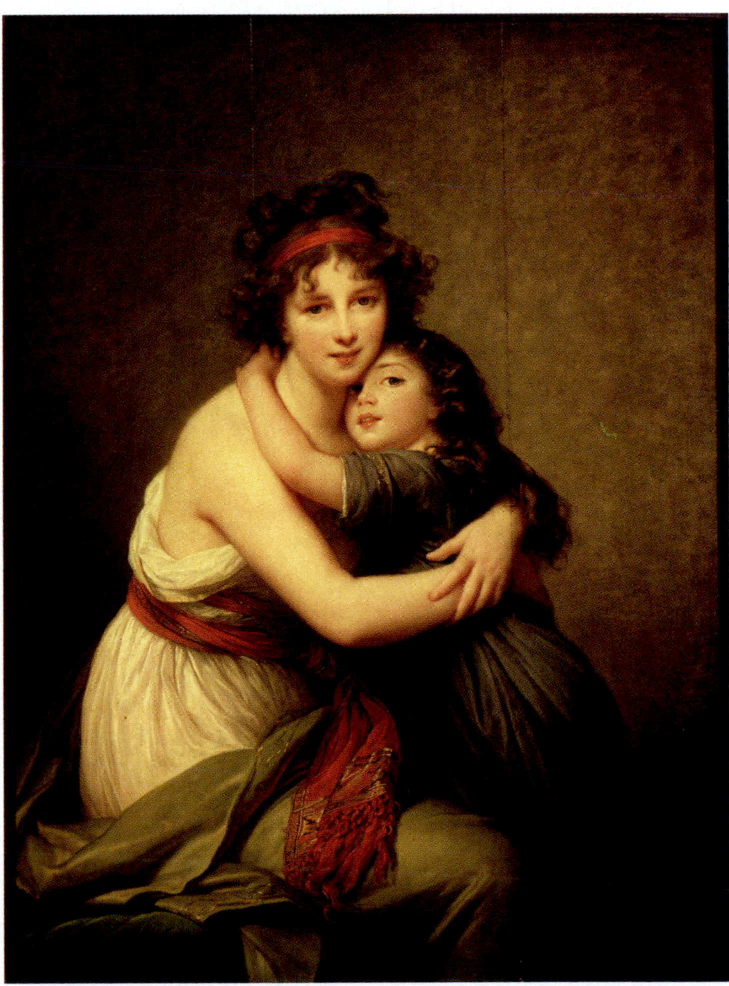

15-40 Marie Louise Élisabeth Vigée-Lebrun, *The Artist and Her Daughter,* c. 1785. Oil on canvas, 51″ × 37″. Louvre, Paris.

CHAPTER 16

The Battle of the Isms: Neoclassicism, Romanticism, and Realism

The birth of Modern Art was a slow one, with many parents over the centuries. From the Middle Ages through most of the seventeenth century, artistic styles had evolved slowly over time, one following another. The Romanesque led to the Gothic, Gothic art was replaced by the Renaissance, the Renaissance by Mannerism, Mannerism by the Baroque. The word *modern* was first used to describe art that was wild and imaginative during the Mannerist period. The Renaissance conception of genius and Rembrandt's emphasis on the artist's personal expression also played parts in defining modernity. In the eighteenth and nineteenth centuries, the last elements were introduced. First, the Baroque was replaced by two distinct styles—the Classical and the Rococo. Proponents of these

	PERIOD	HISTORICAL EVENTS	
1650–1776	The Enlightenment Classicism Georgian Age in England Formation of Academies and Societies for Arts and Sciences	Great Fire of London 1666 Milton, *Paradise Lost* 1667 Locke, *Essay Concerning Human Understanding* 1690	Diderot, *Encyclopedia* 1751 Voltaire, *Candide* 1759
1776–1815	Neoclassicism The Age of Revolutions Industrial and Transportation Revolutions Romanticism in art and literature Napoleonic Age	Jefferson, The Declaration of Independence 1776 The French Revolution 1789–1799 Wollstonecraft, *Vindication of the Rights of Woman* 1792	Napoleon becomes Emperor 1804 Beethoven, Eroica 1804
1815–1860	South American republics break away from Spain The Victorian period in England The Hudson River School – First school of American painting Realism in art and literature	Scott, *Ivanhoe* creates taste for historical novels 1819 Invention of photography 1839	Marx and Engels, *The Communist Manifesto* 1848

movements called themselves the *Rubenistes*—after the flamboyant painter Peter Paul Rubens—and the *Poussinistes*—after the classical master Nicholas Poussin. These eighteenth-century styles were then challenged in the nineteenth century, by a series of almost simultaneous movements jockeying for patronage and prestige. All ending in the suffix "ism": the competing movements of Neoclassicism, Romanticism, and Realism each declared that it was the best expression of the spirit of the age.

THE ENLIGHTENMENT

The **Age of Reason** or the **Enlightenment** stressed the value of rationality over faith, senses, and emotions. The Enlightenment was an age of great scientists and mathematicians, who attempted to unlock the secrets of the universe using the powers of the human intellect. The foremost thinkers of the time embraced the idea of progress—that the world was getting better and that humans were capable of improving their own lives. These ideas would become core beliefs of modernism.

Beginning in England, this intellectual movement spread to France, which in turn spread its influence throughout Europe by the end of the eighteenth century. An important catalyst was the rebuilding of London after the great fire of 1666, which destroyed more than three-quarters of the old city. Christopher Wren's *Saint Paul's Cathedral* (**16-1**) put a new face on the London skyline, one that reflected the best of the Classical, Renaissance, and Baroque traditions. He personally directed the construction of fifty-two new city churches. It was the start of an era that would see for the first time the emergence of an influential native British art.

English Art Becomes Respectable: Reynolds

A career in art in England during the eighteenth century became respectable because of Sir Joshua Reynolds, who became known as an intellectual

ART

Poussin, *Et in Arcadia Ego* c. 1655

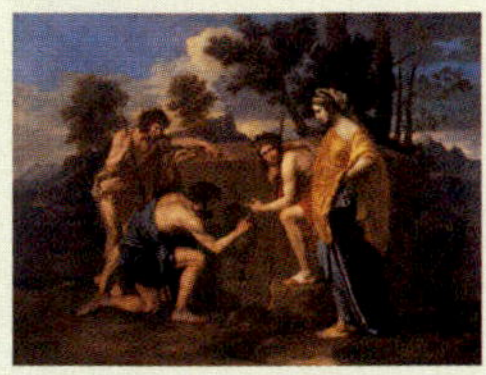

Wren, St. Paul's Cathedral 1675–1710

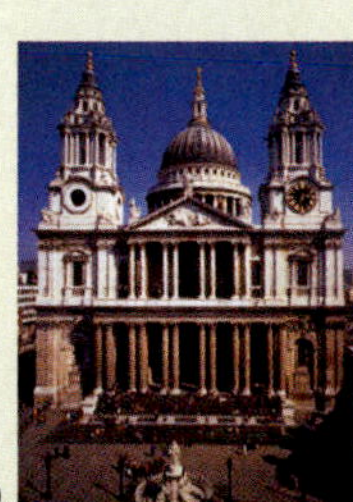

Watteau, *Three Studies of a Youth* c. 1710

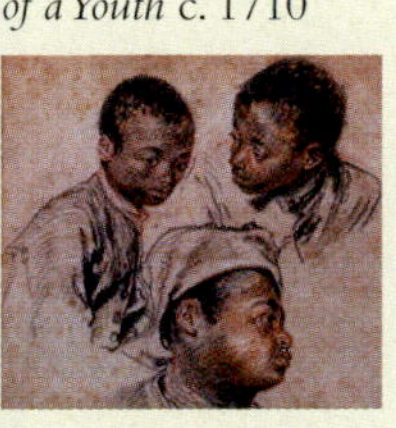

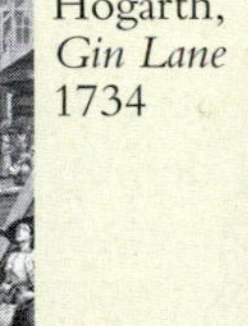

Hogarth, *Gin Lane* 1734

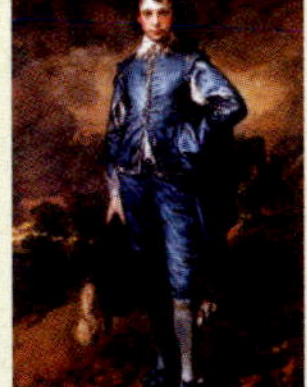

Gainsborough, *The Blue Boy* 1770

Jefferson, Monticello 1770–1806

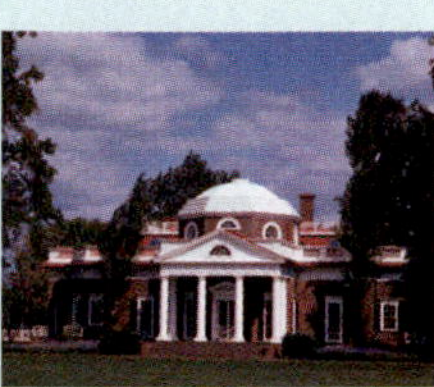

David, *Oath of the Horatii* 1784

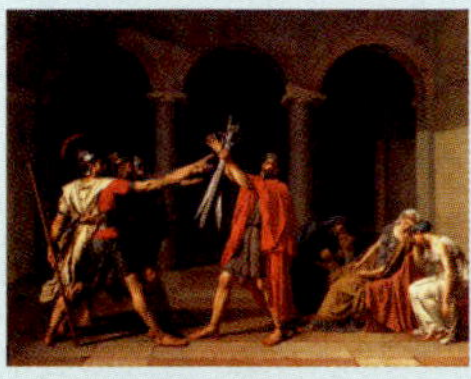

Kauffmann, *Cornelia Pointing to Her Children as Her Treasures* c. 1785

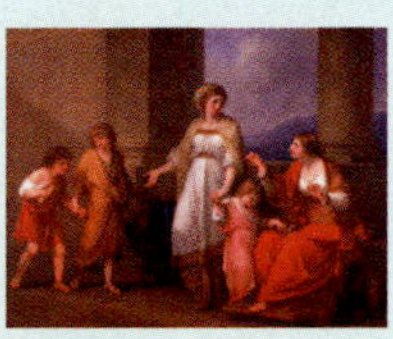

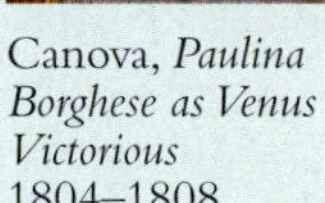

Canova, *Paulina Borghese as Venus Victorious* 1804–1808

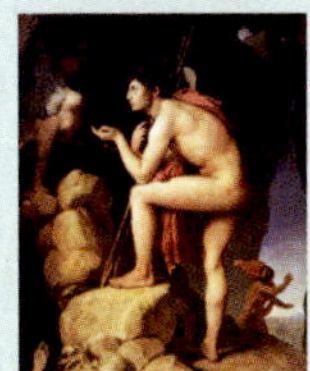

Ingres, *Oedipus and the Sphinx* 1808

Nash, The Royal Pavillion at Brighton 1815–1823

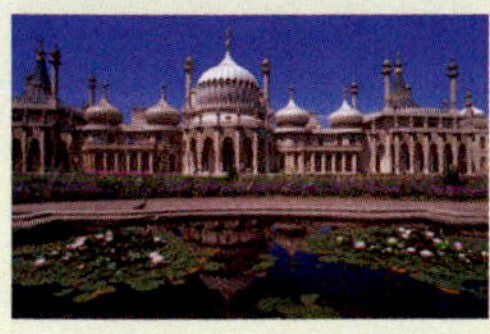

Gericault, *Raft of the Medusa* 1818–1819

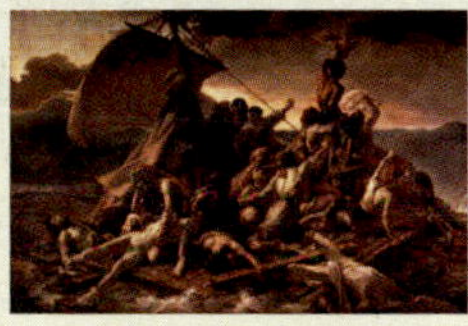

Hokusai, *The Great Wave* c. 1822

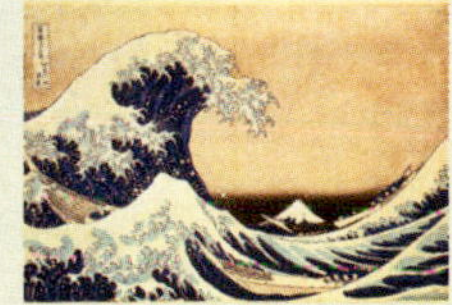

Turner, *Slave Ship* 1840

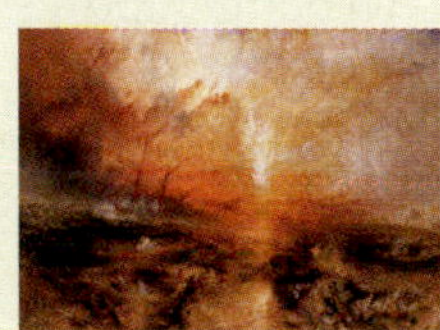

Millet, *The Gleaners* 1857

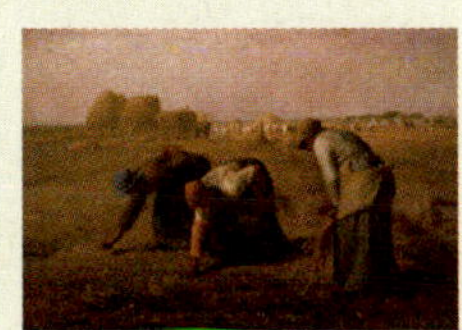

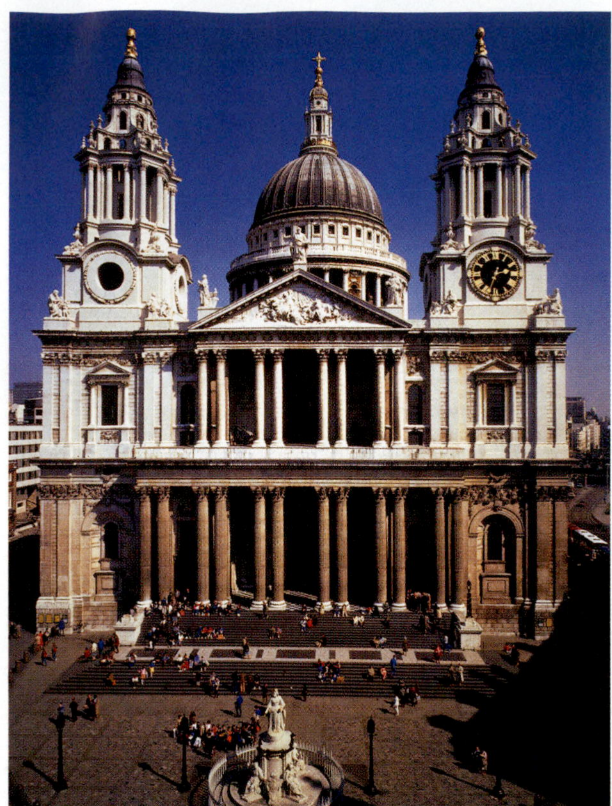

16-1 Christopher Wren, Saint Paul's Cathedral, London, 1675–1710.

figure as well as an artist. Through the interest of wealthy patrons, he was able to study in Italy, an experience that profoundly influenced his views of art and culture. When he returned to London, he immediately became a great success in polite society and the city's most fashionable portrait painter. When the Royal Academy was founded by King George III in 1768, Reynolds became its first president. From this post he was able to dominate "official" art and disseminate his views on aesthetics and the proper training for young painters.

Reynolds taught that all artists should base their work on the Old Masters. He dedicated the Royal Academy to preserving the traditions of the past and believed that an artistic education should begin with technical training, progress to a study of great works of art, and only then attempt to imitate the natural world. Like the French academic and classical artist Poussin, Reynolds believed that great art should concern itself with the ideal rather than the real to express "great and noble ideals." His views were thus directly opposed to those of his countryman and contemporary, William Hogarth (6-7), who believed in useful art that reflected reality.

In his portrayal of the greatest English actress of the period, *Mrs. Siddons as the Tragic Muse* (**16-2**), Reynolds painted a symbolic **allegory** (a form of art in which human characters personify certain qualities or ideals). Because Sarah Siddons was famous for her brilliant acting of tragic roles, particularly Lady Macbeth, Reynolds shows her as the classical muse of tragedy. The artist pays homage not just to the actress but also to the Old Masters in his choices of both style and subject. The actress's pose is copied from that of one of the prophets Michelangelo had painted on the Sistine ceiling, while the dramatic lighting and theatrical contrasts are reminiscent of Rembrandt and Gentileschi. Reynolds's color scheme has a typically reddish brown "old masters" tone that contrasts with the fresher and more natural colors of his rival, Thomas Gainsborough.

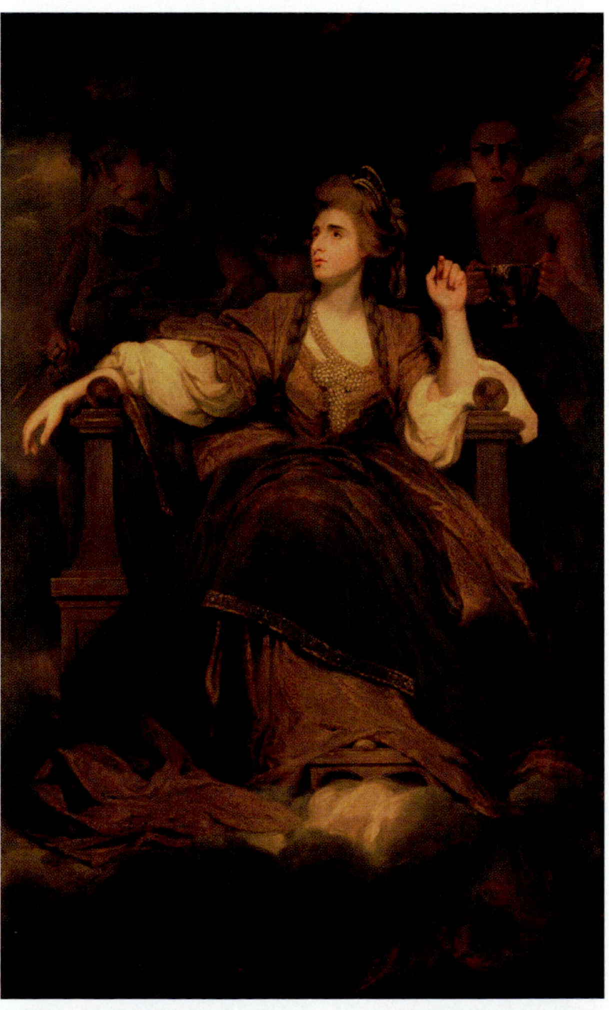

16-2 Sir Joshua Reynolds. *Mrs. Siddons as the Tragic Muse,* 1784. Oil on canvas, 93″ × 51½″. Dulwich Picture Gallery, London.

Thomas Gainsborough

The Blue Boy (**16-3**) is not only Gainsborough's most famous painting but for many years also probably the best-loved picture in English art. Rather than a mythic figure, the boy in the picture is Jonathan Buttall, the son of a wealthy hardware merchant and a friend of the artist. However, the true subject of *The Blue Boy* is a love of painting and perhaps even a bit of Gainsborough's friendly rivalry with Reynolds, who had once painted a boy in a similar brown costume. A popular legend states that it was painted just to disprove one of Reynolds's many aesthetic theories—that it would be impossible to make a great painting using blue as the dominant color.

Despite his fancy dress costume, Jonathan Buttall looks boldly at the viewer and appears vigorously alert and alive. The design is simple and striking. The blues of the costume contrast dramatically with the warm reddish-brown tones of the background. Gainsborough's handling of paint varies from the crisp impasto used to detail the suit to the wispy, feathery lines in the trees and sky.

The two most important English painters of the eighteenth century represented different approaches to art. Reynolds, looking to the artistic models of the past and attempting to portray the ideal rather than the real, was a typical Classicist. Gainsborough, however, introduced many of the attitudes of the movement that later became known as **Romanticism**—a deep love for nature and the landscape and an emphasis on his own personal viewpoint rather than adherence to Classical rules. The contrast between these artists is representative of the conflict between two art movements that would dominate the next one hundred years in Western art: Romanticism and Neoclassicism.

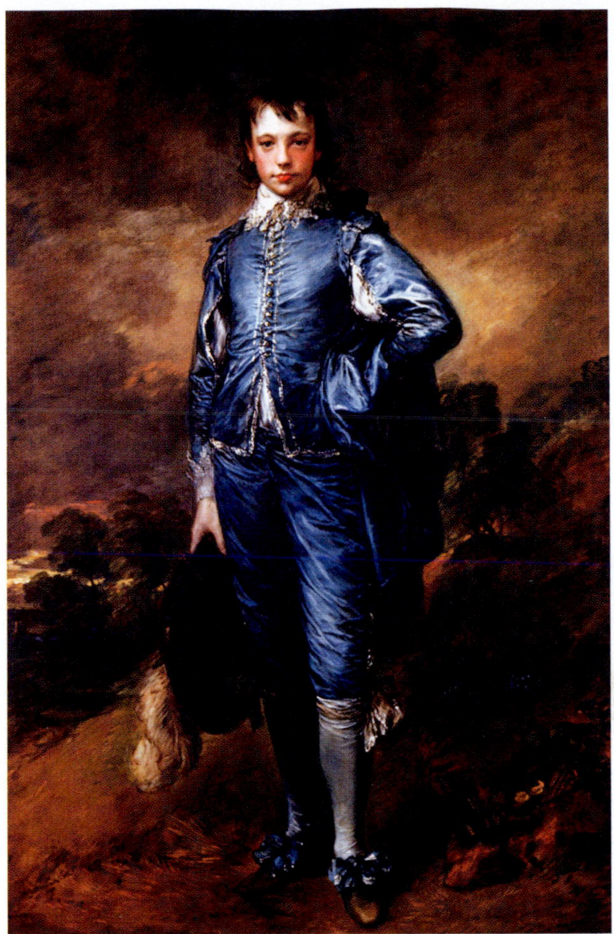

16-3 Thomas Gainsborough, *The Blue Boy,* 1770. Oil on canvas, 70″ × 48″. Henry E. Huntington Library and Art Gallery, San Marino, California.

NEOCLASSICISM

The **Neoclassical** style was a visual expression of the ideals of the Enlightenment. Enlightenment thinkers, both scientists and philosophers, valued order and rationality above all. Similarly, Neoclassical painters rejected both the high drama and murky atmosphere of Baroque art and the misty sentimentality of the Rococo. They searched for clarity of line, color, and form, admiring the simplicity of Greek art.

The supreme object of the Neoclassical artist was to paint a moral lesson that would educate and improve the viewer—what were called "history paintings," generally scenes from the ancient past. They dreamed of creating large works of art that could be used to educate the public to civic virtues, much as stained-glass windows educated peasants in the Middle Ages. In the words of Denis Diderot, an eighteenth-century French philosopher and art critic: "To make virtue attractive, vice odious, ridicule forceful: That is the aim of every honest man who takes up the pen, the brush, or the chisel."

An excellent illustration of this moralizing style of art can be seen in the work of an artist of international reputation, Angelica Kauffman. Like Artemisia Gentileschi, she had been trained by her artist father; like Bernini, she was considered a prodigy. As a young woman Kauffman traveled to Florence and Rome, where she met other Neoclassical artists; she eventually settled in Rome. A good friend of Sir Joshua Reynolds, she was one of only two women who became founding members of the British Royal Academy.

Cornelia Pointing to Her Children as Her Treasures (**16-4**), created in 1785, is a typical Neoclassical painting that both tells a story and points to a moral. Cornelia, a Roman widow, is being visited by a friend who shows off her jewelry. When she asks her hostess to display her own jewels, the proud mother points to her children—two boys on the left and her daughter on the right. Thus the picture demonstrates several values prized by Neoclassicists—modesty, frugality, and pure maternal love. The content and feeling of this painting contrast dramatically with Rococo works about aristocratic sexuality, such as Fragonard's *The Swing* (15-40). Responsibility has replaced frivolity.

The style of the painting reinforces the ideas it expresses. Kauffman's figures are crisp and clean, their outlines set against a plain backdrop. Like other Neoclassical artists, Kauffman prefers clear, bright colors to murky or suggestive shades. Since this is a painted lesson, there is no place for mood, emotion, or atmosphere.

David and the French Revolution

During the eighteenth century, France had lost some of the glory and preeminence she had enjoyed under Louis XIV. Rococo art, patronized by the mistresses of Louis XV, was a style of the boudoir, not the halls of government. Toward the end of the century, the frivolous and playful Rococo was criticized as an art of decadence. French Neoclassical art, modeled more directly on Greek and Roman art than on the work of either Poussin or Reynolds, emerged as a powerful force that seemed to express a new, more serious moral purpose. Discoveries at the recent excavations at Pompeii and Herculaneum also served to inspire a Classical revival in art and fashion in the Western world.

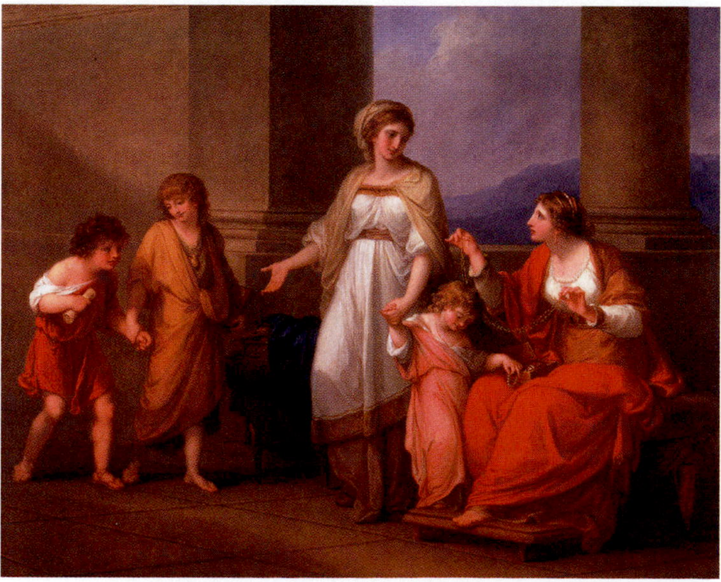

16-4 Angelica Kauffmann, *Cornelia Pointing to Her Children as Her Treasures,* c. 1785. Oil on canvas, 40″ × 50″. Virginia Museum of Fine Arts, Richmond (Adolph D. and Wilkins C. Williams Fund). Acc. #75.22. Photo: Katherine Wetzel.

Although Neoclassicism appealed to many artists throughout Europe and the United States, it found its most perfect expression in the work of the French artist Jacques-Louis David. David took Neoclassical ideals and followed them to their logical conclusions, concentrating their power. His style of painting appeared absolutely brutal when it first appeared. All the fluidity and elegance of the Rococo, echoes of which had remained in the work of Kauffman, were replaced by a new icy-hard surface. In their crystalline purity, David's figures seem to be carved rather than painted. In his enthusiasm for the new Neoclassical style, he revolutionized academic painting.

Success did not come easily to David. When he was denied the prestigious Prix de Rome (a prize of a year's study in Rome given to the most promising student in the French Academy), he even attempted suicide. Happily (and somewhat surprisingly), the Rococo artist Fragonard took pity on him and transferred an important commission to the young artist. Eventually, David did win the prize to study in Rome, which is where his first great masterpiece, *Oath of the Horatii* (**16-5**), was painted.

As in other Neoclassical history paintings, David's painting tells a moral story and seeks to teach proper values. It is based on a legend about the early years of the Roman Republic, when the Romans were about to go to war with the Albans. On the eve of battle, it was decided that the outcome would be determined by single combat in three individual contests. The three brothers of the Horatii family swore to defend the Roman state against three brothers of another family, one of whom was engaged to their sister. David chose to depict the moment when the father calls on his sons to swear to sacrifice their lives, if necessary, for the good of the country. Two brothers would die; so would their sister's fiancé. Thus the virtues David emphasized were patriotism, self-sacrifice, and fidelity to a higher purpose.

The *Oath of the Horatii* shows David's mastery of composition. The geometry of the design is clear: the space is divided by three arches, in front of which are

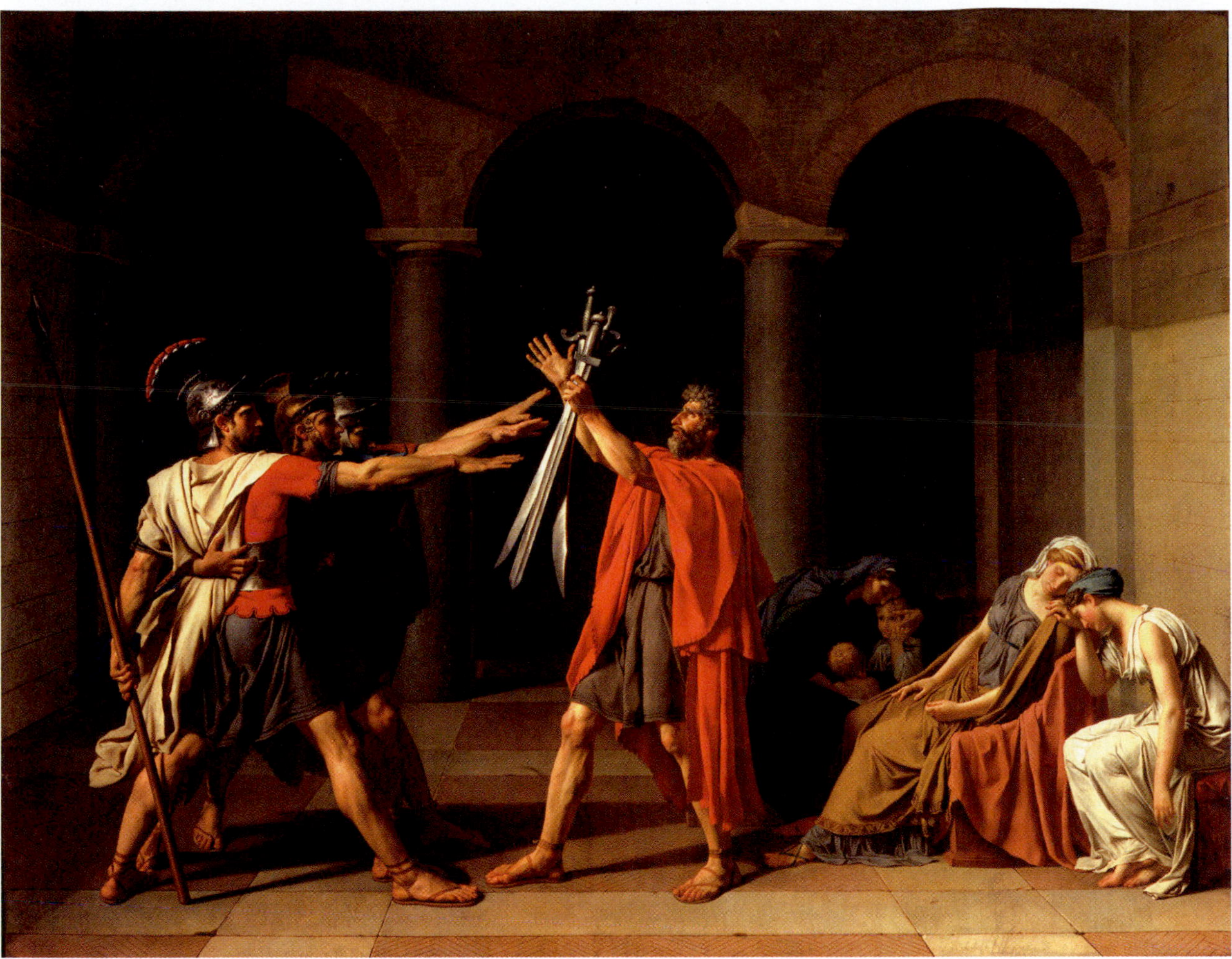

16-5 Jacques-Louis David, *Oath of the Horatii,* 1784. Oil on canvas, 11′ × 14′. Louvre, Paris.

arranged three distinct figure groupings—the sons, the father, and the women. Silhouetted against the simple, darkened background, three arms reaching toward three swords catch the light. David sets up a powerful rhythm of legs, arms, and swords by repeating each form with slight variations. The outlines of the male figures are rigid and strong, in contrast to the soft, melting outlines of the females.

Although the *Oath of the Horatii* was painted before the French Revolution, its style and content put David at the forefront of art and convinced the revolutionaries that he was one of them in spirit. His utter rejection of the Rococo style was seen as an equally strong condemnation of the old regime. David became not only a firm supporter of the Revolution but also one of its leaders, its artist, spokesman, and historian. He organized revolutionary holidays and celebrations. He abolished the Royal Academy and replaced it with what was called the Commune of Art. David also transformed the Louvre, the newly vacant royal palace, into a public art museum. As curator, he named his former benefactor Fragonard, who might otherwise have been in danger because of his past association with aristocrats.

Now David painted contemporary events with the same reverence he had used for historical pictures. Like the ancient Roman Republic, the new French state had heroes and martyrs. What was different was that David knew these men and women; they were his associates and friends. For this reason, *Death of Marat* (**16-6**) has a great immediate impact. Marat was a revolutionary leader who was forced to spend hours in the bath because of a painful skin disease. Because he spent so much time soaking, Marat was accustomed to working and even receiving visitors while in his therapeutic tub. One visitor was a young woman named Charlotte Corday. A revolutionary who disagreed with Marat's policies, she stabbed him while he was at work. The stark painting combines David's emotional intensity with the

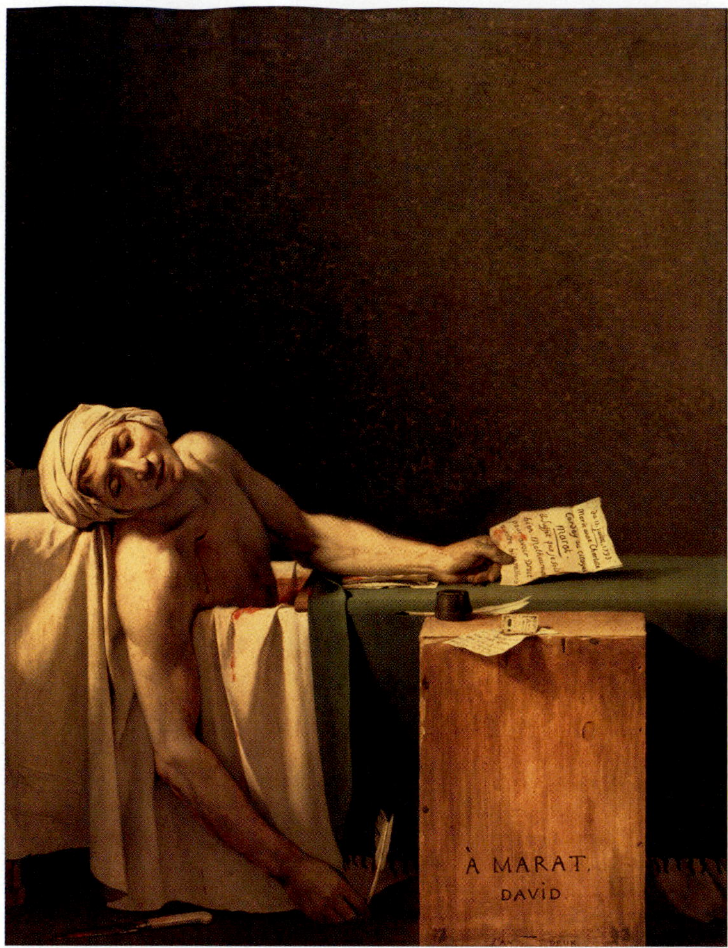

16-6 Jacques-Louis David, *Death of Marat,* 1793. Oil on canvas, approximately 63″ × 49″. Musées royaux des Beaux-Arts de Belgique, Brussels.

simplicity of the Neoclassical style. Like a religious painting by Caravaggio, nothing in the background distracts from the pale corpse of the martyr Marat. With his white, marble-like flesh, Marat is shown as a mythic hero, not a suffering human.

Before Marat's death, revolutionary leaders had inaugurated a series of public executions known as the Reign of Terror, along with it the long chain of events that would lead to the collapse of the Revolution. David was imprisoned as a traitor, but his life was spared. Then, with the rise of Napoleon Bonaparte, David found a new patron. For him, Napoleon became the hero who would bring France back to glory, and he painted his new hero many times.

But Napoleon was a very different kind of leader from Marat. He was a military man. In a dozen years he had not only fought off France's enemies but also conquered much of Europe. This difference in models is obvious when we compare *Bonaparte crossing the Great Saint Bernard Pass* (**16-7**) with *Death of Marat* and *Oath of the Horatii*. Rather than exhibiting classical restraint and purity, David fills his canvas with the dynamic form of a rearing horse. Horizontals and verticals, which create a feeling of stasis, have been replaced by strong diagonals, suggesting movement. Cool harmony and balance were now supplanted by theatricality more reminiscent of Baroque art—foreshadowing the coming Romantic movement.

Canova and Neoclassical Sculpture

As they ascended the thrones of Europe and married into royal families, Napoleon's relatives also became important patrons of Neoclassical art. The greatest sculptor of the period was Antonio Canova, a Venetian who gained international fame at a young age. Like David, Canova studied in Rome and was directly inspired by Classical art. Napoleon's sister, Paulina, had married an Italian Prince of the Borghese family, a Roman dynasty noted for their fabulous art collection and elegant gardens in the heart of the city. It was natural that Paulina would turn to Canova to immortalize her, as he did when he portrayed her as Venus Victorious (Venus after she had been declared the most beautiful of the Greek goddesses in a mythological contest). With nudity echoing that of the *Venus de Milo* (*Aphrodite of Melos*, 12-18), the statue of Paulina lounges on a classical divan (**16-8**). It may seem shocking that a princess asked to have herself shown as the goddess of love in what appears to be a provocative pose—she seems to be either waiting for or relaxing after lovemaking—but Napoleon's sister was known for both her beauty and her scandalous lifestyle. Canova's statue exhibits skill similar to that of Bernini (the Borghese collection still houses both this sculpture and many of Bernini's greatest works), but the effect is far more cool, elegant, and restrained—more Neoclassical. By employing the talents of exceptional artists, the upstart Bonapartes were attempting to catapult their family into the highest society culturally as well as politically.

Soon after working on this statue, Canova was commissioned by Napoleon himself to portray the French leader as Mars, the god of war, although the statue was actually titled *Mars, the Peacemaker.* For this project, the sculptor carved a massive—larger than life-size—naked heroic figure in marble. Unlike his sister, however, Napoleon was embarrassed by a vision of himself as a classical nude. Never publicly

16-7 Jacques Louis-David, *Bonaparte crossing the Great Saint Bernard Pass,* 1801. Oil on canvas, 8′ 6″ × 7′ 3″. Chateaux de Malmaison et Bois-Preau, Rueil-Malmaison, France.

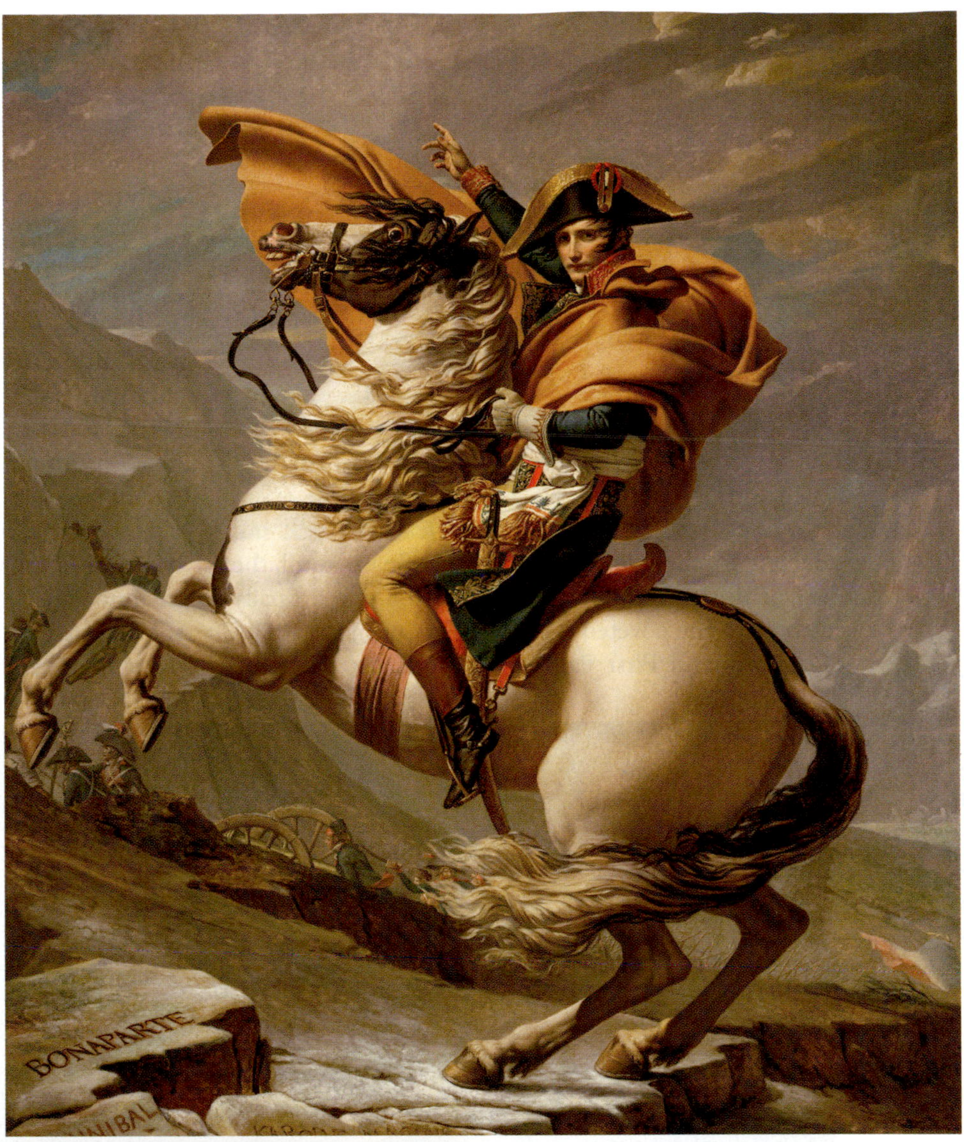

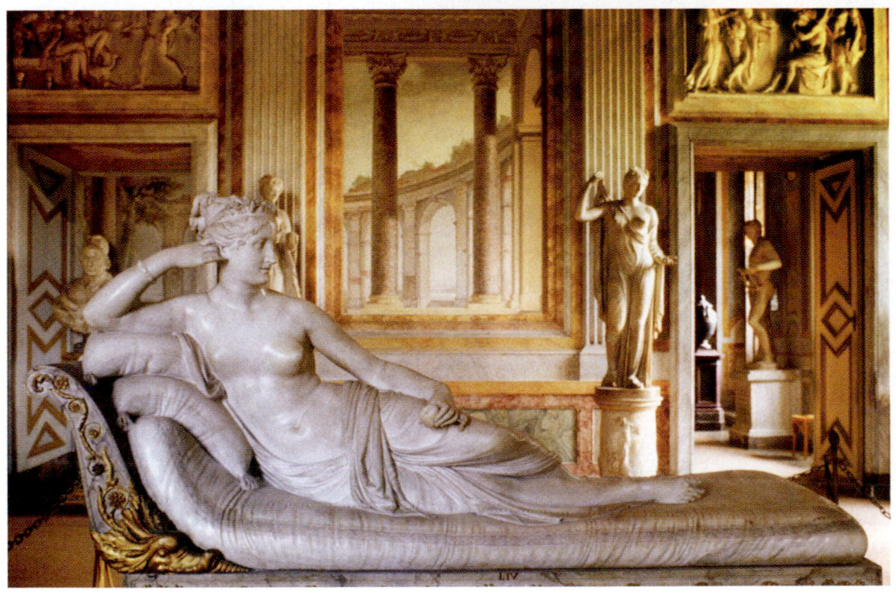

16-8 Antonio Canova, *Portrait of Paulina Borghese as Venus Victorious,* 1804–1808. Marble, height 5′ 3″ (1.6 m), width 6′ 7″ (2 m). Galleria Borghese, Rome.

(**16-11**). A feeling of delicious melancholy pervades many of his evocative images, a sense of yearning and the quest for life's meaning.

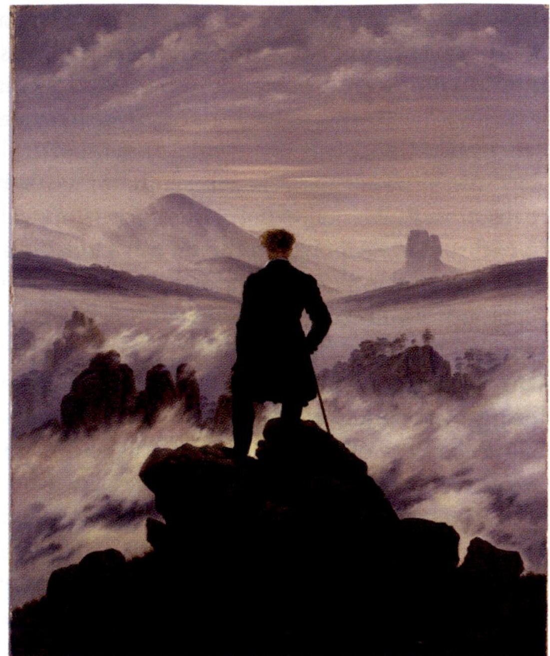

16-11 Caspar David Friedrich, *Wanderer über dem Nebelmeer (Wanderer above a Sea of Fog)*, 1818. Oil on canvas, 37″ × 29″. Kunsthalle Hamburg, Germany.

The English Landscape and Romanticism

England produced great Romantic poets and painters. The works of both groups were centered around nature and the English landscape. J. M. W. Turner's vision of nature was similar to that expressed by Caspar David Friedrich, who gloried in the grandeur and power of the natural world—what was known in the early nineteenth century as the *sublime*. Turner's brilliant career began early. By the age of seventeen, Turner was able to support himself by painting, and he was elected to the British Royal Academy of Art when he was only twenty-four. Turner's favorite themes were dramatic views of storms, fires, sea battles, and sunrises and sunsets over the sea. In *Slave Ship* (**16-12**), Turner exhibits Romanticism of both subject and style. The picture's complete title is *Slave Ship (Slave Throwing Overboard the Dead and Dying, Typhoon Coming On)*. Turner has chosen to show a disaster caused not simply by the destructive power of nature but also by human greed and fear. Here, the slave traders have tossed their human cargo overboard in an attempt to save themselves as the typhoon approaches. The helpless captives sink in the churning waters; on the lower right a chained ankle is visible on a single leg surrounded by swarming fish. *Slave Ship* is the ultimate Romantic scene of wild beauty mixed with horror. But at the same time, Turner conveys a strong antislavery message that appealed to English patrons of the period; England was the center of a strong antislavery movement.

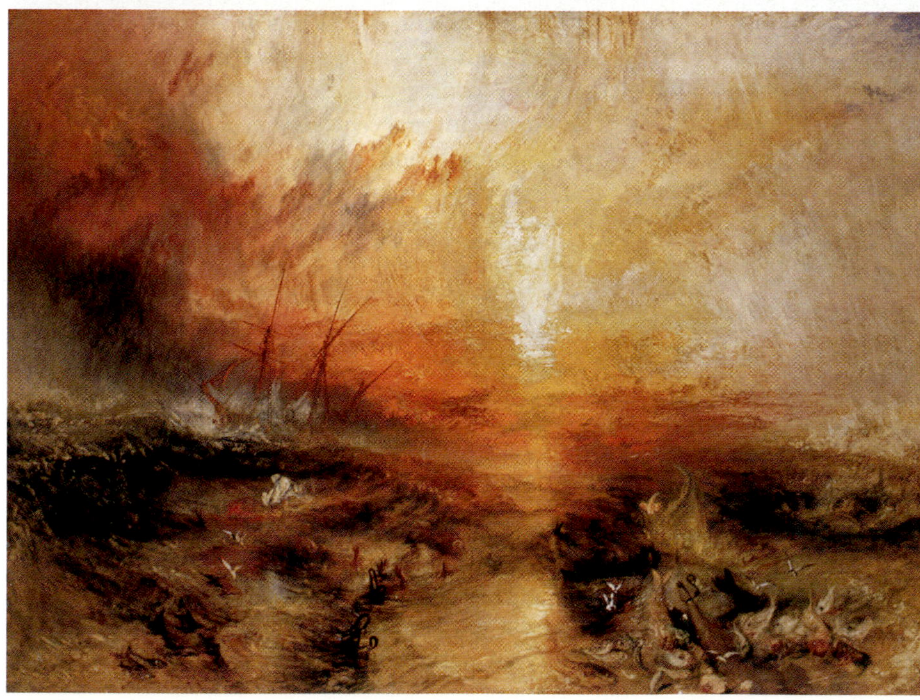

16-12 J. M. W. Turner, *Slave Ship (Slavers Throwing Overboard the Dead and Dying, Typhoon Coming On)*, 1840. Oil on canvas, 35¾″ × 48¼″. Museum of Fine Arts, Boston (Henry Lillie Pierce Fund).

By the end of his career, Turner focused entirely on the raw power of nature and the primal elements of earth, wind, fire, and water. In works like the *Snow Storm* (5-6), he created startling imaginative images, almost totally abstract compositions of color, rich layers of paint, and vigorous brushstrokes that today cannot fail to remind us of the work of the Abstract Expressionists more than a century later.

Romanticism and Politics in France

Théodore Géricault was a young French artist who adopted the Romantic lifestyle. Like the English Romantic Lord Byron, whose poetry he admired, Géricault embraced excess—passionate political convictions, passionate opinions about art, and a passionate taste for adventure. Trained in the academic, Neoclassical style of painting, Géricault traveled to Rome at the age of twenty-five. What caught his attention there were the late works of Michelangelo, especially his *The Last Judgment* (14-27), and the paintings of Caravaggio.

The year Géricault visited Rome, 1816, was also the year of a dramatic historical disaster that caught his imagination and made his reputation. In July, *La Meduse,* a French ship bound for Senegal, was wrecked off the West African coast. The captain and officers boarded the only seaworthy lifeboat and began towing the rest of the one hundred fifty passengers and crew on a raft built from the ship's timbers. After a couple of days, those on the lifeboat cut loose from the raft and abandoned it. By the thirteenth day after the wreck, when the survivors were finally rescued, only fifteen remained alive. The others had died of hunger, thirst, and exposure from the blazing sun as the raft became a living hell where desperate men sickened, became insane, and even ate human flesh.

Géricault threw himself into the immense project of capturing the shocking horror of this event on canvas with enormous energy. In the interest of realism, he had a duplicate raft built in his studio. He interviewed survivors and learned all he could about the disaster. Then he visited hospitals to observe the sick and dying. Yet the final result, the *Raft of the Medusa* (**16-13**), has a unity that overrides incidental details and transforms the picture into an epic statement of the beauty and danger found in humanity and nature.

Searching for the most dramatic moment in the story, Géricault decided to illustrate the instant

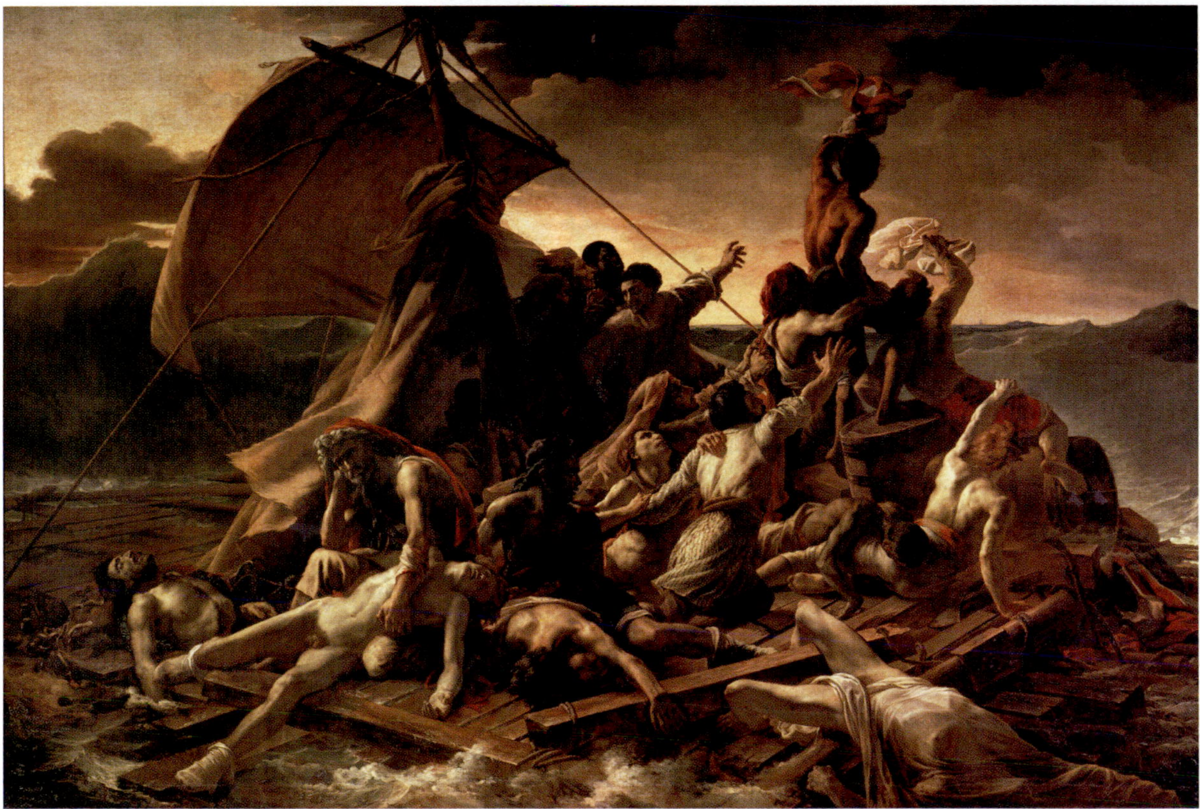

16-13 Théodore Géricault, *Raft of the Medusa,* 1818–1819. Oil on canvas, approximately 16′ × 23′. Louvre, Paris.

A GLOBAL VIEW

Orientalism

In the vicious battle between Neoclassicism and Romanticism, there was one mutual interest—a fascination with exotic foreign lands. **Orientalism,** or the study of Asian art and culture, swept Europe and the United States throughout the nineteenth century. While Americans were most interested in East Asia (China and Japan), Europeans were more attracted to subjects from the Middle East (today's Egypt, Arabia, Turkey, Iraq, and Iran), or in the case of the British, India. What these Orientalists had in common was a view of the peoples, history, and culture of Asia as "other"—the mysterious opposite of Western civilization. Oriental subjects and designs entered Western art at the same time that Europeans were attempting to dominate Asia both economically and politically.

Orientalism influenced all of the fine arts—painting, sculpture, architecture, photography, and design—as well as European literature, music, and philosophy. In some cases, the borrowing was overt, as in the Royal Pavilion at Brighton (**16-20**), built for the Prince Regent (the heir to the British throne and acting king after his father, George III, was declared insane). Known for his active social life and flamboyant taste, the Prince had architect John Nash design a seaside palace that echoes many oriental styles—note the multiple domes, minarets, and Islamic arches—particularly the famous Taj Mahal in India, then a recently acquired British colony. Nash's interpretation stands as a tribute to all of these influences, yet although the exterior and interior of the building have been inspired by the "look" of the Orient, they reflect no real understanding of Asian culture or architecture. The mixing of visual elements from very different societies, separate from their original function and meaning, reflects the European habit of appropriating exotic forms rather than respecting them. Collecting design elements, like trophies, from foreign lands and their imagination of the romantic past, nineteenth-century Europeans remixed periods and civilizations to create a fantasy vision. If Jefferson's Monticello (10-41) is the quintessential Neoclassical ideal, based on Greek and Roman models, Nash's palace is a purely Romantic confection. In Monticello, Jefferson lived the life of the mind; in the Royal Pavilion, the Prince Regent entertained on a lavish scale.

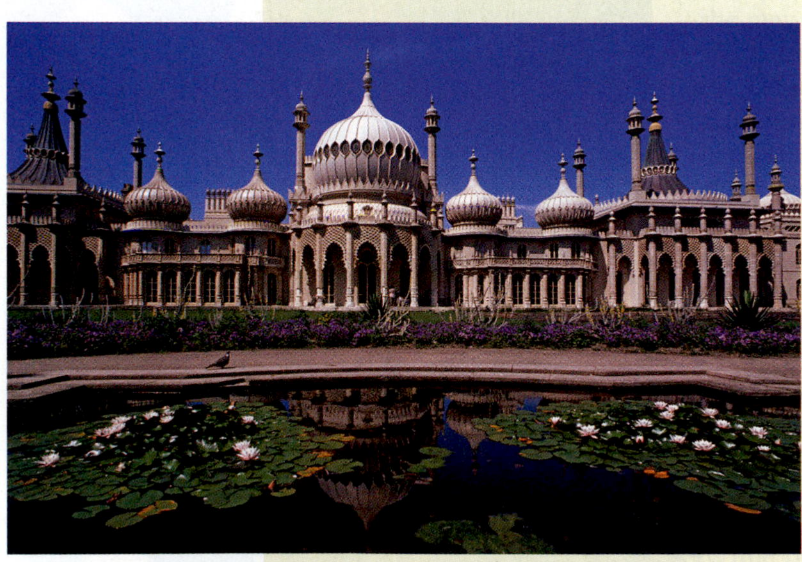

16-20 John Nash, The Royal Pavilion at Brighton, 1815–1823.

The building that inspired The Royal Pavilion was the Taj Mahal of Agra, India (**16-21**), recently selected as one of the new Seven Wonders of the World. The Taj served a very different purpose than Nash's palace. Rather than a personal residence, it was a royal tomb constructed in memory of Mumtaz Mahal, a beloved wife of

A GLOBAL VIEW

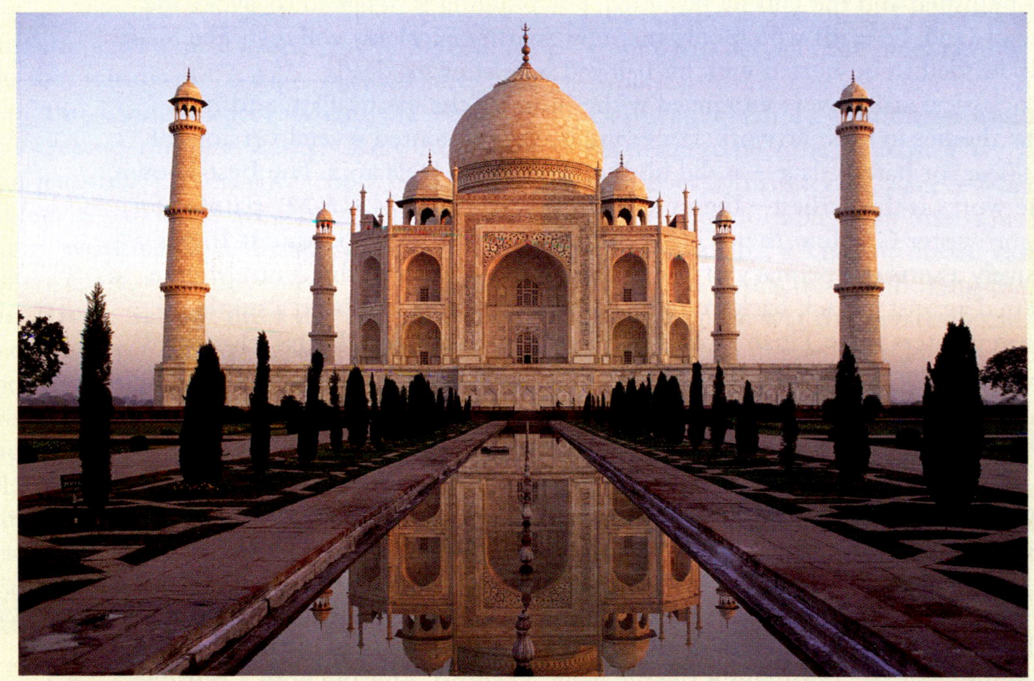

16-21 Taj Mahal, Agra, India. 1623–1647.

the Mughal Emperor Shah Jahan (son of Jahanghir, pictured in 1-21). The famous white marble edifice and its setting took twenty thousand workers seventeen years to complete; one thousand elephants were used on the project. The structure was the result of a collaboration of architects and artists from throughout the Islamic world. No one knows exactly who developed the original concept, but the crown-shaped dome was designed by the Turkish architect Ismail Afandi, while inlaid mosaic designs were supervised by Chiranji Lal, an Indian jewelry artist from Delhi. Persian master Amanat Khan, who decorated the walls with calligraphy, was considered so important that he had a status equal to that of an architect.

The symmetrical structure is made up of precisely balanced shapes: the central block is surmounted by a dome of equal height, while the width of the block and its wings is exactly equal to the height of the block plus the dome. Minarets stand at each corner, their caps miniature versions of the side domes that flank the gently swelling central dome. The whole arrangement is placed on a high platform, reflected in a pool of water set within a garden. This pool is one of four long, narrow pools that criss-crossed the four symmetrical gardens each divided into four sections on the approach to the tomb (four being a holy number in Islam), and the whole is approached through a massive gate indicating that this is a place set apart from daily life, and symbolizing the gate to Paradise.

Despite its Western association with romance, the edifice's symbolism is religious. The entire complex of buildings, waterways, and gardens (which originally included beautiful beds of flowers) was meant to suggest Paradise as described in the Qur'an. Calligraphic inscriptions on the tomb refer to the Day of Judgment, when unbelievers

(continued on next page)

blacks and browns make this a gloomy scene. Yet light falls on their faces, revealing the simple goodness of this family. Despite the obvious clumsiness in van Gogh's early technique, we can already see his ability to transmit strong feelings. This will always be an important strength in his work.

Van Gogh went to Paris to study art, but life there proved difficult. Exposed to all of the most dramatic advances in art, he began to feel the strain. Van Gogh left for the south of France, where he hoped that the warmth of the sun would rejuvenate him. When he got on the train, he did not have a plan for where he would get off. He finally stopped in Arles, which he later called "the country of the sun." There he would have the most productive period of his life. The bright colors of the south would fill his work. He wrote, "I think that after all the future of the new art lies in the south."

In the space of three years, van Gogh went from being a clumsy amateur to a master of line (see 4-8). After ceaseless practice, his drawing had become sure, his lines rhythmic. Some of his advances were due to his study of Japanese art, which he had discovered in Paris (see Global View box). In the house that he rented in Arles, the walls were covered with Japanese prints. Working feverishly, van Gogh would paint for hours, and then collapse and sleep for days.

Van Gogh dreamt of a "school of the south" that he would create in Arles. In June 1888, he invited the living artist he most respected, Paul Gauguin, to come live there with him. Gauguin arrived in October, planning to stay a year, but the visit lasted only nine weeks. At first the men worked well together; they would work all day, and in the evening, exhausted, go off to a café. But Gauguin was not an easy man to get along with, and neither was van Gogh. Tension soon developed between them, and they began to argue. A darker world now entered van Gogh's work. He wrote: "In my painting of *The Night Café* (**17-28**), I have tried to express the idea that the café is a place where one can ruin oneself, go mad, or commit a crime." Van Gogh stayed up three nights to paint this picture, sleeping only during the day. The contrast with his earlier interior, *The Potato Eaters*, is considerable. Dark browns and blacks have been replaced by intense colors. The red walls clash against the green ceiling. The floor is a sickly yellow; the lamps cast a dim light that hovers around them like moths.

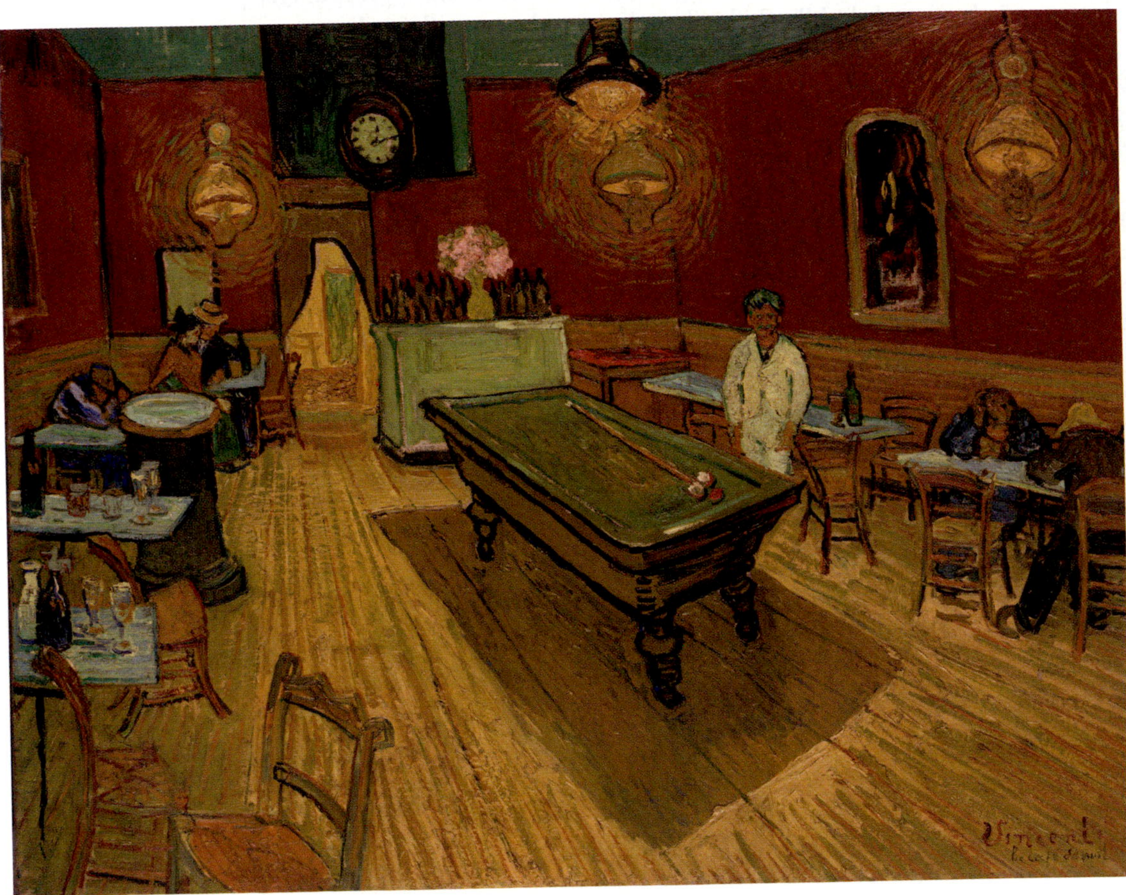

17-28 Vincent van Gogh, *The Night Café,* 1888. Oil on canvas, approximately 28½″ × 36″. Yale University Art Gallery, New Haven, Connecticut.

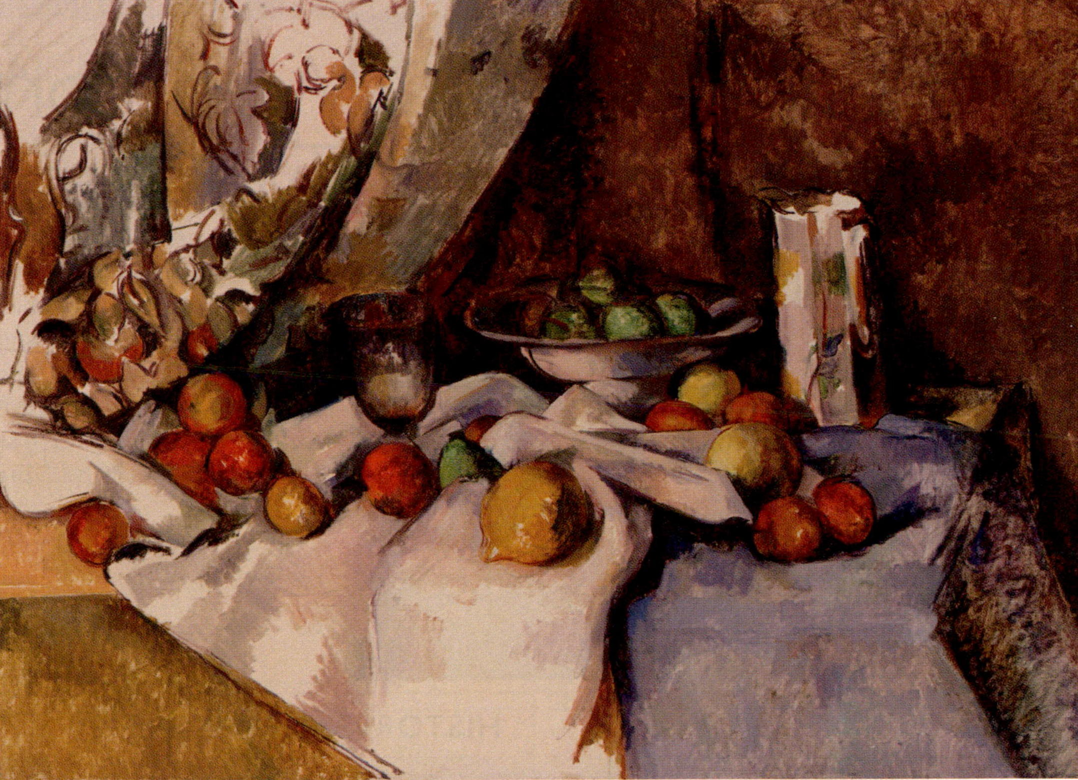

17-32 Paul Cézanne, *Still Life with Apples,* 1895–1898. Oil on canvas, 27″ × 36 ½″. The Museum of Modern Art, New York (Lillie P. Bliss Collection).

arm; he examined the relationship of each part of the vest to the adjacent part of sleeve. After he worked his way down and reached the end of the vest, he probably noticed that the boy's arm was unnaturally long. Most artists would at that point make corrections and make sure that the arm was in proportion to the rest of the body. But to Cézanne that would be dishonest. It was more important to record what he had seen than to have a "logical" picture.

Cézanne's pictures mark the end of the naturalistic approach that Giotto began in the 1300s. By rejecting perspective, the cornerstone of art since the Renaissance, Cézanne opened up a Pandora's box in the twentieth century. Artists became free to pursue their own vision and ignore the fundamental rules of academic art. His influence on the painters of the next generation is profound. The work of the two most important painters of the twentieth century, Henri Matisse and Pablo Picasso (see next chapter), would not be possible if Cézanne had not led the way. His relatively small pictures with the most ordinary of subject matter changed the course of art history.

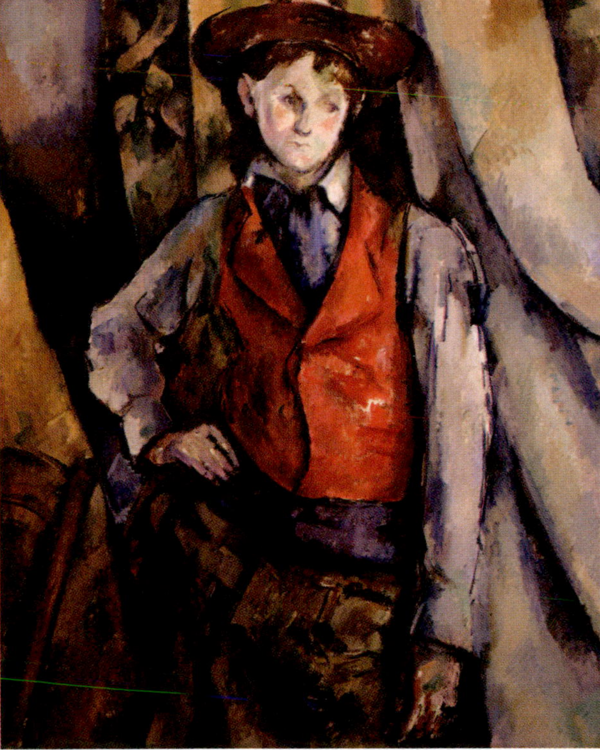

17-33 Paul Cézanne, *Boy in a Red Waistcoat,* 1888–1890. Oil on canvas, 35 ¼″ × 28 ½″. Collection of Mr. and Mrs. Paul Mellon, National Gallery of Art, Washington, DC.

One night, after a particularly violent argument, Gauguin stormed out of the house. Later that night, van Gogh—a little drunk, a little mad perhaps—went into a local house of prostitution and handed his favorite girl a box. Attached to it was a note: "Keep this object carefully." Inside was part of his ear. He almost bled to death. He had severed an artery and was discovered in his bed unconscious. He lay in a coma for three days. Van Gogh had gone mad. From then on, he would paint only in his occasional lucid moments. His *Self-Portrait* of 1889 (**17-29**) is a courageous representation of a man trying to be strong while fighting mental illness. It was painted in the asylum; the world is a confusing mass of blue-green swirls.

In another lucid moment at the asylum, van Gogh painted his greatest picture, *The Starry Night* (**17-30**). We are on a hill, looking below to a small town whose tallest feature is the steeple of a little church. In the distance are mountains. The stars have come out—with a vengeance. Large swirling balls of fire fill the sky. The ground the town rests on is

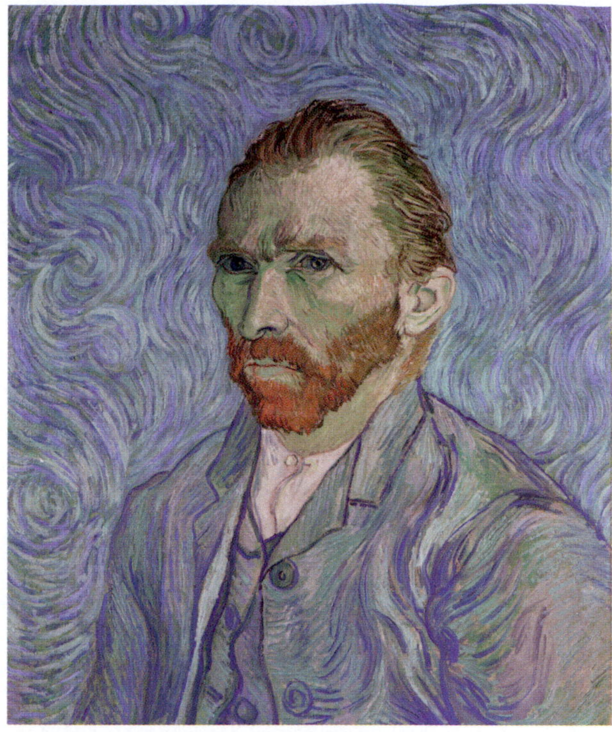

17-29 Vincent van Gogh, *Self-Portrait,* 1889. Oil on canvas, 25 ½″ × 21 ½″. Musée d'Orsay, Paris.

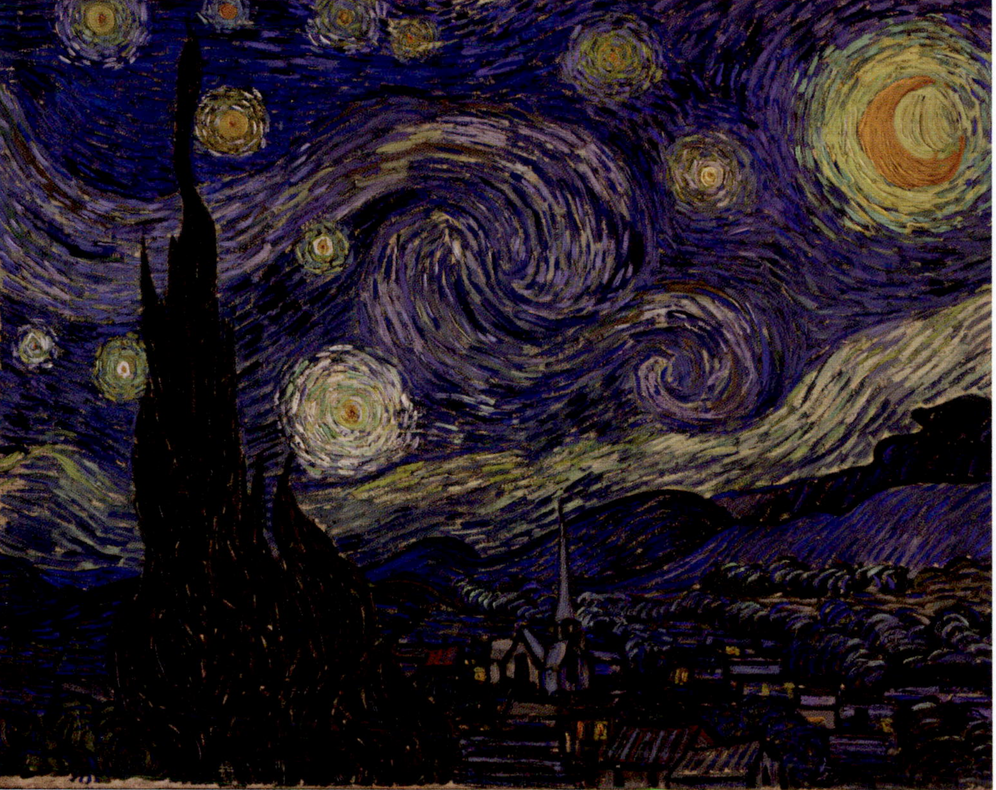

17-30 Vincent van Gogh, *The Starry Night,* 1889. Oil on canvas, 29″ × 36 ¼″. The Museum of Modern Art, New York (acquired through the Lillie P. Bliss Bequest).

unstable; it rolls as if in an earthquake. A large, dark cypress tree rises from the foreground like a brown tongue of fire. All the spiraling shapes are painted by van Gogh with thick lines of paint, sometimes squeezed directly out of a tube (**17-31**). *Starry Night* is a vision, a picture of his mental state. Van Gogh was not satisfied with an imitation of the world but wanted an intense recreation of feeling.

Just two months after he had been discharged from an insane asylum, van Gogh completed his last painting, and then shot himself. He was thirty-seven years old. It had been less than five years since he had painted *The Potato Eaters*. His best work was done in little more than two years. Yet his popularity, fame, and influence would be greater than all but a few artists. When van Gogh declared that artists should "paint things not as they are, but as they feel them," he articulated what would become one of the most important doctrines in twentieth-century art.

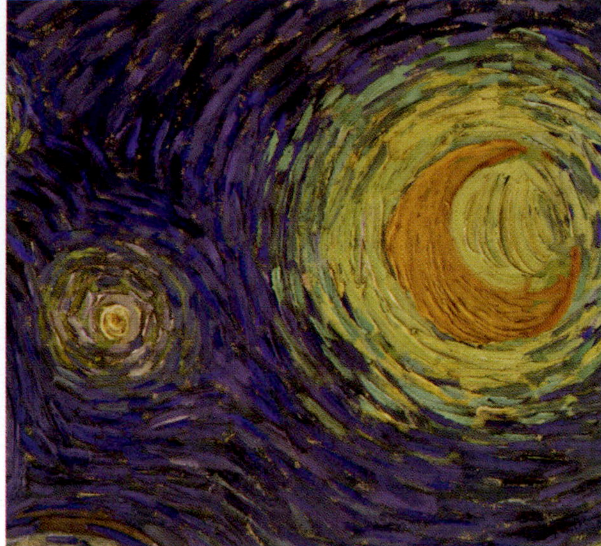

17-31 Detail of figure 17-30.

Cézanne's Revolution

Still, the Postimpressionist who would have the biggest impact on twentieth-century art was Paul Cézanne. Of all the Postimpressionists, Cézanne's work may be the most difficult to appreciate. This is because he *redid the way pictures were made*—a method developed slowly with years of painstaking work. His subject matter was far from revolutionary; he used three of the most ordinary types of painting: still lifes, portraits, and, the favorite of the Impressionists, landscapes. However, if we examine *Still Life with Apples* (**17-32**) closely, what appears at first to be a pleasant still life with some awkward passages proves to be more imaginative. Notice the distortion in the fruit bowl. Its back is tilted forward unnaturally. What you are seeing is not simply a clumsily drawn object. It is a sign that Cézanne is no longer obeying what artists had followed since the beginning of the Renaissance—the mathematical rules of perspective (see Chapter 3).

Cézanne was scrupulously honest. He believed that what the eye saw was the truth, and he realized that perspective was a lie. We do not really see in perspective. None of us is a one-eyed Cyclops, looking in one direction and one direction only. Cameras "see" like that, but people do not. People move their heads and their eyes when they are looking at something.

Perspective, however, had been a very useful lie. It had helped organize paintings and given them the illusion of reality. What could replace it? Cézanne had the courage to try to find out, to go beyond perspective and try to recreate the way we actually see. This is what gives his pictures their fragmented look. His eyes were looking not at the whole scene but at each part separately. That is how we all see; we look from part to part, never really taking in the scene as a whole. Eventually we accumulate a sense of the scene. In fact, the world we know is a carefully constructed web of relationships—approximations of what is there. For example, look at the white of the tablecloth. It appears thick and three dimensional, but the white areas are actually just empty canvas. The darker marks around the white areas make the tablecloth appear to be solid. Cézanne, through his study of color relationships, noticed that we see objects only when they contrast with what is around them.

It is impossible to look at Cézanne's pictures and not be aware of the painter himself. That is part of Cézanne's honesty—he does not conceal his brushstrokes; he reveals how all of the parts of his picture were made. Cézanne used color, not lines, to create forms. He shared with the Impressionists a distaste for conventional drawing, which they associated with the antiquated French Academy. So Cézanne's shapes are constructed by little planes of solid color lying next to each other. In *Boy in a Red Waistcoat* (**17-33**), you can see how Cézanne would narrow his focus to study a specific relationship without paying attention to what could be seen elsewhere. Notice how the arm on the right is much longer than the one on the left. Cézanne never thought of the whole

renewal of the entire Western tradition. Like Futurism, Dada pronounced the icons of the past (exemplified by da Vinci's masterpiece) worthless rubbish to be discarded.

The Dada aesthetic motto was "beautiful as the chance encounter on an operating table of a sewing machine and an umbrella." *Gift* (**18-23**) is an example of the motto put into practice. By creating an unusual combination of everyday items, tacks and an iron, Man Ray, an American friend of Duchamp's, produced a visually powerful creation. His use of juxtaposition—a technique where unrelated objects are taken out of their normal context and joined together, producing a new unique object—opened a new area for artistic exploration. Man Ray called such objects either "indestructible objects" or "objects to be destroyed" and often did smash them. This was the ultimate Dada act, subverting the old notion of art being permanent and deriding the value of immortality. It made the guards in the museums and the notion of masterpieces ridiculous. Other Dadaists caught the iconoclastic mood. One German artist even attached an ax to one of his sculptures with a note encouraging viewers to take a swing at his artwork.

By 1922, there were active centers of Dada activity in Berlin (see Hannah Hoch, 7-16), Paris, Zurich, and New York City. The movement, however, had already crested. The ensuing rapid disintegration of Dada might be seen as the natural culmination of its own manifesto. If anarchy was one's supreme goal, then how could one belong to a movement? Some Dadaists even took actions to encourage its dissolution (for example, sending unsigned insulting letters to their colleagues). By 1923, there were only a few scattered members left in Europe and the United States. The Dada moment had passed.

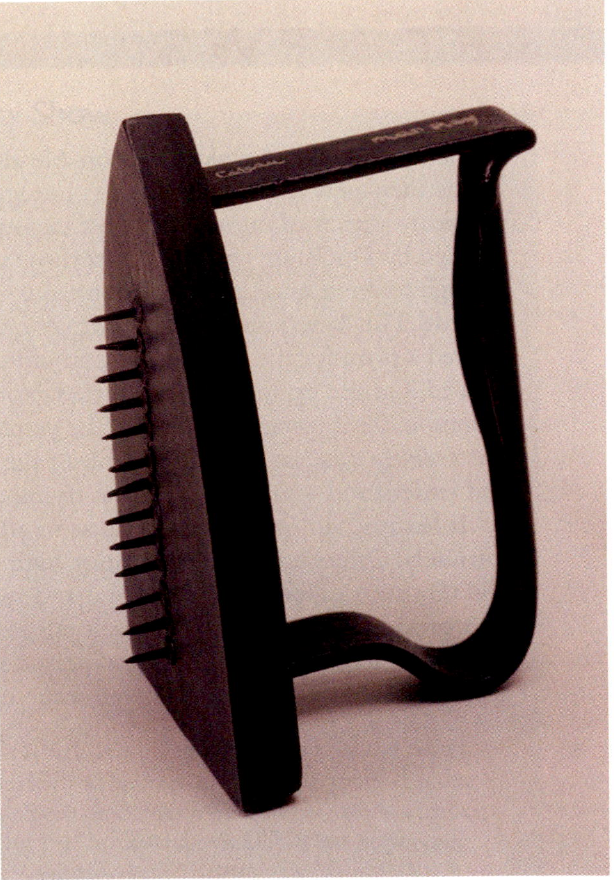

18-23 Man Ray, *Gift*, replica of lost original of 1921. Painted flatiron with nails, 6½″ high. Museum of Modern Art, New York.

The New Objectivity

Embittered by the shattering ordeal of World War I, German Expressionism's very nature changed. Ernst Ludwig Kirchner, its leader, suffered a mental breakdown during the war and was hospitalized. Compare his *Self-Portrait as Soldier* (**18-24**) to his earlier portrait with a model (18-4). The composition is similar: The artist pushed forward on the left with his model behind him on the right. But the toll of the war is now very apparent. The confident, pipe-smoking young bohemian has been replaced by a pale, sunken-cheeked soldier with a butt hanging from his lips. He has aged far more than eight years; his eyes are empty, his look cynical. He holds his painting arm, whose end is a cleanly cut stump, up to the viewer. The only sign of life is the model who now stands shamelessly naked. But she no longer stares lovingly at the symbolically emasculated artist. While never physically injured himself, Kirchner's painting reminds us that the wounds he and many others suffered were both physical and spiritual.

In 1914, Otto Dix had been an "enthusiastic volunteer" of twenty-three. Trained as a machine gunner, he served four years in the front lines. There, Dix was able to see firsthand the results of modern weaponry as the enemy died in his spray of bullets. Like many other veterans who returned from the war, Dix was shocked to see that his homeland seemed unaware of what he had experienced. His countrymen were all too eager to return to the illusions of the previous happier age. In response, Dix became a leading member of a recast Expressionism called

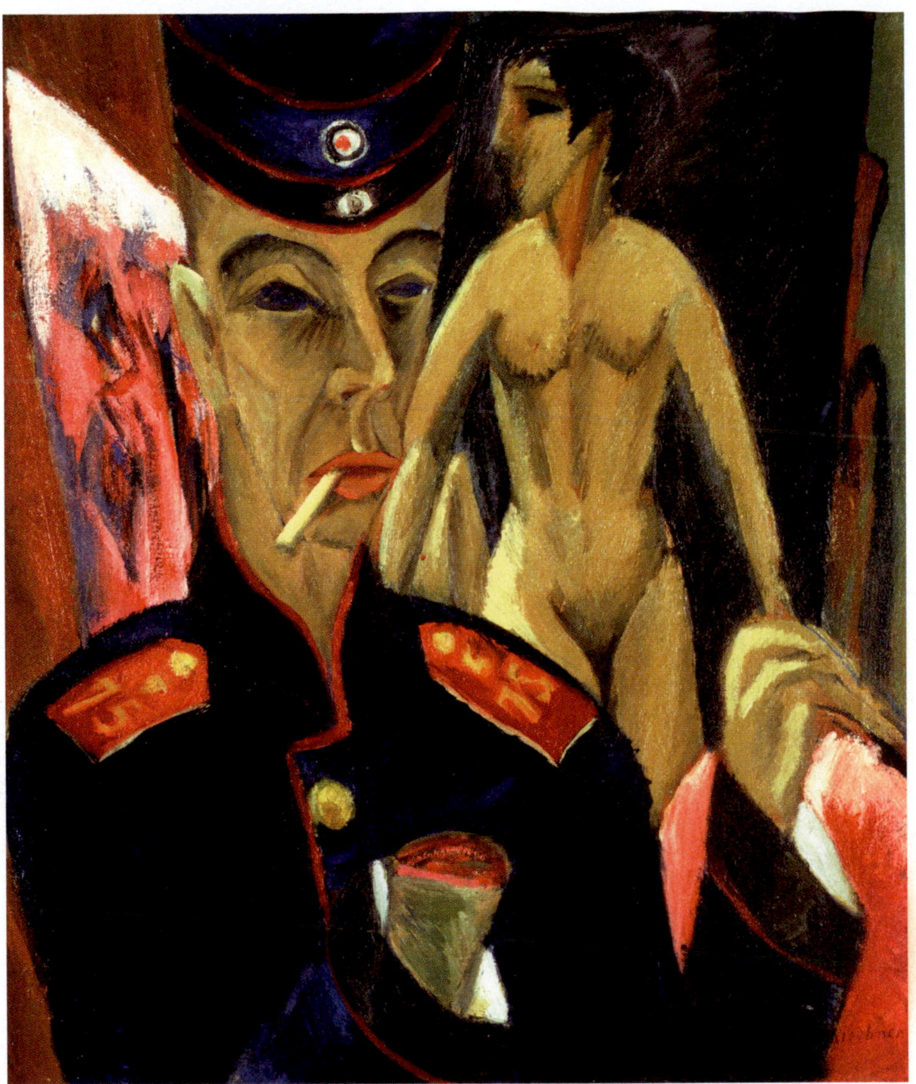

18-24 Ernst Ludwig Kirchner, *Self-Portrait as Soldier,* 1915. Oil on canvas, 27 ¼″ × 24″. © Ingeborg & Dr. Wolfgang Henze-Ketterer, Wichtrach/Bern. Allen Memorial Art Museum, Oberlin College, Ohio (Charles F. Olney Fund).

The New Objectivity. Their goals, he said, were to "show human being in all its grandeur, but also in all its depravity, indeed its brutishness." These Expressionists would have "the courage to portray ugliness, life as it comes."

With *Cardplaying War-Cripples* (**18-25**), Dix confronted his fellow Germans with the real consequences of the Great War and cruelly mocked modern science's pathetic attempts to rebuild the maimed young survivors. The card players in this picture are alive but less human than before. Little more than repulsive half-robots, with clumsily sewn eye sockets and tubes stuck in their faces, they are the useless refuse of war; their lives are over. Dix's grotesque images were meant to cut through the atmosphere of self-delusion and denial among the German populace that he felt was suffocating him.

Käthe Kollwitz (see *Self-Portrait*, 4-4), unlike Dix, was an artist who engaged in the struggles of her time as an outspoken advocate, not as a bitter outsider. She wrote:

> I believe that there must be an understanding between the artist and the people. In the best ages of art that has always been the case. . . . I want to have an effect on my time, in which human beings are so confused and in need of help.

Many of Kollwitz's drawings were designs for posters to be used by humanitarian and socialist organizations. Like Dix, Kollwitz illustrated the suffering that the German government tried to ignore. This did not go without notice. When she won a prestigious prize, a government official canceled it, declaring her work "gutter art."

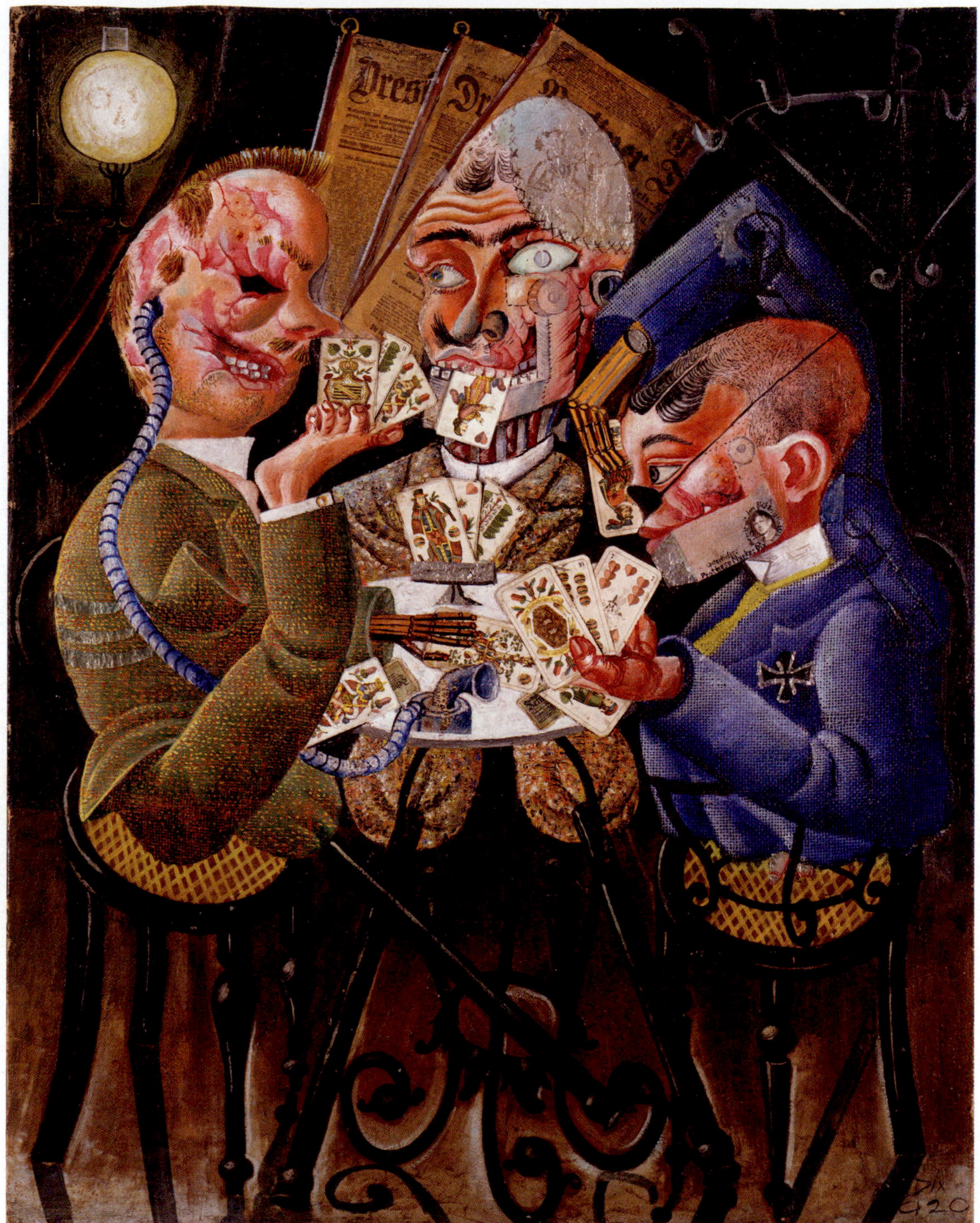

18-25 Otto Dix, *Cardplaying War-Cripples,* 1920. Oil on canvas with montage, 43 ¼″ × 34 ¼″. Nationalgalerie, Staatliche Museen zu Berlin, Germany.

In the 1920s, Germany had its great depression. Devastated financially by the First World War, Germany experienced overwhelming inflation that forced a large part of the population into poverty. There were food riots and starvation. In *Bread!* (**18-26**), Kollwitz shows a mother whose children are hungry but who has nothing to offer them. Kollwitz was unique in her ability to translate abstract social problems into the real burdens that human beings were facing. These problems, unfortunately, remain widespread, which accounts for the enduring power of her art.

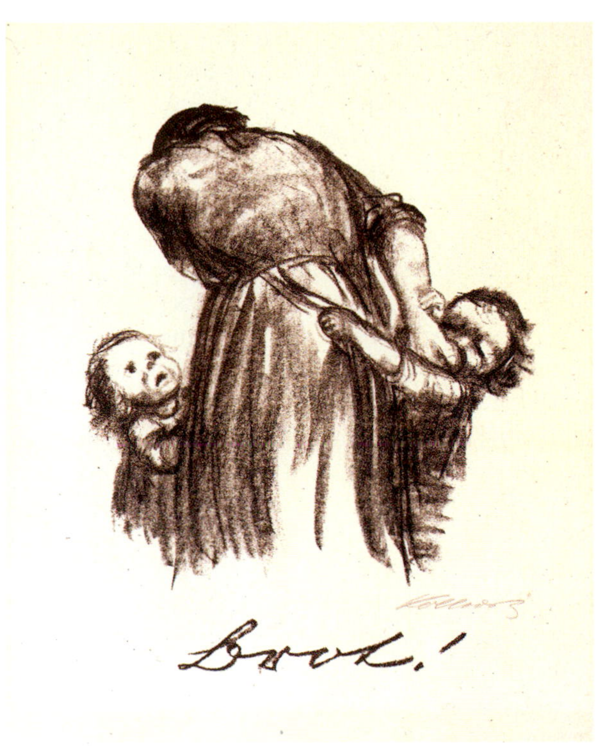

18-26 Käthe Kollwitz, *Bread!,* 1924. Lithograph. Fine Arts Museums of San Francisco, Aschenbach Foundation for Graphic Arts, #1963.30.874

SURREALISM

With the disintegration of the Dada movement, many former Dadaists reorganized under a different flag. Once again they searched for an alternative to a conventional view of reality. They found inspiration in the work of the Viennese psychiatrist, Sigmund Freud, whose discovery of the unconscious and the meaningfulness of dreams had changed the twentieth-century picture of the human mind. This new movement was called **Surrealism,** a word meaning "more real than reality," an art of dreams and the irrational unconscious.

Freud contended that beneath our veneer of rationality, in the unconscious portion of our minds, there lies a world of intense, barely suppressed desires (especially sexual urges). Our dreams, however, give us ways to express feelings that ordinarily have to be suppressed in a symbolic way. So rather than being simply confusing and irrational, dreams are rich in meaning once their symbols are analyzed. In dreams and irrationality, the Surrealists found a fertile world of fantasy and imagination. The unconscious, according to Freud, was also the key to our creativity and emotions. By giving our unconscious a "voice," the Surrealists intended to complete our picture of the world and gain access to the source of imagination. They were therefore confronted with a challenge: How to visualize the irrational unconscious, the unexplainable? How could they make an art of dreams?

The Surrealists of the 1920s found a forerunner of their movement in a relatively unknown Italian painter, Giorgio de Chirico. Without access to the works of Sigmund Freud, he had intuitively created what he called "Metaphysical Pictures" even before World War I. By setting his paintings in landscapes that did not follow the rules of perspective but were painted in a recognizable manner, he was able to evoke the seemingly real but ultimately confusing nature of the dream state. In *Mystery and Melancholy of a Street* (**18-27**), the mathematical certainty of the Renaissance arcade on the left becomes uncertainty when compared to the one on the right. These arcades lead to two irreconcilable vanishing points (see "Linear

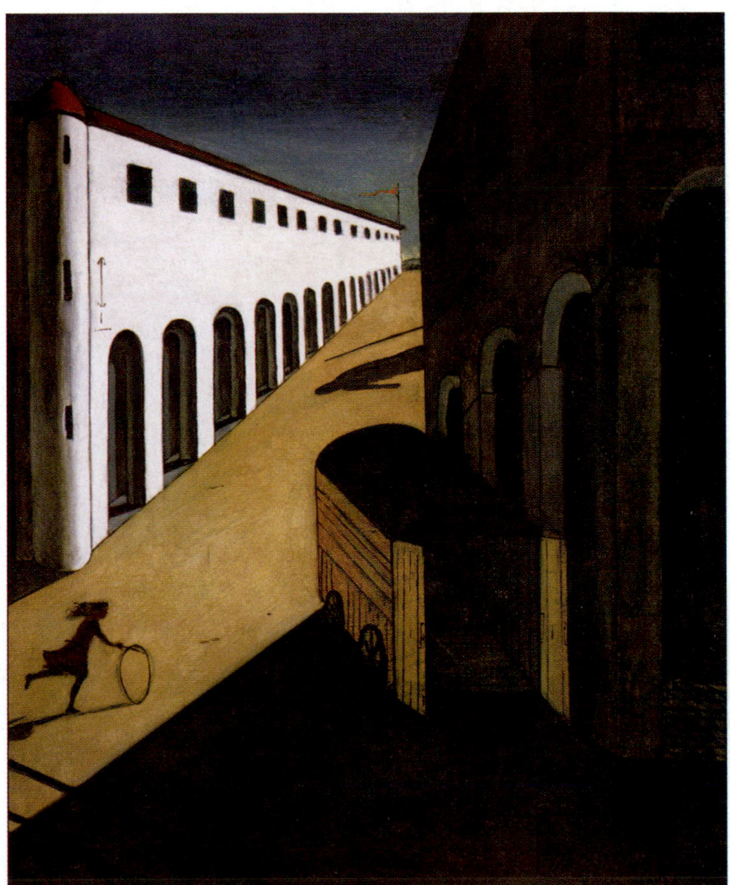

18-27 Giorgio de Chirico, *Mystery and Melancholy of a Street,* 1914. Oil on canvas, 34 ¼″ × 28 ⅛″. Private collection.

Perspective," Chapter 3). An empty boxcar sits in the foreground, enhancing the eerie loneliness of the scene. The frightening quality of a dream is evoked by the interplay between the small girl at play and the long, dark shadow of a figure with a spear above her.

Surrealist Juxtaposition

The Surrealists were committed to the liberation of sexual impulses as the first step in building a better world. Employing the Dadaist technique of illogical juxtaposition, Meret Oppenheim created an unforgettable and oddly sexual Surrealist sculpture—Object *(Le Déjeuner en fourrure),* often known as *Luncheon in Fur* (**18-28**).

By covering a common cup, saucer, and spoon with fur, she altered them profoundly and released many troubling associations. Think of using the fur cup in a conventional way. The connection of two primal urges (thirst and sex) underlies what at first seems only a humorous object but is actually much more disturbing.

Dalí

One of the eerie qualities of dreams is that they look so real while we are asleep. To show dreams in vivid reality, some Surrealists ignored the revolutionary techniques of modern times and returned to the precise techniques of the Baroque masters of Holland and Spain. Salvador Dalí was the greatest master of this style of Surrealism. By bringing a superb realistic technique to Surrealism, he could make bizarre images seem believable.

The setting of Dalí's *The Persistence of Memory* (**18-29**), as in most of his pictures, is a lovely and timeless Mediterranean. In this pleasant landscape reside several strange objects. From left to right, we see a pocket watch with ants crawling on it; a flaccid watch, melted as if made of wax; and another watch hanging limply from a dead tree. An even more disquieting object is placed in the center of this vision—another melted watch hangs over what seems to be a piece of flesh. Complete with eyelashes, it looks as if someone has torn off the side of his or her face and left it on the sand, like a dead fish. In addition to the irrational juxtaposition of these strange objects, their size and scale are confusing, as things often are in dreams.

What does Dalí's picture mean? The artist did not offer much assistance:

> My enemies, my friends and the general public allegedly do not understand the meaning of the images that arise and that I transcribe into my paintings. How can anyone expect them to understand when I myself, the "maker," don't understand my paintings either. The fact that I myself, at the moment of painting, do not understand their meaning doesn't imply that they are meaningless:

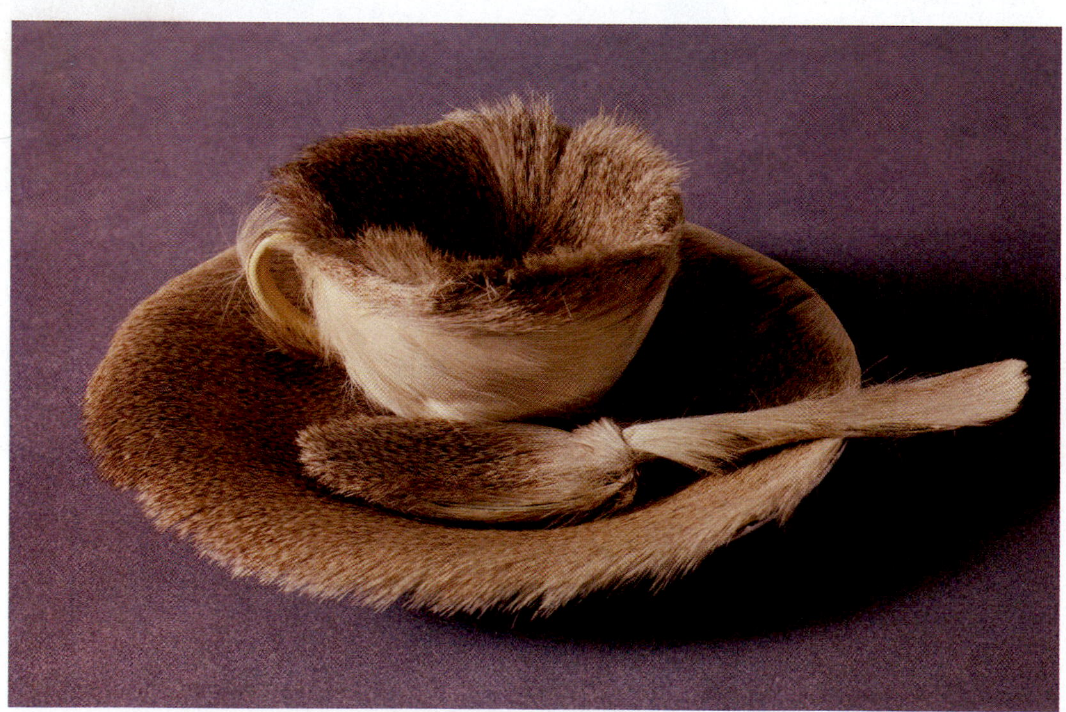

18-28 Meret Oppenheim, *Object (Le Déjeuner en fourrure),* 1936. Fur-covered cup, saucer, and spoon; cup 4 3/8″ diameter; saucer, 9 3/8″ diameter; spoon, 8″ long; overall, 2 7/8″ high. The Museum of Modern Art, New York.

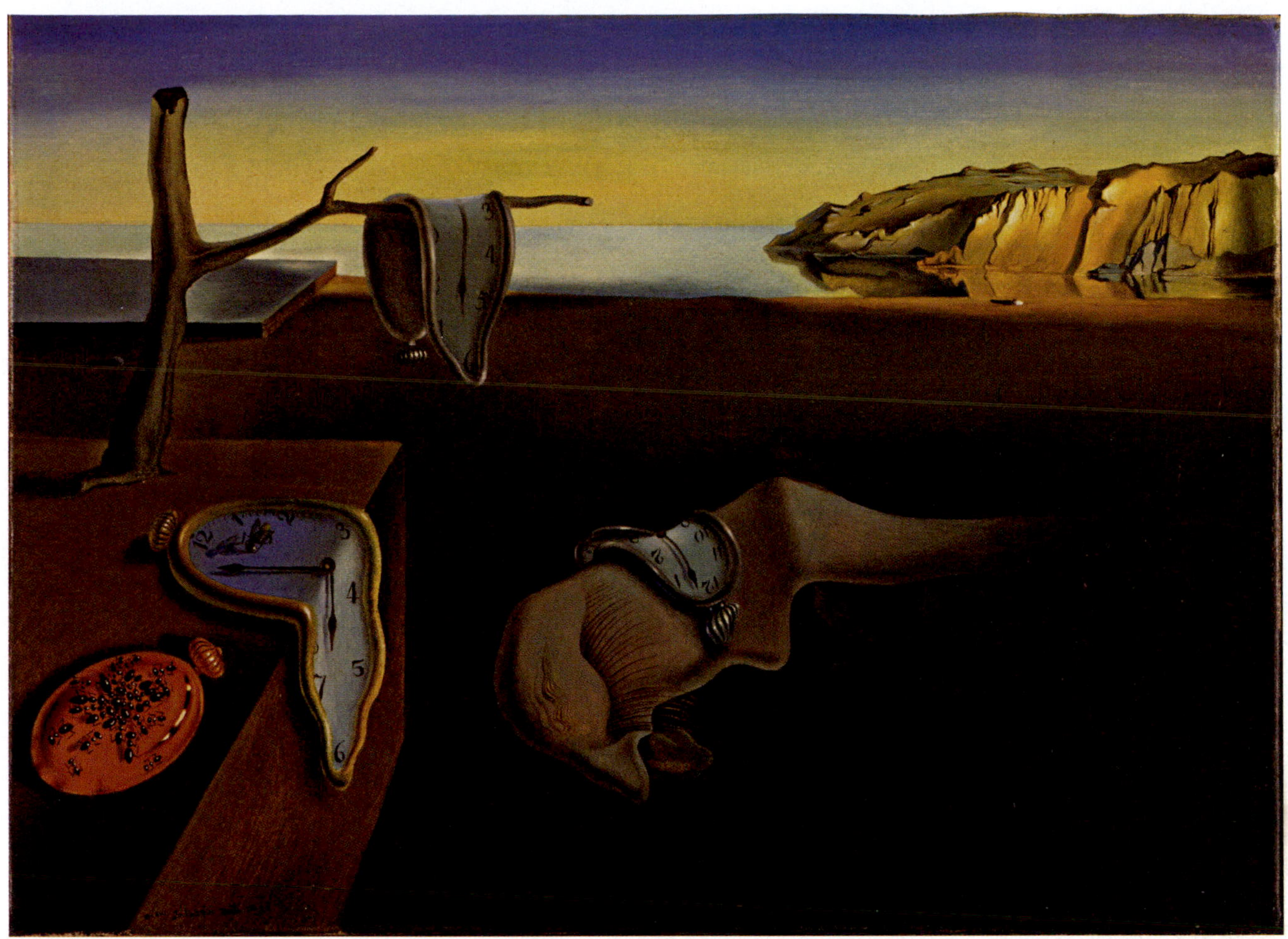

18-29 Salvador Dalí, *The Persistence of Memory,* 1931. Oil on canvas, 9½″ × 13″. The Museum of Modern Art, New York (given anonymously).

> On the contrary, their meaning is so deep, complex, coherent, and involuntary that it eludes simple analysis of logical intuition.

In other words, one should not be surprised that successfully irrational pictures should be incomprehensible. Otherwise, they would not be "images of concrete irrationality."

One of Freud's discoveries in dream analysis was that events and objects could have several meanings at once. Dalí was able to create the visual equivalent of this idea in his *Apparition of Face and Fruit-Dish on a Beach* (**18-30**). Although it may not be initially perceptible, the entire picture is filled with a giant dog. His eye is also a cave (**18-31**), his body also a fruit bowl. The fruit bowl is also a face. Once we understand Dalí's method, this entertaining puzzle manages to lift us out of ordinary existence. We are able to look at the picture with fresh, searching eyes and do not take any part of the image at face value. That is the liberation of Surrealism.

Magritte: The Real World on Trial

René Magritte offered liberation to his viewers by undermining their confidence in the most ordinary things. *The Treachery (or Perfidy) of Images* (**18-32**) borrows the format of a typical children's book. Written below the simple image of a pipe is the sentence *Ceci n'est pas une pipe,* which translated reads, "This is not a pipe." Magritte explained that his titles "were chosen to inspire a justifiable mistrust of any tendency the spectator might have to over-ready self-assurance." Magritte wanted to make the viewer conscious of the limitations of signs, labeling, and language. For

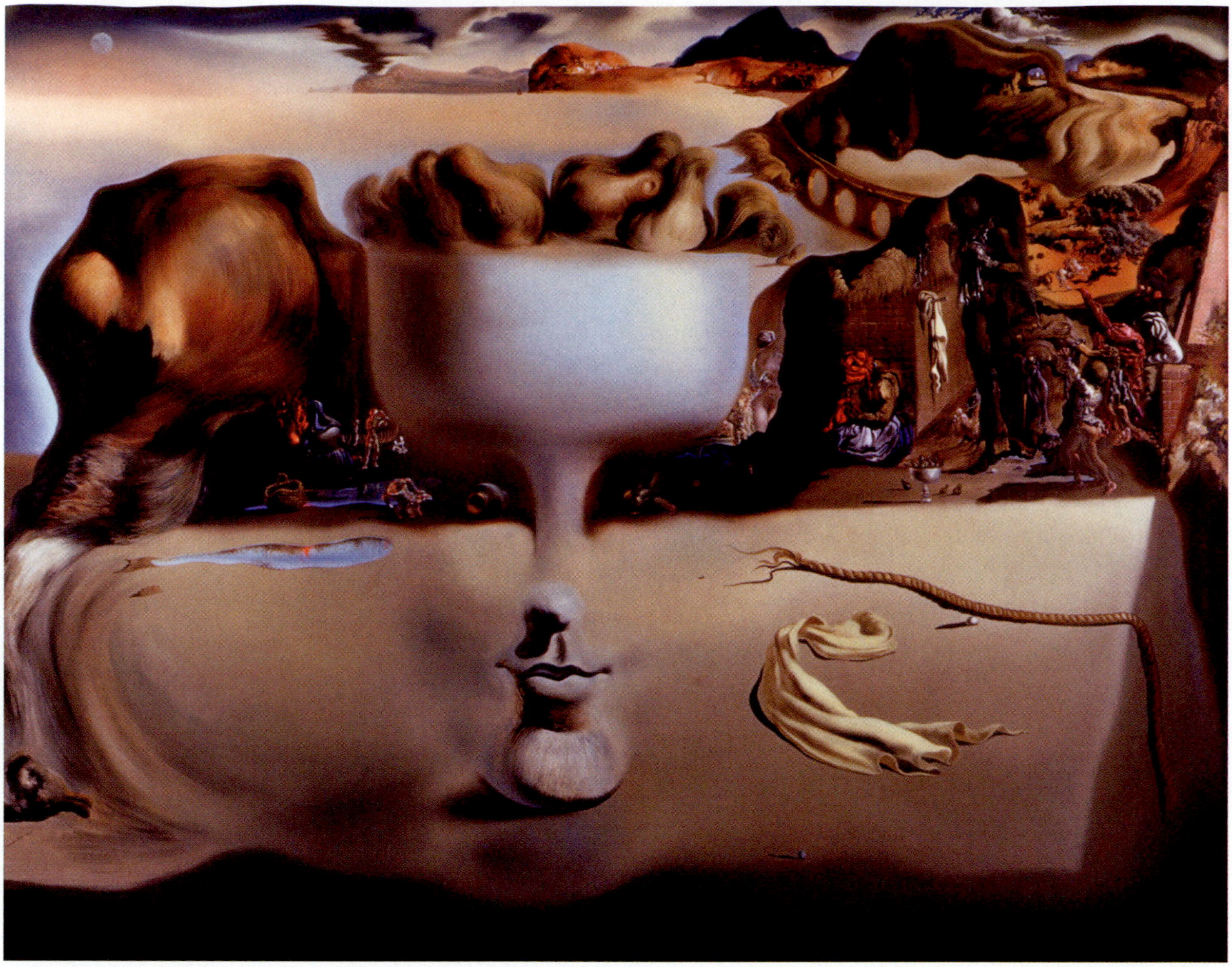

18-30 Salvador Dalí, *Apparition of Face and Fruit-Dish on a Beach,* 1938. Oil on canvas, 45″ × 56⅞″. Wadsworth Atheneum, Hartford, Connecticut (Ella Gallup Sumner and Mary Catlin Sumner Collection).

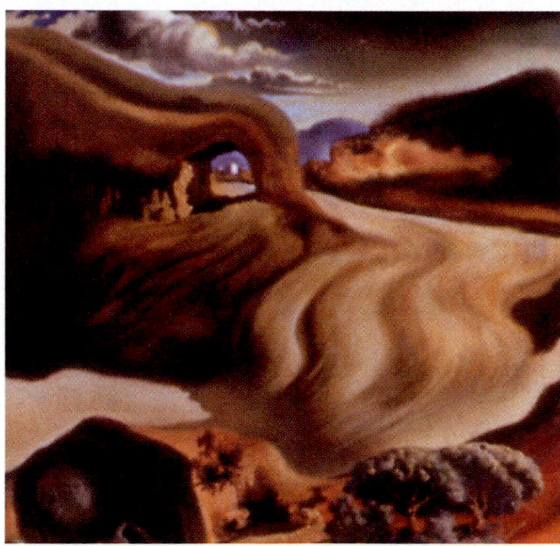

18-31 Detail of figure 18-30.

example, snow has various qualities, so the Eskimos have many names for its different types. Yet in English we lump them all under the word *snow*. What do we miss when we generalize? What have we, by habit, become blind to when we say the word *snow* or *pipe* and stop looking? Simple identification is a prison that prevents us from seeing our world fully.

Magritte felt that our sense of what is normal constrains us. True freedom cannot exist until the fabric of normalcy is destroyed. Like Dalí, Magritte also pictured the impossible realistically. But unlike Dalí's, Magritte's scenes are set not in a distant ideal landscape but in a familiar, almost banal world. In 1939, Magritte explained his approach:

> I painted pictures in which objects were represented with the appearance they have in reality, in a style objective enough to ensure their upsetting effect.

In *L'Empire des lumières* (The Empire of Light) (**18-33**), for example, it is nighttime at street level, but above the trees it is day. Both parts of the picture are absolutely convincing, and the transition between the times of day even seems completely natural. What is portrayed looks normal but cannot be. In this surreal world, nothing is for certain, and things cannot be explained logically. Like ours, perhaps.

When René Magritte undermined language, signs, and conventional perceptions, he undermined all that makes us feel secure. Like many artists of the early twentieth century, he felt obligated to question what was once unquestionable, or, in his words, he was "putting the real world on trial." Along with the other artists in this chapter, he did this not simply to disturb us but to open our eyes to "an infinity of possibilities now unknown in life." His challenge to all of us is to see with fresh eyes, without prejudice. His aim was to return to us the full power of seeing.

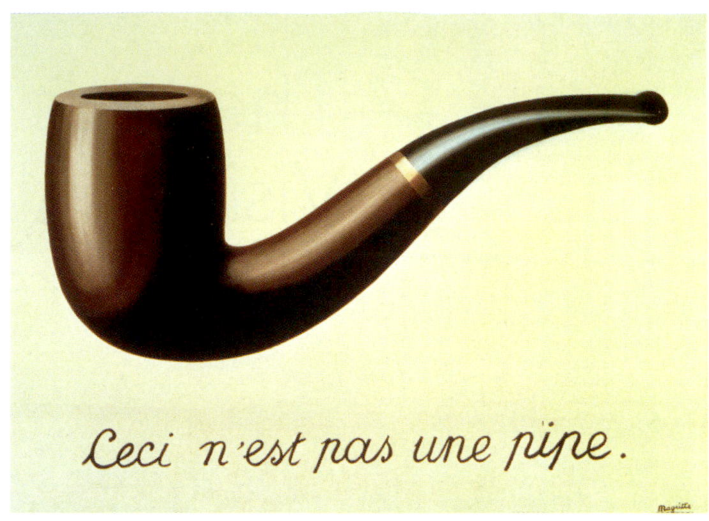

18-32 René Magritte, *The Treachery of Images,* 1928–1929. Oil on canvas, 64.6 × 94.1 cm. Los Angeles County Museum of Art, California.

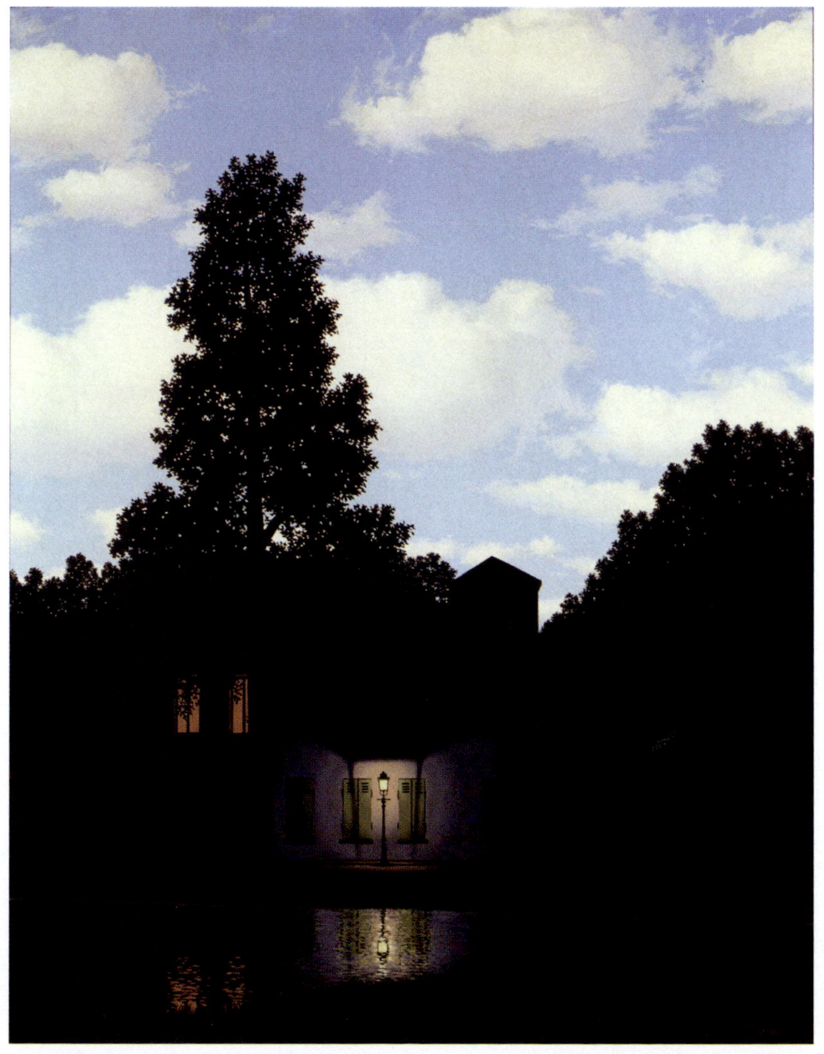

18-33 René Magritte, *L'Empire des lumières,* 1954. Oil on canvas, 4′ 11½″ × 3′ 8⅞″. Músee d'Art Moderne, Brussels, Belgium.

CHAPTER 19

The Invisible Made Visible: Abstract and Nonrepresentational Art

CROSSING THE FRONTIER

Art lovers who followed the avant-garde art movements of the early twentieth century witnessed some shocking changes. Traditional manners of representation that had been considered the essence of art for centuries—beauty, logic, realistic space, literal color, solid objects—were discarded enthusiastically. While many artists broke fresh ground, few were more revolutionary than Pablo Picasso. His treatment of color and form demolished barriers that had seemed impregnable only a few years before. Yet even he respected one

	PERIOD	HISTORICAL EVENTS	
1910–1930	Non-representational art De Stijl The Bauhaus The International Style	World War I 1914–1918 League of Nations founded 1920 Regular radio broadcasts begin 1920 Mahatma Gandhi leads independence movement in India from 1921 James Joyce, *Ulysses* 1922 Louis Armstrong joins King Oliver's band 1922	Gershwin, *Rhapsody in Blue* 1923 Kafka, *The Trial* 1925
1930–1945	The International Style Straight photography Documentary photography Surrealist photography Exodus of artists and intellectuals to the United States from Europe	The Great Depression in United States 1930–1939 Steinbeck, *The Grapes of Wrath* 1939 World War II 1939–1945 Attack on Pearl Harbor 1941 Penicillin discovered 1943	Nuclear bombs exploded over Hiroshima and Nagasaki 1945
1945–1965	Abstract Expressionism The New York School Color field painting The International Style	United Nations founded 1945 Beginning of Cold War 1946–1949 Independence movements in Europe's African and Asian colonies 1940s–1950s–1960s Mao Zedong unites China under Communism 1949	Samuel Beckett, *Waiting for Godot* 1952 Discovery of DNA 1953 Television supplants radio in United States 1950s Building of Berlin Wall 1961

ultimate barrier. While some of his Analytical Cubist compositions were very abstract, Picasso never made a completely nonrepresentational picture. All his art referred to the real, visible world in some way. It was his primary source of inspiration. As a young man, Picasso had seen that Paul Cézanne's work was pointing toward a new, more radical direction for painting—the style of Cubism. Beginning around 1912, other artists began to see that Cubist pictures were pointing toward an even more revolutionary type of art—one that would be completely liberated from the visible world, that could be created only out of pure colors, lines, and shapes. What appeared to be the last frontier for artists was about to be explored.

No one can deny that nonrepresentational art is challenging to the viewer. However, by looking at its first practitioners closely, we will be able to understand the natural progression that led to its creation.

THE SPIRITUAL PATH TO NONREPRESENTATION

Even early in life, Vasily Kandinsky had extraordinary sensitivity to color. When he heard music that moved him, he would close his eyes and see the music in colors. When the young Kandinsky saw a show of Claude Monet's paintings for the first time, he noticed only the colors and did not realize that the pictures were landscapes until he read the catalog. It was one of his first hints that a subject from the visible world would not be necessary for all art.

Kandinsky wanted to show the "inner mystical construction of the world." The latest discoveries in physics seemed to support his own intuition that an underlying invisible force holds our universe together—something called by the physicists "energy." Kandinsky felt that color could show this energy. In paintings like *Blue Mountain* (**19-1**), Kandinsky simplified his drawing to open up wider areas for bright

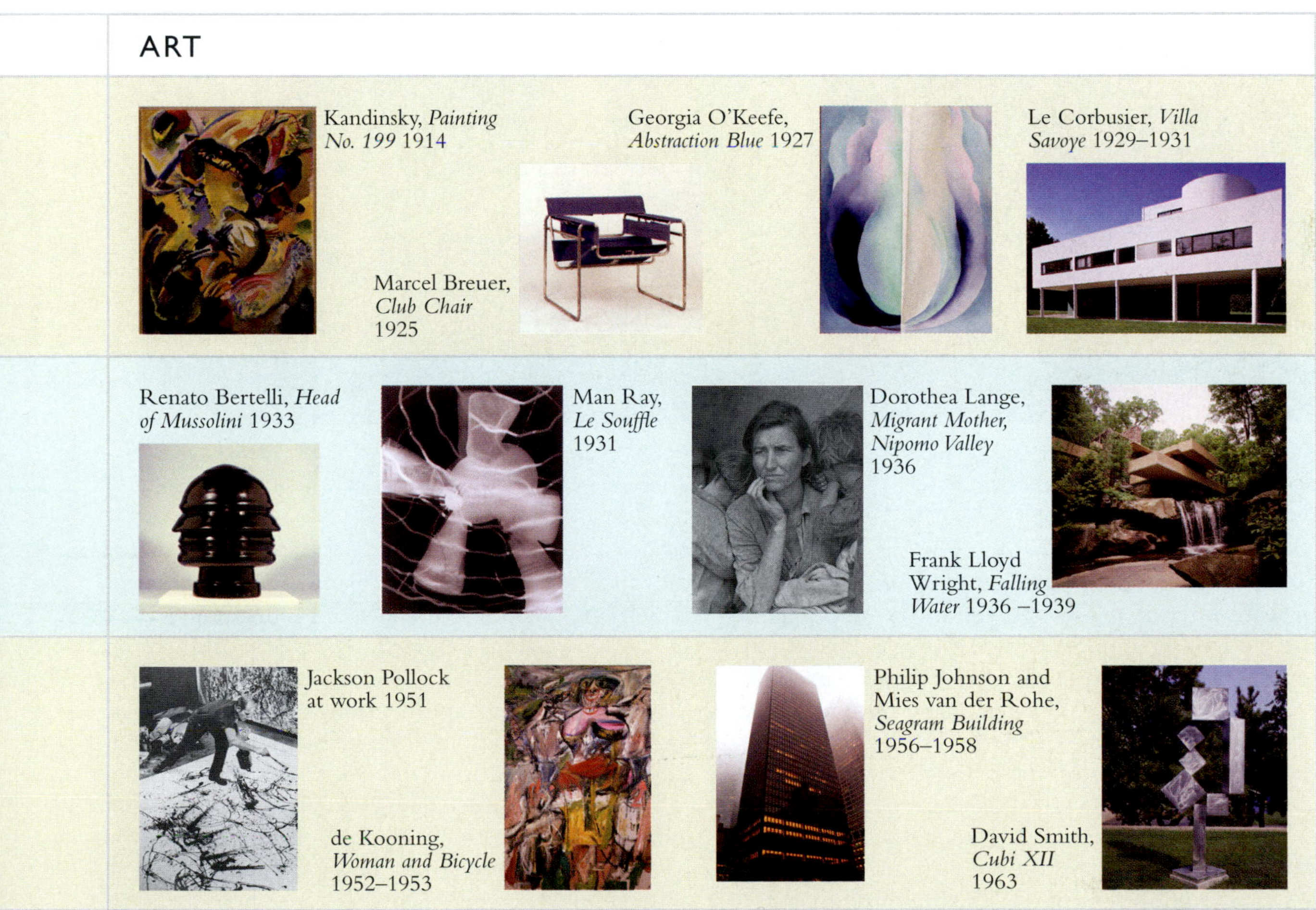

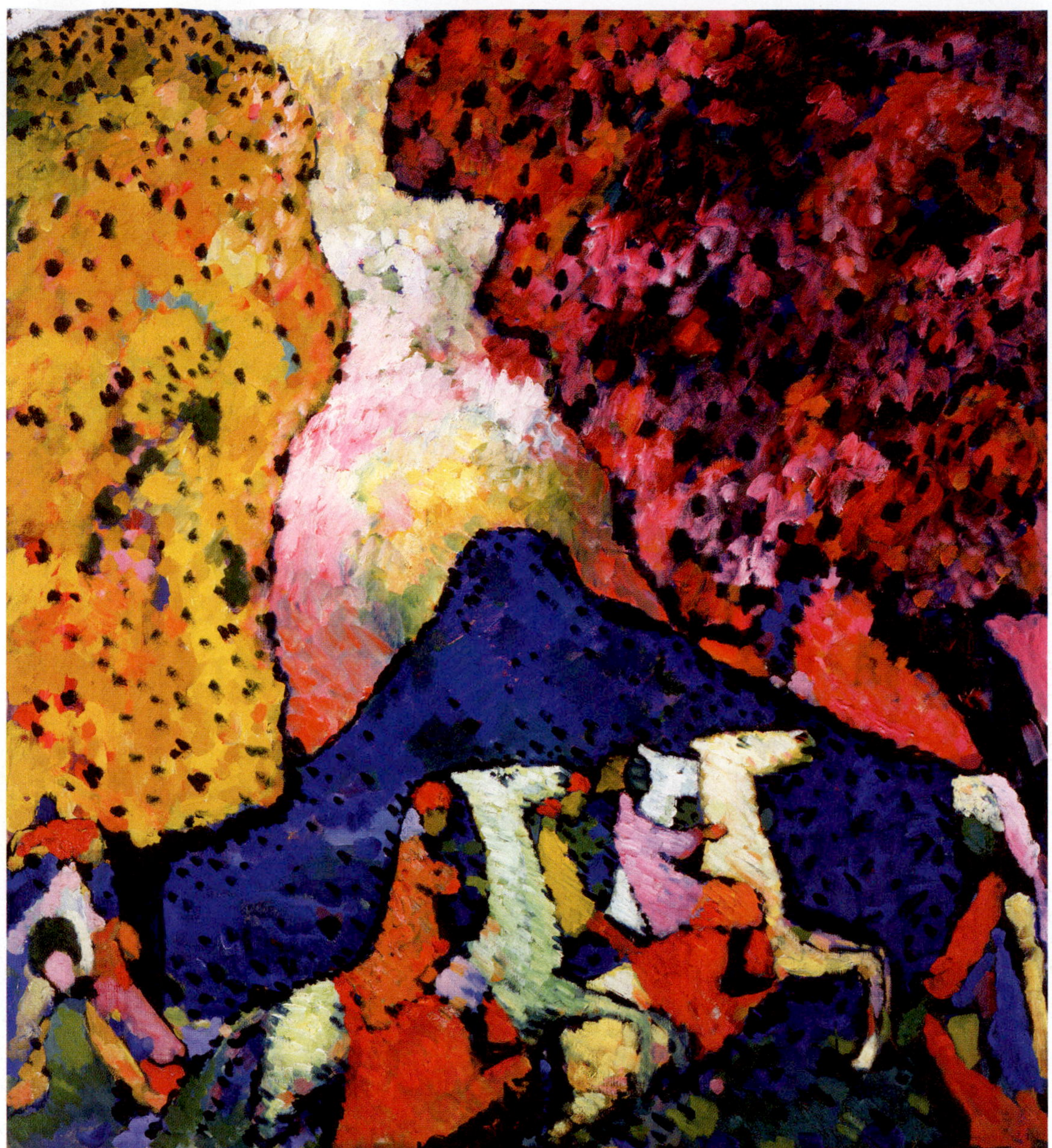

19-1 Vasily Kandinsky, *Blue Mountain,* 1908. Oil on canvas, 41 ¼″ × 37 ¾″. Solomon R. Guggenheim Museum, New York. 41.505.

colors. Life's intensity was evoked by using unmixed, brilliant hues of yellow and red in the trees against the blues of the mountain itself. These colors vibrate vividly together. Despite the obvious power in colorful canvases like *Blue Mountain,* Kandinsky remained dissatisfied. He realized, little by little, that to show the spiritual nature of the cosmos, he needed to abandon all reference to the physical world.

Between 1909 and 1913, elements of the visual world were slowly transformed into more and more abstract symbols. During 1913, Kandinsky painted the first *nonrepresentational* paintings, pictures in which lines, shapes, and colors are independent elements and no longer refer to the real world (**19-2**). Each appears to have a life of its own; lines and shapes move in many directions and almost shove each other aside in an attempt to be noticed. Our eyes are pulled in many directions, and it is difficult to focus on any part of the composition for very long. We are witnessing Kandinsky's own struggle to organize his pictures, to orchestrate energy. His first abstract pictures seem chaotic, because he is painting in a new world where none of the old rules seem to apply. Now, the issue was no longer how to obtain absolute freedom, but how to control it.

Pink Accent (2-27) demonstrates how Kandinsky found ways to organize nonrepresentational painting. He used two large color fields of magenta and gold as a background to unify the picture. To make sure the fields remained in control, he kept the other pictorial elements relatively small in relation to them. By using lively colors and varying the sizes of the circles and squares, Kandinsky was able to achieve a balance that is dynamic but not chaotic. Although *Pink Accent* is a totally nonrepresentational picture, it does have a "natural" feeling to it. The geometric shapes shift like colorful planets in space. They exude animation and energy.

At the end of his life, Kandinsky was in complete command of a totally abstract art. Pictures like *Dominant Curve (Courbe dominante)* (**19-3**), are celebrations. Overflowing with creativity, Kandinsky is now uninhibited by earlier fears of chaos. Each line, color, and shape has its own mood, its own personality. These pictorial elements dance around, floating freely, like many characters joined together in harmony.

MONDRIAN: A LOGICAL APPROACH TO NONREPRESENTATION

The variety in Kandinsky's paintings demonstrates that he had discovered a fertile field for exploration. The Dutch artist Piet Mondrian also created a totally abstract art, nearly simultaneously with Kandinsky. In 1911, he began a series of tree pictures that logically progressed toward abstraction. In a search for nature's underlying geometry, he broke down the trees' limbs into curving lines and the open spaces between them into planes. Over the next three years, in order to bring more order to his canvases, he replaced curves with horizontal and vertical lines, creating an abstract pattern. In the process, Mondrian learned that composition and harmony were more important to him than recording the details of an ordinary subject. Although he once embraced cubism and learned much from Picasso, he soon felt the Cubists had lacked the courage to follow their discoveries to total abstraction—their logical conclusion. He would not hesitate to go further.

Mondrian wanted to make a painting that could be universally understood by people from any culture on earth—a pure painting that would

19-2 Vasily Kandinsky, *Painting No. 199,* (Panel for Edwin R. Campbell No. 2), 1914. Oil on canvas, 64⅛″ × 48⅜″. The Museum of Modern Art, New York (Nelson A. Rockefeller Fund, by exchange).

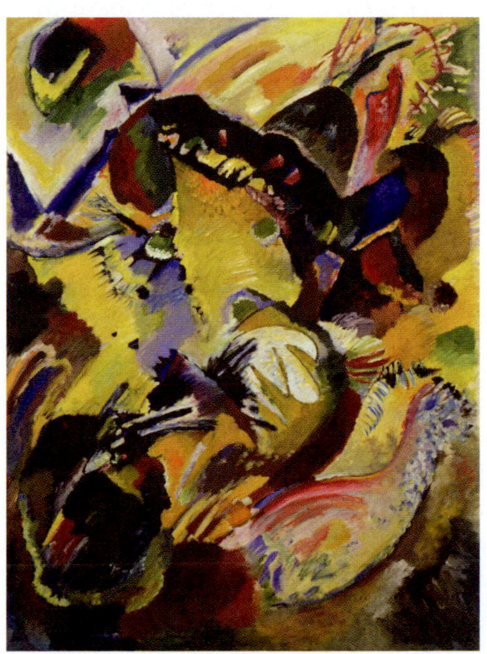

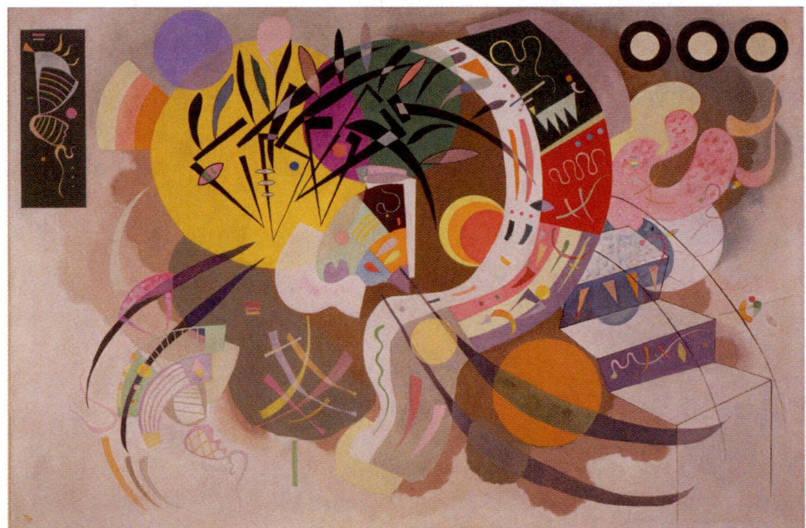

19-3 Vasily Kandinsky, *Dominant Curve (Courbe dominante),* April 1936. Oil on canvas, 50⅞″ × 76½″. Solomon R. Guggenheim Museum, New York. 45.989.

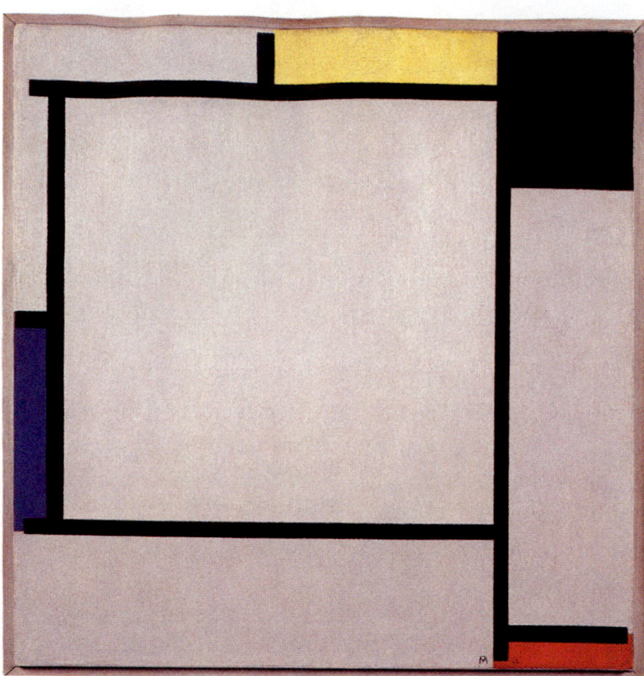

19-4 Piet Mondrian, *Tableau 2, with Yellow, Black, Blue, Red, and Gray,* 1922. Oil on canvas, 21 ⅞″ × 21 ⅛″. Solomon R. Guggenheim Museum. © 2008 Mondrian/Holtzman Trust c/o HCR International Warrenton, VA.

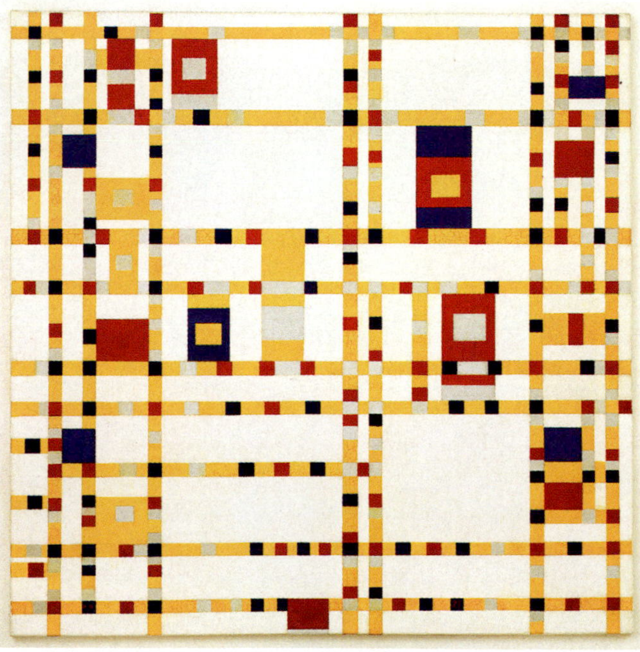

19-5 Piet Mondrian, *Broadway Boogie Woogie,* 1942–1943. Oil on canvas, 50″ × 50″. The Museum of Modern Art, New York. © 2008 Mondrian/Holtzman Trust c/o HCR International Warrenton, VA.

make sense to an Australian aborigine as well as to a European (unlike *The Last Supper,* for example). To create his universal painting, Mondrian decided he needed to simplify visual art to its essence and create perfect images that reflected pure visual harmony. It would have to be an art that depended on no illusions like depth but was flat and direct. He wrote that:

> All painting is composed of line and color. Line and color are the essence of painting. Hence they must be freed from their bondage to the imitation of nature and allowed to exist for themselves.

In the early 1920s, his lines became bolder and firmer, his colors were pure primaries, and his compositions even more simplified (**19-4**). To many viewers, all Mondrian's pictures from this era look exactly the same. However, when they are studied with a sensitive eye, it becomes clear that many different pictures and different feelings can be created even with the simplest elements. While Mondrian reduced art to its pure basics, for him the weight and length of each line and width and area of every color had its effect on the whole mood of the painting. Although there is a mathematical feel to his art, Mondrian despised formulas. He believed that artists had to be intuitive and approached all of his paintings with that attitude.

In 1940, Mondrian left Europe to escape the impending Nazi invasion and came to New York City. It was love at first sight. He adored Manhattan: the rectangular shapes of its skyscrapers, the way its streets were laid out in a grid. He must have been struck with the similarity of the city's appearance to the designs of his pictures. In his New York studio, Mondrian kept a record player on which he played loud "boogie-woogie" music (jazz) while he painted; its upbeat tempo affected his last paintings. The calm and stability of his earlier pictures was replaced by a new spirit, the tones of the modern metropolis. One can almost hear the honking taxi cabs in *Broadway Boogie Woogie* (**19-5**).

DE STIJL

In Holland, during World War I, Mondrian's ideas and approach to art had been translated by followers into a movement called *De Stijl* ("the style"). The Dutch artists proposed "finding practical solutions to universal problems" and believed a pure universal style in art and architecture could be the solution to humanity's misery. They declared that "art and life are no longer two separate domains. . . . We demand the construction of our surroundings according to creative laws." De Stijl artists designed furniture and buildings using flat geometric areas filled with primary colors, like Mondrian's paintings. Gerrit Rietveldt's *Schröder House* (**19-6**) is one of the best examples of De Stijl architecture, a three-dimensional equivalent of Mondrian's pictures. Built in 1924 in Utrecht, Holland, it follows the strict vertical and horizontal orientation of Mondrian's most pure work, but Rietveldt's design has a fluidity that much of Mondrian's work lacked. The rectangular panels seem to float in front of equally rectangular dark windows. All forms are balanced asymmetrically, and a portion of the flat roof seems to move out from the building toward the street. As we look at it, the building seems almost to be in the process of arranging itself. In fact, the interior spaces were designed to be flexible; sliding panels could be moved to accommodate the needs of the occupants. While it seems very modern even today, to really understand its impact in 1924, however, imagine the shocking contrast made by this building painted in white, gray, and primary colors in a neighborhood of nineteenth-century homes.

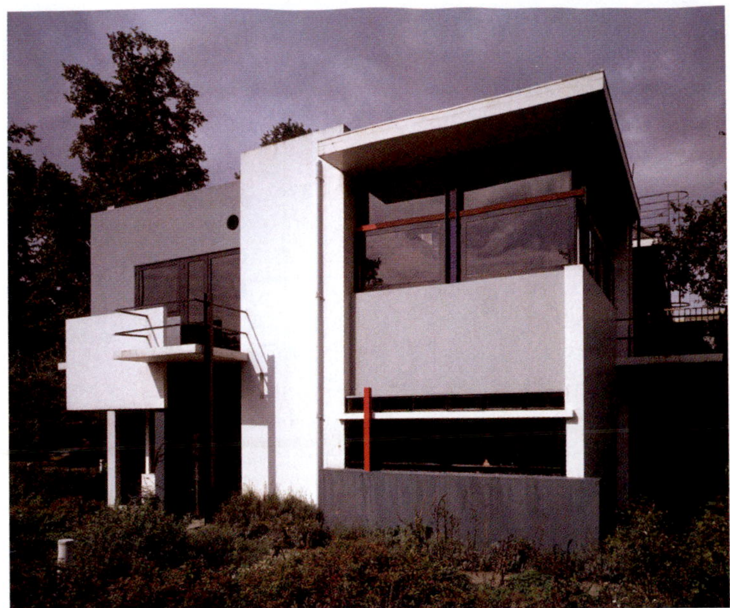

19-6 Gerrit Rietveldt, Schröder House, Utrecht, Netherlands, 1924.

THE INTERNATIONAL STYLE

The Schröder House and De Stijl would eventually be included in a worldwide movement called the **International Style.** Other architects in Europe and the United States shared the Dutch artists' desire for a pure modern counterpart for the Machine Age—constructions that utilized a new language for the arts.

The **Bauhaus,** founded by Walter Gropius (see Chapter 11), was designed to be a home for this new language. Gropius's dictum that "the complete building is the final aim of the visual arts" was one of the central tenets of the movement, and his influential design for the new *Dessau Bauhaus* (**19-7**) epitomizes many of the qualities that would characterize the International Style for decades to come. Finished in 1926, it was the new home for the school after political changes made it impossible for the Bauhaus to remain in its first location.

The building was the antithesis of the heavily ornamented style taught in traditional architectural academies. Flat-roofed and made of modern materials (concrete, steel, and glass), it was free of any superfluous decoration. Boxlike and practical, all spaces were designed for efficient organization. It followed Gropius's directives for the new architecture in 1923:

> We want a clear, organic architecture, whose inner logic will be radiant and naked, unencumbered by lying facades and trickeries; we want an architecture adapted to our world of machines . . . whose function is clearly recognizable in the relation to its form.

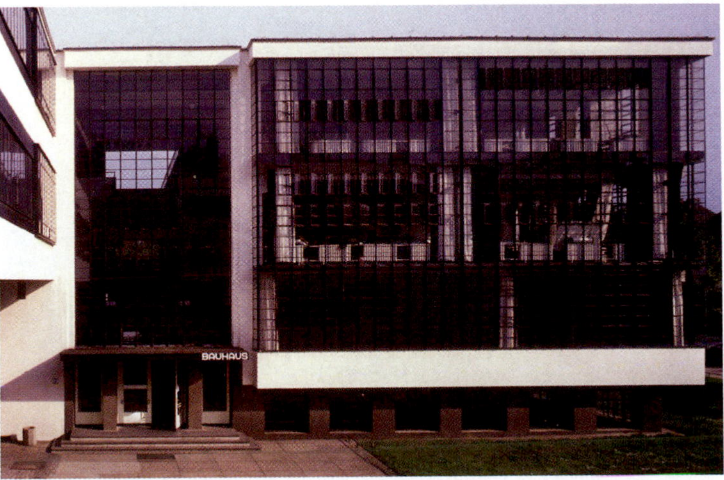

19-7 Walter Gropius, Bauhaus, Dessau, Germany, 1925–1926.

The building was supported by an outer skin of glass and steel, what would be known as a "**glass curtain.**" Notice Gropius's handling of the corners of the building. Instead of the typical heavy stone piers, there was only a sharp edge formed by the meeting of transparent panes of glass. Light poured into the large, open classrooms. The glass-curtain walls also allowed those on the outside to see the activities inside, breaking the age-old tradition of separation between interior and exterior spaces. All aspects of the building were designed and built by instructors and students, from the lamps to the furniture in the dining rooms. Its integration of interior and exterior design became the new tradition for modern architects.

After the Bauhaus was finally closed by the Nazis (see box), Gropius and many of his instructors came to the United States and continued teaching and designing. Their influence on the training of young American artists and architects helped make Modern architecture and design the dominant style for the rest of the twentieth century. One measure of their influence is that the Bauhaus building at Dessau seems like an ordinary building today.

LE CORBUSIER: MASTER OF THE "NEW SPIRIT" IN ARCHITECTURE

Le Corbusier's *Villa Savoye* (**19-8**), however, still seems radical more than a half-century after its construction. Built in 1931 as a weekend house in the suburbs of Paris, it has long since been seen as the embodiment of the International Style. Resting at the top of a hill supported by concrete columns, with horizontal windows providing views in all directions, it is the twentieth century's *Villa Rotonda* (14-24) or *Monticello* (10-38). Unlike Palladio or Jefferson, however, Le Corbusier utilized no Classical elements or historical references. An architectural

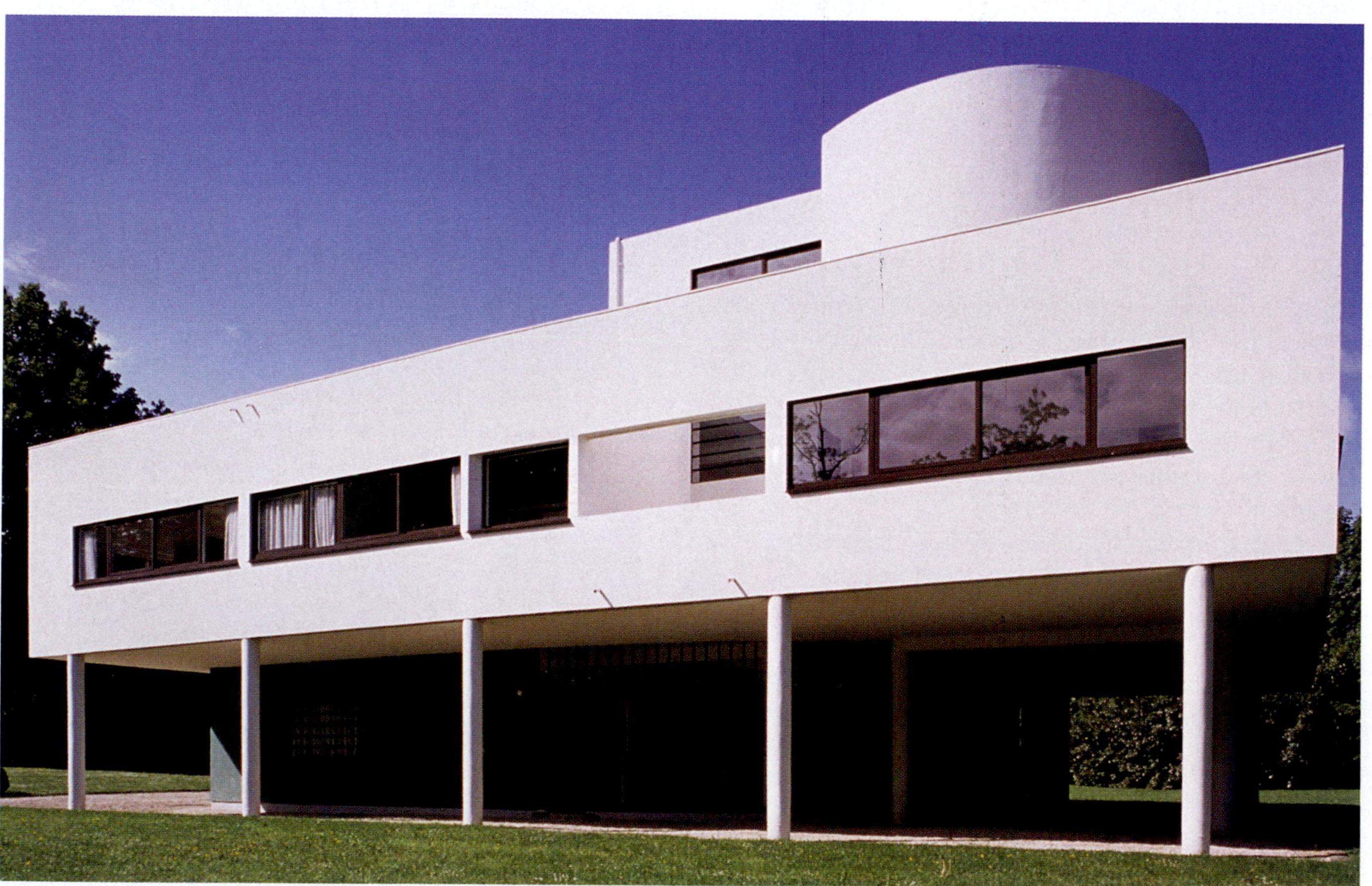

19-8 Le Corbusier, Villa Savoye, Poissy, Ile-De-France, France, 1929–1931.

purist, he believed that Modern buildings should be more rational and scientific than previous styles. According to him, a house was "a machine to be lived in."

In the Villa Savoye, the columns that support the building not only provide a fine view inside and on top but also a convenient place to park one's car. A pure, undecorated skin of windows and smooth stucco surround its inner frame. Inside, ramps lead through large, open, and well-lit rooms and up to a secluded roof garden—a pleasant idiosyncrasy of his buildings. Along with most of the buildings in the International Style, Le Corbusier's buildings have come to be seen as dehumanizing, but that was not their original intention. Like Gropius, Le Corbusier dreamed of an architecture that could create a better world. By utilizing and preaching a new international style, what he called the New Spirit, Le Corbusier hoped that old nationalist boundaries could be broken down, and a new world order devoted to humanitarian goals could be achieved. His "Plan for a Contemporary City for 3 Million Inhabitants" (10-41) was one of a lifetime's worth of projects designed to resolve the intransigent social problems of poverty, homelessness, and class divisions. Le Corbusier imagined such reforms could be achieved through an orderly and perfected architecture. Despite his extraordinarily creative mind (Gropius once said it would take an entire generation of architects to explore all of Le Corbusier's ideas), most of his projects were never built. In the twentieth century, however, this was no longer a hindrance to fame. Because he lived in an age of easily made reproductions, Le Corbusier's blueprints were circulated worldwide, and a younger generation of architects spread his plans and the International Style throughout the world by modifying his ideas and making them less radical.

FRANK LLOYD WRIGHT

Frank Lloyd Wright epitomized the American approach to modern architecture before World War II. Wright, who became the most famous American architect, designed modern buildings that have many similarities to the Bauhaus model but are based on profoundly different ideas. His motto—"Form follows function"—learned in his apprenticeship from the architect Louis Sullivan, remains a slogan of the Modern Art movement.

Wright was born in the beautiful hills of rural Wisconsin just after the end of the Civil War. He learned the lessons of nature, which he called "a wonderful teacher," on his uncle's farm. As a young architect in Chicago, the messages of his childhood were translated into an ideal he would later call "organic architecture": functional buildings designed to work with nature, built from the creative arrangement of simple forms.

For his entire life, Wright refused to be associated with what he felt was the essentially European International Style. In 1932, Wright said of Le Corbusier: "I believe Le Corbusier [is] extremely valuable, especially as an enemy." Wright's *Kaufman House (Fallingwater)*—see drawing, plans, and finished building in Chapter 10—built in 1936, makes a striking comparison with the Villa Savoye. Both homes are designed as country retreats, but their underlying attitudes are quite different. The utter logic and machinelike quality of Le Corbusier's design is opposed by the free forms and natural materials favored by Wright. Wright's building is designed to blend into nature; in fact, it sits on a ledge where a waterfall actually passes under the house. Le Corbusier's villa stands on columns that distance it from nature; its boxlike form has nothing to do with its surroundings. While both architects used concrete to shape simple, geometric forms, Wright's open slabs reach out to nature, while Le Corbusier's box resembles a fortress.

However, both architects shared the modern aesthetic. They believed in the elimination of unnecessary ornament, in letting the function of the building determine its design. Neither approved of the use of historical references. Both believed interiors should be as open as possible. Above all, they were committed to the idea that architects should design every aspect of a building, from the overall plan to the furnishings within. One of the most beautiful results of this aesthetic is Wright's exploration of round shapes at his *Solomon R. Guggenheim Museum* in New York City (**19-9, 19-10**). In a building that is almost a modern sculpture itself, art lovers move smoothly and gradually along a spiral ramp from the top to the ground level without interruption.

Wright was the first American architect to have a truly international influence. While he probably never achieved his intention of being "not only . . . the greatest architect who has ever lived, but the greatest who will ever live," during the middle decades of the twentieth century, there were many in his field who believed he had.

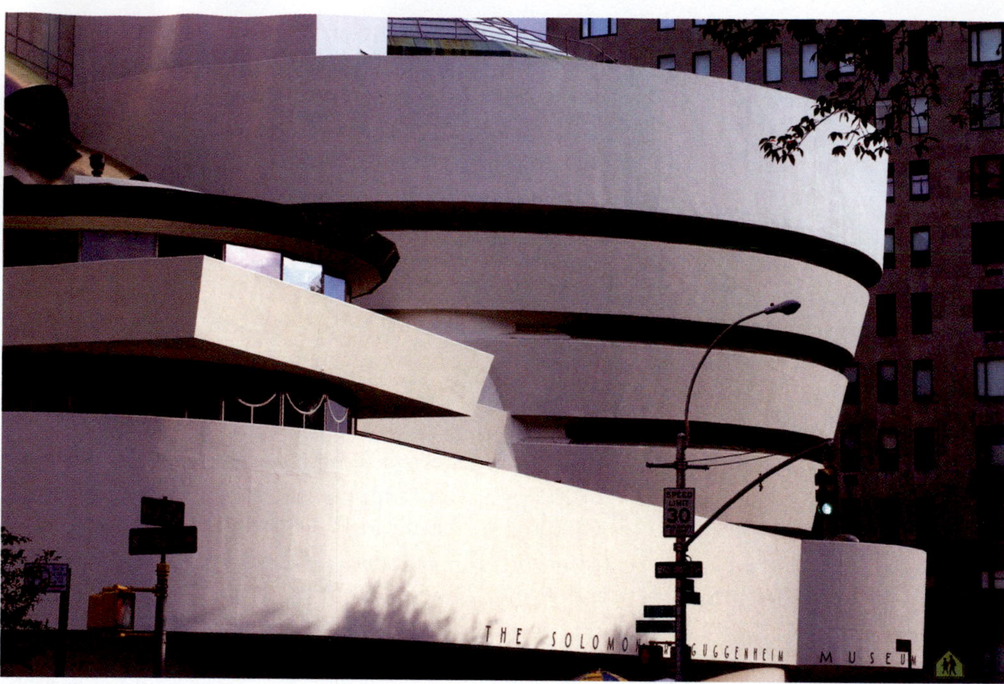

19-9 Frank Lloyd Wright, Solomon R. Guggenheim Museum, New York, 1943–1959.

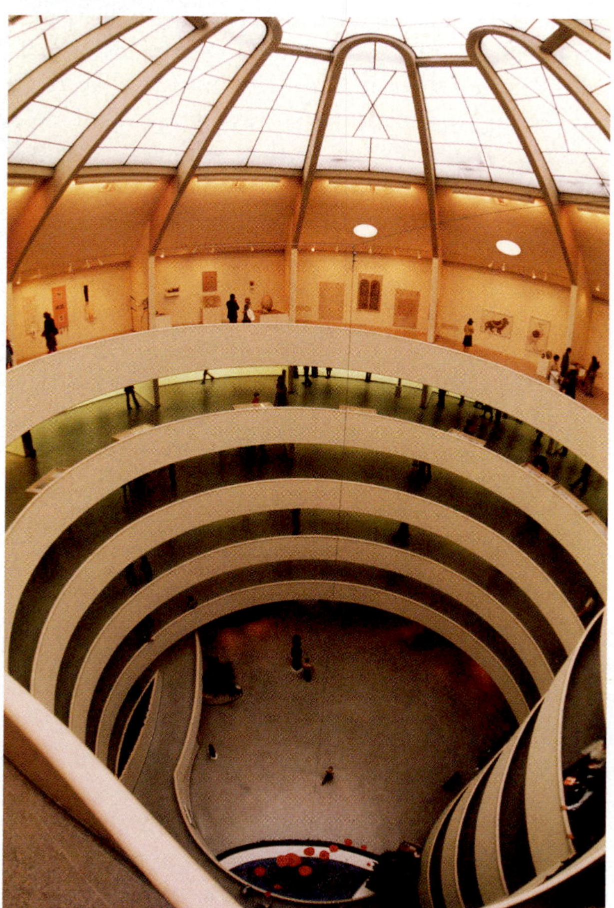

19-10 Frank Lloyd Wright, main rotunda of the Solomon R. Guggenheim Museum, New York, 1943–1959.

ABSTRACT ART IN AMERICA: O'KEEFFE

Georgia O'Keeffe was another American original. Like Wright, O'Keeffe was born in rural Wisconsin and first attracted attention in the early years of the twentieth century. In her old age, she also became a larger-than-life figure in the art world. She said she knew as a child that she wanted to be an artist, even though she had very little idea what that meant. In the early 1900s, however, most American women who wanted a career in art were expected to become teachers; higher ambitions were not considered practical or proper. After years devoted to the study of art, followed by teaching in public schools and colleges, she felt rather discouraged. As she wrote many years later,

> One day I found myself saying to myself, "I can't live where I want to. I can't even say what I want to." I decided I was a very stupid fool not to at least paint as I want to.

She discovered a deep well of inspiration in the abstraction of nature, its creations, and its forces—her most dominant theme during a career that lasted nearly seven decades. *Two Calla Lilies on Pink* is a good example of her sensuous style of synthesizing natural forms (see 3-12).

Radiator Building—Night, New York (**19-11**) was painted in 1927, when she was living in New York

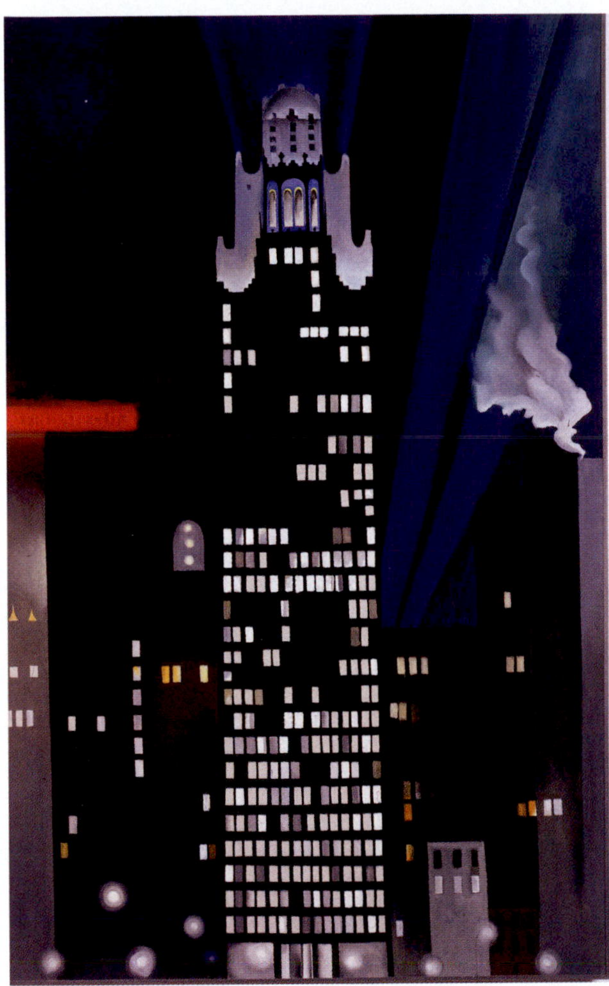

19-11 Georgia O'Keefe, *Radiator Building—Night, New York,* 1927. Oil on canvas, 48″ × 30″. The Carl van Vechten Gallery of Fine Arts, Fisk University, Nashville, Tennessee (Alfred Stieglitz Collection).

City. O'Keeffe focused on the unique experience of artificial light at night in the modern city—a manufactured world filled with unnatural experiences. The home of the American Radiator Company rises like a beacon at the center of the picture; the skyscraper's windows form a grid of whites and grays. Searchlights illuminate an undulating cloud of steam that rises from a rooftop; street lights glow like stars and float mysteriously.

Throughout her career, O'Keeffe followed a pattern that she established at its beginning: taking inspiration from the world around her and reworking it into a personal statement. Sometimes her pictures were quite literal; at other times they would become totally abstract. The simple purity of O'Keeffe at her most nonrepresentational is seen clearly in *Abstraction Blue* of 1927 (**19-12**). What once may have been the interior of a flower is now a series of rounded forms. Arranged symmetrically, they are all brought together in a quiet balance that gives an impression of monumentality. With *Abstraction Blue*'s sharp edges and blue palette, one might have expected it to seem harsh and cool, but O'Keeffe mitigates this sharpness with soft gradations of blue and pink. Such gradual blendings of color combined with crisp edges are hallmarks of her style. Her pictures are accessible to the general public in a way that is rare among the nonrepresentational artists of the twentieth century. Shortly after her death at the age of ninety-eight in 1985, a retrospective of her art in Manhattan drew enormous crowds and solidified O'Keeffe's reputation as one of the most important American artists of the century. As she predicted, when explaining why she made her flowers so big, "I will make even busy New Yorkers take the time to see what I see of flowers."

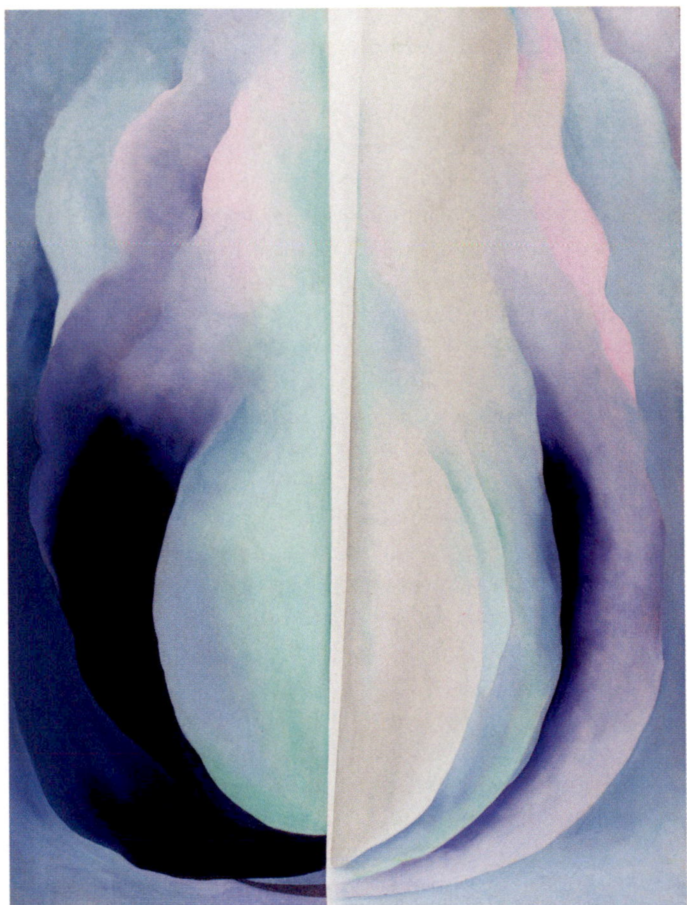

19-12 Georgia O'Keefe, *Abstraction Blue,* 1927. Oil on canvas, 40 ¼″ × 30″. The Metropolitan Museum of Art, New York (acquired through the Helen Acheson Bequest).

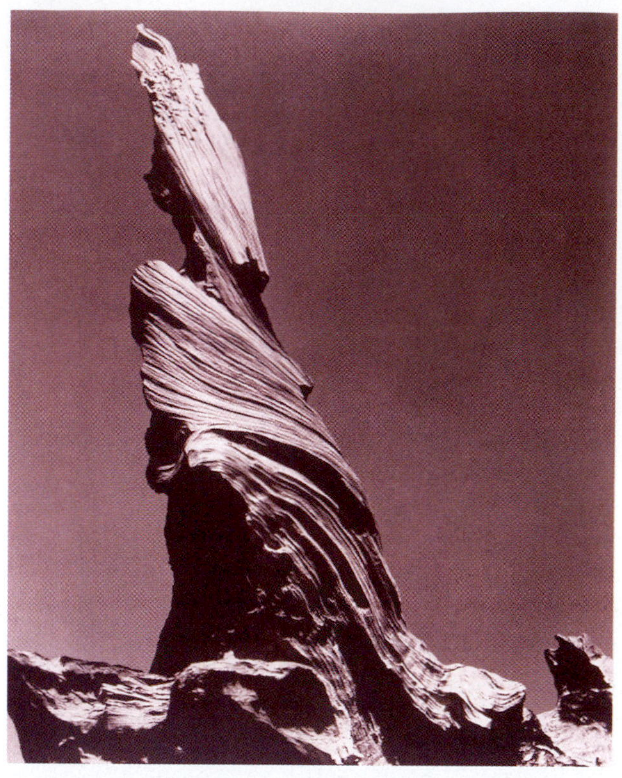

19-13 Edward Weston, *Snag, Point Lobos,* 1930. Gelatin silver print. Center for Creative Photography, University of Arizona.

STRAIGHT PHOTOGRAPHY

When comparing the work of the painter, O'Keeffe, and the photographer, Edward Weston, it seems surprising that they were not close friends. His closely studied vegetables (7-14), sculptural and almost abstract, cannot fail to remind one of similar pictures by O'Keeffe. He also shared with O'Keeffe a love for the wide-open spaces of the American West. Born in Chicago, he visited California for the first time at the age of twenty and stayed virtually for his entire life.

Like many other artists discussed in this chapter, Weston attempted to capture the eternal, but he insisted on doing this "honestly." Disturbed by photographers who tried to imitate painters by using soft focus and other "trickery," he resolved in the 1920s "to present clearly my feeling for life with photographic beauty . . . without subterfuge or evasion." He thus became one of the fathers of *straight photography* (see Chapter 7).

Dismissing interesting accidents produced by rapid shooting, Weston believed photographers should decide on each image they took. Using a large-format camera that allowed him to see exactly what was in the lens, he "previsualized" each image before pressing the shutter release. A time-consuming process, Weston would wait all day if necessary to reveal the "deepest moment of perception." His camera made negatives that were eight by ten inches, and all of his prints were *contact* prints, made directly from a negative without enlargement or reduction. This provided images of the utmost clarity and purity. These prints were also *uncropped* (printed "full-frame"), a tradition established by Weston and followed to this day by many photographers. For him, the need for any alteration to his images implied that he had failed.

Snag, Point Lobos (**19-13**) is ample proof that Weston's patience paid off handsomely. Point Lobos is a state park on the coast of California near Weston's home and one of his favorite sites. The vivid description of the textures on a piece of weathered wood could not be seen so clearly with any other photographic method. It fulfills Weston's ambition to show "the greater mystery of things revealed more clearly than the eyes can see." Photographed against a clear sky, the aged wood seems like an ancient monolith.

THE CENTER OF WESTERN ART SHIFTS

In the 1930s, storm clouds were gathering in Europe that were harbingers of its coming decline. The closing of the Bauhaus by Adolf Hitler's government in Germany was just one small part of his organized plan of censorship, repression, and terror (see box). After Hitler's armies began their attempt at world domination in the 1940s, Europe was no longer capable of providing a nurturing ground for advanced artists. While Picasso and Matisse would stay in France, many artists fled from Europe, looking for a place where they could pursue their art in freedom. Mondrian, Max Ernst, and Salvador Dalí were among the many artists who left Europe for America. They joined other important European artists like Marcel Duchamp, who had already emigrated to the United States before the war.

Their combined presence had a profound effect on American art, especially in New York City where most of them found a home. New York City became the world capital of art in the 1940s and 1950s, replacing Paris, which had been the center of Western art since the age of Louis XIV. The land of Norman Rockwell had been invaded by Modern art.

ART NEWS

The War Against Modern Art: Degenerate Art

As a young man, Adolf Hitler wanted a career as an artist. His student work was far from controversial or threatening. Most of his pictures were architectural drawings and pleasant, sentimental landscapes in watercolor. Unfortunately, when he applied for admission to an art academy in Austria, he was rejected and forced to abandon his dream.

As he rose to power in Germany, Hitler never forgot the insult. He would take his revenge on the art world and decide what was acceptable in art. The Bauhaus was one of the first schools affected by the rise of Nazism. A new Fascist city government appointed a new director, whose view of Bauhaus style was that it was "cosmopolitan rubbish." The school was closed by the government in 1933.

Hitler believed in an art that was elevated and classical, one that anyone could understand. According to him, Modern art was the expression of sick minds. So was modern music like jazz. Modern art was removed from the museums, and private collections were confiscated by the government. While some of these pictures were destroyed in bonfires, many would be sold to raise funds for the Nazi war machine. Artists like the Expressionists, who did not share his views, first lost their teaching positions and later were forbidden to even make any art. Some artists, like Ernst Kirchner, committed suicide. Many were forced into exile. Outside of Germany, the Emergency Rescue Committee was created in Europe to assist fleeing artists, musicians, and writers.

To show the German people his vision of art, in 1937 Hitler opened The House of German Art in Berlin, a museum designed to replace modern art with "a 'German' art and an eternal art." Hitler's chief spokesman declared that the new museum was proof that "the Führer loves art." Along with German masters like Dürer and Holbein, the museum exhibited new works created to glorify the Aryan empire; all part of "a new and vigorous flowering of art."

Across the street, another exhibition opened at the Führer's direction—"Entarte Kunst" (Degenerate Art), **19-14**. Its goal was to educate the people and to cleanse the nation of degenerate influences. More than six hundred works were in the show, which included some of the most important names in the history of Modern art. Among the 112 artists on exhibit were Kandinsky, Mondrian, Klee, Chagall, Ernst, Kollwitz, Nolde, and Kirchner. The works were hung all over the walls at many angles, with slurs like "Bolshevik,"

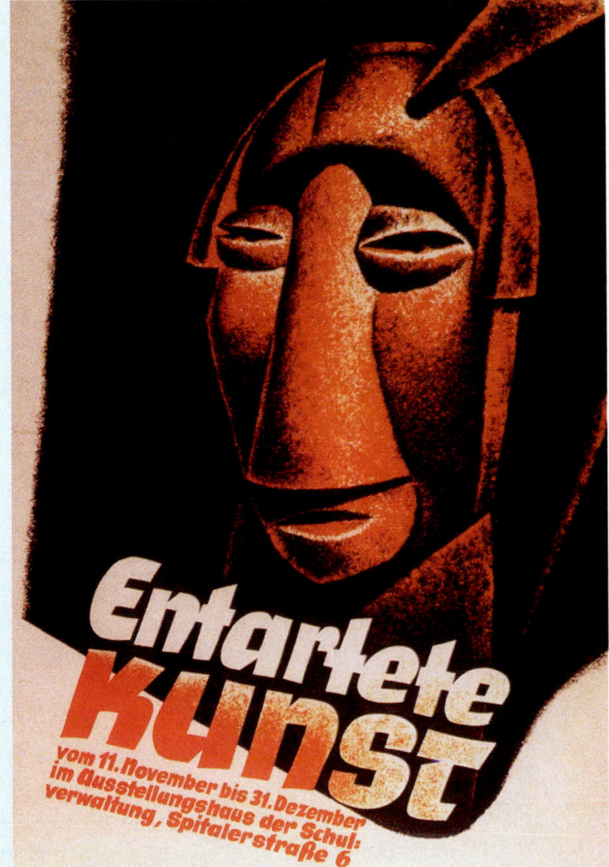

19-14 Degenerate Art Show poster, Hamburg, 1938, Germany.

(continued on next page)

ART NEWS

and "Jew" scrawled next to the pictures. Modern landscapes were described as "Nature as seen by sick minds."

Hitler declared that there were only two possible explanations for these modern artists. He said:

> Either these "artists" really do see things in this way and believe in what they represent. Then one has only to ask how the defect in vision arose, and if it is hereditary, the Minister for the Interior will have to see to it that so ghastly a defect of vision shall not be allowed to perpetuate itself. Or if they do not believe in the reality of such impressions but seek on other grounds to burden the nation with this humbug, then it is a matter for a criminal court.

The Degenerate Art show toured Germany and Austria for four years and would be seen by more than three million people, probably more than any exhibition in history. Most visitors laughed at the works. Artists and art students went to see these masterpieces of twentieth-century art for what they believed was the last time and suffered in silence.

ABSTRACT EXPRESSIONISM: MODERN ART CREATED IN AMERICA

Willem de Kooning, born in Holland, came to this country as a young man. De Kooning's early paintings were portraits, influenced by Picasso but already with a dramatic command of line. Then, in the late 1940s, de Kooning began a series of black-and-white paintings that were totally original (**19-15**). Loose, expressive lines described very complicated and interlocked abstract spaces. It is not clear which shapes are coming forward and which are behind. This was intentional; like the Cubists, de Kooning did not want these pictures to have a conventional background and foreground. His mastery of a gestural, calligraphic line creates powerful rhythms all by itself.

These nonrepresentational, energetic pictures were some of the first of a new kind of painting that would become known as **Abstract Expressionism.** Like many art historical labels, it is a loosely defined one, describing art that combines the potent psychological content of Expressionism with an abandonment of any clear reference to the visual world.

Throughout his career, de Kooning would paint both pictures that referred to the visible world (like *Woman and Bicycle*, 1-41) and those that were more or less completely abstract. He, along with his fellow Abstract Expressionists, believed it was more important to be an honest painter than to stick to a single-minded theory of art. If, while painting, his picture began to look like a woman, then why should he deny it? If it reminded him of looking out a door toward a river, why shouldn't he have the freedom to recognize it? Paintings like *Door to the River* (**19-16**) can be admired either as an imaginative interpretation of a scene or understood on a totally abstract level. The confident, wide, thick brushstrokes and harmony of the colors communicate on a direct emotional plane. The sense of a landscape is intuitive and not compulsory.

Pollock's Action Painting

There were two fathers of this new movement: de Kooning and an American painter, born in Wyoming, Jackson Pollock. Pollock was influenced by the Surrealist artists who came to New York during World War II. He was particularly inspired by the way they gained access to their unconscious through a method called "automatic picturemaking," where all marks were made instinctually, without planning or thought.

Pollock transformed this approach into a revolutionary and nonrepresentational way of painting that would be called his "drip technique" (see photo, **19-17**). On a length of canvas rolled onto the floor of his studio, Pollock would instinctually drip long lines of paint with brushes and sticks. He would hover

over his canvas, sometimes stepping into it, moving constantly. While he was working, his picture would not really have a top or bottom. Not until he was finished would he determine the picture's final size (by cutting the canvas) or where its bottom was (by signing it). His lines were unique not only because of his technique, but also because they did not do what lines had always done in art—describe spaces or shapes. His lines were independent and active, each a lively experience.

The design of a drip painting was also original—an "all-over" picture. This meant that, unlike all previous paintings, in Pollock's work no one part or section dominated the others. No part could be called the subject. All over the canvas, everything was equal in impact. By looking at *Number 1, 1950 (Lavender Mist)* and a detail of it (**19-18, 19-19**), we can see that, whether it is seen at a distance or close up, Pollock's approach created an entirely new kind of space. Nets of lines laid one over another produce a sense of infinity. Looking at a huge Pollock painting is like looking up at a sky full of stars on a clear night.

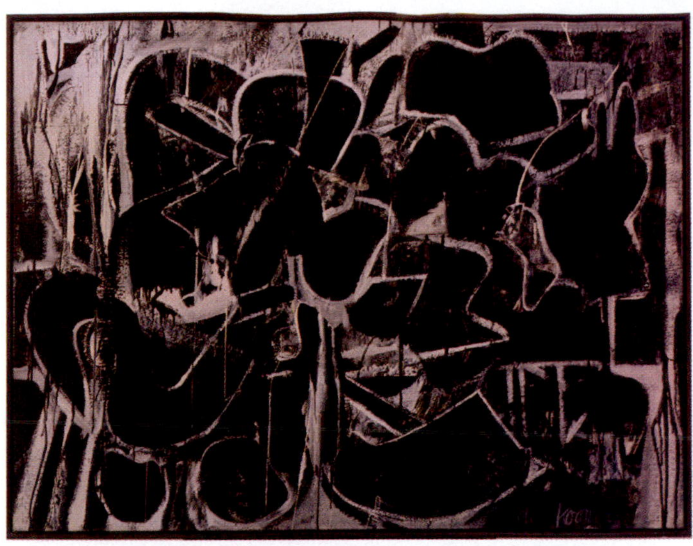

19-15 Willem de Kooning, *Painting,* 1948. Enamel and oil on canvas, 42 ⅝″ × 56 ⅛″. The Museum of Modern Art, New York (purchase).

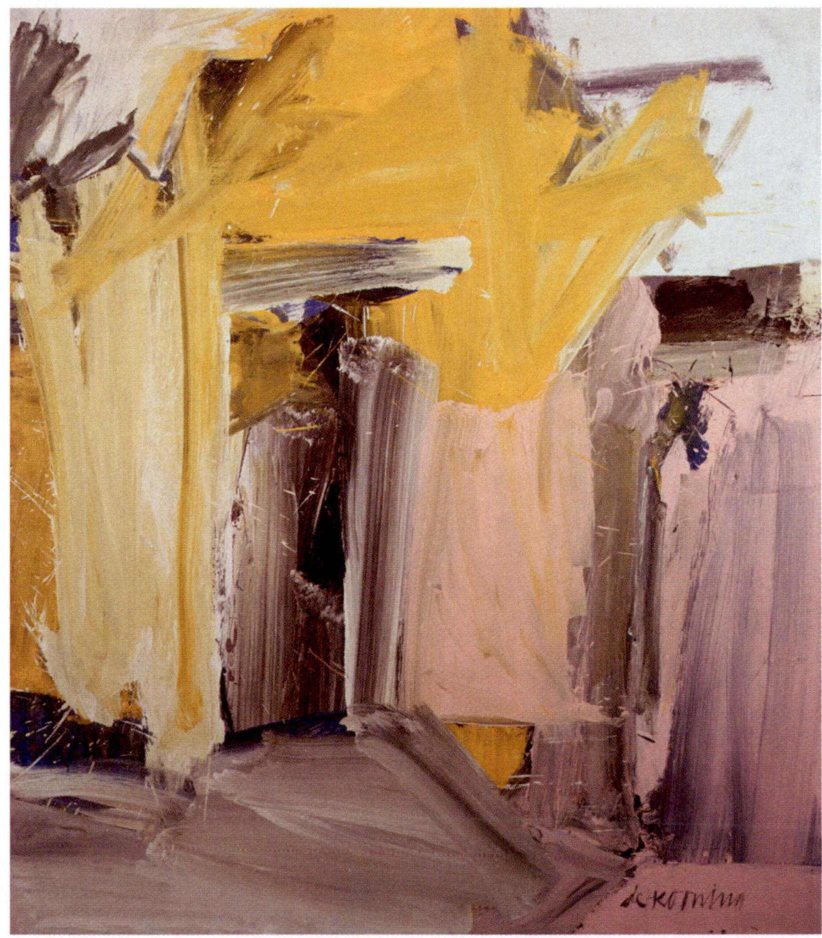

19-16 Willem de Kooning, *Door to the River,* 1960. Oil on canvas, 80″ × 70″. Collection of Whitney Museum of American Art, New York (purchased with funds from the Friends of the Whitney Museum of American Art, 60.63).

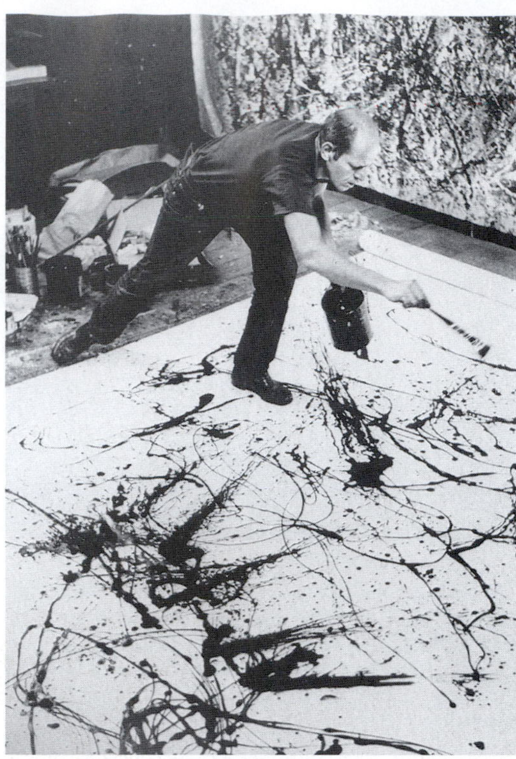

19-17 Jackson Pollock at work, 1951. Photograph by Hans Namuth.

19-19 Detail of figure 19-18.

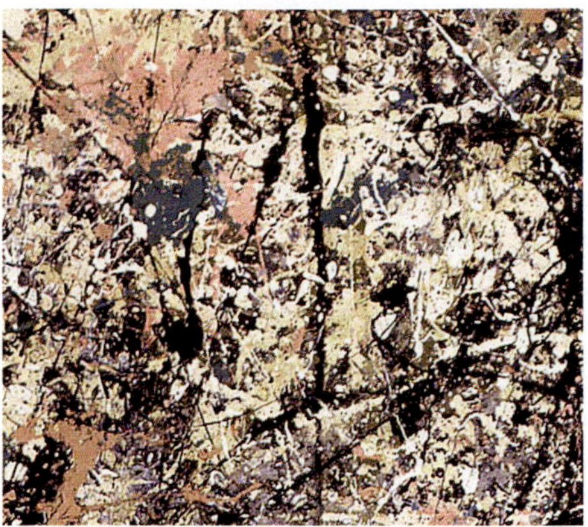

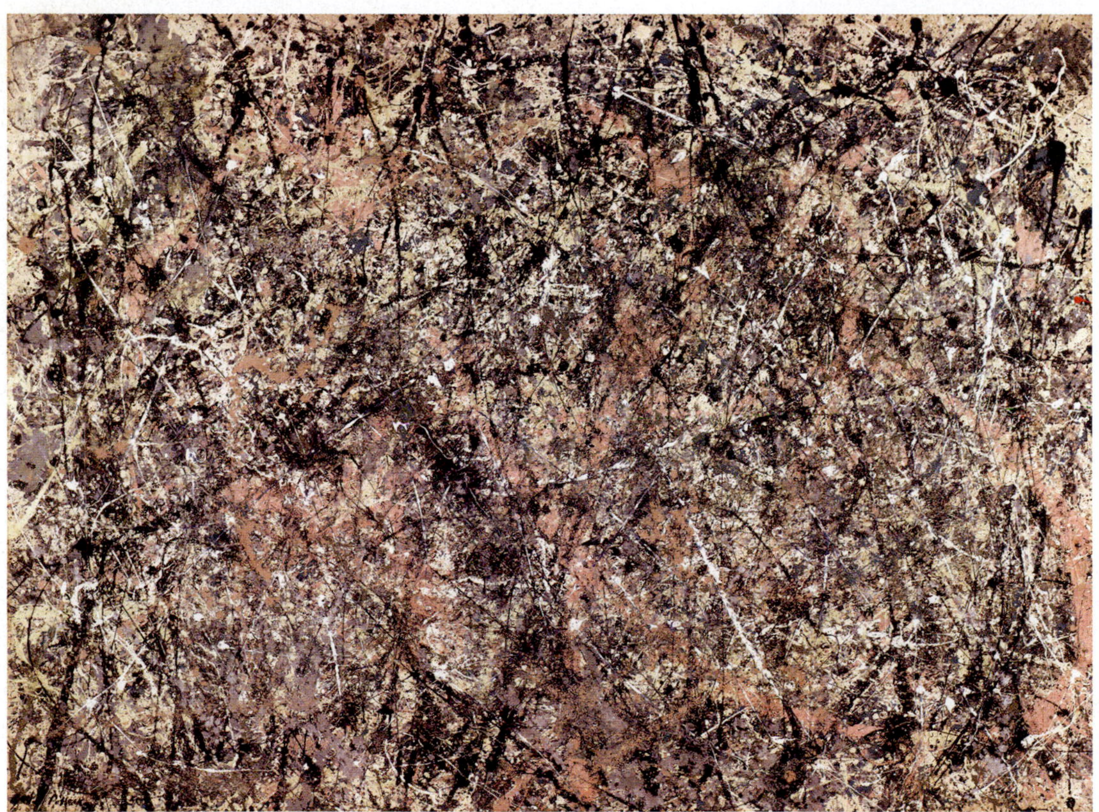

19-18 Jackson Pollock, *Number 1, 1950 (Lavender Mist),* 1950. Oil, enamel, and aluminum on canvas, 88″ × 119″ × 1½″. © DACS. The National Gallery of Art, Washington, D.C. (Ailsa Mellon Bruce Fund).

Pollock is the artist most identified with the term *action painting* because of the energy in his new technique. His action paintings, according to witnesses, were done in fits of intense and often violent activity. He was known to spit at and burn parts of his pictures. Their great size was not a result of any artistic theory but rather Pollock's sense that he needed room to work in. Wall-sized, heroic pictures would become one of the identifying characteristics of Abstract Expressionism.

Jackson Pollock's unusual method of painting and lifestyle transformed him from an unknown to a celebrity. An art critic described Pollock as Picasso's heir, saying he had taken the old master's ideas and made them "speak with an eloquence and emphasis that Picasso himself never dreamed of." For the first time, Pollock was able to survive solely on the sale of his paintings. The paintings of de Kooning and other Abstract Expressionists began to sell, too. Before Pollock's acclaim in the 1950s, the Abstract Expressionists were largely a group of unknown artists living in low-rent apartments in lower Manhattan, barely surviving. As part of a conscious effort to recreate the exciting atmosphere of café life in Paris, they would meet in bars after painting all day and discuss art. Between drinks, they would offer each other consolation and camaraderie—so necessary for the essentially lonely act of making art. Sales were few and far between, but the news media got excited about Jackson Pollock. He was known as a wild man, a real cowboy; when he got drunk, he often was violent. With the attention of the art world and the media, Abstract Expressionism became the dominant style of art worldwide by the late 1950s.

While de Kooning and Pollock were the most influential of the Abstract Expressionists, other members of this group developed their own individual styles. The Abstract Expressionists did not have an all-encompassing style like earlier movements in art history. What they shared was a belief in individual freedom. This individualism is often said to be uniquely American. It may also be seen as a reaction to the totalitarian forces in Europe that led to the horrors of World War II. These artists did not want to share a manifesto, because they believed artists should operate freely.

Color-Field Painting

Mark Rothko was another member of the original group of Abstract Expressionists. Like Pollock, he explored automatic picture-making early in his career; his paintings contained totemic or symbolic shapes produced from the unconscious. In the late 1940s, he generated a new kind of picture, where large areas of color were more dominant than any particular shape. This new way of painting would become known as **Color-Field Painting.**

Rothko had not abandoned his earlier interest in the unconscious. He was simply approaching it from a different direction, by exploring the psychological and spiritual effects of color. In pictures like *Green on Blue* (**19-20**), Rothko creates a living, breathing color field. He applied his colors in thin, transparent layers, one over another. The edges between the rectangular areas are not hard but soft, and they seem to shift, producing a sense of gentle movement.

19-20 Mark Rothko, *Green on Blue,* 1956. Oil on canvas, 89¾″ × 63¼″. Collection of The University of Arizona Museum of Art, Tucson (gift of Edward J. Gallagher, Jr.) Acc. No. 1964.001.001

Many of Rothko's pictures are more than ten feet tall. He wanted viewers to be surrounded by his pictures. It was only on this scale, he felt, that his Color-Field paintings would come alive and affect the spirit of the viewer. He wrote: "I paint large pictures because I want to create a state of intimacy. A large picture is an immediate transaction: It takes you into it."

Teacher to the Next Generation

Hans Hofmann is known primarily as the teacher of the next generation of American Abstract Expressionists. His career in teaching began in his native Germany, and he also lived in Paris, where he witnessed the birth of Fauvism and Cubism. In 1932, he arrived in New York and began teaching. His reputation as a great teacher brought him many students who would become important artists and teachers themselves.

Hofmann believed in what he called "pure painting," which according to him was the only honest painting, "the true realism." What he meant by pure painting was art that would have no reference to the visible world, like his *Memoria in Aeternum* (**19-21**). According to Hofmann, there was more to nature than visual reality. In the Modern era, painting had moved beyond illusionism, which was only a cheap

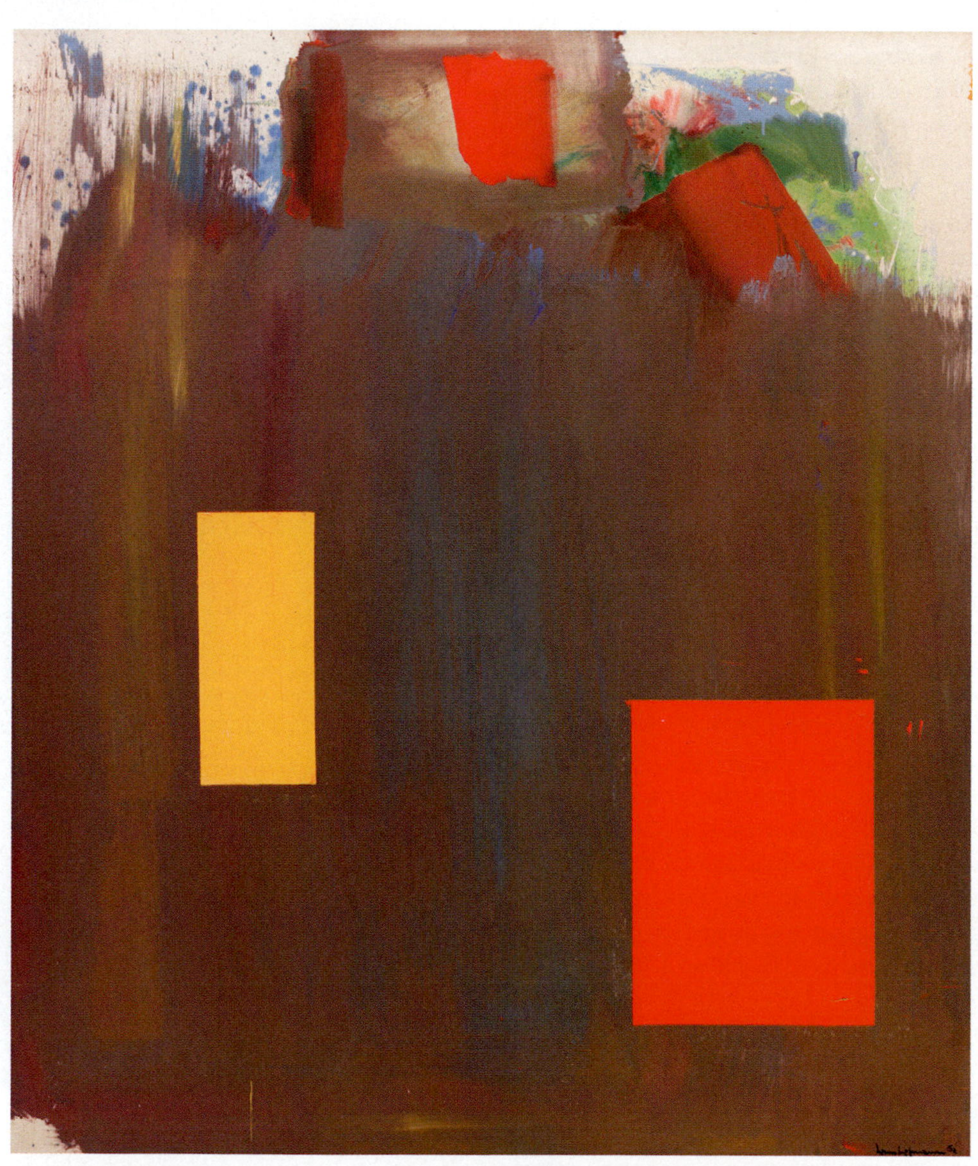

19-21 Hans Hofmann, *Memoria in Aeternum,* 1962. Oil on canvas, 7′ × 6′ ½″. The Museum of Modern Art, New York (gift of the artist).

trick. The activity and excitement on the surface of the painting were enough of a subject for any artist. He talked about "push, pull": how the addition of, say, a rectangle of color creates a whole new dynamic in a picture. It would push the other elements around, necessitating a balancing pull to bring the other parts of the picture into a sense of equilibrium. This push, pull balancing act was what artists, according to Hofmann, had been doing for centuries. It was only with a totally abstract art that the essence of painting could be revealed honestly.

Most of the second generation of Abstract Expressionists were fervent believers in Hofmann's ideas. They believed representational art was dead as fine art, and it should be left to the commercial illustrators. Abstract Expressionism, by the mid-1950s, was the most powerful force in Western art. Its next generation would build on the foundation its creators had built.

The New York School

Helen Frankenthaler was a student of Hans Hofmann and one of the leaders of the next generation (sometimes called *The New York School*). The turning point in her career came during a visit to Jackson Pollock's studio. She watched him at work, spreading his canvas on the floor, circling his picture, painting from every side. She later said, "It was as if I suddenly went to a foreign country but didn't know the language, . . . [I] was eager to live there . . . and master the language."

In 1952, she began to paint in a new way. She spread raw canvas on the floor and began pouring paint from coffee cans, letting it soak into the unprimed canvas. (Most painters *prime* their canvases, which means applying a coat of a special white paint, *gesso*, that seals the fabric.) Her colors stained the canvas, creating unusual effects. The result she called *Mountains and Sea* (**19-22**), a painting more than ten feet tall. Its title came from the colors that reminded her of the Nova Scotia coast she had just visited. Despite its title and great size, there is a sense of intimacy. Because of its soft, gradual transitions, it seems more like watercolor than an oil painting. Unlike "normal" oil paintings, where the paint is clearly on top of the surface, in Frankenthaler's the paint seeped into the canvas, becoming an integral part of it. While she remembers that many who saw her first canvas thought it looked like a "large paint rag," she was convinced she had discovered a new way of working that was rich in possibilities.

She observed that accidents were bound to happen in both her and Pollock's method. Rather than trying to avoid them, she found them to be an important creative stimulus that opened up important new questions for artists. Is all life planned? Doesn't it take true creativity to deal with accidental circumstances, in life and in art? Perhaps an accident would lead her to ideas she would have never thought of on her own. This concept, called *happy accidents,* continues to be popular among contemporary artists. One should not think, however, that Frankenthaler made no attempt to control her paintings. On the contrary, she spent a great deal of time working with her poured paint. She would manipulate the wet areas with brushes, or by blotting. Sometimes she would pour enough paint to create puddles of color—all to create a variety of textures. These different textures gave her work an unusual sense of space, a space that was neither Renaissance nor Cubist.

As mentioned in Chapter 5, Frankenthaler later shifted from oils to the new acrylic polymer paint (see 5-9). This eliminated a faint oily stain that had surrounded each color area in her early work. It also permitted her to experiment with flatter and purer color fields versus the relatively gestural *Mountains and Sea.* These simpler fields would be very influential on later Color-Field painters and the Minimalists of the 1960s and 1970s (see Chapter 20). No matter the medium, her work has a calm, sensuous beauty that sets it apart from the generally anxious works of Abstract Expressionism.

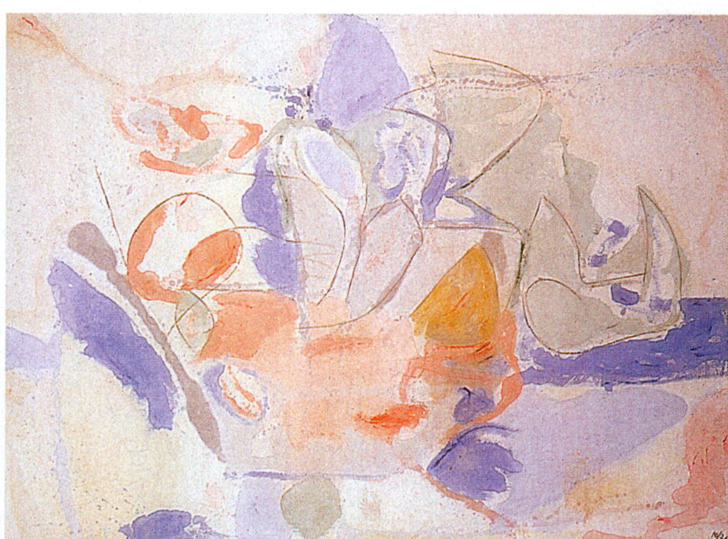

19-22 Helen Frankenthaler, *Mountains and Sea,* 1952. Oil on canvas, 7′ 2⅝″ × 9′ 9¼″. Private Collection

Nonrepresentational Sculpture

Few artists have created a whole new form of art. Most have made their contributions by innovating in traditional forms. In the twentieth century, however, two new forms were invented by artists: Picasso's invention was **collage,** and Alexander Calder's was **kinetic sculpture,** or the *mobile.*

Sculpting was a family tradition for the Calders. His father and grandfather were both successful in the field, his grandfather being best known for the statue of William Penn atop Philadelphia's City Hall. Alexander's first sculptures were not much more than drawings with wire (2-5), but they have a sense of fun and playfulness that was endearing and helped make him one of the most popular artists in the United States and Europe. His miniature circus "performances," with figures made of wire and corks that swallowed knives and walked a tightrope, were the talk of Paris.

His **mobiles,** discussed in Chapter 9, are the sculptures with which he is usually identified. While the mobiles were quite small initially, Calder later in his career built mobiles on an enormous scale in response to public commissions. For example, his mobile designed in the 1970s for the central court of the National Gallery of Art in Washington, D.C. (9-7), spans more than six feet and weighs more than nine hundred pounds. But its gentle movements are able to bring life to the stark, empty space it floats in.

He also made large sculptures he called *stabiles,* like *La Grande Vitesse* (**19-23**), which can be seen in public spaces all over the United States. Despite its huge size (fifty-five feet tall) and weight (forty-two tons), *Vitesse* is not overwhelming, but cheerful and lighthearted. Calder's pleasure in making such works is contagious. Their names rarely mean much; Calder said, "I make the things without any references, but it's necessary to have names, just like cars have license plates." Because of the prevalence of his public work, Calder probably did more to make nonrepresentational art acceptable to the general public than any other artist. The mobile, like Picasso's collage, has become one of the standard art forms. Today, both are even practiced by children in their arts and crafts classes.

The Abstract Expressionist movement in American art during the late 1940s and early 1950s would find its expression in sculpture in the work of David

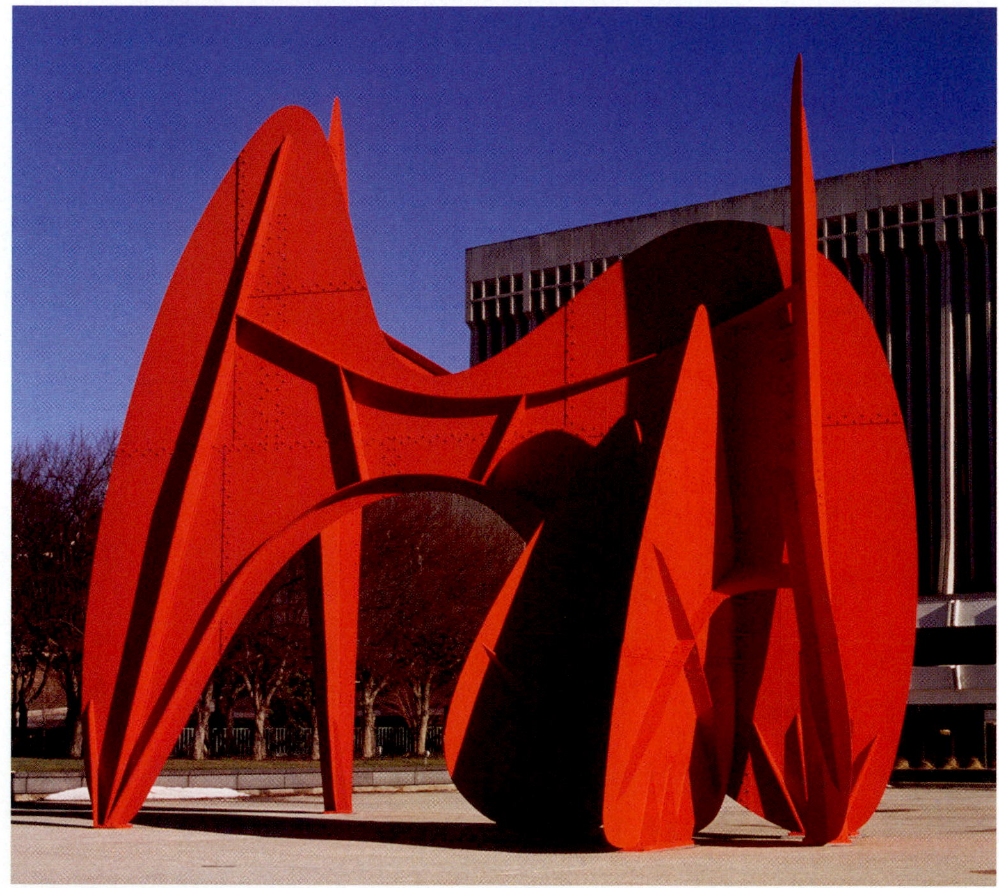

19-23 Alexander Calder, *La Grande Vitesse,* 1969. Painted steel plate, 55′ high. Calder Plaza, Vandenberg Center, Grand Rapids, Michigan.

Smith. He began his artistic career as a painter and was friendly with all of the leading Abstract Expressionists in New York. He shared many of their concerns, especially those of eliminating artificial constraints to artistic freedom and the necessity for an artwork to evolve as it is being made. Smith eventually developed a totally abstract art based on manipulating large geometric solids (see 3-3, 9-22). One of the wonders of Smith's work is how tons of metal are treated lyrically rather than ponderously. His skill as a welder helped him create sculptures that demonstrated that steel can be as flexible a material as the more traditional bronze, stone, and wood.

Mark di Suvero is another sculptor who was inspired by the Abstract Expressionist movement. He has described his work as "painting in three dimensions." If one compares his *Hankchampion* (**19-24**) to the painting of Franz Kline's *New York, New York* (2-4), it is easy to see the connection. Di Suvero's heavy wooden forms seem gestural and intuitively placed. The sculptor used found materials like Louise Nevelson (see Chapter 9), but in his case they were abandoned beams from demolished buildings. Di Suvero left the beams rough and unpolished, wrestled them into position, and connected them with thick bolts and chains.

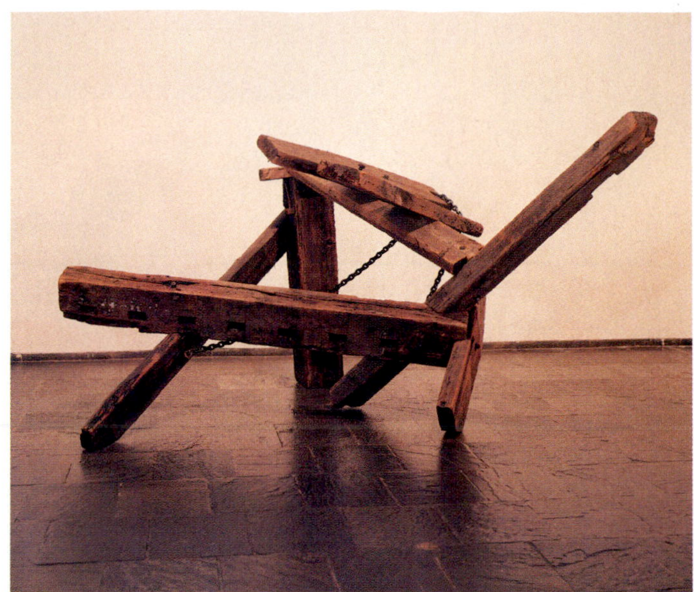

19-24 Mark di Suvero, *Hankchampion,* 1960. Wood and chains, overall: 80″ × 151″ × 112″. Whitney Museum of American Art, New York. Gift of Mr. and Mrs. Robert C. Scull 73.85a–i. Courtesy of Mark di Suvero and Spacetime

Not long after he finished this sculpture in 1960, di Suvero was paralyzed when he was pinned under an elevator in a work-related accident. He was told he might be confined to a wheelchair for the rest of his life. Rather than learning to be satisfied with making small sculptures at a table, he become skilled at handling welding torches, a crane, and a cherry-picker. With these tools, he was able not only to move huge pieces of steel in place, but to bend them as well. This allowed him to make work on an even larger scale than before his accident. He also learned how to walk again in just two years. Today, he continues to work on a monumental scale (often thirty feet tall). His outdoor sculptures can be found all around the world, and he is a member of the crane operator's union.

ARCHITECTURE: THE GLASS BOX

In the twentieth century, modern architects explored the use of glass in ways that would have stunned architects of the past. As a building material, glass has quite different aesthetic possibilities than the traditional media of stone, earth, and metal. Because glass is both transparent and reflective, the standard division between inside and outside is challenged by a building with glass walls. This quality was explored by the American architect Philip Johnson when he built himself an all-glass house in the late 1940s (**19-25**). Except for a central brick core that houses the bathroom, the whole interior space is open, without walls or room dividers. All of the exterior walls are made of glass (although there are built-in shades to be used if desired), so the experience is one of living in the midst of nature, weather, and the trees that surround the site.

The experience within the glass house is far from sleeping under the stars. It retains a building's traditional role of shelter, and its design puts considerable psychological distance between the dweller and nature. Because of Johnson's strict adherence to the tenets of International Style, every aspect of its interior and exterior is integrated, logical, and civilized. The building's purity of design and use of modern materials provide a formal, intellectual vantage point from which to contemplate nature.

For obvious reasons of privacy, as well as expense, solid walls of glass have been more popular for commercial rather than domestic architecture. We associate glass walls with modern office buildings, towers where glass covers a skeleton of steel. Philip Johnson, during his long and distinguished career,

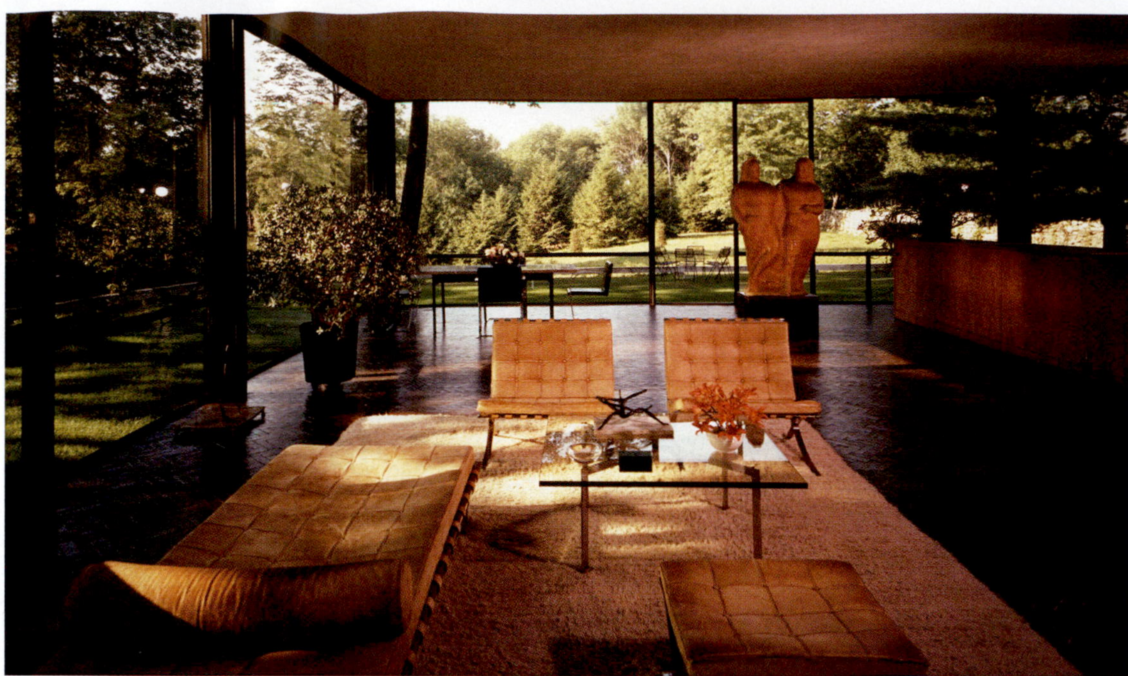

19-25 Philip Johnson, Glass House, New Canaan, Connecticut, 1949.

has designed many fine examples of these goliaths of the International Style, perhaps none better than the *Seagram Building* (10-30), a collaboration with his mentor, Mies van der Rohe (a former director of the Bauhaus). In the 1950s, 1960s, and 1970s, the International Style of architecture dominated large-scale public and corporate architecture around the world, putting an enduring stamp on urban life. Its orderly, disciplined forms are no longer seen as controversial but, in fact, as neutral and nonpartisan. A glass box lacks political or social overtones. Its absence of ornament was also a plus because, as even Johnson admitted in later years, it made building a skyscraper much cheaper.

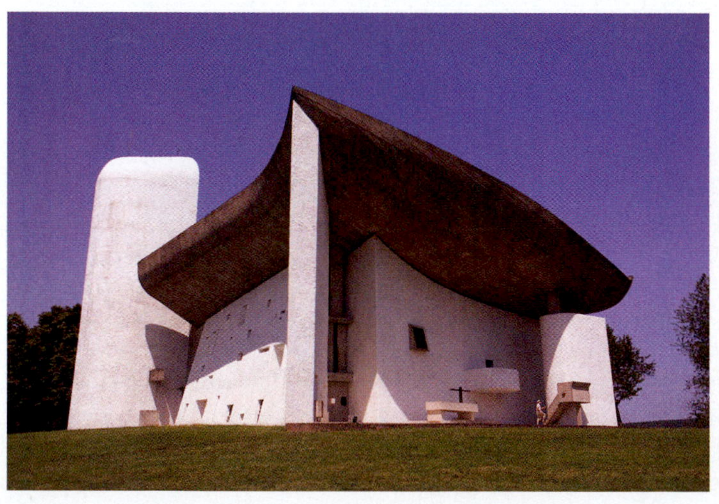

19-26 Le Corbusier, Notre Dame du Haut, Ronchamp, France, 1950–1955.

ORGANIC ABSTRACTION

Nonrepresentation has been pursued in two general directions: the geometric and the organic (see Chapter 2). Johnson's Glass House is a collection of pure right angles, while Buckminster Fuller's geodesic dome (2-9) is a hemisphere, and David Smith's sculptures juggle cubes and cylinders. Those who make geometric works are often interested in evoking pure, transcendent existence, a kind of refined Neoclassical abstraction. Organic abstraction, as in Henry Moore's *Sheep Piece* (2-14), tends to be less cerebral and more spiritual, evocative of natural forces or living things. It could be called a kind of Romantic abstraction.

In the first half of the twentieth century, the highly geometric buildings of Le Corbusier epitomized the beliefs of the International Style and the glorification of the machine. No wonder that the architectural community was stunned by what appeared to be a startling reversal by one of the founding fathers of the International Style in 1950. Le Corbusier's *Notre Dame du Haut* (**19-26**), a small chapel in Ronchamp, France, seems the polar opposite of his earlier buildings, meant to foster a marriage of art and technology and nearer to Moore's sensual sculpture. In the organic, flowing Notre

Dame du Haut, right angles have been replaced by soft curves, rational order with intuitive placement. There is no clear glass curtain filling an interior with even light; instead, small windows with colored glass are placed in deep cuts in the heavy concrete walls (interior, **19-27**).

Le Corbusier had actually given an earlier warning of his change of heart. In 1936, disappointed with the lack of imagination among fellow architects whom he believed were eager only to refine his ideas rather than to go beyond them, he wrote to a group of young architectural students:

> How are we to enrich our creative powers? Not by subscribing to architectural reviews, but by undertaking voyages of discovery into the inexhaustible domain of Nature!

Le Corbusier's chapel is more like a sculpture than a building. It is placed on a hill that looks out onto a river, a site with a long religious history, from the early Christians to pre-Roman pagans. As if challenging less daring followers of the International Style, Le Corbusier exploits the flexibility of concrete with great imagination. The walls are curving, tilted forms that lean toward the center. The roof, shaped like the headdress of a French nun's habit, floats above the outer walls, perched on small columns. It is a building of many original spaces, with a dark, bare inner chapel, as well as an open-air one. An absolutely unique work of architecture, it is extraordinarily free of historical references. Concrete has rarely seemed so sensual or unfettered. Le Corbusier's lesson is that in the hands of creative people, abstract and nonrepresentational art has no boundaries.

THE CHALLENGE OF NONREPRESENTATIONAL ART

Nonrepresentational art has been in existence for more than seventy-five years, the logical development of changes in art during the 1800s. Many of the first totally abstract canvases are antiques; their paint is cracking from the passage of time. Yet abstract art is still often seen as weird or strange.

Most viewers feel more comfortable with artworks that refer to the world they know; many prefer art that tells a story. Nonrepresentational art can do these things, but not in a conventional way. Each work is an expression of the ideals, personality, and mood of the artist. The world they refer to is an inner one. We have seen many artists, all working abstractly, create very different artworks. Some seem passionate and violent, some absolutely logical and calm. If you look closely, there are significant differences even between two emotional Abstract Expressionist artists.

By looking even more closely, one can imagine a story. Each element—each line, shape, volume, and color—is a separate character having its own weight and impact. The tale is one of the relationship of these elements. Who will dominate? Which is weak? How do they connect? Will they ever reconcile their differences? Nonrepresentational artwork is a veritable soap opera. Approach it with an open mind and look carefully; totally abstract paintings and sculptures have scenarios without limit.

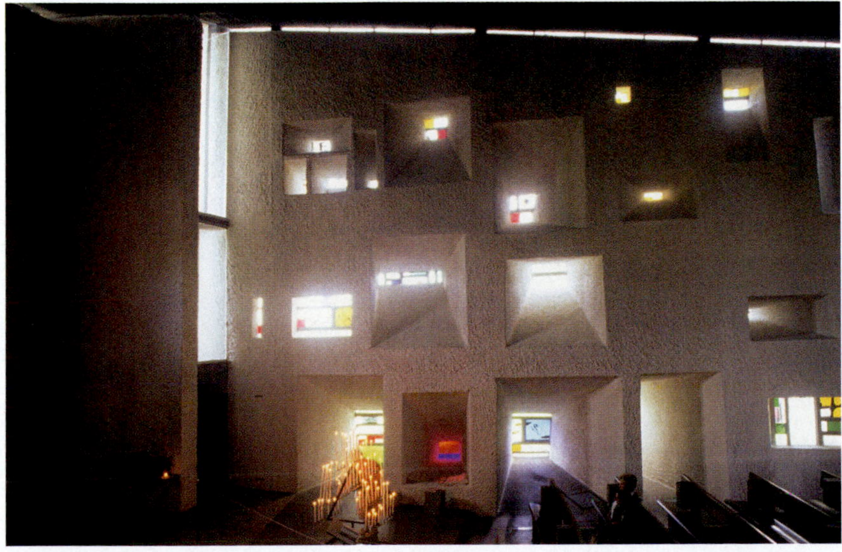

19-27 Le Corbusier, interior of Notre Dame du Haut.

CHAPTER 20

A Storm of Images: Art in the Contemporary World

By the 1950s, New York City was the magnet that drew young, ambitious artists from all over the world, like Paris had a century before. Just as the United States came to be the foremost power in world affairs after World War II, so did America's artists and cultural institutions come to dominate the art world. The School of Abstract Expressionism had dethroned the School of Paris. For the following half-century, artists of every nationality could be found living and working in New York.

Mark Tansey's *Triumph of the New York School* (**20-1**) depicts in tongue-in-cheek manner the surrender of the School of Paris on a smoldering battlefield. On the left, dressed in World War I uniforms are portraits of leading figures of the Modern movement. Picasso in

	PERIOD	HISTORICAL EVENTS	
1945–1960	Abstract Expressionism The New York School The International Style	Jean-Paul Sartre and others develop Existentialism 1940s Churchill describes Soviet domination of Eastern Europe as an "iron curtain" 1946 India and Pakistan become independent states 1947	People's Republic of China united under communist leader Mao Zedong 1949 Korean War begins 1950 New York becomes center of world art 1950s
1960–1980	Pop Art and Happenings Minimalism Earth Art Performance art Video art Superrealism Feminist art	Space race between U.S.S.R. and the United States 1950s–1960s Civil Rights March on Washington 1963 Assassination of President Kennedy 1963 United States fights Vietnam War 1964–1973	First Earth Day 1970 Watergate, President Nixon's resignation 1974 Second wave feminism in the United States 1960s–1970s
1980–present	New Image Neo-Expressionism Post-Modern art and architecture Installation art Digital art	Last remaining European colonies in Africa receive independence 1980s Rise of Islamic fundamentalism 1980s Iran-Iraq war 1980–1990 AIDS first identified 1981 Collapse of Soviet Empire 1991 Nelson Mandela becomes President of South Africa 1994 World Wide Web 1994	Fourth World Conference on Women, Beijing 1995 Introduction of Euro 1999 Attacks on World Trade Center and Pentagon 2001 Growing concern about Global Warming 2000s United States war with Iraq begins 2003

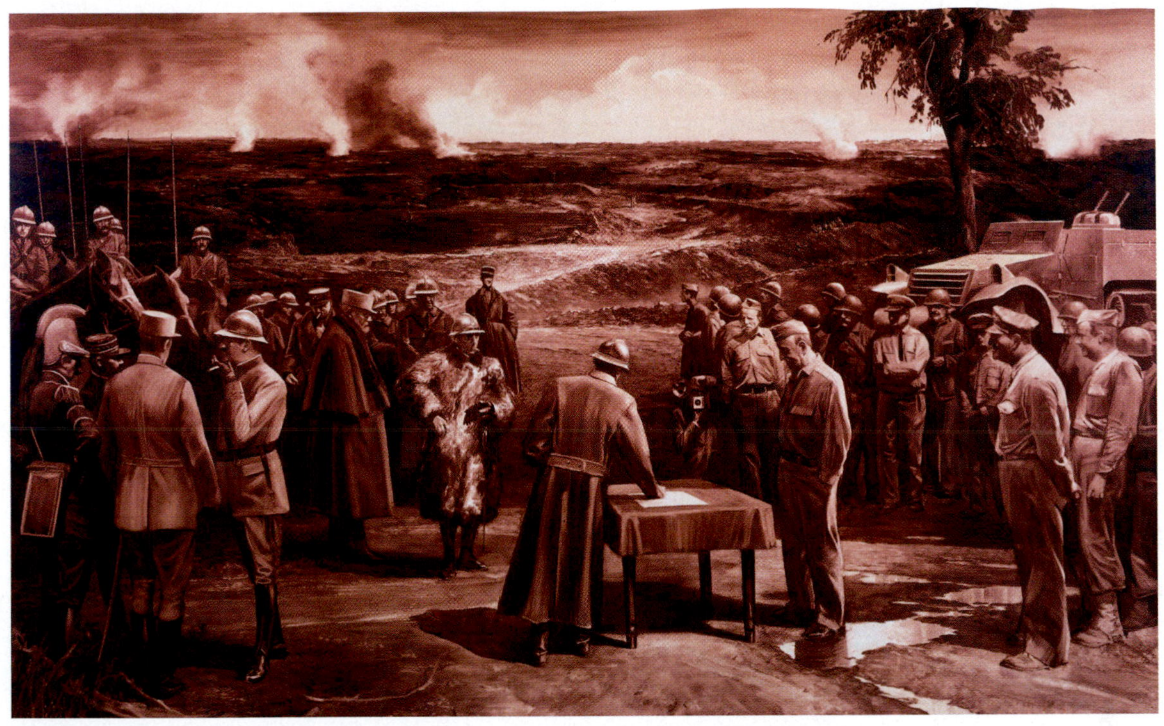

20-1 Mark Tansey, *Triumph of the New York School,* 1984. Oil on canvas, 74″ × 20″. Whitney Museum of Art, New York.

ART

Philip Johnson, Glass House 1949

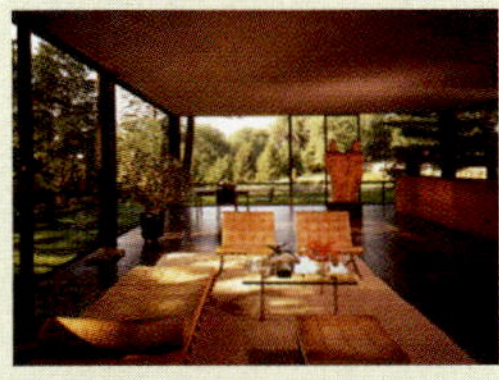

Franz Kline, *New York, New York* 1953

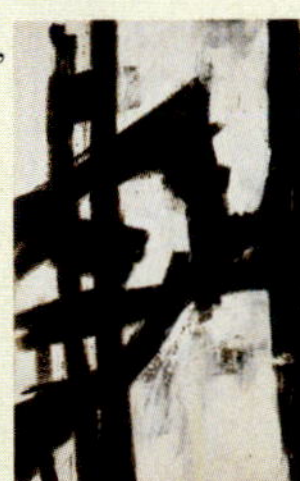

Knoll Showroom in San Francisco 1957

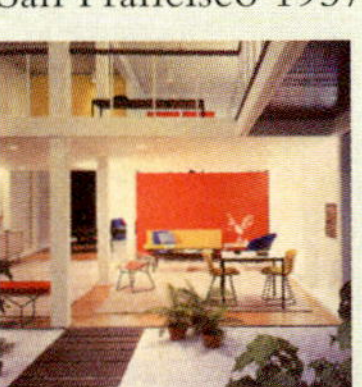

Alberto Giacometti, *Walking Man II* 1960

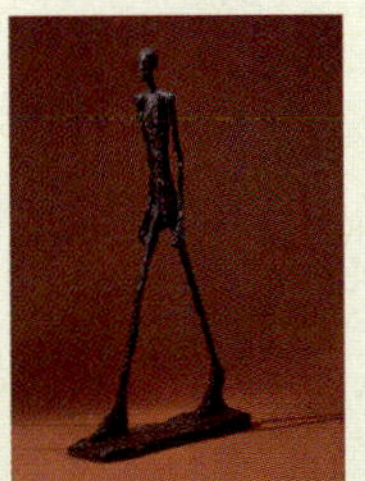

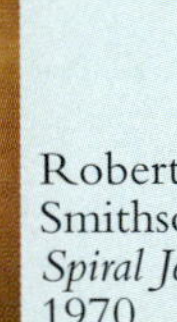

Andy Warhol, *Gold Marilyn Monroe* 1962

Robert Smithson, *Spiral Jetty* 1970

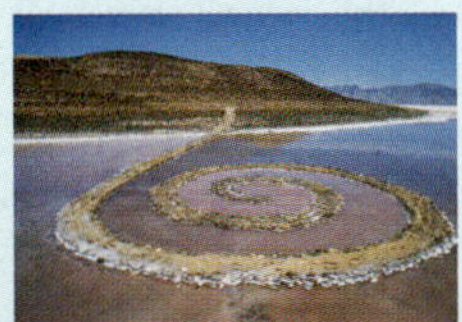

Nam June Paik, *TV Buddha* 1974

SITE, Best Products Showroom 1975

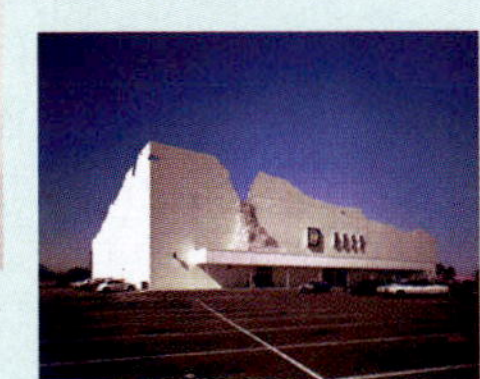

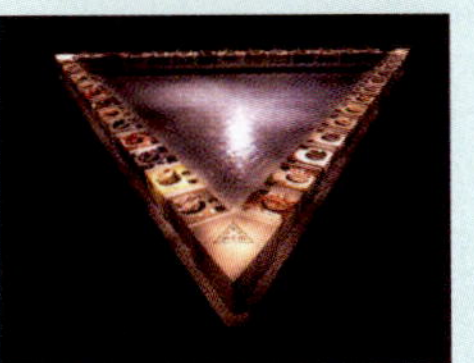

Judy Chicago, *Dinner Party* 1979

Sandy Skogland, *Radioactive Cats* 1980

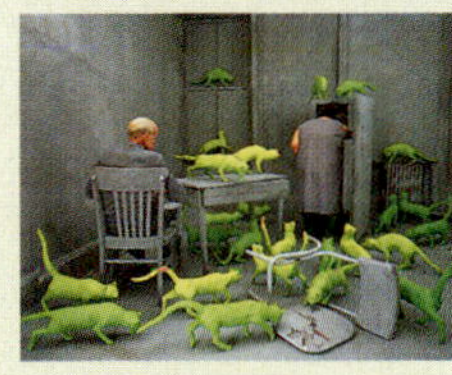

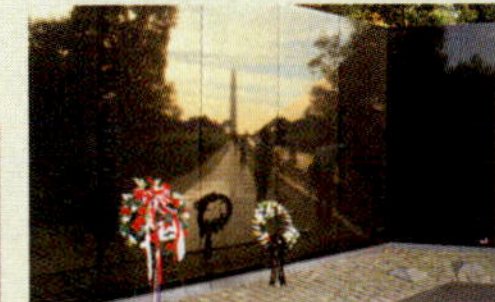

Maya Lin, Vietnam Veterans Memorial 1981–1983

John Lasseter, et al. *Luxo Jr.* 1986

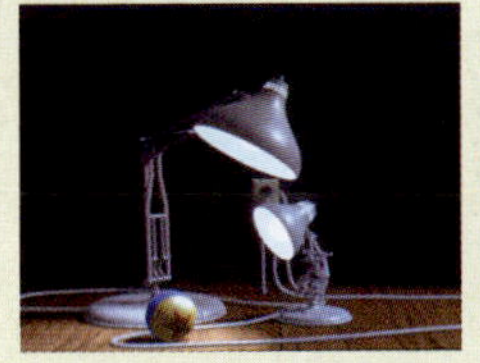

Christo and Jeanne Claude, *The Gates* 2005

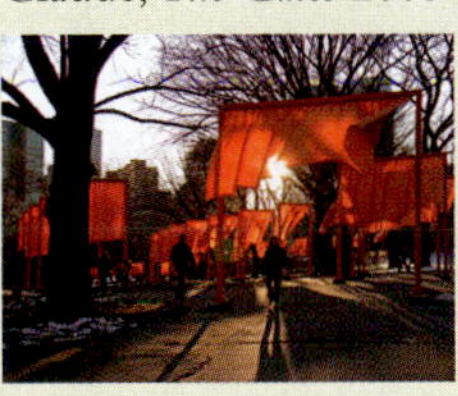

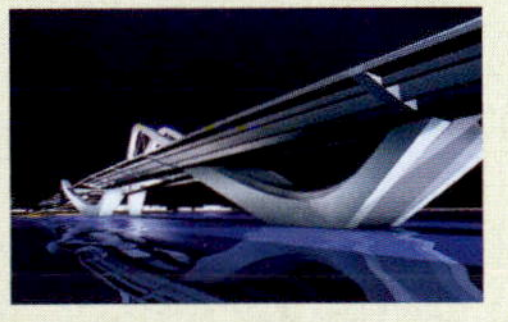

Zaha Hadid, Sheikh Zayed Bridge

a furry aviator's coat stares defiantly, while, to the left of him, Matisse turns his head away. The Americans are dressed in World War II khakis, represented at the signing table by Clement Greenberg, a critic who was their chief supporter. Among the American soldiers are Willem de Kooning and Jackson Pollock.

Born as a movement to open up new territories for art, Abstract Expressionism was quickly trumpeted by critics like Greenberg as the only way to make serious art. In a remarkably short time, academics also embraced the movement and codified it. For the next twenty years, art schools and universities trained students in working abstractly. Drawing realistically was only for beginners, merely a step toward more important concerns. As might be expected, younger artists soon began to feel straitjacketed by the new dogma of Abstract Expressionism.

ALTERNATIVES TO ABSTRACT EXPRESSIONISM: RAUSCHENBERG AND JOHNS

In 1954, Robert Rauschenberg came to New York and met a shy, young artist from rural South Carolina, Jasper Johns. Rauschenberg had grown up in Texas, in a bustling port surrounded by oil refineries, far from the intellectual centers of Paris or New York City. He and Johns became close friends and rented studios in the same building in downtown Manhattan. Like Picasso and Braque during their Analytical Cubist period, for the next few years the two young men worked feverishly and saw each other every day, engaging in an intense dialogue on the nature of art and life. In New York City, the young artists joined in the camaraderie of Pollock, de Kooning, and others. Rauschenberg later said he learned more from drinking with these artists in the taverns of Manhattan than from any of the art schools he attended. But Rauschenberg also witnessed the chilling effect Abstract Expressionism was having on younger artists. Rauschenberg thought that the complete exclusion of our daily visual experience of the world was too high a price to pay for what was said to be a purer, more honest art. He wondered how to get the real world back into painting without totally abandoning the power or achievement of Abstract Expressionism.

Rauschenberg proposed that "a picture is more like the real world when it's made out of the real world" and began the reintroduction of everyday objects as Picasso had, by using the medium of collage, or what Rauschenberg called "**combines.**" In *Bed* (**20-2**), he pulled art and life together by using a bed as his canvas. Across the pillow and sheets and on to the nice quilt, he applied the great colorful gestures and dripping paint of Abstract Expressionism. Despite his use of ordinary materials, the result

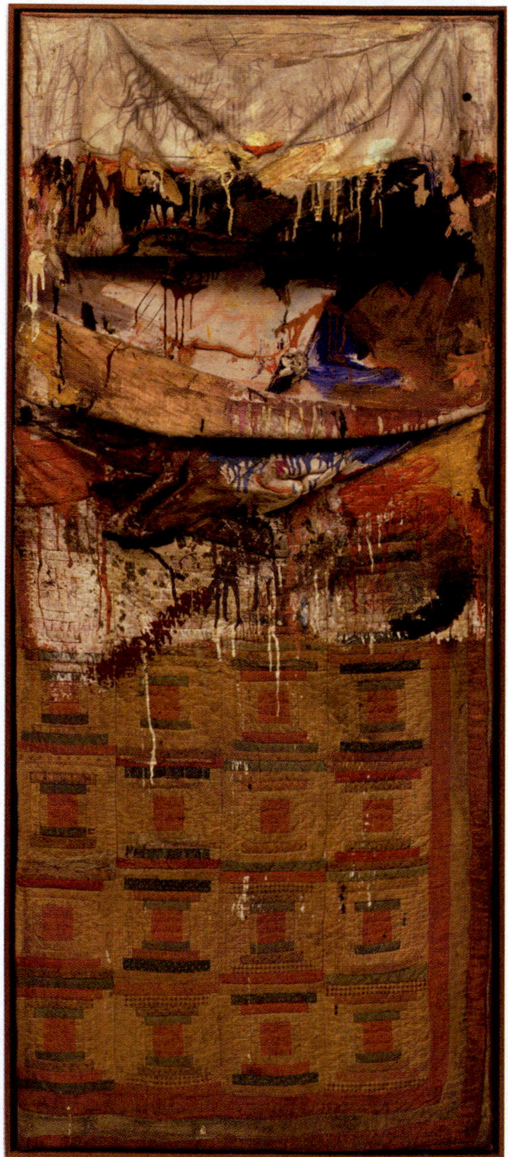

20-2 Robert Rauschenberg, *Bed,* 1955, Combine painting: oil and pencil on pillow, quilt, and sheet on wood supports, 6′ 3¼″ × 31½″ × 8″ (191.1 cm × 80 cm × 20.3 cm). The Museum of Modern Art, New York (Gift of Leo Castelli in honor of Alfred H. Barr, Jr.).

is a shocking combination for anyone raised to keep one's bed clean and crisply made. It is also an unforgettable and powerful image.

Jasper Johns's work, like his personality, was more restrained than Rauschenberg's, but it also challenged the basic premises of Abstract Expressionism. What interested Johns were "things the mind already knows," subjects that were instantly recognizable. For example, his *Flag* (**20-3**) was part of a series of more than twenty-five paintings and many drawings and prints using the same subject. Johns would vary size, number, color, and materials, but the essentially flat flag would be the same in each. Most flags were built by painting thickly over a collage of newspapers, resulting in a very textured surface. The flag paintings seemed to follow the rules of Abstract Expressionism and to slyly undermine them at the same time. Like a typical Abstract Expressionist picture, Johns's images were absolutely flat and nonillusionistic and covered with lively, gestural brushstrokes. But they also had subjects; they were unquestionably, instantly recognizable as flags.

In direct opposition to the romantic search for inner truth found in the action paintings of Pollock and de Kooning, Johns's flag paintings were impersonal. He explains that he chose flags precisely because they are "things which are seen and not looked at, not examined." By using them in atypical ways, Johns is encouraging the viewer to go beyond the conventional reading of flags to see them freshly. He warns of the tendency we all have of thinking we know at one glance what we see. One should be open to new ways of understanding or new uses of ordinary things. His message is reminiscent of René Magritte's *The Treachery of Images* (18-35), a surrealist work in which the illustration of a pipe is subtitled with a message that it is not a pipe.

Done at the peak of Abstract Expressionism's dominance in the late 1950s and early 1960s, Rauschenberg and Johns's work shocked many artists and critics. They reopened the visual world and legitimized borrowing objects and symbols from popular culture. By repeating familiar symbols in lengthy series, Johns had also discarded one of the oldest tests of an artwork's value, one particularly important to the Abstract Expressionists—originality or uniqueness. That, along with the cool tone of Johns's works, appealed to a considerable group of artists who would focus more directly on common household objects and the products of the booming postwar American economy. Their works have become known as **Pop Art.**

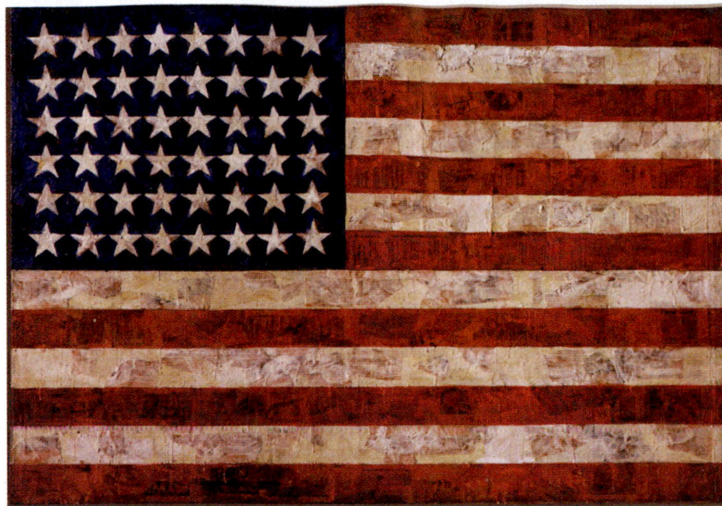

20-3 Jasper Johns, *Flag,* 1954–1955. Encaustic, oil, and collage on fabric mounted on plywood, 42 ¼″ × 60 ⅝″. The Museum of Modern Art, New York (gift of Philip Johnson in honor of Alfred H. Barr, Jr.).

POP ART

The most famous and influential of the Pop artists was Andy Warhol. His early paintings of Campbell's soup cans and cardboard sculptures of Brillo boxes announced that no kind of subject matter was more important than any other. A six-foot canvas devoted to a can of soup seemed to mock the central precepts of Abstract Expressionism, still the dominant force in the art world. When Pollock and Rothko had worked on a large scale, they were announcing that their inner searches and new approaches were important. Few could question the powerful and heroic impact they had. Warhol reminded viewers that anything made large will have a dramatic effect, even a soup can.

Following the success of his first works, Warhol began producing images of celebrities that implied their connection to his images of packaged products. Multiple images of Elvis Presley, Jacqueline Kennedy, and Marilyn Monroe (**20-4**) were given the same treatment as Brillo and Coca-Cola. Even the *Mona Lisa* has become a glamorous commercial product according to Warhol (see Chapter 1). While Jasper Johns's cool attitude seemed revolutionary just a few years earlier, Johns had still applied gestural brushstrokes almost lovingly to his flags and targets. Warhol's approach was more than cool, even neutral. Warhol used photographically created silk-screens of his subjects and printed them directly onto his canvases in order to achieve a more mechanical look.

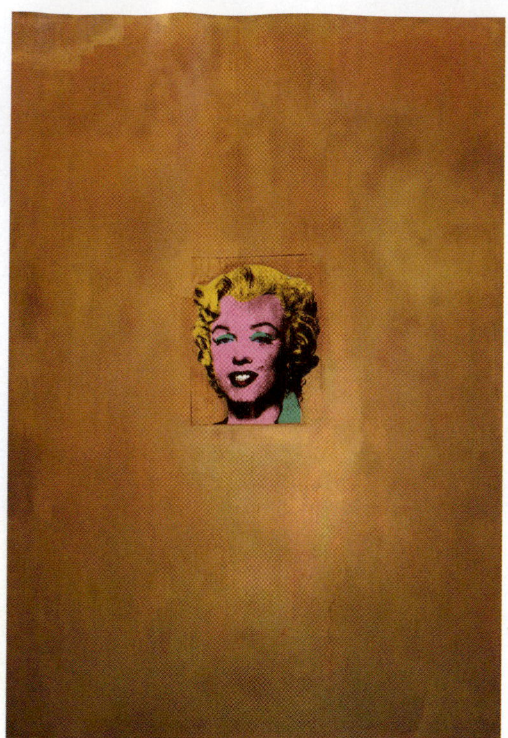

20-4 Andy Warhol, *Gold Marilyn Monroe,* 1962. Synthetic polymer paint, silkscreened, and oil on canvas, 6′ 11 ½″ × 57″. The Museum of Modern Art, New York (gift of Philip Johnson).

He later said: "I want to be a machine. . . . I think everybody should be a machine." His large studio in New York City came to be known, appropriately, as "the Factory." Assistants were reported to be producing his pictures.

Warhol became a celebrity. The Factory was filled every night with famous people and those seeking fame. The artist generally remained silent but listened to conversations and drew inspiration from them. After being shown a dramatic headline and gruesome front-page photograph of a horrible airplane crash, Warhol began his *Disasters* series. Gory automobile wrecks and racist beatings were reproduced several times on single-color canvases. In *Orange Disaster* (**20-5**), a dramatic photograph of the death chamber in a prison is repeated fifteen times. Alone, the electric chair and the small sign that calls for "silence" could move the viewer, but multiplied it loses its effect. The *Disasters* series illustrates the numbing effect that the daily storm of images has on us. When seen over and over again, even the most shocking pictures lose their impact. The Warhol canvases of the 1960s that treat celebrities, tragedies, famous paintings, and products as the same thing recreate the daily experience of watching television news. All are equivalent in importance, each given its few minutes of air time.

By focusing on the things we see every day, Pop Art was following the mandate of Robert Rauschenberg and closing the gap between art and our everyday experience of life. Claes Oldenburg went one step further and called for an art "that does something else than sit on its ass in a museum." He was a founder of *Happenings*, an attempt to use "real" materials and locations as art—theatrical events intended to break down the distance between art and audience, to become, as one artist said, an "all-encompassing art experience." In *Store Days,* for example, Oldenburg rented an abandoned storefront in New York City and filled it with life-size plaster reproductions of hamburgers, cakes, dresses, hardware, and other standard merchandise. Each object was loosely painted in bright colors with drips run-

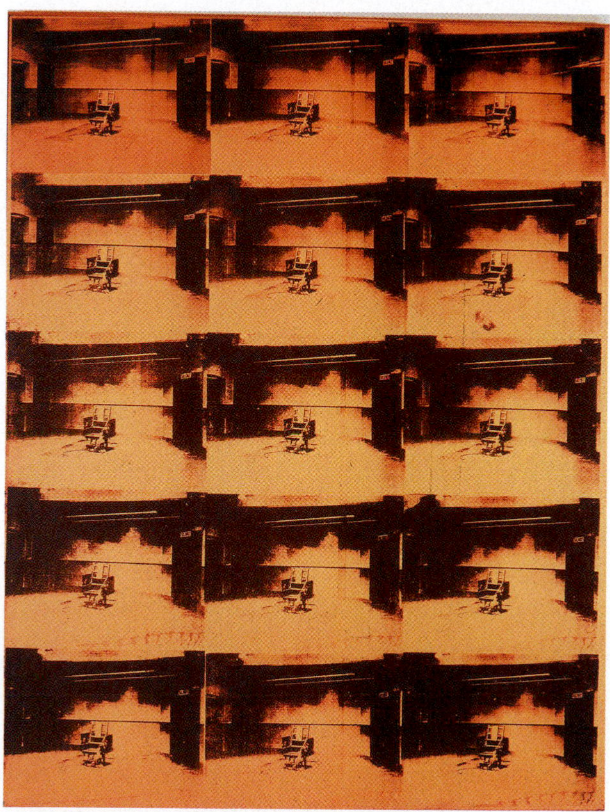

20-5 Andy Warhol, *Orange Disaster,* 1963. Acrylic and silkscreen enamel on canvas, 106″ × 81 ½″. Solomon R. Guggenheim Museum, New York (gift, Harry N. Abrams Family Collection, 1974).

ning over them, a parody of action painting. When the audience entered, they were encouraged to behave like customers. When a sculpture was purchased, in contrast with the custom in fine art galleries, the buyer was permitted to take the object home immediately. Oldenburg replaced sold items from his studio in the back, which served as a storeroom.

Store Days was an examination of the relationship between art and money, an increasing concern among many American artists after World War II. As the American art market gained prominence, art seemed to be becoming more and more a commodity like stocks or precious metals. For the artists who achieved success in the 1950s, the struggle for acceptance, the years spent trying to make ends meet, was part of what gave an artist integrity. They felt that money and early success endangered the honesty and independence of any artist. Not surprisingly, Andy Warhol did not share the older artists' views. He did not find financial rewards disturbing and said "being good in business is the most fascinating kind of art."

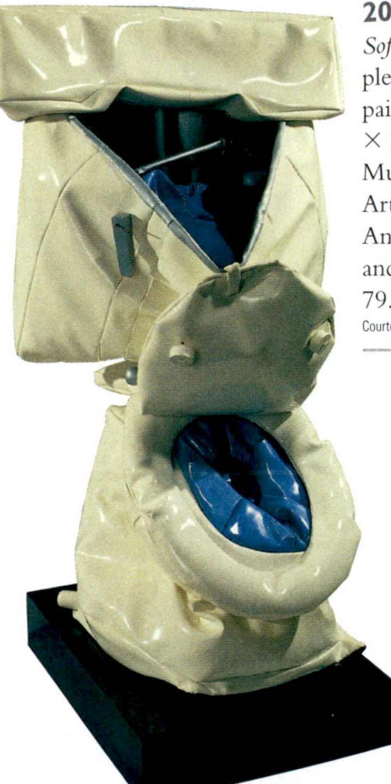

20-6 Claes Oldenburg, *Soft Toilet,* 1966. Vinyl, plexiglass, and kapok, on painted wood base, 57 1/16" × 27 5/8" × 28 1/16". Whitney Museum of American Art, New York. 50th Anniversary Gift of Mr. and Mrs. Victor W. Ganz 79.83a–b. Photograph by Jerry L. Thompson. Courtesy Oldenburg van Bruggen Foundation

Shortly after *Store Days,* Oldenburg's objects began to grow larger in scale. In his one-man exhibition of 1962, the small plaster hamburgers had expanded to soft-cloth ones four feet tall. The gallery was filled with enormous ice cream cones and slices of cakes. Viewers were treated to an *Alice in Wonderland* experience, as if they had shrunk to miniature size. By enlarging the things we see every day to gigantic dimensions, Oldenburg altered their reality and made them strangers to us. This allowed the viewer to examine them freshly, as if seeing them for the first time. Another way to shatter conventional seeing was by changing the materials of commonplace objects. In *Soft Toilet* (**20-6**), the artist substitutes stuffed vinyl for porcelain, and now the familiar bathroom item collapses as if it is fatigued. By making it soft, the toilet is humanized—one can even move its parts around and reshape it.

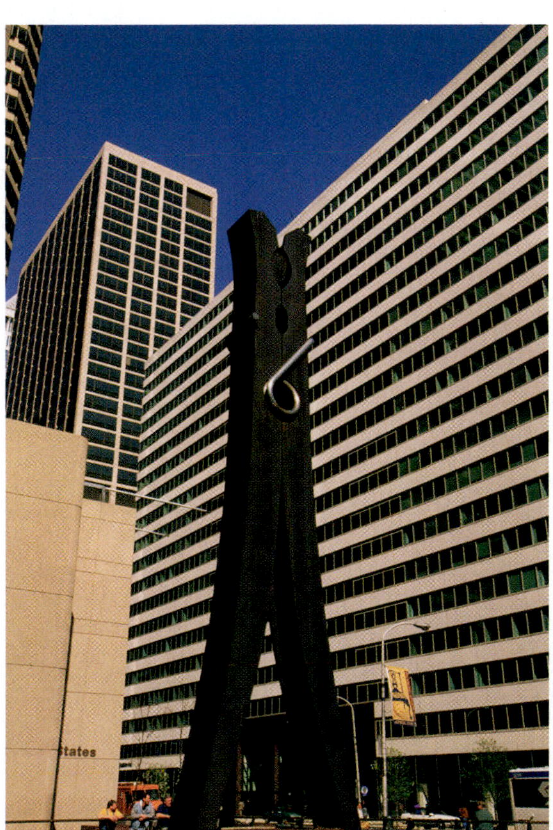

20-7 Claes Oldenburg, *Clothespin,* Philadelphia, 1976. Steel, 45′.

By 1965, Oldenburg had increased the scale of his projects to monumental. At first these were simply sketches of fantasies, but eventually he prepared formal architectural proposals and submitted them to various public and private institutions. In 1967, for example, he proposed to replace the Washington Monument with mammoth scissors that would open and close. Oldenburg has even been successful in realizing some of his monumental dreams. A forty-five-foot clothespin now graces a city square in Philadelphia (**20-7**), and a nearly one-hundred-foot-tall baseball bat is in Chicago.

VENTURI: POP ARCHITECTURE

Just as Abstract Expressionism became the standard form of painting and sculpture in the postwar years, the **International Style** dominated architecture. The buildings and theories of Gropius, Le Corbusier, and Philip Johnson (see Chapter 19), which called for pure, logical designs and prohibited unnecessary ornament or decoration, were the preeminent models for most serious architects around the world. Mies van der Rohe, chief architect of the *Seagram Building* (10-33) and a director of the Bauhaus, spoke for his generation of architects when he said, "Less is more."

Robert Venturi's response, however, was, "Less is a bore." The ideology of the International Style, according to Venturi, was a failure because it ignored the local culture of the locations where its buildings stood. No building could be successful that ignored the interests of the clients and the surrounding architecture. Buildings like the *Villa Savoye* (19-9) were more like alien structures than homes. They spoke a language that no one except sophisticated architectural scholars could understand and had a destructive effect on their environments.

Like the Pop Artists, Venturi felt architects should embrace popular styles of architecture, finding ways to utilize what he called "honky-tonk elements" that spoke in a language anyone could understand. Venturi put his ideas into practice in a design for a firehouse in Columbus, Indiana (**20-8**). Although the simplicity of its form is certainly more reminiscent of the International Style than a Gothic cathedral, several aspects of the building were considered a kind of heresy at the time. Venturi used a variety of windows with different sizes and designs, depending on the needs of the occupants rather than any geometric rules. A loud contrast between glossy white and red brick creates an irregular, not uniform, design. At the top of a seemingly functionless tower (it actually is used for drying hoses), he placed an equally loud sign that announced in bold graphics "FIRE STATION 4" to the public.

Venturi felt strongly that the International Style made a mistake when it rejected the past. The public service nature of his *Fire Station #4* is easily understood because its tower is connected to clock towers and church steeples of the past. It fits into its neighborhood because it is a brick building with a flat front and ordinary glass-windowed garage doors. The front is really a thin façade, an approach Venturi called "the decorated shed . . . a modest building with a big sign," used by supermarkets, department stores, and other commercial buildings all over the country. So unlike the metal-and-glass skyscraper, the Seagram Building, *Fire Station #4* is a truly American building designed to hold its own and live

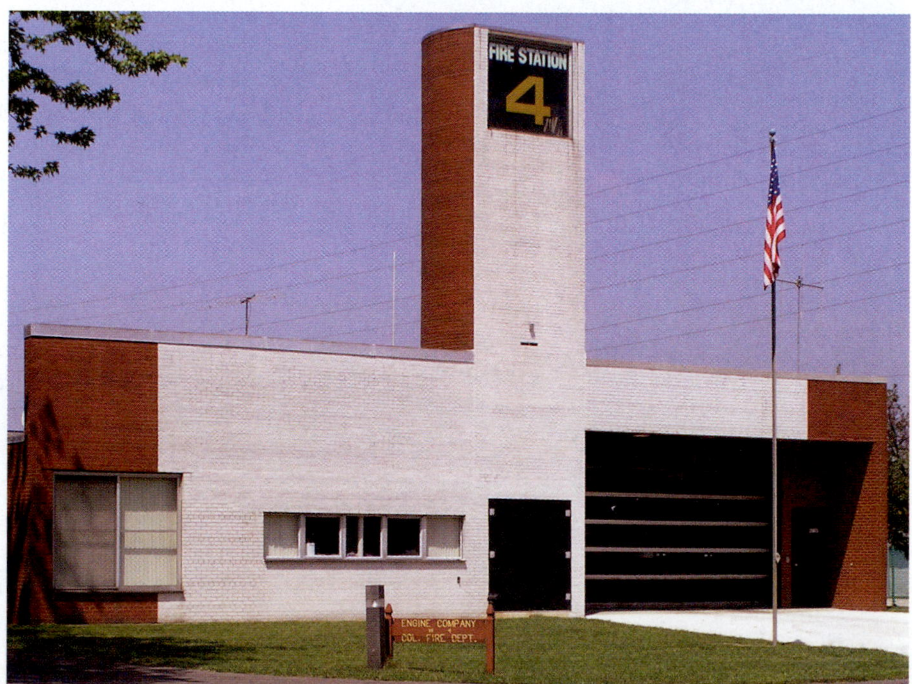

20-8 Robert Venturi (Venturi and Rauch), *Fire Station #4,* Columbus, Indiana, 1965–1967.

with the billboards and gas stations found along any main street or highway. It has what Venturi called the "messy vitality" that the International Style had attempted to eliminate.

THE END OF ART: MINIMALISM

Pop Art was not the only alternative to Abstract Expressionism advanced in the 1960s. A group of serious, intellectual artists disgusted with the emotional outpourings of the Abstract Expressionists and the vulgarity of Pop Art began to make high-minded and refined art known as **Minimalism.** Minimalist art is art stripped down to the essentials, or as one artist said: "what you see is what you see." It is paintings and sculptures that are self-sufficient and have no subject matter, content, or meaning beyond their presence as objects in space. Lauded by some as a return to purity and high ideals, others called Minimalism the end of art. What was occurring was a replay of a battle that we have seen before: the battle among Romanticism, Realism, and Classicism, now in the arena of nonrepresentational and Pop Art. On one side, once again, were the defenders of emotions and expressiveness, on another, ordinary life, and on the third, purity and logic.

Donald Judd was one of the foremost creators and theorists of Minimalism. As an art critic in New York City, the Missouri-born Judd became concerned that art made it difficult to perceive reality. It bothered him that, while contemplating works of art, viewers are inevitably drawn into illusions, emotions not their own, and references to the past. The only way to reconnect the viewer with reality, Judd felt, was to produce works of art with no expressive techniques, free of associations, that could be seen to be simply what they were—plain and honest "matters of fact":

> I wanted work that didn't involve incredible assumptions about everything. I couldn't begin to think about the order of the universe, or, the nature of American society.

Beginning in 1962, Judd made sculptures that were controlled and completely logical, designed to cleanse viewers of whatever concerns or preconceptions they brought into the gallery and allowing them to focus on the situation the artist had created there.

Untitled (**20-9**) is a good example of how Judd resolved his interest in a direct, honest work of art. It is made of ten virtually identical boxes constructed from stainless steel and Plexiglas attached to a wall with even spacing. Because it is internally logical, it is relatively unaffected by what surrounds it. To eliminate any sign of the human hand (which might evoke emotions), Judd had his sculptures manufactured in factories, based on his drawings. Industrial fabrication ensured that his sculptures were also well constructed and as perfect a recreation of his concepts as possible. His boxes were open at two sides, with Plexiglas permitting light to enter so no aspect of their structure was hidden or mysterious. Because *Untitled* contains no allusions or illusions, viewers can focus on what they are truly experiencing. They become aware of being in a unique kind of situation—what

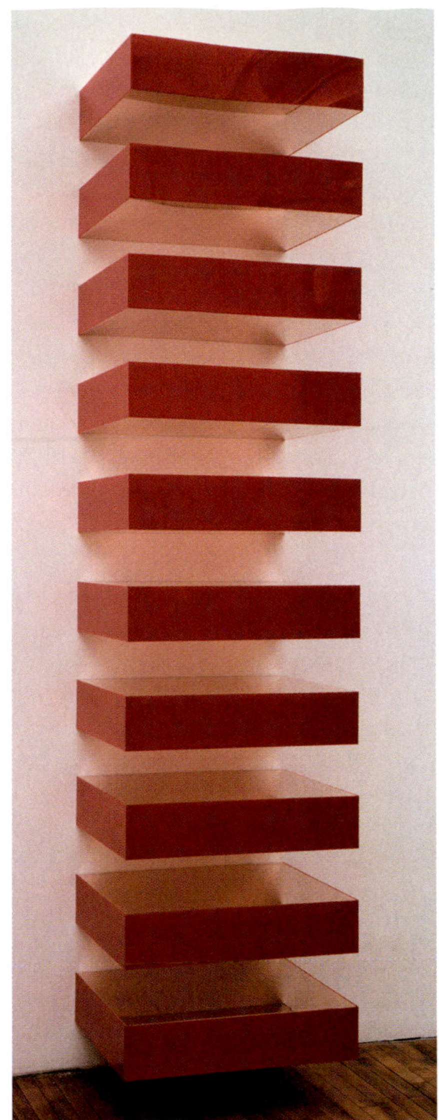

20-9 Donald Judd, *Untitled,* 1967. Stainless steel and Plexiglas, 10 units 9 ⅛″ × 40″ × 30″ each, approximately 16 feet tall overall. Modern Art Museum of Fort Worth. Museum Purchase. The Benjamin J. Tillar Memorial Trust.

Judd would call "art space," an isolated place separated from the commotion of their everyday experience. In such a space, viewers realize the limits of their vision. Although you know logically that each box is the same, as you slowly pass by the work in the gallery, your changing spatial relationships alter its appearance moment by moment. This is what Judd would call a true, unadulterated art experience.

Minimalism appeared to be the final chapter in the refining of purity and truth in the visual arts, a search with a long history, from Ancient Greece to Mondrian. Art had been reduced to one simple, essential experience—the relationship between object and viewer. Yet in Modern Art's long history of radical changes, probably no other movement opened such a wide chasm between the artist and the ordinary viewer. Shell-shocked observers were further startled when one Minimalist artist, Carl Andre, exhibited a pile of 120 bricks called *Equivalent VIII* (**20-10**). The ordinary, mass-produced bricks were neatly arranged, two high, in a rectangle on the gallery floor. In such artwork the conceptual background—the artist's ideas about what art should be—was far more important than any visual attribute. But where would artists go from here, if anywhere?

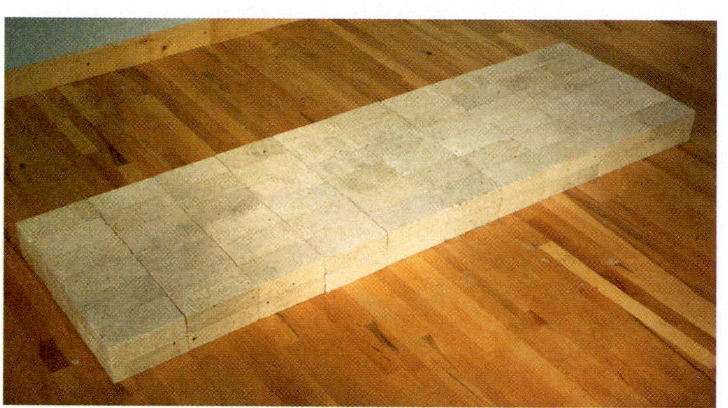

20-10 Carl Andre, *Equivalent VIII,* 1966. View of installation, Tate Gallery, London. Art © Carl Andre/Licensed by VAGA, New York, NY

EXPANDING MINIMALISM

Although Minimalist artists like Judd and Andre continue working within their narrowly devised confines, since 1970 the word *Minimalist* has been enlarged to include a much wider variety of art forms than Judd and Andre would accept. The term is generally used today to refer to any work of art that is refined, simple, and abstract with no references to any subject.

For example, the sculptures of Eva Hesse are described as being fundamentally Minimalist, even though they are much more evocative than Andre's 120 bricks. For example, the forms seen in *Repetition 19, III* (**20-11**) are geometric and nearly as repetitive as a Judd sculpture, but because Hesse used fiberglass, a more flexible material, to make them, they take on a more personal and evocative quality. The

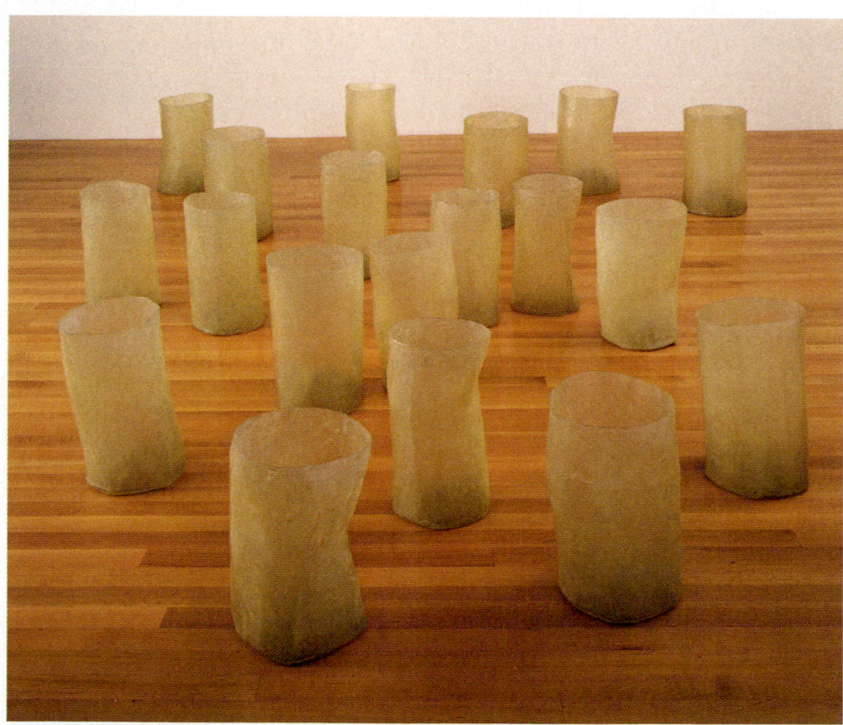

20-11 Eva Hesse, *Repetition 19, III,* 1968. Nineteen tubular fiberglass units, 19″ to 20¼″ high × 11″ to 12¾″ diameter. The Museum of Modern Art, New York (gift of Charles and Anita Blatt). © Estate of Eva Hesse, and Hauser & Wirth, Zürich/London.

translucent, pale, amber-colored shapes in *Repetition 19, III* bend and sag in a naturalistic way. One can see little bubbles in them. While the forms begin as essentially similar, each form becomes unique as it hardens, since fiberglass dries unpredictably. Placed closely together, the columns seem like alien beings interacting. By constructing geometric forms out of materials like hoses, latex rubber, or cord wrapped in fiberglass, Hesse brought a more textured and suggestive aspect to Minimalism. She also helped bridge the gap between crafts and fine arts, laying the groundwork for a more serious evaluation of crafts like ceramics and fibers in the 1970s.

RETURN OF REPRESENTATION: SUPERREALISM

Until Pop Art, for a century the predominant trend in Western art had been away from literal representation toward abstraction. In a related development in the late 1960s, many artists trained as Abstract Expressionists betrayed their teachers with a 180-degree turn toward realism. **Superrealism** (or **photorealism**) was a movement that recreated in two dimensions the look of photographs and in three dimensions used casting to achieve the utmost fidelity to reality. Like the Realists of the nineteenth century, most of the Superrealists avoided drama and concentrated on ordinary life.

At first look, Superrealism appears to be the polar opposite of Minimalism. Richard Estes's *Central Savings* (**20-12**) is an impressive demonstration of the painter's technical skill. Rather than a flat, nonillusionistic canvas, one sees depicted in oil paint a bewildering number of layers of depth, reflection upon reflection of the world behind and within a city restaurant's plate-glass window. However, *Central Savings* does share some qualities with Minimalist art. While Estes's picture is very representational, notice that he is not expressing his feelings about this scene. In a methodical way, he is imitating the way a camera records reality, utilizing the harsh contrasts and precise focus of mechanical vision. Like Minimalist pictures, Superrealist pictures are cool and calculated performances.

Precise images like *Central Savings* are not just technical achievements but compositional ones as well. Estes's design of dense, layered spaces is

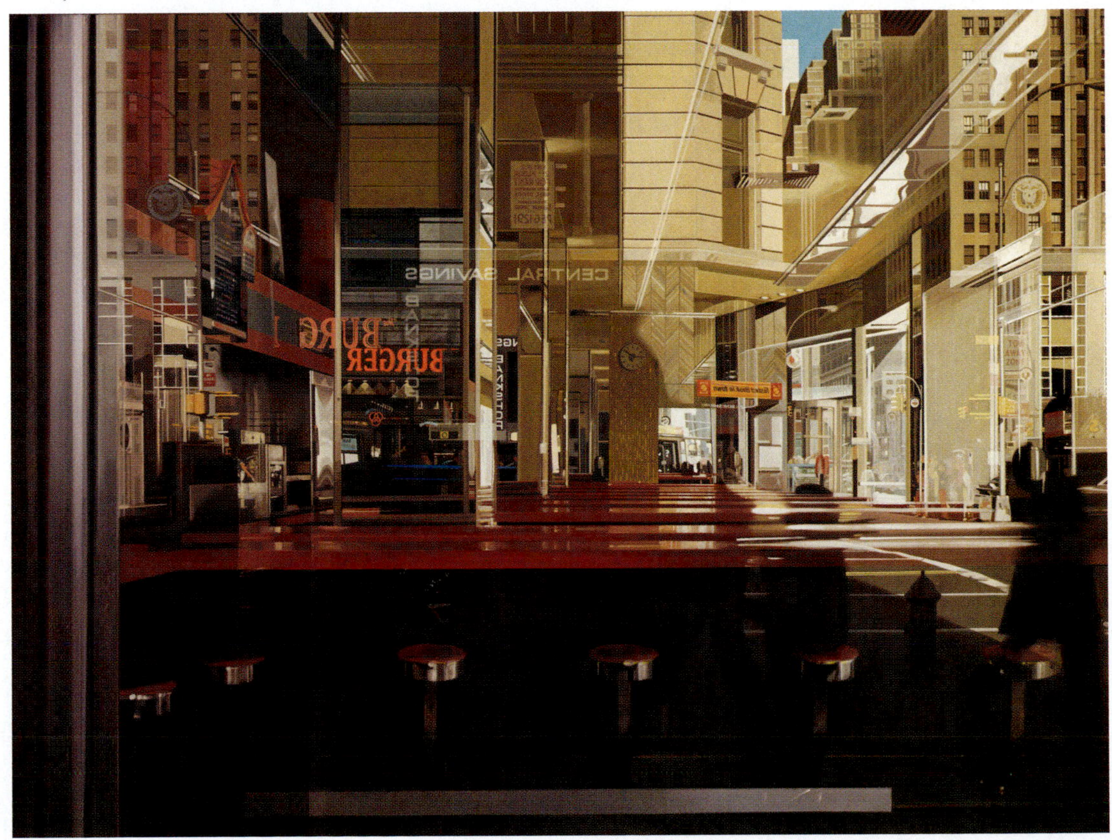

20-12 Richard Estes, *Central Savings,* 1975. Oil on canvas, 36″ × 48″. The Nelson-Atkins Museum of Art, Kansas City, Missouri (gift of the Friends of Art), F75-13. Photograph by Jamison Miller

imaginative: complex but balanced. His subjects are always drawn from the world he lives in, typical American metropolitan scenes, but he never imposes his personal viewpoint or glorifies his cityscapes. As with the Pop artist Warhol and the Minimalist Judd, for Estes "cool" is better than emotional. It is probably no coincidence that in the 1960s "cool" first came to mean "good."

Duane Hanson, however, was a Superrealist artist who was interested in breaking down the barriers between artist and viewers and engaging them. Born in rural Minnesota, he wanted to make an honest art that could communicate with anyone who saw it and not "something that looks nice to hang on a wall." He said, "If art can't reflect life and tell us more about life, I don't think it's an art that will be very lasting." By pouring polyester resin into casts made directly from his models and adding real hair, glass eyes, and clothing, Hanson managed to develop perhaps the most naturalistic sculptures ever created. Museum visitors are usually startled when they encounter one of Hanson's realistic figures.

Hanson generally chose to portray one or two subjects in the midst of an ordinary day. He said, "You can't always scream and holler . . . sometimes a whisper is more powerful." *Janitor* (**20-13**) is typical of his mature works that speak about the emptiness and loneliness of modern life. The janitor's pose reflects exhaustion and dissatisfaction; he is dressed in soiled clothing. When seen in a museum from as little as a few feet away, *Janitor* appears to be just another employee. As one approaches it, one senses that the figure has a natural territory like any living being. However, because it is a sculpture, we are permitted to enter his personal space and stare at him in a way no polite person would ever do. The power of Hanson's sculpture is not limited to his craftsmanship or the verisimilitude of his figures or even his messages. His work taps into the voyeuristic nature of art, the fascination of carefully studying another person and gaining access to his or her private world.

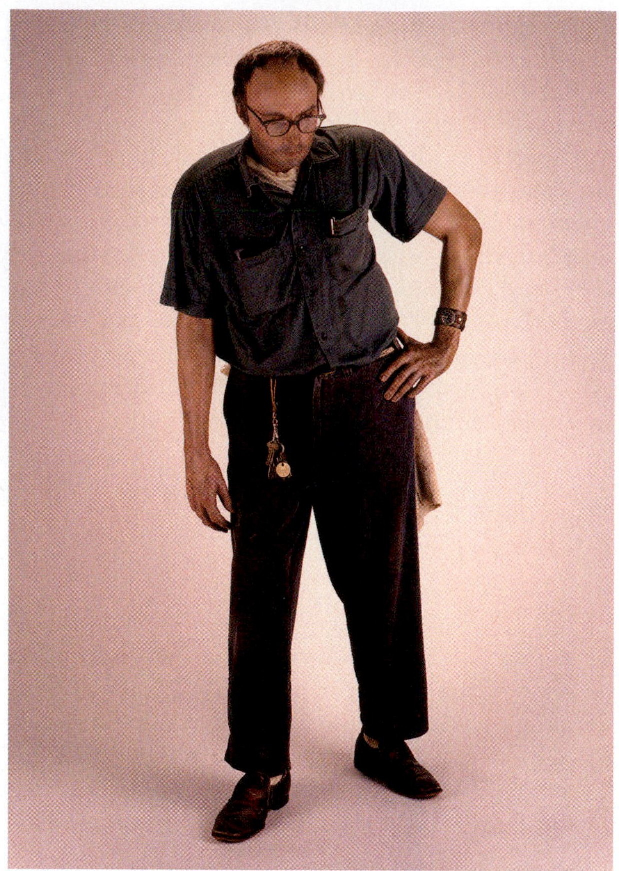

20-13 Duane Hanson, *Janitor,* 1973. Polyester, fiberglass, polychromed in oil, 65 ½″ × 28″ × 22″. Milwaukee Art Museum, Gift of Friends of Art, M1973.91. Photo by Ephraim Le-ver. Art © Duane Hanson/Licensed by VAGA, New York, NY

ARCHITECTURE: BREAKING DOWN BARRIERS

In the late 1960s, a sculpture instructor at New York University, James Wines, became dissatisfied with the direction Modern Art was taking, especially the isolation of artists from the general public. After discovering that he was not alone with this disenchantment, he began meeting regularly with like-minded artists and architects. In 1970, *SITE* (Sculpture in the Environment) was formed to establish a new relationship between art, architecture, and the public. Their goal was to search for a "more . . . socially significant content, a new public imagery drawn from a more integrated fusion of the arts."

SITE members were determined not to use references to the past but to "search for sources of content in the present." Their challenge was to "identify an appropriate iconography for a society with no universal symbols." Their first important commissions were showrooms all across the United States for one of the nation's largest catalog merchandisers, Best Products. Few successful architects would have been enthusiastic about this kind of job—a renovation of a typical box-shaped building in a shopping center along a highway—but the earnest SITE artists went to work analyzing the problem. The challenge would be to find a way to attract the attention of motorists who were speeding down the highway.

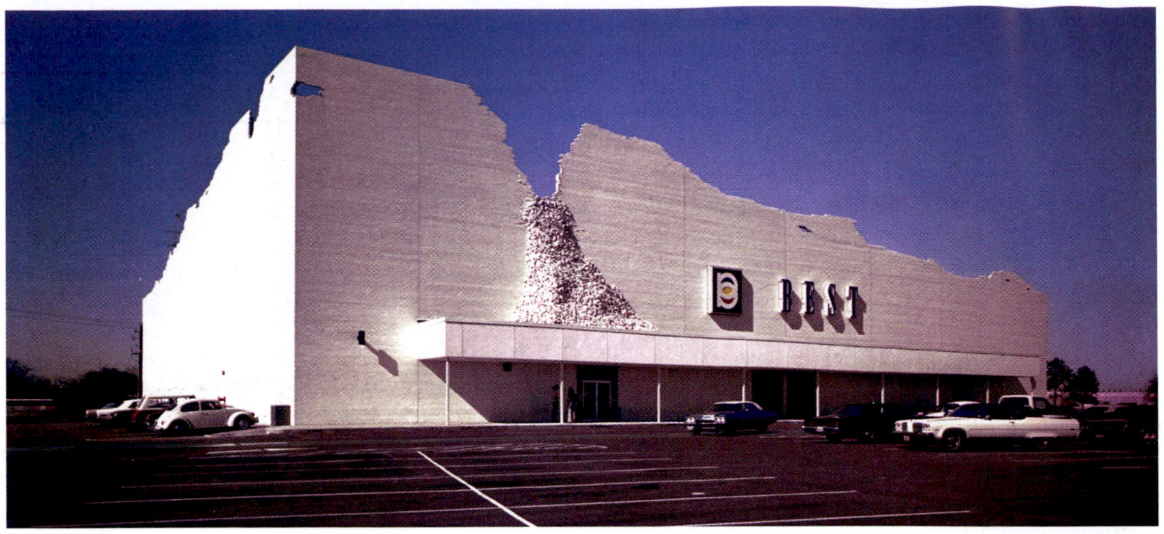

20-14 SITE, Best Products Indeterminate Façade Showroom, Houston, 1975.

Wines and his associates realized that drivers only pay attention to things that are out of the ordinary, that break the pattern of normal life.

Built in 1975, the *Best Products Indeterminate Façade Showroom* (**20-14**) in Houston, Texas, is one of their most famous works. By building a white brick façade higher than the structure's actual roof line (like Venturi's firehouse), the designers gave themselves room for imagination. The startling result was a new building that looks as if it is crumbling into ruin. In the tradition of disaster movies, the edges of the façade have become ragged and broken. Bricks tumble down onto the canopy in front, threatening imminent collapse. The doomsday look of the showroom was hard to ignore; it attracted customers even as it gave notice that American consumer culture was in the process of decay. By looking freshly at architectural problems with an artist's eyes, by ignoring academic approaches but not customer needs, James Wines and SITE continue to create a people-oriented architecture that is stimulating, engaging, and artful.

Renzo Piano of Italy and Richard Rogers of England turned architecture inside out with their design for the *Georges Pompidou National Arts and Cultural Center* (**20-15**). When the city of Paris first gave the commission for a new museum of Modern Art to the architects, it was very controversial. First,

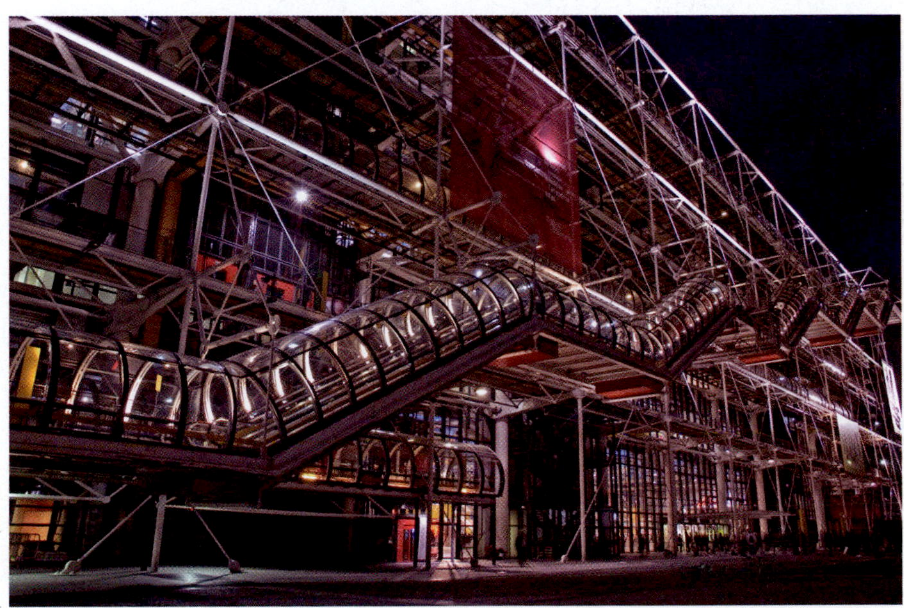

20-15 Renso Piano and Richard Rogers, Georges Pompidou National Arts and Cultural Center, Paris, 1971–1977.

ART ISSUES

Pilgrimages for a New Age

Many of the most important sites in Earth Art are in remote locations that are difficult to reach. While this is not surprising, given the large scale of the works and the cost of land, it does demand a great deal from anyone interested in seeing them in person. In essence, a visitor must make a modern pilgrimage. Like a religious one, it requires time, commitment, and dedication.

To reach Walter De Maria's *Lightning Field* (**20-16**), one has to travel many miles through the desert of New Mexico. The closest town is about 150 miles outside of Albuquerque. Once you arrive there, it is another forty-minute drive to the site. The work itself is four hundred stainless-steel poles spread evenly in a grid over an area of one mile by one kilometer. Each of the poles are about twenty and one-half feet high and two inches in diameter. The organization that maintains the site, the Dia Art Foundation, recommends spending an extended period of time with the work and offers overnight reservations in nearby cabins. While July and August are the best times to see lightning strike the poles, there is no guarantee for any of the pilgrims.

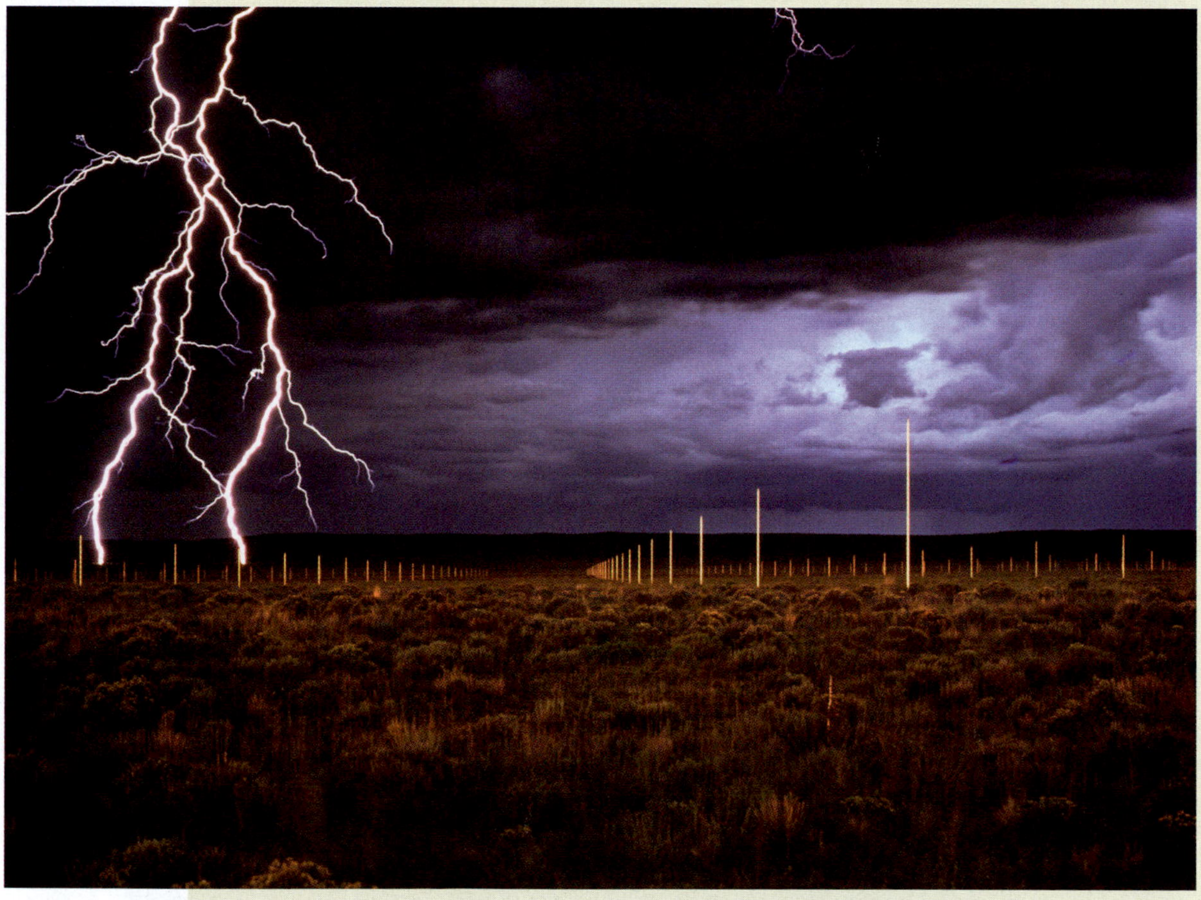

20-16 Walter De Maria, *Lightning Field,* 1977. Four hundred polished stainless-steel poles (2″ diameter and 20′ and 7½″ tall) in a grid of one mile by one kilometer. Southwestern New Mexico. Photo: John Cliett. ©DIA Art Foundation

ART ISSUES

The Dia Art Foundation also maintains Robert Smithson's *Spiral Jetty* (see 9-12). Constructed in 1970, it remains the most famous and archetypal earthwork. This enormous fifteen-hundred-feet-long spiral ramp extends out into an obscure spot of the Great Salt Lake in Utah. In the midst of a state park about ninety miles from Salt Lake City, it can only be reached by driving fifteen miles on rough, dirt roads in an all-terrain vehicle. At the shore, there's a sign that reads, "Spiral Jetty, End of Road." Even after making the long trip, one is not guaranteed a view of it. Because of the water level, it is not always visible, but the chances of glimpsing it are much better than they have been in decades. Two years after its construction in 1972, it disappeared beneath the waters and was assumed gone forever. However, in 2002, much to the surprise and delight of the art world, it reappeared when the water levels of the Salt Lake dropped. The location is not far from another important earthwork. Nancy Holt's *Sun Tunnels* (9-13) can be found in a high-terrain Utah desert two hours driving time to the west.

James Turrell's best-known works like *Atlan* (2-13) use illumination to create a sense of mystery and wonder in a gallery. But for more than twenty-five years, he's been working on a project that uses lighting on a cosmic scale. For his largest work, he says, "the sky is my big studio." The *Roden Crater* is housed in an extinct volcano on the western edge of the Painted Desert of Arizona. Since the 1970s, Turrell has been reshaping the crater into a bowl whose lighting will change based on the movements of the sun, the moon, and the stars. For the viewer, the sky will also become a huge bowl, attached to the rim of the volcano. Nothing else will be visible; it will be a pure experience of light and nature from a 360-degree panorama, what Turrell calls "celestial vaulting." Built twenty-five miles from the nearest electricity, Turrell uses windmills to generate power. Initially intended to be finished in two to three years, it has become his life's work and is only recently nearing completion. When it finally opens, a maximum of fourteen viewers per day will be permitted, eight of whom will stay overnight in rooms inside the crater designed by Turrell. He believes that the pilgrimage to *Roden Crater* will be part of the spiritual experience. "The main thing is to make a journey, so that you actually go to something purposely and have time to settle down and empty out the noise and distractions of daily life."

the architects were not French, a tacit acknowledgement that artistic imagination was no longer solely a French commodity. Second, the construction would require the tearing down of many buildings that were centuries old. But probably most disturbing to French critics was the proposed design itself. It had no visible connection to the Modern movement, whose capital had been Paris and whose masterpieces would be housed there. Instead, the architects provided a new, contemporary approach to architecture. They envisioned an ultramodern cultural center, a reflection of an age of new media and scientific advances.

Unlike typical buildings, the "Beauborg" (nicknamed after its Parisian neighborhood) exposes its inner workings—nothing is hidden. The glass walls are surrounded with a network of white columns and scaffolding. The tubular main escalator is attached to this metal grid, rising up the outside like a mechanical glass worm. The Beauborg's life-support system of pipes and ducts (for plumbing, electricity, air circulation, and heat) is not only visible but also boldly announced, painted in bright colors. Walls are all movable; even the floors can be adjusted. Large video screens and banners can be attached to the grid of pipes anywhere on the building.

GOING BEYOND THE ART WORLD

While the sites used by most Earth artists have been situated in isolated locations (see box), the environmental art of the artists Christo and Jeanne-Claude does not shy away from populated areas. They build their works "NEVER in deserted places, and always sites already prepared and used by people, managed by human beings for human beings." Perhaps that is why they have achieved more widespread fame than either Robert Smithson or Nancy Holt (see Chapter 9).

Christo's earliest efforts were concerned with wrapping objects like cans and oil barrels in cloth and seeing how they were changed by the process. He and Jeanne-Claude became international celebrities when the work grew to a monumental scale—wrapping the Museum of Contemporary Art in Chicago and then a mile-long section of the Australian coast in 1969. It was when the work began to be made outdoors that Jeanne-Claude and he became partners on every project. However, for many years, their partnership was kept private. Christo was the public face of the team.

For Christo and Jeanne-Claude, *Wrapped Coast, Little Bay, Australia* was a success because it allowed viewers to see nature more clearly by drawing a human-made contrast to it. Their even more ambitious *Running Fence, Sonoma and Marin Counties, California, 1972–1976* (**20-17**) of 1976 was planned to draw attention to the glories of the California landscape. Four years in preparation, the final result was an eighteen-foot-high white nylon barrier that

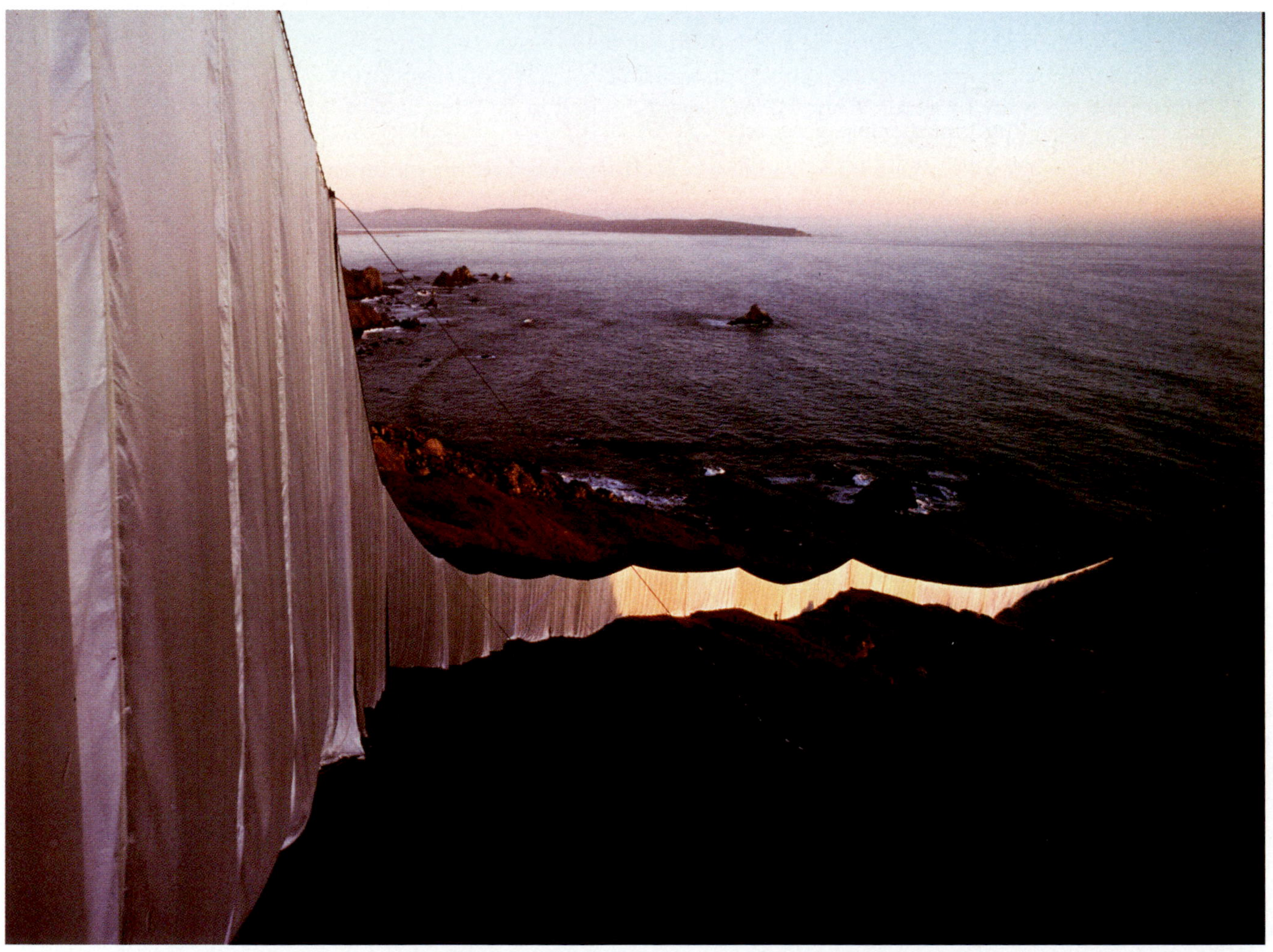

20-17 Christo and Jeanne-Claude, *Running Fence, Sonoma and Marin Counties, California, 1972–1976.* Height: 5.5 meters (18 feet), Length: 39.4 kilometers (24½ miles). 200,000 square meters (240,000 square yards) of woven nylon fabric and 90 miles of steel cable, 2,050 steel poles. Photo: Wolfgang Volz. COPYRIGHT © CHRISTO 1976.

extended for twenty-four and one-half miles across pastures and roads and into the Pacific Ocean. This monumental undertaking cost the artist $3 million, which paid for materials, a team of lawyers, environmental consultants, engineers, workers, and a building contractor.

As with all of Christo and Jeanne-Claude's environmental works, the funds were entirely their own, raised mostly from the sale of Christo's preparatory collages and drawings describing the project. Because the fence was hung on steel poles with cables for only two weeks, many questioned the high cost of such a temporary artwork. Much of the four years were taken up convincing environmental groups that their plan was safe. Why would they be willing to go to all this trouble? Christo said:

> Just as religion was important [in the Renaissance] so are economics, social problems, and politics today. . . . Knowledge of these areas should be an important part of one's work.

The final result *was* breathtaking. Nature cooperated with art by providing innumerable gorgeous settings—sunlight and wind, rolling hills and rocky shore, grazing sheep and grasslands made *Running Fence* a spectacle to behold.

Since then, Christo and Jeanne-Claude have created other environmental works like the *Surrounded Islands,* in Biscayne Bay, Florida, *Umbrellas* in Japan and California, and the recent *Gates* in New York's Central Park, a project that took more than a quarter century to complete (see Chapter 1). Every project has been paid for by the artists. They do not accept grants and they do not use volunteers. For them, "Financing is aesthetic." Every member of the teams that construct the projects is paid. Disposal of the materials used in the projects is also handled by the artists and recycled industrially.

The fact that for decades Jeanne-Claude's artistic partnership with her husband Christo was not made public reflects both the prejudice found in the art world and the difficulty any artist has in achieving success. As they explained it, "The decision to use only the name Christo was made deliberately when we were young because it is difficult for one artist to get established and we wanted to put all the chances on our side." Christo was presented as the artist and Jeanne-Claude as the business manager. It wasn't until 1994 that they revealed that they had been artistic partners on every project since 1961. The ideas for their projects come from either or both of them. According to them, however, there are two clear divisions of labor: "Jeanne-Claude does not make drawings, she was not trained for that. Christo puts their ideas on paper, [and] . . . Christo never had the pleasure of talking to their tax accountant."

MAKING ROOM FOR WOMEN: JUDY CHICAGO

In 1970, an art instructor at Fresno State College in California placed a statement at her solo exhibition that read:

> Judy Gerowitz hereby divests herself of all names imposed upon her through male social dominance and freely chooses her own name,
>
> *Judy Chicago.*

In the same year, she offered a feminist art class that excluded men, in a studio away from her college. The young women not only made works of art but also learned how to use tools. It was the beginning of a career devoted to forcing the inclusion of women in the art world.

The young Judy Cohen grew up in Chicago and was raised in a family that taught equality, so it was a shock for her to learn that America in the 1950s did not share her family's values. Early in her art career, she worked in a Minimalist style (she described this as trying to be "one of the boys") while living in Los Angeles. It was not until 1970 that Chicago made a clean break with the male art world and began making symbolic works using imagery based on female genitalia. During the 1970s, Chicago was a key figure in the birth of the women's movement, organizing Womanspace, a gallery, and the Women's Building, a center for women's culture in Los Angeles. The building housed a multidisciplinary program, called the Feminist Studio Workshop (FSW), where Chicago taught. The FSW encouraged women to explore what it meant to be female and to translate their experiences as women into subjects for artworks. The curriculum included traditional studio classes in art, writing, and video, along with consciousness-raising groups. While the traditional art world was slow to accept the work being done there, Los Angeles became a magnet for talented women from all across the United States and was known as one of the leading centers of the growing feminist movement, and eventually as a world art center.

Chicago's participation in the creation of collaborative artworks that dealt with feminist issues

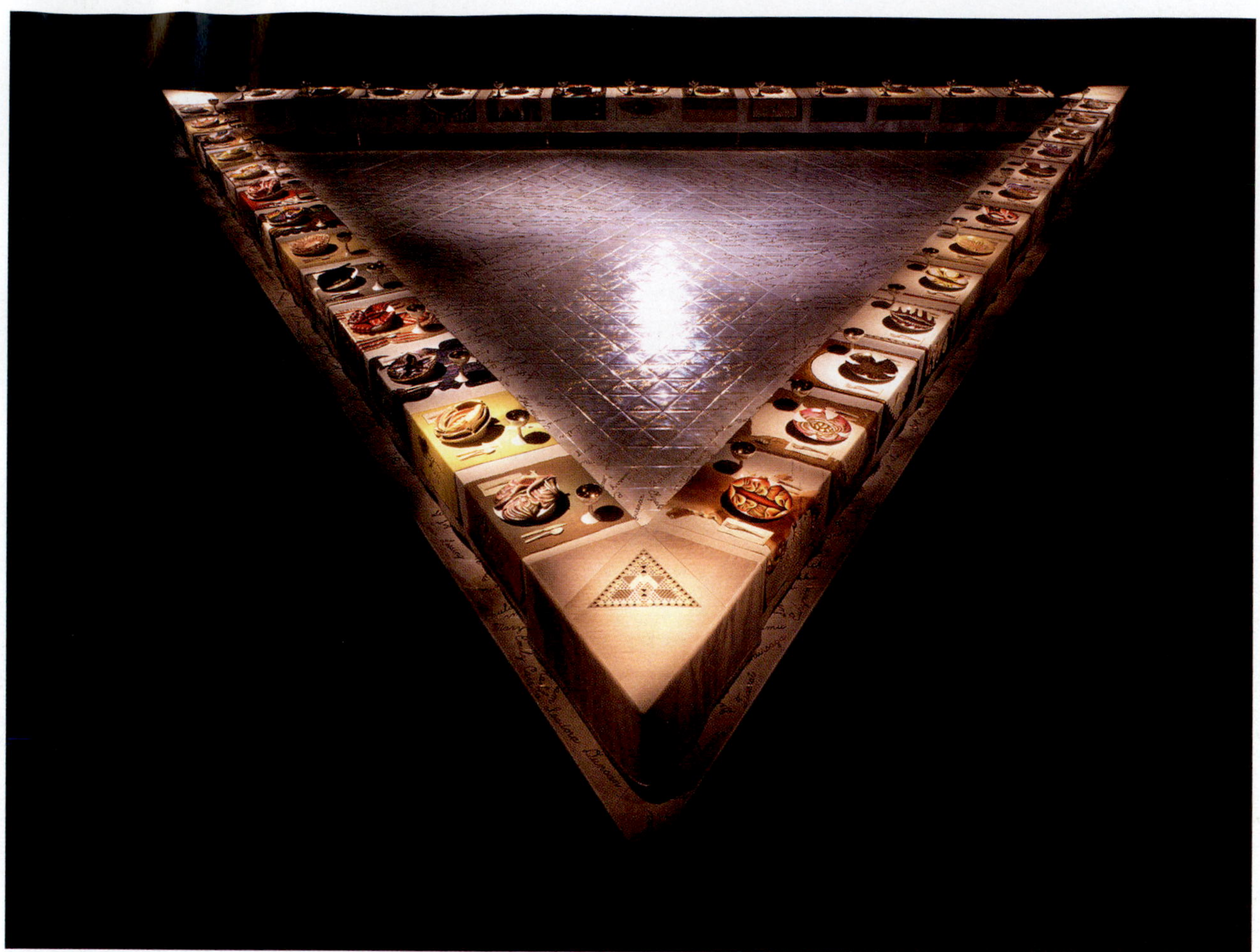

20-18 Judy Chicago, *The Dinner Party,* 1979. Mixed media, 48′ × 48′ × 48′ installed. Brooklyn Museum, New York. photo ©Donald Woodman.

culminated in her most famous work, a room-sized installation called *The Dinner Party* (**20-18**) that was four years in the making. The artist led a team of more than one hundred women in the creation of a triangular table, forty-eight feet on each side. On it were thirty-nine place settings that symbolized the contributions of great women of the past, from prehistoric times to Georgia O'Keeffe. The table rested on a tiled platform on which the names of 999 women were written in gold. *The Dinner Party* utilized crafts media that in the past had been denied consideration as fine art. Each porcelain plate was a symbolic portrait of the woman honored, and her era was evoked in the design of an embroidered runner. Weaving and needlepoint were also employed. The plates all contain Chicago's characteristic vaginal imagery that aims to "make the feminine holy" (**20-19**). A companion book was written to tell about the women represented and to explain the symbols used.

In 1978, *The Dinner Party* was exhibited at the San Francisco Museum (it broke all previous attendance records) and then traveled across the country. At the Brooklyn Museum in 1980, more than seventy-five thousand visitors saw it. Chicago explained the purpose of her work as:

> A people's history—the history of women in Western civilization. . . . This information, however, was . . . certainly unknown to most people. And as long as women's achievements were excluded from our understanding of the past, we would continue to feel as if we had never done anything worthwhile. This absence of any sense of our tradition as women seemed to cripple us psychologically. I wanted to change that, and I wanted to do that through art.

The face of the art world has been changed by the works of Judy Chicago and many other women artists. Not only have the numbers of women artists

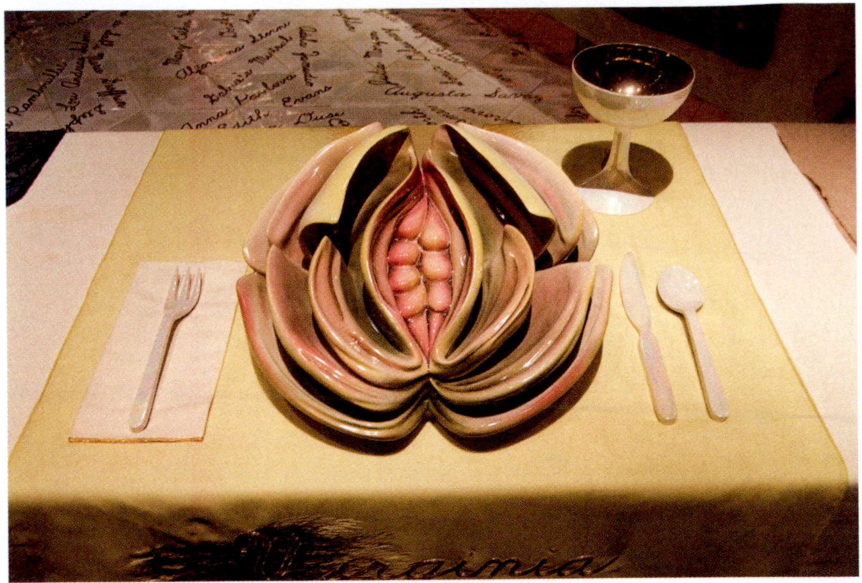

20-19 DETAIL OF: Judy Chicago, *The Dinner Party,* 1979. Mixed media, 48′ × 48′ × 48′ installed. Brooklyn Museum, New York. © James Luciana.

grown, but the kinds of art and strategies they pursued in the 1970s have become important ones for all artists. Political art, collaborative art, performance art, photographing constructed environments, art that deals with the self and fantasy, and appropriation were all unconventional paths originally taken by creative women artists (see box on p. 458).

CHANGING THE NATURE OF THE GALLERY SPACE: PERFORMANCE ART

Performance art (see Chapter 9) is another way twentieth-century avant-garde artists tried to provoke viewers into a reappraisal of art and life. The Futurists, Dadaists, and the Pop Artists all performed art. Some performance art has been very successful in reaching the general public, like the multimedia concerts of Laurie Anderson (9-10), who began performing on streets wearing ice skates embedded in a block of ice while playing cowboy songs on a violin. Joseph Beuys even became a political force in Germany (9-9) as a leader in European environmental and peace movements. Performance artists are interested in producing unexpected repercussions, even dangerous ones.

The Los Angeles artist Chris Burden drew attention to his concepts with works that deliberately tested his own psychological and physical limits. His most famous (or infamous) work was *Shoot* (**20-22**) in 1971. Because Burden believes we live in a culture that is deadened by seeing violent acts portrayed every day on television and in films, he decided to explore and reveal the reality of violence. With inconceivable calm, Burden stood against a wall while a friend standing only twelve feet away shot him in the arm with a rifle. While the plan called for the bullet to simply graze him, the bullet punctured the center of his arm just above the elbow. This did not faze Burden because the performance was about:

> Being shot at to be hit . . . it's something to experience. How can you know what it feels like to be shot if you don't get shot? It seems interesting enough to be worth doing. . . . It was horrible but it was interesting.

Two years later, Burden reenacted the ancient legend of Icarus in a modern way (see Breugel's *Fall of Icarus,* 14-40, for an explanation of the myth). In front of invited spectators, he lay on the floor of his studio naked with a long piece of plate glass balanced on each of his shoulders. Two assistants poured gasoline across the glass and then threw matches at the end of the glass until the gasoline was ignited. In seconds, Burden leapt up and the pieces of fiery glass crashed to the floor.

Burden's horrifying performances are meant to set up an energy between him and his audience. They bring a vividness to danger and violence that he feels our culture has lost. Like many of the artists in this chapter, he is concerned with reestablishing art as a vital, living presence in people's lives. He does this by creating memorable events that challenge our basic assumptions about what an artist is supposed to do and what is art.

ART ISSUES

Why Isn't a Woman's Place in the Museum?

For the past five centuries, an unstated, unofficial, possibly unconscious, but apparent censorship of the artwork of more than half the population in the West has occurred. Although they have been making art as long as it has existed, until recently women have been systematically excluded from most museums and art histories. As women's status has risen in the last 150 years, so have the number of professional women artists. Yet, a visitor to U.S. museums or readers of art history texts from just twenty-five years ago would have seen the almost complete absence of any sign of art created by women. Recently, the censorship of women has begun to slowly subside, mostly as a result of the efforts of women themselves.

However, the traditional measures of success—solo shows in galleries, retrospectives in prominent museums, representation in scholarly works and texts—were slow in coming. For example, before 1987, the National Gallery of Art in Washington, D.C., had in its entire history only one retrospective of a woman artist, Mary Cassatt. Until 1986, the most successful college art survey text in the country did not include the work of a single woman, despite having more than one thousand illustrations. The author stated that unfortunately there had been no women "great enough to make the grade." After his death, his son included twenty-one women in the 1986 edition, out of more than a thousand artworks.

The Guerrilla Girls (**20-20**) are a coalition of artists whose goal is to keep continued pressure on the art establishment to eliminate bias against women. Formed in 1985, they describe themselves as "the conscience of the art world." They began by working secretly, under cover of darkness, plastering posters around Manhattan. Even today, their identities and overall number are unknown; all photographs show them wearing large gorilla masks. They receive mail at a post office box and conduct interviews by phone or email. With simple, well-designed posters (**20-21**), the Guerrilla Girls give status reports on the art world's acceptance (or lack of it) of women. Their first poster listed forty-two of the most well-known contemporary male artists and asked, "What

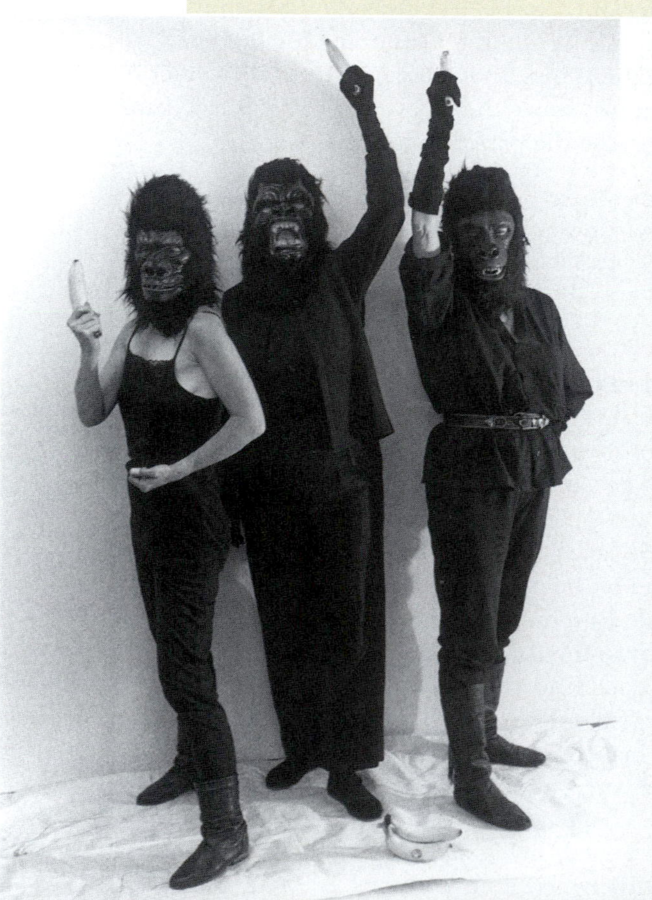

20-20 Guerrilla Girls, 1985. Courtesy Guerrilla Girls, West.

ART ISSUES

do these artists have in common?" The answer was, "They all allow their work to be shown in galleries that show no more than 10 percent women or none at all." A press release warned of more posters ahead, "Simple facts will be spelled out; obvious conclusions can be drawn." The feminist activists were not going to allow male artists to escape responsibility for their galleries' exclusionary policies. Other posters pointed out that in one year, the four major New York City museums had only one retrospective for a woman. Another reminded us that "Women in America earn only 2/3 of what men do. Women artists earn only 2/3 of what men do." A 1989 poster directed to collectors asked:

20-21 Guerrilla Girls poster, c. 1987. Courtesy Guerrilla Girls, New York.

WHEN RACISM & SEXISM ARE NO LONGER FASHIONABLE, WHAT WILL YOUR ART COLLECTION BE WORTH?

The art market won't bestow mega-buck prices on the work of a few white males forever. For the 17.7 million you just spent on a single Jasper Johns painting, you could have bought at least one work by all of these women and artists of color:

Bernice Abbott
Anni Albers
Sofonisba Anguisolla
Diane Arbus
Vanessa Bell
Isobel Bishop
Rosa Bonheur
Elizabeth Bougereau
Margaret Bourke-White
Romaine Brooks
Julia Margaret Cameron
Emily Carr
Rosalba Carriera
Mary Cassatt
Constance Marie Charpentier
Imogen Cunningham
Sonia Delaunay
Elaine de Kooning
Lavinia Fontana
Meta Warwick Fuller
Artemisia Gentileschi
Marguérite Gérard
Natalia Goncharova
Kate Greenaway
Barbara Hepworth
Eva Hesse
Hannah Hoch
Anna Huntingdon
May Howard Jackson
Frida Kahlo
Angelica Kauffmann
Hilma af Klimt
Kathe Kollwitz
Lee Krasner
Dorothea Lange
Marie Laurencin
Edmonia Lewis
Judith Leyster
Barbara Longhi
Dora Maar
Lee Miller
Lisette Model
Paula Modersohn-Becker
Tina Modotti
Berthe Morisot
Grandma Moses
Gabriele Münter
Alice Neel
Louise Nevelson
Georgia O'Keeffe
Meret Oppenheim
Sarah Peale
Ljubova Popova
Olga Rosanova
Nellie Mae Rowe
Rachel Ruysch
Kay Sage
Augusta Savage
Vavara Stepanova
Florine Stettheimer
Sophie Taeuber-Arp
Alma Thomas
Marietta Robusti Tintoretto
Suzanne Valadon
Remedios Varo
Elizabeth Vigée Le Brun
Laura Wheeling Waring

Information courtesy of Christie's, Sotheby's, Mayer's International Auction Records and Leonard's Annual Price Index of Auctions.

Please send $ and comments to: Box 1056 Cooper Sta. NY, NY 10276 GUERRILLA GIRLS CONSCIENCE OF THE ART WORLD

> When Racism & Sexism are no longer fashionable, what will your art collection be worth? The art market won't bestow megabuck prices on the work of a few white males forever. For the 17.7 million you just spent on a single Jasper Johns painting, you could have bought at least one work by all of these women and artists of color:

A list followed with the names of sixty-seven artists, most very well-known and respected, from the Renaissance to the present, including Artemisia Gentileschi, Judith Leyster, Elizabeth Vigee-Lebrun, Angelica Kauffman, Eva Hesse, and Georgia O'Keeffe.

While few would admit it, the posters seem to have had an effect on the prominent art institutions they have targeted. The Whitney Biennial, for example, the most important national survey of contemporary art, had only a 24 percent representation for women in 1987. Two years later, it was 40 percent. In 1999, in an effort to change the way art history is presented, they wrote their *Bedside Guide to the History of Western Art*. The first line is, "Forget the stale, male, Yale textbooks. This is Art Herstory 101!"

Still, equality and an end to sexual discrimination remain distant goals. Although women are having more exhibitions in both galleries and museums than ever before and textbooks are changing, a walk through the permanent collection of any major museum is still fundamentally a tour of the history of male artists. When the Guerrilla Girls revisited the Metropolitan Museum in New York, they found the number of women artists exhibited had actually gone down from 5 percent to 3 percent in the last fifteen years. But 83 percent of the women seen in the artworks were nudes. So they reposed the question from one of their first posters in 1989: "Do women have to be naked to get into the Met. Museum?"

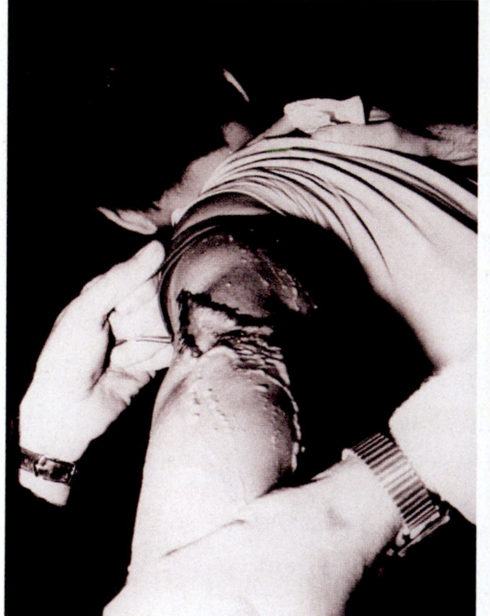

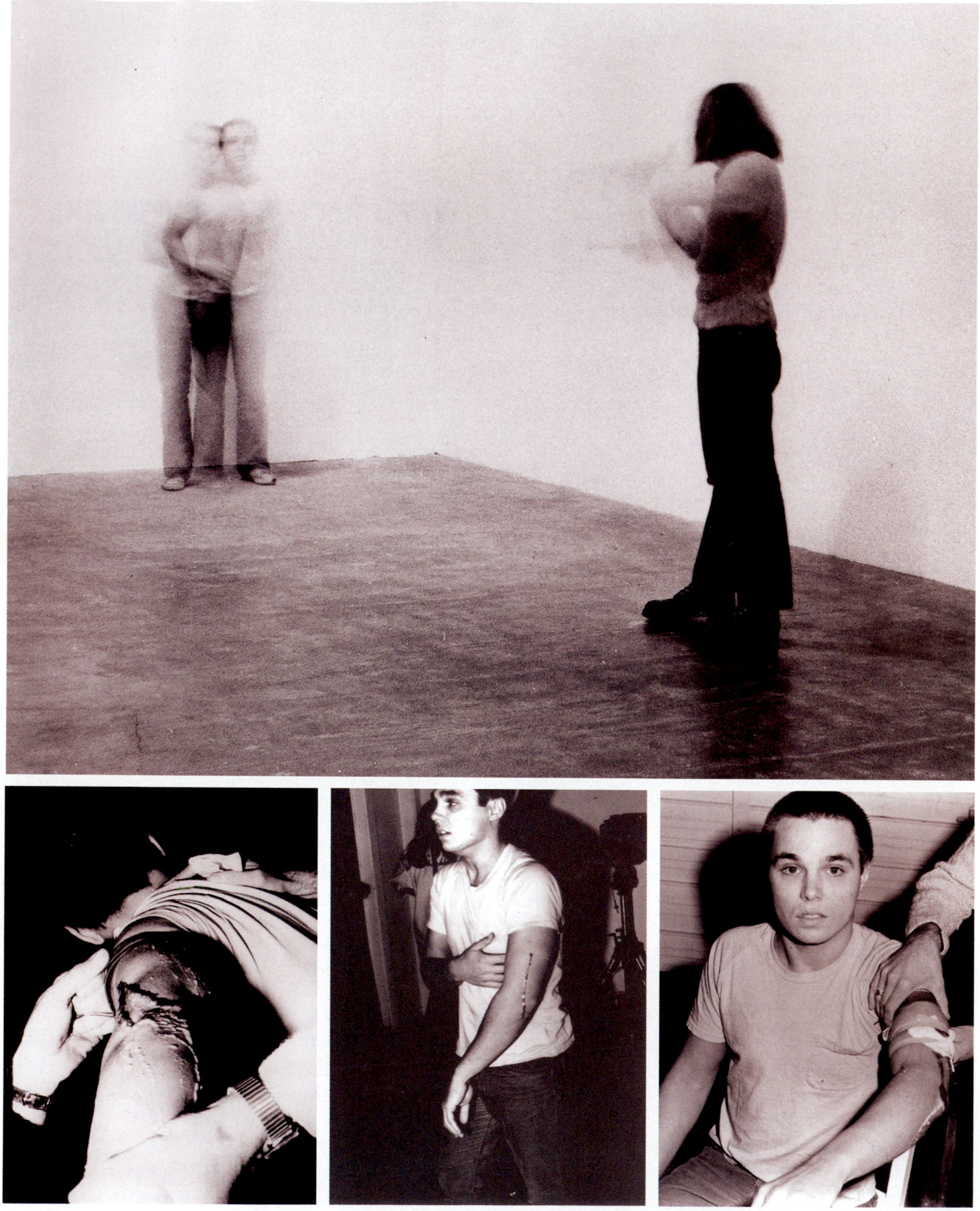

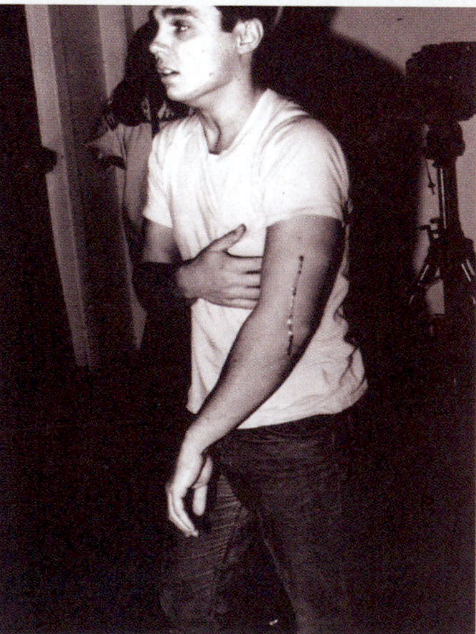

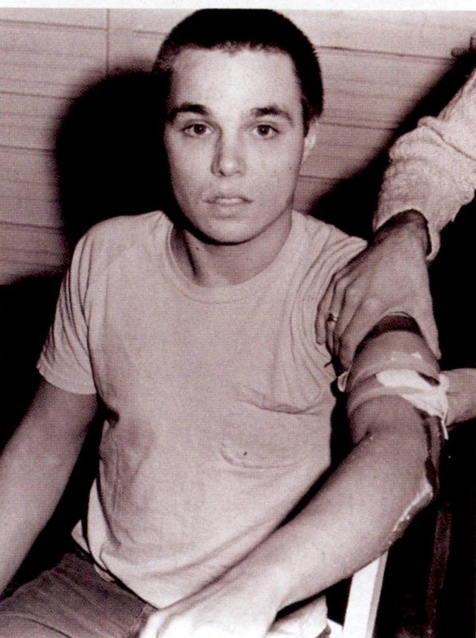

20-22 Chris Burden, *Shoot,* performed at F Space on November 19, 1971. "At 7:45 p.m. I was shot in the left arm by a friend. The bullet was a copper jacket .22 long rifle. My friend was standing about 15 feet from me." Courtesy of the artist.

James Luna reminds us that Native Americans are real, living human beings rather than primitive, innocent tribespeople from a distant past. His *The Artifact Piece* (**20-23**) was exhibited among the collections of Native American artifacts in the Museum of Man of San Diego in 1987. Inside a glass case was the artist himself resting on sand with his name on one label and his scars from injuries listed on three others. Other cases contained ceremonial objects from his reservation. Viewers who had come to the museum to admire the beauty of American Indian culture could not leave without considering the life many contemporary Native Americans live.

THE ART WORLD BECOMES GLOBAL: POSTMODERN ART AND THE NEW IMAGE

In the 1970s, Western Europe had finished its recovery from the devastation of World War II, and new hubs of economic power had emerged. One of the most important was Germany, which returned to its prewar importance in art. The contemporary German artist, Anselm Kiefer, was a student of Josef Beuys. Beuys had urged young artists to begin to meet "the task facing the nation," to confront the "terrible sins and indescribable darkness" and "consummate a process of healing." Even though he was born just as the war was ending for Germany, Kiefer knew the Nazi past was an inescapable part of his heritage. He vowed to deal with the "terror of history" so he would no longer be dislocated from the past and could regain the valuable parts of his culture as well. Kiefer's work is a search for identity, both personal and national.

Märkische Heide (**20-24**) of 1974 focuses on the German landscape. Landscape had been a traditional theme of great German painting since the Romantic Era (see Caspar David Friedrich in Chapter 16). But Kiefer's scene is a desolate panorama. March Heath, southeast of Berlin, has been the site of battles for centuries. Because "you cannot just paint a landscape after tanks have passed through it," Kiefer puts the viewer in the midst of a scorched and blackened land with bare trees. The vista is huge, as is the picture (nearly nine feet long). The sky is distant and gray; the road is broken. Kiefer painted his image on burlap, the roughest, lowest grade of canvas; the surface is as dense and complex as a work by Jackson Pollock. On top of the layers of acrylic and oil paint is thick black shellac that runs like blood over the clods of earth.

Because Kiefer combines vigorous brushstrokes with emotion-laden imagery, his pictures have been labeled **Neoexpressionist,** or a revival of Expressionism. However, unlike the emotionally direct

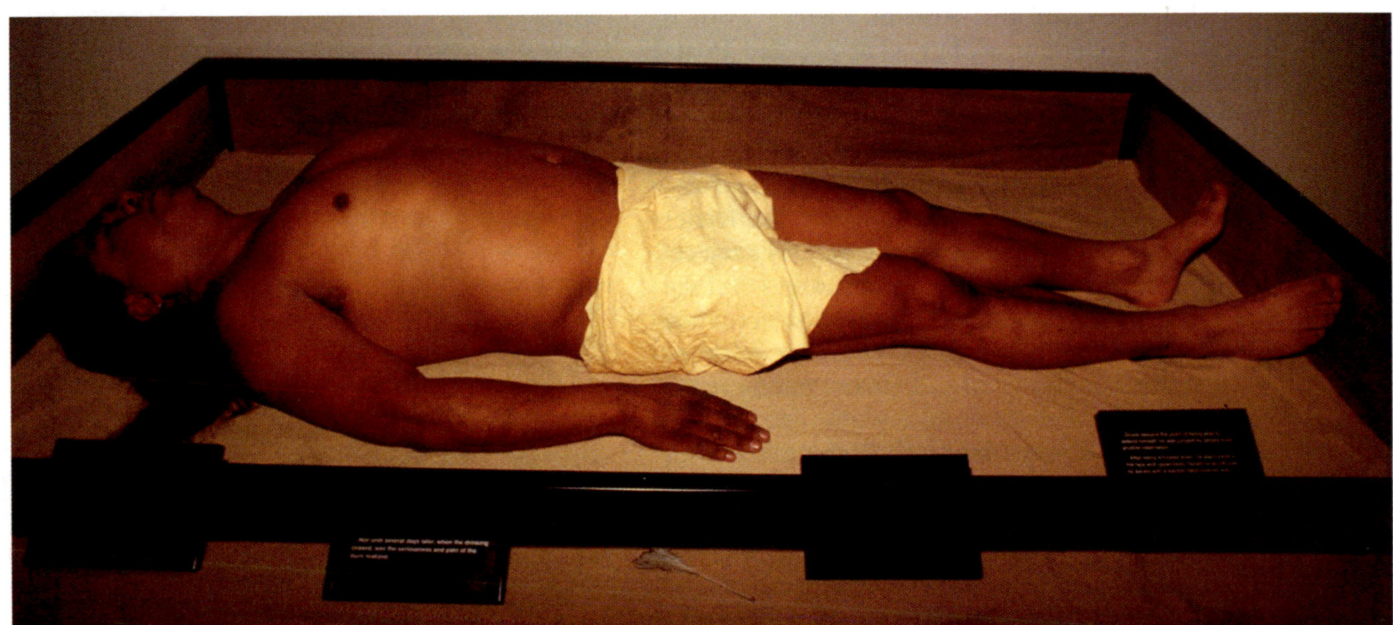

20-23 James Luna, *The Artifact Piece* (detail), 1987. Mixed-media installation and performance at the Museum of Man, San Diego.

CONTEMPORARY INSTALLATIONS

Installations, like those of Kenny Scharf (9-11), continue to be an important art form for contemporary artists. Betye Saar, whose boxed assemblage *The Liberation of Aunt Jemima* we saw in Chapter 1, is one of many sculptors who have recently moved from relatively small-scale sculptures to gallery installations. However, her motivation was unusual. *House of Gris Gris* (**20-34**) was a 1990 collaboration with her daughter, Alison, who is a sculptor most comfortable working on a large scale. The house is a tin shanty with chicken-wire walls filled with brush, leaves, and moss. The ceilings and floors of the house are painted. Its name is from an African charm, and the installation contains African-American ritual objects from Africa, Haiti, Mexico, and the South. For example, the tree branch with bottles at the entrance is known as a "spirit tree"; the empty bottles can capture souls. The hanging wings and oversized body parts outside the shack signify healing. The overall tone of *House of Gris Gris* is both ordinary and metaphysical.

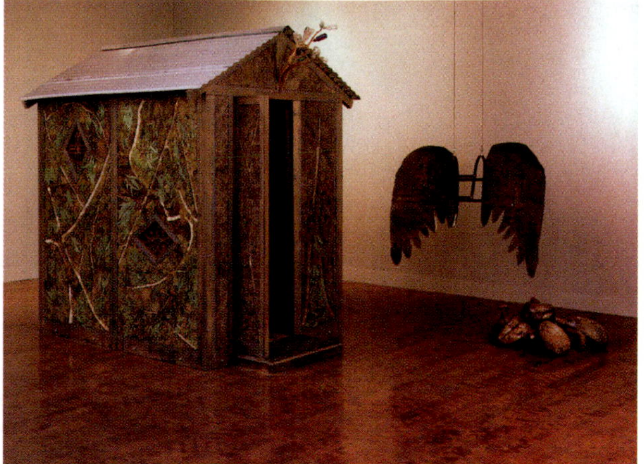

20-34 Betye Saar and Alison Saar, *House of Gris Gris,* 1990. Mixed-media installation at the UCLA Wight Art Gallery, Los Angeles, CA.

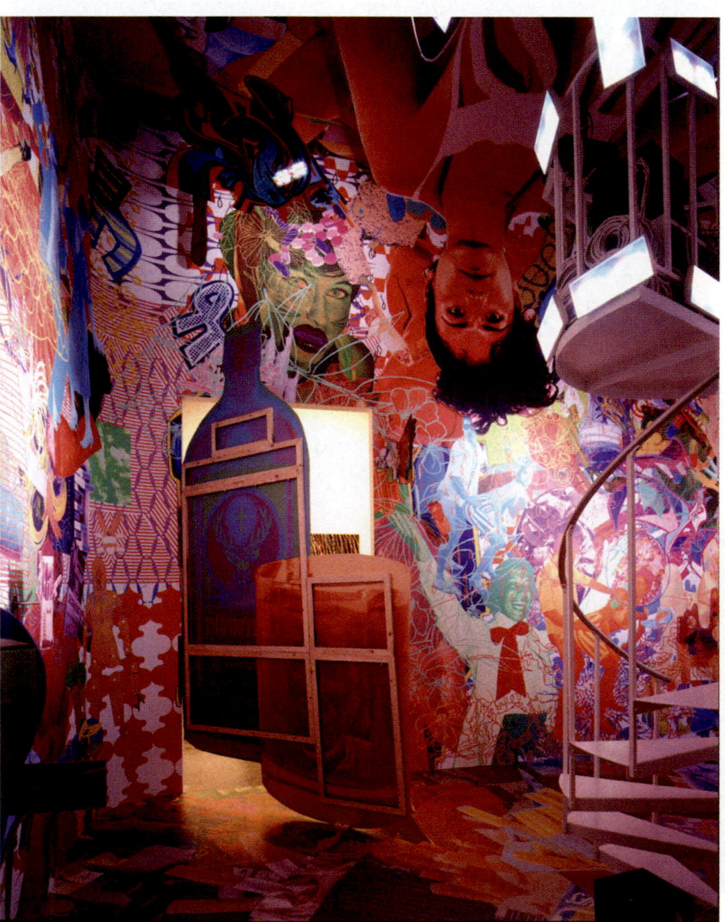

20-35 Assume Vivid Astro Focus, *Assume Vivid Astro Focus 8,* 2004. Installation at 2004 Whitney Biennial.

The mood of the multimedia installations (**20-35**) by Assume Vivid Astro Focus are far from ordinary. Born Eli Sudbrack, the Brazilian artist now makes his home in New York City. His installations (whose titles are the same as his artistic name) are filled with images, music, and moving lights—more like a dance club than a gallery experience. At the center of the version he produced for the 2004 Whitney Biennial was a spiral staircase with colored projecting lights at the top. As a brilliant color changed, different parts of the decorated walls, floors, and ceilings were revealed. The images are a mix of past popular culture, cartoons, gossip, and fashion and girlie magazines. Reminiscent of both the psychedelic era and disco, the effect of all of his installations is high-energy sensory overload. Assume Vivid Astro Focus's goal is to "reach people in ways they don't even know they are being reached."

NEW ELECTRONIC MEDIA

In the last thirty-five years, new electronic media have been added to the list of artists' materials, providing visual artists with tools that apparently have endless possibilities. Electronic media is a rapidly changing area of exploration that includes video art, animation, and digital art. These types of electronic art are often combined with each other and more traditional media.

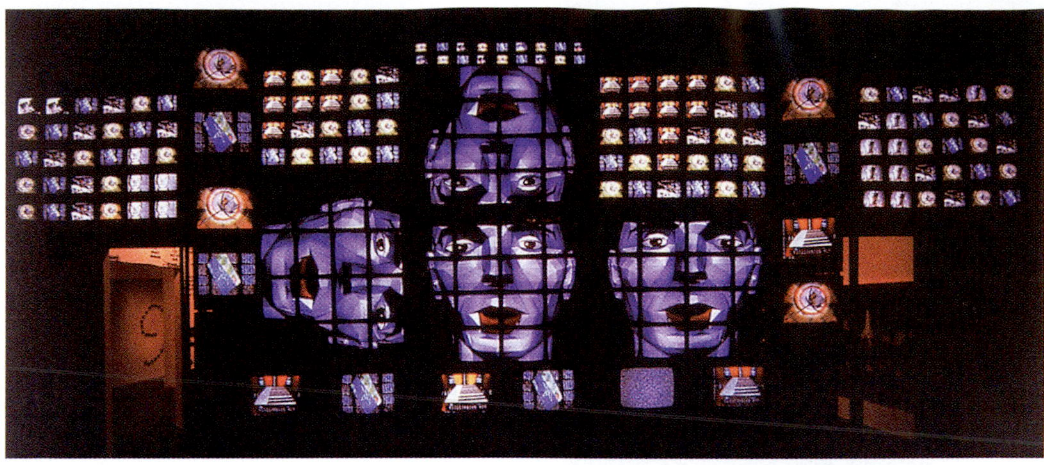

20-36 Nam June Paik, *Fin de Siècle II,* 1989. Video installation, approximately 300 television sets, three-channel color video with sound, dimension variable. Private collection.

Nam June Paik was the father of video art and a leader in its combination with new technologies. In his early *TV Buddha* (8-4), a traditional sculpture of the Buddha appears to be watching his own "live" image intently on a monitor. But Paik's video art was not limited to simple ("single channel") images of sculptures. In 1989 in New York City, his *Fin de Siècle II* ("end of the century," **20-36**) introduced the Whitney Museum's exhibition "Image World—Art and Media Culture." Visitors entering the black room were confronted with a wall of about three hundred television sets launching a barrage of rapidly changing pictures with a loud collage-like soundtrack. The images were a visual stream of consciousness: people dancing, abstract computer imagery, David Bowie singing, and more. At times, groups of twelve or sixteen televisions formed larger pictures, like four three-dimensional computer-generated heads that turned jerkily, ninety degrees at a time. Sometimes the soundtrack connected with the pictures; at other times it became just a clash of white noise and a hundred voices. There was no beginning or end, just the endless bombardment of stimuli that seems to characterize our visual environment, a storm of images.

The medium of video art, like the other artists' media, can take many different forms and present a wide range of visions, depending on the artist's intentions. Matthew Barney's *Cremaster Cycle* is five feature-length films shot in digital video over six years. They are opulent productions filled with elaborate costumes, prosthetic makeup, mythic references, and symbolic and strange imagery. Illogical, like dreams, it is not the stories but the ideas and images that are memorable. *CREMASTER 3* (**20-37**) is three hours long and involves a myth of the construction of New York's Chrysler Building. The artist Richard Serra (see box in Chapter 3) appears as the ancient architect of the Temple of Solomon. Barney plays two roles: an apprentice and the murderer Gary Gilmore. At one point, the scene shifts to the Guggenheim Museum, and the artist is seen climbing up the outside of the circular ramps from level to level. He's dressed in a kilt and has a cloth stuck in his bloody mouth. At the museum's center,

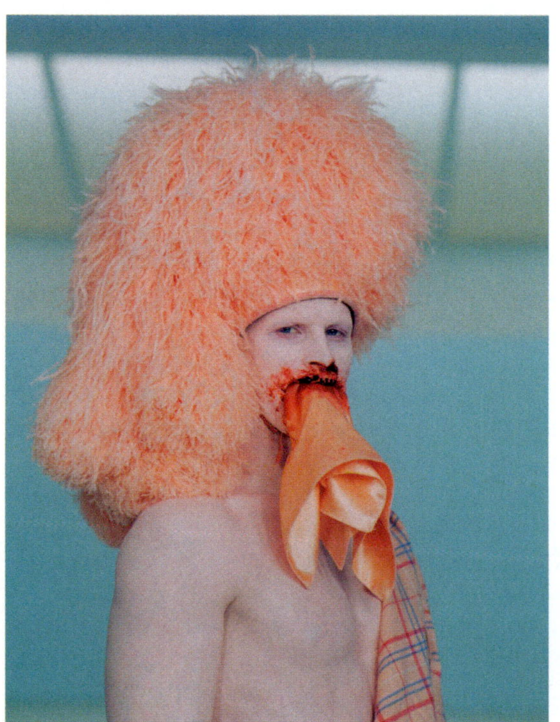

20-37 Matthew Barney, *CREMASTER 3,* 2002. Production still. Two silkscreened digital video disks, stainless steel, internally lubricated plastic, marble, and sterling silver in acrylic vitrine, with 35-mm print; color digital video transferred to film with Dolby Digital sound, 3:01:59, Edition 8/10, vitrine: 43½″ × 47″ × 40″.

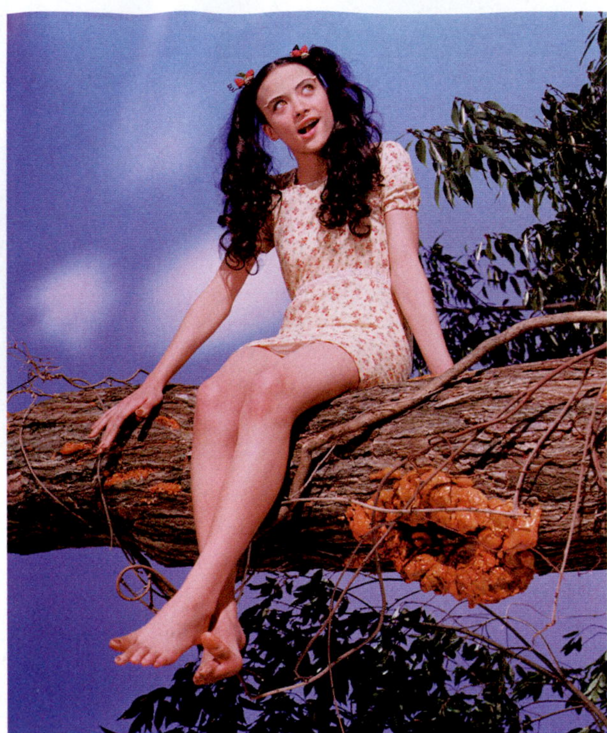

20-38 Motohiko Odani, *Rompers,* 2003. DVD, color video with sound. 2 minutes 52 seconds looped. Courtesy of Yamamoto Gendai, Tokyo, Japan.

a group of Las Vegas showgirls gesture dramatically. Other characters include a half-leopard woman who has glass legs. In another scene at the Saratoga racetrack, the muscles of trotting horses tear off their bodies as they run a race. Throughout the surrealistic film there are many strange sculptures (which Barney also exhibits in galleries) in which Vaseline often plays an important role. He claims the films are simply elaborate vehicles for the sculptures. He prefers to exhibit his sculptures along with related drawings and photographs when screening his films.

Unusual creatures are also featured in Motohiko Odani's *Rompers* (**20-38**), but the mood is playful and sweet. The setting appears to be a natural paradise. An innocent girl sits on a branch swinging her legs and singing a strange melody, with her hair held up by small fruit. The animals and insects all appear to be in harmony. We notice that her eyebrows seem a bit raised, her fingers are very long, and her eyes are unnaturally yellow. The tree has a large orange wound that drips a honey-like sap. But it is not until her tongue flies out like a frog's to catch a fly that we realize she is either not human or we are seeing mutants from our planet's future. Below the girl, frogs with ear-shaped wings circle a puddle.

A different surprise awaits viewers of Eve Sussman's *89 Seconds at Alcázar* (**20-39**). As the film begins, it appears to be an elaborate costume drama. We are looking in on characters dressed in Spanish seventeenth-century costume. They move around the room talking quietly. The lighting is dark but beautiful. We can't quite hear what the characters are saying, but by observing their movements and body language, we begin to understand their relationships. Some are servants. There is a beautifully dressed young girl that everyone defers to. As the high-definition video nears the end after ten minutes, its subject suddenly becomes clear and the whole film takes on added depth. These are the people portrayed in Velazquez's *Las Meninas* (15-17), one of the greatest masterpieces of Baroque painting. They are taking their places for the grand portrait. The girl is the Infanta. We are in the role of the King and Queen of Spain, who are peeking into the court painter's studio and whose presence is revealed (as in the painting) by the mirror on the back wall. Finally, the very moment that Velazquez made immortal comes, and then the characters move back into their lives again.

GLOBAL ART WORLD

While New York remains the center of the art world today, important communities of artists can be found in many cities and on many continents. Takashi Murakami is one of the leading figures in Japanese contemporary art. His art bridges many media, both high and low. In Japan, these distinctions have never been important. Murakami makes paintings, inflatable sculptures, and also designs Louis Vuitton handbags, watches, and collectable figurines. References to Hokusai, anime, and manga (see Chapter 8) are common in his work.

Murakami is best known for his cheerful cartoon characters; his most popular one is Mr. DOB (**20-40**). DOB has been presented in many guises. Sometimes he is simply cute, at other times ferociously angry with razor-sharp teeth. According to the artist, "DOB is a self-portrait of the Japanese people. He is cute but has no meaning and promotes a sarcastic understanding of the truth."

Murakami has studios and factories in both Tokyo and New York. Sometimes grouped with other Japanese artists as part of a Tokyo Pop movement, like Andy Warhol, he uses assistants to produce his work. He has a staff of around eighty people who regularly punch-in at work with timecards. His most recent

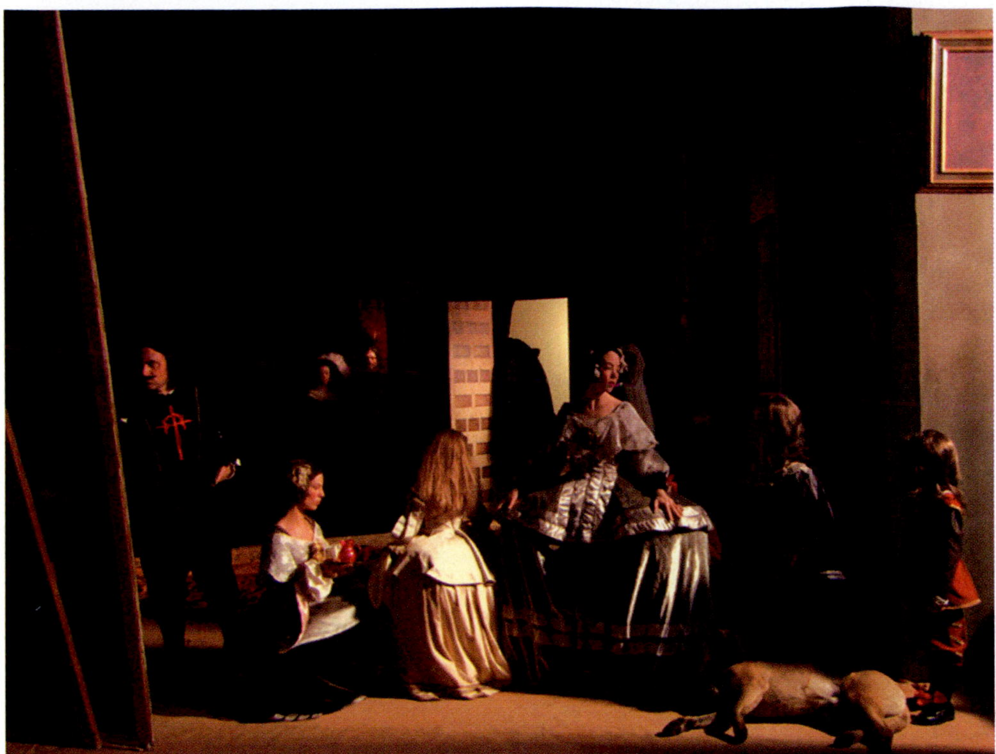

20-39 Eve Sussman, *Her Back to the Camera, 2004.* Screen grab from 89 Seconds at Alcázar. Whitney Museum of American Art, New York. Partial and promised gift of Jeanne L. and Michael L. Klein 2005.86. Courtesy Eve Sussman & The Rufus Corporation

pictures are drawn on a computer and then hand-painted by his assistants. Murakami cheerfully sells his products. He knows that the owners of galleries are concerned that the production of too much work will lower his prices, but he says, "I don't think so. If there is demand, I will keep making them."

Shahzia Sikhander's approach is quite different. The Pakistani artist meticulously handpaints her pictures with a fine squirrel hair brush, mixing the traditional styles of Hindu and Persian painting. She was trained in Islamic court painting at the National College of Art in Lahore, but she uses these techniques to make images with personal imagery. "My whole purpose of taking on the subject was to break the tradition," Sikhander says, "to experiment with it, to find new ways of making meaning."

Many of her pictures, like *Pleasure Pillars* (**20-41**), explore issues of female identity. In the center, ideal images from ancient Western and Eastern cultures are compared. Between them, blue and red hearts are connected. The ancient women seem to be under attack by a flying white hawk-man. The dancing women at the top seem more shocked by the modern fighter plane that is just leaving the scene. By adding personal imagery and references to modern

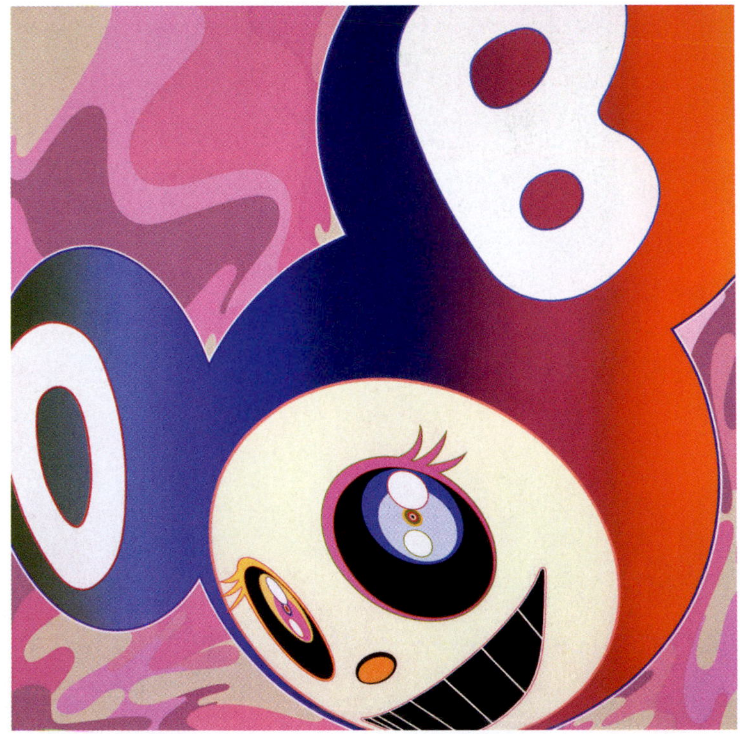

20-40 Takashi Murakami, *AND THEN Rainbow DOB,* 1999. Acrylic on canvas on board. 1000 × 1000 × 50 mm.

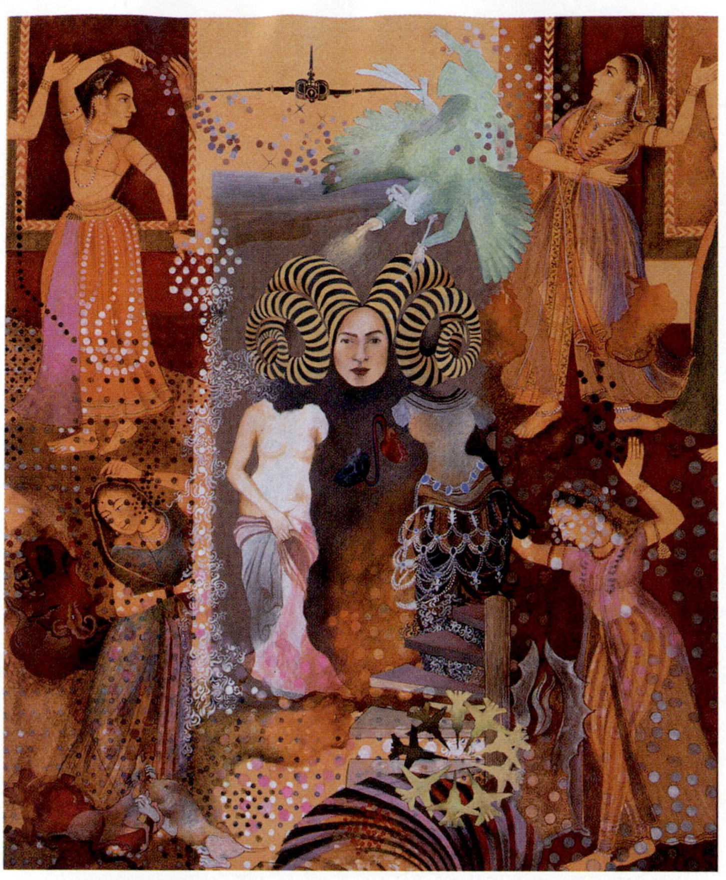

20-41 Shazia Sikander, *Pleasure Pillars,* 2001. Watercolor, dry pigment, vegetable color, tea and ink on wasli paper. Image courtesy of Sikkema Jenkins & Co.

warfare, Sikhander is extending centuries-old artistic traditions and giving them fresh life in the twenty-first century.

Giuseppe Penone has found a unique way to reach back into the past to make a contemporary art form. In 1999, a powerful wind storm knocked down thousands of the huge trees in the Gardens of Versailles (see Chapter 11), trees that had stood for centuries. This terrible loss to a masterpiece of landscape design was bemoaned by the arts community. Penone purchased one of the great fallen Atlas Cedars with the idea of making a sculpture from it. When he began carving into it, he discovered a miraculous thing: behind every knot on the bark, the original branches remain inside the trunk (**20-42**). Over the next two years, Penone dug into the massive eleven-thousand-pound tree and was able to reveal the original slender tree that the great cedar had grown from. His *Cedre de Versailles* (**20-43**) is now a window into a distant past. Inside,

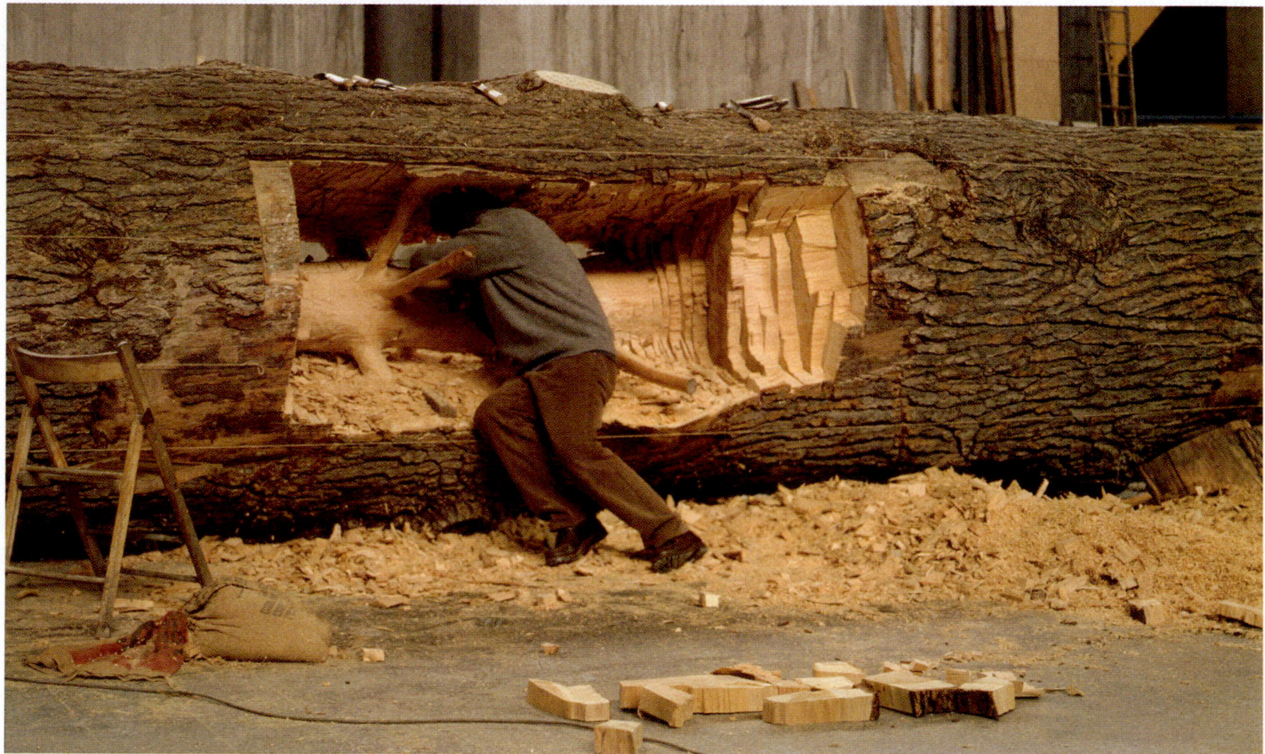

20-42 Giuseppe Penone at work on his *Cedre de Versailles,* 2002. Centre Pompidou.

we can see one of the young trees that were planted in the seventeenth century, during the reign of Louis XIV.

Penone, Sikhander, and Sussman are not alone among today's artists in finding new vitality in old sources. In the twenty-first century, the whole history of art is accessible and available to artists. The mine of the past is a rich and deep one, as are the wide range of media and techniques.

Today's storm of images began with a trickle when the printing press was invented in the fifteenth century. Television, computers, and the World Wide Web are just the most recent developments in a centuries-long history of more and more images becoming available to more and more people. The death of art announced in many obituaries written by artists and art critics during the heyday of Minimalism in the 1960s has come and gone. We are now in what is called a Postmodern and pluralistic era, a period of exploration of seemingly endless possibilities for every medium, new and old. Artists are now justifiably suspicious of anyone who announces that there is only one logical style or approach to making art. The history of the last hundred years—in fact, the whole history of art—is littered with the remains of generations of "true" art. To wait and see what the legions of artists will produce is one of the most pleasurable parts of the power of art today.

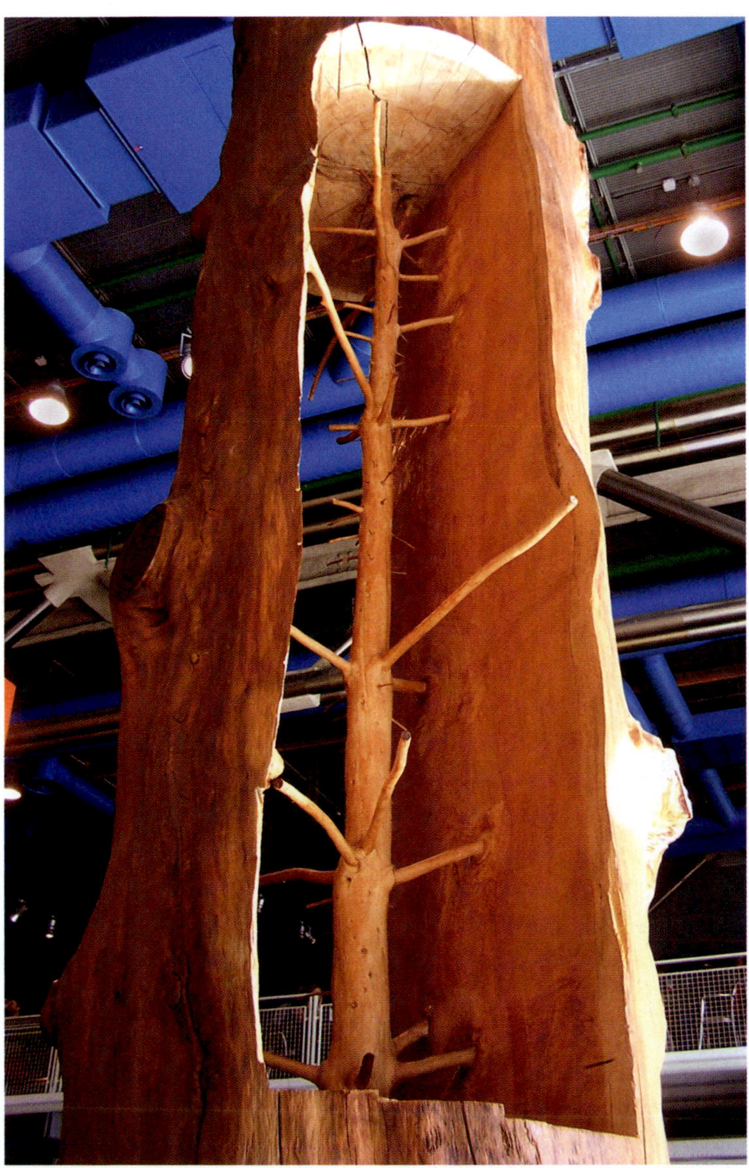

20-43 Giuseppe Penone, *Cedre de Versailles,* 2002.

GLOSSARY

Abstract Expressionism An American art movement that began in the 1950s. Large-scale art that combined Expressionism's potent psychological content and the gestural application of paint with an abandonment of any clear reference to the visual world.

abstract shapes Representational organic or geometric shapes that have been simplified. Even when they have been reduced to their basic underlying forms, distorted or exaggerated, the original sources of abstract shapes remain recognizable.

academic art Art officially sanctioned by the national academies (schools of art) in Europe. In the eighteenth and nineteenth centuries, the academies upheld traditional approaches, encouraging art in Classical or Renaissance styles with epic historical and literary themes. In the modern era, it has come to mean conservative and unimaginative art.

acrylic A water soluble paint that dries quickly and can be applied to most surfaces. Originally made for industrial use in the 1950s, its medium is plastic polymer made from resins.

Action Painting The energetic brushwork of Abstract Expressionism, apparently done in fits of intense and almost violent activity.

additive sculpture As opposed to subtractive, sculpture that is *built up,* such as by modeling a flexible material like clay or plaster, or by building an installation.

adobe A kind of sun-dried brick made of clay mixed with straw, used for building by native tribes of the Southwest and parts of South America.

Age of Reason See **Enlightenment.**

airbrush A spraying device that uses an air compressor to propel paint mist through a nozzle.

alla prima Paintings done quickly and at one sitting, with little or no preparation. Means "at the first."

Allegory A form of art in which human characters personify certain qualities or ideals.

analogous colors Hues adjacent on the color wheel; when placed together, they form pleasant harmonies because they are closely related. An example would be green, blue-green, and blue.

Analytical Cubism The first phase of Cubism. A collection of views from different angles fused into a balanced design with limited color.

anime The Japanese style of animation. Compared to animation in the United States, it has a wider range of themes and subject matter and is enjoyed by all age groups.

aperture (or **diaphragm)** An adjustable opening that controls the amount of light entering a camera.

applied arts The useful media of the visual arts, such as architecture, design, and illustration.

applique In quilting, fabric silhouettes cut out and stitched onto the background of another fabric.

appropriation A method first used in the twentieth-century where imagery from other sources (photographs, past masterpieces) is taken and turned into a new work of art, sometimes with little or no alteration.

aquatint An intaglio printmaking process that creates tonal areas. When powdered resin is applied to a metal plate and then heated, each particle becomes a dot that will resist acid. As with etched lines, the longer an area of aquatint is in the acid bath, the deeper the etch and the darker the tone in the print.

Arcade A covered walkway.

arbitrary colors As opposed to naturalistic or realistic colors, colors that are the invention of the artist.

arch A semicircular construction (usually of stone) that both supports the weight of a building and provides an opening. Used extensively during the Roman Empire, it allowed far wider spaces between columns than post-and-lintel construction. Also known as *rounded arch.*

art nouveau A late nineteenth-century style utilized for furniture, architecture, interiors, and graphic design and characterized by elaborate, rhythmic, and organic decoration. It was the first modern international design style.

assemblage Three-dimensional collages.

asymmetrical balance An intuitive balance of visual weights that results in a more dynamic equilibrium than radial or symmetrical balance.

atmospheric perspective A method of creating a sense of deep space in two-dimensional art based on the effect our atmosphere has on things seen at a distance. Distant forms are portrayed vaguer and closer to the color of the sky than near ones.

avant-garde Literally the "advance guard;" the vanguard or leaders of new directions in the arts.

balance Visually satisfying stability in a work of art. It is created by adjusting the placement of art elements in a field.

Baroque The period in the seventeenth century that included art with dramatic use of light and dark and preferences for dynamic movement and theatrical effects, as well as intense naturalism and the inclusion of elements of ordinary life in religious scenes.

barrel vault A rounded arch that when extended allowed for large and long public spaces in stone buildings, particularly cathedrals built during the Middle Ages.

Bauhaus ("the house of building") A German school devoted to the cause of integrating the arts and modern technology and to transcending the boundaries among craft, design, and art. Founded in 1919 by the architect Walter Gropius, the school stressed a simple, modern, geometrical style.

bearing wall An architectural construction using the walls themselves to support the weight of the roof and floors above.

binder A glue-like substance that holds pigment together, the type of which determines the nature of the medium; for example, oil is the binder in oil paint. Used in all the colored media.

Buddhism A religion founded by Siddhartha Gautama, a prince from Nepal who lived in the sixth century BCE. Through the revelation that all life is an illusion and that the only way to escape pain is to renounce all desires, he attained **nirvana** and became the Buddha.

Byzantine The eastern Roman Empire founded by Constantine. Also an art style of the civilization centered in Constantinople (now Istanbul) during the Middle Ages that was less naturalistic and more symbolic, stylized, flat, and decorative than before the fall of the Empire.

CAD (Computer-Aided Design) A type of three-dimensional modeling software used by designers, engineers, and architects to create models for manufacturing and architecture. The program pictures the objects or buildings in three-dimensions, allowing the viewer to see them from many angles.

camera obscura Literally meaning "dark room," initially a room-sized camera. By preventing all light from entering a room and then cutting a small hole in a shade over a window, a person could project an inverted image of the outside onto the opposite wall. By the 1700s, a table model of the camera obscura with lens and mirror became available, providing a right-side-up projected image on a screen that artists could use for tracing.

capital The crown of an architectural column.

cartoon A preparatory drawing for larger work, such as tapestries or murals.

casting A process that makes one or several lasting copies of sculpture. Often the casts are made of bronze, though other metals or plaster may be used.

ceramics Objects made from clay fired in a kiln for lasting hardness and strength.

chiaroscuro A technique in drawing and painting where a dramatic contrast between light and dark areas creates a convincing illusion of three-dimensional forms. The Italian Baroque painter Michelangelo da Caravaggio is noted for using this technique.

Classical Age The flourishing of Greek culture during the fourth and fifth centuries BCE. Classical Greek art expressed ideals of clarity, order, balance, proportion, harmony, and unity.

Classicism A seventeenth-century movement that, inspired by the Classical art of Greece and Rome, taught that the highest aim of a work of art is to represent noble and serious thoughts. It called for a logical, orderly art with great themes so as to raise viewers up by appealing to their reason, not to their base emotions.

collage The combination of cut-and-pasted paper, photographs, and other materials on a two-dimensional surface.

colonnade A row of columns, usually supporting a roof.

Color-Field Painting A kind of Abstract Expressionism characterized by large areas of color that are more dominant than any particular shape.

color wheel Primary and secondary colors arranged in a circle. The primaries are placed equidistant from each other, with their secondary mixtures between them.

complementary colors Colors that are directly across from each other on the color wheel, such as red and green. When placed together, they accentuate each other's intensity. Considered opposites, or *complements.*

conte crayon A versatile drawing crayon developed in the late 1700s. It comes in a variety of degrees of hardness and can be used to create both subtle tones and dense blacks.

contour lines Lines that describe the edge of a form, sometimes emphasized by changes in weight or width.

cool colors The family of colors based on blue, purple, and green; colors that are associated with calm, order, the sky, and the ocean. They tend to recede away from the viewer.

Counter-Reformation The Roman Catholic church's attempt to combat the Protestant **Reformation** of the sixteenth century. As part of this campaign, the church supported art that would entertain and rouse the faithful.

crafts Traditionally, everyday, useful objects, that were handcrafted. Today, includes non-functional handcrafted objects in **ceramics,** glass, wood, metal, fiber, and other media.

crayon A colored drawing medium with a waxy or oily binder that adheres to paper; does not require fixative.

cross-hatching A drawing technique used to make forms appear three-dimensional. A series of parallel lines cross in a net-like fashion, describing the contours of a surface.

Cubism An alternative to linear perspective organization of space developed by Pablo Picasso and Georges Braque in the early twentieth century. Built from a collection of observations, objects are seen from several angles simultaneously. Each part is equal in importance—there is no conventional foreground and background. The result is a significantly shallower space compared to linear perspective, as well as a less naturalistic appearance.

Dada A meaningless term for an international art movement that began during World War I. Dada manifestos called for the destruction of all values—the end of art, morality, and society. This "anti-art," which took the form of bizarre performances and exhibition of found objects, or "ready-mades," was an effort to evolve a new way of thinking, feeling, and seeing.

daguerreotype The first permanent photographic image, invented by Louis-Jacques-Mande Daguerre in 1839, utilizing silver foil made light sensitive with chemicals. After the foil was exposed to light in a camera, the image was made permanent by bathing in a salt solution.

deductive reasoning The medieval scientific approach to explaining natural phenomena using accepted general rules. Compare to **inductive reasoning.**

design The organization of visual elements into a composition that is visually satisfying.

Die Brucke Literally "the Bridge," a group of German Expressionist artists led by Ernst Kirchner in the early 1900s. By expressing emotions honestly and directly, they hoped to encourage others to abandon the stale hypocritical attitudes of their elders. Clashing hues, strong lines, and aggressive spirit typified their work.

digital arts (or **digital media**) The art forms created with the aid of computer technology.

digitize To translate two-dimensional images (with scanners) and three-dimensional objects (with video cameras) into numbers that a computer can read so the images can appear on the computer's screen.

digitizing or **graphics tablet** A flat, pressure-sensitive input device used by digital artists as an alternative to a mouse. Artists use a pen-shaped stylus to draw directly on the tablet, which can not only sense where lines are being drawn but also the tilt of the pen and how much pressure is being applied.

Earth Art Large-scale environmental sculpture outside of a gallery or museum; interacts directly with nature.

edition The limited number of prints made directly from an image created by an artist on a block, plate, stone, or screen. Once the last print of an edition is "pulled," the block, plate, or other source is destroyed.

egg tempera See **tempera.**

elevation An architectural drawing that shows front and side views of a planned structure on a vertical plane.

engraving The oldest form of intaglio printmaking, developed in Europe during the 1400s. Cuts and scratches dug with tools into a metal plate are filled with ink and print directly onto paper as lines.

Enlightenment An intellectual movement that began in England and spread to France, then spread throughout Europe by the end of the eighteenth century. Great scientists and mathematicians stressed the value of rationality over faith and embraced the idea of progress.

environment See **installation.**

etching An intaglio process using acids rather than tools to cut the metal plate. An acid-resistant wax coating, or **ground,** is applied to the plate. An image is made by cutting through the ground. Then the plate is put in a tray of acid that "bites" into the metal where the wax ground was removed. After the plate is washed with water, it is inked and printed just like an engraving. Lines can be made lighter or darker by the amount of time the plate is in acid.

existentialism A post-World War II philosophy that began in France. It declares that all people are essentially alone, that there is no God in the universe. Each one must face the ultimate meaninglessness of the universe and decide independently how to live one's own life.

Expressionism A Modern Art movement that went beyond an imitation of the world toward an intense re-creation of feeling. Making inner feelings (as dark and deep as they may be) visible was generally achieved with powerful (often clashing) colors and vivid contrasts of light and dark.

facade The outer side of an architectural structure; usually refers to the front of a building.

Fauves Literally the "wild beasts," a group of French artists led by Henri Matisse in the early 1900s. They ignored perspective and used bright colors rreely as a source of pleasure.

figure-ground ambiguity A design whose positive and negative forms are so balanced that it is unclear which part should be called *figure* and which should be called *ground.*

figure triangle Common in Renaissance compositions, a triangular arrangement of elements, often figures.

fine arts The visual arts customarily considered in Western civilization a "high" form of artistic production (in other words, not useful like the **applied arts**). They have traditionally included drawing, painting, and sculpture, but in the last two hundred years have also included outstanding examples of printmaking, photography, design, decorative arts, and crafts.

fixative A spray of shellac or plastic polymer used in charcoal and pastel drawings to ensure a permanent bond to the paper.

flying buttress In a gothic church, an exterior support for stability.

flying logo Via computer animation, a kind of **logo** seen on television that appears to spin in three dimensions and come toward the viewer.

folk art The work of unschooled artists, often working in rural areas. Can include painting, sculpture, and all the decorative arts, but usually created with less expensive materials.

foreshortening In two-dimensional art, the apparent diminishing in size of forms as they seem to recede from the viewer.

forged Metal shaped by heating.

found objects Items from ordinary life that artists use in their works.

frame or ballon-frame construction A supporting skeleton made of vertical and horizontal wooden supports nailed together; used in architectural constructions.

free-standing sculpture Sculpture in the round that the viewer must circle to see completely.

fresco A permanent wall-painting technique in use since ancient times. Pigment and water is brushed directly into fresh, wet plaster (fresco means "fresh" in Italian). As the plaster dries, the pigment is bound into it and literally becomes part of the wall itself.

Futurism An early twentieth-century Italian Modern Art movement led by the poet Filippo Marinetti. A celebration of the age of the machine, it called for a complete and utter rejection of the art of the past.

genre Ordinary and commonplace subject matter; scenes from everyday life.

geometric shapes Enclosed spaces formed by straight lines or curved ones that progress evenly. Squares, rectangles, triangles, and circles are all examples of this kind of two-dimensional shape. Three-dimensional examples are the cube, box, pyramid, and sphere. Sometimes called *hard-edged* shapes.

gesso A thick paint applied to prepare surfaces like wood or canvas for painting. It produces bright white surface impermeable to liquids. Traditionally, a thick paste of gypsum and animal glue, although today many artists replace the glue with an acrylic medium.

glass blowing A craft that transforms hot, molten glass into a finished art object. The glass is picked up in a small spherical blob at the end of a long metal pipe, then blown into bubbles of various shapes, shaped with tools or by rolling on a hard surface, and removed from the pipe to cool slowly.

glaze 1. Paint diluted and made transparent. Often built up in layers on top of **underpainting** to create the illusion of three-dimensional forms. 2. In ceramics, a paint that melts into and fuses with clay while being baked in a kiln.

Gothic Elaborately decorative medieval building style of the twelfth through fifteenth centuries, whose unique features were the **pointed arch,** the ribbed vault, exterior flying **buttresses,** high ceilings, and stained-glass windows.

gouache An opaque watercolor made by adding chalk to pigment and gum arabic. Unlike watercolor, it can be applied more thickly, covers well, and permits changes.

graphic design Once known as "commercial art," it is the manipulation of **typography** and images for advertisements, magazines, books, posters, packages, **logos,** and signs.

grazia During the Renaissance period, art that was beautiful, graceful, and seemingly effortlessly achieved.

Greek orders The three styles that originated in Ancient Greek architecture—Doric, Ionic, and Corinthian. They are most easily identified by their distinctive columns, **capitals** (or decorative tops). and bases.

groin vault The intersection of two barrel vaults at right angles.

ground 1. The visual plane where art elements (or figures) are organized. When elements are added to the ground, it becomes, in itself, a shape (called the negative form), and must be consciously dealt with. 2. The surface of a two-dimensional work of art. 3. A wax coating that resists acid; used in etching.

Hellenistic Age An age that began with the reign of Alexander the Great (356-323 BCE) in Greece. During this time, Greek sculpture became more naturalistic and illusionistic, appealing less to the rational mind and more to the senses than the restrained works of the Classical period.

Hinduism An ancient polytheistic religion native to India in which believers accept that humans experience an unending cycle of birth, life, death, and rebirth. *Karma* determines one's fate; the deeds of one lifetime influence one's status in the next.

horizon line The same as the viewer's eye level, it is where the sky and the earth appear to meet. In linear perspective, it is where parallel lines converge.

Hudson River School A group of nineteenth-century American Romantic painters. These artists saw in America an unspoiled land of great promise and painted many views of the Hudson Valley and other wilderness areas in the Northeast.

hue The name of a color on the color wheel or in the spectrum. For example, violet and green are two different hues.

Humanism The predominant philosophy of the Renaissance and catalyst for the period's great achievements. Its two main ingredients were the study of the ancient cultural achievements of the Greeks and Romans and respect for the individual.

iconoclasm The destruction of religious imagery.

impasto Thick paint that reveals the action of brushstrokes.

Impressionism A Modern Art movement that began around 1870 in France. Based on the idea of conveying an immediate impression of a place and time of day. Impressionist painters worked outdoors, directly studying the moment's light and color. Their typical style achieved heightened color effects by placing colors side by side rather than mixing them.

Impressionists A group of artists who met in cafes and studios and exhibited together in Paris from the 1870s to the end of the nineteenth century. While some, like Claude Monet, worked in the characteristic Impressionist style, others simply joined a rebellion against the dominant academic style of their time.

inductive reasoning A medieval scientific approach where one observes phenomena directly and then uses the gathered information to develop general rules. Compare to **deductive reasoning.**

industrial design The design of manufactured objects such as telephones, typewriters, and automobiles.

installation A room-sized multimedia sculpture constructed in a gallery, museum, or public space. It is meant to surround the viewer with a unique artistic experience. Also known as an *environment.*

intaglio A printmaking method: lines cut into the surface of a metal plate become receptacles for ink after the plate is inked and its surface wiped off. Damp paper and plate are then run through a press; the heavy pressure forces the paper into the ink-filled grooves, and the image is transferred.

intensity The vividness of a particular hue.

International Style The dominant twentieth-century architectural approach in Europe and the United States. The antithesis of the heavily ornamental style taught in nineteenth-century architectural academies, its buildings were flat-roofed, made of modern materials (concrete, steel, and glass), and free of any superfluous decoration. Boxlike and practical, all spaces were designed for efficient organization.

Islam Religion founded by the prophet Mohammed (570-632). The teachings of Mohammed are recorded in The Koran, which tells of the revelations of God through the angel Gabriel. The name "Islam" means "submission to the will of God."

Japonisme The love of all things Japanese, a wave that swept over cultured Western society in the late nineteenth century.

juxtaposition A technique invented by the Dadaists where unrelated objects are taken out of their normal context and joined together, producing a new unique object.

kiln An oven used for drying and baking clay sculptures or ceramics.

kinetic sculpture Sculpture with moving parts.

lens In cameras, the clear, rounded glass or plastic that focuses the light onto the film.

linear perspective The principal means of creating the illusion of the third dimension or depth in Western two-dimensional art since the Renaissance. All parallel lines appear to converge at points in the distance, called **vanishing points.** Forms that seem closer appear larger than those meant to be farther from the viewer. See also **one-point perspective, foreshortening.**

linear style A Neoclassicist approach; typically paintings drawn with sharp outlines, clearly defined forms, and relatively solid areas of color.

lithography A printmaking process where images are drawn or painted directly in grease on a flat stone or metal plate. After the surface is chemically treated and moistened with water, ink will only adhere where there is grease. Wax crayons, soap, and black pigment with *tusche,* a greasy liquid that can be applied with a brush or sprayed on, are the most common materials used to make the images.

local color The general color of anything we see, without considering the effect of lighting or adjacent colors.

logo A symbol or trademark of an organization that is meant to be instantly recognizable.

loom A machine for weaving fibers into cloth.

lost wax method A method, in a series of steps, of using molds to cast hollow metal sculpture or jewelry.

mandala In Buddhist art, an intricate, geometrical design of deities depicted in concentric circles that represent the cosmos.

manga Originally, nineteenth-century printed sketchbooks by Japanese artists that illustrated everyday life, often in a humorous way. Today, it refers to Japanese comic books that are enjoyed by readers of all ages.

Mannerism A sixteenth-century Italian art movement that was a reaction to Renaissance ideals. Mannerist artists used distortion to demonstrate their inventiveness. Their highest aim was elegance.

maquette A sculptural model in clay or wax of a planned larger work or cast work.

matte A dull, nonreflective finish as opposed to a glossy finish.

media, medium Artists' materials, such as oil paint or clay.

metalpoint Drawings with pure, precise lines made by a thin metal wire in a holder; the wire is usually silver, but other metals including lead have been used.

mihrab A niche for prayer in a **mosque,** oriented to face in the direction of Mecca.

minaret A slender tower on the exterior of Islamic buildings.

Minimalism An American art movement that began in the 1960s. Art is stripped down to the essentials; paintings and sculptures are self-sufficient and have no subject matter, content, or meaning beyond their presence as objects in space.

mixed media A method first used in the twentieth-century that mixes materials (manufactured, natural "found objects," as well as conventional art media), often using them in unusual ways, without respect for the traditional borders between two- and three-dimensional media.

mobile A hanging kinetic sculpture, originated by Alexander Calder in the twentieth century, whose parts are moved by air currents.

monotype A one-of-a-kind print made by applying ink or paint directly to a metal plate and then running it through a press with paper. It can also be made without the press by rubbing the back of the paper.

morphing A computer-aided transformation where one image gradually becomes another.

mosaic Picture made of tiles of colored stone, ceramic, or glass.

mosque An Islamic place of worship.

naturalistic Art that is realistic. For example, animals are drawn as if they were alive.

nave The large, central space in a medieval church.

negative form The shape of the space or ground around art elements.

National Treasures In Japan, a system that designates works of art as vitally important to the national heritage because of their historic and aesthetic significance. National Treasures can range from huge statues to fragile decorated boxes, and cannot be sold or taken out of the country. Even accomplished living artists can be given the official title of National Treasure.

Neoclassicism A reaction to Rococo art and the visual expression of the ideals of the Enlightenment of the eighteenth and nineteenth centuries. Its characteristics include clarity of line, color, and form. Its artists sought to create universal moral lessons that would educate and improve the viewer.

Neoexpressionism An international revival of Expressionist methods that began in the 1970s. Combines vigorous paint strokes with emotion-laden figurative imagery.

neutral colors White, black, and gray. Added to colors, they make tints and shades, changing the values but not the hue.

nirvana In Buddhism, a state of eternal bliss.

nonobjective shapes See **nonrepresentational shapes.**

nonrepresentational shapes Shapes that are not meant to refer to anything we can see in the real world. They are sometimes called *nonobjective* or *abstract.* These shapes can be either organic (soft-edged) or geometrical (hard-edged).

oculus "Eye"; round opening or window at the top of a dome.

one-point perspective A system of linear perspective invented by the Renaissance artist Filippo Brunelleschi. All parallel lines appear to converge at one point in the distance, the *vanishing point,* which is exactly on the **horizon line.** As in all linear perspective, the sizes of objects shrink as they increase in distance from the viewer.

Op Art A nonrepresentational style, introduced in the 1960s, that explored optical illusions.

organic shapes Enclosed spaces formed by uneven curves. They are sometimes called **naturalistic,** biomorphic, or soft-edged. Examples are shapes that look like amoebas or treetops.

Orientalism A fascination with or the study of Middle Eastern and Asian art and culture. A taste for exoticism that swept Europe and the United States in the nineteenth century; it viewed the peoples, history, and culture of the Middle East and Asia as "other"—the mysterious opposite of Western civilization.

painterly style An approach to painting promoted by the nineteenth-century Romantics, utilizing broad strokes, indistinct outlines between shapes, and colors blended into each other. It is a style intended to reach viewers' emotions rather than their minds.

pastels Colored chalks in sticks that are a combination of loose dry pigment and a **binder** of paste or methylcellulose.

Pax Romanus Roman peace during the reign of Augustus, when citizens could travel safely anywhere within the Roman Empire.

performance art Contemporary events designed to be ephemeral, lasting only in memory.

perspective An architectural drawing that gives a three-dimensional impression of a new building in its setting.

photomontage The imaginative combination of more than one photographic image.

photorealism See **Superrealism.**

piazza Large courtyard.

picture plane A flat two-dimensional surface within which art elements are organized.

plastic Moldable material, like wet clay, rather than rigid.

pointed arch A Gothic arch that allowed larger openings in the outer wall and higher ceilings in the interior than the Roman rounded arch.

pointillism The Post impressionistic style developed by Georges Seurat. By placing small spots of pure color side by side, Seurat let the viewer's eye optically mix the colors and thereby increase their luminosity.

Pop Art An American and English art movement of the 1960s that celebrated the commodities and celebrities of the time.

porcelain A type of **ceramic** developed in China. By baking clay at a high temperature it is transformed into a translucent material of glasslike hardness, sometimes known as "china."

positive form The shape of an art element.

Postimpressionism Separate expressions of dissatisfaction with Impressionism at the end of the nineteenth century by artists who had initially worked in that style. The most important figures of this new movement were Georges Seurat, Paul Gauguin, Vincent van Gogh, and Paul Cezanne.

post-and-lintel A form of architectural construction in which posts or columns support horizontal lintels (cross beams).

Post-Modern Art A contemporary movement that began in the 1980s. The dominant trends of Modern Art—a rejection of the past and of decorative elements and a steady movement towards nonrepresentational images—are reversed. Post-Modern Artists are interested in rediscovering the past, not rejecting it, and see history as a vast menu from which to select.

primary colors Red, yellow, and blue, the three colors that cannot be made from any others, and that are the sources for all other colors.

proportion The relative sizes of the parts of an object to each other.

quill Pens made from bird feathers, most commonly goose. Variation in the pressure applied to the pen will smoothly change a line's width. Popular since the medieval period.

radial balance All elements revolve around a central point.

raku Hand-shaped Japanese ceramics associated with the tea ceremony. Irregular and asymmetrical, with glazes thick and rough, their imperfection is prized as a mark of mastery.

Realism A nineteenth-century movement that rejected the idealized historical and mythological subjects of academic Neoclassicism; instead it focused on unembellished ordinary contemporary life as the source of truth and meaning.

Reformation A rebellion led by Martin Luther against the Roman Catholic church in the sixteenth century resulting in the creation of Protestantism.

registration In color prints, the proper alignment of each color with the other inked colors.

reinforced concrete (or **ferroconcrete**) Concrete reinforced with thin iron rods to provide added strength. It enables architects to design structures with dramatic shapes.

relief printmaking A method of printmaking where the negative spaces of a design are cut away, leaving the positive areas raised. The print's marks are made from inking what is left in "relief" on the block. Woodcuts, linoleum cuts, and rubber stamps fall into this category.

relief sculpture A sculptural image that projects from a flat, two-dimensional background. The back of a relief sculpture is not meant to be seen; the entire design can be understood from a frontal view.

Renaissance Meaning "rebirth," a period famous for art and architecture and generally considered to mark the beginning of the modern world. Spanning the fourteenth to sixteenth centuries in Europe, it was marked by renewed interest in Classical culture as well as the development of capitalism, the rise of the nation-state, scientific investigation, and individualism. Also known as the "Age of Exploration."

rendering 1. A synonym for drawing. 2. In 3D computer design, modeling, or animation, the final stage when all objects, backgrounds, lights, shadows, reflections, special effects, and movements in a scene are generated by the computer.

rhythm Repetition of similar shapes, as in *patterns.*

rock art Painting on and carving in rock walls. An art form for tens of thousands of years, it can be found in North America, Asia, Australia, and all across Africa.

Rococo An eighteenth-century lighthearted and decorative style of art whose subject matter is typically about lovers. It was a reaction to the formality of Classicism.

Romanesque Medieval building style of the ninth through twelfth centuries based on the Roman round arch. Heavy stone geometric buildings were supported by thick walls with few windows and dark interiors.

Romanticism A nineteenth-century reaction to **Neoclassicism,** by rejecting logic and order and looking for the inner truth of intuition and passions. Romantic artists admired the untamed power of nature and used a painterly style.

rotunda A completely round building or a circular interior with a dome.

Salon An annual exhibition in Paris, begun in 1737, of art chosen by members of the French Academy. It was the only important public exhibition available to artists in the mid-nineteenth century.

saturated colors Colors that have a high level of intensity.

scale The relative size between an object and a constant, usually the size of the average person.

secondary colors Orange, green, and purple, created by mixing two primary colors.

secondary symbolism Common in Medieval and Northern Renaissance art, where details have additional meanings, such as a white lily in a vase representing the Virgin Mary.

serpentinata In Mannerism, the most elegant pose for a body—when the limbs and torso resembled the letter "S." It refers to the twisting of a snake.

sfumato lighting In Italian, "the soft mist of a fountain." Soft lighting in Renaissance paintings originally used by Leonardo da Vinci. It makes both edges and details unclear. The lack of definite edges forces viewers to use their imagination, making portraits like the *Mona Lisa* seem more lifelike.

shades Hues that have been darkened by the neutral color black. Navy blue is a very dark shade of blue.

shutter The part of the camera that is triggered by the photographer and controls the time of the exposure.

silkscreen (or **serigraphy**) An inexpensive method of producing very large editions of prints. A stencil is attached to silk tightly stretched over a wooden frame. Paper or cloth is placed underneath the screen and ink is spread across the screen with a rubber blade or squeegee. The areas of silk not covered with a stencil let the ink come through and print onto the medium.

simultaneous contrast The effect of two colors meeting. Differences between them are accentuated; their similarities are not apparent.

steel frame (or **cage construction)** A form of architectural construction developed in the 1890s using a steel interior skeleton that resembles a bird cage. Used today for building skyscrapers. Its facade is often a simple "skin" of glass.

stigmata Bloody signs of the nails that held Christ to the cross.

De Stijl ("the Style") Early twentieth-century Dutch artists who believed a pure universal style in art and architecture could be the solution to humankind's misery. Followers of Piet Mondrian, they designed furniture and buildings using flat geometric areas filled with primary colors.

stoicism A Greek philosophy that encouraged dignity, rational thought, and control over one's emotions.

stupa A Buddhist religious shrine in the shape of a mound. Pilgrims walk around it, symbolizing the Path of Life around the World Mountain. The walking is a form of meditation and worship.

subtractive sculpture As opposed to **additive,** sculpture carved out of materials such as wood or stone.

Superrealism (or **photorealism**) A movement that began in the 1970s that in two dimensions, re-creates the look of photographs. In three dimensions, casting is often used to achieve the utmost fidelity to reality.

Surrealism An art movement begun in the 1920s that depicted dreams and visions of the irrational unconscious and was inspired by Sigmund Freud's theories.

symmetrical balance Sometimes known as *bilateral symmetry,* a balance where there is general equivalence of shape and position on opposite sides of a central axis; if folded in half, the forms would match.

Synthetic Cubism The second phase of Cubism, where more colorful and playful visual symbols replaced the limited colors and angular planes of analytical cubism.

tempera A painting medium in which pigments are mixed with egg yolks (sometimes called **egg tempera**).

tenebroso Literally, the "dark manner." A technique of the followers of Michelangelo da Caravaggio.

terra-cotta Clay baked in a kiln and hardened to a rich red-earth tone.

texture mapping In computer art, the wrapping of a texture around a wire-grid form drawn by an artist to create a realistic or imaginative surface.

three-dimensional space The kind of space we actually live in. It contains objects that can be viewed from all sides, objects that have height, width, and depth. Sculpture and architecture are examples of three-dimensional art forms.

throwing The action of a potter using a wheel to build a round vessel. A lump of clay is lifted and shaped by hand as the wheel turns.

tints Hues that have been lightened by the neutral color white. Pink is a pale tint of red.

transept In a medieval church, the short rectangular space that ran perpendicular to the **nave,** forming the Latin-cross floor plan.

trompe l'oeil Art that fools our eyes into believing that what we see is real.

trumeau The central pillar of the main doorway of a church.

two-dimensional space Flat space that can only be viewed from one side. Anything that exists in this space will have height and width but no depth. However, two-dimensional art forms often create the *illusion* of depth. Drawing and painting are examples of two-dimensional art forms.

typography The manipulation and selection of styles and sizes of letters *(type)* in graphic design.

Ukiyo-e Literally "pictures of the floating world"; Japanese woodcut prints that depicted brothels, the theater, and scenes of travelers and ordinary life among the middle class of Japan. The style and subjects of these prints influenced the development of Impressionism and Postimpressionism.

underpainting Painting done as a foundation for subsequent transparent glazes. Usually establishes basic composition and tonal relationships.

unity A sense of coherence or wholeness in a work of art. Unity alone is unlikely to sustain the interest of a viewer. It must be balanced with *variety.*

value The relative lightness and darkness of a color.

vanishing point In linear perspective, a point where parallel lines appear to converge on the horizon, like railroad tracks meeting at a point in the distance.

vernacular architecture The architecture of ordinary buildings built in a traditional, local style, without the assistance of a professional architect.

video art Art works that are created with video cameras or are constructed with video monitors.

visual weight The relative importance of an element in a picture plane. Visual weight is dependent on the position, color, size, shape, or texture of the element.

volume A three-dimensional shape, although sometimes implied, such as a drawing of a vase.

volute A decorative spiral on a column.

warm colors The family of colors based on yellow, orange, and red; colors that are associated with extreme emotions, chaos, fire, and the sun. They tend to advance towards the viewer.

warp In weaving, vertical parallel threads arranged in a **loom.**

wash Diluted ink applied with a brush to add tonal values to a drawing.

watercolor Transparent paint that is a quick-drying combination of pigment and gum arabic. Diluted with water, it is usually applied to paper.

weft (or **woof**) In weaving, horizontal parallel threads passed at right angles to the **warp** and interlaced with them in a **loom.**

wood engraving A relief process similar to **woodcut,** but that uses the endgrain on blocks of hard wood. The endgrain's density permits very fine, precise lines to be created, and, compared to woodcuts, many more prints can be made before the block begins to deteriorate.

woodcut A type of **relief printmaking** made by carving directly into a smooth piece of wood and removing any parts of the surface not meant to be part of the image.

wrought Metal shaped by hammering.

PHOTO CREDITS

CHAPTER 1

1-1 ©Réunion des Musées Nationaux (R.G. Ojeda)/ Art Resource, NY
1-2 ©Roger-Viollet, Paris, Private Collection/The Bridgeman Art Library
1-3 ©Réunion des Musées Nationaux/Art Resource, NY
1-4 ©Réunion des Musées Nationaux/Art Resource, NY
1-5 ©Alinari Archives/Art Resource
1-6 ©Archivo Iconografico, S.A./CORBIS
also Chapter 13 map
1-7 ©Robert Harding Picture Library Ltd/Alamy
1-8 ©Erich Lessing/Art Resource, NY
also Chapter 12 map
1-9 Jean Vertut
also Chapter 12 map
1-10 Jean Vertut
1-11 ©Yale University Art Gallery/Art Resource, NY
1-12 ©CuboImages srl/Alamy
1-13 ©Werner Foreman/Topham/The Image Works
1-14 ©Malcolm Kirk
1-15 ©Dennis Cox/Alamy
1-16 ©Art Resource, NY
1-17 ©Erich Lessing /Art Resource, NY
1-18 ©Scala/Art Resource, NY
also Chapter 15 timeline and Chapter 14 map
1-19 Imperial War Museum
1-20 Freer Gallery of Art, Smithsonian Institution, Washington, D.C. F1942.15a
also Chapter 19 timeline
1-21 University of California, Berkeley Art Museum; purchased with the aid of funds from the National Endowment for the Arts (selected by The Committee for the Acquisition of Afro-American Art). Photograph courtesy of Michael Rosenfeld Gallery, LLC, New York, NY. Photograph by Joshua Nefsky.
1-22 Private Collection, ©DACS /Photo ©Boltin Picture Library/The Bridgeman Art Library. ©2008 Artists Rights Society (ARS), New York/ADAGP, Paris/Succession Marcel Duchamp.
1-23 ©Bill Helsel/Alamy
also Chapter 20 timeline
1-24 ©Rob Crandall/The Image Works
1-25 ©Ansel Adams Publishing Rights Trust/CORBIS
1-26 ©1978 The Imogen Cunningham Trust
1-27 Photo by Stephen White, Pékin Fine Arts Co. Ltd.
1-28 ©Ian Goodrick/Alamy
1-29 The Gates, Project for Central Park, New York City. Photo: Wolfgang Volz. ©Christo and Jeanne-Claude 2003
1-30 The Gates, Central Park, New York City, 1979-2005. Photo: Wolfgang Volz. ©Christo and Jeanne-Claude 2005
also Chapter 20 timeline
1-31 Private Collection, Courtesy of David Tunkl Fine Art.
1-32 Solomon R. Guggenheim Museum, New York, Gift, Solomon R. Guggenheim, 1938. Accession #38.508. ©2008 Artists Rights Society (ARS), New York/VG Bild-Kunst, Bonn.
1-33 ©Digital Image ©The Museum of Modern Art/Licensed by SCALA/Art Resource, NY. ©2008 Artists Rights Society (ARS), New York/ADAGP, Paris.
1-34 Art Image copyright ©The Metropolitan Museum of Art/Art Resource, NY
also Chapter 18 timeline
1-35 Acquired 1949, The Phillips Collection, Washington, D.C. ©1973 (renewed 2001) Grandma Moses Properties Co., New York.
1-36 Courtesy of Museum of Northern Arizona Photo Archives, E3176. (Negative number 81C.7) Photographer, Mark Middleton .
1-37 Courtesy of The Coca-Cola Company
1-38 Courtesy Reserve Bank of New Zealand. Courtesy of the artist, Herb Kawainui Kane
1-39 ©Scala/Art Resource, NY
also Chapter 17 timeline
1-40 © Geoffrey Clements/CORBIS. ©2008 The Willem de Kooning Foundation/Artists Rights Society (ARS), New York.
also Chapter 19 timeline
1-41 ©Scala/Art Resource, NY
1-42 © Geoffrey Clements/CORBIS. ©2008 The Willem de Kooning Foundation/Artists Rights Society (ARS), New York.
1-43 ©Gjon Mili, Time & Life Pictures/Getty Images.
1-44 ©The Andy Warhol Foundation, Inc./Art Resource, NY. ©2008 Andy Warhol Foundation for the Visual Arts/Artists Rights Society (ARS), New York.

1-45 ©Réunion des Musées Nationaux/Art Resource, NY
1-46 ©Tony Oursler
1-47 Courtesy Marianne Boesky Gallery, New York

CHAPTER 2

2-1 Museum of Fine Arts, Boston. Zoe Oliver Sherman Collection given in memory of Lillie Oliver Poor, 1938. 38.1838. Photograph ©2008 Museum of Fine Arts, Boston.
2-2 ©Bildarchiv Preussischer Kulturbesitz/Art Resource, NY
2-3 Library of Congress, Prints and Photographs Division
2-4 ©Albright-Knox Art Gallery/CORBIS . ©2008 The Franz Kline Estate/Artists Rights Society (ARS), New York.
also Chapter 20 timeline
2-5 Solomon R. Guggenheim Museum, New York. Accession #65.1738. Photograph by David Heald ©The Solomon R. Guggenheim Foundation, New York. ©2008 Calder Foundation, New York/Artists Rights Society (ARS), New York.
2-8 Digital Image ©The Museum of Modern Art/Licensed by SCALA/Art Resource, NY. ©2008 Estate of Pablo Picasso/Artists Rights Society (ARS), New York.
2-9 ©Arcaid/Alamy
2-10 ©Cleveland Museum of Art, Leonard C. Hanna, Jr. Fund. 2002.29. Photo: Allan Finkelman. Art © Louise Bourgeois/Licensed by VAGA, New York, NY
2-11 ©Alinari/Art Resource, NY
2-12 ©Yale University Art Gallery/Art Resource, NY
2-13 Solomon R. Guggenheim Museum, Panza Collection, Gift, 1991. 91.408. Photograph by Erika Barahona ©Solomon R. Guggenheim Foundation, New York. ©James Turrell
2-14 ©Robert Estall Photo Agency/Alamy. Reproduced by permission of the Henry Moore Foundation.
2-15 © SSPL/The Image Works
2-16 © Erich Lessing/Art Resource, NY
2-18 Courtesy Paula Cooper Gallery, New York
2-19 © Pat Behnke/Alamy
2-20 © guichaoua/Alamy
2-21 © Bildarchiv Preussischer Kulturbesitz (Elke Walford)/Art Resource, NY
2-25 Digital Image ©The Museum of Modern Art/Licensed by SCALA/Art Resource, NY. ©2008 Artists Rights Society (ARS), New York/ADAGP, Paris.
2-26 © Gift of Mrs Joseph B. Schlotman, The Detroit Institute of Arts, USA/The Bridgeman Art Library
2-27 © Alinari Archives/The Image Works. ©2008 Artists Rights Society (ARS), New York/ADAGP, Paris. © 2008 Artists Rights Society (ARS), New York/ADAGP, Paris.

CHAPTER 3

3-1 Whitney Museum of American Art, New York. Purchase 96.53.4a-b ©Ellsworth Kelly.
3-2 Courtesy Donald Young Gallery, Chicago.
3-3 © Paul Almasy/CORBIS
3-4 © Massimo Listri/CORBIS
3-6 © Scala/Art Resource, NY
also Chapter 12 timeline and Chapter 12 map
3-7 Image copyright ©The Metropolitan Museum of Art/Art Resource, NY
3-8 © Scala/Art Resource, NY
3-9 © The Philadelphia Museum of Art/Art Resource, NY
3-10 Courtesy of ACE Gallery Los Angeles.
3-11 ©Lauros/Giraudon, Pantheon, Paris, France/The Bridgeman Art Library
also Chapter 15 timeline
3-12 ©The Philadelphia Museum of Art/Art Resource, NY. ©2008 Georgia O'Keeffe Museum/Artists Rights Society (ARS), New York.
3-13 ©Galleria dell'Accademia, Venice, Italy/The Bridgeman Art Library
3-14 Gift of Enid A. Haupt. 1977.47.7. Image ©2007 Board of Trustees, National Gallery of Art, Washington, DC. ©2008 Artists Rights Society (ARS), New York/ADAGP, Paris.
also Chapter 20 timeline
3-15 ©Scala/Art Resource, NY
3-16 ©age fotostock/SuperStock
also Chapter 13 timeline
3-17 Courtesy the artist and Hauser & Wirth, Zürich/London.
3-18 Therrien, Robert, Under the Table, 1994, wood, metal and enamel, 117 x 312 x 216 inches overall, The Broad Art Foundation, Santa Monica, CA. Photography: Douglas M. Parker Studio, Los Angeles. ©2008 Robert Therrien/Artists Rights Society (ARS), New York.
3-19 AP Images/Mario Cabrera. ©2008 Richard Serra/Artists Rights Society (ARS), New York.
3-20 Digital Image ©The Museum of Modern Art/Licensed by SCALA/Art Resource, NY. ©2008 Artists Rights Society (ARS), New York/SOMAAP, Mexico City.
3-21 ©Giraudon, Louvre, Paris, France/The Bridgeman Art Library

3-22 ©Brooklyn Museum of Art, New York, USA, Gift of Anna Ferris/The Bridgeman Art Library
3-23 The Court of Gayumars(2005.1.165; M200) © Aga Khan Trust for Culture, Geneva *also Chapter 14 timeline*
3-24 ©Scala/Art Resource, NY
3-25 Solomon R. Guggenheim Museum, New York. Accession #54.1412-Georges Braque ©2008 Artists Rights Society (ARS), New York/ ADAGP, Paris. ©2008 Artists Rights Society (ARS), New York/ADAGP, Paris.
3-26 CArt Resource, NY. ©1961 M.C. Escher Foundation-Baarn-Holland. All rights reserved.

CHAPTER 4

4-1 ©Réunion des Musées Nationaux /Art Resource, NY
4-2 Harvard University Art Museums, Fogg Art Museum, Gift of Charles E. Dunlap, 1954.110 Photo: Allan Macintyre ©President and Fellows of Harvard College
4-3 ©James Luciana
4-4 Image ©2005 Board of Trustees, National Gallery of Art, Washington DC Rosenwald Collection. ©2008Artist's Rights Society (ARS), New York/VG Bild-Kunst, Bonn
4-5 ©Burstein Collection/CORBIS *also Chapter 16 timeline*
4-6 Digital Image ©The Museum of Modern Art/ Licensed by SCALA/Art Resource, NY
4-7 The Metropolitan Museum of Art, New York, Robert Lehman Collection, 1975. (1975.1.862) Photograph ©1997 The Metropolitan Museum of Art
4-8 Rijksmuseum, Amsterdam
4-9 Museum of Fine Arts, Boston. Special Chinese and Japanese Fund, 15.907. Photograph ©2008 Museum of Fine Arts, Boston. *also Chapter 14 timeline*
4-10 ©Réunion des Musées Nationaux/Art Resource, NY
4-11 Marian Goodman Gallery, New York
4-12 Image courtesy of Sikkema Jenkins & Co.
4-13 Digital Image ©The Museum of Modern Art/Licensed by SCALA/Art Resource, NY. Courtesy of Cai Studio.

CHAPTER 5

5-1 Digital Image ©The Museum of Modern Art/ Licensed by SCALA/Art Resource, NY. Art ©Jasper Johns/Licensed by VAGA, New York, NY
5-2 ©Erich Lessing/Art Resource, NY
5-3 San Francisco Art Institute, gift of William Gerstle. Photo: David Wakely.
5-4 Digital Image ©The Museum of Modern Art/Licensed by SCALA/Art Resource, NY. Copyright ©Andrew Wyeth.
5-5 ©Erich Lessing/Art Resource, NY
5-6 ©Clore Collection, Tate Gallery, London/Art Resource, NY
5-7 The Art Institute of Chicago (Mr. and Mrs. Lewis Larned Coburn Memorial Collection, 1954.183). Photography ©The Art Institute of Chicago.
5-8 Kronos Collection, New York.
5-9 ©The Detroit Institute of Arts, USA, Founders Society Purchase, Dr & Mrs Hilbert H. DeLawter Fund/The Bridgeman Art Library. Copyright ©Helen Frankenthaler.
5-10 ©Journal-Courier/Clayton Stalter/The Image Works
5-11 Hirshhorn Museum and Sculpture Garden, Smithsonian Institution. Photo: Lee Stalsworth. Art ©Romare Bearden Foundation/Licensed by VAGA, New York, NY
5-12 Courtesy Paula Cooper Gallery, New York
5-13 V&A Images/Victoria and Albert Museum, London. Art ©Vik Muniz/Licensed by VAGA, New York, NY

CHAPTER 6

6-2 ©British Museum/HIP/Art Resource, NY
6-3 ©Victoria & Albert Museum, London/Art Resource, NY
6-4 ©Mary Evans Picture Library/The Image Works
6-6 ©Scala/Art Resource, NY
6-7 ©Topham/The Image Works *also Chapter 16 timeline*
6-9 ©British Museum/HIP/Art Resource, NY
6-10 ©Worcester Art Museum, Massachusetts, USA/ The Bridgeman Art Library *also Chapter 17 timeline*
6-12 ©British Museum/HIP/Art Resource, NY
6-13 Digital Image ©The Museum of Modern Art/ Licensed by SCALA/Art Resource, NY *also Chapter 17 timeline and Chapter 18 timeline*
6-14 ©Private Collection/The Bridgeman Art Library. Courtesy of the artist.
6-16 Mary Boone Gallery, NY
6-17 Museum of Fine Arts Boston. Denman Waldo Ross Collection, 1909. 09.295. Photograph ©2008 Museum of Fine Arts, Boston.

6-18 ©Private Collection/The Bridgeman Art Library. Copyright ©David Hockney.
6-19 ©Kiki Smith, Courtesy PaceWildenstein, New York. Photography by Gregory Heins.

CHAPTER 7

7-2 Conservatoire Nationale des Arts et Métiers, Paris.
7-3 ©NMPFT/SSPL/The Image Works
7-4 ©Private Collection, The Stapleton Collection/ The Bridgeman Art Library
7-6 ©Private Collection, The Stapleton Collection/ The Bridgeman Art Library
7-7 The Minneapolis Institute of Arts, The Kate and Hall J. Peterson Fund, Acc. #72.118.8
7-8 Copyright ©Henri Cartier-Bresson/ Magnum Photos
7-9 Library of Congress, Prints and Photographs Collection
also Chapter 19 timeline
7-10 ©NMeM/Royal Photographic Society Collection/SSPL/The Image Works. ©2008 Georgia O'Keeffe Museum/Artists Rights Society (ARS), New York.
also Chapter 18 timeline
7-11 ©Library of Congress, Washington D.C., USA/The Bridgeman Art Library. Permission Joanna T. Steichen.
7-12 Digital Image ©The Museum of Modern Art/Licensed by SCALA/Art Resource, NY. ©2008 Man Ray Trust/Artists Rights Society (ARS), New York.
also Chapter 19 timeline
7-13 Digital Image ©The Museum of Modern Art/ Licensed by SCALA/Art Resource, NY
7-14 ©Bildarchiv Preussischer Kulturbesitz/Art Resource, NY. ©2008 Artists Rights Society (ARS), New York/VG Bild-Kunst, Bonn.
also Chapter 18 timeline
7-15 Copyright © 1984 The Estate of Robert Mapplethorpe.
7-16 ©Sebastiao Salgado/Contact Press Images
7-17 © 1980 Sandy Skoglund.
also Chapter 20 timeline
7-18 Courtesy of the Artist and Metro Pictures
7-19 Courtesy of Jerry Uelsmann

CHAPTER 8

8-1 ©Image Select/Art Resource, NY
8-2 ©DACS/The Bridgeman Art Library. ©2008 Artists Rights Society (ARS), New York/ SIAE, Rome.
8-3 ©ArenaPal/Topham/The Image Works. ©2008 Salvador Dali, Gala-Salvador Dali Foundation/Artists Rights Society (ARS), New York.
8-4 Digital Image ©The Museum of Modern Art/ Licensed by SCALA/Art Resource, NY
also Chapter 20 timeline
8-5 Bill Viola, The Crossing, 1996, Video/sound installation. Photo: Kira Perov
8-6 Bill Viola, The Crossing, 1996, Video/sound installation. Photo: Kira Perov
8-7 Collection Museum of Contemporary Art, Chicago. Courtesy the artist and Hauser & Wirth, Zürich/London.
8-8 Lincoln Laboratory, MIT, Roger Sudbury
8-9 Courtesy of A. Michael Noll
8-10 Courtesy of Maggie Taylor
8-11 Courtesy of Stephanie Syjuco
8-12 House Industries
8-13 Courtesy the artist and The Project, New York.
8-14 Copyright 1986 by Pixar. All rights reserved. "Luxo" is a trademark of Jac. Jacobson Industries.
also Chapter 20 timeline
8-15 ©Touhoku Shinsha/The Kobal Collection
8-16a Peter Edmunds, www.swarmsketch.com.
8-16b Peter Edmunds, Unclaimed Baggage, 05/12/2005, online collaborative drawing from www.swarmsketch.com.
8-17 bitforms gallery, nyc

CHAPTER 9

9-1 ©Danny Lehman/CORBIS
also Chapter 12 timeline and Chapter 12 map
9-2 ©Private Collection/The Bridgeman Art Library. Permission Joanna T. Steichen.
9-3 ©Erich Lessing/Art Resource, NY
also Chapter 12 map
9-4 Metropolitan Museum of Art, Michael C. Rockefeller Memorial Collection, Gift of Nelson A. Rockefeller, 1965. (1987.412.309) Photograph ©1983 The Metropolitan Museum of Art
also Chapter 15 timeline and Chapter 13 map
9-5 ©Alinari Archives/Art Resource, NY
also Chapter 15 map
9-6 ©Alinari Archives/Art Resource, NY
9-7 Gift of the Collectors Committee, Photograph © 2001 Board of Trustees, National Gallery of Art, Washington. ©2008 Calder Foundation, New York/Artists Rights Society (ARS), New York.
9-8 Museum Jean Tinguely, photo by David Gahr. ©2008 Artists Rights Society (ARS), New York/ADAGP, Paris
9-9 ©2008 Artists Rights Society (ARS), New York VG Bild-Kunst, Bonn
9-10 Copyright: Laurie Anderson. Photograph: Perry Hoberman. Courtesy of Sean Kelly Gallery, New York

9-11 Courtesy of Scharf Studio, photography by Tseng Kwong Chi.
9-12 Art ©Estate of Robert Smithson/Licensed by VAGA, New York, NY
9-13 ©Scott T. Smith/CORBIS. Art ©Nancy Holt/ Licensed by VAGA, New York, NY
9-14 ©Robert Preston Photography/Alamy
also Chapter 13 timeline
9-15 Hirshhorn Museum and Sculpture Garden, Smithsonian Institution. Photo: Lee Stalsworth
9-17 Image copyright ©The Metropolitan Museum of Art/Art Resource, NY
9-18 Image copyright ©The Metropolitan Museum of Art/Art Resource, NY
9-19 ©Jtb Photo Communications Inc./Photolibrary
also Chapter 13 timeline
9-20 ©Scala/Art Resource, NY
9-21 Hirshhorn Museum and Sculpture Garden, Smithsonian Institution. Photo: Lee Stalsworth. Art ©Estate of David Smith/Licensed by VAGA, New York, NY
also Chapter 19 timeline
9-22 Digital Image ©The Museum of Modern Art/Licensed by SCALA/Art Resource, NY. ©2008 Estate of Louise Nevelson/Artists Rights Society (ARS), New York.
9-23 Solomon R. Guggenheim Museum, New York. Purchased by exchange with funds contributed by Dakis Joannou and with a special International Director's Council fund in honor of Dakis Joannou, 2003. Accession #2003.79. Photograph by David Heald ©The Solomon R. Guggenheim Foundation, New York
9-24 Courtesy of the Artist and Metro Pictures
9-25 "A Cappella" by Patrick Dougherty, Villa Montalvo, Saratoga, CA, Photo by Ron Johnson.

CHAPTER 10

10-1 ©2008 Frank Lloyd Wright Foundation, Scottsdale, AZ/Artists Rights Society (ARS), New York.
10-2 ©2008 Frank Lloyd Wright Foundation, Scottsdale, AZ/Artists Rights Society (ARS), New York.
10-3 ©2008 Frank Lloyd Wright Foundation, Scottsdale, AZ/Artists Rights Society (ARS), New York.
10-4 ©age fotostock/SuperStock. ©2008 Frank Lloyd Wright Foundation, Scottsdale, AZ/Artists Rights Society (ARS), New York.
also Chapter 19 timeline
10-5 ©Yoram Lehman/Peter Arnold, Inc.
10-6 ©Erich Lessing/Art Resource, NY
10-7 ©Vanni/Art Resource, NY
also Chapter 14 timeline
10-8 ©Wolfgang Kaehler/Alamy
10-9 ©Brian Brake/Photo Researchers, Inc.
10-10 ©Georg Gerster/Photo Researchers, Inc.
10-11 ©Vanni/Art Resource, NY
10-12 ©Borromeo/Art Resource, NY
also Chapter 12 timeline and Chapter 12 map
10-14 Courtesy Saskia Ltd., ©Dr. Ron Wiedenhoeft
10-17 ©Cosmo Condina/Alamy
also Chapter 13 map
10-20 Index/Artphoto
also Chapter 12 timeline
10-22 ©La Madeleine, Vezelay, France/The Bridgeman Art Library
10-23 ©Anthony Scibilia/Art Resource, NY
10-26 ©Scala/Art Resource, NY
also Chapter 12 timeline and Chapter 12 map
10-27 ©Peter Aaron/Esto
10-28a ©Réunion des Musées Nationaux/Art Resource, NY
10-28b ©Réunion des Musées Nationaux/Art Resource, NY
10-30 ©Rob Kavanagh/Alamy
also Chapter 19 timeline
10-31 Ezra Stoller ©Esto
10-32 ©VIEW Pictures Ltd (Nathan Willock)/Alamy
10-33 ©David Burton/Alamy
10-34 ©Vincenzo Lombardo/Getty Images
also Chapter 14 map
10-36 ©DeA Picture Library/Getty Images
10-37 ©Alinari/Art Resource, NY
10-38 ©Robert Llewellyn/SuperStock
also Chapter 16 timeline
10-39 Robert Lautman Photography Collection, Courtesy National Building Museum
10-40 ©William S. Helsel/Getty Images/Stone
10-41 From Urbanisme, Cres, Paris, 1925, page 301. ©2008 Artists Rights Society (ARS), New York/ADAGP, Paris/FLC.
10-42 Courtesy Zaha Hadid Architects
also Chapter 20 timeline
10-43 Diller Scofidio + Renfro

CHAPTER 11

11-1 ©Réunion des Musées Nationaux/Art Resource, NY
also Chapter 13 timeline and Chapter 13 map
11-2 ©National Museum of Women in the Arts, Washington, DC. Gift of Wallace and Wilhelmina Hollady
11-3 ©Scala/Art Resource, NY
also Chapter 12 timeline
11-4 ©British Museum/HIP/Art Resource, NY
11-5 ©Topham/The Image Works
also Chapter 14 timeline

11-6 ©Smithsonian American Art Museum, Washington, DC/Art Resource, NY
also Chapter 17 timeline
11-7 Digital Image ©The Museum of Modern Art/Licensed by SCALA/Art Resource, NY
11-8 ©Bildarchiv Preussischer Kulturbesitz/Art Resource, NY
also Chapter 13 map
11-9 ©Topham/The Image Works
11-10 ©Victoria & Albert Museum, London/Art Resource, NY
11-11 ©Museum of Fine Arts, Boston, Massachusetts, USA, Bequest of Maxim Karolik/The Bridgeman Art Library
11-12 Image copyright ©The Metropolitan Museum of Art/Art Resource, NY
11-13 Photo: © schoppleinstudio.com. Courtesy of the Voulkos & Co. Catalogue Project, www.voulkos.com
11-14 San Francisco Museum of Modern Art (gift of the Modern Art Council). Art ©Estate of Robert Arneson/Licensed by VAGA, New York, NY
11-15 Courtesy of the artist.
11-16 ©Indianapolis Museum of Art, USA, Gift of Marilyn and Eugene Glick/The Bridgeman Art Library
11-17 Copyright ©Magdalena Abakanowicz. Courtesy of the Marlborough Gallery, New York.
11-18 ©Smithsonian American Art Museum, Washington, DC/Art Resource, NY
11-19 ©Smithsonian American Art Museum, Washington, DC/Art Resource, NY
11-20 Private Collection. Courtesy Tibor de Nagy Gallery, New York
11-21 ©Ellen McKnight/Alamy
11-22 ©Myra Mimlitsch-Gray. Courtesy of Rotasa Collection Trust.
11-23 Courtesy of TAI Gallery, Santa Fe, New Mexico. Photo by Mochizuki Akira, Japan.
11-24 ©Victoria & Albert Museum, London/Art Resource, NY
11-25 Designed by Milton Glaser
11-26 ©Private Collection/The Bridgeman Art Library
also Chapter 19 timeline
11-27 Digital Image ©The Museum of Modern Art/Licensed by SCALA/Art Resource, NY. ©2008 Artists Rights Society (ARS), New York/VG Bild-Kunst, Bonn.
11-28 ©Arcaid/Alamy
11-29 ©Erich Lessing/Art Resource, NY
also Chapter 18 timeline
11-30 Courtesy of Knoll International
also Chapter 20 timeline
11-31 ©Glyn Thomas/Alamy
11-32 ©Art Kowalsky/Alamy
also Chapter 15 timeline and Chapter 15 map
11-33 ©2008 The Isamu Noguchi Foundation and Garden Museum, New York/Artists Rights Society (ARS), New York.

CHAPTER 12

12-1 ©Gary Cook/Alamy
also Chapter 12 timeline and Chapter 12 map
12-2 ©Erich Lessing/Art Resource, NY
12-3 ©Araldo de Luca
also Chapter 12 timeline
12-4 ©Bildarchiv Preussischer Kulturbesitz/Art Resource, NY
also Chapter 12 timeline and Chapter 12 map
12-5 Egyptian National Museum, Cairo, Egypt, Photo ©Boltin Picture Library/The Bridgeman Art Library
12-6 ©Carmen Redondo/CORBIS
12-7 ©Giraudon/Art Resource, NY
12-8 ©Erich Lessing/Art Resource, NY
12-9 ©View Stock/Alamy
also Chapter 12 timeline and Chapter 12 map
12-10 Image copyright ©The Metropolitan Museum of Art/Art Resource, NY
12-11 Cella rendering from The Parthenon Project, www.debevec.org/Parthenon, ©2004 University of Southern California
12-13 ©World Religions Photo Library/Alamy
also Chapter 12 map
12-14 ©Christophe Loviny/CORBIS
also Chapter 14 timeline
12-15 ©Ancient Art & Architecture Collection
12-16 ©Araldo de Luca/CORBIS
12-17 ©Scala/Art Resource, NY
also Chapter 12 timeline
12-18 ©Erich Lessing/Art Resource, NY
12-19 ©Robert Harding Picture Library Ltd (Richard Ashworth)/Alamy
also Chapter 12 timeline and Chapter 12 map
12-20 ©Réunion des Musées Nationaux/Art Resource, NY
also Chapter 12 map
12-21 ©Araldo de Luca/CORBIS
12-22 ©Scala/Art Resource, NY
12-23 ©Robert Harding Picture Library Ltd (John Ross)/Alamy
also Chapter 12 timeline
12-24 ©Robert Harding Picture Library (Roy Rainford)/Alamy
also Chapter 12 timeline and Chapter 12 map
12-25 Canali Photobank
12-26 ©Visual Arts Library (London)/Alamy
12-27 ©Wendy Kay/Alamy
12-28 ©Robert Harding Picture Library (Roy Rainford)/Alamy

12-29 ©Robert Harding Picture Library (John Miller)/Alamy
12-30 ©Scala/Art Resource, NY
12-31 ©Araldo de Luca/CORBIS
12-32 ©Alinari/Art Resource, NY

CHAPTER 13

13-1 ©Scala/Art Resource, NY
also Chapter 13 timeline
13-2 Image copyright ©The Metropolitan Museum of Art/Art Resource, NY
13-3 ©Erich Lessing/Art Resource, NY
also Chapter 13 timeline
13-4 ©Cameraphoto Arte, Venice/Art Resource, NY
also Chapter 13 map
13-5 ©Cameraphoto Arte, Venice/Art Resource, NY
13-6 ©Adam Eastland/Alamy
13-7 ©Rolf Richardson /Alamy
also Chapter 13 timeline
13-9 ©The British Museum/Topham-HIP/The Image Works
also Chapter 13 timeline and Chapter 13 map
13-10 ©The British Library/Topham-HIP/The Image Works
also Chapter 13 timeline and Chapter 13 map
13-11 ©The British Library/Topham-HIP/The Image Works
13-12 ©Steve Taylor/Alamy
also Chapter 13 timeline and Chapter 13 map
13-13 ©Westend 61 (Andreas M. Gross)/Alamy
also Chapter 13 timeline
13-14 ©Werner Forman/Art Resource, NY
also Chapter 14 timeline
13-15 ©Adam Woolfitt/CORBIS
13-16 ©John and Lisa Merrill/CORBIS
13-17 ©Robert Harding Picture Library Ltd (Adam Woolfitt)/Alamy
also Chapter 13 timeline and Chapter 13 map
13-18 ©Reiner Elsen/Mauritius Die Bildagentur Gmbh/Photolibrary
also Chapter 13 map
13-19 ©John C. Huntington
also Chapter 13 timeline
13-20 Robert L. Brown
also Chapter 13 map
13-21 ©Erich Lessing/Art Resource, NY
also Chapter 13 timeline and Chapter 13 map
13-22 ©coolangie/Alamy
13-23 ©David Crossland/Alamy
13-24 ©Erich Lessing/Art Resource, NY
also Chapter 13 map
13-25 ©Bildarchiv Monheim GmbH (Florian Monheim)/Alamy
also Chapter 13 map
13-26 Courtesy of the author
13-27 ©Photos 12 (Anne Joudiou)/Alamy
13-29 ©Bildarchiv Monheim GmbH (Florian Monheim)/Alamy
also Chapter 13 timeline and Chapter 13 map
13-30 ©Jon Arnold Images/Alamy
13-31 ©Bildarchiv Monheim GmbH (Jochen Helle)/Alamy
13-32 ©Erich Lessing/Art Resource, NY
13-33 ©Erich Lessing/Art Resource, NY
13-34 ©Erich Lessing/Art Resource, NY
13-35 ©Arcaid (Richard Bryant)/Alamy
13-36 ©Scala/Art Resource, NY
13-37 ©Scala/Art Resource, NY
13-38 ©Scala/Art Resource, NY
also Chapter 13 map

CHAPTER 14

14-1 ©Scala/Art Resource, NY
also Chapter 14 timeline
14-2 ©Erich Lessing/Art Resource, NY
14-3 ©Erich Lessing/Art Resource, NY
14-4 ©Duomo, Florence, Italy/Ken Welsh/The Bridgeman Art Library
also Chapter 14 timeline and Chapter 14 map
14-5 ©Scala/Art Resource, NY
14-6 ©Erich Lessing/Art Resource, NY
also Chapter 14 timeline
14-7 ©Scala/Art Resource, NY
14-8 ©Erich Lessing/Art Resource, NY
14-9 ©Scala/Art Resource, NY
also Chapter 14 timeline
14-10 Bodleian Library
14-11 ©imagebroker/Alamy
14-12 ©Fratelli Fabbri, Milan, Italy/The Bridgeman Art Library
14-13 ©Erich Lessing/Art Resource, NY
14-14 ©Alinari/Art Resource, NY
also Chapter 14 timeline and Chapter 14 map
14-15 © Araldo de Luca/CORBIS
14-16 ©Scala/Art Resource, NY
also Chapter 14 timeline
14-17 ©Jim Zuckerman/Corbis
14-18 ©Erich Lessing/Art Resource, NY
14-19 ©Vittoriano Rastelli/CORBIS
14-20 ©Vittoriano Rastelli/CORBIS
14-21 ©Scala/Art Resource, NY
14-22 ©Alinari/Art Resource, NY
also Chapter 14 timeline
14-23 ©Alinari/Art Resource, NY
also Chapter 15 timeline
14-24 ©Villa Rotonda, Vicenza, Italy/Merilyn Thorold/The Bridgeman Art Library
also Chapter 15 timeline and Chapter 14 map
14-25 ©Scala/Art Resource, NY
14-26 ©Art Resource, NY

14-27 ©Giraudon/Art Resource, NY
also Chapter 14 timeline
14-28 © SuperStock, Inc./SuperStock
also Chapter 14 timeline and Chapter 14 map
14-29 ©Erich Lessing/Art Resource, NY
14-30 ©Scala/Art Resource, NY
14-31 ©British Museum/HIP/Art Resource, NY
also Chapter 14 map
14-32 ©Cleveland Museum of Art, Leonard C. Hanna, Jr. Fund. 1984.37
14-33 ©SuperStock, Inc.
14-34 ©Erich Lessing/Art Resource, NY
14-35 ©Musee d'Unterlinden, Colmar, France/The Bridgeman Art Library
14-36 ©Erich Lessing/Art Resource, NY
14-37 ©Erich Lessing/Art Resource, NY
14-38 ©Erich Lessing/Art Resource, NY
14-39 ©Prado, Madrid, Spain/Giraudon/The Bridgeman Art Library
14-40 ©Scala/Art Resource, NY
14-41 ©Erich Lessing/Art Resource, NY

CHAPTER 15

15-1 ©Ali Meyer/The Bridgeman Art Library
15-2 The Art Archive/Galleria degli Uffizi Florence/Dagli Orti (A)
also Chapter 15 timeline
15-3 ©Scala/Art Resource, NY
15-4 ©Erich Lessing/Art Resource, NY
15-5 © SuperStock, Inc./SuperStock
15-6 ©Nimatallah/Art Resource, NY
15-7 ©Scala/Art Resource, NY
15-8 ©The Detroit Institute of Arts, USA/Gift of Mr Leslie H. Green/The Bridgeman Art Library
also Chapter 15 timeline
15-9 ©Scala/Art Resource, NY
also Chapter 15 timeline
15-10 ©Scala/Art Resource
15-11 ©Erich Lessing/Art Resource, NY
15-12 ©Scala/Art Resource, NY
15-13 ©Joseph Martin/The Bridgeman Art Library
15-14 ©Lightworks Media/Alamy
15-15 ©Hemis (Bertrand Gardel)/Alamy
15-16 ©CuboImages srl (Riccardo Lombardo/Alamy
15-17 ©Erich Lessing/Art Resource
also Chapter 15 map
15-18 ©Prado, Madrid, Spain/The Bridgeman Art Library
15-19 ©Peter Willi/The Bridgeman Art Library
also Chapter 15 map
15-20 ©Erich Lessing/Art Resource, NY
15-21 ©Giraudon/The Bridgeman Art Library
15-22 ©Scala/Art Resource, NY
15-23 The Metropolitan Museum of Art Marquand Collection, Gift of Henry G. Marquand, 1889 (89.15.21) Photograph ©The Metropolitan Museum of Art
also Chapter 15 timeline
15-24 © Wallace Collection, London, UK/The Bridgeman Art Library
15-25 ©Bildarchiv Preussischer Kulturbesitz/Art Resource, NY
15-26 ©Scala/Art Resource, NY
15-27 Rijksmuseum, Amsterdam
15-28 © National Gallery Collection; By kind permission of the Trustees of the National Gallery, London/CORBIS
also Chapter 15 map
15-29 ©Archivo Iconografico, S.A./CORBIS
15-30 ©Erich Lessing/Art Resource, NY
15-31 Andrew W. Mellon Collection, 1937.1.72. Image ©2007 Board of Trustees, National Gallery of Art, Washington, DC.
15-32 ©Réunion des Musées Nationaux/Art Resource, NY
also Chapter 16 timeline
15-33 ©Réunion des Musées Nationaux/Art Resource, NY
also Chapter 15 timeline
15-34 ©Reunion des Musees Nationaux (Robert Polidori)/Art Resource.
15-35 ©Réunion des Musées Nationaux/Art Resource, NY
15-36 ©Réunion des Musées Nationaux/Art Resource, NY
15-37 ©Réunion des Musées Nationaux (Harry Bréjat)/Art Resource, NY
15-38 ©Réunion des Musées Nationaux (Gérard Blot)/Art Resource, NY
also Chapter 15 timeline
15-39 ©SuperStock, Inc./SuperStock
also Chapter 15 timeline
15-40 ©Giraudon/The Bridgeman Art Library
also Chapter 15 timeline

CHAPTER 16

16-1 ©ImageState (Pictor International)/Alamy
also Chapter 16 timeline
16-2 ©Dulwich Picture Gallery, London, UK/The Bridgeman Art Library
16-3 ©Francis G. Mayer/CORBIS
also Chapter 16 timeline
16-4 ©Virginia Museum of Fine Arts, Richmond, VA. The Adolph D. and Wilkins C. Williams Fund. Acc. #75.22. Photo: Katherine Wetzel.
also Chapter 16 timeline

16-5 ©Réunion des Musées Nationaux (G. Blot/ C. Jean)/Art Resource, NY
also Chapter 16 timeline
16-6 ©Musees Royaux des Beaux-Arts de Belgique, Brussels, Belgium/The Bridgeman Art Library
16-7 ©Erich Lessing/Art Resource, NY
16-8 ©Art Kowalsky/Alamy
also Chapter 16 timeline
16-9 ©Erich Lessing/Art Resource, NY
16-10 ©British Museum/Art Resource, NY
16-11 ©Bildarchiv Preussischer Kulturbesitz (Elke Walford)/Art Resource, NY
16-12 © Burstein Collection/CORBIS
also Chapter 16 timeline
16-13 ©Erich Lessing/Art Resource, NY
also Chapter 16 timeline
16-14 ©Réunion des Musées Nationaux/Art Resource, NY
16-15 Image copyright ©The Metropolitan Museum of Art/Art Resource, NY
16-16 ©Pierre Barbier/Roger-Viollet/The Image Works
also Chapter 16 timeline
16-17 ©Geoffrey Clements/CORBIS
16-18 ©Geoffrey Clements/CORBIS
16-19 ©Private Collection/The Bridgeman Art Library
16-20 ©Gus/Alamy
also Chapter 15 timeline
16-21 ©Iconotec (Hugo Canabi)/Alamy
also Chapter 16 timeline
16-22 ©Giraudon/The Bridgeman Art Library
16-23 Metropolitan Museum of Art, New York. Gift in memory of Jonathan Sturges by his children, 1895 (95.13.3). Photograph ©2001 The Metropolitan Museum of Art
16-24 ©Bridgeman Art Library, London/SuperStock
also Chapter 17 timeline
16-25 ©British Museum/HIP/Art Resource, NY
16-26 ©Erich Lessing/Art Resource, NY
16-27 ©Erich Lessing/Art Resource, NY
also Chapter 16 timeline
16-28 Image copyright ©The Metropolitan Museum of Art/Art Resource, NY
16-29 ©Adoc-photos/Art Resource, NY
16-30 ©Phoenix Art Museum, Arizona, USA/The Bridgeman Art Library

CHAPTER 17

17-1 ©Lauros/Giraudon/The Bridgeman Art Library
17-2 ©Erich Lessing/Art Resource, NY
also Chapter 17 timeline
17-3 Sterling and Francine Clark Art Institute, Williamstown, Massachusetts. Acquired by Sterling and Francine Clark, 1942. 1955.658
17-4 ©Erich Lessing/Art Resource, NY
also Chapter 17 timeline
17-5 Image copyright ©The Metropolitan Museum of Art/Art Resource, NY
17-6 Image copyright © The Metropolitan Museum of Art/Art Resource, NY
17-7 Image copyright © The Metropolitan Museum of Art/Art Resource, NY
17-8 ©Réunion des Musées Nationaux/Art Resource, NY
also Chapter 17 timeline
17-9 The Art Institute of Chicago, Gift of Arthur M. Wood in memory of Pauline Palmer Wood, 1985.1103. Photography ©The Art Institute of Chicago
17.10 Image copyright ©The Metropolitan Museum of Art/Art Resource, NY
also Chapter 17 map
17-11 ©Burstein Collection/CORBIS
17-12 ©Erich Lessing/Art Resource, NY
also Chapter 17 map
17-13 ©Francis G. Mayer/CORBIS
also Chapter 17 timeline
17-14 ©Erich Lessing/Art Resource, NY
17-15 ©Erich Lessing/Art Resource, NY
also Chapter 17 timeline
17-16 Image copyright ©The Metropolitan Museum of Art/Art Resource, NY
17-17 ©National Gallery of Art, Washington DC, USA, Index/The Bridgeman Art Library
17-18 ©Erich Lessing/Art Resource, NY
17-19 Courtesy of the author
17-20 Courtesy of the author
also Chapter 17 timeline
17-21 ©SuperStock, Inc./SuperStock
17-22 ©Erich Lessing/Art Resource, NY
also Chapter 17 timeline
17-23 ©Erich Lessing/Art Resource, NY
17-24 ©Albright Knox Art Gallery, Buffalo, New York, USA/The Bridgeman Art Library
17-25 ©Stedelijk Museum, Amsterdam, The Netherlands/The Bridgeman Art Library
17-26 ©Mary Evans Picture Library/The Image Works
17-27 ©Réunion des Musées Nationaux (Richard Lambert)/Art Resource, NY
17-28 ©Yale University Art Gallery/Art Resource, NY
also Chapter 16 timeline
17-29 ©Erich Lessing/Art Resource, NY
also Chapter 17 timeline
17-30 Digital Image © The Museum of Modern Art/ Licensed by SCALA/Art Resource, NY
also Chapter 17 map

17-31 Digital Image © The Museum of Modern Art/ Licensed by SCALA/Art Resource, NY
17-32 Digital Image © The Museum of Modern Art/ Licensed by SCALA/Art Resource, NY
17-33 Collection of Mr. and Mrs. Paul Mellon, in Honor of the 50th Anniversary of the National Gallery of Art. 1995.47.5. Image courtesy of the Board of Trustees, National Gallery of Art, Washington, DC.
also Chapter 17 timeline

CHAPTER 18

18-1 ©JLImages/Alamy
also Chapter 18 timeline
18-2 ©Erich Lessing/Art Resource, NY. ©2008 The Munch Museum/The Munch-Ellingsen Group/Artists Rights Society (ARS), New York.
18-3 Digital Image ©The Museum of Modern Art/Licensed by SCALA/Art Resource, NY. ©2008 The Munch Museum/The Munch-Ellingsen Group/Artists Rights Society (ARS), New York.
also Chapter 18 timeline
18-4 ©Hamburger Kunsthalle, Hamburg, Germany/ The Bridgeman Art Library. ©Ingeborg & Dr. Wolfgang Henze-Ketterer, Wichtrach/Bern
18-5 Statens Museum for Kunst, Copenhagen. © Nolde Stiftung Seebüll
18-6 San Francisco Museum of Modern Art, Collection SFMOMA . Bequest of Harriet Lane Levy 50.6075. © 2008 Artists Rights Society (ARS), New York/ADAGP, Paris.
18-7 ©SuperStock, Inc./SuperStock . ©2008 Succession H. Matisse, Paris/Artists Rights Society (ARS), New York.
also Chapter 18 timeline
18-8 Digital Image ©The Museum of Modern Art/Licensed by SCALA/Art Resource, NY. ©2008 Succession H. Matisse, Paris/Artists Rights Society (ARS), New York.
18-9 Helen Birth Bartlett Memorial Collection. 1926.253. Photography ©The Art Institute of Chicago.. ©2008 Estate of Pablo Picasso/Artists Rights Society (ARS), New York
18-10 The Brooklyn Museum, New York, Frank L. Babbott Fund. Acc. #52.160
18-11 Art Institute of Chicago, Major Acquisitions Centennial Fund. 1984.550. Photography © The Art Institute of Chicago.
18-12 Digital Image ©The Museum of Modern Art/Licensed by SCALA/Art Resource, NY. ©2008 Estate of Pablo Picasso/Artists Rights Society (ARS), New York.
also Chapter 18 timeline
18-13 ©Réunion des Musées Nationaux (R.G. Ojeda)/ Art Resource, NY. ©2008 Estate of Pablo Picasso/Artists Rights Society (ARS), New York.
18-14 Digital Image ©The Museum of Modern Art/Licensed by SCALA/Art Resource, NY. ©2008 Estate of Pablo Picasso/Artists Rights Society (ARS), New York.
18-15 Digital Image ©The Museum of Modern Art/Licensed by SCALA/Art Resource, NY. ©2008 Estate of Pablo Picasso/Artists Rights Society (ARS), New York.
18-16 ©Art Resource, NY. ©2008 Estate of Pablo Picasso/Artists Rights Society (ARS), New York.
also Chapter 18 timeline
18-17 Digital Image ©The Museum of Modern Art/Licensed by SCALA/Art Resource, NY. © 2008 Artists Rights Society (ARS), New York/ADAGP, Paris.
also Chapter 18 timeline
18-18 Digital Image © The Museum of Modern Art/ Licensed by SCALA/Art Resource, NY
18-19 Digital Image © The Museum of Modern Art/ Licensed by SCALA/Art Resource, NY
also Chapter 18 timeline
18-20 ©The Philadelphia Museum of Art/Art Resource, NY. ©2008 Artists Rights Society (ARS), New York/ADAGP, Paris/Succession Marcel Duchamp.
18-21 Digital Image ©The Museum of Modern Art/ Licensed by SCALA/Art Resource, NY
18-22 ©Tate Gallery, London/Art Resource, NY. ©2008 Artists Rights Society (ARS), New York/ADAGP, Paris/Succession Marcel Duchamp.
also Chapter 18 timeline
18-23 Digital Image ©The Museum of Modern Art/Licensed by SCALA/Art Resource, NY. ©2008 Man Ray Trust/Artists Rights Society (ARS), New York.
18-24 ©SuperStock, Inc./SuperStock. ©Ingeborg & Dr. Wolfgang Henze-Ketterer, Wichtrach/Bern
also Chapter 18 timeline
18-25 ©Bildarchiv Preussischer Kulturbesitz (Joerg P. Anders)/Art Resource, NY. ©2008 Artists Rights Society (ARS), New York/VG Bild-Kunst, Bonn.
18-26 Fine Arts Museums of San Francisco, Achenbach Foundation for Graphic Arts, #1963.30.874. ©2008 Artists Rights Society (ARS), New York/VG Bild-Kunst, Bonn.
also Chapter 18 timeline
18-27 ©Private Collection/The Bridgeman Art Library. ©2008 Artists Rights Society (ARS), New York/SIAE, Rome.
also Chapter 18 timeline
18-28 Digital Image ©The Museum of Modern Art/Licensed by SCALA/Art Resource, NY. ©2008 Artists Rights Society (ARS), New York/ProLitteris, Zurich.
also Chapter 18 timeline

18-29 Digital Image ©The Museum of Modern Art/Licensed by SCALA/Art Resource, NY. ©2008 Salvador Dali, Gala-Salvador Dali Foundation/Artists Rights Society (ARS), New York.
also Chapter 18 timeline

18-30 ©Francis G. Mayer/CORBIS. ©2008 Salvador Dali, Gala-Salvador Dali Foundation/Artists Rights Society (ARS), New York.

18-31 ©Francis G. Mayer/CORBIS. ©2008 Salvador Dali, Gala-Salvador Dali Foundation/Artists Rights Society (ARS), New York.

18-32 ©Banque d'Images, ADAGP/Art Resource, NY. ©2008 C. Herscovici, Brussels/Artists Rights Society (ARS), New York.

18-33 ©Banque d'Images, ADAGP/Art Resource, NY. ©2008 C. Herscovici, Brussels/Artists Rights Society (ARS), New York.

CHAPTER 19

19-1 Solomon R. Guggenheim Museum, New York. Solomon R. Guggenheim Founding Collection, Gift, Solomon R. Guggenheim. 41.505. ©2008 Artists Rights Society (ARS), New York/ADAGP, Paris.

19-2 Digital Image ©The Museum of Modern Art/Licensed by SCALA/Art Resource, NY. ©2008 Artists Rights Society (ARS), New York/ADAGP, Paris.
also Chapter 19 timeline

19-3 Solomon R. Guggenheim Museum, New York. Solomon R. Guggenheim Founding Collection, Gift, Solomon R. Guggenheim. 45.989. ©2008 Artists Rights Society (ARS), New York/ADAGP, Paris.
also Chapter 19 timeline

19-4 ©2008 Mondrian/Holtzman Trust c/o HCR International Warrenton, VA

19-5 Digital Image ©The Museum of Modern Art/Licensed by SCALA/Art Resource, NY. ©2008 Mondrian/Holtzman Trust c/o HCR International Warrenton, VA

19-6 ©VIEW Pictures Ltd (Nathan Willock)/Alamy. ©2008 Artists Rights Society (ARS), New York/Beeldrecht, Amsterdam.

19-7 ©Vanni/Art Resource, NY

19-8 © Edifice (Adrian Forty)/CORBIS. ©2008 Artists Rights Society (ARS), New York/ADAGP, Paris/FLC.

19-9 ©Timothy McCarthy/Art Resource, NY. ©2008 Frank Lloyd Wright Foundation, Scottsdale, AZ/Artists Rights Society (ARS), New York.
also Chapter 19 timeline

19-10 ©Paolo Koch/Photo Researchers, Inc. ©2008 Frank Lloyd Wright Foundation, Scottsdale, AZ/Artists Rights Society (ARS), New York.

19-11 Fisk University Galleries, Nashville, Tennessee. ©2008 Georgia O'Keeffe Museum/Artists Rights Society (ARS), New York.

19-12 Digital Image ©The Museum of Modern Art/Licensed by SCALA/Art Resource, NY. ©2008 Georgia O'Keeffe Museum/Artists Rights Society (ARS), New York.
also Chapter 20 timeline

19-13 Collection, Center for Creative Photography, University of Arizona, Tucson. ©1981 Arizona Board of Regents

19-14 ©The Granger Collection, New York

19-15 Digital Image ©The Museum of Modern Art/Licensed by SCALA/Art Resource, NY. ©2008 The Willem de Kooning Foundation/Artists Rights Society (ARS), New York.

19-16 ©Geoffrey Clements/CORBIS. ©2008 The Willem de Kooning Foundation/Artists Rights Society (ARS), New York.

19-17 ©1991 Hans Namuth Estate, Courtesy, Center for Creative Photography, The University of Arizona, Tucson.

19-18 National Gallery of Art, Washington DC, USA, ©DACS/The Bridgeman Art Library. ©2008 The Pollock-Krasner Foundation/Artists Rights Society (ARS), New York.
also Chapter 19 timeline

19-19 National Gallery of Art, Washington DC, USA, ©DACS/The Bridgeman Art Library. ©2008 The Pollock-Krasner Foundation/Artists Rights Society (ARS), New York.

19-20 Collection of The University of Arizona Museum of Art, Tucson. Gift of Edward J. Gallagher, Jr. Acc. No. 1964.001.001. ©2008 Kate Rothko Prizel & Christopher Rothko/Artists Rights Society (ARS), New York.

19-21 Digital Image ©The Museum of Modern Art/Licensed by SCALA/Art Resource, NY. ©2008 Renate, Hans & Maria Hofmann Trust/Artists Rights Society (ARS), New York.

19-22 ©SuperStock, Inc./SuperStock. Copyright ©Helen Frankenthaler.

19-23 ©Panoramic Images/Getty Inc. ©2008 Calder Foundation, New York/Artists Rights Society (ARS), New York.

19-24 Whitney Museum of American Art, New York. Gift of Mr. and Mrs. Robert C. Scull 73.85a-i. Courtesy of Mark di Suvero and Spacetime

19-25 © Bill Maris/Arcaid/CORBIS

19-26 © new photo service/Alamy. ©2008 Artists Rights Society (ARS), New York/ADAGP, Paris/FLC.
also Chapter 20 timeline

19-27 © wim wiskerke/Alamy. ©2008 Artists Rights Society (ARS), New York/ADAGP, Paris/FLC.

CHAPTER 20

20-1 ©Geoffrey Clements/CORBIS
20-2 Digital Image ©The Museum of Modern Art/ Licensed by SCALA/Art Resource, NY. Art © Robert Rauschenberg/Licensed by VAGA, New York, NY
20-3 Digital Image ©The Museum of Modern Art/ Licensed by SCALA/Art Resource, NY. Art © Jasper Johns/Licensed by VAGA, New York, NY
20-4 Digital Image ©The Museum of Modern Art/ Licensed by SCALA/Art Resource, NY. ©2008 Andy Warhol Foundation for the Visual Arts/Artists Rights Society (ARS), New York.
also Chapter 20 timeline
20-5 ©The Andy Warhol Foundation, Inc./Art Resource, NY. ©2008 Andy Warhol Foundation for the Visual Arts/Artists Rights Society (ARS), New York.
20-6 Whitney Museum of American Art, New York. 50th Anniversary Gift of Mr. and Mrs. Victor W. Ganz 79.83a-b. Photograph by Jerry L. Thompson. Courtesy Oldenburg van Bruggen Foundation.
20-7 © Robert Holmes/CORBIS. Courtesy Oldenburg van Bruggen Foundation.
20-8 ©Don DiBernardo/Artifice Images.
20-9 ©Geoffrey Clements/CORBIS. Art © Judd Foundation. Licensed by VAGA, New York, NY
20-10 ©Tate Gallery, London/Art Resource, NY. Art ©Carl Andre/Licensed by VAGA, New York, NY
20-11 Digital Image ©The Museum of Modern Art/Licensed by SCALA/Art Resource, NY. ©Estate of Eva Hesse, and Hauser & Wirth, Zürich/London.
20-12 The Nelson-Atkins Museum of Art, Kansas City, Missouri. Gift of the Friends of Art, F75-13. Photograph by Jamison Miller.
20-13 Milwaukee Art Museum, Gift of Friends of Art, M1973.91. Photo by Ephraim Le-ver. Art ©Duane Hanson/Licensed by VAGA, New York, NY
20-14 Courtesy of SITE, New York
also Chapter 20 timeline
20-15 ©Mehdi Chebil/Alamy
20-16 Photo: John Cliett. ©DIA Art Foundation
20-17 Photo: Wolfgang Volz. COPYRIGHT ©CHRISTO 1976.
20-18 photo ©Donald Woodman. ©2008 Judy Chicago/ Artists Rights Society (ARS), New York.
also Chapter 20 timeline
20-19 ©James Luciana. ©2008 Judy Chicago/Artists Rights Society (ARS), New York.
20-20 Courtesy Guerrilla Girls, West
20-21 Courtesy Guerrilla Girls, New York
20-22 ©Chris Burden. Courtesy Gagosian Gallery
20-23 Courtesy of James Luna, Luiseno Tribe
20-24 Collection Van Abbemuseum, Eindhoven, Netherlands . Photograph: Peter Cox, Eindhoven, The Netherlands. Copyright ©Anselm Kiefer.
20-25 Collection of the Artist, courtesy Cheim & Read, New York. Photo © by Peter Moore. Art © Louise Bourgeois/Licensed by VAGA, New York, NY
20-26 Lucas Samaras
20-27 Courtesy of Acquavella Galleries, Inc. and the artist.
20-28 © Dave Jepson/Alamy
20-29 ©Art on File/CORBIS
20-30 © Wim Wiskerke/Alamy
20-31 ©The Philadelphia Museum of Art/Art Resource, NY. ©Estate of Richard Diebenkorn
20-32 The Nelson-Atkins Museum of Art, Kansas City, Missouri. Purchase: the Renee C. Crowell Trust, F95-16 A-C. Photograph by Robert Newcombe.
20-33 Courtesy of the author
20-34 Courtesy of Michael Rosenfeld Gallery, LLC, New York, NY and the Hammer Museum, Los Angeles.
20-35 Courtesy of Peres Projects, Los Angeles and John Connelly Presents, New York
20-36 Courtesy of the artist.
20-37 ©2002 Matthew Barney. Photo: Chris Winget. Courtesy Gladstone Gallery
20-38 Courtesy the artist and Yamamoto Gallery, Tokyo
20-39 Whitney Museum of American Art, New York. Partial and promised gift of Jeanne L. and Michael L. Klein 2005.86. Courtesy Eve Sussman & The Rufus Corporation.
20-40 Courtesy Galerie Emmanuel Perrotin, Paris & Miami. ©2006 Takashi Murakami/Kaikai Kiki Co., Ltd. All Rights Reserved.
20-41 Image courtesy of Sikkema Jenkins & Co.
20-42 Giuseppe Penone et Dina Carrara, 2003. ©2008 Artists Rights Society (ARS), New York/ ADAGP, Paris.
20-43 Courtesy of the author. ©2008 Artists Rights Society (ARS), New York/ADAGP, Paris.

INDEX

NOTE: Page references in **bold** indicate artwork, illustrations or photos.

A

H

N

Q

R

S

T

U

V

W

Y

Z